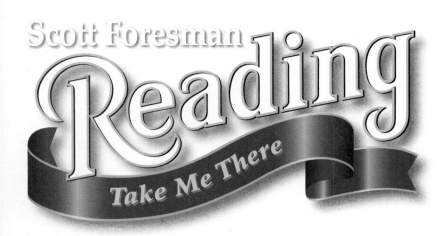

Scott Foresman Reading
Take Me There

Grade 1, Unit 5

Take Me There

SCIENTIFICALLY RESEARCH BASED
Scott Foresman Reading AND Reading First
SCIENTIFICALLY RESEARCH BASED

Scott Foresman

scottforesman.com

Editorial Offices: Glenview, Illinois • Parsippany, New Jersey
New York, New York
Sales Offices: Parsippany, New Jersey • Duluth, Georgia
Glenview, Illinois • Coppell, Texas • Ontario, California

Contents

Week 1
A Real Gift/Arthur's Reading Race

Week 2
A Big Day for Jay/Lost!

Week 3
Baby Otter Grows Up/Foal

GRADE 1 UNIT 5

Week 4
What a Sight!/Lost in the Museum

Week 5
Chompy's Afternoon/Dinosaur Babies

Week 6
Abbie Burgess/The Bravest Cat!

Overview of Links to Reading First

The **Links to Reading First** were developed based on scientifically-based research and incorporate proven methods of reading instruction to ensure that all children learn to read well by the end of grade 3. They are linked to existing Teacher's Edition instruction in *Scott Foresman Reading.* Links to Reading First should be used to provide more explicit instruction and systematic practice on critical elements of early reading. For each week, you will find Instructional Routines that link to the phonemic awareness, phonics, and story reading skills for that week. The Links to Reading First manuals include the following features:

Instructional Handbook The Instructional Handbook for Grade 1 discusses four areas of instruction—phonological and phonemic awareness, phonics, word structure, and fluency—and recommended instructional practices in *Scott Foresman Reading.*

Using the Instructional Routines A typical lesson is used to walk you through each day's Instructional Routines and to explain what they are and when to use them. The routines for each day are predictable, that is, the same set of routines appears on every Day 1, another set appears on every Day 2, and so on. They will quickly become familiar to you.

5-Day Instructional Plans A color-coded Plan for each week shows the five critical areas of Reading First that are covered in each day's instruction and indicates when to turn to the Instructional Routines during the course of each day. Use the 5-Day Instructional Plans in Links to Reading First instead of the 5-Day Planners in the Teacher's Edition.

Instructional Routines The daily Instructional Routines provide differentiated instruction and text recommendations and incorporate more intensive, explicit teaching; additional teacher modeling; more student practice; systematic, cumulative review; and scaffolded instruction in the critical areas of Reading First for all children. The degree of explicitness in the Routines will contribute to children's reading success.

Phonological and Phonemic Awareness:
The Sounds of Language

For children to learn to read, they must be able to think about language separate from its meaning. They must understand that spoken language is made up of a series of sounds. This ability is called **phonological awareness**. Phonological awareness skills may be sequenced into three levels of development. The most complex of these levels is known as **phonemic awareness**. Children who are aware of individual sounds in words are developing phonemic awareness. Phonemic awareness is one of the strongest predictors of a child's future reading ability. Teachers who understand how to increase phonemic awareness will help young learners achieve reading success.

> **phonological awareness**
> an awareness of the sounds that make up spoken language
>
> **phonemic awareness**
> one kind of phonological awareness which includes the ability to hear individual sounds in words and to identify and manipulate those sounds

The First Level of Phonological Awareness

What Are Children at This Level Learning?

Children at the first level of phonological awareness are learning to

- segment a sentence into words
- recognize rhyme and produce rhyming words
- segment a word into syllables

How Do I Support Learning at This Level?

Activities that develop phonological awareness are oral. You can support children working at this level by having them

- listen to stories and poems and sing songs that incorporate language play, such as rhyme and rhythm
- sort pictures whose names rhyme
- repeat a sentence, changing just one word, such as the first or last word
- move counters to identify the number of words in a sentence
- pronounce a whole word when you've supplied its syllables
- say and clap the syllables of words of varying lengths

How Do I Assess Children's Skills at This Level?

Assessments of phonological and phonemic awareness should be administered orally, one child at a time. They may include informal assessments you've constructed, published checklists, or more formal tests. Assessment should focus on the skills listed for each level of development.

Assess children's progress by determining if they can

- count the number of words they hear in a spoken sentence
- identify the first word or the last word of a sentence
- consistently identify pairs of rhyming words and generate rhyming words
- readily identify the number of syllables in spoken words

The Second Level of Phonological Awareness

What Are Children at This Level Learning?

Children at the second level of phonological awareness are learning to

- identify spoken words that begin with the same sound
- notice similarities and differences in the sounds that make up words
- combine onset and rime to produce a word and separate a spoken word into its onset and rime

Lily and Louis like lemonade.

How Do I Support Learning at This Level?

You can support children working at this level by having them

- listen to stories and poems and sing songs that incorporate elements of language such as alliteration (the repetition of initial consonant sounds) and assonance (the repetition of vowel sounds within words)
- repeat and create tongue twisters, exaggerating the repeated initial sound
- sort pictures according to initial consonant sounds

- select from sets of several spoken words the one that begins/ends with a different sound
- separate spoken words into onset and rime. If you say *pick,* they say /p/ *ick.*
- combine examples of onset and rime into words. If you say /ch/ *ip,* they say *chip.*

How Do I Assess Children's Skills at This Level?

Assess children's progress by determining if they can

- hear which of several pictured items begin with the same sound
- use initial, final, or medial sounds to choose a spoken word or to mark a picture that is unlike others in a group
- combine onset and rime to say a word and separate spoken words into their onset and rime

Phonemic Awareness:
The Third Level of Phonological Awareness

What Are Children at This Level Learning?

Children at the phonemic awareness level are developing the skills they will need to benefit from phonics instruction. They are learning to

- isolate individual sounds at the beginning, in the middle, or at the end of words
- segment a spoken word into its individual sounds
- blend individual sounds to make words
- add, delete, or substitute sounds in spoken words

Children's phonemic awareness abilities will continue to grow in a reciprocal fashion as they learn phonics.

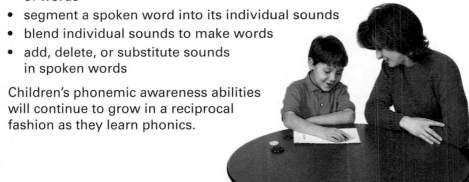

How Do I Support Learning at This Level?

You can support children working at this level by providing adequate modeling for each of these activities. Have children

- place a marker in a sound box to show where a sound occurs in a spoken word
- count sounds in spoken words by moving markers into sound boxes
- blend individual sounds to form words. For example, if you say /b/ /a/ /th/, they say *bath.*
- segment spoken words into their individual sounds. For example, if you say *me,* they say /m/ /ē/.
- delete sounds from spoken words. For example, *Say* late *without the* /l/. *Say* bite *without the* /t/.
- add sounds to spoken words. For example, *Say* ear *with* /f/ *at the beginning. Say* plan *with* /t/ *at the end.*
- change a sound in a spoken word to make a new word. For example, *Change the first sound in* ham *to* /j/. *Change the last sound in* ham *to* /d/.

How Do I Assess Phonemic Awareness?

Children who are able to hear and manipulate individual sounds in words can

- segment a word into its individual sounds
- blend individual sounds to make words
- manipulate sounds when directed to add, delete, or substitute a sound in a word

Phonics:
Sounds and Symbols

When we help children relate the sounds of spoken language to the symbols of written language, we are teaching **phonics**. Phonics instruction helps children learn the alphabetic principle, the understanding of the systematic relationships between letters and sounds. Becoming familiar with these letter-sound relationships will help children become successful readers and writers.

> **phonics**
> instruction that stresses the relationship between letters and sounds

What Is Blending and Why Is It Important?

Once children learn several individual letter-sounds, they are ready for the next step—blending sounds to decode words. When modeling blending, each sound should be pronounced separately before it is blended with the sounds that precede it. For example, to model blending the word *sat:*

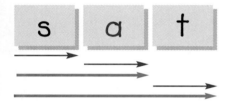

1. Write the letter *s,* and ask children for the sound, /s/.
2. Add the letter *a.* Ask for its sound, /a/.
3. Put your hand under *s,* and as you move your hand to *a,* say and blend the sounds sequentially, with no pause between letter-sounds, /sa/.
4. Add the letter *t,* and ask children for the sound, /t/. As you move your hand across the letters, blend the sounds in *sat.*
5. Then pronounce the word *sat* normally.

In this way, children learn two important things:

- to consider each sound in sequence when decoding
- to expect blended phonemes to sound like a meaningful word

How Do Children Learn to Write What They Hear?

Reading and writing reflect and support each other. Making the connection between the two reinforces children's knowledge of regularly spelled patterns and expands their ability to recognize new words.

Asking children to write for sounds will strengthen their grasp of the letter-sounds being learned. Writing for sounds forces children to think about the sounds they hear in a word, the sequence of those sounds, and which letters stand for those sounds. When having children write for sounds, say each word clearly and distinctly to enable them to segment the sounds and write what they hear. Guide them in writing the words sound by sound. Model this process frequently for children when you write.

How Do Children Move from Sounding Out to Making Sense?

Children make sense of written symbols when they expect print to make sense. This is an expectation children develop by watching adults read for meaning and by seeing others get information from print. One important factor in children's understanding that print should make sense is the feedback they get as they make their own attempts to read. When children sound out words and blend the sounds, ask questions such as "Does that sound like a word you know? Does that sound right?" By questioning rather than correcting or supplying the word, you will keep learners attentive and engaged.

Children will learn to use these strategies until they come up with a word that makes sense. As children respond to your questions, they reevaluate and adjust until they are successful. That success encourages them to ask themselves the same questions when they read on their own.

What Is a Chunking Wall and How Is It Used?

The objective of phonics instruction is for children to apply what they learn about letter-sounds to unfamiliar words as they read. One way to support them in this task is to provide useful visual reminders.

One tool that encourages phonics application is a chunking wall. A chunking wall organizes words by sound-spelling patterns. It helps children move from relying on individual letter-sounds to recognizing common vowel patterns in words. Children participate by adding words to the wall. Take every opportunity to model using the chunking wall as a reference during reading and writing. Then, when decoding an unfamiliar word, children can refer to the chunking wall to search for familiar word parts and apply those sounds to the new word.

How Do I Measure Children's Progress?

Assessment is the key to knowing what children understand, what they are just beginning to grasp, and what is still ahead of them. Information gained from assessment will help you plan instruction to meet each child's needs.

To assess children's knowledge of sound-symbol correspondences, you may use flashcards, word lists, or formal inventories. In these assessments, children may be presented with single letters, groups of letters, or words that they must pronounce correctly. Make a record of letter-sounds that have been mastered and those that are still being learned.

Phonics should also be assessed by monitoring children's ability to apply phonics skills as they read actual text. Checklists and fluency assessments can be used for this purpose. Combining the assessment of phonics in isolation with the assessment of phonics in context will provide a more complete picture of children's phonics ability.

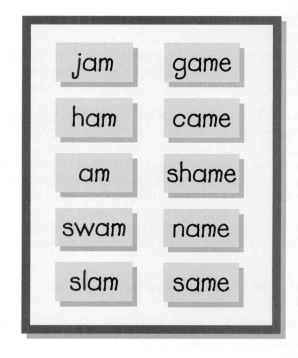

Using Word Structure

The purpose of all decoding strategies is to get meaning from the printed word. Along with an awareness of letter-sound relationships, children must develop an awareness of morphemes. **Morphemes** are the smallest meaningful units of language and include word parts such as base words, inflected endings, prefixes, and suffixes. A morpheme may be a single syllable, as *peach,* or more than one syllable, as *banana.* A morpheme may be a whole word, as *happy,* or a part of a word, as *-est.* A word may be made up of one or more morphemes. *Friend* consists of one morpheme; *friendly,* two; *unfriendly,* three; *unfriendliest,* four. Children who learn to examine these important word parts will possess another powerful strategy for identifying unfamiliar words as they read, for expanding their vocabularies, and for spelling.

> **morpheme**
> the smallest meaningful unit of language, including base words, prefixes, and suffixes
>
> **morpheme awareness**
> the ability to attend to the structure of words and to the word parts that convey meaning

How Does Word Structure Aid Decoding?

For morphemes to be useful to children, they must be taught explicitly, sequentially, and systematically. Instruction in grades 1 and 2 includes inflected endings, such as *-s, -es, -ed, -ing;* compound words; the most frequent suffixes and prefixes; spelling changes; and the application of this knowledge to unfamiliar words.

Model for children how to

- examine a word for its word parts
- take off first any prefixes, then the endings or suffixes
- determine if the base word is known or can be decoded
- add back the endings, suffixes, and prefixes and pronounce the word in sequence, part by part

The ability to examine words and to see their parts will allow children to read multisyllabic words more efficiently and will improve their fluency.

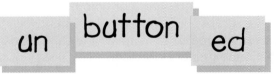

How Does Word Structure Give Clues to Meaning?

Since morphemes are meaningful units, instruction must include the meaning conveyed by each word part and how it affects the meaning of the word to which it is attached. For example, children should understand that *-s* or *-es* may convey "more than one," *-ed* signals an action that happened in the past, and *un-* means "not" or "the opposite of."

Teaching meaning-related words together will help children's vocabularies expand more rapidly, will help them determine the meaning of new words, and will allow them to read with greater comprehension.

loud

loudly

louder

loudest

Fluency

What Is Fluency?

Fluency is the ability to read quickly and accurately. Fluency develops over time and with considerable practice. Fluent readers decode words automatically. This freedom from decoding allows them to concentrate on understanding their reading. Without fluency, children are unable to comprehend what they have read.

How Do I Help Children Become Fluent Readers?

There are two ways to develop children's fluency: by modeling fluent reading and by having children engage in repeated oral reading as you monitor them and provide guidance and feedback. When children are provided with models of fluent reading, they are able to hear how a fluent reader sounds. Fluent reading is effortless and with expression. When children engage in repeated oral reading, they have the opportunity to practice until they can read a text with few or no mistakes.

Teacher modeling of fluent reading should include explicit instruction in such things as reading with accuracy, using an appropriate pace, dividing the text into meaningful phrases, attending to punctuation, and reading with expression. Daily teacher read-alouds provide additional opportunities for children to hear models of fluent reading.

Methods of practicing repeated oral reading include

- Child-adult reading—A child reads one-on-one with an adult who models fluent reading, assists with word recognition, and provides feedback.
- Choral reading—Children read aloud as a group with a fluent adult reader.
- Tape-assisted reading—Children read aloud from their books as they follow an audio-taped model or as they echo it.
- Paired reading—Children read aloud with a partner who is more fluent or who has equal ability.
- Readers theater—Children read a dialogue-rich script derived from a story. One child reads the narrator's part while other children read the dialogue of story characters.

What Should Children Read to Develop Fluency?

Since fluency develops when children practice reading with a high degree of success, it is important for them to reread a variety of short texts that are relatively easy. The texts should be at their independent reading level, that is, readers should have a 95% success rate (misreading only about 1 in 20 words). When instructing children, you may use an instructional level text—a challenging but manageable text—with which children will have a 90% success rate (misreading only about 1 in 10 words). Text that is too difficult does not allow children to develop fluency or to experience success.

How Do I Assess Fluency?

Informal and formal assessments of fluency should be conducted regularly. Informal assessment consists of monitoring children's oral reading and judging their progress. To assess children formally, take timed samples of their oral reading, measure words read correctly per minute, and set goals for their progress.

Using the Instructional Routines

Instructional Routines

The Nap *and* Oh, Cats!
Teacher's Edition, pages 10i–43d

 Day 1

If children cannot remember the sequence of sounds, **then** add letters to the activity to help them manipulate sounds.

Phonemic Awareness
Substitute Final Phonemes
Say:
- We've been learning how to say the sounds in words. Now we're going to learn how to make new words by changing last sounds.
- Listen as I say the sounds in *cat*, /k/ /a/ /t/. Now listen as I change the /t/ in *cat* to /p/. First, I take off the /t/. Then I add /p/: *cap*.
- Now I will change the /p/ in *cap* to /n/. First, I say the sounds in *cap*, /k/ /a/ /p/. Then I take off the /p/. Then I add /n/: *can*.
- Change the /p/ in *map* to /t/. What's the word? (mat)
- Change the /t/ in *mat* to /n/. What's the word? (man)
- Change the /n/ in *man* to /d/. What's the word? (mad)
- Change the /m/ in *mad* to /h/. What's the word? (had)
- Change the /d/ in *had* to /m/. What's the word? (ham)

Connect Sound to Letter
Introduce a/a/
Display Alphabet Card *Aa*. **Say:**
- The name of this letter is *a*. What is the name of this letter?

Model writing *Aa* on the board and point out the capital and lowercase forms. Have children write *Aa* on their papers. Then **say:**
- The sound for *a* is /a/. What is the sound for *a*?

If children need additional instruction for a/a/, **then** use the Connect Sound to Letter routine at the right.

Practice until children can say the letter name and sound. Then **say:**
- Listen as I say three sounds and blend them into a word: /k/ /a/ /t/, *cat*. Say it with me: /k/ /a/ /t/, *cat*.

Display *c, a,* and *t*.
- What is the sound for *c?* What is the sound for *a?* Let's blend the sounds for *c* and *a*: /ka/.

Continue with *t*.
- What is the sound for *t?* Let's blend the sound for each letter into a word.

Touch under each letter as you say the sound.
- The word is *cat*.

Continue with *man;* then have children blend the sounds for *bad, had, can,* and *cab*.

The Nap / Oh, Cats!

Use the Day 1 Routines to provide more explicit instruction, teacher modeling, and student practice for phonemic awareness and for each week's new phonics skills. More support for reading the Phonics Story also appears on Day 1. These routines should be incorporated into the Day 1 instruction as shown on the 5-Day Instructional Planner.

Phonemic Awareness Daily phonemic awareness routines offer additional practice in segmenting, blending, and manipulating sounds in spoken words. Early success in phonemic awareness prepares children to relate sounds to letters. Phonemic awareness is highly related to early reading and spelling success. The phonemic awareness routines link to the phonics skills that are practiced that day and replace the Phonics Songs and Rhymes Chart activity in the Teacher's Edition.

Connect Sound to Letter Children who are still struggling with letter-sounds need more instruction to help them connect sounds to letters. Use this routine in place of the Teacher's Edition instruction for this letter-sound.

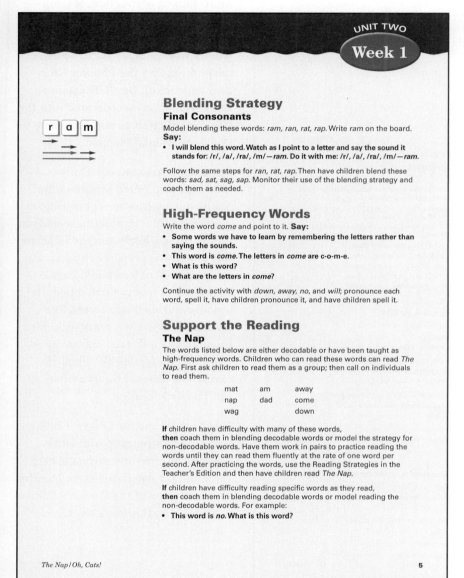

Blending Strategy
Final Consonants

Model blending these words: *ram, ran, rat, rap.* Write *ram* on the board. **Say:**

• I will blend this word. Watch as I point to a letter and say the sound it stands for: /r/, /a/, /ra/, /m/ — *ram.* Do it with me: /r/, /a/, /ra/, /m/ — *ram.*

Follow the same steps for *ran, rat, rap.* Then have children blend these words: *sad, sat, sag, sap.* Monitor their use of the blending strategy and coach them as needed.

High-Frequency Words

Write the word *come* and point to it. **Say:**

• Some words we have to learn by remembering the letters rather than saying the sounds.
• This word is *come.* The letters in *come* are c-o-m-e.
• What is this word?
• What are the letters in *come*?

Continue the activity with *down, away, no,* and *will*; pronounce each word, spell it, have children pronounce it, and have children spell it.

Support the Reading
The Nap

The words listed below are either decodable or have been taught as high-frequency words. Children who can read these words can read *The Nap.* First ask children to read them as a group; then call on individuals to read them.

mat	am	away
nap	dad	come
wag		down

If children have difficulty with many of these words, **then** coach them in blending decodable words or model the strategy for non-decodable words. Have them work in pairs to practice reading the words until they can read them fluently at the rate of one word per second. After practicing the words, use the Reading Strategies in the Teacher's Edition and then have children read *The Nap.*

If children have difficulty reading specific words as they read, **then** coach them in blending decodable words or model reading the non-decodable words. For example:

• This word is *no.* What is this word?

The Nap/Oh, Cats!   5

Blending Strategy Children need opportunities to practice blending every day. Frequent letter-by-letter blending when reading words improves children's word reading. The blending model used in the Instructional Routines is the same as the one in the Teacher's Edition. When one of the week's target skills is a word structure skill, a **Review Word Parts** routine appears at this point.

The five **High-Frequency Words** for the week are introduced in this routine. High-frequency words may be decodable, that is, children have previously learned all the letter-sounds in the word, or non-decodable, that is, there may be one or more letter-sounds in the word which children have not yet learned. Decodable high-frequency words should be blended; non-decodable high-frequency words are learned by spelling and saying the words. Using these strategies consistently will aid children's word reading.

Support the Reading Use this routine following Build Oral Language and Vocabulary in the Teacher's Edition. The list of words that children can practice prior to reading provides additional scaffolding for reading the Phonics Story. This routine also identifies appropriate word-reading strategies for problem words. Turn to the Reading Strategies in the Teacher's Edition before having children read the story.

Day 2

If children cannot remember the sequence of sounds, **then** add letters to the activity to help them manipulate sounds.

Phonemic Awareness
Substitute Final Phonemes
Say:
- We've been learning how to say the sounds in words. Now we're going to learn how to make new words by changing last sounds.
- Listen as I change the /t/ in *pat* to /d/. First, I take off the /t/. Then I add /d/: *pad.*
- Now I will change the /d/ in *pad* to /n/. First, I take off the /d/. Then I add /n/: *pan.*
- Change the /d/ in *bad* to /t/. What's the word? (bat)
- Change the /p/ in *tap* to /n/. What's the word? (tan)
- Change the /d/ in *sad* to /t/. What's the word? (sat)

Blending Strategy
Phonics Review
To practice this week's letter-sounds, have children make these words with the letter cards from the Small Group Manipulatives Package. Have them segment each word to spell it. **Say:**
- Listen as I say a word: *can.* Now I will say each sound in *can*: /k/ /a/ /n/. I will find cards to spell those sounds: /k/-*c*, /a/-*a*, /n/-*n*. Now I'll blend the word to read it: /k/, /a/, /ka/, /n/ — *can.*

Have children segment each word to spell it. Have them blend each word to read it.

cab	mat	dad
map	bag	Sam
ran	sad	fat

Review High-Frequency Words
In addition to practicing this week's words, have children review the words *and, look, see, go, to.* **Say:**
- We talked about these words before. Some of these words may have letters whose sounds we can blend. We can blend the sounds in *and.*

Model blending the decodable word *and.* Use the blending model pictured at the left. Then have children blend it with you. Then **say:**
- Some words we have to learn by remembering the letters instead of saying the sounds.

For the non-decodable words, pronounce each non-decodable word, spell it, and then have children pronounce it and spell it.

6

The Nap / Oh, Cats!

Use the Day 2 Routines to practice the phonics skills of the week, to systematically review previously taught phonics skills and high-frequency words, to build fluency, and to expand children's oral language. Use the **Day 2 Routines** through Build Fluency in place of the Phonics Practice Activities in the Teacher's Edition.

Blending Strategy The Blending Strategy routines frequently incorporate the use of letter cards to allow children to manipulate letter-sounds. A "spelling for sounds" activity such as this one requires children to listen to each sound in a word and identify the letter that stands for that sound. This practice contributes to both their reading and spelling success.

Review High-Frequency Words The Instructional Routines include a daily review of the week's five new high-frequency words and a systematic review of previously taught high-frequency words. The Instructional Routines also remind students of the strategies they can use to read decodable words and non-decodable words.

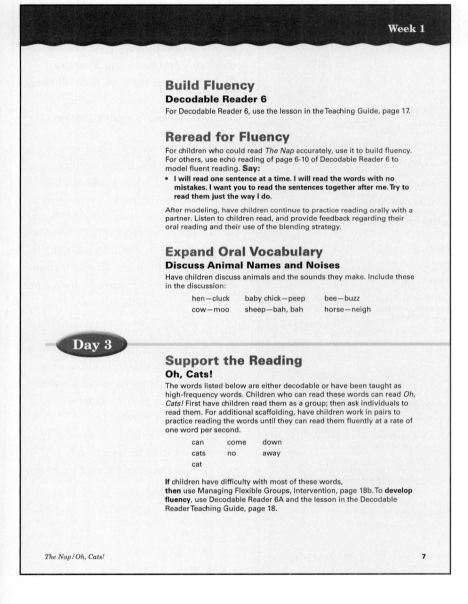

Build Fluency
Decodable Reader 6

For Decodable Reader 6, use the lesson in the Teaching Guide, page 17.

Reread for Fluency

For children who could read *The Nap* accurately, use it to build fluency. For others, use echo reading of page 6-10 of Decodable Reader 6 to model fluent reading. **Say:**

- **I will read one sentence at a time. I will read the words with no mistakes. I want you to read the sentences together after me. Try to read them just the way I do.**

After modeling, have children continue to practice reading orally with a partner. Listen to children read, and provide feedback regarding their oral reading and their use of the blending strategy.

Expand Oral Vocabulary
Discuss Animal Names and Noises

Have children discuss animals and the sounds they make. Include these in the discussion:

hen—cluck	baby chick—peep	bee—buzz
cow—moo	sheep—bah, bah	horse—neigh

Day 3

Support the Reading
Oh, Cats!

The words listed below are either decodable or have been taught as high-frequency words. Children who can read these words can read *Oh, Cats!* First have children read them as a group; then ask individuals to read them. For additional scaffolding, have children work in pairs to practice reading the words until they can read them fluently at a rate of one word per second.

can	come	down
cats	no	away
cat		

If children have difficulty with most of these words, **then** use Managing Flexible Groups, Intervention, page 18b. To **develop fluency**, use Decodable Reader 6A and the lesson in the Decodable Reader Teaching Guide, page 18.

The Nap / Oh, Cats!

7

Build Fluency Use the Decodable Readers instead of the Phonics Readers. The Decodable Readers include a larger number of words to which the phonics skills can be applied—80 to 100 percent—and few or no irregular words, thus providing intensive application of letter-sounds and blending. Lessons for the Decodable Readers appear in the *Decodable Readers Teaching Guide* and in the back of the Teacher's Editions.

Reread for Fluency This routine may replace or may be used in addition to the Day 2 Reread for Fluency activity in the Teacher's Edition. You can help improve children's fluency by modeling fluent reading and by providing guidance and feedback as you monitor their repeated oral readings. Fluency routines like this one appear on Days 2, 3, 4, and 5. Use **Expand Oral Vocabulary** following Reread for Fluency.

Use the Day 3 Routines to provide more support in reading the Main Selection, for guidance in choosing an alternative text, for a cumulative review of phonics skills, and for building fluency.

Support the Reading Use this routine after Build Oral Language and Vocabulary in the Teacher's Edition. It provides scaffolding for reading the Main Selection and will help you identify children who should use a differentiated text. Turn to Reading Strategies in the Teacher's Edition before having children read the story.

Before reading *Oh, Cats!*, introduce the following words: *say, play, jump, be, so.* Children have not learned all the letter-sounds for these words. Point to each word, identify it, spell it, and then have children read it.

Page 21: say, play
Page 30: jump
Page 36: be
Page 37: so

After introducing the words, use the Reading Strategies in the Teacher's Edition and then have children read *Oh, Cats!*
If children have difficulty reading specific words as they read, **then** coach them in blending decodable words or model reading non-decodable words. For example:
- **This word is** *away.* **What's this word?**

Phonemic Awareness
Segment Phonemes
- **Now I'm going to separate the sounds in a word I say.**
- **Listen as I say the word:** *nap.* **Now I will say each sound in** *nap:* **/n/ /a/ /p/. Now say the sounds in** *nap* **with me, /n/, /a/, /p/.**

Have children say the word and segment the sounds in the following words.

cap /k/ /a/ /p/	cat /k/ /a/ /t/	cats /k/ /a/ /t/ /s/
mad /m/ /a/ /d/	bat /b/ /a/ /t/	dad /d/ /a/ /d/

Blending Strategy
Review Consonants *b, f, m, r, s*

To **review consonants**, have children blend the words listed here. Write the words on the board and **say:**
- **I will blend this word. Watch as I point to a letter and listen as I say its sound: /b/, /a/, /ba/, /t/ —** *bat.* **Do it with me: /b/, /a/, /ba/, /t/ —** *bat.*

bag	man	sad	fan	rat	mad
fat	ran	mat	map	sat	Sam

Monitor their use of the blending strategy and coach them as needed.

Review High-Frequency Words
In addition to practicing this week's words, have children review the words *blue, three,* and *yellow.* Write the word *blue* on the board and **say:**
- **Some words we have to learn by remembering the letters instead of saying the sounds.**
- **This word is** *blue.* **The letters in** *blue* **are b-l-u-e.**
- **What is this word?**
- **What are the letters in** *blue?*

8   *The Nap / Oh, Cats!*

Support the Reading Replace the Leveled Readers with Decodable Readers as recommended in the routine to provide more opportunities for children to apply what they are learning about letters and sounds. To use the Main Selection with children, first introduce the non-decodable story vocabulary that is identified for you. This routine also identifies appropriate word-reading strategies for problem words.

The remaining Day 3 Routines should be used in place of the Phonics Practice Activities in the Teacher's Edition.

Phonemic Awareness Activities that practice segmenting sounds help children hear individual sounds in words and improve their spelling.

Blending Strategy A systematic review of phonics skills and word structure skills appears on Days 1 through 4 in a Blending Strategy and/or a Review Word Parts routine.

Review High-Frequency Words Routines for both non-decodable and decodable high-frequency words continue each day to help children achieve automaticity with these words.

Follow the same steps for *three* and *yellow*. Pronounce each word, spell it, then have children pronounce it and spell it.

Reread for Fluency
Decodable Reader 6
Say:
- I am going to read this story aloud. I will read the words with no mistakes. I want you to read it aloud with me. Try to read the words just as I do.

Use your oral reading to model for children where to pause, when to change pitch, and which words to stress. Then have children reread orally three to four times, or until they can read with few or no mistakes.

Day 4

Phonemic Awareness
Add Phonemes
Say:
- We've been learning how to say the sounds in words. Now we're going to learn how to make new words by adding sounds.
- Listen as I add /p/ to the beginning of the word *at*. When I add /p/ to /at/, I get *pat*.
- Now I'll add /s/ to the beginning of the word *am*. When I add /s/ to /am/, I get *Sam*.
- Add /t/ to the beginning of *an*. (tan)
- Add /f/ to the beginning of *it*. (fit)
- Add /s/ to the beginning of *it*. (sit)
- Add /h/ to the beginning of *is*. (his)

If children cannot remember the sequence of sounds, **then** add letters to the activity to help them manipulate sounds.

Blending Strategy
Review Initial Consonants *c*/k/, *g*/g/, *n*, *p*, *t*
Write *tag* on the board and **say:**
- I will blend this word. Watch as I point to a letter and listen as I say its sound: /t/, /a/, /ta/, /g/ —*tag*. Do it with me: /t/, /a/, /ta/, /g/ —*tag*.

Write these words on the board and have children blend them. Monitor their use of the blending strategy and coach them as needed.

t	a	g

cat	gal	nag
pan	tam	cap

The Nap/Oh, Cats!

9

Reread for Fluency Use the Decodable Reader instead of the Phonics Reader to provide the most practice with the letter-sounds children are learning.

Use the **Day 4 Routines** to practice the phonics skills of the week, to systematically review previously taught phonics skills and high-frequency words, to build fluency, and to expand children's oral language. Use the Day 4 Routines before using the Phonics lesson in the Teacher's Edition.

Review High-Frequency Words

In addition to practicing this week's words, have children review the words *blue*, *at*, and *can*. **Say:**

• **We talked about these words before. Some of these words may have letters whose sounds we can blend. We can blend the sounds in *at* and *can*.**

Model blending the words *at* and *can*. Then have children blend them with you. Then **say:**

• **Some words we have to learn by remembering the letters instead of saying the sounds.**

For the non-decodable word *blue*, pronounce the word, spell it, and then have children pronounce it and spell it.

Reread for Fluency

For children who could accurately read *Oh, Cats!*, use it to build fluency. For others, use Decodable Reader 6A in place of *Oh, Cats!* **Say:**

• **I will read one sentence at a time. I will read just the way I speak. I want you to read each sentence together after me. Try to read just as if you are speaking.**

Use your oral reading to model reading with an appropriate rate. Then have children take turns reading orally with a partner. Listen to them read, and provide feedback regarding their oral reading and their use of the blending strategy.

Expand Oral Vocabulary
What Cats Can Do

Have children discuss what cats can do. Have them tell about the cats they have seen doing these things.

run	meow	purr	play	slide
eat	climb	jump	hide	

Day 5

Ongoing Assessment
Word Reading

Use these words to assess children's ability to read words with short *a* and final consonants *n, t, d, p, g, m:*

ran	mat	rag	lad
fad	rap	Pam	tag

If children cannot read the words,
then use the **Reteach** lessons for Short *a* and/or Final Consonants on page AR11 of the Teacher's Edition.

10   *The Nap / Oh, Cats!*

Reread for Fluency This routine continues the recommended practices for improving fluency: teacher modeling and monitoring of children's repeated oral readings. Choose the appropriate text for children to practice. Four rereadings are sufficient for most children to improve significantly their fluency with a text.

Expand Oral Vocabulary Children who understand words orally can connect meanings to print more readily. Routines for expanding children's oral vocabulary appear on Days 2 and 4 of the Instructional Routines. Use this routine after completing the day's phonics instruction. (Similar oral vocabulary lessons in the Teacher's Edition should be used on Days 1 and 3.)

The primary purpose of the Day 5 Routines is to monitor children's progress. Use the Ongoing Assessments for Word Reading and Fluency instead of Assess Oral Reading on Day 5 of the Teacher's Edition.

Ongoing Assessment: Word Reading Word reading assesses children's ability to apply their knowledge of the week's phonics elements. This assessment must be conducted one-on-one. Write the tested words on flashcards or in a list. The assessment contains at least four items for each letter-sound to be assessed. Record children's progress on the blackline master that appears on page xxiii. Reteaching for these phonics skills can be found in the back of each Teacher's Edition.

Ongoing Assessment

Fluency

Materials Children should read grade-level text that they have not practiced. This text should be similar in difficulty to the selections children have practiced this week. Assess fluency by taking a timed sample of the child's oral reading; record the number of words read correctly per minute. See Monitoring Fluency page xxi.

Spelling

Segment Phonemes

When administering the Spelling Test, use only the first six words: *sat, at, am, cat, ran,* and *man.* Encourage children to segment sounds as they spell.

Review High-Frequency Words

In addition to practicing this week's words, have children review *the, a, look,* and *my.* Write the word *the* on the board and **say:**

- **Some words we have to learn by remembering the letters instead of saying the sounds.**
- **This word is *the*. The letters in *the* are t-h-e.**
- **What is this word?**
- **What are the letters in *the*?**

Continue the activity with *a, look,* and *my.* Pronounce each word, spell it, and then have children pronounce it and spell it.

Build Fluency

Repeated Readings

Have children practice reading aloud Take-Home Decodable Reader 6 and/or 6A with a partner before taking it home. Children should reread the text three to four times for optimal fluency.

The Nap/Oh, Cats!

11

Ongoing Assessment: Fluency It is important to assess fluency to be sure children are making appropriate progress. Directions for monitoring fluency appear on page xxi and in the Teacher's Edition on page AR22. Use the blackline master on page xxii to record children's reading growth. By the end of first grade, children should be able to read approximately sixty words per minute correctly.

Spelling The first six spelling words each week reflect one of the week's target phonics skills so that children are learning to write the same letter-sounds they are learning to read. It is recommended that you test just those first six words. Segmenting routines that appear throughout the week will help children prepare for the spelling test.

Build Fluency Use the Take-Home Decodable Readers for repeated readings instead of the Take-Home Phonics Reader. To demonstrate their reading skill at home, children should take home a copy of a selection that they have been reading during the week.

Monitoring Fluency

To assess fluency formally, take timed samples of children's oral reading and measure the number of words read correctly per minute. By the end of first grade, children should be able to read approximately forty to sixty words correctly per minute on unpracticed, grade-level texts.

How to Measure Words Correct Per Minute Choose two or three texts for the child to read. The texts should be narrative, not informational or expository. Make copies for yourself. Have the child read each text aloud to you for one minute. Follow along in your copy of the text, marking words that are read incorrectly. Self-corrections are counted as correct; omissions, substitutions, and mispronunciations are counted as incorrect. At the end of one minute, draw a line after the last word that was read. Repeat this process with the remaining texts. Then count the total number of correct words the child read in each text and compute the average number of words correct per minute for all passages read. Use the Fluency Progress Chart on the following page to record each child's progress. Repeat this process periodically to monitor growth.

Setting Fluency Goals A first-grade child who is reading 20 words correctly per minute at week 15 will have to gain an additional 40 words per minute by the end of the school year. To reach the target of 60 words correct per minute, a child must increase his or her oral reading rate by 2.6 correct words per minute per week.

Children who significantly exceed the goals that have been set do not have to be monitored as frequently and, instead, that time should be allocated to more complex skills and strategies such as comprehension. For those children who read significantly below the goals that have been set, confirm that they are using text that they can read with 90 to 95 percent accuracy.

Monitoring Word Reading

The Day 5 Ongoing Assessment for word reading includes four to eight items for each phonics skill to be assessed that week. Display the words on flashcards or in a list. Have the child read the words aloud to you. Use the Word Reading Chart on page xxiii to record the number of words read correctly for each phonics skills. If a child cannot read the words, use the Reteach lesson for that phonics skill. Reteach lessons are found at the back of the Teacher's Editions. After reteaching, assess the child's word reading again.

Name_____

Fluency Progress Chart, Grade 1

Words Correct Per Minute (vertical axis): 100, 95, 90, 85, 80, 75, 70, 65, 60, 55, 50, 45, 40, 35, 30, 25, 20, 15, 10, 5

Timed Reading (horizontal axis): 1, 2, 3, 4, 5, 6, 7, 8, 9, 10, 11, 12, 13, 14, 15, 16, 17, 18, 19, 20, 21, 22, 23, 24, 25, 26, 27, 28, 29, 30

Note to the Teacher Use this chart to monitor children's progress on the Day 5 Fluency Assessment.

Name_____

Word Reading Chart   Unit 5

	Total Words	Words Correct	Reteach ✔	Reassess: Words Correct
Week 1				
Long *e: ea*	4			
Ending *-ed* (double final consonant)	4			
Week 2				
Long *a: ai*	4			
Long *a: ay*	4			
Contractions	4			
Week 3				
Long *o: oa*	4			
Long *o: ow*	4			
Ending *-ing* (double final consonant)	5			
Week 4				
Long *i: ie*	4			
Long *i: igh*	4			
Singular Possessives	4			
Week 5				
Long *i: y*	4			
Long *e: y*	4			
Compound Words	4			
Week 6				
Vowel Pattern *ew*	4			
Vowel Pattern *ue*	4			
Ending *-es*	4			

Note to the Teacher Use this chart to monitor children's progress on the Day 5 Word Reading Assessment.

Reading First

5-Day Instructional Plan

Instructional Routines

See the **Reading First Instructional Routines for Unit 5, Week 1,** pages 4–11 for daily Routines in
- Working with Phonemes
- Using Blending Strategies
- Building Fluency
- Expanding Vocabulary

Day 1

Activate Prior Knowledge p. 10j
Big Book *Rabbits and Raindrops*

Phonics pp. 10k–10l

Instructional Routines
- Phonemic Awareness

Connect Sounds to Letters
Long *e: ea*
Inflected Ending *-ed*

Instructional Routines
- Connect Sound to Letter
- Blending Strategy

Spelling: Inflected Ending *-ed* Words
ask   call   clean
asked   called   cleaned

High-Frequency Words
buy   only   or   right   think

Instructional Routines
- High-Frequency Words

Reading pp. 10m–17
Build Oral Language Vocabulary
people   soft   signs

Instructional Routines
- Support the Reading

Reading Strategies
Read the Phonics Story
A Real Gift

Oral Language p. 17a
Expand Vocabulary: Discuss Multiple-Meaning Words

Writing pp. 17a–17b
Shared Writing: List
- List Gifts You Appreciate
- Independent Writing

Handwriting: *Zz*

Read Aloud, p. 17b
Read aloud *Don't Tease the Guppies* by Pat Lowery Collins.

Day 2

Phonics pp. 17c–17d

Long *e: ea*
Inflected Ending *-ed*
Phonics Practice Activities

Instructional Routines
- Blending Strategy
- Review Phonics
- Review High-Frequency Words

Use Decodable Reader 33 instead of the Phonics Reader.
Use Teaching Guide, p. 53.
- Build Fluency

Spelling: Inflected Ending *-ed* Words

High-Frequency Words

Reading pp. 17e–17f
Comprehension: Predicting Listening Comprehension
- Read Aloud "The Ice-Cream Problem"

Instructional Routines
- Reread for Fluency *A Real Gift* or Decodable Reader 33
- Expand Oral Vocabulary

Oral Language p. 17g
Speaking: Retell a Story
Discuss a Movie, Play, or TV Show

Writing pp. 17g–17h
Modeled Writing: Take a Stand
Write to Take a Stand
- Independent Writing

Grammar: Adjectives (Describing Words)

Read Aloud, p. 17h
Read aloud *Not the Piano, Mrs. Medley* by Evan Levine.

Day 3

Reading pp. 18a–41

Build Oral Language

Vocabulary

almost	curb	prove
bought	eight	shook
could	paint	spy

Instructional Routines

- Support the Reading
Use Leveled Reader 19A.

Reading Strategies
Read *Arthur's Reading Race*
Comprehension: Predicting
Flexible Groups, p. 18b

Use Leveled-Reader 19A.

Use the Teacher's Edition, pp. LR1–LR2

Phonics pp. 41a–41b

Long *e: ea*
Inflected Ending -*ed*

Instructional Routines

- Phonemic Awareness
- Blending Strategy
- Review High-Frequency Words

Use Decodable Reader 33 instead
of the Phonics Reader.

- Reread for Fluency

Review Phonics: Long *o* (CVCe)
Spelling: Inflected Ending -*ed* Words

High-Frequency Words

Oral Language p. 41c

Expand Vocabulary: Identify and Use
Multiple-Meaning Words

Writing pp. 41c–41d
Modeled Writing: Write About a
Movie, Play, or TV Show
- Independent Writing
- Peer Conference
Grammar: Adjectives
(Describing Words)

Read Aloud, p. 41d
Read aloud *Night City* by Monica
Wellington.

Day 4

Reading pp. 42–43

Reader Response
Leveled Practice, Easy, *Leveled
Practice and Test Link,* p. 55
Review: Plot

Instructional Routines

- Phonemic Awareness
- Review Word Parts
- Review High-Frequency Words
- Reread for Fluency *Arthur's Reading
Race* or Decodable Reader 33

Phonics pp. 43a–43b

Long *e: ea*
Inflected Ending -*ed*
Reteach
Review Compound Words
Spelling: Inflected Ending -*ed* Words

High-Frequency Words

Oral Language pp. 44–45

Instructional Routines

- Expand Oral Vocabulary

Language Arts

Grammar: Adjectives
(Describing Words)

Speaking: Talk About Adjectives

Writing pp. 44–45
Grammar: Adjectives
(Describing Words)

Writing: Identify Adjectives

Study Skill: Map

Read Aloud, p. 44
Read aloud *You Can Learn Sign
Language!* by Jackie Kramer.

Day 5

Reading pp. 45a–45b

Assess Oral Reading
Prepare for the Assessment

Instructional Routines

- Use the Ongoing Assessments
instead of the Oral Reading
Checklist.
- Word Reading
- Fluency

Comprehension Check, p. 45a

Phonics p. 45c

Long *e: ea*
Inflected Ending -*ed*
Phonics Practice Activities

Instructional Routines

- Spelling
- Review High-Frequency Words

Use Take-Home Decodable Reader
33 instead of the Phonics
Take-Home Reader.

- Build Fluency

Oral Language p. 45d
Speaking: Retell a Story

Writing p. 45d
Interactive Writing: Poster
Make a Poster

- Independent Writing
- Portfolio

Read Aloud, p. 45d
Ask children for a favorite book
you have shared with them and
read it aloud.

Instructional Routines

A Real Gift *and* Arthur's Reading Race

Teacher's Edition, pages 10i–45d

Day 1

If children cannot remember the sequence of sounds, **then** add letters to the activity to help them manipulate sounds.

Phonemic Awareness
Substitute Medial Phonemes
Say:

- Today we are going to make new words by changing the middle sound.
- Listen as I say the sounds in *tame,* /t/ /ā/ /m/. Now listen as I change the /ā/ in *tame* to /ē/. /t/ /ē/ /m/, *team.*
- Now I will take /a/ from *cram,* and change it to /ē/. The word I get is *cream.*
- Change /e/ in *Ben* to /ē/. (bean)
- Change /e/ in *peck* to /ē/. (peak)
- Change /ō/ in *woke* to /ē/. (weak)
- Change /ā/ in *snake* to /ē/. (sneak)
- Change /ō/ in *mole* to /ē/. (meal)

If children need additional instruction for long *e* spelled *ea,* **then** use the Connect Sound to Letters routine at the right.

Connect Sound to Letters
Introduce Long *e: ea*

Write the word *team.* **Say:**

- Listen as I blend the sounds in this word, /t/ /ē/ /m/—*team.*
- The letters *ea* often stand for the sound /ē/.
- What sound do you hear in the middle of *team?* (/ē/)
- Now blend the sounds with me, /t/ /ē/ /m/—*team.*

Continue modeling with *bean.* Then have children blend the sounds for *meat, cheap, beat, eat, tea, peach, treat,* and *clean.* Remind them that the letters *ea* often stand for the /ē/ sound.

Review Word Parts
Inflected Ending *–ed*

Write the sentence *He treated us all well.* Have the sentence read. Remind children that endings are sometimes added to words, and have them find the word that has an ending. **Say:**

- The word *treated* has an ending. If I cover up the *–ed* ending, I see that the base word is *treat.* I can read the base word with its ending: *treat, -ed, treated.*

Write the sentence *Tom tapped the drum.* Have the sentence read. Remind children that endings are sometimes added to words, and have them find the word that has an ending. **Say:**

A Real Gift/Arthur's Reading Race

- The word *tapped* has an ending. What ending does it have? (-ed)
- In the word *tapped,* the last consonant, *p,* is doubled before *–ed* is added. Many words have this spelling change before an ending is added.
- To read a word like this I cover up the added consonant and the ending to see what the base word is.
- Now I can read the base word with its ending: *tap, ped, tapped.*

Continue modeling with *hugged.* Then call on children to read these words, point out the ending, and frame the base word. Use the following words: *packed, jumped, hopped, tripped, cleaned, begged, grinned.* Have them identify the words in which the last consonant is doubled before *–ed* is added. If children have difficulty reading the base words, then coach them in blending.

High-Frequency Words

To teach the words *buy, or, only, think,* and *right,* **say:**

- We talked about these words before. Some words we have to learn by remembering the letters rather than saying the sounds. Some of these words may have letters whose sounds we can blend. We can blend the sounds in *think.*

Model blending the decodable word *think.* Then have children blend it with you. For the non-decodable words *buy, or, only,* and *right,* pronounce each word, spell it, have children pronounce it, and have children spell it.

Support the Reading

A Real Gift

The words listed below are either decodable or have been taught as high-frequency words. Children who can read these words can read *A Real Gift.* First ask children to read them as a group; then call on individuals to read them.

real	petted	right	or
reads	stopped	buy	walked
speak	passed	only	

If children have difficulty with many of these words,
then coach them in blending decodable words, or model the strategy for non-decodable words. Have them work in pairs to practice reading the words until they can read then fluently at the rate of one word per second.

Before reading *A Real Gift,* introduce the following words: *country, school, loud, mind, sounds, hard, signs, doctor's.* Children have not learned all the letter-sounds for these words. Point to each word, identify it, and then have children point to it and read it.

Page 11:   country, school, loud, mind, sounds, hard

Page 12:   signs

Page 17:   doctor's

After introducing the words, use the Reading Strategies in the Teacher's Edition and then have children read *A Real Gift.*

If children have difficulty reading specific words as they read, **then** coach them in blending decodable words, or model reading non-decodable words. For example, **say:**

- **This word is *something.* What is this word?**

Day 2

Blending Strategy
Phonics Review

To practice this week's letter-sounds, have children make these words using the letter cards from the Small Group Manipulatives Package. Have children segment each word to spell it. Have them blend each word to read it.

seat	treat
flea	lean
leaf	clean
pea	dream

Review Phonics
Long *a, i, o, u* (CVCe)

Write these words on the board and have children blend them. Use the blending model at the left. Remind children that the *e* at the end of a word makes the vowel say its name.

wave	hide	those
cube	fame	froze
kite	fuse	smile

Monitor their use of the blending strategy, and coach them as needed.

Review High-Frequency Words

In addition to practicing this week's words, have children review the words *after, as, call, laugh.* First model blending the decodable word *as.* Then have children blend it with you. **Say:**

- **Some words we have to learn by remembering the letters rather than saying the sounds.**

For the non-decodable words *after, call,* and *laugh,* pronounce each word, spell it, then have children pronounce it and spell it.

Build Fluency

Decodable Reader 33

For Decodable Reader 33, use the lesson in the Teaching Guide, page 53.

Reread for Fluency

For children who could read *A Real Gift* accurately, use it to build fluency. For others, use Decodable Reader 33 to model fluent reading. **Say:**

- **I will read this story. I want you to read the sentences together after me. I am going to read with expression. Try to read just the way I do.**

Use your oral reading to model expressive reading, showing the excitement of the story characters. Then have children practice reading the story orally with a partner. Listen to children read, and provide feedback regarding their oral reading and their use of the blending strategy.

Expand Oral Vocabulary

Discuss Multiple-Meaning Words

Write the sentence pairs below. Discuss the two meanings of the underlined words.

> The dog was in a backyard <u>pen</u>.
> That <u>pen</u> has blue ink.
> Stepping on a flower will <u>squash</u> it.
> We had <u>squash</u> for dinner.
> The play will <u>last</u> two hours.
> I was <u>last</u> in line.
> Dan is a sports <u>fan</u>.
> A <u>fan</u> cooled the room.

Day 3

Support the Reading

Arthur's Reading Race

The words listed below are either decodable or have been taught as high-frequency words. Children who can read these words can read *Arthur's Reading Race*. First have children read them as a group; then ask individuals to read them. For additional scaffolding, have children work in pairs to practice reading words until they can read them fluently at the rate of one word per second.

read	eat	stepped	buy
teach	cream	asked	right
deal		laughed	only

If children have difficulty with most of these words, **then** use Managing Flexible Groups, Intervention, page 18b. To **develop fluency**, use Leveled Reader 19A and the lesson in the Teacher's Edition, pages LR1–LR2.

Before reading *Arthur's Reading Race*, introduce the following words: *learned, sister, already, pointed, easy, pie, money, today, strawberry, chocolate*. Children have not learned all the letter-sounds for these words. Point to each word, identify it, and then have children point to it and read it.

Page 19:	learned
Page 21:	sister
Page 22:	already, pointed, easy, pie
Page 33:	money
Page 34:	today
Page 37:	strawberry, chocolate

After introducing the words, use the Reading Strategies in the Teacher's Edition and then have children read *Arthur's Reading Race*.

If children have difficulty reading specific words as they read, **then** coach them in blending decodable words, or model reading non-decodable words. For example, say:
- **This word is *sister*. What's this word?**

Phonemic Awareness
Substitute Medial Phonemes
Say:
- **Today we are going to make new words by changing the middle sound.**
- **Listen as I say the sounds in *rob*, /r/ /o/ /b/. Now listen as I change the /o/ in *rob* to /ō/: /r/ /ō/ /b/, *robe*.**
- **Change the /o/ in *tot* to /ō/. (tote)**
- **Change the /o/ in *rod* to /ō/. (rode)**
- **Change the /o/ in *hop* to /ō/. (hope)**
- **Change the /o/ in *cod* to /ō/. (code)**
- **Change the /o/ in *not* to /ō/. (note)**

If children cannot remember the sequence of sounds, **then** add letters to the activity to help them manipulate sounds.

Blending Strategy
Review Long and Short Vowels (CVCe, CVC)
To **review long and short vowels (CVCe, CVC)**, have children blend the words listed here. Use the blending model for *globe*. Coach them in blending as needed.

globe	glob	huge	hug
hope	hop	cute	cut
spine	spin	scrape	scrap
slate	slat	quite	quit

Review High-Frequency Words

In addition to practicing this week's words, have children review the words *something*, *every*, *made*, and *mother*. First model blending the decodable word *made*. Then have children blend it with you. For the non-decodable words, **say:**

- **Some words we have to learn by remembering the letters rather than saying the sounds.**

Pronounce each word, spell it, then have children pronounce it and spell it.

Reread for Fluency
Decodable Reader 33
Say:

- **I will read one sentence at a time. I will read the words with no mistakes. I want you to read the sentences together after me. Try to read them just as I do.**

Then Have children reread orally three or four times, or until they can read the story with few or no mistakes.

Day 4

Phonemic Awareness
Add Initial Phonemes
Say:

- **Listen as I say the sounds in *eat*, /ē/ /t/. Now listen as I add /b/ to the beginning of *eat*: /b/ /ē/ /t/ . What is the word? (beat)**
- **Add /m/ to *eat*: /m/ /ē/ /t/. What's the word? (meat)**
- **Add /s/ to *eat*: /s/ /ē/ /t/. What's the word? (seat)**
- **Now I will say the sounds in *each*, /ē/ /ch/. Listen as I add /t/ to the beginning of *each*: /t/ /ē/ /ch/. What is the word? (teach)**
- **Add /b/ to *each*: /b/ /ē/ /ch/. What's the word? (beach)**
- **Add /r/ to *each*: /r/ /ē/ /ch/. What's the word? (reach)**

Review Word Parts
Compound Words
To **review compound words**, write *cupcake* on the board. **Say:**

- **This is a compound word. I can see two smaller words in *cupcake*: *cup* and *cake*.**

Draw a line through *cup/cake* on the board. **Say:**

- When I see a compound word, first I read the two smaller words. Then I blend them together to read the whole word.
- I can blend each part, /k/ /u/ /p/ *cup* and /k/ /ā/ /k/ *cake*. Do it with me: /k/ /u/ /p/ *cup* and /k/ /ā/ /k/ *cake*. Now blend the two parts together: /k/ /u/ /p/ /k/ /ā/ /k/ *cupcake*.

Continue the activity with these words: *beanbag, weekend, sunrise, meatball, teapot, seashell,* and *mealtime*. If children have difficulty in decoding these word parts, then coach them in blending.

Review High-Frequency Words

In addition to practicing this week's words, have children review the non-decodable words *of, was, father,* and *going*. **Say:**

- **Some words we have to learn by remembering the letters rather than saying the sounds.**

Pronounce each word, spell it, then have children pronounce it and spell it.

Reread for Fluency

For children who could accurately read *Arthur's Reading Race,* use it to build fluency. For others, use Leveled Reader 19A. **Say:**

- **I will read one page at a time. I will read just the way I speak. I want you to read each page together after me. Try to read just as if you are speaking.**

Use your oral reading to model reading with an appropriate rate. Then have children practice reading the story orally with a partner. Listen to them read, and provide feedback regarding their oral reading and their use of the blending strategy.

Then conduct three or four timed one-minute readings of the first four pages. Have children reread with the goal of reading more words with fewer errors in each successive reading.

Expand Oral Vocabulary
Discuss Multiple-Meaning Words

Write these words on the board and have children choose a word that will work in two sentences you read: *fall, bee, sink, fall, rose.*

Put the dishes in the _____.
Our feet will _____ in that mud.

A _____ buzzed around the flower.
We had a spelling _____ at school.

Steam _____ from the kettle.
Dad gave Mom a _____ for Valentine's Day.

School starts in the _____.
Don't trip on that rug and _____.

Day 5

Ongoing Assessment
Word Reading

Use these words to assess children's ability to read words with long *e* (ea) and inflected ending *–ed*.

peach	dream	shopped	planned
jeans	steal	grabbed	petted

If children cannot read the words,
then use the **Reteach** lessons for Long *e* (ea) and/or Inflected Ending *-ed* on page AR11 of the Teacher's Edition.

Ongoing Assessment
Fluency

Materials Children should read grade-level text that they have not practiced. This text should be similar in difficulty to the selections children have practiced this week.

Assess fluency by taking a timed sample of the child's oral reading; record the number of words read correctly per minute. See Monitoring Fluency, page xxi.

Spelling
Segment Phonemes

When administering the Spelling Test, use only the first six words: *clean, asked, call, cleaned, ask, called*. Encourage children to segment sounds as they spell.

Review High-Frequency Words

In addition to practicing this week's words, have children review the words *has, thank, very, be*. First model blending the decodable words *has, thank*, and *be*. Then have children blend them with you. Then **say:**

• **Some words we have to learn by remembering the letters rather than saying the sounds.**

For the non-decodable word *very*, pronounce it, spell it, then have children pronounce it and spell it.

Build Fluency
Repeated Readings

Have children practice reading aloud the Take-Home Decodable Reader 33 with a partner before taking it home. Children should reread the text three to four times for optimal fluency.

Reading First

5-Day Instructional Plan

Key to Instruction in

Phonemic Awareness

Phonics

Fluency

Vocabulary

Text Comprehension

Instructional Routines

See the **Reading First Instructional Routines for Unit 5, Week 2,** pages 14–21 for daily Routines in
- Working with Phonemes
- Using Blending Strategies
- Building Fluency
- Expanding Vocabulary

Day 1

Activate Prior Knowledge p. 46j
Song "Oh Where, O Where . . . ."
Phonics pp. 46k–46l

Instructional Routines
- Phonemic Awareness

Connect Sounds to Letters
Long *a: ai, ay*
Contractions

Instructional Routines
- Connect Sound to Letter
- Blending Strategy

Spelling: Long *a: ai, ay*
say	may	wait
play	way	rain

High-Frequency Words
don't	from	hear	live	when

Instructional Routines
- High-Frequency Words

Reading pp. 46m–53
Build Oral Language Vocabulary
noisy	knew	found
crowded	opened	

Instructional Routines
- Support the Reading

Reading Strategies
Read the Phonics Story *A Big Day for Jay*

Oral Language p. 53a
Expand Vocabulary: Discuss Words That Have Opposite Meanings

Writing pp. 53a–17b
Shared Writing: List
- List Ways to Stay Safe
- Independent Writing

Handwriting: *Yy*

Read Aloud, p. 53b
Read aloud *First Flight* by David McPhail.

Day 2

Phonics pp. 53c–53d
Long *a: ai, ay*
Contractions
Phonics Practice Activities

Instructional Routines
- Blending Strategy
- Review Word Parts
- Review High-Frequency Words

Use Decodable Reader 34 instead of the Phonics Reader.
Use Teaching Guide, p. 54.
- Build Fluency

Spelling: Long *a* Words

High-Frequency Words

Reading pp. 53e–53f
Comprehension: Compare and Contrast
Listening Comprehension
- Read Aloud "Do Animals Get Lost?"

Instructional Routines
- Reread for Fluency *A Big Day for Jay* or Decodable Reader 34
- Expand Oral Vocabulary

Oral Language p. 53g
Speaking: Discuss How to Solve a Problem
What Shoud You Do When You Get Lost?

Writing pp. 53g–53h
Modeled Writing: Interesting Sentences
Write About Getting Lost
- Independent Writing

Grammar: Adjectives That Tell Color and Shape

Read Aloud, p. 53h
Read aloud *Angus, Lost* by Marjorie Flack.

Day 3

Reading pp. 54a–81

Build Oral Language
Vocabulary

across	crying	library
buildings	disappears	through
climbed	hurt	worry

Instructional Routines

- Support the Reading
Use Decodable Reader 35 instead
of Leveled Reader 20A.

Reading Strategies
Read *Lost!*
Comprehension: Compare and
Contrast
Flexible Groups, p. 54b

Decodable Reader 35
and Teaching Guide, p 55.

Phonics pp. 81a–81b

Long *a: ai, ay*
Contractions

Instructional Routines

- Phonemic Awareness
- Blending Strategy
- Review High-Frequency Words

Use Decodable Reader 34 instead
of the Phonics Reader.

- Reread for Fluency

Review Phonics: Long Vowels (CVCe)
Spelling: Long *a: ai, ay* Words

High-Frequency Words

Oral Language p. 81c

Expand Vocabulary: Antonyms

Writing pp. 81c–81d

Modeled Writing: Description of a
Story Illustration
- Independent Writing
- Peer Conference
Grammar: Adjectives that Tell Color
and Shape

Read Aloud, p. 81d,
Mrs. Potter's Pig by Phyllis Root.

Day 4

Reading pp. 82–83

Reader Response
Leveled Practice, Easy, *Leveled
Practice and Test Link,* p. 58
Review: Setting

Instructional Routines

- Phonemic Awareness
- Review Phonics
- Review High-Frequency Words
- Reread for Fluency *Lost!*
or Decodable Reader 35.

Phonics pp. 83a–83b

Long *a: ai, ay*
Contractions
Reteach
Review Initial Digraphs
Spelling: Long: *a: ai, ay* Words

High-Frequency Words

Oral Language pp. 84–85

Instructional Routines

- Expand Oral Vocabulary

Language Arts

Grammar: Adjectives That Tell
Color and Shape
Speaking: Talk About Adjectives

Writing p. 84–85

Grammar: Adjectives That Tell
Color and Shape
Writing: Identify Adjectives That
Tell Color and Shape

Study Skill: Glossary: Guide Words

Read Aloud, p. 84
Read aloud *Make Way for Ducklings*
by Robert McCloskey.

Day 5

Reading pp. 85a–85b

Assess Accuracy and Comprehension
Prepare for the Assessment

Instructional Routines

- Use the Ongoing Assessments
instead of the Accuracy and
Comprehension Assessment.
- Word Reading
- Fluency

To **Check Comprehension,** use
Listen to Individual Readers, p. 85a.

Phonics p. 85c

Long *a: ai, ay*
Contractions
Phonics Practice Activities

Instructional Routines

- Spelling
- Review High-Frequency Words

Use Take-Home Decodable Reader
34 and/or 35 instead of the Phonics
Take-Home Reader.

- Build Fluency

Oral Language p. 85d

Speaking: Discuss How to Solve
a Problem

Writing p. 85d

Interactive Writing: Postcard

- Independent Writing
- Portfolio

Read Aloud, p. 85d
Ask children for a favorite book
you have shared with them and
read it aloud.

Instructional Routines

A Big Day for Jay *and* Lost!

Teacher's Edition, pages 46i–85d

Day 1

Phonemic Awareness

Segment Phonemes

Say:

- Listen as I say each sound in *tail*. I will say the word slowly to hear all the sounds: /t/ /ā/ /l/. Say it with me: /t/ /ā/ /l/.
- Now I will say each sound in *stay:* /s/ /t/ /ā/. Say it with me: /s/ /t/ /ā/.
- Say each sound in *main*. (/m/ /ā/ /n/)
- Say each sound in *trail*. (/t/ /r/ /ā/ /l/)
- Say each sound in *day*. (/d/ /ā/)
- Say each sound in *play*. (/p/ /l/ /ā/)
- Say each sound in *maid*. (/m/ /ā/ /d/)

Connect Sound to Letters

Introduce Long *a*: *ai, ay*

Write the word *tail*. **Say:**

- Listen as I say the sounds in this word, /t/ /ā/ /l/—*tail*.
- The letters *ai* stand for the long *a* sound, /ā/.
- What sound do you hear in the middle of *tail*? (/ā/)
- Now blend the sounds with me, /t/ /ā/ /l/—*tail*.

Write the word *day* on the board and point to the letters. **Say:**

- Say each sound with me, /d/ /ā/.
- Yes, now blend the sounds with me, /d/ /ā/—*day*.
- The letters *ay* stand for the long *a* sound, /ā/.
- The letters *ai* and *ay* can stand for the long *a* sound, /ā/.

Have children blend the sounds for *main, fail, paid, trail, rail, maid; stay, tray, stray, say, hay; afraid, explain, someday*. Remind them that the letters *ai* and *ay* can stand for the long *a* sound.

If children need additional instruction for long *a* spelled *ai, ay*,

then use the Connect Sound to Letters routine at the right.

Review Word Parts
Contractions
Write the following contractions on the board and have children tell what two words each contraction takes the place of.

can't (cannot)	didn't (did not)	isn't (is not)
don't (do not)	I'll (I will)	let's (let us)
I'm (I am)	it's (it is)	he's (he is)
won't (will not)	aren't (are not)	

High-Frequency Words

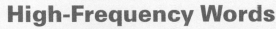

To teach the words *from, don't, hear, when, live* (/liv/ and /līv/), **say:**

- **We talked about these words before. Some words we have to learn by remembering the letters rather than saying the sounds. Some of these words may have letters whose sounds we can blend. We can blend the sounds in *when*.**

Model blending the decodable words *when* and *live* (/līv/). Then have children blend them with you. For the non-decodable words *from, don't,* and *live* (/liv/), pronounce each word, spell it, have children pronounce it, and have children spell it.

Support the Reading
A Big Day for Jay
The words listed below are either decodable or have been taught as high-frequency words. Children who can read these words can read *A Big Day for Jay*. First ask children to read them as a group; then call on individuals to read them.

wait	today	can't	when
afraid	okay	it's	hear
Jay		let's	live

If children have difficulty with many of these words,
then coach them in blending decodable words or model the strategy for non-decodable words. Have them work in pairs to practice reading the words until they can read them fluently at the rate of one word per second.

Before reading *A Big Day for Jay*, introduce the following words: *Fire Dragon, jars, cow, police officer, opened.* Children have not learned all the letter-sounds for these words. Point to each word, identify it, spell it, and then have children read it.

Page 46:   Fire Dragon

Page 47:   jars

Page 48:   cow

Page 51:   police officer

Page 53:   opened

After introducing the words, use the Reading Strategies in the Teacher's Edition and then have children read *A Big Day for Jay*.

If children have difficulty reading specific words as they read, **then** coach them in blending decodable words, or model reading non-decodable words. For example, **say:**

• **This word is** *from*. **What is this word?**

Day 2

Blending Strategy
Phonics Review

Write these words on the board and have children blend them. Use the blending model at the left.

stain	may	team	week
meet	we	be	clay
paid	chain	ray	peak
free	clean	she	seed

Monitor their use of the blending strategy, and coach them as needed.

Review Word Parts
Contractions

Write these words on the board and have children point out the apostrophe. Then have them tell the two words that each contraction stands for.

let's (let us)	can't (cannot)	didn't (did not)
it's (it is)	I'll (I will)	she's (she is)

Review High-Frequency Words

In addition to practicing this week's words, have children review the non-decodable words *our*, *walk*, *who*. Pronounce each word, spell it, then have children pronounce it and spell it.

Build Fluency

Decodable Reader 34

For Decodable Reader 34, use the lesson in the Teaching Guide, page 54.

Reread for Fluency

For children who could read *A Big Day for Jay* accurately, use it to build fluency. For others, use Decodable Reader 34. First turn to page 27. **Say:**

*   **I will read this story. I want you to read the sentences together after me. I am going to read with expression. Try to read just the way I do.**

Then model reading the rest of the story. Then have children practice reading using Readers Theater: One child reads the narrator's part while the other children read the dialogue of story charcters.

Expand Oral Vocabulary

Antonyms

Read the following words and ask children to supply an opposite:

cry (laugh)	old (new)	slow (fast)
dirty (clean)	ugly (beautiful)	healthy (sick)
over (under)	asleep (awake)	down (up)
loud (soft)	hard (soft)	easy (hard)
wrong (right)	quiet (noisy)	buy (sell)

Day 3

Support the Reading

Lost!

The words listed below are either decodable or have been taught as high-frequency words. Children who can read these words can read *Lost!* First have children read them as a group; then ask individuals to read them. For additional scaffolding, have children work in pairs to practice reading words until they can read them fluently at the rate of one word per second.

say	afraid	don't	when
way	explain	I'll	hear
		it's	live
		won't	

If children have difficulty with most of these words,
then use Managing Flexible Groups, Intervention, page 54b. To
develop fluency, use Decodable Reader 35 and the lesson in the
Teaching Guide, page 55.

Before reading *Lost!*, point out the following words: *people*, *friendly*,
either, *idea*, *elevator*, *pointing*, *playground*, *finally*. Children have not
learned all the letter-sounds for these words. Point to each word,
identify it, spell it, and then have children read it.

Page 57:	people
Page 58:	friendly
Page 61:	either
Page 62:	idea
Page 63:	elevator
Page 64:	pointing
Page 69:	playground
Page 76:	finally

After introducing the words, use the Reading Strategies in the Teacher's
Edition and then have children read *Lost!*

If children have difficulty reading specific words as they read,
then coach them in blending decodable words, or model reading non-
decodable words. For example, **say:**

- **This word is *hear*. What's this word?**

Phonemic Awareness
Segment Phonemes
Say:
- **Listen as I say the sounds in *wait*. I will say the word slowly to hear all
  the sounds: /w/ /ā/ /t/. Say it with me: /w/ /ā/ /t/.**
- **Now I will say each sound in *tray*: /t/ /r/ /ā/. Say it with me: /t/ /r/ /ā/.**
- **Say each sound in *bait*. (/b/ /ā/ /t/)**
- **Say each sound in *day*. (/d/ /ā/)**
- **Say each sound in *paint*. (/p/ /ā/ /n/ /t/)**
- **Say each sound in *stay*. (/s/ /t/ /ā/)**

Blending Strategy

Review Long Vowels (CVCe)

To **review long vowels (CVCe)**, have children blend the words listed here. Use the blending model at the left. Monitor their use of the strategy and coach them in blending as needed.

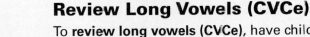

brave	smile	tote
huge	shake	time
stone	cute	made
kite	rode	cube

Some children can try two-syllable decodable words. For example:

reptile	fireside	classmate
namesake	misplace	cupcake

Review High-Frequency Words

In addition to practicing this week's words, have children review the non-decodable words *four*, *funny*, *long*, and *watch*. Pronounce each word, spell it, then have children pronounce it and spell it.

Reread for Fluency

Decodable Reader 34

Say:

- **I will read this story. I want you to read the sentences together after me. I am going to read with expression. Try to read just the way I do.**

Use your oral reading to model appropriate intonation, showing the excitement of the story charcters. Then have children practice reading orally with a partner. Listen to the children read, and provide feedback regarding their oral reading and their use of the blending strategy.

Phonemic Awareness

Add Initial Phonemes

Say:

- **Listen as I say the sounds in *eat*, /ē/ /t/. Now listen as I add /w/ to the beginning of *eat*: /w/ /ē/ /t/. What is the word? (wheat)**
- **Add /th/ to *ink*: /th/ /i/ /n/ /k/. What's the word? (think)**
- **Add /sh/ to *ape*: /sh/ /ā/ /p/. What's the word? (shape)**
- **Add /ch/ to *in*: /ch/ /i/ /n/. What's the word? (chin)**
- **Add /ch/ to *air*: /ch/ /â/ /r/. What's the word? (chair)**

Review Phonics

Initial Digraphs

To review initial digraphs, have children blend the words listed here. Use the blending model at the left. Monitor their use of the blending strategy and coach them in blending as needed.

| champ | wheel | shake | three | chose | whip |
| cheese | whale | shine | thump | shelf | thank |

Review High-Frequency Words

In addition to practicing this week's words, have children review the non-decodable words *were*, *about*, and *any*. Pronounce each word, spell it, then have children pronounce it and spell it.

Reread for Fluency

For children who could read accurately *Lost!*, use it to build fluency. For others use Decodable Reader 35 in place of *Lost!* **Say:**

- **I am going to read one page at a time. I will read just the way I speak. I want you to read each page together after me. Try to read just as if you are speaking.**

Use your oral reading to model reading with an appropriate rate. Then have children practice reading the story orally with a partner. Listen to them read, and provide feedback regarding their oral reading and their use of the blending strategy. Children should be reading at 40 to 50 correct words per minute.

Expand Oral Vocabulary

Antonyms

Say:

- **I will read a sentence and repeat one of the words.**
- **You will think of an opposite of the repeated word and say the sentence with the new word.**
- **I will do the first one for you.**
- *Our homework was <u>easy</u>. easy*
- *Hard is an opposite of <u>easy</u>.*
- *Our homework was hard.*

Continue with the following sentences:

> The dog was <u>unfriendly</u>. unfriendly (friendly)
> The package was <u>heavy</u>. heavy (light)
> I got to the party <u>early</u>. early (late)
> The book was on a <u>high</u> shelf. high (low)
> This towel is <u>dry</u>. dry (wet)

Day 5

Ongoing Assessment
Word Reading

Use these words to assess children's ability to read words with long *a* *(ai, ay)* and contractions.

rain	say	didn't	snail
stay	he'll	paint	gray
braid	pay	she's	aren't

If children cannot read the words,
then use the **Reteach** lessons for Long *a (ai, ay)* and/or Contractions on pages AR12 and AR13 of the Teacher's Edition.

Ongoing Assessment
Fluency

Materials Children should read grade-level text that they have not practiced. This text should be similar in difficulty to the selections children have practiced this week.

Assess fluency by taking a timed sample of the child's oral reading; record the number of words read correctly per minute. See Monitoring Fluency, page xxi.

Spelling
Segment Phonemes

When administering the Spelling Test, use only the first six words: *rain, way, may, say, wait, play*. Encourage children to segment sounds as they spell.

Review High-Frequency Words

In addition to practicing this week's words, have children review the words *ask, kind, over*. First model blending the decodable word *ask*. Then have children blend it with you. For the non-decodable words *kind* and *over*, pronounce each word, spell it, then have children pronounce it and spell it.

Build Fluency
Repeated Readings

Have children practice reading aloud the Take-Home Decodable Reader 34 and/or 35 with a partner before taking it home. Children should reread the text three to four times for optimal fluency.

Reading First

5-Day Instructional Plan

Key to Instruction in

Phonemic Awareness

Phonics

Fluency

Vocabulary

Text Comprehension

Instructional Routines

See the **Reading First Instructional Routines for Unit 5, Week 3,** pages 24–31 for daily Routines in
- Working with Phonemes
- Using Blending Strategies
- Building Fluency
- Expanding Vocabulary

Day 1

Activate Prior Knowledge p. 86j
Poem "Foal"

Phonics pp. 86k–86l

Instructional Routines
- Phonemic Awareness

Connect Sounds to Letters
Long *o: oa, ow*
Inflected Ending *-ing*

Instructional Routines
- Connect Sound to Letter
- Blending Strategy

Spelling: Inflected Ending *-ing*

grow	float	show
growing	floating	showing

High-Frequency Words

around	her	new	old	show

Instructional Routines
- High-Frequency Words

Reading pp. 86m–93

Build Oral Language Vocabulary

baby	months	otter

Instructional Routines
- Support the Reading

Reading Strategies
Read the Phonics Story *Baby Otter Grows Up*

Oral Language p. 93a

Expand Vocabulary: Discuss Unfamiliar Words

Writing pp. 93a–93b
Shared Writing: Award
- Create an Award
- Independent Writing

Handwriting: *Gg*

Read Aloud, p. 93b
Read aloud *Verdi* by Janell Cannon.

Day 2

Phonics pp. 93c–93d

Long *o: oa, ow*
Inflected Ending *-ing*
Phonics Practice Activities

Instructional Routines
- Blending Strategy
- Review Word Parts
- Review High-Frequency Words

Use Decodable Reader 36 instead of the Phonics Reader.

Use Teaching Guide, p. 56.
- Build Fluency

Spelling: Inflected Ending *-ing*

High-Frequency Words

Reading pp. 93e–93f

Comprehension: Sequence
Listening Comprehension
- Read Aloud
"The Nightcrawler Hunt"

Instructional Routines
- Reread for Fluency *Baby Otter Grows Up* or Decodable Reader 36
- Expand Oral Vocabulary

Oral Language p. 93g
Listening: Listen for the Main Idea

Writing pp. 93g–93h
Modeled Writing: Write Facts
Write About Growing Up
- Independent Writing

Grammar: Adjectives That Tell Size

Read Aloud, p. 93h
Read aloud *Hermit Crab Moves House* by Linda Hartley.

Day 3

Reading pp. 94a–111

Build Oral Language
Vocabulary

beneath	neigh	stronger
field	newborn	struggle
hooves	ponies	wobbly

Instructional Routines

- Support the Reading
Use Leveled Reader 21A.

Reading Strategies
Read *Foal*
Comprehension: Sequence
Flexible Groups, p. 94b

Use Leveled Reader 21A.

Use the Teacher's Edition, pp. LR13–LR14

Phonics pp. 111a–111b

Long *o: oa, ow*
Inflected Ending *-ing*

Instructional Routines

- Phonemic Awareness
- Blending Strategy
- Review High-Frequency Words
Use Decodable Reader 36 instead of the Phonics Reader.
- Reread for Fluency

Review Phonics: Long *e: e, ee, ea*
Spelling: Inflected Ending *-ing*

High-Frequency Words

Oral Language p. 111c

Expand Vocabulary: Understand Unfamiliar Words

Writing pp. 111c–111d
Modeled Writing: Animal Fact Cards
- Independent Writing
- Peer Conference
Grammar: Adjectives That Tell Size

Read Aloud, p. 111d.
Read aloud *Every Autumn Comes the Bear* by Jim Arnosky.

Day 4

Reading pp. 112–113

Reader Response
Leveled Practice, Easy, *Leveled Practice and Test Link,* p. 61
Review: Setting

Instructional Routines

- Phonemic Awareness
- Review Word Parts
- Review High-Frequency Words
- Reread for Fluency *Foal* or Leveled Reader 21A.

Phonics pp. 113a–113b

Long *o: oa, ow*
Inflected Ending *-ing*
Reteach
Review Single and Double Medial Consonants
Spelling: Inflected Ending *-ing*

High-Frequency Words

Oral Language pp. 114–115

Instructional Routines

- Expand Oral Vocabulary

Language Arts
Grammar: Adjectives That Tell Size
Speaking: Talk About Adjectives

Writing p. 114–115
Grammar: Adjectives That Tell Size

Writing: Identify Adjectives That Tell Size

Study Skill: Illustrations and Captions

Read Aloud, p. 114
Read aloud *Cheetah* by Taylor Morrison.

Day 5

Reading pp. 115a–115b

Assess Oral Reading
Prepare for the Assessment

Instructional Routines

- Use the Ongoing Assessments instead of the Oral Reading Checklist.
- Word Reading
- Fluency

Comprehension Check, p. 115a

Phonics p. 115c

Long *o: oa, ow*
Inflected Ending *-ing*
Phonics Practice Activities

Instructional Routines

- Spelling
- Review High-Frequency Words
Use Take-Home Decodable Reader 36 instead of the Phonics Take-Home Reader.
- Build Fluency

Oral Language p. 115d
Listening: Listen for the Main Idea

Writing p. 115d
Interactive Writing: Journal Entry

- Independent Writing
- Portfolio

Read Aloud, p. 115d
Ask children for a favorite book you have shared with them and read it aloud.

Instructional Routines

Baby Otter Grows Up *and* Foal

Teacher's Edition, pages 86i–115d

Day 1

If children cannot remember the sequence of sounds,
then add letters to the activity to help them manipulate sounds.

Phonemic Awareness
Substitute Medial Phonemes
Say:
- Today we are going to make new words by changing the middle sound.
- Listen as I say the sounds in *bait*: /b/ /ā/ /t/. Now listen as I change the /ā/ in *bait* to /o/: /b/ /ō/ /t/, *boat*.
- Change the /ā/ in *grain* to /ō/. *(groan)*
- Change the /ē/ in *feel* to /ō/. *(foal)*
- Change the /ē/ in *green* to /ō/. *(grown)*
- Change the /ā/ in *main* to /ō/. *(moan)*
- Change the /ē/ in *lead* to /ō/. *(load)*

If children need additional instruction for long *o: oa, ow,*
then use the Connect Sound to Letter routine at the right.

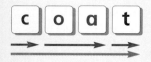

Connect Sound to Letter
Introduce Long *o: oa, ow*
Write the word *coat*. **Say:**
- Listen as I blend the sounds in /k/ /ō/ /t/ — *coat*.
- What sound do you hear in the middle of *coat*? *(/ō/)*
- The letters *oa* stand for the sound /ō/.
- Now blend the sounds with me: /k/ /ō/ /t/ — *coat*.

Continue modeling with *crow*. Then have children blend the sounds for *goat, oak, road, soap, bowl, glow, slow* and *show*.

Review Word Parts
Inflected Ending *-ing*
Write this sentence: *Jake is sleeping on the cot.* Have the sentence read aloud. Remind children that endings are sometimes added to words, and have them find the word that has an ending. **Say:**
- The word *sleeping* has an ending. What ending does it have? *(-ing)* If I cover up the *-ing* ending, I see that the base word is *sleep.* I can read the base word with its ending: *sleep, -ing — sleeping.*

Write this sentence on the board: *May is skipping down the block.* Have the sentence read. Have children find the word that has an ending. **Say:**
- The word *skipping* has an ending. What ending does it have? *(-ing)* If I cover up the *-ing* ending, I see the word *skip* has an extra *p.* For some short vowel words, I know that the last consonant is doubled before adding an ending.

- **To read a word like this, I cover up the doubled consonant and the ending to see what the base word is. Then I can read the base word and the ending: *skip, ping, skipping*.**

Call on children to read these words, to point out the endings, and to frame the base words. If children have difficulty reading the base words, then coach them in blending. Have them identify the words in which the last consonant is doubled before *-ing* is added.

hugging	kicking	digging	mixing
growing	slipping	swimming	sticking

High-Frequency Words

To teach the words *her, show, old, new,* and *around,* **say:**

- **We have talked about these words before. Some words we have to learn by remembering the letters rather than saying the sounds. Some of these words may have letters whose sounds we can blend. We can blend the sounds in *show*.**

Model blending the decodable words *show* and *old*. Have children blend them with you. For the non-decodable words, *her, new,* and *around,* pronounce each word, spell it, have children pronounce it, and have children spell it.

Support the Reading
Baby Otter Grows Up

The words listed below are either decodable or have been taught as high-frequency words. Children who can read these words can read *Baby Otter Grows Up*. First ask children to read them as a group; then call on individuals to read them.

growing	float	sailing	old	around
holding	show	boat	her	
coat	swimming	grown	new	

If children have difficulty with many of these words,
then coach them in blending decodable words or model the strategy for non-decodable words. Have them work in pairs to practice reading the words until they can read them fluently at the rate of one word per second.

Before reading *Baby Otter Grows Up,* introduce the following words: *could, almost*. Children have not had all the letter-sounds for these words. Point to each word, identify it, spell it, and then have children read it.

Page 91: could   Page 92: almost

After introducing the words, use the Reading Strategies in the Teacher's Edition and then have children read *Baby Otter Grows Up.*

If children have difficulty reading specific words as they read, **then** coach them in blending decodable words, or model reading non-decodable words. For example say:

- **This word is *around*. What is this word?**

Day 2

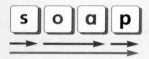

Blending Strategy

Phonics Review

To practice long *o* spelled *oa* , *ow* and to **review long *o,* (CVCe and CV)** have children blend each word and read it.

soap	mow	globe	so	coach
toad	go	own	robe	

Review Word Parts

Ending *-ing*

Write the word *eating* on the board. **Say:**

- **The word *eating* has an ending. If I cover up the *-ing* ending, I see that the base word is *eat*. I can read the base word with its ending: *eat, -ing, eating*.**

Write these words on the board. Have children cover the *-ing* ending, read the base word, and then read the whole word. If children have difficulty reading the base words, then coach them in blending. Have them tell which words have the last consonant doubled.

reading	clapping	picking	toasting
towing	dreaming	sitting	playing

Review High-Frequency Words

In addition to practicing this week's words, have children review the words *water, again, small,* and *what.* **Say:**

- **Some words we have to learn by remembering the letters rather than saying the sounds**
- **This word is *small*. The letters in *small* are s–m–a–l–l.**
- **What is this word? What are the letters in *small*?**

Continue with the remaining non-decodable words.

Build Fluency
Decodable Reader 36

For Decodable Reader 36, use the lesson in the Teaching Guide, page 56.

Reread for Fluency

For children who could read *Baby Otter Grows Up* accurately, use it to build fluency. For others, use Decodable Reader 36 to model fluent reading. **Say:**

- **I will read this story. I want you to read the sentences together after me. I am going to read with expression. Try to read just the way I do.**

Use your oral reading to model appropriate intonation, showing excitement of the story characters. Then have children take turns reading orally with a partner. Listen to children read, and provide feedback regarding their oral reading and their use of the blending strategy.

Expand Oral Vocabulary
Unfamiliar Words
Say:

- **Listen to this sentence:** *Mother used compost to help her garden grow.*
- *Compost* **is a word I don't know. I will say the sentence again to try to figure out what** *compost* **means.** *Mother used compost to help her garden grow.*
- *Compost* **must mean a special thing you put on soil at planting time.**
- **When you come across a word you don't know, use the words around it to help you figure out the meaning.**

Say the following sentences to children. Have them tell what the underlined word means and how they figured it out.
The rain turned to <u>sleet</u> and became a layer of ice. *(partly frozen rain)*
I will <u>stow</u> my books in my school bag. *(pack)*
The story about a man from Mars is just a <u>hoax</u>. *(made-up story passed off as true)*

Day 3

Support the Reading
Foal

The words listed below are either decodable or have been taught as high-frequency words. Children who can read these words can read *Foal*. First have children read them as a group; then ask individuals to read them. For additional scaffolding, have children work in pairs to practice reading the words until they can read them fluently and at a rate of one word per second.

foal	mother	show	graze
milk	close	friend	running
grow	teeth	around	jumping

If children have difficulty with most of these words,
then use Managing Flexible Groups, Intervention, page 94b. To **develop fluency**, use Leveled Reader 21A and the lesson in the Teacher's Edition, pages LR13–LR14.

Before reading *Foal*, introduce the following words: *bigger, cuddle, together, wonder, sturdy,* and *enough.* Children have not learned all the letter-sounds for these words. Point to each word, identify it, spell it and then have children read it.

Page 96:	bigger	Page 103:	wonder
Page 97:	cuddle	Page 104:	sturdy
Page 101:	together	Page 107:	enough

After introducing the words, use the Reading Strategies in the Teacher's Edition and then have children read *Foal*.

If children have difficulty reading specific words as they read,
then coach them in blending decodable words, or model reading the non-decodable words. For example, **say:**

• **This word is** *her.* **What's this word?**

Phonemic Awareness
Substitute Final Phonemes
Say:

• **We are going to make new words by changing the last sound,**
• **Listen as I say the sounds in** *glee*: **/g/ /l/ /ē/. Now listen as I change the /ē/ in** *glee* **to /ō/: /g/ /l/ /ō/,** *glow.* **Say the sounds with me: /g/ /l/ /ō/,** *glow.*
• **Change the /ō/ in** *flow* **to /ē/. What's the word?** *(flee)*
• **Change the /ō/ in** *throw* **to /ē/. What's the word?** *(three)*
• **Change the /ō/ in** *know* **to /ē/. What's the word?** *(knee)*
• **Change the /ō/ in** *show* **to /ē/. What's the word?** *(she)*

Blending Strategy
Review Long *e: e, ee, ea*

To **review long** *e*, have children blend the long *e* words listed here. Use the blending model pictured at the left. Remind children that *e, ea,* and *ee* can all stand for long *e*. Coach them in blending as needed.

If children cannot remember the sequence of sounds,
then add letters to the activity to help them manipulate sounds.

dream	sweet	speak	meet	teach
be	she	leash	wheel	three

Review High-Frequency Words

In addition to practicing this week's words, have children review the words *after, call, something, made, every,* and *mother.* For the decodable word *made,* **say:**

- **We have talked about these words before. Some of these words may have letters whose sounds we can blend. We can blend the sounds in *made.***

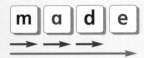

Model blending the decodable word *made,* and have children blend it with you. For the non-decodable words *after, call, something, every,* and *mother,* pronounce each word, spell it, and then have children pronounce it and spell it.

Reread for Fluency
Decodable Reader 36

Read the first 5 pages of Decodable Reader 36 to model fluent reading at an appropriate rate. **Say:**

- **I will read one page at a time. I will read just the way I speak. I want you to read each page together after me. Try to read just as if you are speaking.**

Then have children reread orally three to four times, or until they can read with few or no mistakes. Children should be reading at a rate of 40 to 50 correct words per minute.

Day 4

Phonemic Awareness
Segment Phonemes

Have children segment the sounds in the following words:

boast (/b/ /ō/ /s/ /t/)	sweet (/s/ /w/ /ē/ /t/)
both (/b/ /ō/ /th/)	sprain (/s /p/ /r/ /ā/ /n/)
egret (/ē/ /g/ /r/ /e/ /t/)	slowpoke (/s/ /l/ /ō/ /p/ /ō/ /k/)

Review Word Parts
Syllables

Write the word *rabbit* on the board. **Say:**

- **When you read longer words like this one, first divide the word into smaller parts.**
- **If there are two consonants in the middle, divide the word between the consonants. I see two *b*'s together, so I'll divide between them.** (Draw a line between the letters.)

- **Next, I read each part *rab bit*. Then I blend the parts together: *rabbit*. Blend them with me: *rab bit, rabbit***

Have children divide these words, read the two parts, and blend the parts together to read the word.

ad|vice	cac|tus	plas|tic	pup|pet	hel|met
bas|ket	hid|den	mag|net	gal|lop	mit|ten

Review High-Frequency Words

In addition to practicing this week's words, have children review the words *laugh, of, was, father,* and *going*. Blend the decodable word *going*. Then have children blend it with you. For the remaining non-decodable words *laugh, of, was,* and *father,* pronounce each word, spell it, and then have children pronounce it and spell it.

Reread for Fluency

For children who could accurately read *Foal*, use it to build fluency. For others, use pages 14 and 15 of Leveled Reader 21A to model fluent reading. **Say:**

- **I will read one sentence at a time. I will read the words with no mistakes. I want you to read the sentences together after me. Try to read them just the way I do.**

After modeling reading with accuracy, have children choral read aloud as a group with a fluent adult reader. Listen to children read, and provide feedback regarding their oral reading and their use of the blending strategy.

Expand Oral Vocabulary
Unfamiliar Words

Discuss with children how they can figure out the meaning of a word that they don't know as they read. Remind them that they can use the words around or near the word they don't know. Read the following sentences. Have children tell what the underlined word means and how they figured out the meaning.

John plays the viola in music class. *(a musical instrument)*
Mary watered the petunia to help it grow. *(a plant or flower)*
We ate zucchini for dinner. *(a kind of food)*
The horse loped along in an easy gallop. *(ran at an easy pace)*

Day 5

Ongoing Assessment
Word Reading

Use these words to assess children's ability to read words with long *o* and inflected ending *-ing*:

toad	flowing	foam	row	snowing
blow	soak	running	moaning	planning

If children cannot read the words,
then use the **Reteach** lessons for Long *o* and/or Ending *-ing* on page AR14 of the Teacher's Edition.

Ongoing Assessment
Fluency

Materials Children should read grade-level text that they have not practiced. This text should be similar in difficulty to the selections children have practiced this week.

Assess fluency by taking a timed sample of the child's oral reading; record the number of words read correctly per minute. See Monitoring Fluency, page xxi.

Spelling
Segment Phonemes

When administering the Spelling Test, use only the first six words: *grow, show, floating, growing, float,* and *showing*. Encourage children to segment sounds as they spell.

Review High-Frequency Words

In addition to practicing this week's words, have children review the words *has, thank, very,* and *be*. Model blending the decodable words *has, thank,* and *be*. Then have children blend them with you. For the non-decodable word *very,* pronounce it, spell it, and then have children pronounce it and spell it.

Build Fluency
Repeated Readings

Have children practice reading aloud Take-Home Decodable Reader 36 with a partner before taking it home. Children should reread the text three to four times for optimal fluency.

Reading First

5-Day Instructional Plan

Key to Instruction in

Phonemic Awareness

Phonics

Fluency

Vocabulary

Text Comprehension

Instructional Routines

See the **Reading First Instructional Routines for Unit 5, Week 4,** pages 34–41, for daily Routines in
- Working with Phonemes
- Using Blending Strategies
- Building Fluency
- Expanding Vocabulary

Day 1

Activate Prior Knowledge p. 116j
  Poem "Behind the Museum Door"

Phonics pp. 116k–116l

Instructional Routines
- Phonemic Awareness

Connect Sounds to Letters
Long *i: igh, ie*
Singular Possessives

Instructional Routines
- Connect Sound to Letter
- Blending Strategy

Spelling: Long *i* Words
  lie   tie   light
  pie   night   right

High-Frequency Words
  been   first   found   start   together

Instructional Routines
- High-Frequency Words

Reading pp. 116m–123

Build Oral Language Vocabulary
  museum   fur

Instructional Routines
- Support the Reading

Reading Strategies
Read the Phonics Story *What a Sight!*

Oral Language p. 123a

Expand Vocabulary: Discuss Place Names

Writing pp. 123a–123b

Shared Writing: List
- List Places
- Independent Writing

Handwriting: *Jj*

Read Aloud, p. 123b
Read aloud *Bill and Pete Go Down the Nile* by Tomie dePaola.

Day 2

Phonics pp. 123c–123d

Long *i: igh, ie*
Singular Possessives
Phonics Practice Activities

Instructional Routines
- Blending Strategy
- Review Word Parts
- Review High-Frequency Words

Use Decodable Reader 37 instead of the Phonics Reader.
Use Teaching Guide, p. 57.
- Build Fluency

Spelling: Long *i* Words

High-Frequency Words

Reading pp. 123e–123f

Comprehension: Cause and Effect
Listening Comprehension
- Read Aloud "Goldilocks and the Three Bears"

Instructional Routines
- Reread for Fluency *What a Sight!* or Decodable Reader 37
- Expand Oral Vocabulary

Oral Language p. 123g

Speaking: Large Group Discussion
Discuss Places to Learn

Writing pp. 123g–123h

Modeled Writing: Ad
Write an Ad for a Special Place
- Independent Writing

Grammar: Adjectives

Read Aloud, p. 123h
Read aloud a suspense story.

Day 3

Reading pp. 124a–151

Build Oral Language
Vocabulary

cafeteria	fierce	hurried
dinosaur	fooling	penguins
else	happened	scared

Instructional Routines

- Support the Reading
Use Decodable Reader 38 instead of Leveled Reader 22A.

Reading Strategies
Read *Lost in the Museum*
Comprehension: Cause and Effect
Flexible Groups, p. 124b

Decodable Reader 38 and Teaching Guide, p. 58

Phonics pp. 151a–151b

Long *i: igh, ie*
Singular Possessives

Instructional Routines

- Phonemic Awareness
- Blending Strategy
- Review High-Frequency Words

Use Decodable Reader 37 instead of the Phonics Reader.

- Reread for Fluency

Review Phonics: Long *a: ai, ay*
Spelling: Long *i* Words

High-Frequency Words

Oral Language p. 151c

Expand Vocabulary: Name Items Found in Specific Places

Writing pp. 151c–151d

Modeled Writing: My Favorite Trip
- Independent Writing
- Peer Conference
Grammar: Adjectives

Read Aloud, p. 151d.
Read aloud *My Map Book* by Sara Fanelli.

Day 4

Reading pp. 152–153

Reader Response
Leveled Practice, Easy, *Leveled Practice and Test Link,* p. 64
Review: Character

Instructional Routines

- Phonemic Awareness
- Review Word Parts
- Review High-Frequency Words
- Reread for Fluency *Lost in the Museum* or Decodable Reader 38.

Phonics pp. 153a–153b

Long *i: igh, ie*
Singular Possessives
Reteach
Review Contractions
Spelling: Long *i* Words

High-Frequency Words

Oral Language pp. 154–155

Instructional Routines

- Expand Oral Vocabulary

Language Arts
Grammar: Adjectives
Speaking: Talk About Adjectives

Writing p. 154–155

Grammar: Adjectives
Writing: Identify Adjectives That Tell What Kind

Study Skill: Map

Read Aloud, p. 154
Read aloud *My Visit to the Aquarium* by Aliki.

Day 5

Reading pp. 155a–155b

Assess Word Reading
Prepare for the Assessment

Instructional Routines

- Use the Ongoing Assessments instead of the Word Recognition Checklist.
- Word Reading
- Fluency

Comprehension Check, p. 155a

Phonics p. 155c

Long *i: igh, ie*
Singular Possessives
Phonics Practice Activities

Instructional Routines

- Spelling
- Review High-Frequency Words

Use Take-Home Decodable Reader 37 and/or 38 instead of the Phonics Take-Home Reader.

- Build Fluency

Oral Language p. 155d

Speaking: Large Group Discussion

Writing p. 155d

Interactive Writing: Thank-You Note
Thank a Farmer

- Independent Writing
- Portfolio

Read Aloud, p. 155d
Ask children for a favorite book you have shared with them and read it aloud.

Instructional Routines

What a Sight! *and* Lost in the Museum

Teacher's Edition, pages 116i–155d

Day 1

If children cannot remember the sequence of sounds, **then** add letters to the activity to help them manipulate sounds.

Phonemic Awareness
Substitute Medial Phonemes

Say:

*   Today we are going to make new words by changing the middle sound.
*   Listen as I say the sounds in *tot*: /t/ /o/ /t/. Now listen as I change the /o/ in *tot* to /ī/: /t/ /ī/ /t/, *tight*.
*   Change the /i/ in *lit* to /ī/. What's the word? *(light)*
*   Change the /ō/ in *note* to /ī/. What's the word? *(night)*
*   Change the /a/ in *flat* to /ī/. What's the word? *(flight)*
*   Change the /ē/ in *seat* to /ī/. What's the word? *(sight)*
*   Change the /ō/ in *tote* to /ī/ What's the word? *(tight)*

If children need additional instruction with long *i* spelled *igh* and *ie*, **then** use the Connect Sound to Letter routine at the right.

Connect Sound to Letter
Introduce Long *i*: *igh*, *ie*

Write the word *high*. **Say:**

*   This word is *high*. Say the word with me—*high*. What sound do you hear at the end of *high*? Yes, /ī/, the letters *igh* stand for /ī/.
*   Blend this word with me: /h/ /ī/.
*   When *i* is followed by *gh*, the *i* usually stands for its long sound. The *g* and *h* are silent.

Write these words on the board and have children blend them: *flight, sigh, slight, thigh, light,* and *sight*.

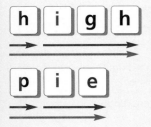

Write the word *pie*. **Say:**

*   This word is *pie*. Say the word with me—*pie*. What sound do you hear at the end of *pie*? Yes, /ī/, the letters *ie* stand for /ī/.
*   Blend this word with me: /p/ /ī/.
*   When two vowels appear together in a word, the first one usually stands for its long vowel sound and the second is silent.

Write these words on the board and have children blend them: *tie, die, lie,* and *fries*.

Review Word Parts
Singular Possessives

Write these sentences. *Jack has three books. These are Jack's books.* Read the sentences to the class. **Say:**

- **These sentences are about Jack. Both sentences are about something that Jack owns—books.**
- **Look at the second sentence.** (Underline *Jack's* and circle the apostrophe and *s*.)
- **When we talk or write about a thing that someone or something has or owns, we add an apostrophe and *s* to the name.**

Write the following sentences on the board. Read them with the class and have children underline the possessive noun.

The <u>boy's</u> jacket is new.
May we go to <u>Jane's</u> house?
The <u>cat's</u> bowl is green.
One <u>baby's</u> sock came off.

High-Frequency Words

To teach the non-decodable words *been*, *first*, *start*, *found*, and *together*, **say:**

- **Some words we have to learn by remembering the letters rather than saying the sounds.**
- **This word is *been*. The letters in *been* are b–e–e–n.**
- **What is the word? What letters are in *been*?**

Continue with the words *first*, *start*, *found*, and *together*.

Support the Reading
What a Sight!

The words listed below are either decodable or have been taught as high-frequency words. Children who can read these words can read *What a Sight!* First ask children to read them as a group; then call on individuals to read them.

right	Jim's	pie	first	found
Tiger's	Dad's	lie	together	
sighed	bright	sight	start	
might	high	fright	been	

If children have difficulty with many of these words,
then coach them in blending decodable words, or model the strategy for non-decodable words. Have them work in pairs to practice reading the words until they can read them fluently at a rate of one word per second.

Before reading *What a Sight!*, introduce the following words: *Nicky*, *could*, *lion*, and *move*. Children have not learned all the letter sounds for these words. Point to each word, identify it, spell it, and then have children read it.

Page 116:   Nicky
Page 117:   could
Page 120:   lion
Page 121:   move

After introducing the words, use the Reading Strategies in the Teacher's Edition and then have children read *What a Sight!*

If children have difficulty reading specific words as they read, **then** coach them in blending decodable words, or model reading the non-decodable words. For example **say:**

• **This word is** *together.* **What is this word?**

Day 2

Blending Strategy
Phonics Review

To practice long *i, (igh, ie)* and to **review long e (ee, ea, e)** and **long o (oa, ow, o)**, have children segment each word to spell it. Remind them that some sounds are spelled with two or three letters. Have them blend each word to read it.

fright	screams	magpie	so
he	growing	upright	hello
moat	blowhole	indeed	

Review Word Parts
Singular Possessives

Write the sentence *Dad's hat is black.* Read the sentence with the class. Remind children that the apostrophe and *s* shows that something belongs to someone. Circle the apostrophe and *s* and **say:**

• **The apostrophe and *s* in the word *Dad's* means that something belongs to Dad. The hat belongs to Dad.**

Write these phrases on the board. Have children read each phrase aloud, circle the apostrophe and *s*, and then use the phrase in a sentence. You may want to write the sentences on the board and read them together.

Nat's lunchbox   Mike's coat   the dog's leash
the cat's tail   the fish's tank   Mom's dress

Review High-Frequency Words

In addition to practicing this week's words, have children review the non-decodable words *have, around, new,* and *does.* **Say:**

• **This word is *have*. The letters in *have* are h–a–v–e.**
• **What is this word? What are the letters in *have*?**

Continue with *around, new,* and *does.*

Build Fluency

Decodable Reader 37

For Decodable Reader 37, use the lesson in the Teaching Guide, page 57.

Reread for Fluency

For children who could read *What a Sight!* accurately, use it to build fluency. For others, use Decodable Reader 37 to model fluent reading. **Say:**

• **I will read one sentence at a time. I will read just the way I speak. I want you to read each sentence together after me. Try to read just as if you are speaking.**

Use your oral reading to model reading at an appropriate rate. Then conduct three to four one-minute readings of pages 62–65. Have children reread with the goal of reading more words with fewer errors in each successive reading. Children should be reading at a rate of 40 to 50 correct words per minute.

Expand Oral Vocabulary

Place Names

Have children discuss places they have visited on vacation or on school trips. Include the following words in your discussion.

park	sports stadium	library
zoo	airport	concert hall
museum	train station	auditorium

Day 3

Support the Reading

Lost in the Museum

The words listed below are either decodable or have been taught as high-frequency words. Children who can read these words can read *Lost in the Museum*. First have children read them as a group; then ask individuals to read them. For additional scaffolding, have children work in pairs to practice reading the words until they can read them fluently at a rate of one word per second.

right	whale's	dinosaur's	started
night	Jim's	all	found
tight	fried	together	

If children have difficulty with most of these words, **then** use Managing Flexible Groups, Intervention, page 124b. To **develop fluency**, use Decodable Reader 38 and the lesson in the Teaching Guide, page 58.

Before reading *Lost in the Museum*, introduce the following words: *teacher, turned, worry, hurt, others, toe, before, tired, foot, air, dark, great, head, stew, choose, vegetables.* Children have not learned all the letter-sounds for these words. Point to each word, identify it, spell it, and then have children read it.

Page 124:	teacher	Page 138:	before
Page 129:	room	Page 140:	tired
Page 133:	turned	Page 141:	foot, air
Page 134:	worry, hurt	Page 142:	dark
Page 135:	others	Page 143:	great, head
Page 136:	toe	Page 149:	choose, stew, vegetables

After introducing the words, use the Reading Strategies in the Teacher's Edition and then have children read *Lost in the Museum*.

If children have difficulty reading specific words as they read, **then** coach them in blending decodable words, or model reading the non-decodable words. For example **say:**

• **This word is *first*. What's this word?**

Phonemic Awareness
Segment Phonemes

Have children segment the sounds in the following words.

fries /f/ /r/ /ī/ /z/	flee /f/ /l/ /ē/	tie /t/ /ī/
flight /f/ /l/ /ī/ /t/	gloat /g/ /l/ /ō/ /t/	light /l/ /ī/ /t/

Blending Strategy
Review Long *a (ai, ay,* CVCe)

To **review long *a* (*ai, ay,* CVCe)**, have children blend and segment each word to spell it. As they work, remind them that some sounds are spelled with two letters and that silent *e* at the end of a word makes a vowel say its name. Have children blend each word to read it.

pain	shave	daylight	stain	dates	strain
saying	wayside	wake	fate	grain	scrape

Review High-Frequency Words

In addition to practicing this week's words, have children review the words *friend, pretty, four, funny, long,* and *watch*. Blend the decodable word *long*. Have children blend it with you. For the non-decodable words *friend, pretty, four, funny* and *watch*, pronounce each word, spell it, and then have children pronounce it and spell it.

Reread for Fluency
Decodable Reader 37

Use Decodable Reader 37 to model fluent reading and attending to quotation marks. First turn to page 67. **Say:**

- **I will read page 67. In this part of the story, Jill and her father are talking. Quotation marks tell me that. Listen to me read this page, and notice if I read the way Jill and her father would speak.**
- **Now read this page aloud with me. Try to read the words in quotations the way the characters would say them.**

Then model reading the rest of the story. Have children reread orally three to four times, or until they can read with few or no mistakes.

Day 4

Phonemic Awareness
Segment Phonemes

Have children segment the sounds in the following words.

might /m/ /ī/ /t/	lie /l/ /ī/	crow /k/ /r/ /ō/
stay /s/ /t/ /ā/	sigh /s/ /ī/	claim /k/ /l/ /ā/ /m/
bright /b/ /r/ /ī/ /t/	oath /ō/ /th/	tie /t/ /ī/
tree /t/ /r/ /ē/	cold /k/ /ō/ /l/ /d/	high /h/ /ī/

Review Word Parts
Contractions

Write this sentence on the board: *Jay can't reach that high.* **Say:**

- **Read this sentence with me: *Jay can't reach that high.***
- **I look at the word *can't*. I know that *can't* is a short way of saying *can not*. The apostrophe shows where the *n* and *o* were taken out to make a new word.**

Have children write the two words for each contraction from below. Have them use their contractions in sentences. If children have difficulty reading the contractions, then coach them in blending.

it's *(it is)*	let's *(let us)*	I'll *(I will)*
she'll *(she will)*	isn't *(is not)*	she's *(she is)*
he'll *(he will)*	I'm *(I am)*	he's *(he is)*

Review High-Frequency Words

In addition to practicing this week's words, have children review the non-decodable words *soon*, *your*, *were*, and *about*. **Say:**

- **Some words we have to learn by remembering the letters rather than saying the sounds.**

- This word is *soon*. The letters in *soon* are s–o–o–n.
- What is this word? What are the letters in *soon*?

Continue with the remaining non-decodable words.

Reread for Fluency

For children who could accurately read *Lost in the Museum,* use it to build fluency. For others, use Decodable Reader 38 to model fluent reading. **Say:**

- I will read one sentence at a time. I will read just the way I speak. I want you to read each sentence together after me. Try to read just as if you are speaking.

Use your oral reading to model reading at an appropriate rate. Then conduct three to four one-minute readings of pages 76–79. Have children reread with the goal of reading more words with fewer errors in each successive reading. Children should be reading at a rate of 40 to 50 correct words per minute.

Expand Oral Vocabulary

Name Items in Specific Places

Recall with the children the places they named earlier in the week. Choose two of the places, such as a zoo and library. Have children name things they might see at each place. Include the words listed below.

zoo			library		
animals	lions	gorillas	books	tables	posters
cages	tigers	dolphins	magazines	computers	desks
signs	bears	seals	chairs	maps	shelves

Day 5

Ongoing Assessment

Word Reading

Use these words to assess children's ability to read words with long *i* *(igh, ie)* and singular possessives:

light	man's	lie	high
cat's	tie	pie	die
dog's	sigh	Mike's	right

If children cannot read the words,
then use the **Reteach** lessons for Long *i (igh, ie)* and/or Singular Possessives on pages AR15 and AR16 of the Teacher's Edition.

Ongoing Assessment
Fluency

Materials Children should read grade-level text that they have not practiced. This text should be similar in difficulty to the selections children have practiced this week.

Assess fluency by taking a timed sample of the child's oral reading; record the number of words read correctly per minute. See Monitoring Fluency, page xxi.

Spelling
Segment Phonemes

When administering the Spelling Test, use only the first six words: *night*, *pie*, *tie*, *right*, *light*, and *lie*. Encourage children to segment sounds as they spell.

Review High-Frequency Words

In addition to practicing this week's words, have children review the words *ask*, *kind*, and *over*. **Say:**

- **We have talked about these words before. Some of these words may have letters whose sounds we can blend. We can blend the sounds in *ask*.**

Blend the decodable word *ask*. Then have children blend it with you. For the non-decodable words *kind* and *over*, pronounce each word, spell it, and then have children pronounce it and spell it.

Build Fluency
Repeated Readings

Have children practice reading aloud Take-Home Decodable Readers 37 and/or 38 with a partner before taking it home. Children should reread the text three to four times for optimal fluency.

Reading First

5-Day Instructional Plan

Key to Instruction in

Phonemic Awareness

Phonics

Fluency

Vocabulary

Text Comprehension

Instructional Routines

See the **Reading First Instructional Routines for Unit 5, Week 5,** pages 44–51, for daily Routines in
- Working with Phonemes
- Using Blending Strategies
- Building Fluency
- Expanding Vocabulary

Day 1

Activate Prior Knowledge p. 156j
Poem "A Dinosaur Baby"

Phonics pp. 156k–156l

Instructional Routines
- Phonemic Awareness

Connect Sounds to Letters
Vowel Sounds of *y*
Compound Words

Instructional Routines
- Connect Sound to Letter
- Blending Strategy

Spelling: Vowel Sounds of *y*
baby   many   why
funny   my   fly

High-Frequency Words
animals even heard most their

Instructional Routines
- High-Frequency Words

Reading pp. 156m–163

Build Oral Language Vocabulary
thought   roar

Instructional Routines
- Support the Reading

Reading Strategies
Read the Phonics Story *Chompy's Afternoon*

Oral Language p. 163a

Expand Vocabulary: Create Homonym Titles

Writing pp. 163a–163b

Shared Writing: Word Bank
- Dinosaur Days Word Bank
- Independent Writing

Handwriting: *Bb*

Read Aloud, p. 163b
Read aloud a book about dinosaurs.

Day 2

Phonics pp. 163c–163d

Vowel Sounds of *y*
Compound Words
Phonics Practice Activities

Instructional Routines
- Blending Strategy
- Review Word Parts
- Review High-Frequency Words

Use Decodable Reader 39 instead of the Phonics Reader.
Use Teaching Guide, p. 59.
- Build Fluency

Spelling: Vowel Sounds of *y*

High-Frequency Words

Reading pp. 163e–163f

Comprehension: Main Idea
Listening Comprehension
- Read Aloud "No Escape!"

Instructional Routines
- Reread for Fluency *Chompy's Afternoon* or Decodable Reader 39
- Expand Oral Vocabulary

Oral Language p. 163g

Speaking: Tell an Original Story in Order

Writing pp. 163g–163h

Modeled Writing: Choose Vivid Words
Write About Dinosaur Days
- Independent Writing

Grammar: Adjectives

Read Aloud, p. 163h
Read aloud *Dinosaur Bob and His Adventures with the Family Lizardo* by William Joyce.

Day 3

Reading pp. 164a–187

Build Oral Language
Vocabulary
break   enemies   herds   millions
breathed guarded human
Earth   heavy   hunters

Instructional Routines

- Support the Reading
Use Leveled Reader 23A.

Reading Strategies
Read *Dinosaur Babies*
Read "Something Big Has
Been Here" and "Unfortunately"
Comprehension: Main Idea
Flexible Groups, p. 164b

Use Leveled Reader 23A.

Use the Teacher's Edition,
pp. LR25–LR26

Phonics pp. 187a–187b

Vowel Sounds of *y*
Compound Words

Instructional Routines

- Phonemic Awareness
- Blending Strategy
- Review High-Frequency Words

Use Decodable Reader 39 instead
of the Phonics Reader.

- Reread for Fluency

Review Phonics: Long *i: igh, ie*
Spelling: Vowel Sounds of *y*

High-Frequency Words

Oral Language p. 187c

Expand Vocabulary: Name Types of
Dinosaurs

Writing pp. 187c–187d

Modeled Writing: My Favorite Trip
- Independent Writing
- Peer Conference
Grammar: Adjectives

Read Aloud, p. 187d
I Met a Dinosaur by Jan Wahl

Day 4

Reading pp. 188–189

Reader Response
Leveled Practice, Easy, *Leveled
Practice and Test Link,* p. 67
Review: Cause and Effect

Instructional Routines

- Phonemic Awareness
- Review Word Parts
- Review High-Frequency Words
- Reread for Fluency *Dinosaur Babies*
or Leveled Reader 23A.

Phonics pp. 189a–189b

Vowel Sounds of *y*
Compound Words
Reteach
Review Endings *-ed* and *-ing*
Spelling: Vowel Sounds of *y*

High-Frequency Words

Oral Language pp. 190–191

Instructional Routines

- Expand Oral Vocabulary

Language Arts
Grammar: Adjectives
Speaking: Talk About Adjectives

Writing pp. 190–191

Grammar: Adjectives
Writing: Identify Adjectives That

Tell How Many

Study Skill: Take Notes

Read Aloud, p. 190
Read aloud *An Alphabet of Dinosaurs*
by Peter Dodson.

Day 5

Reading pp. 191a–191b

Assess Accuracy and Comprehension
Prepare for the Assessment

Instructional Routines

Use the Ongoing Assessments
instead of the Accuracy and
Comprehension Assessment.

- Word Reading
- Fluency

To **Check Comprehension,** use
Listen to Individual Readers, p. 191a.

Phonics p. 191c

Vowel Sounds of *y*
Compound Words
Phonics Practice Activities

Instructional Routines

- Spelling
- Review High-Frequency Words

Use Take-Home Decodable Reader
39 instead of the Phonics
Take-Home Reader.

- Build Fluency

Oral Language p. 191d

Speaking: Tell an Original Story
in Order

Writing p. 191d

Interactive Writing: E-mail Note
E-mail a Friend

- Independent Writing
- Portfolio

Read Aloud, p. 191d
Ask children for a favorite book
you have shared with them and
read it aloud.

Instructional Routines

Chompy's Afternoon *and* Dinosaur Babies
Teacher's Edition, pages 156i–191d

Day 1

If children cannot remember the sequence of sounds,
then add letters to the activity to help them manipulate sounds.

Phonemic Awareness
Substitute Initial Phonemes
Say:
- Today we are going to make new words by changing the first sound.
- Listen as I say the sounds in *bunny*, /b/ /u/ /n/ /ē/. Now listen as I change /b/, the first sound in *bunny*, to /s/. First, I take off the /b/. Then I add /s/: *sunny*.
- Now I will change /s/, the first sound in *sunny*, to /f/. First, I say the sounds in *sunny*, /s/ /u/ /n/ /ē/. Then I take off the /s/. Then I add /f/: *funny*.
- Change the /y/ in *yummy* to /t/. What's the word? *(tummy)*
- Change the /b/ in *berry* to /ch/. What's the word? *(cherry)*
- Change the /t/ in *tiny* to /sh/. What's the word? *(shiny)*
- Change the /b/ in *bunny* to /r/. What's the word? *(runny)*

If children need additional instruction for the vowel sounds of *y*,
then use the Connect Sound to Letter routine at the right.

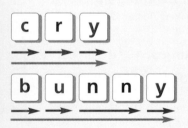

Connect Sound to Letter
Introduce Vowel Sounds of *y*

Write the word *cry*. **Say:**
- This word is *cry*. Say the word with me—*cry*. What sound do you hear at the end of *cry?* Yes, /ī/. The letter *y* stands for /ī/.
- Now listen as I blend the sounds in *cry*: /k/ /r/ /ī/—*cry*. Say it with me: /k/ /r/ /ī/—*cry*.
- When *y* comes at the end of a word, it sometimes stands for /ī/, the long *i* sound.

Write the word *bunny*. **Say:**
- This word is *bunny*. Say the word with me—*bunny*. What sound do you hear at the end of *bunny?* Yes, /ē/. The letter *y* at the end of *bunny* stands for /ē/ and makes up the last syllable.
- Now listen as I blend the sounds in the first syllable of *bunny*: /b/ /u/ /n/ /bun/. Say it with me: /b/ /u/ /n/ /bun/. Now I'll add the last syllable, /ē/: /bunē/, *bunny*. Say it with me: /bunē/—*bunny*.
- When *y* comes at the end of a word, it sometimes stands for /ē/, the long *e* sound.

Continue with *yummy, happy, lucky* and *dry, fly, sky*. Remind children that the *y's* at the end of words make either the long *e* or long *i* sound.

Review Word Parts

Compound Words

Write the word *eggshell* on the board. Frame the words *egg* and *shell* as you **say:**

- **When I see a long word made of two smaller words, first I read the two smaller words. Then I blend them together to read the whole word.**
- ***Eggshell* is a compound word. The word *eggshell* is a made up of two smaller words, *egg* and *shell*, *eggshell*. Read the word with me: *egg–shell*, *eggshell*.**

Write *sunset* and **say:**

- ***Sunset* is another compound word. What are the two smaller words that make up the word *sunset*? (*sun* and *set*) Now read the word with me: *sun–set*, *sunset*.**

Call on children to point out the two smaller words in each of these compound words and then read the compound word.

nearby	nightlight	Sunday
meatloaf	backpack	mailman

High-Frequency Words

To teach the words *animals*, *most*, *even*, *heard*, and *their*, **say:**

- **Some words we have to learn by remembering the letters rather than saying the sounds.**
- **This word is *animals*. The letters in *animals* are a-n-i-m-a-l-s.**
- **What is this word? What are the letters in *animals*?**

For the remaining words, pronounce each word and spell it. Then have children pronounce it and spell it.

Support the Reading

Chompy's Afternoon

The words listed below are either decodable or have been taught as high-frequency words. Children who can read these words can read *Chompy's Afternoon*. First ask children to read them as a group; then call on individuals to read them.

Chompy	happy	carry	everything	very	most
pretty	my	lucky	hilltop	even	animal
hungry	try	anything	somewhere	there	heard

If children have difficulty with many of these words,
then coach them in blending decodable words, or model the strategy for non-decodable words. Have them work in pairs to practice reading the words until they can read them fluently at the rate of one word per second.

Before reading *Chompy's Afternoon*, introduce the following words: *afternoon, food, could, put, here, bully, far*. Children have not learned all the letter-sounds for these words. Point to each word, identify it, spell it, and then have children read it.

Page 156:	afternoon
Page 157:	food, could
Page 158:	put
Page 159:	here
Page 162:	bully
Page 163:	far

After introducing the words, use the Reading Strategies in the Teacher's Edition and then have children read *Chompy's Afternoon*.

If children have difficulty reading specific words as they read *Chompy's Afternoon*,

then coach them in blending decodable words, or model reading the non-decodable words. For example, **say:**

- **This word is *even*. What is this word?**

Day 2

Blending Strategy
Phonics Review

To practice this week's letter-sounds and to **review initial blends and digraphs**, have children segment each word to spell it. Have them blend each word to reread it.

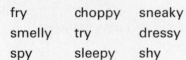

fry	choppy	sneaky
smelly	try	dressy
spy	sleepy	shy

Review Word Parts
Contractions

Write the word *didn't* on the board. Beneath write *did not*. Remind children that the contraction *didn't* is a short way of writing *did not*. Point to the apostrophe and **say:**

- **The apostrophe in *didn't* takes the place of a letter that has been left out. What letter has been left out of *didn't?* Yes, the letter *o* has been left out of *didn't*. The apostrophe takes the place of *o*.**

Call on children to write the two words for these contractions. Then have them tell which letters have been left out of each contraction:

aren't	you'll	let's	he's
that's	isn't	we'll	I'm

Review High-Frequency Words

In addition to practicing this week's words, have children review the non-decodable words *many*, *live* (pronounced /liv/), and *walk*. Pronounce each word and spell it. Then have children pronounce it and spell it.

Build Fluency
Decodable Reader 39

For Decodable Reader 39, use the lesson in the Teaching Guide, page 59.

Reread for Fluency

For children who could read *Chompy's Afternoon* accurately, use it to build fluency. For others, use Decodable Reader 39 to model fluent reading. **Say:**

- **I am going to read this story aloud. I want you to read the sentences together after me. I am going to read with expression. Try to read just the way I do.**

Use your oral reading to model appropriate intonation, showing where to pause, when to change pitch, and which words to stress. Then have children practice reading the story orally with a partner. Listen to children read, and provide feedback regarding their oral reading and their use of the blending strategy.

Expand Oral Vocabulary
Story Homonyms

Write these words from *Chompy's Afternoon* and their homonym pairs. Remind children that both words in a pair sound the same but are spelled differently and have different meanings. Discuss the meanings for both words in each pair.

for	so	by	too	here
four	sew	buy	two	hear

Day 3

Support the Reading
Dinosaur Babies

The words listed below are either decodable or have been taught as high-frequency words. Children who can read these words can read *Dinosaur Babies*. First have children read them as a group; then ask individuals to read them. For additional scaffolding, have children work in pairs to practice reading the words until they can read them fluently at the rate of one word per second.

baby	inside	lucky	most	animals
nobody	outside	heard	their	maybe
very	hungry	even		

If children have difficulty with most of these words,
then use Managing Flexible Groups, Intervention, page 164b. To **develop fluency**, use Leveled Reader 23A and the instructional support in the Teacher's Edition, pages LR25 and LR26.

Before reading *Dinosaur Babies*, introduce the following words: *sound, were, quarter, warm, grew, brought, heads, eyes, berries, circle, changing*. Children have not learned all the letter-sounds for these words. Point to each word, identify it, spell it, and then have children read it.

Page 164:	sound	Page 173:	heads, eyes
Page 167:	were, quarter	Page 174:	berries
Page 169:	warm	Page 181:	circle
Page 171:	grew	Page 183:	changing
Page 172:	brought		

After introducing the words, use the Reading Strategies in the Teacher's Edition and then have children read *Dinosaur Babies*.

If children have difficulty reading specific words as they read *Dinosaur Babies*,
then coach them in blending decodable words, or model reading non-decodable words. For example, **say:**

• **This word is *heard*. What's this word?**

Phonemic Awareness
Segment Phonemes

To help children distinguish the two vowel sounds for final *y*, have them segment the sounds in the following words.

by /b/ /ī/	rusty /r/ /u/ /s/ /t/ /ē/	funny /f/ /u/ /n/ /ē/
sunny /s/ /u/ /n/ /ē/	my /m/ /ī/	sly /s/ /l/ /ī/

Blending Strategy
Review Long Vowels

To **review long *i* spelled *igh*, *ie*, and CVCe**, have children segment each word to spell it and blend each word to read it. Use the blending model pictured at the left. Coach them in blending as needed.

lie	die	sigh	right	hide	tie
light	dime	side	rice	high	tight

Review High-Frequency Words

In addition to practicing this week's words, have children review the non-decodable words *after*, *call*, *laugh*, *something*, and *every*. **Say:**

- **Some words we have to learn by remembering the letters rather than saying the sounds.**
- **This word is *after*. The letters in *after* are a-f-t-e-r.**
- **What is this word? What are the letters in *after*?**

Pronounce each word and spell it. Then have children pronounce it and spell it.

Reread for Fluency
Decodable Reader 39

Use pages 88-91 of Decodable Reader 39 to model fluent reading with appropriate rate. **Say:**

- **I am going to read one page at a time. I will read just the way I speak. I want you to read each page together after me. Try to read just as if you are speaking.**

Then have children reread orally three or four times, or until they can read with few or no mistakes. Children should be reading at a rate of 40 to 50 correct words per minute.

Day 4

If children cannot remember the sequence of sounds, **then** add letters to the activity to help them manipulate sounds.

Phonemic Awareness
Substitute Initial Phonemes

- **Today we are going to make new words by changing the first sound.**
- **Listen as I say the sounds in *cry*, /k/ /r/ /ī/. Now listen as I change the /k/ in *cry* to /t/. First, I take off the /k/. Then I add /t/: *try*.**
- **Now I will change the /t/ in *try* to /f/. First, I say the sounds in *try*, /t/ /r/ /ī/. Then I take off the /t/. Then I add /f/: *fry*.**
- **Change the /f/ in *fry* to /d/. What's the word?** *(dry)*
- **Change the /sh/ in *shy* to /w/. What's the word?** *(why)*
- **Change the /w/ in *why* to /b/. What's the word?** *(by)*
- **Change the /b/ in *by* to /m/. What's the word?** *(my)*

Review Word Parts
-ed, *-ing* with Spelling Change

To **review *-ed* and *-ing* with a spelling change,** write each base word below. Have children read the word, add the endings *-ed* and *-ing*, and read the new words. If children have difficulty reading the base words, then coach them in blending. Remind them to double the final consonant of the base word before adding the ending.

skip (skipped, skipping)   jog (jogged, jogging)
pet (petted, petting)   hop (hopped, hopping)
grab (grabbed, grabbing)   step (stepped, stepping)

Review High-Frequency Words

In addition to practicing this week's words, have children review the words *made*, *mother*, *of*, *was*, and *father*. **Say:**

- **We talked about these words before. Some of these words may have letters whose sounds we can blend. We can blend the sounds in *made*.**

Model blending the word *made*. Use the blending model at the left. Then have children blend it with you. For the non-decodable words *mother*, *of*, *was*, and *father*, pronounce each word and spell it. Then have children pronounce it and spell it.

Reread for Fluency

For children who could read accurately*Dinosaur Babies*, use it to build fluency. For others, use Leveled Reader 23A in place of *Dinosaur Babies*. **Say:**

- **I will read one sentence at a time. I will read the words with no mistakes. I want you to read the sentences together after me. Try to read them just the way I do.**

After modeling reading with accuracy, have children continue to practice reading orally with a partner. Listen to children read, and provide feedback regarding their oral reading and their use of the blending strategy.

Expand Oral Vocabulary
Homonym Sentences

Write these homonym pairs. Read the first two words. Then have children read them. Discuss the meanings of both words. Then have children suggest a sentence that includes both words in the pair and write it on the board. (e.g., *Dan blew a blue horn.*) Continue this procedure with each homonym pair.

blew	ate	there	be
blue	eight	their	bee

Day 5

Ongoing Assessment
Word Reading

Use these words to assess children's ability to read words with *y:* /ē/, /ī/ and compound words:

sly	rosebud	puppy	fry	dusty	why
hobby	sky	cupcake	bedtime	hilly	teapot

If children cannot read the words,
then use the Reteach lessons for Vowel Sounds of *y* and/or Compound Words on page AR17 of the Teacher's Edition

Ongoing Assessment
Fluency

Materials Children should read grade-level text that they have not practiced. This text should be similar in difficulty to the selections children have practiced this week.

Assess fluency by taking a timed sample of the child's oral reading; record the number of words read correctly per minute. See Monitoring Fluency, page xxi.

Spelling
Segment Phonemes

When administering the Spelling Test, use only the first six words: *funny, why, baby, my, many, fly*. Encourage children to segment sounds as they spell.

Review High-Frequency Words

In addition to practicing this week's words, have children review the words *going, has, thank, very,* and *be*. **Say:**

• **We talked about these words before. Some of these words may have letters whose sounds we can blend. We can blend the sounds in *be*.**

Model blending the word *be*. Use the blending model at the left. Then have children blend it with you. Repeat the procedure for the decodable words *going, has,* and *thank*. For the non-decodable word *very*, pronounce the word and spell it. Then have children pronounce it and spell it.

Build Fluency
Repeated Readings

Have children practice reading aloud Take-Home Decodable Reader 39 with a partner before taking it home. Children should reread the text three to four times for optimal fluency.

Reading First

5-Day Instructional Plan

Key to Instruction in

Phonemic Awareness

Phonics

Fluency

Vocabulary

Text Comprehension

Instructional Routines

See the **Reading First Instructional Routines for Unit 5, Week 6,** pages 54–63, for daily Routines in
- Working with Phonemes
- Using Blending Strategies
- Building Fluency
- Expanding Vocabulary

Day 1

Activate Prior Knowledge p. 192j
Fable "The Lion and the Mouse"

Phonics pp. 192k–192l

Instructional Routines
- Phonemic Awareness

Connect Sounds to Letters
Vowel Patterns *ew, ue*
Inflected Ending *-es* and Plural *-es*

Instructional Routines
- Connect Sound to Letter
- Blending Strategy

Spelling: *ew, ue* Words
new	drew	true
grew	blue	glue

High-Frequency Words
because better give people put

Instructional Routines
- High-Frequency Words

Reading pp. 192m–199

Build Oral Language Vocabulary
safely   hero

Instructional Routines
- Support the Reading

Reading Strategies
Read the Phonics Story *The True Story of Abbie Burgess*

Oral Language p. 199a

Expand Vocabulary: Discuss Comparatives

Writing pp. 199a–199b
Writing Process: Prewrite
Class Research Report

Handwriting: *Pp*

Read Aloud, p. 199b
Read aloud *Hazel's Amazing Mother* by Rosemary Wells.

Day 2

Phonics pp. 199c–199d

Vowel Patterns *ew, ue*
Inflected Ending *-es* and Plural *-es*
Phonics Practice Activities

Instructional Routines
- Blending Strategy
- Review Word Parts
- Review High-Frequency Words

Use Decodable Reader 40 instead of the Phonics Reader.

Use Teaching Guide, p. 60.
- Build Fluency

Spelling: *ew, ue* Words

High-Frequency Words

Reading pp. 199e–199f

Comprehension: Cause and Effect
Listening Comprehension
- Read Aloud "The Accidental Hero"

Instructional Routines
- Reread for Fluency *The True Story of Abbie Burgess* or Decodable Reader 40
- Expand Oral Vocabulary

Oral Language p. 199g
Speaking: Small Group Discussion
Discuss the Class Report

Writing pp. 199g–199h
Writing Process: Draft
Class Research Report
Grammar: Adjectives

Read Aloud, p. 199h
Read aloud a story about bravery.

Day 3

Reading pp. 200a–223

Build Oral Language
Vocabulary
accident except minds
believe garage reporters
burns hospital special

Instructional Routines

- Support the Reading
Use Decodable Reader 41 instead
of Leveled Reader 24A.

Reading Strategies
Read "The Bravest Cat!"
Read "Kittens"
Comprehension: Cause and Effect
Flexible Groups, p. 200b

Decodable Reader 41 and Teaching
Guide, p. 61

Phonics pp. 223a–223b

Vowel Patterns *ew, ue*
Inflected Ending *-es* and Plural *-es*

Instructional Routines

- Phonemic Awareness
- Blending Strategy
- Review High-Frequency Words

Use Decodable Reader 40 instead
of the Phonics Reader.

- Reread for Fluency

Review Phonics: Vowel Sounds of *y*
Spelling: *ew, ue* Words

High-Frequency Words

Oral Language p. 223c

Expand Vocabulary: Unfamiliar Words

Writing pp. 223c–223d

Writing Process: Revise and Edit
Class Research Report
Grammar: Adjectives

Read Aloud, p. 223d
Read aloud *A Trip to the Firehouse*
by Laura Driscoll.

Day 4

Reading pp. 224–225

Reader Response
Leveled Practice, Easy, *Leveled
Practice and Test Link,* p. 70
Review: Main Idea

Instructional Routines

- Phonemic Awareness
- Review Phonics
- Review High-Frequency Words
- Reread for Fluency *The Bravest Cat!*
or Decodable Reader 41.

Phonics pp. 225a–225b

Vowel Patterns *ew, ue*
Inflected Ending *-es* and Plural *-es*
Reteach
Review Final Digraphs *-ng, -nk*
Spelling: *ew, ue* Words

High-Frequency Words

Oral Language pp. 226–227

Instructional Routines

- Expand Oral Vocabulary

Language Arts
Grammar: Adjectives
Speaking: Talk About Adjectives

Writing pp. 226–227

Grammar: Adjectives
Writing: Identify Adjectives
Study Skill: Periodicals

Read Aloud, p. 226
Read aloud *The Bravest Dog Ever:
The True Story of Balto*
by Natalie Standiford.

Day 5

Reading pp. 227a–227b

Assess Oral Reading
Prepare for the Assessment

Instructional Routines

Use the Ongoing Assessments
instead of the Oral Reading
Checklist.

- Word Reading
- Fluency

Comprehension Check, p. 227a

Phonics p. 227c

Vowel Patterns *ew, ue*
Inflected Ending *-es* and Plural *-es*
Phonics Practice Activities

Instructional Routines

- Spelling
- Review High-Frequency Words

Use Take-Home Decodable Reader
40 and/or 41 instead of the Phonics
Take-Home Reader.

- Build Fluency

Oral Language p. 227d

Speaking: Small Group Discussion

Writing p. 227d

Writing Process: Publish
Class Research Report

- Conference
- Portfolio

Read Aloud, p. 227d
Read aloud *Balto and the Great Race*
by Elizabeth Cody Kimmel.

Instructional Routines

Abbie Burgess *and* The Bravest Cat!
Teacher's Edition, pages 192i–227d

Day 1

If children cannot remember the sequence of sounds,
then add letters to the activity to help them manipulate sounds.

Phonemic Awareness
Substitute Initial Phonemes
Say:

- Today we are going to make new words by changing the first sound.
- Listen as I say the sounds in *blew*, /b/ /l/ /ü/. Now listen as I change /b/, the first sound in *blue*, to /k/. First, I take off the /b/. Then I add /k/: *clue*.
- Now I will change /k/, the first sound in *clue*, to /f/. First, I say the sounds in *clue*, /k/ /l/ /ü/. Then I take off the /k/. Then I add /f/: *flew*.
- Change the /f/ in *flew* to /g/. What's the word? *(glue)*
- Change the /k/ in *crew* to /d/. What's the word? *(drew)*
- Change the /d/ in *drew* to /g/. What's the word? *(grew)*
- Change the /f/ in *few* to /n/. What's the word? *(new)*

If children need additional instruction for the vowel patterns *ew, ue,*
then use the Connect Sound to Letters routine at the right.

Connect Sound to Letters
Introduce Vowel Patterns *ew, ue*

Write the word *grew*. **Say:**

- This word is *grew*. Say the word with me—*grew*. What sound do you hear at the end of *grew*? Yes, /ü/; the letters *ew* stand for /ü/.
- Now listen as I blend the sounds in *grew*: /g/ /r/ /ü/ /grü/—*grew*. Say it with me: /g/ /r/ /ü/ /grü/—*grew*.
- The letters *ew* can stand for the sound /ü/.

Write the word *clue*. **Say:**

- This word is *clue*. Say the word with me—*clue*. What sound do you hear at the end of *clue*? Yes, /ü/; the letters *ue* stand for /ü/.
- Now listen as I blend the sounds in *clue*: /k/ /l/ /ü/ /klü/—*clue*. Say it with me: /k/ /l/ /ü/ /klü/—*clue*.
- The letters *ue* can also stand for the sound /ü/.

Continue with *blew, crew* and *glue, true*. Remind children that the *ew* or *ue* in these words stand for the sound /ü/.

Review Word Parts
Inflected Ending *-es* and Plural *-es*

Write the sentence *Jane reaches the bushes.* Read the sentence and point to the word *reaches* as you **say:**

- The word *reaches* has an ending. If I cover up the *-es* ending, I see that the base word is *reach*. I can read the base word with its ending: *reach, -es, reaches.* The *-es* ending on the word *reaches* adds an extra syllable—*reach–es, reaches.* Say it with me—*reach–es, reaches.*

Now point to the word *bushes* and **say:**

- The word *bushes* has an ending too. If I cover up the *-es* ending, I see that the base word is *bush*. I can read the base word with its ending: *bush, -es, bushes.* The *-es* ending on the word *bushes* makes it mean "more than one bush." The *-es* ending also adds an extra syllable—*bush–es, bushes.* Say it with me—*bush–es, bushes.*

Call on children to read these words, point out the endings, and frame the base words. Coach them in blending the base words as needed.

pitches	ranches	tosses
wishes	rushes	branches

High-Frequency Words

To teach the words *because, better, give, people,* and *put,* **say:**

- **Some words we have to learn by remembering the letters rather than saying the sounds.**
- **This word is *because*. The letters in *because* are b-e-c-a-u-s-e.**
- **What is this word? What are the letters in *because?***

For the remaining words, pronounce each word and spell it. Then have children pronounce it and spell it.

Support the Reading
Abbie Burgess

The words listed below are either decodable or have been taught as high-frequency words. Children who can read these words can read *Abbie Burgess*. First ask children to read them as a group; then call on individuals to read them.

true	branches	dashes	give	people
watches	blue	washes	because	better
few	tosses	crews	put	

If children have difficulty with many of these words,
then coach them in reading decodable words, or model the strategy for non-decodable words. Have them work in pairs to practice reading the words until they can read them fluently at the rate of one word per second.

Before reading *Abbie Burgess*, introduce the following words: *lighthouse, storm*. Children have not learned all the letter-sounds for these words. Point to each word, identify it, spell it, and then have children read it.

Page 193: lighthouse

Page 194: storm

After introducing the words, use the Reading Strategies in the Teacher's Edition and then have children read *Abbie Burgess*.

If children have difficulty reading specific words as they read *Abbie Burgess*,

then coach them in blending decodable words, or model reading the non-decodable words. For example, **say:**

• **This word is *people*. What is this word?**

Blending Strategy
Phonics Review

To practice this week's letter-sounds and to **review long *u* (CVCe)**, have children segment each word to spell it. Have them blend each word to reread it. Coach them in blending as needed.

flew	newest	dewdrop	truce
bluebird	flutes	glued	chewy

Review Word Parts
Inflected and Plural *-es*

Write the sentence *Tom catches the tosses*. Have the sentence read. Remind children that endings are sometimes added to words, and have them find the two words that have endings. **Say:**

• **The word *catches* has an ending. If I cover up the *-es* ending, I see that the base word is *catch*. I can read the base word with its ending: *catch, -es, catches*.**

• **What is the other word with an ending? Yes, *tosses* has an ending. *Toss* is the base word, and *-es* is the ending. Read the word with me: *toss, -es, tosses*.**

Call on children to read these words, point out the endings, and frame the base words. Coach them in blending the base words as needed.

crashes	fixes	teaches
dashes	passes	sixes

Review High-Frequency Words

In addition to practicing this week's words, have children review the non-decodable words *out*, *water*, and *around*. **Say:**

- **Some words we have to learn by remembering the letters rather than saying the sounds.**
- **This word is *out*. The letters in *out* are o-u-t.**
- **What is this word? What are the letters in *out*?**

Continue the activity with the non-decodable words *water* and *around*. Pronounce each word and spell it. Then have children pronounce it and spell it.

Build Fluency

Decodable Reader 40

For Decodable Reader 40, use the lesson in the Teaching Guide, page 60.

Reread for Fluency

For children who could read *Abbie Burgess* accurately, use it to build fluency. For others, use Decodable Reader 40 to model fluent reading. **Say:**

- **I will read one sentence at a time. I will read the words with no mistakes. I want you to read the sentences together after me. Try to read them just the way I do.**

After modeling reading with accuracy, have children continue to practice reading the story orally with a partner. Listen to children read, and provide feedback regarding their oral reading and their use of the blending strategy.

Expand Oral Vocabulary

Comparatives

Have children discuss comparative words. Have them name something that is big. Then ask them to name something that is even bigger. Finally, have them name something that is the biggest of all. Explain that the words *big*, *bigger*, and *biggest* are used to compare big things. Have children offer the comparatives for other words. Include these words in your discussion.

clean *(cleaner, cleanest)*	high *(higher, highest)*
small *(smaller, smallest)*	soft *(softer, softest)*
wet *(wetter, wettest)*	hard *(harder, hardest)*

Support the Reading
The Bravest Cat!

The words listed below are either decodable or have been taught as high-frequency words. Children who can read these words can read *The Bravest Cat!* First have children read them as a group; then ask individuals to read them. For additional scaffolding, have children work in pairs to practice reading the words until they can read them fluently at the rate of one word per second.

true	give	people
new	because	better
put		

If children have difficulty with most of these words,
then use Managing Flexible Groups, Intervention, page 200b. To **develop fluency**, use Decodable Reader 41 and the lesson in the Teaching Guide, page 61.

Before reading *The Bravest Cat!*, introduce the following words: *building, engines, firefighters, eyes, scared, touches, doctor, newspapers, slowly, room, hurt, letters, world*. Children have not learned all the letter-sounds for these words. Point to each word, identify it, spell it, and then have children read it.

Page 201:	building, engines, firefighters	Page 211:	newspapers
Page 207:	eyes, scared	Page 212:	slowly, room
Page 208:	touches	Page 213:	hurt
Page 209:	doctor	Page 214:	letters, world

After introducing the words, use the Reading Strategies in the Teacher's Edition and then have children read *The Bravest Cat!*

If children have difficulty reading specific words as they read *The Bravest Cat!*,
then coach them in blending decodable words, or model the strategy for reading non-decodable words. For example, **say:**

• **This word is *better*. What's this word?**

Phonemic Awareness
Segment Phonemes

To help children distinguish the two vowel sounds for final *y,* have them segment the sounds in the following words.

shy /sh/ /ī/	sandy /s/ /a/ /n/ /d/ /ē/	jumpy /j/ /u/ /m/ /p/ /ē/
mighty /m/ /ī/ /t/ / /ē/	fly /f/ /l/ /ī/	why /w/ /ī/

Blending Strategy
Phonics Review

To **review initial consonant blends and the vowel sounds of y**, have children blend the words listed here. Use the blending model pictured at the left. Coach them in blending as needed.

| sky | sneaky | cry | spotty | creepy |
| sleepy | creamy | try | sloppy | dry |

Review High-Frequency Words

In addition to practicing this week's words, have children review the words *friend*, *pretty*, *soon*, and *your*. **Say:**

- We talked about these words before. Some of these words may have letters whose sounds we can blend. We can blend the sounds in *pretty*.

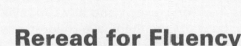

Model blending the decodable word *pretty*. Then have children blend it with you. For the non-decodable words *friend*, *soon*, and *your*, pronounce each word and spell it. Then have children pronounce it and spell it.

Reread for Fluency
Decodable Reader 40

Use Decodable Reader 40 to model fluent reading at an appropriate rate. **Say:**

- I am going to read one page at a time. I will read just the way I speak. I want you to read each page together after me. Try to read just as if you are speaking.

Then have children reread orally three or four times, or until they can read with few or no mistakes.

Day 4

If children cannot remember the sequence of sounds, **then** add letters to the activity to help them manipulate sounds.

Phonemic Awareness
Substitute Final Phonemes
Say:

- Today we are going to make new words by changing the last sound.
- Listen as I say the sounds in *back*, /b/ /a/ /k/. Now listen as I change /k/, the last sound in *back*, to /ng/. First, I take off the /k/. Then I add /ng/: *bang*.
- Now I will change the /p/ in *sip* to /ng/. First, I say the sounds in *sip*, /s/ /i/ /p/. Then I take off the /p/. Then I add /ng/: *sing*.

- Change the /m/ in *brim* to /ng/. What's the word? *(bring)*
- Change the /m/ in *clam* to /ng/. What's the word? *(clang)*
- Change the /t/ in *lot* to /ng/. What's the word? *(long)*
- Change the /d/ in *rid* to /ng/. What's the word? *(ring)*

Review Phonics
Final Digraphs

To **review final digraphs**, have children make each word below with the letter cards from the Small Group Manipulatives Package. Have them segment each word to spell it. Then have them blend the word to read it. Remind them that the last two letters of each word make one sound. Use the blending model at the left. Coach them in blending as needed.

| sang | much | with | think |
| crash | ranch | ring | sink |

Review High-Frequency Words

In addition to practicing this week's words, have children review the words *four*, *long*, *watch*, and *were*. To review the decodable word *long*, blend the word and then have children blend it with you. For the non-decodable words *four*, *watch*, and *were*, pronounce each word and spell it. Then have children pronounce it and spell it.

Reread for Fluency

For children who could read accurately *The Bravest Cat!*, use it to build fluency. For others, use Decodable Reader 41 in place of *The Bravest Cat!* **Say:**

- **I am going to read this story aloud. I want you to read the sentences together after me. I am going to read with expression. Try to read just the way I do.**

Use your oral reading to model appropriate intonation, showing children where to pause. Then have children practice rereading using Readers Theater: one child reads the narrator's part while other children read the dialogue of story characters.

Expand Oral Vocabulary
Unfamiliar Words
Say:

- **Listen to this sentence:** *The book was interesting from the first page to the final page.*

- I don't know what the word *final* means, but I can use the other words in the sentence to figure it out.
- I can think about how I read a book—from the first page to the last page. So, the word *final* must mean about the same thing as the word *last*.
- If the other words in the sentence don't help me understand what *final* means, I can look up the word in a dictionary.
- If I don't have a dictionary or I can't find the word in the dictionary, I can ask a friend, a parent, or a teacher for help.

Have children use the other words in each sentence below to figure out the meaning of each underlined word:

> When Lilly tripped and broke the cup, she knew it was an <u>accident</u>.
>
> Ted was <u>miserable</u> when he fell and lost the race.
>
> When Mike finally reached the top of the hill, he was <u>delighted</u>.

Day 5

Ongoing Assessment
Word Reading

Use these words to assess children's ability to read words with the vowel patterns *ew*, *ue* and inflected and plural *-es:*

glue	chew	clashes	crew	fixes	true
messes	Sue	stew	due	few	patches

If children cannot read the words,
then use the **Reteach** lessons for Vowel Patterns *ew*, *ue* and/or Inflected Ending and Plural *-es* on pages AR18 and AR19 of the Teacher's Edition.

Ongoing Assessment
Fluency

Materials Children should read grade-level text that they have not practiced. This text should be similar in difficulty to the selections children have practiced this week.

Assess fluency by taking a timed sample of the child's oral reading; record the number of words read correctly per minute. See Monitoring Fluency, page xxi.

Spelling
Segment Phonemes

When administering the Spelling Test, use only the first six words: *drew*, *grew*, *blue*, *new*, *true*, *glue*. Encourage children to segment sounds as they spell.

Review High-Frequency Words

In addition to practicing this week's words, have children review the non-decodable words *about*, *any*, *kind,* and *over*. Pronounce each word and spell it. Then have children pronounce it and spell it.

Build Fluency
Repeated Readings

Have children practice reading aloud Take-Home Decodable Reader 40 and/or 41 with a partner before taking it home. Children should reread the text three to four times for optimal fluency.

Children will

- use letter-sound knowledge to read decodable text
- decode words with long *e* spelled *ea*
- decode words with inflected ending *-ed* (with and without spelling change: double the final consonants)
- segment and blend words with long *e* spelled *ea*

Connect to Spelling

Decodable Reader 33 practices the spelling words *clean, asked,* and *called.*

Decodable Reader 33
Dean's Neat Green Cast

Materials Decodable Readers 33–41, pages 5–17

Introduction

Show Decodable Readers 33–41. Turn to page 5. Ask a volunteer to read the title, *Dean's Neat Green Cast.*

Say: **This is a story about a boy named Dean and what happens to him when he has a sled accident.**

Segment and Blend Sounds

Practice segmenting and blending the long *e* word *neat.*

Say: **Listen as I say this word slowly: /n/ /ē/ /t/.**
Now you say the word slowly: /n/ /ē/ /t/.
Touch your cheek when you hear the long *e*, /ē/.

Repeat /n/ /ē/ /t/ until all children successfully identify long *e*.

Say: **First I said the word slowly: /n/ /ē/ /t/.**
Now I'll blend the sounds together: /nnnēēēt/, *neat.*
Now you blend the sounds together: /nnnēēēt/, *neat.*

Read the Story

Have children turn to page 6, which is the first page of the story.

Say: **Let's read this page together.**
　　　Dean and Sid like to ride sleds.
　　　Dean and Sid can race on sleds.
　　　Dean likes to beat Sid.

Ask: **In which words do you hear long *e*, /ē/?**
Touch your cheek when you hear /ē/.

Read each word slowly. Be sure that children hear long *e* in *Dean* and *beat.*

Children may read the rest of the story aloud. For children who are having difficulty identifying long *e* spelled *ea* in words, continue reading the story following the model above.

After Reading

Activity 1 Write the word *Dean* on the board and have a volunteer read it. Have children think of words that rhyme with *Dean* and suggest their spelling. Remind children that long *e* can be spelled in several ways.

Activity 2 Have children go back through the story and list all of the words that end with the inflected ending *-ed.* The list should include: *tipped, needed, called, checked, asked, picked, yelled, seemed,* and *grinned.*

Children will

- use letter-sound knowledge to read decodable text
- decode words with long *a* spelled *ai, ay*
- decode words with contractions
- segment and blend words with long *a*

Connect to Spelling

Decodable Reader 34 practices the spelling words *play, may,* and *wait.*

Decodable Reader 34 Ray's Fire Bell

Materials Decodable Readers 33–41, pages 19–31

Introduction

Show Decodable Readers 33–41. Turn to page 19. Ask a volunteer to read the title, *Ray's Fire Bell.*

Say: **The fire bell keeps ringing in Miss Fay's classroom. Why? Let's find out.**

Segment and Blend Sounds

Practice segmenting and blending the long *a* word *Ray's.*

Say: **Listen as I say this word slowly: /r/ /ā/ /z/.**

Now you say the word slowly: /r/ /ā/ /z/.

Raise your hand when you hear the long *a*, /ā/.

Repeat /r/ /ā/ /z/ until all children successfully identify long *a.*

Say: **First I said the word slowly: /r/ /ā/ /z/.**

Now I'll blend the sounds together: /rrrāāāzzz/, *Ray's.*

Now you blend the sounds together: /rrrāāāzzz/, *Ray's.*

Read the Story

Have children turn to page 20, which is the first page of the story.

Say: **Let's read this page together.**

> **Ray is our pet.**
> **He will not stay in his tank.**
> **He may walk all over this class.**

Ask: **In which words do you hear long *a*, /ā/?**

Raise your hand when you hear /ā/.

Read each word slowly. Be sure that children hear the long *a* in *Ray, stay,* and *may.*

Children may read the rest of the story aloud. For children who are having difficulty identifying long *a,* continue reading the story following the model above.

After Reading

Activity 1 Create two columns on the chalkboard. One column should have the heading *ay* and the other *ai.* Have children pair up and go through the story, first finding all the long *a* words spelled *ay,* then the long *a* words spelled *ai.* Column one words should include: *Ray, stay, may, Fay, May, Clay, day, play,* and *Jay.* Column two words should include: *Vail, painting, paint, wait, Bails, pail,* and *Faith.*

Activity 2 Write the following words on the board and ask children to find the contraction in the story that matches one of them:

has not   I would   did not   he will   (didn't)

Children will

- use letter-sound knowledge to read decodable text
- review decoding words with long *e* spelled *ea*
- review decoding words with inflected ending *-ed*
- review decoding words with long *a* spelled *ai, ay*
- review decoding words with contractions

Connect to Spelling

Decodable Reader 35 practices the spelling words *ask, asked, call, called, clean, cleaned, play, may, wait,* and *rain.*

Decodable Reader 35 Let's Play!

Materials Decodable Readers 33–41, pages 33–45

Review Phonics Skills

Write *cleaned* on the board.

Say: **Read this word with me: /k/ /l/ /ē/ /n/ /d/, cleaned.**

What sound does *ea* make in *cleaned*? (/ē/)

Do you hear the *-ed* ending? /d/, cleaned.

Now I'm going to read three words.

Speak up when you hear a word with long *e: creak, bark, meal.*

Repeat each word slowly until all children speak up when they hear *creak* and *meal.* Point out the *-ed* ending in *cleaned* again. Ask children to read the word with and without the ending.

Introduction

Show Decodable Readers 33–41. Turn to page 33. Ask a volunteer to read the title, *Let's Play!* Point out the contraction *Let's* in the title and ask children to tell you its two-word form, *(Let us).* Tell children that this is a story about two friends. It is full of long *e* words and words that end in *-ed.*

Read the Story

Have children turn to page 35, which is the second page of the story.

Say: **Let's read the second page of this story together:**

> **"May I play with Beth?" asked Kay.**
> **"Yes," said Mom, "but we**
> **will eat at six. Be cleaned up then."**

Ask: **Which words have /ē/ spelled *ea*?**

Raise your hand when you hear a word with /ē/ spelled *ea*.

Read each word again slowly. Children should identify *eat* and *cleaned* as having long *e* spelled *ea.* Children may go back to page 34 and read the story aloud. For those who are having difficulty identifying long *e* spelled *ea,* continue reading the story following the model above.

After Reading

Activity 1 Write *real* on the board. Remind children that *real* has a long *e* /ē/ spelled *ea.* Invite children to think of other words that rhyme with *real.* They might mention *meal, deal, seal, steal, squeal,* and *heal.* Have children go back through the story to find long *e* words spelled *ea.* Their list should include: *eat, cleaned, deal, teach, please, treats,* and *clean.*

Activity 2 Write *play* on the board. Remind children that *play* has a long *a* /ā/ spelled *ay.* Ask children to find words in the story that rhyme with *play.* Their list should include *Kay, may, stay, clay,* and *day.*

Children will

- use letter-sound knowledge to read decodable text
- decode words with long *o* spelled *oa* and *ow*
- decode words with inflected ending *-ing*
- segment and blend words with long o spelled *oa*

Connect to Spelling

Decodable Reader 36 practices the spelling words *grow, show,* and *floating.*

Decodable Reader 36 Duck's Coat

Materials Decodable Readers 33–41, pages 47–59

Introduction

Show Decodable Readers 33–41. Turn to page 47. Ask a volunteer to read the title, *Duck's Coat.*

Say: **This is a story about a duck and her new coat.**

Segment and Blend Sounds

Practice segmenting and blending the long *o* word *coat.*

Say: **Listen as I say this word slowly: /k/ /ō/ /t/.**
Now you say the word slowly: /k/ /ō/ /t/.
Touch your nose when you hear the long *o,* /ō/.

Repeat /k/ /ō/ /t/ until all children successfully identify long *o.*

Say: **First I said the word slowly: /k/ /ō/ /t/.**
Now I'll blend the sounds together: /kōōōt/, *coat.*
Now you blend the sounds together: /kōōōt/, *coat.*

Read the Story

Have children turn to page 48, which is the first page of the story.

Say: **Let's read this page together.**
Duck had a coat.
It didn't fit.
The coat will not grow.
Duck needed a coat that fit.

Ask: **In which words do you hear long *o,* /ō/?**
Touch your nose when you hear /ō/.

Read each word slowly. Be sure that children hear long *o* in *coat* and *grow.* Point out the spelling of each word.

Children may read the rest of the story aloud. For children who are having difficulty identifying long *o* spelled *oa* and *ow* in words, continue reading the story following the model above.

After Reading

Activity 1 Draw a large coat on the chalkboard. Have children go back through the story and find all of the words with long *o* spelled *oa* and *ow.* As the children find a long *o* word, have them write it on the chalkboard coat. The list should include: *coat, grow, showed, show, moaned, Goat, floating, rowboat, Crow, Toad, road, towing,* and *loading.*

Activity 2 Have children go back through the story and find all of the words with inflected ending *-ing.* Have them sort the words according to which words have a spelling change and which do not. You may also wish to have the children dramatize the words. The list should include: *shopping, missing, floating, fixing, towing, loading, digging, sitting,* and *getting.*

Objectives

Children will

- use letter-sound knowledge to read decodable text
- decode words with long *i* spelled *igh, ie*
- decode words with possessives
- segment and blend words with long *i* spelled *igh*

Connect to Spelling

Decodable Reader 37 practices the spelling words *pie, tie(d), light,* and *right.*

Decodable Reader 37 It's Just Right!

Materials Decodable Readers 33–41, pages 61–73

Introduction

Show Decodable Readers 33–41. Turn to page 61. Ask a volunteer to read the title, *It's Just Right!*

Say: **This is a story about a girl, Pam, who longs to have a cat like her friend Jill's.**

Segment and Blend Sounds

Practice segmenting and blending the long *i* word *right.*

Say: **Listen as I say this word slowly: /r/ /ī/ /t/.**

Now you say the word slowly: /r/ /ī/ /t/.

Raise your right hand when you hear the long *i*, /ī/.

Repeat /r/ /ī/ /t/ until all children successfully identify long *i*.

Say: **First I said the word slowly: /r/ /ī/ /t/.**

Now I'll blend the sounds together: /rrrīīt/, *right*.

Now you blend the sounds together: /rrrīīt/, *right*.

Read the Story

Have children turn to page 62, which is the first page of the story.

Say: **Let's read this page together.**

> **Jill is Pam's pal.**
> **Jill and Pam have fun.**
> **Jill's cat plays with its tail.**

Ask: **Which two words show that a person has or owns something?**

Point to yourself when you hear such a word.

Read each word slowly. Be sure that children can identify the possessives *Pam's* and *Jill's.*

Children may read the rest of the story aloud. For children who are having difficulty identifying long *i* words spelled *igh* or *ie* or possessives, continue reading the story following the model above.

After Reading

Activity 1 Read the story aloud to children, asking them to purr softly like a cat when they hear words that show possession. Children should purr when hearing *Pam's, Jill's, cat's,* and *Dad's.*

Activity 2 Ask children to go back through the story and find all the words with long *i* spelled *-igh* and *-ie.* The list should include: *right, sighs, night, pie, tied, bright, light, right,* and *tight.* Ask children to look on the word wall and see if they can find any other words with /ī/ spelled *-igh* and *-ie.*

Children will

- use letter-sound knowledge to read decodable text
- review decoding words with long *o* spelled *oa, ow*
- review decoding words with long *i* spelled *igh, ie*
- review decoding words with inflected ending *-ing*
- review decoding words with singular possessives

Connect to Spelling

Decodable Reader 38 practices the spelling words *grow, float, show, growing, lie, pie, night, light,* and *right.*

Decodable Reader 38 Night Sights

Materials Decodable Readers 33–41, pages 75–85

Review Phonics Skills

Write *night* and *coat* on the board.

Say: **Read this word with me: /n/ /ī/ /t/, night.**
What sound does igh make in night? (/ī/)

Continue the procedure with the long *o* word *coat.*

Say: **Now I'm going to read three words.**
Tell me whether each word has /ī/ or /ō/: boat, fight, float.

Repeat each word slowly until all children name the vowel they hear.

Introduction

Show Decodable Readers 33–41. Turn to page 75. Ask a volunteer to read the title, *Night Sights.* Tell children that this story is about a girl and her father on a nighttime adventure. This story is full of long *i* words spelled *igh* and *ie* and long *o* words spelled *oa* and *ow.*

Read the Story

Have children turn to page 76, which is the first page of the story.

Say: **Let's read the first page of this story together:**
> *Let's go on a night ride!*
> *We'll need coats and flashlights.*
> *We'll need mittens and hats.*

Ask: **Which words have /ī/? Which have /ō/?**
Raise your hand high when you hear a word with /ī/.
Wiggle your fingers when you hear a word with /ō/.

Read each word again slowly. Children should identify *night, ride,* and *flashlights* as having long *i* and *go* and *coats* as having long *o.* Point out the different spelling patterns in each. Children may read the rest of the story aloud. For those who are having difficulty identifying long *i* and *o,* continue reading the story following the model above.

After Reading

Activity 1 Have children look back through the story for inflected ending *-ing* words. Have them write the words on the board. Invite the children to name the base word for each. Words and base words should include: *hopping, hop; jumping, jump; croaking, croak; growing, grow; eating, eat.*

Activity 2 Ask two students to stand up. Write their names on the board. Add an *'s* to their names to create the possessive. Have children read through the story to find the three possessive words *(night's, plant's, tree's).* Ask them to read these words.

Children will

- use letter-sound knowledge to read decodable text
- decode words ending in *y* (long *e*, long *i*)
- decode compound words
- segment and blend words ending in *y* (long *i*)

Connect to Spelling

Decodable Reader 39 practices the spelling words *funny, many, my,* and *fly.*

Decodable Reader 39 My Mail

Materials Decodable Readers 33–41, pages 87–99

Introduction

Show Decodable Readers 33–41. Turn to page 87. Ask a volunteer to read the title, *My Mail.*

Say: **In this story, Molly sends notes to her friends and learns how mail is delivered.**

Segment and Blend Sounds

Practice segmenting and blending the long *i* sound in the word *my.*

Say: **Listen as I say this word slowly: /m/ /ī/.**
Now you say the word slowly: /m/ /ī/.
Raise your hand when you hear the long *i*, /ī/.

Repeat /m/ /ī/ until all children successfully identify long *i*.

Say: **First I said the word slowly: /m/ /ī/.**
Now I'll blend the sounds together: /mmmīīī/, *my*.
Now you blend the sounds together: /mmmīīī/, *my*.

Read the Story

Have children turn to page 88, which is the first page of the story.

Say: **Let's read this page together.**
My name is Molly. I like getting mail.
Each day I check my mailbox. Many
times I don't get mail. It is still fun to check.

Ask: **In which word does *y* have a long *i* sound, /ī/?**
In which words does *y* have a long *e* sound, /ē/?

Read each word slowly. Be sure that children can identify the long *i* in *My* and the long *e* in *Molly* and *Many*. Children may read the rest of the story aloud. For children who are having difficulty identifying the long *i* or long *e* sound for *y*, continue reading the story following the model above.

After Reading

Activity 1 Have children go back through the story and list all of the words ending in *y* that have a long *e* or long *i* sound. Long *e* words should include: *Molly, many, Kathy, City* and *funny.* Long *i* words should include: *my, Ty, by,* and *fly.* Have them write a sentence using two of these words.

Activity 2 Have children go back through the story and look for compound words. Ask them to identify each word in the compound. The list should include *mailbox, without, Seaside, pickup,* and *inside.*

Children will

- use letter-sound knowledge to read decodable text
- decode words with vowel patterns *ew* and *ue*
- decode words with inflected ending *-es* and plural *-es*
- segment and blend words with vowel pattern *ue*

Connect to Spelling

Decodable Reader 40 practices the spelling words *new, grew, Drew, blue, true,* and *glue.*

Decodable Reader 40
What's New with Sue?

Materials Decodable Readers 33–41, pages 101–113

Introduction

Show Decodable Readers 33–41. Turn to page 101. Ask a volunteer to read the title, *What's New with Sue?*

Say: **This is a story about Sue, a girl who learned to blow a bubble with her gum.**

Segment and Blend Sounds

Practice segmenting and blending the vowel pattern *ue* word *Sue.*

Say: **Listen as I say this word slowly: /s/ /ü/.**

Now you say the word slowly: /s/ /ü/.

Raise your hand when you hear the long *u*, /ü/.

Repeat /s/ /ü/ until all children successfully identify the long *u.*

Say: **First I said the word slowly: /s/ /ü/.**

Now I'll blend the sounds together: /sssüüü/, *Sue.*

Now you blend the sounds together: /sssüüü/, *Sue.*

Read the Story

Have children turn to page 102, which is the first page of the story.

Say: **Let's read this page together.**

This is Sue. What is new with Sue?

Sue can chew gum. She is big.

Ask: **In which words do you hear long *u*, /ü/?**

Raise your hand when you hear /ü/.

Read each word slowly. Be sure that children can identify long *u* in *Sue, new,* and *chew.*

Children may return to the beginning of the story and read it aloud. For children who are having difficulty identifying long *u* vowel patterns *ew* and *ue* in words, continue reading the story following the model above.

After Reading

Activity 1 Draw thirteen "bubble gum bubbles" on the board. Have children reread the story and find words with vowel pattern *ew* and *ue.* Have them write the words inside the bubbles. The *ew* words should include *new, chew, few, chews, Drew, blew, grew,* and *flew.* The *ue* words should include *Sue, clue, blue, true,* and *glue.*

Activity 2 Have children go back through the story and list all of the words with inflected ending *-es* and plural *-es.* The list should include: *wishes, boxes, teaches,* and *kisses.*

Decodable Reader 41
Ty's New Baseball

Materials Decodable Readers 33–41, pages 115–127

Review Phonics Skills

Write *Ty* and *Betty* on the board.

Say: **Read this word with me: /t/ /ī/, *Ty*.**
What sound does *y* make in *Ty?* (/ī/)

Continue the procedure with *Betty*. (long *e*, /ē/)

Say: **Now I'm going to read three words.**
Tell me whether each word has /ī/ or /ē/: *fly, baby, cry*.

Repeat each word slowly until all children name the vowels.

Introduction

Show Decodable Readers 33–41. Turn to page 115. Ask a volunteer to read the title, *Ty's New Baseball.* Tell children that this story is about friends who need a new baseball. The story has many words that end in *y* as well as long *u* words spelled *ew* and *ue*.

Read the Story

Have children turn to page 116, which is the first page of the story.

Say: **Let's read the first page of this story together:**

> *"I can't pitch," said Ty. "My baseball is*
> *busted. We can't play a ballgame with it."*
> *"We can see if we can fix it," said Betty,*
> *Jessy, and Lew.*

Say: **Write an *i* in the air when you hear a word in which *y*
stands for /ī/; write an *e* in the air when you hear a
word in which *y* stands for /ē/.**

Read each word again slowly. Children should identify *Ty* and *my* as having long *i* and *Betty* and *Jessy* as having long *e*. Children may read the rest of the story aloud. For those who are having difficulty identifying the vowel sounds that *y* stands for, continue reading the story following the model above.

After Reading

Activity 1 Have children page through the story to find compound words. As they name a word, write it on the board. Words should include: *baseball, ballgame, inside, maybe, mailboxes, handstands,* and *handprint.* Ask children to compare the two plural words and their endings (*handstands* ends in *-s; mailboxes* ends in *-es*).

Activity 2 Write these two headings on the board: *ew* and *ue*. Have children identify words from the story that fit these vowel patterns. Words should include: *Lew, glue, new, clue, Lew's, few, blue,* and *chewing.*

Arthur's Reading Race

Long *e: ea*

Teach

Pronounce /ē/ and have children say the sound with you. Ask what long vowel sound this is. Write the words *bend* and *bean* on the board. Guide children in blending the words. Ask which word has the long *e* sound. Explain that the letters *ea* can stand for the long *e* sound.

Read the following sentences aloud. Ask children to name the word in each sentence that has the long *e* sound. Say:

Our team scored six goals in the game.

The seal played with a big red ball.

As children identify the words *team* and *seal*, write them on the board and underline the letters *ea* in each word. Ask children which letters stand for the long *e* sound.

Practice and Assess

Say the following words one at a time: *wheat, pet, clean, tent, bead, nest,* and *steam*. Tell children to say "write it" when they hear a word with the sound /ē/. Then write those words on the board.

> wheat   bead   clean   steam

After writing the words, ask a volunteer to underline the letters that stand for the long *e* sound in each word.

Then ask children to suggest rhyming words for those on the board. Write each word they say, and ask them if the word uses the letters *ea* for the sound /ē/. If yes, leave it up. If not, erase it.

Inflected Ending *-ed*

Teach

Write the word *pick* on the board and have children read it. Then say:

I pick up my dog.

Explain that the word *pick* shows that you are doing the action now. Write the word *picked* on the board and say:

I picked up my dog last night.

Point out that when you add *-ed* to a word, it means that the action happened in the past.

Write the following words on the board: *lock, locked* and *stop, stopped*. Have children read the words aloud and identify the ending that means something has already happened. Then ask children how *stopped* is different from *stop*. Guide children to understand that in some words that end with one vowel followed by a consonant, the final consonant is written again before adding the *-ed*.

Practice and Assess

Write the following words: *packed, jogged, wished, bumped, petted,* and *zipped*. Have children read each word and tell which have a final consonant that was doubled when *-ed* was added.

Tell children to write the following words on their paper: *hop, hug, stamp, clap, watch*. Have children change each word to show an action that happened in the past. Ask volunteers to write the new words on the board and use them in a sentence.

> hopped   hugged   stamped
> clapped   watched

Check to make sure children have doubled the final consonants in *hop, hug*, and *clap* before adding *-ed*.

Arthur's Reading Race

Predicting

Teach

Explain to children that when they read, they can often figure out what might happen next in the story. Point out that children can use the words and pictures in a story, their own experience, and other things they have read to predict what might happen next.

Reread several pages of *Arthur's Reading Race* aloud. For pages 18–21, model using clues from the story to show how you might make a prediction. Say:

I read about Arthur learning to read. I learned that he reads in the car and in bed. In the pictures, Arthur looks happy. I think that the story will tell me about how much Arthur likes to read.

Practice and Assess

Cut out pictures from magazines or newspapers. Display each picture and read any captions. Ask children what they think might happen next. Have them identify clues they used to make their predictions.

Read the following sentences. Tell children to use what you read and what they know to predict what might happen next.

The boys and girls read a story. They put their books away. The school bell rang. The children put on their jackets.

What do you think happened next? (Accept logical answers. Children might predict that the boys and girls will go home, line up for the school bus, or go out for recess.)

What words in the story helped you make your prediction?
Did you use your own experience to make your prediction?

Use the Selection Audio for an additional Reteach lesson.

CD 6/Tape 21, Side 2

Lost!

Long *a: ai, ay*

Teach

Write the letters *ai* on the board and tell children that these letters can stand for the sound /ā/. Add the letters *m* and *l* to write the word *mail*, and model blending it as you underline the letters *ai*. Ask children to suggest words that rhyme with *mail* and write them on the board. Have children blend each word.

mail	may

Write the letters *ay* on the board and tell children that these letters can also stand for the sound /ā/. Add the letter *m* to make the word *may* and model blending it as you underline the letters *ay*. Ask children to name words that rhyme with *may* and write them on the board. Have children blend each word.

Practice and Assess

Write the words *hay* and *paid* on the board. Ask children what vowel sound they hear in *hay* and *paid*. Then have them identify the letters that stand for the sound /ā/.

Display the following words with double-sided tape on the back of each.

Have children read each word and identify the vowel sound. If the word does not have the long *a* sound, remove it from the board.

Then have children sort the words into those with long *a* spelled *ai* and those with long *a* spelled *ay*.

Lost!

Contractions

Teach

Write the following words on the board:

I am   I'm

Tell children that *I'm* is a shorter way of writing the words *I am*. The apostrophe takes the place of the letter *a*. Explain that when two words are shortened and put together, the new word is called a contraction. A contraction always has an apostrophe to show where some letters were left out.

Practice and Assess

Write the following words and their contractions on the board. Have children read each contraction. Ask a volunteer to draw a line to match the words used to make it.

isn't	cannot
let's	is not
it's	I am
I'll	let us
can't	it is
I'm	I will

Have children copy the following words on a sheet of paper: *we'll, he's, don't, they're*. Next to each contraction they should write the two words used to make it.

Compare and Contrast

Teach

Hold up two different pencils and ask children to tell how they are alike and how they are different. Remind children that another way you can learn about two things is to find how the things are alike and how they are different. Tell children you will say some sentences. They should then tell you whether the sentence is showing how things are alike or how they are different. Say:

A cat and a tiger are both cats. (alike)
A cat is much smaller than a tiger. (different)
A pencil and a crayon both write. (alike)
A pencil and a crayon are made of different materials. (different)

Practice and Assess

Reread *Lost!* and discuss with children the ways that the boy and the bear are alike and ways they are different. Explain that when you tell how characters in a story are alike and different, it helps you understand the story and the characters better.

Draw a large Venn diagram on the board and label the one circle *bike* and the other *car*. Ask volunteers to describe a bike, and jot their suggestions in that circle. Repeat the process for a car. Ask children if they notice any details that are the same. As children note similarities, erase them from the circle area and rewrite them in the center overlapped part.

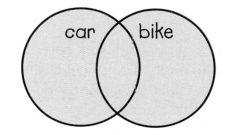

Selection Audio
CD 6/Tape 22, Side 2

Use the Selection Audio for an additional Reteach lesson.

Foal

Long o: *oa, ow*

Teach

Write the word *goat* on the board and blend the word, emphasizing the sound /ō/. Underline the letters *oa* and explain to children that the letters *oa* stand for the long *o* sound in *goat*.

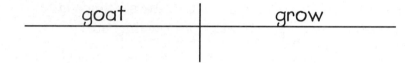

goat	grow

Have children suggest words that rhyme with *goat* and *grow*. Write the rhyming words on the board and have children blend them.

Practice and Assess

Write the following words on the board: *sock, mow, boat, loan, flow, hot, low, soap, top, toad, own, job.*

Create a chart as shown. Tell children that they will sort the words into those that have the long *o* sound spelled *oa*, those with the long *o* sound spelled *ow*, and those with the short *o* sound. Have a volunteer point to a word, read it, and then write it in the appropriate column. Continue until all the words have been entered correctly on the chart.

Long o (oa)	Long o (ow)	Short o

Ask children to suggest other words that have the long *o* sound and write them on the board. Let children decide if they belong in either the *oa* or *ow* column or if the long *o* sound is spelled another way.

Inflected Ending *-ing*

Teach

Write the following sentence and have it read.

Bob is running and jumping.

Remind children that the letters *-ing* can be added to many action words to make a new word. Have a volunteer read the action words in the sentence and underline the *-ing*.

Frame *run* in *running*. Point out that *run* ends with one vowel followed by a consonant. Tell children that in words like *run*, the final consonant is doubled before adding *-ing*. Then circle the two *n*'s in running.

Practice and Assess

Remind children that the letters *-ing* are added to action words. Write the following words on the board and have children read them. Have a volunteer point out which words had the final consonant doubled before *-ing* was added.

walking   swimming   dropping   hearing

Write these words on the board:

skip   stop   wish
want   chop   tip

Have volunteers add the *-ing* ending to each word, being careful to add another consonant when needed.

Foal

Sequence

Teach

Explain to children that many things they do every day must be done in a certain order. Ask children to share some activities they do on a school day and list them on the board. Read the list with children and then ask:

What comes first?

Help children order the events. (See sample below)

> get on school bus
> wake up and get dressed
> eat breakfast

Point out that events in stories also happen in a certain order. Clue words, such as *first, next,* and *last* sometimes signal the order of events. Reread the activities on the board, using clue words to tell the sequence of events. (For example, "First you wake up and get dressed.")

Practice and Assess

Reread *Baby Otter Grows Up* and have volunteers tell what comes first, next, and last in the story. Remind children to use clue words when they retell a story.

Display the following sentences on strips of paper with double-faced tape on the back of each. Read them and have children reorder them to show the sequence.

> Lee watered the small plants.
>
> Lee planted seeds.
>
> Lee picked flowers in the garden.

Tell children to rewrite the sentences, using the words *first, next,* and *last* to show the order of events. Have children draw pictures to show the story sequence.

Selection Audio Use the Selection Audio for an additional Reteach lesson.
CD 6/Tape 23, Side 2

Lost in the Museum

Long *i: igh, ie*

Teach

Write the word *night* on the board and read it. Ask:

What vowel sound is heard in *night*?

Say /ī/ and have the children repeat it. Underline the letters *igh* and tell children that these letters stand for the long *i* sound in night. Follow the same procedure with *pie* and the letters *ie*.

| ni<u>gh</u>t | p<u>ie</u> |

Practice and Assess

Tell children that you are going to read some sentences. After each sentence, children should say the word that has the long *i* sound. Say:

The bird's nest is high in the tree. (high)

Dad might take me to the show. (might)

If you don't water the plants, they will die. (die)

Display the following word cards with double-sided tape on the back of each:

swim   fight   tie   sit   tight
lie   right   light   crib   rib

Have children take turns selecting a card and reading the word. If the word has long *i*, ask them to identify the letters that stand for the long *i* sound. Have the children sort the words into three groups: *ie* words, *igh* words, and words with short *i*.

Lost in the Museum

Singular Possessives

Teach

Write the following on the board and read it:

the book that belongs to Pat

Pat's book

Explain to children that these words have the same meaning. They tell who owns the book. Point to 's and remind children that the apostrophe plus s shows something belongs to someone.

Practice and Assess

Reread *What a Sight!* aloud as children track the print. Tell children to raise their hand when they see a word that signals ownership, identify it, and tell what is owned. Then write the words on the board: *Nicky's, Tiger's, Jim's, Dad's.* Have children underline the 's in each word to reinforce the idea of ownership.

Write the lists below. Have a child read a phrase in the first column. Then have the child find and read a phrase in the second column that has the same meaning. If the child has correctly matched two phrases, have him or her draw a line that connects the phrases. Continue until all the phrases have been matched.

the dog of Mike	Mike's dog
Juan's bike	the pet of my friend
the wheel of the bike	the bike of Juan
Bill's pen	the pen of Bill
the father of Amy	the dog's bone
my friend's pet	the tail of the cat
the cat's tail	the bike's wheel
the bone of the dog	Amy's father

Cause and Effect

Teach

Explain to children that one thing sometimes makes something else happen. To find out if one event makes another one happen, children can ask themselves "Why did this happen?" as they read. Clue words such as *because* may help them answer their question.

Reread page 121 in *What a Sight!* Ask children what Tiger did. (Tiger jumped out of Jim's backpack.) Then ask why Tiger jumped out of Jim's backpack. (Tiger jumped out because he saw a painting of a very large dog.) Guide children to understand that seeing the picture of the dog made Tiger jump. In other words, one thing made another happen.

Practice and Assess

Tell children you will read some sentences and ask some questions about why things happened. Say:

The sun came out, and the snowman started to melt. (he melted)

What happened to the snowman? (he melted)

Why did the snowman start to melt? (the sun came out)

Continue asking similar questions using the following sentences:

The baby cried because his cookie fell on the floor.

There was no wind. The kite would not fly.

Have children work in pairs to write two cause-and-effect sentences using the word *because*. Have them share their sentences with the class, who should identify what happened in each sentence and why it happened.

Use the Selection Audio for an additional Reteach lesson.

Selection Audio

CD 7/Tape 24, Side 2

Dinosaur Babies

Vowel Sounds of *y*

Teach

Write the word *lucky* on the board. Say it slowly, emphasizing the ending sound /ē/. Ask:

What sound is heard at the end of *lucky*? (ē)

What letter stands for the ending sound? (*y*)

Write the word *my* on the board. Say it slowly, emphasizing the ending sound /ī/. Ask:

What sound is heard at the end of *my*. (ī)
What letter stands for the long *i* sound? (*y*)

Explain to children that *y* at the end of the word can stand for the long *e* sound or the long *i* sound. It usually stands for the long *e* sound at the end of words that have two or more syllables.

Practice and Assess

Write the following words on the board:

cry   shy   windy   pretty
silly   sunny   by   dry

Have children read each word aloud and tell what sound the letter *y* stands for at the end of the word.

Then give the following clues. Have volunteers frame and read the correct word on the board. Say:

When the wind is blowing, it is… (windy)

The opposite of wet is… (dry)

Someone who is uncomfortable around new people is… (shy)

When the sun is shining it is… (sunny)

Babies sometimes… (cry)

Another word for goofy is… (silly)

Then make a chart as shown. Have children sort the words into those in which the *y* spells the long *e* sound and those in which the *y* spells the long *i* sound.

y = long e	*y* = long i

Compound Words

Teach

Write the words *cupcake* and *handshake* on the board and have them read. Remind children that compound words are made of two whole words that were put together. Have children draw a line between the two words in each compound.

Create the following chart:

in	prints
any	side
foot	more

Point to and read a word from the first column. Ask a volunteer to find a word from the second column that makes a compound word. Have him or her draw a line connecting the two words and say the compound word aloud. Then write the compound word. Repeat the process with the other words.

Practice and Assess

Reread *Chompy's Afternoon* aloud with children. As you read, have children identify compound words. Write the words on the board and have volunteers identify the two words that make each compound word.

Display these word cards with double-face tape on the back of each.

Have children choose two word cards to make a compound word. Point out that words can be used more than once. Challenge children to make as many compound words as they can and write them on their paper. After children have written the compound words, have them share their lists.

Dinosaur Babies

Main Idea

Teach

Remind children that *every* story has one big idea that tells what the whole story is about. Have children recall *Dinosaur Babies*. Ask children to tell what the big or most important idea is. (how baby dinosaurs lived and grew) If children offer responses that include details, such as "Dinosaurs are good mothers" or "Baby dinosaurs ate leaves, berries, and seeds," guide children to understand that these are only small parts of the story. They do not tell what the whole story is about.

Practice and Assess

Write the following sentences on the board.

> Ted and I set up the tent.
>
> Mom brought food from the car.
>
> Dad started a campfire.
>
> We toasted marshmallows.
>
> We sang songs.
>
> Our family likes to camp.

Ask children to identify which sentence tells the main idea. (Our family likes to camp.)

Review selections from *Take Me There* with children and remind them that *every* story has one idea that is the most important. As you review each selection, ask children to tell the main idea in their own words.

Use the Selection Audio for an additional Reteach lesson.

Selection Audio
CD 7/Tape 25, Side 2

The Bravest Cat!

Vowel Patterns *ew, ue*

Teach

Write the words *blew* and *true* on the board and read them aloud. Ask how the words are alike. (They rhyme; they end with the same sound.) Ask what vowel sound is heard in both words. Frame *ew* in *blew* and *ue* in *true*. Explain that these letters can stand for the sound /ü/.

Practice and Assess

Have children write *blew* on a sheet of paper. Tell them to follow your instructions to make new words. Say:

Change *bl* to *n*. What's the word? (new)

Change *n* to *st*. What's the word? (stew)

Change *st* to *cr*. What's the word? (crew)

Change *cr* to *fl*. What's the word? (flew)

Then have children write the word *true*. Continue giving these instructions in the same manner.

Change *tr* to *bl*. What's the word? (blue)

Change *b* to *c*. What's the word? (clue)

Change *cl* to *S*. What's the word? (Sue)

Change *S* to *d*. What's the word? (due)

The Bravest Cat!

Inflected Ending *-es*

Teach

Write this sentence on the board and have it read:

Bill mix the paint.

Ask if the sentence sounds right. Ask why not. If children do not make any suggestions, add *-es* to *mix*. Then read the sentence again. Explain that sometimes we need to add *-es* at the end of an action word to make it sound right in a sentence.

Write the word *box* on the board. Ask children to say the word that means "more than one box." Write *boxes* on the board and read it aloud, emphasizing both syllables. Tell children that *-es* can also be added to a word to mean more than one.

Practice and Assess

Display the following word cards:

kiss dish duck lunch pet
bike father beach watch

Put the cards for *-es* and *-s* facedown. Have children take turns selecting a card and then choosing a word that can have that ending. Have the child write the word with the ending on the board and read it. Ask another child to use the word with the ending in a sentence.

If needed, ask volunteers to suggest a base word and then have another child say what ending it would get: *-s* or *-es*. Write the new words on the board.

Cause and Effect

Teach

Remind children that they can figure out if one thing in a story makes another thing happen by asking "Why?" They can also look for clue words such as *because*. Review the selection *The Bravest Cat!* Guide children to understand that the mother cat is burned because she went into the burning building to rescue her kittens. Ask why the doctors named the mother cat Scarlett. (because she had red burns)

Practice and Assess

Make a chart as shown. Display the sentences below on strips of paper. Have each pair read. Have children place sentences under the correct columns.

What Happened	Why Did It Happen

It began to rain.

Jana put up her umbrella.

Daniel missed the bus.

He did not hear the alarm clock.

Dolores wanted a pet.

Her grandpa bought her a dog.

Jon's clothes were too small.

He grew five inches last year.

Divide the class into groups. Have children cut out pictures from magazines or newspapers and write sentences about their pictures that tell what happened and why it happened.

Use the Selection Audio for an Additional Reteach lesson.

CD 7/Tape 26, Side 2

Matching Students to Texts

Providing children with reading materials they can and want to read is the first step toward developing fluent readers. A running record allows you to determine each child's instructional and independent reading level. Information on how to take a running record is provided on pp. AR22–AR23.

Instructional Reading Level

Only approximately 1 in 10 words will be difficult when reading a selection from the Student Edition for children who are at grade level. (A typical first-grader reads approximately 60–80 words per minute.)

- Children reading at grade level should read regularly from the Student Edition with teacher support as suggested in the Teacher's Editions.

- Children reading below grade level can read the A and B Leveled Readers. The Leveled Reader Resource Guide provides instructional plans for supporting children reading the A and B Leveled Readers.

- Children reading at or above grade level can use Set C/Challenge Leveled Readers, which provide literature and activities for these children.

Independent Reading Level

Children should read regularly in independent-level material, text in which no more than approximately 1 in 20 words is difficult for the reader. Other factors that make a book easy to read include the child's interest in the topic, the amount of text on a page, how well illustrations support meaning, and the complexity and familiarity of the concepts. Suggested books for self-selected reading are provided with each lesson and on pp. AR24–AR25 in this Teacher's Edition.

Guide children in learning how to self-select books at their independent reading level. As you talk about a book with children, discuss the challenging concepts in it, list new words children find in sampling the book, and ask children about their familiarity with the topic. A blackline master to help children evaluate books for independent reading is provided on p. AR21.

Self-Selected/Independent Reading

While oral reading allows you to assess children's reading level and fluency, independent reading is of crucial importance to children's futures as readers and learners. Children need to develop their ability to read independently for increasing amounts of time.

- Schedule a regular time for sustained independent reading in your classroom. During the year, gradually increase the amount of time devoted to independent reading.

- More fluent readers may choose to read silently during independent-reading time. Other children might read to a partner, to a stuffed animal, or to an adult volunteer.

- Help children track the amount of time they read independently and the number of pages they read in a given amount of time. Tracking will help motivate them to increase their duration and speed gradually. A blackline master for children to use to track independent reading is provided on p. AR21.

Name _____

Choosing a Book to Read by Yourself

These questions can help you pick a book to read.

_____ **1.** Is this book about something that I like?

_____ **2.** This book may be about a real person, about facts, or a made-up story. Do I like reading this kind of book?

_____ **3.** Have I read other things by this author? Do I like the author?

If you say "yes" to question 1, 2, or 3, go on.

_____ **4.** Were there fewer than 5 hard words on the first page?

_____ **5.** Does the number of words on a page look about right to me?

If you say "yes" to questions 4 and 5, the book is right for you.

Silent Reading

Write the date, the title of the book, and the number of pages you read.

Date	Title	Pages

© Scott Foresman

Taking a Running Record

A running record is an assessment of a child's oral reading accuracy and oral reading fluency. Reading accuracy is based on the number of words read correctly. Reading fluency is based on the reading rate (the number of words read per minute) and the degree to which a child reads with a "natural flow."

How to Measure Reading Accuracy

1. Choose a grade-level text of about 80 to 120 words that is unfamiliar to the child.

2. Make a copy of the text for yourself. Make a copy for the child or have the child read aloud from a book.

3. Give the child the text and have the child read aloud. (You may wish to tape-record the child's reading for later evaluation.)

4. On your copy of the text, mark any miscues or errors the child makes while reading. See the Running Record Sample on page AR23, which shows how to identify and mark miscues.

5. Count the total number of words in the text and the total number of errors made by the child. Note: If a child makes the same error more than once, such as mispronouncing the same word multiple times, count it as one error. Self-corrections do not count as actual errors. Use the following formula to calculate the percentage score, or accuracy rate:

$$\frac{\text{Total Number of Words} - \text{Total Number of Errors}}{\text{Total Number of Words}} \times 100 = \text{percentage score}$$

Interpreting the Results

- A child who reads **95–100%** of the words correctly is reading at an **independent level** and may need more challenging text.

- A child who reads **90–94%** of the words correctly is reading at an **instructional level** and will likely benefit from guided instruction.

- A child who reads **89%** or fewer of the words correctly is reading at a **frustrational level** and may benefit most from targeted instruction with lower-level texts and intervention.

See the Scott Foresman Leveling System on pages 205 and 206 of the Leveled Reader Resource Guide to help you select materials that are appropriate for the child's reading level.

How to Measure Reading Rate

1. Follow Steps 1–3 above.

2. Note the exact times when the child begins and finishes reading.

3. Use the following formula to calculate the number of words per minute (wpm), or reading rate:

$$\frac{\text{Total Number of Words Read}}{\text{Total Number of Seconds}} \times 60 = \text{words per minute}$$

Interpreting the Results

An appropriate rate is roughly equal to the student's age x 10, plus or minus 10. For example, a 7-year-old student should read 60–80 words per minute.

Running Record Sample

"Take your _bath_, Fay." [H]

"I'm May," said the baby.

"Oops!" said Mother. [the ^]

"Take your nap, Kay."

"I'm Fay," said the baby.

"Oops!" said Mother.

One day Kay was not _good_. Off she [/fensē/]
went, under the fence.

"Kay!" said Mother. "I told you
(once) before! Don't go under the fence!"

"But, Mother! I'm Fay!"

And the little pig cried.

Mother Pig had a plan. She turned
them around. And she curled their tails. [the pigs] [(sc)]

Fay's tail curled up. May's tail curled
down. Kay's tail curled once. Then it curled
once more. Kay's went round and round.

—From *Which is Which?*,
Leveled Reader 27A
Grade 1

Total Number of Words: **94**

Number of Errors: **5**

Accuracy Percentage Score: **95%**

Reading Time: **80 sec**

Reading Rate: **71 wpm**

Miscues

Hesitation

The student hesitates over a word, and the teacher provides the word. Wait several seconds before telling the student what the word is.

Insertion

The student inserts words or parts of words that are not in the text.

Mispronunciation/Misreading

The student pronounces or reads a word incorrectly.

Omission

The student omits words or word parts.

Substitution

The student substitutes words or parts of words for the words in the text.

Self-Correction

The student reads a word incorrectly but then corrects the error. Do not count self-corrections as actual errors. However, noting self-corrections will help you identify words the student finds difficult.

$$\frac{94 - 5}{94} = \frac{89}{94} = .946 = 95\%$$

$$\frac{94}{80} \times 60 = 70.5 = 71 \text{ words per minute}$$

Unit 5 Take Me There

Easy	On-Level	Challenge

Arthur's Reading Race

Anansi Does the Impossible: An Ashanti Tale by Verna Aardema (Atheneum, 1997) Assisted by his wife, Anansi accomplishes three "impossible" deeds to gain the Sky God's stories.

Arthur Tricks the Tooth Fairy by Marc Brown (Random House, 1998) Arthur poses as the Tooth Fairy to placate the irrepressible D.W.

Fire Race: A Karuk Coyote Tale retold by Jonathan London (Chronicle Books, 1993) Superb illustrations and exciting text relate the tale of Coyote's efforts to bring light to the world.

Lost!

Corduroy by Don Freeman (Viking, 1985) In this classic, a stuffed bear in a store finally gains a real home when a little girl buys him.

The Great Race by David McPhail (HarperCollins, 1997) A group of eleven friends need to use division to figure out how many cars they will need on the rollercoaster.

Mrs. Potter's Pig by Phyllis Root (Candlewick, 1996) Immaculate Mrs. Potter has a baby who just can't stay clean—and who appears to have turned into a pig!

Foal

Is This a House for Hermit Crab? by Megan McDonald (Orchard, 1990) When Hermit Crab becomes too large for his house, he emerges to secure a new one.

The Very Quiet Cricket by Eric Carle (Philomel, 1990) In this sweet story, a very quiet cricket learns to express himself.

Happy Birthday, Biscuit! by Alyssa Satin Capucilli (HarperCollins, 1999) Biscuit is celebrating his first birthday, and the little girl he lives with invites his friends Puddles and Daisy over for a birthday party.

Lost in the Museum

McDuff Comes Home by Rosemary Wells (Hyperion, 1997) While in hot pursuit of a bunny, McDuff the terrier becomes lost and requires help finding his way home.

It's George! by Miriam Cohen (Greenwillow, 1988) George may not be the best student in the class, but his presence of mind during an emergency proves lifesaving.

Humphrey, the Lost Whale: A True Story by Wendy Tokuda (Heian, 1986) Humphrey, a migrating whale, becomes lost in the San Francisco Bay and requires human intervention.

Dinosaur Babies

Dinosaur Dress-Up by Allen L. Sirois (Tambourine, 1992) Professor Saurus reveals the real cause of dinosaur extinction—their slavish devotion to fashion!

The True Story of Pocahontas by Lucille Recht Penner (Random House, 1994) This book presents a quick overview of the life of the Powhatan princess.

Dinosaur Bob and His Adventures with the Family Lizardo by William Joyce (Harper, 1995) The Lizardo family returns home from their vacation in Africa with a very friendly dinosaur.

The Bravest Cat

Frogs by Laura Driscoll (Grosset & Dunlap, 1998) This is an easy introduction to the amphibian.

Hazel's Amazing Mother by Rosemary Wells (Dutton, 1992) Hazel's mother ingeniously comes to Hazel's assistance when bullies strike.

All About Dogs and Puppies by Laura Driscoll (Grosset & Dunlap, 1998) Readers learn about various dog breeds, their care, and their talents.

Read Aloud

Not the Piano, Mrs. Medley

by Evan Levine (Orchard, 1991) Mrs. Medley, Max's grandmother, lugs armloads of provisions and supplies to the beach and finally enjoys the simple pleasures of the sand and waves.

Read Aloud

Angus Lost

by Marjorie Flack (Farrar Straus & Giroux, 1997) Angus the dog is lost in the dark night!

Read Aloud

Verdi

by Janell Cannon (Harcourt Brace, 1997) A young python fears growing old.

Read Aloud

My Map Book

by Sara Fanelli (HarperCollins, 1995) This is a wonderful collection of child-centered maps.

Read Aloud

I Met a Dinosaur

by Jan Wahl and Chris Sheban (Harcourt Brace, 1997) After she sees them in a museum, a little girl sees dinosaurs wherever she goes.

Read Aloud

Slugger Season

by Laura Driscoll (Grosset & Dunlap, 1998) This book presents information about baseball's great hitters, including Mark McGwire and Sammy Sosa.

D.E.A.R. Drop Everything And Read

Suggestions for Self-Selected Reading

The rationale for self-selected reading is two-fold. It helps foster the idea of reading for enjoyment while it provides opportunities to practice reading and develop fluency. A common practice for self-selected reading is to begin with ten minutes per day and gradually increase that time. Your state or district may have guidelines in place for self-selected reading.

Reading aloud to children provides an opportunity to expose them to a range of literary genres and text types to guide them in thinking about text. Reading aloud also provides children with a model of fluent reading and shows them how to read with expression. Books selected for reading aloud should appeal to children's interests, be appropriate to their developmental level, and engage their imaginations.

Use the following management suggestions to help maximize self-selected reading time in your classroom.

- Talk with children about what they like to read. Encourage them to choose books based on these preferences and to explore other types of books.
- If you set aside a day for children to share their books, encourage creative presentations. If more than one child is reading the same title, they may want to work together on a presentation.
- Ideas for presenting books are limitless, but extra classroom time is often at a premium. Consider the time involved in presentation activities.

Use the following activity suggestions to add variety to self-selected reading time.

- Children may have a favorite story, poem, or short passage to share. Provide time for children to prepare their choices for sharing and then to read them aloud.
- Children may want to encourage others to read their books. Suggest that they create an advertisement for the book that will persuade others to read it.

DK Unit 5 Theme-Related Titles

Eyewitness Reader Dinosaur Dinners
Lee Davis and Barbara Taylor
New York: DK Publishing, 1999

Eyewitness Explorers Seashore
David Burnie
New York: DK Publishing, 1997

See the 5-Day Planner for each lesson for daily suggestions for self-selected reading and read alouds.

Using a Computer

Computer Vocabulary

cursor a flashing mark to show a position on the screen

highlight to select a specific amount of text

icon a symbol on the screen that stands for something, such as the Trash or a software program

keyboard a device with rows of numbers, letters, and other keys used for typing

mouse a device used to move a pointer around on a computer screen

software programs for the computer, such as word processing or games

toolbar or **menu** options that can be selected in order to do certain things, such as make a New file, Open a file, and Close a file

word processing typing in order to create a document, such as a letter or report

Photocopy the reproducible student page on AR27 and distribute it to your students.

STEP 1 Creating a Document
Show children how to start the computer and launch its word processing program.

- Show them how to click on the word *File* at the top of the computer screen and to hold the mouse button down.
- Use the mouse to drag the pointer to *New*.
- Let go of the mouse button. A blank page should open on the screen.
- Help students complete the Practice activity on their own.

STEP 2 Keyboarding
Have children look at the keyboard.

- Point out that the top row of keys has numbers and other symbols.
- Point out that the next three rows contain letters and most punctuation marks.
- Explain three other important keys.
  The *space bar* adds spaces between words.
  The *return* or *enter* key begins a new line.
  The *shift* key makes capital letters.
- Have children practice typing on the keyboard.

STEP 3 Making Changes
Have children look at the three pictures.

Picture 1 shows a writer's first draft. The writer knew she had made mistakes. She also wanted to make other changes. Picture 2 shows that the writer used the mouse to put the cursor where she wanted to make a change. She also used the mouse to highlight parts she wanted to change. She did this many times until she made the changes she wanted.

She italicized words by clicking on I .

She underlined a word by clicking on U .

She made a word boldfaced by clicking on B .

The writer also used the space bar between the words *really* and *liked*.

Allow students to practice making changes.

STEP 4 Saving Files
Show children how to save their files.

- Go to the *File* toolbar at the top of the screen. Click and scroll down until you see the words *Save As* and release the mouse button.
- Click on *New Folder* and name the new folder; click *Save*.
- Explain that to open the file later, they can open the folder and click on the file with the correct name.
- Have students complete the Practice activity.

Extend Skills

Draw Children can use the DRAWING feature of the word processing program to draw pictures and place them in their documents. Help them label their pictures and print the finished document.

E-mail Children who are familiar with the school's e-mail system can send a message to two people at once.

Cut/Copy/Paste Demonstrate using the cut, copy, and paste features to make changes.

Spreadsheets Make a chart on the blackboard with places for children to add their names, favorite colors, and favorite foods. Demonstrate how this information can be put on the computer using a spreadsheet program.

NOTE: To complete this lesson, students should have access to one or more computers.

Tech Time Using a Computer

Technology

1 Creating a Document

Follow your teacher's directions to create a new document.

- Click on *File*.
- Use the mouse to drag the pointer to *New*.
- Let go of the mouse button.

2 Keyboarding

Look at the keyboard with your teacher.

- The top row of keys has numbers and symbols.
- The next three rows have letters and punctuation.
- Three other important keys are the *space bar*, *return* or *enter*, and *shift*.
- Practice typing sentences with the keyboard.

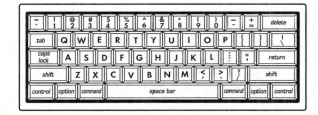

3 Making Changes.

Look at the three pictures below with your teacher.

Frog and Dog	Frog and Dog	*Frog and Dog*
I reallyliked this book. The title sounds silly, but the dog is cool.	I reallyliked this book. The title sounds silly, but the dog is cool.	I really liked this book. The title sounds silly, but the dog is **cool.**
Picture 1	**Picture 2**	**Picture 3**

- Practice making changes to your sentences.

4 Saving Files

Follow your teacher's directions to save a file.

- Go to the *File* toolbar and select *Save As*.
- Click on *New Folder*, name the new folder, and click on *Save*.
- To open the file, open the folder, and click on the file with the correct name.

Practice

- Make a new file, or page.
- Type this:
    - A. Computers are fun!
    - B. United States
    - C. $49.99
    - D. "Be good," she said.
- Type a sentence. Use the mouse and keyboard to fix any errors. Change the way a word looks.
- Name and save your file.

May be reproduced for classroom use. Guide your students through the activities.

The goal of *Scott Foresman Reading* is the development and encouragement of fluent readers, articulate writers and speakers, and discerning listeners and viewers.

Reading Benchmarks

The Reading Benchmarks recognize that students do not progress at the same rate toward the goal of being mature, skilled communicators. Within the same classroom are students at varying stages in their journey toward that goal. The teacher can gauge their progress in general ways by comparing student behaviors against these benchmark guidelines.

Scope and Sequence

The major strands and individual learning expectations in the Scope and Sequence are supported by research on how children develop and learn and by expectations held for learners by national and state guidelines.

Reading

The goal of reading is that a reader construct the meaning of a text. This goal is achieved through the interaction of a reader's prior knowledge and the key features of the text. These features—graphophonic, syntactic, and semantic—offer clues that readers can use to help themselves understand what they read. Research has shown that children understand the role of word order (syntax) and meaning (semantics) in oral language, but to develop reading fluency, they need instruction in graphophonic features in written words and visual text. This instruction includes phonemic awareness (words are made of sounds), phonics (letters represent these sounds in words), and spelling (common spelling patterns can be found in words).

Proficient readers learn to interact with all three kinds of features so that they can "make sense" of their reading, recognize when they don't, and use strategies to get back on the meaning track.

Literature

Readers, listeners, and viewers who know the characteristics of different genres know what to expect of an author or playwright and therefore are better able to comprehend the writer's message. When readers can discern the techniques and literary devices authors use, they can better appreciate not only what the author is communicating but how the message is conveyed and how response is evoked.

Language and Communication
Research and Study Skills
Habits and Attitudes

While each language art is stressed more strongly at different times depending on the task, effective communication is often a meshing and interaction of them. *Scott Foresman Reading* encourages students to develop in their ability to communicate both orally and in writing. Skilled communicators do many kinds of writing. Informally, they write letters and notes and record their thoughts in journals and diaries. Formally, they formulate questions about which to communicate answers or ideas, research to find answers or support for their ideas, and present their ideas in an effective organization and a strong yet appealing manner. Success in school and the workplace requires that able communicators know how to locate and synthesize information and know how to present that information and its implications to an audience, whether orally, in writing, or visually. In our diverse world, communication best takes place when the communicator uses common and traditional rules of grammar, usage, spelling, capitalization, and punctuation.

Grade 1

Novice indicates that the child is at an introductory level. Learners are at a Novice developmental level when they:

Reading Success Indicators for **Decoding and Word Recognition**	All students will develop the knowledge and skills necessary to fluently decode and recognize printed words.	• demonstrate knowledge of concepts of print: that words are separated by spaces, that words have one-to-one correspondence with speech and print, that print preserves meaning • identify some high-frequency words, recognize some letters, and begin to write and spell conventionally • recognize that words are composed of sounds, which are represented by letters • demonstrate phonemic awareness by knowing rhyming words, recognizing word family patterns, hearing syllables, isolating and matching initial sounds, blending phonemes and syllables, recognizing short vowels and CVC word patterns • apply picture clues and initial consonant sounds for decoding
Reading Success Indicators for **Strategies for Fluency and Understanding**	All students will develop the strategies, skills, and knowledge necessary to fluently read, comprehend, and respond to a range of general and technical material.	• predict and comprehend details when stories are read to them • locate the beginning and end of the text • track speech to print, locate a place in the text where someone left off reading, and locate particular words • use pictures to "read" a story • generally read orally with an adult or independently with familiar material • read 3–5 little books or stories independently per week • respond to text read to them by drawing pictures and writing at least one word • develop penmanship skills (grip, stroke, position)
Reading Success Indicators for **Enhancing Understanding and Learning from Text**	All students will read to investigate important issues in depth. They read across a variety of genres or within one genre, and demonstrate their understanding of issues and problems about the world they live in.	• compare and contrast ideas related to one issue when presented orally from several texts and from teacher-led discussion • discuss the most important details when looking at pictures • categorize key concepts and related ideas presented in oral discussion • communicate their ideas through pictures, transitional spelling, and some conventional spelling • choose several characters across various texts, compare and contrast these characters to find similarities and differences

Developing

Developing means that progress is being made toward achieving proficiency. Learners are at a Developing developmental level when they:

- recognize at least 50 high-frequency words
- develop concepts of print (sentence and paragraph)
- recognize and can write most upper- and lowercase letters, know the order of the alphabet
- recognize most initial consonant sounds and some vowel sounds (including short and long) for decoding new words
- demonstrate phonemic awareness with rhyming words, word family patterns, hearing syllables, matching and segmenting initial consonant and consonant blend sounds, blending syllables, and word patterns (CVC and CVCe)
- apply decoding strategies (contextual, phonics, structural analysis)

- predict, comprehend details, make connections, begin to self-question, and self-monitor for sense when reading simple books and short stories
- track speech to print, locate a place in the text where someone left off reading, and locate particular words
- are becoming fluent with oral reading of familiar text, are beginning to apply decoding strategies to unfamiliar grade-appropriate texts (5–7 little books and stories per week)
- become familiar with vocabulary building concepts (synonyms, antonyms)
- respond to text they read by writing a sentence or more in a literature log or journal, or by discussing orally

- distinguish a question from a statement
- compare and contrast ideas related to one issue by reading one book and comparing this to teacher-led discussion and to books presented orally by others
- discuss the most important details presented in pictures and text of grade-appropriate books
- categorize key concepts and related ideas found in text or presented in oral discussion
- identify sequence
- make connections to other text
- name the steps in a process
- identify problems and solutions in stories
- synthesize ideas from several books read into a drawing, diagram, or project
- develop test-taking strategies (multiple choice)
- communicate ideas in one or two sentences

Proficient

Proficient means that the child has achieved the advanced developmental level for that particular grade and is ready to move on to the next grade's success indicators. Learners are at a Proficient developmental level when they:

- use high-frequency words and phonetic analysis for decoding
- recognize and can spell at least 75 high-frequency words
- develop concepts of print (paragraphs, types of sentences)
- recognize and can order all letters in upper- and lowercase and alphabetize by first letter
- recognize complex letter/sound correspondences, including long and r-controlled vowels, diphthongs and vowel digraphs, word families, and patterns (CVC, CVCe, CVVC)
- segment and blend initial, final, and medial phonemes; substitute phonemes; and blend syllables
- use a range of decoding strategies for more complex words
- distinguish meaning and recognize spelling patterns for possessive nouns, contractions, compound words, and simple inflectional endings

- use prediction, context clues, making connections to their background, and other comprehension strategies (self-question, self-monitor, cross check) to read grade-appropriate texts
- sort out the important text to read, set purpose (read for meaning), and preview with grade-appropriate texts
- are becoming fluent with oral and silent reading of unfamiliar grade-appropriate texts (5–10 little books, picture books, stories, magazine articles, and news stories per week)
- are becoming familiar with vocabulary-building concepts (synonyms, antonyms, homonyms, multiple meanings)
- comprehend both fiction and nonfiction grade-appropriate text
- respond to text read by writing several sentences or more in a literature log or journal, or by discussing orally
- identify problems and solutions in stories

- ask questions about a topic
- select point at which they want to begin reading in a book by using the table of contents and chapter titles
- use a picture dictionary for spelling
- read and comprehend one book on a topic and compare this to teacher-led discussion and to books presented orally by others on the same topic
- discuss the most important details presented in pictures and text of grade-appropriate books
- categorize key concepts and related ideas found in text or presented in oral discussion and label these categories
- draw conclusions based on different perspectives or ideas presented in texts
- identify sequence
- interpret bar graphs, lists, and maps
- write labels, notes, and captions

Novice indicates that the child is at an introductory level. Learners are at a Novice developmental level when they:

Reading Success Indicators for
Literature and Appreciation

All students will read texts representing a wide range of literary genres for different purposes and will demonstrate their appreciation of literature through responses that indicate their ability to connect text to their world yesterday, today, and tomorrow.

- discuss basic plot of simple stories and respond through drama and by oral retelling
- predict what will happen next in the middle of a story being read aloud
- are beginning to distinguish between real and imaginary
- express feelings about selections read aloud, including literature from different cultures
- actively listen to both classic and contemporary literature
- understand concepts of author and illustrator
- write class innovations based on selections read (using patterned literature)

Success Indicators for
Application and Action

All students will apply what they learn from texts to their lives and to the lives of others through the following themes:

- Good Times We Share (Myself and Others)
- Take a Closer Look (The World Around Us)
- Let's Learn Together (Learning and Working)
- Favorite Things Old and New (Traditions)
- Take Me There (Journeys in Time and Space)
- Surprise Me! (Creativity)

At this level, children are almost always dependent on the teacher or other adults for locating materials, reading to them, taking dictation, and helping them draw conclusions about what was read. For example, if children are planning a trip or gathering information about community workers, the teacher would help with narrowing the topic, asking the questions, locating resources, analyzing steps in an action plan, and providing assistance in accomplishing most tasks. Children work independently on oral or graphic presentations by drawing their favorite things, creating three-dimensional models of animals, or writing their own book. They also:

- work in a whole-class situation on projects outlined by the teacher, brainstorm ideas as the teacher takes dictation, complete simple one-step tasks in project, name steps completed in a project
- share materials and resources, respect others' space as they participate together in groups, practice careful use of materials and resources
- communicate ideas through pictures, transitional spelling, and some conventional spelling; role-play and use creative movement to express ideas

Developing

Developing means that progress is being made toward achieving proficiency. Learners are at a Developing developmental level when they:

- discuss basic plot of simple stories and respond through drama, retellings, and art
- predict what will happen next in the middle of a story they are reading
- distinguish between real and imaginary
- compare and contrast characters and different cultures in literature
- recognize rhyme, rhythm, repetition, narration, and simple dialogue
- write innovations based on selections with repetitive patterns
- select both classic and contemporary literature to read or be read to
- identify with role of author and illustrator

Children are becoming more social and enjoy working with others in small groups, although they need considerable teacher guidance. They may work together on a class or group project such as a play or planning a presentation of family favorites. With assistance, they can share the responsibilities such as parts, scenery, props, and costumes. Children reflect on steps they took in carrying out a project such as painting a mural of a desert or rain forest to help them formulate their own action plans in the future. They also:

- participate in group projects (as above); participate in decision making on projects; complete simple two- to three-step tasks in projects; name and sequence the steps completed in a project, performance, or event; read some nonfiction material independently
- cooperate with others (as above), assist other group members with tasks, control own behavior in a group situation
- communicate ideas (as above) with an increasing use of transitional spelling and conventional spelling; create detailed and recognizable art through drawing, painting, and models

Proficient

Proficient means that the child has achieved the advanced developmental level for that particular grade and is ready to move on to the next grade's success indicators. Learners are at a Proficient developmental level when they:

- discuss basic plot of simple stories and respond through drama, retellings, art, and writing
- predict what will happen next in the middle of a story they are reading
- distinguish between real and imaginary and fact and fiction
- compare and contrast characters, plots, and different cultures in literature
- recognize rhyme, rhythm, repetition, narration, and dialogue
- read picture books, stories, poetry, expository articles, and fantasy
- select both classic and contemporary literature to read or be read to
- begin recognizing author's craft and language
- identify with the role of author and illustrator
- make a chart of how animals or persons grow over time or through experiences

Children can now write short nonfiction pieces such as preparing a picture brochure plus captions for visitors to their classroom. They conduct rudimentary research (e.g., a travel destination) from one or two sources and compare and contrast their information with that of others in the class. They present their information by creating a video, class book, display, poster, or multimedia presentation, though all projects still require considerable teacher or adult guidance. They also:

- participate in group projects (as above), decide on group research topic, suggest resources for investigation, learn to take simple notes
- cooperate with others (as above), take responsibility for own actions, manage resources and materials on an elementary level, work with group members toward a common goal
- communicate ideas (as above), write 5–8 sentences with some editing for spelling, produce detailed art and models that have more recognizable forms, attempt neatness in displays, learn how to add graphic aids to text such as maps, graphs, and charts

Scope and Sequence

Reading

Foundations of Literacy	K	1	2	3	4	5	6
Phonemic Awareness							
Identify and isolate initial and final sounds of spoken words	•C	•C					
Recognize and produce rhyming words	•C	•C					
Segment one-syllable words into initial, medial, and final sounds, and recombine sounds into words	•C	•C					
Identify, segment, and combine syllables in spoken words (e.g., by clapping syllables, moving manipulatives)	•C	•C					
Understand that spoken words are composed of sounds which are represented by alphabetic letters	•C	•C					
Print Knowledge and Concepts of Print							
Develop print awareness (concept of letter, word)	•C	•C					
Develop print awareness (concept of sentence, paragraph)	•	•C					
Track print: left to right on line, top to bottom on page, front to back of book	•C	•C					
Recognize that capitalization and punctuation are used for comprehension	•	•C					
Recognize environmental print	•	•					
Match spoken to printed words	•C	•C					
Develop awareness that print conveys and preserves meaning	•C	•C					
Emerging Reading/Writing Skills							
Show an interest in and respond to text read aloud	•	•					
Hold book right side up	•C	•C					
Identify parts of a book (cover, title page) and their functions	•C	•C					
Understand terms *author* and *illustrator* and distinguish their roles	•C	•C					
Describe how illustrations contribute to the text	•C	•C					
Know the order of the alphabet	•	•					
Know capital and lower case letter names and distinguish between the two	•C	•C					
Know letter/sound relationships	•C	•C					
Develop skill in gross and fine motor functioning and hand/eye coordination	•	•					
Gain increasing control of penmanship (e.g., holding pencil, paper position, stroke, posture)	•	•					
Write letters of the alphabet, both capitals and lower case	•	•					
Print own name	•	•					
Dictate messages/stories for others to write	•	•					
Write using pictures, some letters, transitional spelling if appropriate	•C	•					
Write labels, notes, and captions (e.g., for illustrations, charts, possessions)	•	•					
Use conventional spelling of familiar words in final drafts		•C					
Write messages that move left to right on a line, top to bottom on a page	•	•C					

Phonics, Word Analysis, Spelling, Vocabulary, and Fluency	K	1	2	3	4	5	6
Decoding strategy: Use phonics and structural analysis to decode words	•	•	•	•	•	•	•
Decoding strategy: Use semantic, syntactic, and graphophonic clues to identify words and their meanings	•	•	•	•	•	•	•
Vocabulary-in-context strategy: Use punctuation, explanatory phrases, and overall sense to gain and monitor word meanings		•	•	•	•	•	•
Process strategy: Know to ask and answer, What do I do when I come to a word I don't know?		•	•	•	•	•	•
Process strategy: Read fluently on development level with appropriate rate, stress, intonation, and style		•	•	•	•	•	•

Phonics and Decoding Skills

Phonics/Phonic Elements

	K	1	2	3	4	5	6
Letter/sound correspondence	•T	•T					
Blend sounds to make words	•C	•C	•	•			
Consonants	•T	•T	•T	•T	•	•	•

• = instructional opportunity   C = formal one-on-one teacher/child assessment conference   T = tested in standardized test format

Phonics, Word Analysis, Spelling, Vocabulary, and Fluency *Continued*

	K	1	2	3	4	5	6
Consonant blends	•	•T	•T	•T	•		
Consonant digraphs		•T	•T	•T			
Short and long vowels	•	•T	•T	•T			
r-Controlled vowels (vowel + r)		•T	•T	•T	•	•	•
Vowel digraphs and diphthongs		•T	•T	•T	•	•	•
Phonograms (word families)	•T	•T	•T	•			
Common word patterns (CVC, CVCe, etc.)	•	•T	•	•	•	•	•
Schwa sound			•	•	•	•	•

Word Analysis

	K	1	2	3	4	5	6
Plurals and possessives	•	•T	•T	•T	•T	•T	•T
Contractions		•T	•T	•	•	•	•
Compound words		•T	•T	•T	•	•	•
Base words, endings, prefixes, and suffixes	•	•T	•T	•T	•T	•T	•T
Syllabication and common syllable patterns for word identification		•	•T	•T	•T	•T	•T

Spelling

Sound and Letter Patterns

	K	1	2	3	4	5	6
Phonograms (word families)		•					
Vowels: short, long, r-controlled, digraphs, diphthongs, and unusual vowel spellings		•	•	•	•	•	•
Schwa sound				•	•	•	•
Consonants: single, double, blends, digraphs, silent, and unusual consonant spellings		•	•	•	•	•	•

Word Structure

	K	1	2	3	4	5	6
Endings on nouns and verbs		•	•	•	•	•	•
Irregular plurals						•	•
Syllable constructions			•	•	•		•
Affixes		•	•	•	•	•	•
Compound words		•		•	•	•	•
Apostrophes in contractions and possessives			•	•	•	•	•
Capital letters and abbreviations					•	•	
Greek and Latin word parts					•	•	•

Meaning Relationships

	K	1	2	3	4	5	6
Homophones				•	•	•	•
Easily confused words					•	•	•
Words related to each other					•	•	•
Words from other languages							•

Common Spelling Errors

	K	1	2	3	4	5	6
				•	•	•	•

Vocabulary and Fluency

Context Clues

	K	1	2	3	4	5	6
Picture clues	•	•	•				
Synonyms	•	•T	•T	•T	•T	•T	•T
Antonyms	•	•T	•T	•T	•T	•T	•T
Homonyms/homophones/homographs		•T	•T	•T	•T	•T	•T
Multiple-meaning words		•T	•T	•T	•T	•T	•T
Unfamiliar words		•T	•T	•T	•T	•T	•T
Specialized/technical/topical words				•	•	•	•

Vocabulary Building

	K	1	2	3	4	5	6
Classify words	•	•	•	•	•	•	•
Use graphic organizers to group, study, and retain vocabulary	•	•	•	•	•	•	•
Know abbreviations, acronyms, and shortened forms of words			•	•	•	•	•

• = instructional opportunity   T = tested in standardized test format

	K	1	2	3	4	5	6
Understand easily confused words and idioms			•	•	•	•	•
Understand connotation and denotation				•T	•T	•T	•T
Use etymologies for meaning (including Greek and Latin roots and affixes)					•	•	•
Develop vocabulary through listening and discussing	•	•	•	•	•	•	•
Develop vocabulary through meaningful and concrete experiences	•	•	•	•	•	•	•
Develop vocabulary through reading	•	•	•	•	•	•	•
Develop vocabulary through the use of grade-appropriate reference materials	•	•	•	•	•	•	•
Recognize words in the environment	•	•					
Recognize regular and irregular high-frequency words	•	•T	•T				
Understand selection vocabulary	•	•T	•T	•T	•T	•T	•T
Understand content-area vocabulary				•T	•T	•T	•T
Make analogies					•	•	•T

Comprehension

	K	1	2	3	4	5	6
Comprehension strategy: Know and use the reading process: preview and activate prior knowledge, predict, read, self-monitor, use fix-up strategies, summarize, reflect and respond	•	•	•	•	•	•	•
Comprehension strategy: Construct meaning using all possible avenues: text, knowledge of selection and topic, illustrations, text features, other print and technological/software resources, resource people	•	•	•	•	•	•	•
Formal assessment strategy: Develop test-taking strategies and answer test-like questions (multiple choice, true/false, short answer)		•	•	•	•	•	•

Strategies and Skills

	K	1	2	3	4	5	6
Activate prior knowledge and preview	•	•	•	•	•	•	•
Self-question to assess overall understanding		•	•	•	•	•	•
Self-monitor and use fix-up strategies		•	•	•	•	•	•
Author's possible viewpoint/bias			•	•	•	•T	•T
Author's purpose (e.g., inform, entertain, persuade, express)	•	•T	•T	•T	•T	•T	•T
Cause and effect	•T	•T	•T	•T	•T	•T	•T
Classify/categorize	•T	•T	•T	•	•	•	•
Compare and contrast	•	•T	•T	•T	•T	•T	•T
Context clues for understanding words, phrases, and word referents		•T	•T	•T	•T	•T	•T
Draw conclusions	•T	•T	•T	•T	•T	•T	•T
Fact and opinion			•T	•T	•T	•T	•T
Generalize	•	•	•	•T	•T	•T	•T
Graphic sources (e.g., charts, maps, lists, pictures, etc.)	•	•	•T	•T	•T	•T	•T
Make judgments about ideas and text			•T	•T	•T	•T	•T
Main idea or main idea with supporting details	•	•T	•T	•T	•T	•T	•T
Paraphrase					•T	•T	•T
Persuasive devices and propaganda						•	•T
Predict and verify or refine predictions	•T	•T	•T	•T	•T	•T	•T
Realism/fantasy or fact/nonfact/fantasy	•	•T	•T	•T	•		
Recall and retell	•T	•T	•	•	•	•	•
Sequence of events	•	•T	•T	•T	•T	•T	•T
Steps in a process			•T	•T	•T	•T	•T
Story elements							
Character	•T	•T	•T	•T	•T	•T	•T
Plot and plot structure	•	•T	•T	•T	•T	•T	•T
Setting	•	•T	•T	•T	•T	•T	•T
Theme	•	•T	•T	•T	•T	•T	•T
Summarize	•	•	•T	•T	•T	•T	•T
Text structure or method of presenting information					•T	•T	•T
Visualize		•	•	•T	•T	•T	•T

• = instructional opportunity   T = tested in standardized test format

Comprehension *Continued*	K	1	2	3	4	5	6
Critical Thinking							
Infer		•T	•T	•T	•T	•T	•T
Analyze		•T	•T	•T	•T	•T	•T
Organize ideas and information		•	•T	•T	•T	•T	•T
Make judgments		•	•T	•T	•T	•T	•T
Hypothesize		•	•	•	•	•	•T
Synthesize ideas within a text	•	•	•T	•T	•T	•T	•T
Synthesize ideas from different texts and media	•	•	•T	•T	•T	•T	•T
Compare and contrast across selections, genres, and cultures (intertextuality)	•	•	•T	•T	•T	•T	•T
Evaluate and critique ideas and text		•	•T	•T	•T	•T	•T
Make analogies		•	•	•	•	•	•T

Literature

Genres and Literary Craft	K	1	2	3	4	5	6
Genres							
Fiction							
Animal fantasy	•	•	•	•	•	•	
Drama/play		•	•	•T	•T	•T	•T
Fantasy	•	•	•	•T	•T	•T	•T
Historical fiction			•	•T	•T	•T	•T
Humorous fiction	•		•	•	•	•	•
Mystery			•			•	
Picture book	•	•	•	•			
Realistic fiction	•	•	•	•T	•T	•T	•T
Science fiction				•			•T
Short story					•	•	•
Traditional stories: fable, fairy tale, folk tale, tall tale, legend, myth		•	•	•T	•T	•T	•T
Nonfiction							
Almanac entry				•	•	•	•
Biography/autobiography		•	•	•T	•T	•T	•T
Diary/journal						•	
Encyclopedia article (print or CD-ROM)				•	•	•	•
Expository article		•	•	•T	•T	•T	•T
How-to article		•		•	•	•	•
Internet article				•	•	•	•
Interview			•				
Magazine article				•	•	•	•
Narrative writing	•	•	•	•T	•T	•T	•T
Newsletter		•	•				
Newspaper article				•	•	•	•
Personal essay				•	•	•	•
Persuasive essay							•
Photo essay		•	•	•	•	•	•
Textbook				•	•	•	•
Poetry and Song	•	•	•	•	•	•	•

• = instructional opportunity   T = tested in standardized test format

Genres and Literary Craft *Continued*

Literary Devices

	K	1	2	3	4	5	6
Allusion							•
Dialect					•	•	•
Dialogue and narration		•	•	•	•	•	•
Exaggeration/hyperbole				•	•	•	•T
Figurative language							
Simile			•	•T	•T	•T	•T
Metaphor	•	•	•	•T	•T	•T	•T
Idiom		•	•	•T	•T	•T	•T
Slang				•	•	•	•
Jargon				•	•	•	•
Invented words							•
Flashback					•	•	•T
Foreshadowing						•	•T
Humor					•	•	•
Imagery and sensory words					•T	•T	•T
Irony							•
Mood						•T	•T
Personification				•	•	•	•T
Point of view			•	•	•T	•T	•T
Puns and word play					•	•	•
Sound devices and poetic elements							
Rhyme	•	•	•	•	•	•	•
Rhythm and cadence	•	•	•	•	•	•	•
Repetition			•	•	•	•	•
Onomatopoeia			•	•	•	•	•
Alliteration				•	•	•	•
Line length						•	•
Symbolism				•	•	•	•T
Tone							•T
Understatement							•

Author's Craft/Style

	K	1	2	3	4	5	6
Recognize/analyze author's craft, style, language		•	•	•	•	•	•
Analyze the effect of author's perspective/viewpoint/bias on text and choice of genre			•	•	•	•	•

Illustrator's Craft/Style

	K	1	2	3	4	5	6
Recognize/analyze illustrator's craft or style		•	•	•	•	•	•
Analyze how art complements text				•	•	•	•
Analyze/appreciate fine art							•

Literary Response and Appreciation

	K	1	2	3	4	5	6
Reflect on reading and respond in various ways	•	•T	•T	•T	•T	•T	•T
Recognize evocation—the thoughts and feelings aroused during reading or listening	•	•	•	•	•	•	•
Relate own experience and other literary experience to what is being read	•	•	•	•	•	•	•
Assume alternate points of view to explore a literary selection	•	•	•	•	•	•	•
Reflect upon the relevance of the literary experience to the reader's own life	•	•	•	•	•	•	•
Synthesize and extend the literary experience, e.g., through drawing, dramatizing, miming, storytelling, etc.	•	•	•	•	•	•	•
Evaluate the quality of the literary experience	•	•	•	•	•	•	•
Seek additional literary experience through varied voluntary reading	•	•	•	•	•	•	•
Make connections between literature and other curriculum areas	•	•	•	•	•	•	•

• = instructional opportunity   T = tested in standardized test format

Language and Communication

Grammar and Usage in Speaking and Writing	K	1	2	3	4	5	6
Parts of speech							
Verbs and verb tenses	•	•T	•T	•T	•T	•T	•T
Nouns	•	•T	•T	•T	•T	•T	•T
Pronouns		•T	•T	•T	•T	•T	•T
Adjectives	•	•T	•T	•T	•T	•T	•T
Adverbs			•T	•T	•T	•T	•T
Conjunctions				•T	•T	•T	•T
Prepositions				•T	•T	•T	•T
Interjections							•T
Phrases	•	•T			•	•	•
Sentences: kinds, types, parts, fragments, run-ons, complete, combining	•	•T	•T	•T	•T	•T	•T
Paragraphs			•T	•	•	•	•
Misplaced modifiers							•T

Writing Process, Strategies, and Skills	K	1	2	3	4	5	6
Engage in modeled, shared, interactive writing	•	•	•				
Use the five-step writing process		•	•	•	•	•	•
Prewrite using various strategies	•	•	•	•	•	•	•
Use published pieces as models for writing		•	•	•	•	•	•
Decide on audience, purpose, and kind of writing		•	•	•	•	•	•
Write based on a picture	•	•	•	•	•		
Write based on literature		•	•	•	•	•	•
Write about a TV show, movie, or play			•	•	•	•	•
Take notes during research			•	•	•	•	•
Organize ideas (graphic organizer, outline, etc.)	•	•	•	•	•	•	•
Evaluate research and raise new questions		•	•	•	•	•	•
Develop draft	•	•	•	•	•	•	•
Descriptive writing		•	•	•	•	•	•
Narrative writing		•	•	•	•	•	•
Expository writing		•	•	•	•	•	•
Persuasive writing		•	•	•	•	•	•
Write in a variety of appropriate forms (sentences, paragraphs, stories, letters, reports, sketches, etc.)	•	•	•	•	•	•	•
Revise drafts in various ways	•	•	•	•	•	•	•
Edit for correct spelling, grammar, usage, and mechanics		•	•	•	•	•	•
Publish	•	•	•	•	•	•	•
Take pride in neat and correct visual appearance	•	•	•	•	•	•	•
Use correct penmanship	•	•	•	•	•	•	•
Give multimedia presentation						•	•
Use technology in writing		•	•	•	•	•	•
Write for personal use (response logs, notes for comprehension, etc.)		•	•	•	•	•	•
Evaluate writing	•	•	•	•	•	•	•
Apply criteria for evaluation		•	•	•	•	•	•
Respond constructively to others' writing		•	•	•	•	•	•
Self-evaluate on whether own purposes were met		•	•T	•	•	•	•
Review own collection of writing to monitor growth	•	•	•	•	•	•	•

Mechanics in Writing	K	1	2	3	4	5	6
Capitalization	•	•T	•T	•T	•T	•T	•T
Punctuation	•	•T	•T	•T	•T	•T	•T

• = instructional opportunity   T = tested in standardized test format

Listening and Speaking	K	1	2	3	4	5	6
Expand vocabulary by listening and speaking	•	•	•	•	•	•	•
Connect experiences, ideas, and cultural traditions with those of others through speaking and listening	•	•	•	•	•	•	•
Listen for various purposes	•	•	•	•	•	•	•
Listen carefully and critically to oral reading, discussions, and spoken messages	•	•	•	•	•	•	•
Use comprehension skills and strategies while listening to oral text and messages	•	•	•	•	•	•	•
Understand and retell text and messages heard	•	•	•	•	•	•	•
Understand the major ideas and supporting evidence in spoken messages					•	•	•
Identify and analyze a speaker's opinions and persuasive techniques					•	•	•
Self-monitor understanding of a spoken message and seek clarification as necessary					•	•	•
Respond appropriately to questions, directions, text read aloud, and oral presentations	•	•	•	•	•	•	•
Participate in rhymes and songs	•	•	•	•			
Participate in conversations and discussions	•	•	•	•	•	•	•
Speak for various purposes	•	•	•	•	•	•	•
Speak to a group or audience in appropriate ways and with appropriate delivery	•	•	•	•	•	•	•
Read orally with appropriate fluency (accuracy, expression, style, and attention to phrasing and punctuation)		•	•	•	•	•	•
Present dramatic interpretations of literature and literary experiences	•	•	•	•	•	•	•
Give precise directions, accurate information, and convincing ideas while speaking	•	•	•	•	•	•	•
Gain increasing control of conventional grammar and usage when speaking	•	•	•	•	•	•	•

Viewing	K	1	2	3	4	5	6
Develop awareness and understanding of the importance of the media	•	•	•	•	•	•	•
Interact with a variety of print and non-print media for a range of purposes (e.g., to learn, to receive information, to evaluate, to interpret, to appreciate)	•	•	•	•	•	•	•
Use comprehension skills and strategies to understand messages conveyed by the media	•	•	•	•	•	•	•
Use critical thinking to analyze and synthesize ideas and viewpoints in the media	•	•	•	•	•	•	•
Recognize bias, propaganda, and persuasive techniques in the media					•	•	•
Compare and contrast print, visual, and electronic media					•	•	•
Respond to the media (discussion, writing, multimedia presentations, etc.)	•	•	•	•	•	•	•

Research and Study Skills

Research Strategies and Skills	K	1	2	3	4	5	6
State the steps of the research process (set purpose, frame questions, choose sources, collect information, organize and present information)					•	•	•
Form and revise relevant questions for inquiry	•	•	•	•	•	•T	•T
Distinguish between and evaluate reference sources				•T	•T	•T	•T
Use specific study strategy (K-W-L, skim and scan, etc.) to find or learn information				•	•	•	•
Locate and collect information	•	•	•	•	•	•	•
Highlight				•	•	•	•
Take notes/record findings			•	•	•	•	•
Evaluate, interpret, and draw conclusions about key information					•	•	•T
Make outline					•T	•T	•T
Organize content systematically (e.g., sequentially or around main ideas)		•	•	•	•	•	•
Record knowledge, write report, or present orally		•	•	•	•	•	•
Credit primary and secondary reference sources					•	•	•
Select, organize, and incorporate visual aids					•	•	•
Know and use parts of a book	•	•T	•T	•T	•T	•T	•T
Use alphabetical order		•T	•T	•T	•T	•	
Follow directions	•	•	•	•	•	•	•

• = instructional opportunity   T = tested in standardized test format

Understanding and Using Reference Sources

Understanding and Using Reference Sources	K	1	2	3	4	5	6
Almanac				•	•	•T	•T
Atlas				•T	•T	•T	•T
Card catalog/library database				•	•T	•T	•T
Dictionary/glossary		•	•	•T	•T	•T	•T
Encyclopedia		•	•	•T	•T	•T	•T
Magazine/periodical				•	•T	•T	•T
Manual				•	•	•	•
Newsletter		•	•	•			
Newspaper	•			•T	•T	•T	•T
Readers' Guide to Periodical Literature						•	•T
Technology (non-computer electronic media–e.g., cassettes, TV, videotape, CD-ROM; computer programs and services; Internet)	•	•	•	•	•	•	•
Telephone directory				•	•	•T	•T
Textbook				•T	•T	•T	•T
Thesaurus		•	•	•	•	•	•
Trade book		•	•	•	•	•T	•T

Understanding and Using Graphic Sources	K	1	2	3	4	5	6
Advertisement				•	•	•	•
Chart/table	•	•T	•T	•T	•T	•T	•T
Diagram/scale drawing				•	•	•	•T
Graph	•	•T	•T	•T	•T	•T	•T
Illustration (photograph or art) and/or caption	•	•	•	•	•	•	•
List	•	•	•	•			
Map	•	•T	•T	•T	•T	•T	•T
Order form					•T	•	•
Poster/announcement				•	•T	•T	•
Recipe						•	•
Schedule				•	•T	•T	•T
Sign		•			•	•	
Time line			•	•T	•T	•T	•T

Habits and Attitudes

	K	1	2	3	4	5	6
Derive pleasure from reading, listening, viewing	•	•	•	•	•	•	•
Value print as a means of gaining information	•	•	•	•	•	•	•
Value print as a means of assessing various opinions and points of view	•	•	•	•	•	•	•
Develop an appreciation of different genres and authors	•	•	•	•	•	•	•
Connect experiences and ideas with those from other perspectives, experiences, customs, and cultures	•	•	•	•	•	•	•
Develop attitudes and abilities to interact with members of other groups and cultures	•	•	•	•	•	•	•
Work cooperatively with others	•	•	•	•	•	•	•
Recognize that all peoples and cultures, native and immigrant, have made valuable contributions to the common culture of the United States	•	•	•	•	•	•	•
Recognize and study themes and connections that cross cultures and bind them together in their common humanness	•	•	•	•	•	•	•
Develop lifelong reading and writing habits	•	•	•	•	•	•	•
Read independently from a wide variety of genres (for enjoyment, to understand self and others, for information and utility, etc.)	•	•	•	•	•	•	•
Keep reading log/reading journal or have a list of favorite authors and works		•	•	•	•	•	•
Write and discuss independently (for enjoyment, to seek information, to understand, etc.)	•	•	•	•	•	•	•
Share reading and writing with others	•	•	•	•	•	•	•

• = instructional opportunity   T = tested in standardized test format

Program Themes

	Myself and Others	**The World Around Us**	**Learning and Working**
	We read about others to see ourselves and to discover the hopes, dreams, and concerns people share. We learn positive ways to work out differences.	We learn about living things in their environments. We gain respect for them so we can assume some responsibility for protecting them.	People learn and work together to accomplish things great and small. We read about these activities to value learning, to understand ways problems can be solved, and to respect the accomplishments of others.
K	**Getting to Know Us** **Look at Me Now!** Where do we grow from here? **Meet Family and Friends** Who are the people we love?	**A World of Wonders** **Claws, Paws, Sun, and Seeds** How do things grow? **Bears and Bunnies** What is your world like?	**So Much to Do!** **Finding Our Way** Where do I fit in? **In Our Big Backyard** What can we learn close to home?
1	**Good Times We Share** How are our families and friends special?	**Take a Closer Look** Look closely! *Now* what can we see?	**Let's Learn Together** What can we learn when we all work together?
2	**You + Me = Special** What makes us all special?	**Zoom In!** What can we learn from looking at the world around us?	**Side by Side** How can we learn and work well together?
3	**Finding My Place** How do friends and family help us grow?	**The Whole Wide World** How can we learn about and care for the world?	**Getting the Job Done** How can we learn from everything we do?
4	**Focus on Family** Who helps us find our talents, abilities, and dreams?	**A Wider View** What place do plants and animals have in the world around us?	**Keys to Success** How do learning and working lead to success?
5	**Relating to Others** What are the important things in life?	**My World and Yours** How do we show that we care about our surroundings?	**A Job Well Done** What do we learn from our experiences?
6	**Discovering Ourselves** How do our relationships with others help us learn about ourselves?	**The Living Earth** What can we learn from observing the world around us?	**Goals Great and Small** How do people accomplish their ambitions?

Traditions

We read about ways people are linked together and to the past. We grow in appreciation of who we are and what we value and in understanding others.

Every Day Is Special

All Together
Why is it better being together?

Let's Go
How did we get where we are?

Favorite Things Old and New
How do things get to be favorites?

Ties Through Time
What things do we do together in the same special way?

From Past to Present
How can our traditions and the traditions of others make our lives more interesting?

Timeless Stories
How do stories from the past help us live in the present?

Time and Time Again
What things are worth repeating over time?

The Way We Were– The Way We Are
How can understanding the past help us live in the present?

Journeys in Time and Space

We read about and learn to appreciate people and places in our world today and in the past. We speculate about the future.

Off We Go!

Let's Explore
How do we get from here to there?

Make a Wish
How do dreams keep us going?

Take Me There
Where will we go? How will we grow?

All Aboard!
What can we learn by traveling?

Are We There Yet?
How can visits to other times and other places make our lives better?

Other Times, Other Places
What can we learn from reading about times and places we've never been?

Traveling On
Where do people's journeys take them?

Into the Unknown
What can we learn from visiting real and imaginary times and places?

Creativity

We learn about ways people use their creativity to solve problems, make decisions, create works of art, and express new ideas.

Open the Doors

Anything Is Possible
How do we think in new ways?

Imagine That!
How do we use our thinking caps?

Surprise Me!
How do we get all those great ideas?

Just Imagine!
How do we use our imaginations to do things?

Imagination.kids
How many ways can we use our imaginations?

Express Yourself!
How many forms can creativity take?

Think of It!
How do we find a new way?

I've Got It!
How many ways can people be creative?

Scoring Rubrics

Expository Writing

6-Point Scoring Rubric

6	5	4	3	2	1
• expository writing is well focused on the topic • contains clear ideas • logically organized; uses transitions • voice is engaging; well suited to purpose and audience • demonstrates varied, precise word choice • sentences are complete and varied • shows excellent control of writing conventions	• expository writing is focused on the topic • most ideas are clear • logically organized; uses some transitions • voice comes through well; suited to purpose and audience • generally demonstrates varied, precise word choice • most sentences are complete and varied • shows very good control of writing conventions	• expository writing is generally focused on the topic • ideas are generally clear • logically organized with some lapses; has transitions • voice comes through occasionally; suited to purpose and audience • often demonstrates varied, precise word choice • many sentences are complete and varied • shows good control of writing conventions	• expository writing may stray from topic • ideas may be somewhat unclear • somewhat organized; may lack transitions • voice uneven; not always suited to purpose or audience • word choice could be more varied, precise • some incomplete sentences; little variety • shows fair control of writing conventions	• expository writing is minimally related to the topic • ideas are often unclear • minimally organized; no transitions • slight evidence of voice; little sense of purpose or audience • poor choice of words; limited vocabulary • sentences are incomplete; show little or no variety • shows little knowledge of writing conventions	• expository writing is not focused on the topic • ideas are unclear • unorganized; no transitions • weak voice; no sense of purpose or audience • limited vocabulary • gross errors in sentence structure • shows no knowledge of writing conventions

5-Point Scoring Rubric

5	4	3	2	1
• expository writing well focused on the topic • contains clear ideas • logically organized; uses transitions • voice is engaging; well suited to purpose and audience • demonstrates varied, precise word choice • sentences are complete and varied • shows excellent control of writing conventions	• expository writing is focused on the topic • most ideas are clear • logically organized; uses some transitions • voice is fairly strong: suited to purpose and audience • generally demonstrates varied, precise word choice • most sentences are complete and varied • shows very good control of writing conventions	• expository writing is generally focused on the topic • ideas are generally clear • logically organized with some lapses; transitions weak • voice comes through occasionally; may not suit purpose and audience • word choice could be more varied, precise • many sentences are complete; generally varied • shows fairly good control of writing conventions	• expository writing strays from topic • many ideas are unclear • little organization; few or no transitions • voice comes through rarely; poorly suited to purpose or audience • choice of words limited • incomplete sentences; little variety • shows frequent errors in writing conventions	• expository writing is not focused on topic • ideas are unclear • unorganized; no transitions • weak voice; no sense of audience or purpose • choice of words very limited • incomplete sentences; no variety • shows many serious errors in writing conventions

3-Point Scoring Rubric

3	2	1
• expository writing is well focused on the topic • contains clear ideas • logically organized; uses transitions • voice is engaging; well suited to purpose and audience • demonstrates varied, precise word choice • sentences are complete and varied • shows excellent control of writing conventions	• expository writing is generally focused on the topic • ideas are sometimes unclear • logically organized with lapses; transitions need improvement • voice comes through fairly well; may not suit purpose or audience • word choice could be more varied, precise • some sentences are complete and varied • shows fair control of writing conventions	• expository writing is not focused on the topic • ideas are unclear • unorganized; no transitions • weak voice; no sense of purpose or audience • choice of words very limited • incomplete sentences; no variety • shows little or no control of writing conventions

Narrative Writing

6-Point Scoring Rubric

6	5	4	3	2	1
• narrative writing is well focused on the topic • contains clear ideas • logically organized; uses transitions • voice is engaging; well suited to purpose, and audience • demonstrates varied, precise word choice • sentences are fluent and varied • shows excellent control of writing conventions	• narrative writing is focused on the topic • most ideas are clear • logically organized; uses some transitions • voice comes through well; suited to purpose and audience • generally demonstrates varied, precise word choice • most sentences are complete and varied • shows very good control of writing conventions	• narrative writing is generally focused on the topic • ideas are generally clear • logically organized with some lapses; has transitions • voice comes through occasionally; suited to purpose and audience • often demonstrates varied, precise word choice • many sentences are complete and varied • shows good control of writing conventions	• narrative writing is generally focused but may stray from topic • ideas may be somewhat unclear • somewhat organized; may lack transitions • voice uneven; not always suited to purpose or audience • word choice could be more varied, precise • some incomplete sentences; little variety • shows fair control of writing conventions	• narrative writing is minimally related to topic • ideas are often unclear • minimally organized; no transitions • slight evidence of voice; little sense of purpose or audience • poor choice of words; limited vocabulary • sentences are incomplete; show little or no variety • shows little knowledge of writing conventions	• narrative writing is not focused on the topic • ideas are unclear • unorganized; no transitions • weak voice; no sense of purpose or audience • limited vocabulary • gross errors in sentence structure • shows no knowledge of writing conventions

5-Point Scoring Rubric

5	4	3	2	1
• narrative writing is well focused on the topic • contains clear ideas • logically organized; uses transitions • voice is engaging; well suited to purpose and audience • demonstrates varied, precise word choice • sentences are complete and varied • shows excellent control of writing conventions	• narrative writing is focused on the topic • most ideas are clear • logically organized; uses some transitions • voice is fairly strong; suited to purpose and audience • generally demonstrates varied, precise word choice • most sentences are complete and varied • shows very good control of writing conventions	• narrative writing is generally focused on the topic • ideas are generally clear • logically organized with some lapses; transitions weak • voice comes through occasionally; may not suit purpose and audience • word choice could be more varied, precise • many sentences are complete; generally varied • shows fairly good control of writing conventions	• narrative writing strays from topic • many ideas are unclear • little organization; few or no transitions • voice comes through rarely; poorly suited to purpose or audience • choice of words limited • incomplete sentences; little variety • shows frequent errors in writing conventions	• narrative writing is not focused on topic • ideas are unclear • unorganized; no transitions • weak voice; no sense of audience or purpose • choice of words very limited • incomplete sentences; no variety • shows many serious errors in writing conventions

3-Point Scoring Rubric

3	2	1
• narrative writing is well focused on the topic • contains clear ideas • logically organized; uses transitions • voice is engaging; well suited to purpose and audience • demonstrates varied, precise word choice • sentences are complete and varied • shows excellent control of writing conventions	• narrative writing is generally focused on the topic • ideas are sometimes unclear • logically organized with lapses; transitions need improvement • voice comes through fairly well; may not suit purpose or audience • word choice could be more varied, precise • some sentences are complete and varied • shows fair control of writing conventions	• narrative writing is not focused on the topic • ideas are unclear • unorganized; no transitions • weak voice; no sense of audience • choice of words very limited • incomplete sentences; no variety • shows little or no control of writing conventions

Descriptive Writing

6-Point Scoring Rubric

6	5	4	3	2	1
• descriptive writing is well focused on the topic • contains clear ideas • logically organized; uses transitions • voice is engaging; well suited to purpose and audience • precise, vivid language paints strong pictures • sentences are fluent and varied • shows excellent control of writing conventions	• descriptive writing is focused on the topic • most ideas are clear • logically organized; uses some transitions • voice comes through well; suited to purpose and audience • generally demonstrates varied, precise word choice • most sentences are complete and varied • shows very good control of writing conventions	• descriptive writing is generally focused on the topic • ideas are generally clear • logically organized with some lapses; has transitions • voice comes through occasionally; suited to purpose and audience • often demonstrates varied, precise word choice • many sentences are complete and varied • shows good control of writing conventions	• descriptive writing may stray from the topic • ideas may be somewhat unclear • somewhat organized; may lack transitions • voice uneven; not always suited to purpose or audience • word choice could be more varied, precise • some incomplete sentences; little variety • shows fair control of writing conventions	• descriptive writing is minimally related to the topic • ideas are often unclear • minimally organized; no transitions • slight evidence of voice; little sense of purpose or audience • poor choice of words; limited vocabulary • sentences are incomplete; show little or no variety • shows little knowledge of writing conventions	• descriptive writing is not focused on the topic • ideas are unclear • unorganized; no transitions • weak voice; no sense of purpose or audience • limited vocabulary • gross errors in sentence structure • shows no knowledge of writing conventions

5-Point Scoring Rubric

5	4	3	2	1
• descriptive writing is well focused on the topic • contains clear ideas • logically organized; uses transitions • voice is engaging; well suited to purpose and audience • demonstrates varied, precise word choice • sentences are complete and varied • shows excellent control of writing conventions	• descriptive writing is focused on the topic • most ideas are clear • logically organized; uses some transitions • voice is fairly engaging; suited to purpose and audience • generally demonstrates varied, precise word choice • most sentences are complete and varied • shows very good control of writing conventions	• descriptive writing is generally focused on the topic • ideas are generally clear • logically organized with some lapses; transitions somewhat weak • voice comes through occasionally; may not suit purpose or audience • word choice could be more varied, precise • many sentences are complete; generally varied • shows fairly good control of writing conventions	• descriptive writing strays from topic • many ideas are unclear • little organization; few or no transitions • voice comes through rarely; poorly suited to purpose or audience • word choice limited • incomplete sentences; little variety • shows frequent errors in writing conventions	• descriptive writing is not focused on the topic • ideas are unclear • unorganized; no transitions • weak voice; no sense of audience or purpose • word choice very limited • incomplete sentences; no variety • shows many serious errors in writing conventions

3-Point Scoring Rubric

3	2	1
• descriptive writing is well focused on the topic • contains clear ideas • logically organized; uses transitions • voice is engaging; well suited to purpose and audience • demonstrates varied, precise word choice • sentences are complete and varied • shows excellent control of writing conventions	• descriptive writing is generally focused on the topic • ideas are sometimes unclear • logically organized with lapses; transitions need improvement • voice comes through fairly well; may not suit purpose or audience • word choice could be more varied, precise • some sentences are complete and varied • shows fair control of writing conventions	• descriptive writing is not focused on the topic • ideas are unclear • unorganized; no transitions • weak voice; no sense of purpose or audience • choice of words very limited • incomplete sentences; no variety • shows little or no control of writing conventions

Persuasive Writing

6-Point Scoring Rubric

6	5	4	3	2	1
• persuasive writing is well focused on the topic • contains clear ideas • logically organized; presents reasons in order • voice is engaging; well suited to purpose and audience • demonstrates precise, persuasive wording • sentences are fluent and varied • shows excellent control of writing conventions	• persuasive writing is focused on the topic • most ideas are clear • logically organized; presents reasons in some order • voice comes through well; suited to purpose and audience • generally demonstrates precise, persuasive word choice • most sentences are complete and varied • shows very good control of writing conventions	• persuasive writing is generally focused on the topic • ideas are generally clear • logically organized with some lapses, presents most reasons in order • voice comes through occasionally; suited to purpose and audience • often demonstrates precise, persuasive word choice • many sentences are complete and varied • shows good control of writing conventions	• persuasive writing is generally focused but may stray from topic • ideas may be somewhat unclear • somewhat organized; reasons may not be in proper order • voice uneven; not always suited to purpose or audience • word choice is not always precise or persuasive • some incomplete sentences; little variety • shows fair control of writing conventions	• persuasive writing is minimally related to topic • ideas are often unclear • minimally organized; reasons are not in order • slight evidence of voice; little sense of purpose or audience • poor choice of words; not very persuasive • sentences are incomplete; show little or no variety • shows little knowledge of writing conventions	• persuasive writing is not focused on topic • ideas are unclear • unorganized; reasons, if any, are not in order • weak voice; no sense of purpose or audience • limited vocabulary; fails to persuade • gross errors in sentence structure • shows no knowledge of writing conventions

5-Point Scoring Rubric

5	4	3	2	1
• persuasive writing is well focused on the topic • contains clear ideas • logically organized; presents reasons in order • voice engaging; well suited to purpose and audience • demonstrates precise, persuasive wording • sentences are complete and varied • shows excellent control of writing conventions	• persuasive writing is focused on the topic • most ideas are clear • logically organized; presents reasons in some order • voice is fairly engaging; suited to purpose and audience • generally demonstrates precise, persuasive word choice • most sentences are complete and varied • shows very good control of writing conventions	• persuasive writing is generally focused on the topic • ideas are generally clear • logically organized with some lapses, presents most reasons in order • voice comes through occasionally; may not suit purpose and audience • word choice could be more precise, persuasive • many sentences are complete; generally varied • shows fairly good control of writing conventions	• persuasive writing strays from topic • many ideas are unclear • little organization; reasons are not in order • voice comes through rarely; poorly suited to audience or purpose • word choice limited, not persuasive • incomplete sentences; little variety • shows frequent errors in writing conventions	• persuasive writing is not focused on the topic • ideas are unclear • unorganized; reasons, if any, are not in order • weak voice; no sense of audience or purpose • word choice very limited; fails to persuade • incomplete sentences; no variety • shows many serious errors in writing conventions

3-Point Scoring Rubric

3	2	1
• persuasive writing is well focused on the topic • contains clear ideas • logically organized; presents reasons in order • voice is engaging; well suited to purpose and audience • demonstrates precise, persuasive word choice • sentences are complete and varied • shows excellent control of writing conventions	• persuasive writing is generally focused on the topic • ideas are sometimes unclear • logically organized with lapses; presents most reasons in order • voice comes through fairly well; may not suit audience or purpose • word choice could be more precise, persuasive • some sentences are complete and varied • shows fair control of writing conventions	• persuasive writing is not focused on the topic • ideas are unclear • unorganized; reasons, if any, are not in order • weak voice; no sense of audience or purpose • word choice very limited; fails to persuade • incomplete sentences; no variety • shows little or no control of writing conventions

Handwriting

Position for Writing

Left-handed and right-handed writers slant their papers differently from one another, but they sit and hold their pencils the same way.

Body Position
- Children should sit tall, with both feet flat on the floor and arms relaxed on a table or desk.
- Children should hold their papers at the top with their non-writing hand.

Paper Slant
- Paper should be positioned at a slant that is approximately parallel to the writing arm.
- For left-handed children, the paper should slant from the right at the top to the left at the bottom.
- Right-handed children should slant the paper from the left at the top to the right at the bottom.

Pencil Grip
- Children should grasp the pencil lightly between the thumb and index finger, usually about an inch above the pencil point.
- For a child who grasps the pencil too close to the point, a simple remedy is to wrap a rubber band around the pencil about an inch above the point. Have the child hold the pencil above the rubber band.

Legibility

Legibility should be the goal of handwriting instruction. Children should be praised for writing legibly, even though their writing may deviate from a perfect model. Legibility is based on flexible but standard criteria for letter form, size, and slant, and for letter and word spacing.

Letter Form
- Standards for letter form enable each letter to be distinguished clearly from other letters.
- In the letter *a*, for example, the round part of the letter must be open, and the letter must be closed at the top. The letter *a* must not be confused with *u, d,* or *o.*
- The letters *t* and manuscript *f* must be crossed; the letters *i* and *j* dotted.

Letter Size
- Small letters sit on the bottom line and touch the middle line.
- Tall letters sit on the bottom line and touch the top line.
- Letters with descenders have tails that go down under the bottom line and, in D'Nealian™, touch the line below.

Letter Slant
- Letter slant should be consistent.
- All letters may slant to the right, to the left, or be straight up and down.

Letter and Word Spacing
- Letters in a word should be evenly spaced. They should not be written too close together or too far apart.
- There should be more space between words in a sentence than between letters in a word. This allows each word to stand out.

D'Nealian™ Alphabet

a b c d e f g h i
j k l m n o p q r s t
u v w x y z

A B C D E F G
H I J K L M N O
P Q R S T U V
W X Y Z . , ' ?

1 2 3 4 5 6
7 8 9 10

Manuscript Alphabet

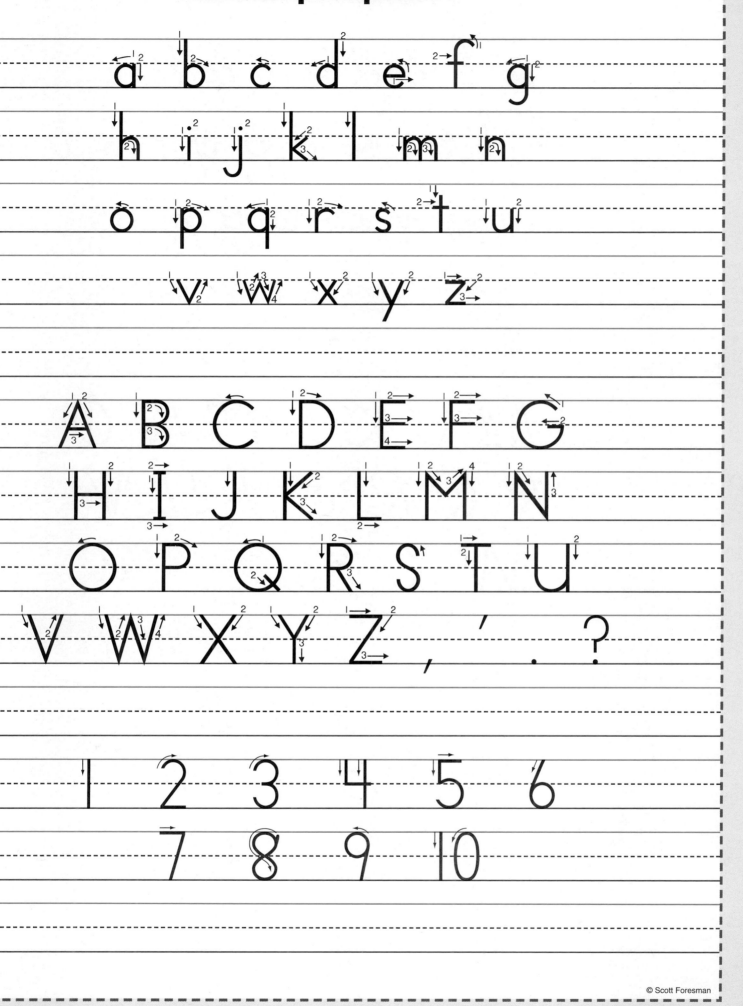

Word List

	Phonics Words		High-Frequency/ Tested Words	Spelling Words

Unit 2   **Phonics Words**   **High-Frequency/ Tested Words**   **Spelling Words**

The Nap / Oh, Cats!

Short a

am	ham	sag
at	hat	Sam
bad	lap	sap
bag	mad	sat
bam	man	tan
bat	map	that
cab	mat	wag
can	nap	
cap	pan	
cat	pat	
cats	rag	
dad	ram	
fan	ran	
fat	rap	
glad	rat	
had	sad	

Final Consonants n, t, d, p, g, m

am	in	sad
at	lap	sag
bad	mad	Sam
bag	man	sat
bam	map	tan
bat	mat	that
big	nap	up
can	not	wag
cap	on	
cat	pan	
dad	pat	
fan	rag	
fat	ram	
glad	ran	
had	rap	
ham	rat	
hat	red	

High-Frequency/Tested Words:
away, come, down, no, will

Spelling Words:
at, sat, cat, ran, an, man

Look at That! / Can You Find It?

Short a

am	hat	tags
an	jab	taps
and	Jan	that
ant	laps	wags
at	man	zaps
bad	map	
bag	mats	
bat	naps	
cab	Nat	
can	pan	
caps	Pat	
cat	rags	
Dan	raps	
fan	sad	
fat	Sam	
had	snack	
has	tag	

Final Consonants b, k, s, r, f, l

bear	star
book	tub
bus	us
cab	wear
chair	web
cub	
four	
has	
if	
is	
jab	
leaf	
look	
our	
pail	
snail	
spider	

High-Frequency/Tested Words:
all, are, find, make, play

Spelling Words:
am, had, sad, bad, fan, can

What Did I See? / I Went Walking

Short i

big	lick	swims
brick	Nick	tick
click	pick	tin
did	pig	trick
dig	pin	trip
hid	pink	wick
hill	pit	will
hit	sick	win
in	sit	
it	slick	
kick	slip	
kids	stick	

Final -ck

back	sack
black	sick
brick	slick
click	stick
duck	tack
kick	tick
lick	trick
Nick	wick
pick	
quack	
Rick	
rock	

High-Frequency/Tested Words:
did, me, saw, walk, went

Spelling Words:
it, sit, hit, pick, sick, kick

Word List

Unit 2	Phonics Words		High-Frequency/ Tested Words	Spelling Words

Fish Mix

How Many Fish?

Short *i*			Final *-x*		High-Frequency/Tested Words	Spelling Words
big	is	will	ax		how	fix
did	it	wink	box		many	mix
fin	its	winks	fix		on	six
fish	mitt		Max		they	in
fit	mix		mix		why	him
fix	pink		six			did
grin	six		tax			
him	spin		wax			
ill	swim					
in	swish					

Jog, Frog, Jog

Tadpole to Frog

Short *o*		*-s* Plurals		High-Frequency/Tested Words	Spelling Words
box	log	cats	pots	does	job
dog	lot	dots	rocks	he	log
dots	mop	eggs	tadpoles	into	dog
fog	not	frogs	tops	this	jobs
fox	on	hogs		water	logs
frog	pop	jobs			dogs
hog	pot	legs			
hop	rock	logs			
hot	stop	pigs			
job					
jog					

A Big Job

Sweet Potato Pie

Short *o*			Inflected Endings *-s* and *–ing*			High-Frequency/Tested Words	Spelling Words
block	hot	pot	bakes	jumps	sings	by	hot
Bob	job	rock	chops	licking	sips	eat	not
box	lock	sock	cooking	locking	socks	sing	got
chop	lot	stop	digs	locks	starts	stop	mop
clock	mob	Tom	eating	picking	stops	them	hop
crop	Mom	top	eats	picks	swinging		top
frog	mop		filling	rocking	washing		
got	not		gets	rocks	watering		
hop	pop		jumping	singing			

	Phonics Words		High-Frequency/ Tested Words	Spelling Words

The Big Mess
The Little Red Hen

Short e

bed	led	spell
bell	less	Ted
Ben	let	tell
Bess	mess	ten
dress	met	Tess
fed	Ned	then
fell	next	well
get	pen	wet
help	pet	yes
hen	red	
Jen	set	
jet	shed	

Double Final Consonants

ball	hall	well
bell	less	will
Bess	mall	yell
call	Matt	
class	mess	
dress	miss	
fall	pass	
fell	sell	
fill	spell	
glass	tell	
grass	Tess	
guess	wall	

High-Frequency/Tested Words:
help
now
said
so
who

Spelling Words:
red
bed
fed
well
tell
mess

Yes, We Want Some Too!
Cat Traps

Short e

bed	let	ten
beg	men	them
bell	met	well
bless	net	yell
deck	next	yes
dress	peck	
fell	pen	
get	pet	
hen	red	
jet	sets	
leg	tell	

Initial r and l Blends

black	crows	play
bless	draw	please
block	dress	plot
blot	drip	trap
blue	crop	trip
clams	drum	trot
clap	flies	
claw	frog	
clip	gray	
club	green	
cluck	plan	

High-Frequency/Tested Words:
for
good
some
too
want

Spelling Words:
get
let
met
pet
ten
yes

My Buddy, Stan
Biscuit

Short u

brush	mud	stuff
bug	puff	sun
bun	Pug	tub
but	pup	tuck
cub	puppy	tug
cup	rub	up
cut	rug	us
fun	run	yum
hug	Russ	
jug	slug	
jump	snug	

Initial s Blends

scat	stay
sled	step
sleep	stick
sleepy	story
slip	
slug	
small	
smell	
snack	
snug	
Stan	

High-Frequency/Tested Words:
jump
more
sleep
time
with

Spelling Words:
cup
fun
puff
run
stuff
up

Word List

Unit 3	Phonics Words		High-Frequency/ Tested Words	Spelling Words

Trucks

Communities

Short u

bus	luck	sub
but	mud	truck
club	mug	tub
cup	pup	tuck
cut	rub	tug
duck	rug	us
dump	run	
fun	rut	
grub	scrub	
hug	stub	
hut	stuck	

c /s/ and g /j/

cell	Geri's
cement	giant
cent	officers
Cindy	police
city	
garbage	
gem	
Gene	
George	

High-Frequency/Tested Words:
bring
carry
hold
our
us

Spelling Words:
bus
but
cut
hug
rug
us

Fox and Bear

Fox and Bear Look at the Moon

Short Vowels

am	fun	pet
at	get	ran
back	glad	red
bell	got	run
big	had	Sam
bill	has	sat
bit	ill	sit
can	in	spot
chat	is	tap
cup	it	that
cut	Jill	Tom
did	lot	trucks
dot	met	up
fat	nap	web
fell	not	well
fill	pals	wet
fix	Pam	will
Fox	pat	yes

Final Consonant Blends

and	land
band	lump
best	milk
brand	must
bump	nest
cast	past
cent	pest
chest	pond
clump	pump
dump	rest
fast	sand
fist	stand
hand	stump
help	tent
hump	test
jump	want
just	
lamp	

High-Frequency/Tested Words:
came
know
out
she
there

Spelling Words:
and
best
fast
hand
just
must

I Can Read

Lilly Reads

Short Vowels

an	eggs	on
and	elf	pest
band	fish	plump
bed	Fred	rest
bend	fun	rust
best	get	sand
black	ham	send
block	hand	shut
box	hug	snack
bump	hut	sock
bus	in	spell
but	jump	spill
can	just	still
caps	land	stop
cats	let	sun
clap	lock	test
cribs	Mom	when
dad	much	will

Contractions

can't
don't
he'll
he's
I'll
it's
let's
she'll
that's
we'll

High-Frequency/Tested Words:
again
please
read
say
word

Spelling Words:
clap
drop
drum
sled
spot
trip

Unit 4	Phonics Words			High-Frequency/ Tested Words	Spelling Words

Unit 4 — Phonics Words — High-Frequency/Tested Words — Spelling Words

The Red Stone Game
The Gingerbread Man

Long a

ate	hate	take
bake	lake	wake
cake	late	
came	made	
date	make	
face	Nate	
fake	plate	
Gale	rake	
game	rate	
gate	skate	
gave	slate	

Inflected Ending -ed

asked	peeled
boiled	picked
called	pulled
cleaned	walked
cooked	wanted
helped	washed
jumped	
kicked	
laughed	
listed	
looked	

High-Frequency/Tested Words:
after
as
call
laugh
something

Spelling Words:
ate
bake
gave
late
make
take

The Same as You
Cherry Pies and Lullabies

Long a

bake	lake	same
brave	late	take
cake	made	tape
cape	make	
game	name	
gave	page	
grades	plates	

Initial Digraphs ch and th

chairs	chin	this
champ	chocolate	thought
chat	that	
checkers	the	
cherry	thick	
chick	thin	
chicken	things	

High-Frequency/Tested Words:
every
made
mother
of
was

Spelling Words:
tap
tape
cap
cape
mad
made

Rose and Grandma Make the Sun Shine
Our Family Get-Together

Long o

bone	nose	stone
close	poke	stove
cone	pole	stroke
dome	pose	those
doze	rode	tone
home	role	woke
hope	rope	wrote
hose	rose	
joke	shone	
lone	stole	

Initial Digraphs sh and wh

shade	shovel	while
shake	show	whine
shaped	showed	whip
sheep	whales	whistle
shells	wharf	white
shine	what	
ships	wheels	
shoe	when	
shone	where	
shop	which	

High-Frequency/Tested Words:
father
going
has
thank
very

Spelling Words:
rode
those
hope
home
joke
stone

Word List

Unit 4	Phonics Words		High-Frequency/ Tested Words	Spelling Words

The Rolling Rice Cake

The Rat and the Cat

Long *i*			**Medial Consonants**		**High-Frequency/ Tested Words**	**Spelling Words**
bike	like	size	after	never	be	like
bite	lime	slice	apple	picnic	friend	nice
dime	line	time	basket	polite	pretty	time
dine	mice	white	better	present	soon	ride
file	mine	wife	bottom	ribbon	your	white
fine	nice	wipe	cherry	yogurt		five
fire	nine		closer	yummy		
five	pine		happen			
hide	rice		little			
hike	ride		melon			
kite	ripe		muffin			

June and the Mule

Slim, Luke, and the Mules

Long *u*			**Final Digraphs**			**High-Frequency/ Tested Words**	**Spelling Words**
cute			bang	inch	sang	four	fish
dude			batch	long	sing	funny	long
flute			bath	lunch	stretch	long	such
huge			both	mash	such	watch	that
Jules			bring	match	think	were	the
June			brush	math	watch		with
Luke			catch	patch	with		
mule			clang	path			
plume			crash	ranch			
rules			ding	rich			
tune			fish	ring			
use			flash	rush			

Riddle-dee Fiddle-dee-dee

The Riddles

Long *e: ee, e*		**Compound Words**			**High-Frequency/ Tested Words**	**Spelling Words**
be	see	airplane	honeybee	sunlight	about	we
bee	seen	anything	honeycomb	sunrise	any	she
breeze	she	bumblebee	inside	sunshine	ask	me
feet	sleep	butterfly	jellyfish		kind	he
green	three	cannot	pancakes		over	see
he	tree	cowboy	peanut			green
Lee	we	doorbell	scarecrow			
me		football	sunflowers			

Unit 5	Phonics Words				High-Frequency/ Tested Words	Spelling Words
A Real Gift **Arthur's Reading Race**	**Long *e: ea***			**Inflected Ending *-ed***	buy only or right think	ask asked call called clean cleaned
	beach beak beam beans beat bleach clean cream deal dream ease easy eat heat	leaf meal meat neat peach peas please reach read real seam seat speak steal	steam tea teach team treat wheat	asked boiled called cleaned cooked grabbed jumped kicked laughed learned listed passed peeled petted	picked pointed pulled signed sounded stepped stopped walked wanted	
A Big Day for Jay **Lost!**	**Long *a: ai, ay***			**Contractions**	don't from hear live when	say play may way wait rain
	bay day gain gray hail hay Jay lay mail may	nail okay pail pain pay play rail rain say snail	stay tail today train wait way	aren't can't didn't don't he'll he's I'll I'm isn't it's	let's she's there'll there's they'll we'll won't	

Word List

Unit 5	Phonics Words		High-Frequency/ Tested Words	Spelling Words

Baby Otter Grows Up
Foal

Long o: oa, ow

blow	load	toad
boat	low	tow
bow	mow	
coat	road	
crow	roam	
float	row	
foal	show	
glow	slow	
goat	snow	
grow	soak	
grown	soap	

Inflected Ending -ing

blowing	running
feeling	sailing
floating	showing
growing	singing
holding	sinking
hopping	skipping
jumping	slipping
looking	snowing
playing	soaking
roaming	swimming
rowing	

High-Frequency/Tested Words

around
her
new
old
show

Spelling Words

grow
growing
float
floating
show
showing

What a Sight!
Lost in the Museum

Long i: igh, ie

bright	might
die	night
Dwight	pie
flight	right
fried	sigh
fright	sight
high	thigh
lie	tie
light	tight

Singular Possessives

Amy's	Katie's
bird's	Margaret's
Dad's	Mom's
Dean's	museum's
dinosaur's	Sam's
dog's	Tiger's
Dwight's	Tran's
friend's	whale's
Jim's	

High-Frequency/Tested Words

been
first
found
start
together

Spelling Words

lie
pie
tie
night
light
right

	Phonics Words		High-Frequency/ Tested Words	Spelling Words
Chompy's Afternoon **Dinosaur Babies**	**Vowel Sounds of _y_**	**Compound Words**		

Chompy's Afternoon
Dinosaur Babies

Vowel Sounds of _y_

any	fly	runny
baby	fry	shiny
berry	funny	sky
Bobby	happy	sunny
bony	heavy	tiny
bully	hungry	try
bunny	lucky	very
by	many	why
carry	my	yummy
Chompy	nobody	
cry	only	
dry	pretty	

Compound Words

afternoon	inside	sunset
anymore	nearby	tiptoe
anything	nobody	waterfall
baseball	outside	water-
bedroom	pathway	melons
breakfast	rainbow	without
cupcakes	raindrop	
eggshell	redbird	
everything	rosebud	
football	snowflake	
footprints	something	
hilltop	somewhere	

High-Frequency/Tested Words:
animals
even
heard
most
their

Spelling Words:
baby
funny
many
my
why
fly

Abbie Burgess
The Bravest Cat!

Vowels Patterns _ew, ue_

blew	Dewey	news
blue	drew	newspapers
bluebird	few	stew
Bluey	flew	Sue
clue	glue	true
crews	grew	
dew	new	

Inflected Ending _-es_/Plural _-es_

branches	ranches	watches
bushes	reaches	wishes
crashes	rushes	
dashes	teaches	
fixes	tosses	
marches	touches	
passes	washes	

High-Frequency/Tested Words:
because
better
give
people
put

Spelling Words:
new
grew
drew
blue
true
glue

Word List

Unit 6	Phonics Words		High-Frequency/ Tested Words	Spelling Words

Bluebirds in the Garden

The Garden

r-Controlled ar

art	darkly	start
backyard	far	tar
bar	garden	yard
bark	hard	yarn
barn	jar	
car	large	
card	mark	
charge	part	
Clark	smart	
dark	star	

Suffix -ly

brightly	softly
darkly	suddenly
hardly	
loudly	
nearly	
quickly	
quietly	
really	
sadly	
slowly	

High-Frequency/Tested Words

much
shall
these
wish
work

Spelling Words

car
far
star
dark
yard
start

Jordan Makes a New Friend

Ice-Cold Birthday

r-Controlled or

before	more	stork
born	morning	storm
core	Mort	stormy
cork	or	story
for	popcorn	tore
fork	pork	torn
fort	port	wore
horn	short	
horse	sport	
Jordan	store	

Inflected Endings -s, -es, -ed, -ing

baking	hopped	skated
blowing	jumped	sledding
called	laughed	snowed
coming	liked	snowing
cooked	likes	spilled
crying	looked	stared
falling	named	started
fixes	needed	stepped
forms	played	stopped
going	playing	teaches
happened	rained	
having	runs	
hoping	sharing	

High-Frequency/Tested Words

before
cold
full
off
would

Spelling Words

born
for
fork
or
short
torn

Unit 6	Phonics Words		High-Frequency/ Tested Words	Spelling Words

Show Time: Your First Play

Do You Live in a Nest?

r-Controlled *er, ir, ur*

birch	girl	third
bird	her	turkeys
birth	hurt	turn
blurt	jerk	turtle
burn	nurse	twirl
burst	person	whirl
chirp	purple	
clerk	purse	
fern	shirt	
fir	sir	
first	skirt	
fur	stir	

Comparative Endings *-er, -est*

bigger	slower
biggest	slowest
faster	smaller
higher	smallest
longer	softer
longest	softest
louder	sweetest
loudest	taller
quicker	tallest
quickest	warmer
rounder	warmest
roundest	

High-Frequency/Tested Words:
each
once
other
under
which

Spelling Words:
her
turn
hurt
girl
first
bird

What's New in Mrs. Powell's Class?

Fox on Stage

Vowel Diphthong *ow* /ou/

bow	meow
brown	now
clown	owl
cow	plow
crowd	pow
crown	Powell
down	prowls
drown	town
frown	vow
gown	wow
growl	
how	
howl	

Medial Consonants

along	ever	parents
apart	forget	pencil
began	forgot	posters
begins	funny	princess
behind	Jason	riddles
better	jester	river
broken	jolly	salad
Carmen	Lola	shiny
costumes	Monday	today
curtain	morning	yellow
Danny	mummy	
Dexter	never	
dragon	paper	

High-Frequency/Tested Words:
along
goes
great
idea
pull

Spelling Words:
how
now
town
down
brown
clown

Word List

	Phonics Words		High-Frequency/ Tested Words	Spelling Words

Doggy Art

The Snow Glory

Vowel Diphthong *ou*

around	outside
bound	pound
clouds	pout
crouch	round
found	scout
ground	shout
hound	sound
hour	south
house	sprout
mound	stout
mouse	trout
mouth	
out	

Medial Consonants

artist	happy	puzzle
balloons	Henry	sofa
belly	kitten	sparkle
bottle	little	table
cattle	many	whisper
collar	middle	
cover	Molly	
cozy	paper	
fiddle	petal	
flower	pocket	
fuzzy	pretty	
giggle	puppy	
glory	purple	

High-Frequency/Tested Words:
almost
knew
picture
thought
took

Spelling Words:
pretty
happy
little
kitten
puppy
better

I'll Join You

Leon and Bob

Vowel Diphthongs *oi, oy*

boil	Roy
boy	soil
broil	spoil
coil	toy
coin	Troy
cowboy	voice
enjoy	
foil	
join	
joy	
Moy	
noise	
oil	

Multisyllabic Words

acted	lazy	something
airplane	moving	sometimes
anymore	opened	spaceship
become	opening	suddenly
breakfast	outside	suitcase
cannot	over	thinking
cattle	planted	Thursday
couldn't	popcorn	tiptoe
cowboy	pretended	townhouse
didn't	pretending	waited
downhill	quickly	waiting
downtown	quietly	wanted
galloped	redbird	wasn't
going	rounded	zebra
grandma	shouted	
halfway	somehow	

High-Frequency/Tested Words:
always
boy
move
open
school

Spelling Words:
cannot
outside
grandma
something
popcorn
tiptoe

 # Awards

Index

46m, 93h, 116m, 156m, 192m, **1.6** 36m, 83a, 106m, 131d, 132m, 162m, 169a

Graphic sources
announcement, **1.6** 105
calendar, **1.4** 109, **1.6** 75
chart/table, **1.6** 35, 101, 131
diagram/scale drawing, **1.2** 171, **1.3** 135
graph, **1.1** 102, **1.3** 136h, **1.4** 43, 80h, 110h, 162–163, 199
illustration (photograph or art) and/or caption, **1.5** 115
map, **1.2** 68, **1.4** 167, **1.5** 45, 82, 150–151, 155, 156h
poster, **1.6** 105
recipe, **1.3** 77
schedule, **1.4** 79d, 167d
sign, **1.3** 162h, 185, **1.5** 10g

Grouping students, **1.1** 9, 21, 37, 55, 67, 85, 101, 119, 131, 149, 167, 185, 197, **1.2** 18b, 52b, 80b, 124b, 158b, 180b, **1.3** 18b, 48b, 86b, 107, 120b, 144b, 170b, 189b, **1.4** 9, 18b, 52b, 88b, 118b, 140g, 148b, 176b, 203a, **1.5** 9, 18b, 54b, 94b, 124b, 164b, 200b, **1.6** 18b, 44b, 84b, 112b, 140b, 170b

Groups, working in, **1.1** 21, 55, 85, 119, 149, 185, **1.2** 9d, 39a, 43, 43d, 44g, 44h, 67a, 68, 72h, 79g, 111a, 116g, 116h, 123g, 145a, 149, 150g, 150h, 157g, 167a, 172g, 172h, 197a, 198, **1.3** 35a, 39, 40g, 40h, 47g, 73a, 74, 78h, 107, 107a, 108, 112g, 131a, 136g, 136h, 143f, 157a, 161, 162g, 162h, 181a, 183, **1.4** 9, 10h, 39a, 39c, 43, 44g, 80g, 80h, 87f, 105a, 106, 109, 110g, 110h, 117g, 135a, 136, 139d, 140g, 163a, 164, 168h, 195a, 199, 201, **1.5** 9, 10h, 41a, 42, 46h, 81a, 85d, 86g, 86h, 111, 111a, 115, 116g, 116h, 123g, 151a, 152, 155d, 156h, 187a, 187c, 191, 192g, 199b, 199g, 199h, 223a, 223c, 227, 227d, **1.6** 10g, 10h, 31a, 35, 36h, 43f, 71a, 72, 76g, 76h, 101a, 105, 105d, 106g, 106h, 127a, 157a, 161d, 162h, 191a, 199b

Guided reading, **1.2** 18b, 52b, 80b, 124b, 158b, 180b, **1.3** 18b, 48b, 86b, 107, 120b, 144b, 170b, 189b, **1.4** 9, 10n, 18b, 52b, 88b, 118b, 140n, 148b, 176b, 203a, **1.5** 9, 18b, 54b, 94b, 124b, 164b, 200b, **1.6** 18b, 44b, 84b, 112b, 140b, 170b. *See also* **Grouping students.** Guided reading and leveled readers are a part of every lesson plan.

H

Habits and attitudes
consequences of actions/behaviors/choices (as demonstrated in literary selections). *See* **Character education.**
humanity and compassion (as demonstrated in literary selections). *See* **Character education.**
toward other groups and people (multicultural values) **1.1** 8, **1.2** 8, 10h, 44g, 72h, 116g, 150g, 172g, **1.3** 8, 40h, 112h, 136g, 162h, **1.4** 8, 10g, 44h, 80h, 110h, 140h, **1.5** 8, 9a–9d, 10h, 46h, 86h,

116h, **1.6** 8, 10g, 36g, 76h, 106g, 132g, 162h
toward reading, writing, listening, speaking, viewing, **1.1** 98, 159, 168–169, **1.2** 138–139, 156–157, 190–191, **1.3** 20–21, 32–33, 58–59, 73, 88–89, 104–105, 168–169, 172–173, **1.4** 146–147, 154–155
See also **Oral language and concepts.**

Handwriting
letter form/size/slant, **1.1** 97, 127, 163, 193, AR65, **1.2** 17b, 51b, 79b, 123b, 157b, 179b, AR57, **1.3** 17b, 47b, 85b, 119b, 143b, 169b, AR48, **1.4** 17b, 51b, 87b, 117b, 147b, 175b, AR48, **1.5** 17b, 53b, 93b, 123b, 163b, 199b, AR48, **1.6** 17b, 43b, 83b, 111b, 139b, 169b, AR48
letter, word, and sentence spacing, **1.1** AR65, **1.2** 17b, 51b, 157b, AR57, **1.3** 17b, 47b, 85b, 119b, 143b, 169b, AR48, **1.4** 51b, 87b, 117b, 147b, 175b, AR48, **1.5** 17b, 53b, 93b, 123b, 163b, 199b, AR49–AR50, **1.6** 17b, 43b, 83b, 111b, 139b, 169b, AR49–AR50
manuscript, **1.1** 97, 127, 163, 193, AR66–AR67, **1.2** 17b, 51b, 79b, 123b, 157b, 179b, AR58–AR59, **1.3** 17b, 47b, 85b, 119b, 143b, 169b, AR49–AR50, **1.4** 17b, 51b, 87b, 117b, 147b, 175b, AR49–AR50, **1.5** 17b, 53b, 93b, 123b, 163b, 199b, AR49–AR50, **1.6** 17b, 43b, 83b, 111b, 139b, 169b, AR49–AR50
pencil grip, **1.1** 63, AR65, **1.2** AR57, **1.3** AR48, **1.4** AR48, **1.5** AR48, **1.6** AR48
posture/paper position, **1.1** 33, AR65, **1.2** AR57, **1.3** AR48, **1.4** AR48, **1.5** AR48, **1.6** AR48

Health activities. *See* **Cross-curricular activities.**

High-frequency words, 1.1 31, 33, 36, 44, 61, 63, 66, 71, 75, 95, 97, 100, 105, 109, 125, 127, 130, 135, 139, 161, 163, 166, 171, 175, 191, 193, 196, 205, **1.2** 10m, 44m, 72m, 116m, 150m, 172m, **1.3** 10m, 40m, 78m, 112m, 136m, 162m, **1.4** 10m, 44m, 80m, 110m, 140m, 168m, **1.5** 10m, 46m, 86m, 116m, 156m, 192m, **1.6** 10m, 36m, 76m, 106m, 132m, 162m

Higher-order thinking skills. *See* **Critical thinking.**

Home-school connection. *See* **School-home connection.**

Homonyms, 1.3 85a, 107c, 112m, 119a, **1.4** 87a–87b, **1.5** 46m, 163a

Humanity. *See* **Character education.**

Humor. *See* **Literary devices.**

I

Idioms. *See* **Figurative language, Literary devices.**

Illustrations. *See* **Graphic sources,** illustration and/or caption; **Prereading strategies.**

Implied message. *See* **Main idea, Theme.**

Inclusion. *See* **Other ways to learn.**

Independent reading. *See* **Bibliographies, D.E.A.R., Self-selected reading.**

Inferences. *See* **Author's purpose; Conclusions, drawing; Fiction and nonfiction, distinguishing; Predicting.** In addition, inferential thinking questions appear throughout Guiding Comprehension in each lesson.

Inflected endings. *See* **Spelling,** word structure; **Structural analysis.**

Informal assessment. *See* **Assessment.**

Informational text. *See* **Functional reading.**

Integrated curriculum. *See* **Cross-curricular activities.**

Internet (as reference source). *See* **Reference sources, Technology.**

Intervention, 1.1 37, 68, 102, 163, 198, **1.2** 18b, 52b, 80b, 124b, 158b, 180b, **1.3** 18b, 48b, 86b, 120b, 144b, 170b, **1.4** 18b, 52b, 88b, 118b, 148b, 176b, **1.5** 18b, 54b, 94b, 124b, 164b, 200b, **1.6** 18b, 44b, 84b, 112b, 140b, 170b
comprehension support, **1.1** 38, 136, 159, 176, 198, **1.2** 17f, 51f, 79f, 123f, 157f, 179f, **1.3** 17f, 47f, 85f, 119f, 143f, 169f, **1.4** 17f, 51f, 87f, 117f, 147f, 175f, **1.5** 17f, 53f, 93f, 123f, 163f, 199f, **1.6** 17f, 43f, 83f, 139f, 169f
grammar support, **1.2** 39d, 67d, 111d, 145d, 167d, 197d, **1.3** 35d, 73d, 107d, 131d, 157d, 181d, **1.4** 39d, 75d, 105d, 135d, 163d, 195d, **1.5** 41d, 81d, 111d, 151d, 187d, 223d, **1.6** 31d, 71d, 101d, 127d, 157d, 191d
phonics support, **1.2** 10k, 17d, 41a, 44k, 51d, 69a, 72k, 79d, 113a, 116k, 123d, 147a, 150k, 157d, 169a, 172k, 179d, 199a, **1.3** 10k, 17d, 37a, 40k, 47d, 75a, 78k, 85d, 109a, 112k, 119d, 133a, 136k, 143d, 159a, 162k, 169d, 183a, **1.4** 10k, 17d, 41a, 44k, 51d, 77a, 80k, 87d, 107a, 110k, 117d, 137a, 140k, 147d, 165a, 168k, 175d, 197a, **1.5** 10k, 17d, 43a, 46k, 53d, 83a, 86k, 93d, 113a, 116k, 123d, 153a, 156d, 163d, 189a, 192k, 199d, 225a, **1.6** 10k, 17d, 33a, 36k, 43d, 73a, 76k, 83d, 103a, 106k, 129a, 132k, 139d, 159a, 162k, 169d, 193a
vocabulary support, **1.1** 31, 61, 95, 125, 191

Interview. *See* **Oral language and concepts,** oral language activities.

J

Journal. *See* **Log, Writing forms/products.**

Judgments, making. *See* **Conclusions, drawing; Fiction and nonfiction, distinguishing; Predicting; Theme (as a story element).**

K

K-W-L reading strategy, 1.3 120a, **1.5** 86m, 94a, **1.6** 76m

L

Language arts. *See* **Creative/dramatic activities, Grammar and usage, Mechanics, Oral language and concepts, Spelling, Writing forms/products, Writing modes, Writing process.**

Language, oral. *See* **Oral language and concepts.**

Large group discussion. *See* **Oral language and concepts.**

Learning centers. *See* **Cross-curricular work stations.**

Learning styles. *See* **Other ways to learn.**

Less-able readers. *See* **Intervention.**

Leveled readers. *See* **Bibliographies, Guided reading.**

Levels of thinking. *See* **Critical thinking.**

Life skills. *See* **Own life, text's relation to.**

Limited English proficient children. ESL notes throughout Guiding Comprehension in the lesson plan point out idioms, multiple meaning words, and other language features that may be difficult for children with limited English proficiency.

Listening. *See* **Oral language and concepts.**

Literal comprehension. Literal comprehension questions appear throughout Guiding Comprehension in each lesson.

Literary craft
author's craft/style/language, **1.3** 172–173, **1.4** 154–155

Literary devices
dialogue, **1.3** 20–21, 172–173
humor, **1.4** 154–155
idiom, **1.4** 146–147
narration, **1.3** 20–21
point of view, **1.3** 131d, 169f
See also **Figurative language, Sound devices and poetic elements.**

Literary genres. *See* **Genres.**

Literary response and appreciation
appreciation of author's craft/style, **1.3** 172–173, **1.4** 154–155
enjoyment of literature, **1.1** 98, 159, 168–169, **1.2** 138–139, 156–157, 190–191, **1.3** 32–33, 58–59, 73, 88–89, 104–105, 168–169, **1.4** 146–147, 154–155
See also **Habits and attitudes.**

Literature selections
"Arthur's Reading Race," Marc Brown, **1.5** 18–41
"Biscuit," Alyssa Satin Capucilli, **1.3** 86–106
"Bravest Cat!, The" Laura Driscoll, **1.5** 200–221
"Can You Find It?," Sharon Fear, **1.2** 52–67
"Cat Traps," Molly Coxe, **1.3** 48–73
"Cherry Pies and Lullabies," Lynn Reiser, **1.4** 52–75
"Communities," Gail Saunders-Smith, **1.3** 120–131

"Dinosaur Babies," Lucille Recht Penner, **1.5** 164–185
"Do You Live in a Nest?," Carmen Tafolla, **1.6** 84–101
"Foal," Mary Ling, **1.5** 94–109
"Fox and Bear Look at the Moon," David McPhail, **1.3** 144–157
"Fox on Stage," James Marshall, **1.6** 112–127
"Garden, The," Arnold Lobel, **1.6** 18–30
"Gingerbread Man, The," Sally Bell, **1.4** 18–39
"How Many Fish?," Caron Lee Cohen, **1.2** 124–144
"I Went Walking," Sue Williams, **1.2** 80–110
"Ice-Cold Birthday," Maryann Cocca-Leffler, **1.6** 44–69
"Leon and Bob," Simon James, **1.6** 170–190
"Lilly Reads," Laurie Krasny Brown, **1.3** 170–180
"Little Red Hen, The," Patricia and Fredrick McKissack, **1.3** 18–35
"Lost!," David McPhail, **1.5** 54–81
"Lost in the Museum," Miriam Cohen, **1.5** 124–151
"Lunch," Denise Fleming, **1.1** 22–27
"My Family's Market," Theresa Volpe, **1.1** 87–91
"Oh, Cats!," Nola Buck, **1.2** 18–39
"Our Family Get-Together," Carmen Tafolla, **1.4** 88–104
"Rat and the Cat, The," Edward Marshall, **1.4** 118–133
"Riddles, The," Bernard Wiseman, **1.4** 176–195
"Slim, Luke, and the Mules," Stewart Christopher, **1.4** 148–163
"Snow Glory, The," Cynthia Rylant, **1.6** 140–157
"Sweet Potato Pie," Anne Rockwell, **1.2** 180–197
"Tadpole to Frog," Fay Robinson, **1.2** 158–166
"Tumble Bumble," Felicia Bond, **1.1** 151–157
See also **Phonics stories, Poetry selections.**

Log
journal, **1.1** 20, 54, 84, 118, 148, 184, **1.2** 10i, 44i, 72i, 116i, 150i, 172i, **1.3** 10i, 40i, 78i, 112i, 136i, 162i, **1.4** 10i, 44i, 80i, 110i, 140i, 168i, **1.5** 10i, 46i, 86i, 116i, 156i, 192i, **1.6** 10i, 36i, 76i, 106i, 132i, 162i
response, **1.2** 14–15, 38, 64–65, 76–77, 108–109, 120–121, 140–141, 154–155, 162–163, 176–177, 196, **1.3** 14–15, 34, 72, 82–83, 102–103, 116–117, 128–129, 140–141, 156, 166–167, 178–179, **1.4** 14–15, 48–49, 72–73, 100–101, 114–115, 130–131, 144–145, 172–173, 192–193, **1.5** 14–15, 38–39, 50–51, 90–91, 106–107, 120–121, 148–149, 160–161, 220–221, **1.6** 14–15, 40–41, 68–69, 80–81, 110, 124–125, 136–137, 152–153, 166–167, 186–187

M

Main idea, 1.1 46, 92–93, 98, 102, 106, AR21, **1.2** 50–51, **1.3** 85e–85f, 104–105, AR15, **1.4** 87e–87f, 102–103, 137, AR15, **1.5** 92–93, 163e–163f, 182–183, 225, AR18, **1.6** 111

Managing Scott Foresman Reading, 1.1 4–5, **1.2** 8d–8e, **1.3** 8d–8e, **1.4** 8d–8e, **1.5** 8d–8e, **1.6** 8d–8e

Map/globe. *See* **Graphic sources.**

Mapping selections. *See* **Graphic organizers.**

Mass media. *See* **Cross-curricular activities, Viewing.**

Mathematics activities. *See* **Cross-curricular activities.**

Mechanics (of English grammar and writing)
capitalization
nouns, proper, **1.1** 97, **1.3** 85h, 107d, 110–111, 169h, 181d, 184–185, **1.4** 16–17
sentence, **1.1** 41, 71, 105, 135, 161, 171, 201, **1.2** 17h, 39d, 42–43, 157h, 170–171, 179h, 200–201, **1.4** 9c, **1.6** 31d, 34–35, 43h, 74–75, 101d, 104–105
titles, **1.3** 119h, 131d, 134–135
paragraph features, **1.4** 12–13, 82–83
punctuation
apostrophe, **1.4** 175h, 195d, 198–199
end marks, **1.1** 41, 71, 105, 135, 161, 171, 201, **1.2** 17h, 39d, 42–43, 110–111, 157h, 167, 170–171, 179h, 200–201, **1.3** 84–85, **1.4** 86–87, 124–125, 194–195, **1.5** 80–81, 92–93, **1.6** 31d, 34–35, 43h, 71d, 74–75, 83h, 101d, 104–105, 126–127
quotation marks, **1.3** 20–21, 142–143, 172–173

Media. *See* **Cross-curricular activities, Viewing.**

Metacognition. *See* **Self-monitoring.**

Modeling. Teacher modeling and think-alouds are presented throughout Skills in Context lessons and After Reading lessons.

Modern realistic fiction. *See* **Genres.**

Multi-age classes, suggestions for, 1.1 28, 58, 92, 122, 158, 188, **1.2** 17e, 51e, 79e, 123e, 157e, 179e, **1.3** 17e, 47e, 85e, 119e, 143e, 169e, **1.4** 17e, 51e, 87e, 117e, 147e, 175e, **1.5** 17e, 53e, 93e, 123e, 163e, 199e, **1.6** 17e, 43e, 83e, 111e, 139e, 169e

Multicultural connections, 1.2 8, 10h, 44g, 72h, 116g, 150g, 172g, **1.3** 8, 10h, 40h, 104–105, 112h, 136g, 162h, **1.4** 8, 10g, 44h, 80h, 110h, 112–113, 140h, **1.5** 8, 9a–9d, 10h, 40–41, 46h, 86h, 116h, **1.6** 8, 10g, 36g, 76h, 106g, 132g, 162h

Multiple intelligences. *See* **Other ways to learn.**

Multiple meaning words, 1.3 80–81, **1.4** 51a, 75c, **1.5** 17a, 41c, **1.6** 43a, 71c, 83a, 101c

Music activities. *See* **Cross-curricular activities.**

N

T

Acknowledgments

Text

K-W-L Strategy: The K-W-L Interactive Reading Strategy was developed and is used by permission of Donna Ogle, National-Louis University, Evanston, Illinois, co-author of *Reading Today and Tomorrow,* Holt, Rinehart & Winston Publishers, 1988. (See also *The Reading Teacher,* February 1986, pp. 564–570.)

Page 46j: "Oh Where, Oh Where Has My Little Dog Gone?" Public domain.

Page 86j: "Foal" from *Menagerie* by Mary Britton Miller. Copyright estate of Mary Britton Miller. Reprinted by permission.

Page 116j: "Behind the Museum Door" from *Good Rhymes, Good Times* by Lee Bennett Hopkins. Copyright © 1973, 1995 by Lee Bennett Hopkins. Now appears in *Good Rhymes, Good Times,* published by HarperCollins Publishers. Reprinted by permission of Curtis Brown, Ltd.

Page 156j: "A Dinosaur Baby" from *Wee Sing Dinosaurs* by Pamela Conn Beall, Susan Hagen Nipp and Nancy Spence Klein. Copyright © 1991 by Pamela Conn Beall, Susan Hagen Nipp and Nancy Spence Klein. Used by permission of Price Stern & Sloan, Inc., a division of Penguin Putnam Inc.

The Know Zone™ is a registered trademark of Addison Wesley Longman, Inc.

Scott Foresman Phonics System™ is a registered trademark of Addison-Wesley Educational Publishers, Inc.

Page 9a: *Aunt Flossie's Hats (and Crab Cakes Later)* Clarion Books a Houghton Mifflin Company imprint. Text copyright ©1991 by Elizabeth Fitzgerald Howard.

Selected text and images in this book are copyrighted © 2002.

Artists

Cover illustration © Maryjane Begin
Maryjane Begin: i, 8a
Tony Nuccio: pages 10g, 46h, 86g, 116h, 123d, 156g, 163d
Mike Dammer: pages 10h, 10j, 46g, 123e, 156j, 163e, 192g
Gwen Connelly: pages 17e, 46h, 83b, 189b, 199e
Reggie Holladay: pages 46j, 86j, 192j
Rusty Fletcher: page 93a
Linda Howard Bittner: page 93e
Doug Knutson: pages 116j, 156j
Elizabeth Allen: page 123h
Bernard Adnet: page 199a

Photographs

Every effort has been made to secure permission and provide appropriate credit for photographic material. The publisher deeply regrets any omission and pledges to correct, in subsequent editions, errors called to its attention.

Unless otherwise acknowledged, all photographs are the property of Scott Foresman, a division of Pearson Education. Page abbreviations are as follows: (t) top, (c) center, (b) bottom, (l) left, (r) right, (ins) inset, (s) spot, (bk) background.

Page 10n: © Lawrence Migdale
Page 46j: Michael Newman/PhotoEdit
Page 46n: Courtesy, Lily Toy Hong
Page 53e: Henry R. Fox/Animals Animals/Earth Scenes
Page 54b: Photo by Richard Hutchings
Page 86j: SuperStock
Page 86n: Courtesy, Susan McCloskey
Page 116j: A. Ramey/PhotoEdit
Page 116n: Photo by Richard Hutchings
Page 124b: (T) Courtesy, Miriam Cohen, (B) Courtesy, William Morrow
Page 123a: VCG/FPG International LLC
Page 192j: PhotoDisc
Page 192n: Photo by Ron Davis
Page 200b: Photo by Brent Jones

Notes

Notes

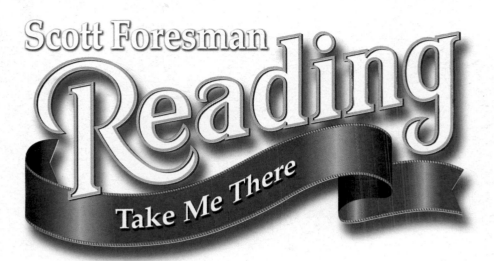

Scott Foresman
Reading
Take Me There

Grade 1, Unit 5

Take Me There

PEARSON

Scott
Foresman

scottforesman.com

DORLING KINDERSLEY

Editorial Offices: Glenview, Illinois • Parsippany, New Jersey • New York, New York
Sales Offices: Parsippany, New Jersey • Duluth, Georgia • Glenview, Illinois
Coppell, Texas • Ontario, California • Mesa, Arizona

About the Cover Artist

Maryjane Begin and her family live in Providence, Rhode Island, where she teaches college students when she is not working on her own art. Many of her illustrations—even of imaginary places—show how things in Providence look.

Cover illustration © Maryjane Begin

ISBN 0-328-03953-5

345678910V0631009080706050403

Program Authors

Peter Afflerbach, Ph.D.

Professor, Department of Curriculum and Instruction, Director of the Reading Center, University of Maryland at College Park; Member of the Board of Directors of the National Reading Conference; Advisor to the National Assessment of Educational Progress and the Voluntary National Test of Reading

Research Contributions: Assessment, Reading Comprehension, Strategic Reading

James W. Beers, Ph.D.

Professor, School of Education, College of William & Mary, Williamsburg, Virginia; Director of the Eastern Virginia Writing Project of the National Writing Project; Author of Scott Foresman-Addison Wesley's *Everyday Spelling*

Research Contributions: Intervention Strategies, Phonics and Spelling in Literacy Development, Writing for Critical Thinking

Camille L. Z. Blachowicz, Ph.D.

Professor of Education, Codirector of the Reading Leadership Institute, National College of Education, National-Louis University, Evanston, Illinois

Research Contributions: Comprehension Development, Vocabulary Instruction, Staff Development

Candy Dawson Boyd, Ph.D.

Professor, School of Education, Saint Mary's College, Moraga, California; Founder and Director of the Master's and Specialist Credential and Certificate Programs in Reading/Language Arts; Award-Winning Children's Author

Research Contributions: Cultural Diversity, Early Literacy, Intervention Strategies, Multicultural Literature

Wendy Cheyney, Ed.D.

Professor of Special Education, Department of Educational Psychology and Special Education, Associate Dean for Academic Affairs, College of Education, Florida International University, University Park Campus, Miami

Research Contributions: Phonological and Phonemic Awareness, Early Literacy

Deborah Diffily, Ph.D.

Assistant Professor, Early Childhood Education, Southern Methodist University, Dallas, Texas

Research Contributions: Early Childhood Education, Family Involvement

Dolores Gaunty-Porter, Ph.D.

Professor of Literacy, Language, and Learning, School of Education, Chapman University, Orange County, California

Research Contributions: English as a Second Language, Inclusion, Staff Development

Connie Juel, Ph.D.

Professor of Education, Director of the Jeanne Chall Reading Lab, Graduate School of Education, Harvard University, Cambridge, Massachusetts

Research Contributions: Literacy Development, Word Recognition Instruction, Reading Difficulties

Donald J. Leu, Ph.D.

John and Maria Neag Endowed Chair in Literacy and Technology, Neag School of Education, University of Connecticut, Storrs-Mansfield; Member of the Board of Directors for the National Reading Conference; Member of the Research Committee for the International Reading Association

Research Contributions: Reading Comprehension, Technology in the Classroom

Jeanne R. Paratore, Ed.D.

Associate Professor of Education, Department of Developmental Studies, Boston University; Founder of the Intergenerational Literacy Project; Member of the Board of Directors of the International Reading Association

Research Contributions: Intervention Strategies, Grouping Practices, School-Home Partnerships

Sam L. Sebesta, Ed.D.

Professor Emeritus, College of Education, University of Washington, Seattle

Research Contributions: Children's Literature, Decoding in Linguistic Development, Oral Reading Fluency, Reader Response

Karen Kring Wixson, Ph.D.

Dean of the School of Education and Professor of Education, University of Michigan, Ann Arbor; Advisor to the National Research Council; Codirector of the Michigan English Language Arts Framework Project

Research Contributions: Alignment of Reading Curriculum and Assessment, Instruction for Reading and Writing Disabilities, Development of Thematic Units

Consultants and Reviewers

Consultants

Consulting Authors

Carol Berkin, Ph.D. Professor of History
Baruch College, City University of New York:
Reading in the Content Areas

Anna Uhl Chamot, Ph.D. Associate Professor of ESL
George Washington University, Washington, D.C.:
English as a Second Language

Jim Cummins, Ph.D. Professor
Modern Language Centre and Curriculum Department
Ontario Institute for Studies in Education, Toronto, Canada:
English as a Second Language

Karen Erickson, Ph.D. Assistant Professor
Department of Education, University of New Hampshire,
Durham: *Intervention Strategies, Learning Styles*

Lily Wong Fillmore, Ph.D. Professor
Graduate School of Education, University of California, Berkeley:
English as a Second Language

George González, Ph.D. Professor (Retired)
School of Education, University of Texas Pan-American,
Edinburg: *Bilingual Education, English as a Second Language*

Priscilla Griffith, Ph.D. Chair
Instructional Leadership and Academic Curriculum
University of Oklahoma, Norman:
Phonemic Awareness, Phonics Instruction, Writing

Carolyn Kessler, Ph.D. Professor Emerita of ESL
University of Texas, San Antonio: *English as a Second Language*

Jackson Lee, Jr., Ed.D. Professor of Education
Francis Marion University, Florence, South Carolina:
Reading in the Content Areas

Senior Consultants

Margaret Gritsavich, C.A.S. Faculty Associate
Arizona State University, Tempe: *Writing, Assessment*

Nancy Reeves Radcliffe, Ph.D.
Houston Baptist University, Houston, Texas: *Gifted and Talented*

Reviewers

Student Edition

Connie Barnhart Second and Third Grade Teacher
Gilder Elementary School, Bellevue, Nebraska

Cheryl Borovitcky Second Grade Teacher and President
Mahoni Valley Council, Ohio Council IRA, Poland City Schools
Youngstown, Ohio

Gail F. Brown Reading Specialist
Perrymont Elementary School, Lynchburg, Virginia

Julia M. Chaney Reading Specialist
Taylor Elementary School, Hobbs, New Mexico

Ynette Colyer Third Grade Teacher
Bel Air Elementary School, Albuquerque, New Mexico

Barbara Giese Fourth Grade Teacher
Rocky Run Elementary School, Fredericksburg, Virginia

Lloyd Hardesty CCIRA President 2002–2003
Colorado Springs, Colorado

Jeannene A. Henry Reading Methods Instructor
Prescott SD, Prescott, Arizona

Karen R. Jackson Third Grade Teacher
Joseph Leidy Elementary School, Philadelphia, Pennsylvania

Laura Kaiser Literacy Staff Developer
PS 222, Brooklyn, New York

Collette M. Martin Reading Specialist
Mary Carr Creer Elementary School, Charlottesville, Virginia

Louise McGinnis First Grade Teacher
Golden Grove Elementary School, West Palm Beach, Florida

Sherri Moss First Grade Teacher
Bethune Elementary School, Hollywood, Florida

Catherine M. Radu Reading and Language Arts
Consultant, Traverse City Schools, Traverse City, Michigan

Tamara Jo Rhomberg
Rockwood School District, Eureka, Missouri

Amy D. Taylor First Grade Teacher
Twinbrook Elementary School, Rockville, Maryland

Sharon B. Webber Fifth Grade Teacher
Davis Magnet School, Jackson, Mississippi

Christine Woods First Grade Teacher
Hillrise Elementary School, Las Cruces, New Mexico

Teacher's Edition

Robin Atwood First Grade Teacher
Taylorsville Elementary School, Taylorsville, Mississippi

Mari Carlson Reading Coordinator
Waukegan School District, Waukegan, Illinois

Paul A. Coleman Assistant Principal
Montview Elementary School, Aurora, Colorado

Catherine Fox
Englishtown, New Jersey

Judith W. Gillette Title One Director
Standish Elementary School, Bay City, Michigan

Charlotte Hall Teacher on Assignment
Grinnett County Curriculum Center, Lawrenceville, Georgia

Linda Hinton First Grade Teacher
Soldier Creek Elementary School, Midwest, Oklahoma

Carol Ann Hulton Reading Coordinator
Talmadge School, Springfield, Massachusetts

Nicki Johnson First Grade Teacher
Wildewood Elementary School, Ralston, Nebraska

Kim King Sixth Grade Teacher
Soldier Creek Elementary School, Midwest, Oklahoma

Catherine Kuhns First Grade Teacher
Country Hill School, Coral Springs, Florida

Pamela J. McAtee First Grade Teacher
Target Range Elementary School, Missoula, Montana

Dr. Janet Perrin
Thomas J. Lahey Elementary School, Greenlawn, New York

Tamara Jo Rhomberg
Rockwood School District, Eureka, Missouri

Dr. Mae S. Sheftall Title I Coordinator
Bibb County Public School, Macon, Georgia

Dr. Maureen Siera Professor of Education
St. Martins College, Kent, Washington

Linda Squires Reading Specialist
Southern Heights Elementary School, Hobbs, New Mexico

Scheneithia Stickler First Grade Teacher
Signal Hills Elementary School, Manassas, Virginia

Dr. Margaret Timmons Language Arts Supervisor
Paterson Public Schools, Paterson, New Jersey

Janet Titensor deHoyos Second Grade Teacher
Joaquin Elementary School, Provo, Utah

Anita R. Turner District Reading Specialist
Carver Educational Center, Gambrills, Maryland

Joetta Whiteley First Grade Teacher
Crosby Park Elementary, Lawton, Oklahoma

Kindergarten

Ellen M. Christie Kindergarten Teacher
Holland Elementary School, Satellite Beach, Florida

Leslie Coburn Kindergarten Teacher
Middleburg Elementary School, Middleburg, Virginia

Sandra Connolly Kindergarten Teacher
Ralph Blevins Elementary School, Eureka, Missouri

Trisha Evans Kindergarten Teacher
Madison Elementary School, Ocala, Florida

Debra R. Friedman Kindergarten and First Grade Teacher
Welleby Elementary School Sunrise, Florida

Cynthia Giovo Kindergarten Teacher
Millard Hawk Primary School, Central Square, New York

Gwen Mora Kindergarten Teacher
Hillsborough County, Temple Terrace, Florida

Rebecca Pickard Kindergarten Teacher
Arrowhead Elementary School, Glendale, Arizona

Robin Robb Kindergarten Teacher
Indialantic Elementary School, Indialantic, Florida

Marilyn Russell Kindergarten Teacher
Southside Estates Elementary School, Jacksonville, Florida

Dr. Mae S. Sheftall Title I Coordinator
Bibb County Public School, Macon, Georgia

Linda Sholar Kindergarten Teacher
Sangre Ridge Elementary School, Stillwater, Oklahoma

Dot Solenski Kindergarten Teacher
Riverglades Elementary School, Parkland, Florida

Consultants and Reviewers

Scott Foresman Reading

Every child will succeed.

Dear Educator,

There is no greater legacy we can leave our children than to ensure their ability to read. In spite of this, we are keenly aware of the fact that in our schools today many children are struggling to effectively learn how to read.

The purpose of **Reading First** is to admit that although there are no easy, quick solutions for optimizing reading achievement, there is an extensive knowledge base that shows us the skills children must learn in order to read well. These five critical areas of explicit instruction are: *Phonemic Awareness, Phonics, Fluency, Vocabulary, and Text Comprehension.*

Scott Foresman Reading supports the research base that is critical for student success in each of these five important **Reading First** areas. In addition, it embraces evidence that describes other important elements of a high-quality, comprehensive, scientifically based research approach to reading instruction: Oral Language, Alphabetic Knowledge, Decodable Text, Listening Comprehension, Informational Text, and Ongoing Assessment.

We at Scott Foresman have been dedicated to helping educators teach students to read for more than 100 years. The combination of this important federal legislation and our carefully crafted, research-based program puts you in the best position ever to realize this tremendous goal.

We look forward to working with you to capitalize on this momentous opportunity. Together, we will help every child succeed.

Sincerely,

Paul L. McFall

Paul L. McFall
President, Scott Foresman

Scott Foresman Reading aligns to the scientifically based research of Reading First.

$\mathcal{E}$very child is like no other child in the world.

With Scott Foresman Reading, every child succeeds because test preparation is built into every part of the program.

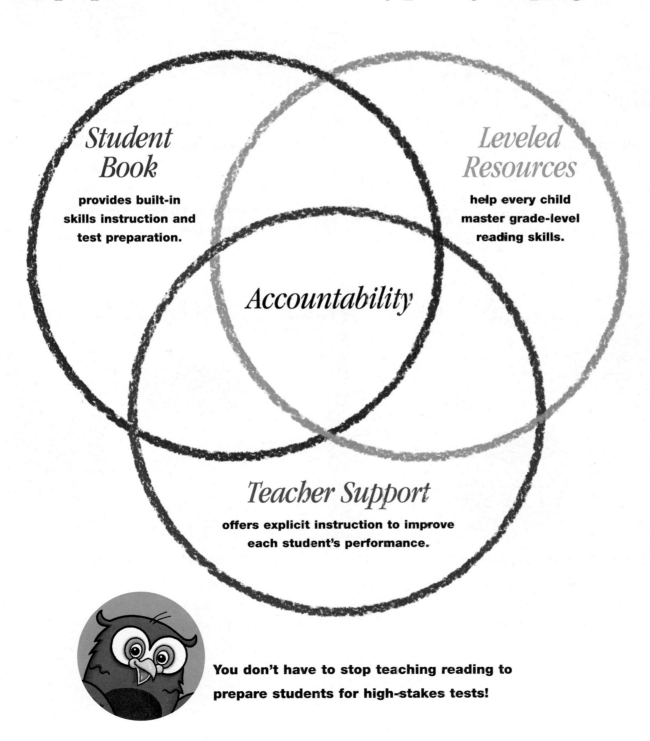

Student Book
provides built-in skills instruction and test preparation.

Leveled Resources
help every child master grade-level reading skills.

Accountability

Teacher Support
offers explicit instruction to improve each student's performance.

You don't have to stop teaching reading to prepare students for high-stakes tests!

$\mathcal{S}$tudent Book: For Built-in Instruction

Weekly preparation for reading and test-taking success

Begin with the Phonics Story

- Right in the student book!
- Accessible to all children
- Introduces the phonics skills and the high-frequency words each week

Then read the Main Selection

- Applies the same phonics skills and high-frequency words introduced in the Phonics Story
- Targets the weekly comprehension skill and tested vocabulary

Follow up with Reader Response

- Opportunities for personal, critical, and written response after each lesson
- Test preparation to improve short written responses on tests

Finish the week with Language Arts

- Directly tied to the reading selection
- Integrates language arts instruction and includes a writing application
- No need for a separate language book!

Review vocabulary with Words I Know

- Reviews tested words in each unit
- Makes children (and parents) aware of words they need to know

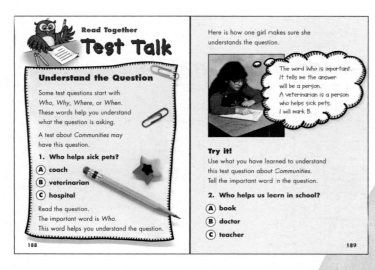

Prepare for tests with Test Talk

- Lesson that develops a key test-taking strategy in each unit
- Reading and writing practice for tests
- Transparencies to support instruction

Every child deserves the very best.

Student Book: Grades 1 and 2

ix

Leveled Resources: For Every Reader

Leveled Readers and practice for every week

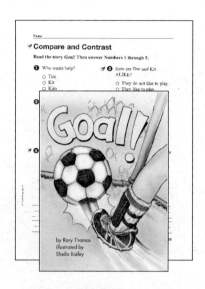

Easy Reader (A)

- For students reading one year to one-and-a-half years below grade level

- Additional direct instruction on the same comprehension skill and tested vocabulary taught each week

- Lesson plans in the Teacher's Edition and in a separate Resource Guide

- Practice master in test format

On-Level Reader (B)

- For students reading on grade level to one-half year below grade level

- Additional direct instruction on the same comprehension skill and tested vocabulary taught each week

- Lesson plans in the Teacher's Edition and in a separate Resource Guide

- Practice master in test format

Challenge Reader (C)

- For students reading at or above level

- Thematically related articles and stories that expand target comprehension skills, vocabulary, and critical thinking

- Lesson plans in the Teacher's Edition and in a separate Resource Guide

- Research projects and cross-curricular activities for practice

Leveled practice in test format for each main selection

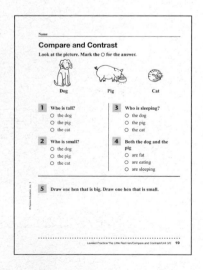

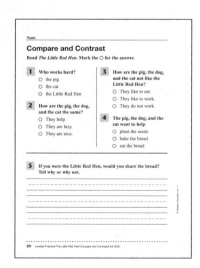

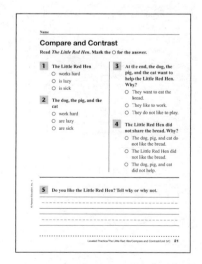

Easy

On-Level

Challenge

Additional leveled resources

Phonics Reader

- Reinforces weekly phonics skills and high-frequency words
- Applies phonics skills to a new selection
- Available in a reproducible take-home format

Decodable Reader

- Decodable text that supports the phonics instruction of the week
- Lesson plans in the Teacher's Edition and in a separate Teaching Guide
- Available in a reproducible take-home format

Adding English/ESL

- Parallel lessons for each main selection based on the most effective ESL strategies

Ten Important Sentences

- Reinforces comprehension skills through key sentences in each selection

Every child shines like a little star.

Teacher Support: For Test Success

Direct, explicit instruction every day of the week

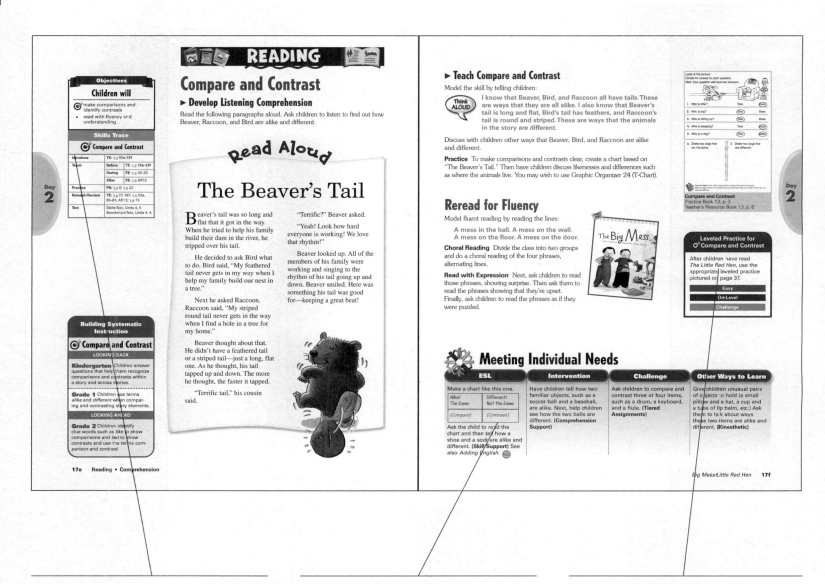

Teach

Each week targets a comprehension skill that's commonly found on standardized tests.

Manage

Management tools help you address individual needs, flexible grouping, and guided reading.

Assess

Ongoing assessment includes leveled practice and reteaching for targeted instruction.

Test prep opportunities

Improving your students' test scores

With Scott Foresman Reading, you don't have to stop teaching reading to prepare students for high-stakes tests. Test preparation is built into the program to ensure success. During the year students will learn key tested skills and test-taking strategies, as well as become familiar with the language and format of standardized tests.

- **A target skill each week** that's commonly assessed on standardized tests

- **Multiple exposures to critical skills** before the unit test

- **Reader Response** with short response questions in test format after each selection and a scoring rubric

- **"Test Talk" icons** in the lesson plan to identify daily opportunities for using test language

- **"Test Talk" lesson** that teaches specific test-taking strategies in each unit

- **"Test Talk" transparencies** to support instruction in test language and format

- **"If/Then" guidelines** for ongoing assessment with specific reteach opportunities and leveled practice

- **Test prep highlighted** in the Unit Skills Overview, Assessment Overview, and Reaching Every Student chart

- **Leveled Practice and Test Link** for weekly leveled practice in test format

Every child needs a hand to hold.

Teacher Support: Grades 1 and 2

Program Organization

Kindergarten

22 Big Books (Including an Alphabet Big Book)

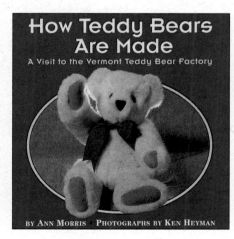

15 Read Aloud Trade Books

Oral Language Chart

Phonics Songs and Rhymes Chart

6 Teacher's Editions (1 per unit)

Grade 1

Kindergarten Review

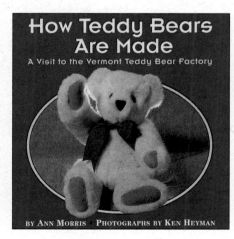

13 Big Books

5 Student Books

6 Teacher's Editions (1 per unit)

Grades 2–3

2 Student Books

**6 Teacher's Editions
(1 per unit)**

Grades 4–6

1 Student Book

**6 Teacher's Editions
(1 per unit)**

*Every child
matters most
of all.*

Program Components

Assessment

Assessment Handbook contains information about conference records, self-assessment, portfolio analysis, reading progress summaries, and running records.

Benchmark Assessment and Skill Development Checklists in the Kindergarten and Grade 1 (Unit 1) Teacher's Editions track skill development over the course of the year.

Individual Reading Inventory and Running Record provides diagnostic information about individual students and helps with instructional and placement decisions.

Kindergarten Skills Assessment collects information about a child's reading, writing, and language skills development.

Leveled Practice and Test Link provides leveled practice in test format for each main selection, practice tests, and test-taking strategies.

Placement Tests identify instructional needs and establish a baseline for each student.

Running Record and Miscue Analysis guidelines are included in each Teacher's Edition.

Selection Tests help you assess student abilities and monitor progress.

"Test Talk" Transparencies contain additional short response, extended response, and multiple-choice questions with answers.

Unit and End-of-Year Benchmark Tests help assess students' progress at the end of each unit and at the end of the school year.

Unit and End-of-Year Skills Tests measure students' ability to apply unit skills in a standardized test format.

Leveled Resources

Wordless Stories develop phonemic awareness, oral language skills, and key story concepts for kindergartners.

Kindergarten Reader provides targeted practice of phonics skills and high-frequency words for on-level readers.

Independent Readers reinforce early reading behaviors and allow children to practice skills and strategies independently.

Independent Reader Resource Guide contains lesson plans for every Independent Reader, management ideas, ways to extend the reading, and an assessment chart.

Collection for Readers (Very Easy Reader) provides intervention for students reading two levels below grade level.

Easy Reader (A) provides additional direct instruction for each week's target comprehension skill and tested vocabulary and is written one to one-and-a-half years below grade level.

On-Level Reader (B) provides additional direct instruction for each week's target comprehension skill and tested vocabulary and is written on grade level to one-half year below grade level.

Challenge Reader (C) is a collection of thematically related articles, stories, and projects for each unit that can be used with students reading at or above grade level.

Leveled Reader Resource Guide A and B provides lesson plans for Leveled Readers A and B, guided reading, activity sheets, and comprehension and vocabulary support.

Leveled Reader Resource Guide C contains lesson plans for Leveled Readers C, pacing guides, research projects, comprehension support, and scoring guides.

Intervention Handbook includes strategy routines, selection summaries, lesson plans, and an answer key for the Collection for Readers.

Adding English/ESL is a companion program that provides parallel ESL lessons, strategies, full-color vocabulary posters, comprehension strategy posters, and blackline masters.

Ten Important Sentences is a booklet of blackline masters, strategies, and activities that build comprehension skills for each selection.

Trade Book Library for self-selected reading features a thematically related On-Level and Challenge book for each unit.

Phonics

Decodable Readers provide decodable text for blending practice, application of sound-spelling patterns, and cumulative review.

Decodable Readers Teaching Guide contains lessons for each Decodable Reader, blending practice, spelling connections, and activities to apply decoding skills.

Phonemic Awareness and Phonics Manipulatives Kit helps you teach phonics with a variety of hands-on, word-building resources and multisensory phonics games.

Phonemic Awareness Audiocassette presents standard pronunciations of all target sounds plus blending and segmenting of sounds.

Phonics and Word-Building Board (Student) helps students build words and sentences using the magnetic word-building cards.

Phonics and Word-Building Board (Teacher) can be used with magnetic word-building cards for modeling or group work in building words and sentences.

Phonics Handbook details current research and best practices in teaching phonics and phonemic awareness.

Phonics Readers reinforce each week's target phonics skills and high-frequency words.

Phonics Songs and Rhymes Audiocassettes/CDs provide recordings of all songs and rhymes in the program plus instrumental tracks.

Phonics Songs and Rhymes Flip Chart develops phonemic awareness and phonics skills with songs and rhymes set to familiar tunes.

Phonics Songs and Rhymes Posters build phonemic awareness and help review kindergarten skills at the beginning of first grade.

Phonics Sourcebook consists of reproducible blackline master game boards, cards, and words and letters from the Phonemic Awareness and Phonics Manipulatives Kit.

Phonics Take-Home Readers are reproducible blackline versions of the Phonics Readers that students can share with their families.

Phonics Workbook contains additional paper-and-pencil practice to reinforce weekly phonics target skills.

Phonics Workbook Blackline Masters and Answer Key provides all Phonics Workbook pages in a reproducible format.

Small Group Manipulative Package provides magnetic letters, phonograms, and high-frequency word cards for working with small groups of students.

Word Wall Cards help children practice high-frequency words and can be displayed on the magnetic Word-Building Wall using magnetic clips.

Word-Building Wall is a large magnetic board you can use to make your own word wall.

Program Components

Program Components

Teacher Support

Classroom Routines Kit provides research-based routines for instruction, students, school/home, and the classroom environment.

Daily Word Routines Flip Chart provides a quick, daily review of phonics/word study, vocabulary, and language skills.

Family Reading Activities Calendar is a daily activity calendar with literacy activities for students and their families.

Family Reading Guide explains key reading terms and provides effective activities to develop reading skills at home.

Grammar Practice Book provides extra practice in grammar, usage, and mechanics each week.

Graphic Organizer Flip Chart has a write-on, wipe-off surface to demonstrate reading comprehension techniques.

Graphic Organizer Transparencies model higher-level thinking skills and organize information to build comprehension.

My Read, Write, and Listen Practice Book is a full-color workbook for kindergartners and first graders.

Oral Language Flip Chart contains rhymes to build oral language skills and activate prior knowledge each week.

Practice Book provides weekly practice to reinforce target skills along with tests for each main reading selection.

Professional Development Series helps school districts implement research-based best practices for reading instruction.

Spelling Workbook contains a weekly spelling pretest along with three practice worksheets for each week.

Teacher's Resource Book contains blackline masters of all Practice Book pages, Selection Tests, and family activities.

Topic/Theme Posters can introduce unit themes, build background, and assess prior knowledge as well as develop students' vocabulary and phonics skills.

Vocabulary Flip Chart displays selection vocabulary in context sentences for practice and review.

Writing Transparencies model steps of the writing process for practice and discussion.

Technology

AstroWord CD-ROM reinforces phonics, vocabulary, and word study skills using an exciting intergalactic theme.

Background-Building Audiocassettes/CDs support concept development for every main selection.

Book Builder CD-ROM motivates students to practice target comprehension skills as they create their own books.

Computer Assessment Management System lets teachers and administrators monitor, evaluate, and plan instruction based on criterion-referenced materials.

Internet Guide unlocks the power of the Web with clear explanations, projects, troubleshooting tips, and more.

The Know Zone™ provides test preparation practice online. Also available on CD-ROM for Grades K–1.

Multimedia Studio CD-ROM helps students create dynamic multimedia presentations with illustrations, photos, video clips, sound effects, and Web connections.

Reading Road Show contains skill-building videos, audio-cassettes, hand puppets, and activities from Children's Television Workshop, the creators of *Sesame Street*.

Reading Together: The School-Home Connection Video demonstrates techniques parents can use at home to support their child's literacy development.

Scott Foresman Reading Web Site provides instant access to information, activities, and projects for students, teachers, and parents.

Selection Audiocassettes/CDs allow students to listen to each selection and follow along word for word.

Staff Development Videos (5) highlight the latest research and demonstrate best practices of master teachers.

Teacher's Resource Planner CD-ROM is a scheduling and planning tool that can print worksheets and correlate curriculum to specific objectives.

Teacher's Technology Companion CD-ROM offers an easy tutorial for integrating technology into your curriculum.

TestWorks™ **CD-ROM** can create personalized, multiple-choice tests, free-response tests, and practice worksheets.

Components by Grade Level

All this and more!

	K	1	2	3	4	5	6
Student Editions		•	•	•	•	•	•
Teacher's Editions	•	•	•	•	•	•	•
Big Books	•	•	•	•			
Read Aloud Trade Books	•						
Assessment							
Assessment Handbook	•	•	•	•	•	•	•
Kindergarten Skills Assessment	•						
Placement Tests	•	•	•	•	•	•	•
Selection Tests		•	•	•	•	•	•
"Test Talk" Transparencies		•	•	•	•		
Unit and End-of-Year Benchmark Tests		•	•	•	•	•	•
Unit and End-of-Year Skills Tests		•	•	•	•	•	•
Leveled Resources							
Collection for Readers (Very Easy Reader)				•	•	•	•
Easy Reader (A)		•	•	•	•	•	•
On-Level Reader (B)		•	•	•	•	•	•
Challenge Reader (C)		•	•	•	•	•	•
Leveled Reader Resource Guides		•	•	•	•	•	•
Leveled Practice and Test Link	•	•	•	•	•	•	•
Adding English/ESL		•	•	•	•	•	•
Ten Important Sentences		•	•	•	•	•	•
Trade Book Library		•	•	•	•	•	•
Phonics							
Phonemic Awareness and Phonics Manipulatives Kit	•	•	•	•			
Phonics and Word-Building Boards	•	•	•	•	•	•	•
Phonics Readers		•	•	•			
Phonics Songs and Rhymes Audiocassettes/CDs	•	•	•	•			
Phonics Songs and Rhymes Flip Chart	•	•	•	•			
Phonics Workbook	•	•	•	•	•	•	•
Teacher Support							
Daily Word Routines Flip Chart				•	•	•	•
Grammar Practice Book		•	•	•	•	•	•
Oral Language Flip Chart	•						
Practice Book	•	•	•	•	•	•	•
Spelling Workbook				•	•	•	•
Teacher's Resource Book	•	•	•	•	•	•	•
Writing Transparencies		•	•	•	•	•	•
Technology							
Background-Building Audiocassettes/CDs		•	•	•	•	•	•
Book Builder CD-ROM	•	•	•	•			
The Know Zone™	•	•	•	•	•	•	•
Selection Audiocassettes/CDs	•	•	•	•	•	•	•
Scott Foresman Reading Web Site	•	•	•	•	•	•	•
TestWorks™ CD-ROM	•	•	•	•	•	•	•

Contents

Take Me There

Unit 4
Favorite Things Old and New

Unit 5
Take Me There

Unit 6
Surprise Me!

Contents

Unit 5

Unit 5

Take Me There

**Where will we go?
How will we grow?**

Unit 5 Skills Overview

	Week 1	Week 2	Week 3
Reading	A Real Gift/ Arthur's Reading Race	A Big Day for Jay/ Lost!	Baby Otter Grows Up/ Foal
Comprehension Target Skills	✔ ⊙ **Predicting,** 17e–17f, 32–33, 45a–45b	✔ ⊙ **Compare and Contrast,** 53e–53f, 60–61, 85a–85b	⊙ **Sequence,** 93e–93f, 108–109, 115a–115b
Comprehension Review **Vocabulary**	(Review) Plot, 43 High-Frequency Words, 10l, 17d, 41b, 43b, 45c	(Review) Setting, 83 High-Frequency Words, 46l, 53d, 81b, 83b, 85c	(Review) Setting, 113 High-Frequency Words, 86l, 93d, 111b, 113b, 115c
Phonics/Word Study			
Phonics Target Skills	✔ ⊙ **Long e: ea,** 10k, 17c, 41a, 43a, 45c ✔ ⊙ **Inflected Ending -ed,** 10l, 17c, 41a, 43a, 45c	✔ ⊙ **Long a: ai, ay,** 46k–46l, 53c, 81a, 83a, 85c ✔ ⊙ **Contractions,** 46l, 53c, 81a, 83a, 85c	✔ ⊙ **Long o: oa, ow,** 86k–86l, 93c, 111a, 113a, 115c ✔ ⊙ **Inflected Ending -ing,** 86l, 93c, 111a, 113a, 115c
Phonics Review **Spelling**	(Review) Long o (CVCe), 41a (Review) Compound Words, 43a Spelling Words with Inflected Ending -ed, 10l, 17d, 41b, 43b, 45c	(Review) Long Vowels with Final e, 81a (Review) Initial Digraphs ch, sh, th, wh, 83a Spelling Words with Long a: ai, ay, 46l, 53d, 81b, 83b, 85c	✔ (Review) Long e: e, ee, ea, 111a (Review) Single and Double Medial Consonants, 113a Spelling Words with Long o; Inflected Ending -ing, 86l, 93d, 111b, 113b, 115c
Oral Language **Speaking** **Listening** **Viewing**	Expand Vocabulary: Multiple-Meaning Words, 17a, 41c Retell a Story, 17g, 45d Listen to a Big Book, 10j Listening to Predict, 17e Reread for Fluency, 17f, 41a, 43	Expand Vocabulary: Antonyms, 53a, 81c Discuss How to Solve a Problem, 53g, 85d Listen to a Poem, 46j Listening to Compare and Contrast, 53e Reread for Fluency, 53f, 81a, 83	✔ **Expand Vocabulary: Unfamiliar Words,** 93a, 111c Listening for Main Idea, 93g, 115d Listen to a Poem, 86j Listening for Sequence, 93e Reread for Fluency, 93f, 111a, 113
Writing **Grammar, Usage, and Mechanics** **Genre and Literary Skills** **Research and Study Skills**	Write About a Movie, Play or TV Show, 41c ✔ **Adjectives,** 17h, 41d, 44 ✔ **Study Skill: Map,** 45	Description of a Story Illustration, 81c ✔ **Adjectives,** 53h, 81d, 84 Genre: Fantasy, 56–57 Study Skill: Glossary: Guide Words, 85	Write Facts, 93g, 111c ✔ **Adjectives,** 93h, 111d, 114 Genre: Narrative Nonfiction, 96–97 Study Skill: Illustrations and Captions, 115

⊙ Target Skill   (Review) Review Skill

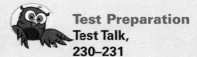

Week 4	**Week 5**	**Week 6**
What a Sight!/ Lost in the Museum	**Chompy's Afternoon/ Dinosaur Babies**	**Abbie Burgess/ The Bravest Cat!**
✔ ⓖ **Cause and Effect,** 123e–123f, 146–147, 155a	✔ ⓖ **Main Idea,** 163e–163f, 182–183, 191a–191b	✔ ⓖ **Cause and Effect,** 199e–199f, 210–211, 227a–227b
(Review) Character, 153 High-Frequency Words, 116l, 123d, 151b, 153b, 155c	✔ (Review) Cause and Effect, 189 High-Frequency Words, 156l, 163d, 187b, 189b, 191c	✔ (Review) Main Idea, 225 High-Frequency Words, 192l, 199d, 223b, 225b, 227c
✔ ⓖ **Long i: igh, ie,** 116k–116l, 123c, 151a, 153a, 155c ✔ ⓖ **Singular Possessives,** 116l, 123c, 151a, 153a, 155c	✔ ⓖ **Vowel Sounds of y (Long e, Long i),** 156k–156l, 163c, 187a, 189a, 191c ⓖ **Compound Words,** 156l, 163c, 187a, 189a, 191c	✔ ⓖ **Vowel Patterns ew, ue,** 192k–192l, 199c, 223a, 225a, 227c ✔ ⓖ **Inflected Ending -es; Plural -es,** 192l, 199c, 223a, 225a, 227c
✔ (Review) Long a: ai, ay, 151a ✔ (Review) Contractions, 153a Spelling Words with Long i, 116l, 123d, 151b, 153b, 155c	✔ (Review) Long i: igh, ie, 187a ✔ (Review) -ed and -ing Endings, 189a Spelling Words with Vowel y, 156l, 163d, 187b, 189b, 191c	✔ (Review) Vowel Sounds of y, 223a (Review) Final Digraphs -ng, -nk, 225a Spelling Words with ew, ue, 192l, 199d, 223b, 225b, 227c
Expand Vocabulary: Place Names, 123a Name Items Found in Specific Places, 151c Large Group Discussion, 123g, 155d Listen to a Poem, 116j Listening for Cause and Effect, 123e Reread for Fluency, 123f, 151a, 153	Expand Vocabulary: Homonyms, 163a Dinosaur Names, 187c Tell an Original Story in Order, 163g, 191d Listen to a Poem, 156j Listening for the Main Idea, 163e Reread for Fluency, 163f, 187a, 189	**Expand Vocabulary:** Comparatives, 199a ✔ **Unfamiliar Words,** 223c Small Group Discussion, 199g, 227d Listen to a Fable, 192j Listening for Cause and Effect, 199e Reread for Fluency, 199f, 223a, 225
Write About a Favorite Trip, 151c ✔ Adjectives, 123h, 151d, 154 Genre: Realistic Fiction, 126–127 ✔ Study Skill: Map, 155	Writing a Description, 163g–163h, 187c ✔ Adjectives, 162–163, 163h, 187d, 190 Genre: Expository Nonfiction, 166–167 Study Skill: Take Notes, 191	✔ **Writing Process,** 199a–199b, 199g–199h, 223c–223d, 227d ✔ **Writing with Adjectives,** 199h, 223d, 226, 227d Study Skill: Periodicals, 227

✔ Skill tested on Unit 5 Benchmark Test and/or Unit 5 Skills Test

Reaching Every Student

	Teach			Assess
	Teacher's Edition Pupil Edition Target Comprehension and Phonics Skills	**Phonics Readers and Decodable Readers** Phonics Skills	**Leveled Readers** Target Skills and Vocabulary	**Ongoing Assessment**
◉ Predicting	**Lesson 1** Predicting: 17e–17f, 32–33 Phonics Story: 10–17 Long *e: ea*/Inflected Ending *-ed:* 10k–10l, 17c, 41a, 43a, 45c	Phonics Reader: *The Neat Green Cast* Decodable Reader 33: *Dean's Neat Green Cast*	**Easy:** That Is Right, Walrus (19A) **On-Level:** Texas Eggs (19B) **Challenge:** Take Me There (5C)	**Teacher's Edition:** Predicting: 32–33 Long *e: ea:* 12–13, 41b Inflected Ending *-ed:* 41b
◉ Compare and Contrast	**Lesson 2** Compare and Contrast: 53e–53f, 60–61 Phonics Story: 46–53 Long *a: ai, ay*/Contractions: 46k–46l, 53c, 81a, 83a, 85c	Phonics Reader: *Who Rang the Bell?* Decodable Reader 34: *Ray's Fire Bell* Decodable Reader 35: *Let's Play*	**Easy:** From Dad (20A) **On-Level:** House of Wood, House of Snow (20B) **Challenge:** Take Me There (5C)	**Teacher's Edition:** Compare and Contrast: 60–61 Long *a: ai, ay:* 48–49, 81b Contractions: 48–49, 80–81, 81b
◉ Sequence	**Lesson 3** Sequence: 93e–93f, 108–109 Phonics Story: 86–93 Long *o: oa, ow*/Inflected Ending *-ing:* 86k–86l, 93c, 111a, 113a, 115c	Phonics Reader: *Duck Gets a New Coat* Decodable Reader 36: *Duck's Coat*	**Easy:** Mary Goes Walking (21A) **On-Level:** Desert Fox (21B) **Challenge:** Take Me There (5C)	**Teacher's Edition:** Sequence: 108–109 Long *o: oa, ow:* 100–101, 111b Inflected Ending *-ing:* 88–89, 104–105, 111b
◉ Cause and Effect	**Lesson 4** Cause and Effect: 123e–123f, 146–147 Phonics Story: 116–123 Long *i: igh, ie*/Singular Possessives: 116k–116l, 123c, 151a, 153a, 155c	Phonics Reader: *Dad's Gift* Decodable Reader 37: *It's Just Right!* Decodable Reader 38: *Night Sights*	**Easy:** All Together Now! (22A) **On-Level:** How Bill Found Rain (22B) **Challenge:** Take Me There (5C)	**Teacher's Edition:** Cause and Effect: 146–147 Long *i: igh, ie:* 122–123, 138–139, 151b Singular Possessives: 151b
◉ Main Idea	**Lesson 5** Main Idea: 163e–163f, 182–183 Phonics Story: 156–163 Vowel Sounds of *y* (long *e*, long *i*)/Compound Words: 156k–156l, 163c, 187a, 189a, 191c	Phonics Reader: *My Mail* Decodable Reader 39: *My Mail*	**Easy:** Pandas (23A) **On-Level:** What Lilly Pup Heard (23B) **Challenge:** Take Me There (5C)	**Teacher's Edition:** Main Idea: 182–183 Vowel Sounds of *y* (long *e*, long *i*): 158–159, 170–171, 187b Compound Words: 158–159, 170–171, 187b
◉ Cause and Effect	**Lesson 6** Cause and Effect: 199e–199f, 210–211 Phonics Story: 192–199 Vowel Patterns *ew, ue*/Inflected Ending *-es* and Plural *-es:* 192k–192l, 199c, 223a, 225a, 227c	Phonics Reader: *Sue Blew a Big Bubble* Decodable Reader 40: *What's New with Sue?* Decodable Reader 41: *Ty's New Baseball*	**Easy:** Why Little Possum's Tail Is Bare (24A) **On-Level:** Many Little Beads (24B) **Challenge:** Take Me There (5C)	**Teacher's Edition:** Cause and Effect: 210–211, 214–215 Vowel Patterns *ew, ue:* 198–199, 214–215, 223b Inflected Ending *-es* and Plural *-es:* 198–199, 223b

Assess	Intervention		Test Prep
Selection Tests and Unit Tests	**Reteach and Review Skills** Differentiate Instruction	**Leveled Practice**	**Test Talk**
Practice Book 1.5: 13–14 Teacher's Resource Book 1.5: 13–14 Unit 5 Skills Test Unit 5 Benchmark Test	**Teacher's Edition** 16–17, 41a, 43, 43a, AR11–AR12 **Links to Reading First 1.5** 2–11	Teacher's Edition: 10b, 43 Leveled Practice and Test Link: 55–57	Pupil Edition: 230–231 Teacher's Edition: 16–17, 26–27, 32–33, 42, 230–231
Practice Book 1.5: 29–30 Teacher's Resource Book 1.5: 31–32 Unit 5 Skills Test Unit 5 Benchmark Test	**Teacher's Edition** 52–53, 81a, 83, 83a, AR12–AR13 **Links to Reading First 1.5** 12–21	Teacher's Edition: 46b, 83 Leveled Practice and Test Link: 58–60	Pupil Edition: 230–231 Teacher's Edition: 52–53, 60–61, 66–67, 78–79, 82, 230–231
Practice Book 1.5: 45–46 Teacher's Resource Book 1.5: 49–50 Unit 5 Skills Test Unit 5 Benchmark Test	**Teacher's Edition** 92–93, 111a, 113, 113a, AR14–AR15 **Links to Reading First 1.5** 22–31	Teacher's Edition: 86b, 113 Leveled Practice and Test Link: 61–63	Pupil Edition: 230–231 Teacher's Edition: 92–93, 102–103, 108–109, 112, 230–231
Practice Book 1.5: 61–62 Teacher's Resource Book 1.5: 67–68 Unit 5 Skills Test Unit 5 Benchmark Test	**Teacher's Edition** 118–119, 151a, 153, 153a, AR15–AR16 **Links to Reading First 1.5** 32–41	Teacher's Edition: 116b, 153 Leveled Practice and Test Link: 64–66	Pupil Edition: 230–231 Teacher's Edition: 118–119, 144–145, 146–147, 150–151, 152, 230–231
Practice Book 1.5: 77–78 Teacher's Resource Book 1.5: 85–86 Unit 5 Skills Test Unit 5 Benchmark Test	**Teacher's Edition** 162–163, 187a, 189, 189a, AR17–AR18 **Links to Reading First 1.5** 42–51	Teacher's Edition: 156b, 189 Leveled Practice and Test Link: 67–69	Pupil Edition: 230–231 Teacher's Edition: 162–163, 166–167, 182–183, 188, 230–231
Practice Book 1.5: 93–94 Teacher's Resource Book 1.5: 103–104 Unit 5 Skills Test Unit 5 Benchmark Test	**Teacher's Edition** 194–195, 223a, 225, 225a, AR18–AR19 **Links to Reading First 1.5** 52–64	Teacher's Edition: 192b, 225 Leveled Practice and Test Link: 70–72	Pupil Edition: 230–231 Teacher's Edition: 194–195, 210–211, 212–213, 224, 230–231

More Assessment Resources

Assessment Handbook contains information about conference records, self-assessment, portfolio analysis, reading progress summaries, and running records.

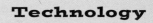

Technology

The Know Zone™ provides test preparation techniques and reinforcement online.

Computer Assessment Management System lets teachers and administrators monitor, evaluate, and plan instruction based on criterion-referenced materials.

TestWorks can create personalized multiple-choice tests, free-response tests, and practice worksheets.

Teacher's Resource Planner CD-ROM is a scheduling and planning tool that can print worksheets and correlate curriculum to specific objectives.

National Computer Systems (NCS) provides management software, training, staff development, and communication tools for the school and home. NCS also provides standards-based assessments and resources to support achievement gaps.

Assessment Overview

Formal Assessment

Selection Tests
Practice Book
pp. 13, 29, 45, 61, 77, 93

Unit 5
Skills Test
Skills Tests
Teacher's Manual

Unit 5
Benchmark Test
Benchmark Tests
Teacher's Manual
Available in TerraNova
and SAT-9 formats.

Ongoing Assessment

"If . . . then . . . " statements throughout the lessons guide the instruction.

Ongoing Assessment

Summarizing

If... children have trouble summarizing what is happening,	**then...** use the **Think Aloud** below to model how to summarize.

Informal Assessment

Observable Behaviors
By the end of this unit, most of your children should be able to demonstrate that they can:

Listening and Speaking
- Listen to broaden vocabulary, identify main idea, solve problems
- Participate in large and small group discussions

Word Identification and Word Knowledge
- Decode words with long vowel patterns with increasing fluency
- Use structural cues to expand knowledge of words with inflected endings, compound words, and–'s possessive
- Use strategies such as context clues to unlock the meanings of unfamiliar words, with teacher modeling

Variety of Texts and Genres
- Participate in listening to, reading, and discussing a variety of texts and genres, including fantasy
- Identify some features of fiction and nonfiction

Reader Response
- Respond to text by predicting; identifying setting, main idea, and cause and effect; constructing models; developing rules; and making a time line

Writing
- Write about a movie or TV show, write a news story, write a class report
- Revise and edit to use vivid adjectives, with teacher guidance

Research and Study Skills
- Use a map, with teacher direction

See pages AR30–AR33 of this Teacher's Edition for complete grade-level benchmarks.

National Test Correlation

Skills Tested in Unit 5	ITBS Form M	TerraNova 5th Ed.	CAT 5th Ed.	SAT 9th Ed.	MAT 7th Ed.	Your Test
Comprehension						
Cause and Effect	●	●	●	●	●	
Compare and Contrast	●		●	●	●	
Main Idea	●	●	●	●	●	
Predicting	●	●	●	●	●	
Phonics and Word Study						
Unfamiliar Words		●			●	
Long Vowels *a, e, i, o;* Sound of Vowel Patterns *ew, ue*	●	●	●	●	●	
Inflected Endings *-ed, -ing, -es;* Plural *-es*			●	●	●	
Contractions *('s, n't, 'm, 'll)*	●			●	●	
Genre and Literary Skills						
Genre: Fantasy, Realistic Fiction, Expository and Narrative Nonfiction						
Grammar, Usage, and Mechanics Skills						
Adjectives	●		●			
Using Adjectives to Improve Sentences					●	
Research and Study Skills						
Maps						

Key

ITBS Iowa Tests of Basic Skills
TerraNova Comprehensive Test of Basic Skills
CAT California Achievement Test

SAT Stanford Achievement Test
MAT Metropolitan Achievement Test

Theme Launch

Value of the Theme

The stories in Take Me There refer to children's expanding horizons, both physical and intellectual.

Discuss the Theme Question

Read the theme question on page 9. Encourage children to talk about things they will do when they get older. Guide children as they discuss

- what they can do that a younger child can't do
- how they solve problems
- how they have changed since they were babies

Launch the Theme

Use the Big Book

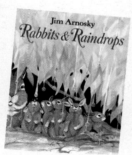

The Big Book, *Rabbits and Raindrops*, can be used to begin exploring the theme of Take Me There. Read the book with children and discuss these questions:

- Have the baby bunnies been out in the field before? Tell why you answered the way you did.

- Why was Mother Rabbit worried about her babies? Who worries about you?

- Do you think the baby rabbits will always wait for their mother before they go out into the field? Explain.

See page 10j in the Teacher's Edition for another way to use the Big Book.

Use the Read Aloud

For another activity to help launch the theme, use the Read Aloud on pages 9a–9d of this Teacher's Edition.

Crossing Cultures

You can use the following selection to help children learn about their own and other cultures and explore common elements of culture.

Arthur's Reading Race Children can take a "walk" down the main street of their own community and tell what they would see. Children who have visited other regions can share what they have seen.

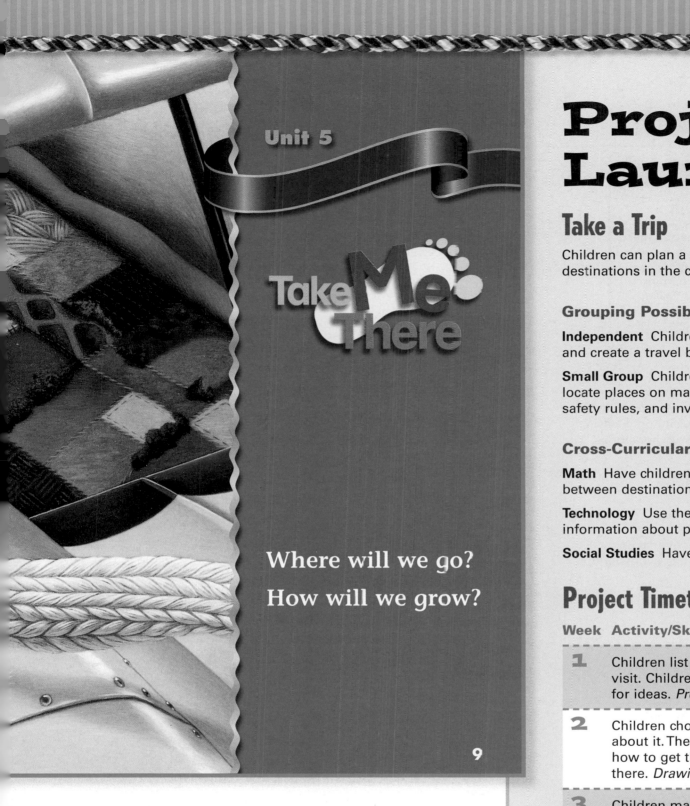

Take Me There

Where will we go?
How will we grow?

9

Project Launch

Take a Trip

Children can plan a pretend trip to explore destinations in the country or in the world.

Grouping Possibilities

Independent Children can work alone to research and create a travel brochure.

Small Group Children can work in a group to locate places on maps, make posters of travel safety rules, and invite guest speakers.

Cross-Curricular Connections

Math Have children compare the distances between destinations.

Technology Use the Internet to find maps and information about places.

Social Studies Have children study maps.

Project Timetable

Week	Activity/Skill Connection
1	Children list places they would like to visit. Children interview family members for ideas. *Prewrite*
2	Children choose a place to visit and read about it. They draw conclusions about how to get there and what they will do there. *Drawing Conclusions*
3	Children make lists of the things they would have to do to get ready for a trip. Children put the items in sequential order. *Sequencing*
4	Children mark their travel destinations on a map. They write invitations to travel agents or airline or train personnel to be guest speakers for the class. *Organizing Ideas and Information*
5	Children prepare their travel plans and present them to the class. *Publish*

Presentation options and a scoring guide can be found on page 231c.

Objectives

Children will

- apply a listening behavior: making connections
- use comprehension strategies: recognizing author's purpose and summarizing or retelling
- expand vocabulary

Theme Connection

The unit *Take Me There* poses the questions, "Where will we go? How will we grow?" In this story, Sarah and Susan visit Aunt Flossie, where they learn and grow from her stories.

Introduce the Read Aloud

Listening Behavior:
Make Connections

Ask the children to listen for events and people in the story that are like events and people in their own lives.

Explain that this is a *realistic* story; it could happen in real life.

Set a Purpose:
Listen to Appreciate Cultures

Invite the children to listen to the story to learn about what life was like long ago, including what people wore and what they did.

Read aloud *Aunt Flossie's Hats (and Crab Cakes Later).* You may wish to read the whole story and then reread to build comprehension and listening skills. The notes on the following pages suggest learning activities.

Aunt Flossie's Hats

(and Crab Cakes Later)

BY ELIZABETH FITZGERALD HOWARD

On Sunday afternoons, Sarah and I
go to see Great-great-aunt Flossie.
Sarah and I love Aunt Flossie's house.
It is crowded full of stuff and things.
Books and pictures and lamps and pillows . . .
Plates and trays and old dried flowers . . .
And boxes
and boxes
and boxes
of HATS!
On Sunday afternoons when Sarah and I
go to see Aunt Flossie, she says,
"Come in, Susan. Come in, Sarah.
Have some tea. Have some cookies.
Later we can get some crab cakes!"
We sip our tea and eat our cookies,
and then Aunt Flossie lets us look
in her hatboxes.
We pick out our hats and try them on.
Aunt Flossie says they are her memories,
and each hat has its story.
Hats, hats, hats, hats!
A stiff black one with bright red ribbons.
A soft brown one with silver buttons.
Thin floppy hats that hide our eyes.
Green or blue or pink or purple.
Some have fur and some have feathers.
Look! This hat is just one smooth soft rose,
but here's one with a trillion flowers!
Aunt Flossie has so many hats!
One Sunday afternoon, I picked out
a wooly winter hat, sort of green, maybe.
Aunt Flossie thought a minute.

Aunt Flossie almost always thinks a minute
before she starts a hat story.
Then she sniffed the wooly hat,
"Just a little smoky smell now," she said.
Sarah and I sniffed the hat too.
"Smoky smell, Aunt Flossie?"
"The big fire," Aunt Flossie said.
"The big fire in Baltimore.
Everything smelled of smoke for miles around.
For days and days.
Big fire. Didn't come near our house
on Centre Street, but we could hear
fire engines racing down St. Paul.
Horses' hooves clattering.
Bells! Whistles!
Your great-grandma and I couldn't sleep.
We grabbed our coats and hats and ran outside.
Worried about Uncle Jimmy's grocery store,
worried about the terrapins and crabs.
Big fire in Baltimore."
Aunt Flossie closed her eyes.
I think she was seeing long ago.
I wondered about crab cakes.
Did they have crab cakes way back then?
Then Sarah sniffed Aunt Flossie's hat.
"No more smoky smell," she said.
But I thought I could smell some,
just a little.
Then Sarah tried a different hat.
Dark, dark blue, with a red feather.
"This one, Aunt Flossie! This one!"
Aunt Flossie closed her eyes and thought a minute.
"Oh my, yes, my, my. What an exciting day!"

We waited, Sarah and I.
"What happened, Aunt Flossie?" I asked.
"Big parade in Baltimore."

"Ooh! Parade!" said Sarah. "We love parades."

"I made that hat," Aunt Flossie said,
"to wear to watch that big parade.
Buglers bugling. Drummers drumming.
Flags flying everywhere. The boys—
soldiers, you know—back from France.

Listening Comprehension

Author's Purpose
These questions can help children recognize
the author's purpose.

- Why do you think the author chose to
  have Aunt Flossie tell stories about her
  past? (To teach something about the past.)
  Inferential

- Does the author want her story to make
  you feel happy or sad? Explain how you
  can tell. (She wants us to feel happy
  because the girls in the story are happy.)
  Critical

Ongoing Assessment

Author's Purpose

If... children are not able to understand how the story is supposed to make them feel,	then... reread the part where the girls try on hats and hear Aunt Flossie's memories. Ask if the story is happy or sad.

Summarizing or Retelling
Help children decide what the main parts of
the story are so far.

- Tell what happens in the beginning and in
  the middle of the story. (In the beginning,
  Sarah and her sister visit Aunt Flossie. In
  the middle, they try on hats and listen to
  Aunt Flossie's memories.) Summarizing

Listening Behavior

Make Connections

Invite children to tell of events and people in the story that are like events and people in their own lives.

Visualize

Ask children to close their eyes and listen as you reread the event when Aunt Flossie's best Sunday hat blows away. Encourage them to form a mental image of the day as they listen. Suggest that they picture the weather, how the people are dressed, and so on. Ask volunteers to share their mental images.

Listening and Language

Expand Vocabulary

Discuss the meanings of the following words with children.

crab cakes: small, round patties made of chopped crab meat and spices
clattering: making a loud noise
buglers: people who play bugles, musical instruments like small trumpets or horns

Marching up Charles Street. Proud.
Everyone cheering, everyone shouting!
The Great War was over!
The Great War was over!"
"Let's have a parade!" I said.
Sarah put on the dark blue hat.
I found a red one with a furry pompom.
We marched around Aunt Flossie's house.

"March with us, Aunt Flossie!" I called.
But she was closing her eyes.
She was seeing long ago.
"Maybe she's dreaming about crab cakes,"
Sarah said.

Then we looked in the very special box.
"Look, Aunt Flossie! Here's your special hat."
It was the big straw hat
with the pink and yellow flowers
and green velvet ribbon.
Aunt Flossie's favorite best Sunday hat!
It's our favorite story,
because we are in the story,
and we can help Aunt Flossie tell it!

Aunt Flossie smiled.
"One Sunday afternoon," she said, "we were
going out for crab cakes.
Sarah and Susan . . . ."
"And Mommy and Daddy," I said.
"And Aunt Flossie," said Sarah.
Aunt Flossie nodded. "We were walking
by the water. And the wind came."

"Let me tell it," I said. "The wind came
and blew away your favorite best Sunday hat!"
"My favorite best Sunday hat," said Aunt Flossie.
"It landed in the water."
"It was funny," said Sarah.
"I didn't think so," said Aunt Flossie.

"And Daddy tried to reach it," I said,
"but he slid down in the mud. Daddy looked
really surprised, and everybody laughed."
"He couldn't rescue my favorite, favorite
best Sunday hat," said Aunt Flossie.

"And Mommy got a stick and leaned far out.
She almost fell in, but she couldn't reach
it either. The water rippled, and your
favorite best Sunday hat just floated by
like a boat!"

"Now comes the best part, and I'll tell it!"
said Sarah. "A big brown dog came.
It was walking with a boy.
'May we help you?' the boy asked.
'My dog Gretchen can get it.'
The boy threw a small, small stone.
It landed in Aunt Flossie's hat!
'Fetch, Gretchen, fetch!
Fetch, Gretchen, fetch!'
Gretchen jumped into the water
and she swam. She swam and she got it!
Gretchen got Aunt Flossie's hat!
'Hurray for Gretchen!'
We all jumped up and down.
'Hurray for Aunt Flossie's hat!'"

"It was very wet," said Aunt Flossie,
"but it dried just fine . . . almost like new.
My favorite, favorite best Sunday hat."

"I like that story," I said.
"So do I," said Sarah.
"And I like what happened next!
We went to get crab cakes!"

"Crab cakes!" said Aunt Flossie.
"What a wonderful idea! Sarah, Susan,
telephone your parents.
We'll go get some crab cakes right now!"

I think Sarah and I will always agree
about one thing: Nothing in the whole wide
world tastes as good as crab cakes.

But crab cakes taste best after stories . . .
stories about Aunt Flossie's hats! ■

About the Author
*Elizabeth Fitzgerald Howard, who lives in Pittsburgh,
really did have a ninety-eight-year-old Aunt Flossie
whose favorite hat blew away one day.*

Respond to the Read Aloud

Discuss the Story
You may want to use these discussion questions. Other possible response activities follow.

1. Why do you think the author wrote this story? Do you think she wanted to show how much fun it can be to visit with older people and hear stories, or do you think she wanted to show how brave dogs can be? (She wanted to show how much fun it can be to visit with older people and hear stories.) **Author's Purpose**

2. Tell in your own words the story about the hat with the smoky smell. (There was a big fire in Baltimore. You could smell smoke and hear fire engines. Aunt Flossie's family ran outside.) **Retelling**

Creative Response
Ask children to recall the various hats that Aunt Flossie told stories about. Invite children to draw a picture of their favorite hat from the story. **Visual Representation**

Written Response
Tell children to divide a sheet of paper into three parts. Children should draw three pictures that show portions of the scene on the day when Aunt Flossie lost her hat in the water. Have them write under each picture what is happening. **Summarizing**

Assessing the Written Response
Pictures with descriptions might include (1) Aunt Flossie wearing her hat by the water, (2) the hat in the water, and (3) Gretchen rescuing the hat.

Lesson Overview

Phonics Story

A Real Gift
pages 10–17

The **Phonics Story** . . .

- introduces 🔄 **Long *e: ea*** and **Inflected Ending *-ed***

- introduces the high-frequency words

  buy only or right think

- builds fluency

- builds decoding skills

> **Use the Phonics Story to prepare children for reading the Main Selection.**

Main Selection

Arthur's Reading Race
pages 18–41

The **Main Selection** . . .

- introduces 🔄 **Predicting**

- practices 🔄 **Long *e: ea*** and **Inflected Ending *-ed***

- practices the high-frequency words

  buy only or right think

Leveled Practice
in Test Format
for *Arthur's Reading Race*

MARC BROWN
ARTHUR'S READING RACE

TARGET SKILL Predicting

Leveled Readers

TARGET SKILL

Predicting
Tested Vocabulary

Easy	On-Level	Challenge

That Is Right, Walrus
by Kana Riley
Illustrated by Mircea Catusanu

Leveled Reader 19A

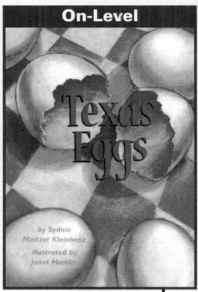

Texas Eggs
by Sydnie Meltzer Kleinhenz
Illustrated by Janet Hamlin

Leveled Reader 19B

Take Me There
Collected Readings

Leveled Reader 5C

For instruction and leveled practice answers, see Teacher's Edition, pp. LR39–LR45.

For Guided Reading
see Teacher's Edition, pp. LR1–LR6.

Practice for Leveled Readers

Easy

Predicting

Read the story *That is Right, Walrus.* Then answer Numbers 1 through 5.

❶ Walrus does NOT go
○ to the playground.
○ to the beach.
○ to Grandma's house.

❷ Look at page 7. Walrus should buy cowboy boots. Why?
○ She is going to a cold place.
○ She is going to a ranch.
○ She is going to the beach.

❸ Look at page 11. Will Walrus think of the bed first or the sleeping bag?
● She will think of the bed first.
○ She will think of the sleeping bag first.
○ She will ask her Grandma first.

❹ What is the right gift for Grandma?
○ flowers
○ a book
● a book and flowers

✎ ❺ Look at page 2. How do you know Walrus will buy the bathing suit?

She is going to the beach.

Teacher's Edition, p. LR3

On-Level

Predicting

Read the story *Texas Eggs.* Then answer Numbers 1 through 5.

❶ Look at pages 2 and 3. How did the girl get to Texas?
○ by boat
○ by plane
○ by car

❷ Look at page 11. How do you know Grandpa will play with the shell next?
● Grandpa played with the she is on the other days.
○ Grandpa likes to play with things to eat.
○ All grandpas use shells for fun.

❸ Why does Grandpa save the shells?
● He fills the shells with bits of paper.
○ He wants to give them to the cat.
○ He makes pictures with the shells.

❹ The girl breaks the shell over Grandpa a head. What happens?
○ Grandpa gets mad.
○ The children stop playing.
● The bits of paper fall on Grandpa.

✎ ❺ The girl asks, **"Why do you want the shells?"** What will Grandpa say next? Write the words from the story

"Only for fun."

Teacher's Edition, p. LR6

Challenge

The Places I Go

In "Ode to My Shoes," the poet's shoes rest under the bed and dream of the places they have been. What if your shoes could tell a story? What would they tell about you? Think back as far as you can. You can tell your own story.

Collect Facts and Ideas
❶ Find out about your life. What were you like as a baby? Talk to your family.
❷ Look at a map. Find where you were born. Look for places that you have been.

Put It All Together
❸ Draw pictures and write sentences that show and tell what you were like growing up.
❹ Draw a picture and write about yourself now.
❺ Draw a picture of yourself as an older person. Write about it.

Prepare and Share
❻ Make a time line using your pictures and writings. Share your time line with your classmates.

Take Me There **3**

Leveled Reader 5C, p. 3

Easy

Predicting
Look at the picture. Mark the ○ for the answer.

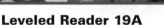

1 What does the boy want?
○ something little
● ice cream
○ a friend

3 What will the boy do?
○ drink water
○ eat a hot dog
● eat the ice cream

2 What will the father do?
○ Father will buy the ice cream.
● Father will sell the ice cream.
○ Father will sit.

4 What does the boy carry?
○ a bear
○ an ice cream
● a ball

5 What will the boy play? Draw a picture that shows him playing.
Children should conclude that the boy is going to play basketball. Drawings should show him playing basketball.

On-Level

Predicting
Read *Arthur's Reading Race.* Mark the ○ for the answer.

1 Arthur will give D. W. an ice cream if she
○ sees a hot dog
○ keeps off the grass
● reads ten words

3 Look at page 31. What makes you think D. W. will get an ice cream?
● She can read many signs.
○ She sees the police.
○ She keeps off the grass.

2 Look at pages 24 to 25. What clue shows that D. W. can read?
● She reads a sign.
○ She reads a book.
○ She walks with Arthur.

4 Look at page 35. You know D. W. will get an ice cream because
● she read ten words
○ Arthur had ten cents
○ she saw an ice cream store

5 Write what you think will happen when Arthur gets home.

Answers will vary, but they should indicate an ability to
make predictions based on clues in the story.

Challenge

Predicting
Read *Arthur's Reading Race.* Mark the ○ for the answer.

1 Read pages 18 to 21. You can tell this story will be about reading because
● each page is about reading
○ D. W. reads in bed
○ Arthur is in school

3 What clue tells you D. W. will read ten words?
● She can read many signs.
○ She sees the police.
○ She buys Arthur ice cream.

2 Read pages 26 to 29. How do you know that D. W. is more careful than Arthur?
○ She sees three words.
○ She walks before she sees the sign.
● She sees the sign that says not to walk.

4 Look at page 39. What is a clue that Arthur will get paint on his pants?
● A sign says WET PAINT.
○ Arthur is reading a book.
○ Arthur is eating an ice cream.

5 What do you think Arthur will tell his mother about his pants? Write what he might say.

Answers will vary. Possible answer: Arthur might say, "I
didn't see the WET PAINT sign."

Leveled Practice and Test Link, pp. 55–57, *Arthur's Reading Race*

Additional Leveled Resources

Phonics Resources

Phonics Reader 25

Phonics Take-Home Readers in Reproducible Format

Book 25

Decodable Reader 33

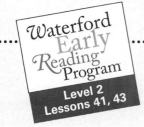

Waterford Early Reading Program
Level 2
Lessons 41, 43

Language Support

Adding English
pp. 161–168

Ten Important Sentences
p. 31

Trade Books for Self-Selected Reading

Easy	On-Level	Challenge

Harriet Reads Signs and More Signs
by Betsy & Giulio Maestro. Crown, 1981

This Is the Way We Go to School
by Edith Baer. Scholastic, 1992
Trade Book Library Title

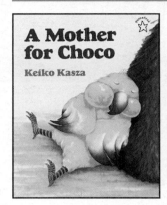

A Mother for Choco
by Keiko Kasza. Paper Star, 1996
Trade Book Library Title

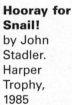

Hooray for Snail!
by John Stadler. Harper Trophy, 1985

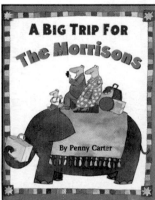
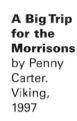

A Big Trip for the Morrisons
by Penny Carter. Viking, 1997

Away from Home
by Anita Lobel. Greenwillow, 1994

I Go with My Family to Grandma's
by Ricki Levinson. Dutton, 1986

Glasses for D.W.
by Marc Brown. Random House, 1996

When Will I Read?
by Miriam Cohen. Greenwillow, 1977

Self-Selected Reading

- Allow 10–20 minutes per day for self-selected reading.
- For additional titles and for a read-aloud suggestion, see pp. AR24–AR25.
- For daily self-selected reading suggestions, see the 5-Day Planner, pp. 10e–10f.
- For activity ideas and management tips, see p. AR25.

- Have children select materials to read for pleasure, such as favorite books and stories.

Developmental Reading Assessment (DRA) from Celebration Press, an imprint of Pearson Learning, helps teachers by providing and documenting students' development as readers over time.

Links to Reading First 1.5, pp. 2–11

5-Day Planner

Reading

Comprehension

Vocabulary

Fluency

Independent Reading

Phonics/Word Study

Phonemic Awareness

Phonics

Spelling

High-Frequency Words

Oral Language

Speaking, Listening, Viewing

Oral Vocabulary

Writing

Grammar, Usage, Mechanics

Your State Standards

Customize your week with the Teacher's Resource Planner CD-ROM!

Day 1

Activate Prior Knowledge, p. 10j

Phonics pp. 10k–10l

Phonemic Awareness: Long *e: ea*

✓ ⌖ **Phonics:** Introduce Long *e: ea*, Inflected Ending *-ed*
PHONICS SONGS AND RHYMES CHART "Eat a Treat!"

Spelling: Inflected Ending *-ed* Words
⌖ Pretest
Work with Spelling Pattern

High-Frequency Words: Introduce **buy, only, or, right, think**

Reading pp. 10m–17

Story Vocabulary

Read Pupil Edition PHONICS STORY: *A Real Gift*

Independent Reading
Self-Selected Reading, pp. 10d; AR24

Oral Language pp. 10m, 17a

Build Oral Language

Expand Vocabulary: Discuss Multiple-Meaning Words

Writing pp. 10i, 17a–17b

Shared Writing: List

Handwriting: *Zz*

Daily Writing Prompt: Write about a new place you went or a new thing you did.

Day 2

Phonics pp. 17c–17d

✓ ⌖ **Phonics:** Practice Long *e: ea*, Inflected Ending *-ed*

Apply Phonics: Read the **PHONICS READER** *The Neat Green Cast* or **DECODABLE READER** 33

Spelling: Writing for Sounds

High-Frequency Words: Practice

PB 1.5: Phonics, pp. 3, 4; High-Frequency Words, p. 5
TRB 1.5: Phonics, pp. 3, 4; High-Frequency Words, p. 5

Reading pp. 17e–17f

✓ ⌖ **Comprehension:** Predicting **READ ALOUD** "The Ice-Cream Problem"

Fluency: Reread the **PHONICS STORY:** *A Real Gift*

PB 1.5: Predicting, p. 6
TRB 1.5: Predicting, p. 6

Independent Reading
Self-Selected Reading, pp. 10d; AR24

Oral Language p. 17g

⌖ **Speaking:** Retell a Story

Writing pp. 10i, 17g–17h

Modeled Writing: Take a Stand

✓ ⌖ **Grammar:** Adjectives (Describing Words)

PB 1.5: p. 7; **TRB 1.5:** p. 7

Daily Writing Prompt: Write about a time someone helped you do something new.

10e   5-Day Planner

 Target Skill    **Review Skill**    **Assessment**

PB Practice Book
TRB Teacher's Resource Book

pp. 55–57

Leveled Practice and Test Link in TerraNova, SAT9, or ITBS format

Target Skills of the Week

Day 3

Reading pp. 18a–41

Story Vocabulary

Read Pupil Edition MAIN SELECTION: *Arthur's Reading Race*

✓ **Comprehension:** Predicting

Guided Reading Resources/Flexible Groups, pp. 18b; LR1–LR6
Leveled Readers 19A, 19B, 5C

PB 1.5: Vocabulary, p. 8
TRB 1.5: Vocabulary, p. 8

Independent Reading
Self-Selected Reading, pp. 10d; AR24

Phonics pp. 41a–41b

✓ **Phonics:** Practice Long *e: ea,* Inflected Ending *-ed*

Review Long *o* (CVCe)

Fluency: Reread the PHONICS READER *The Neat Green Cast*

Spelling: Practice with Writing

High-Frequency Words: Practice

PB 1.5: Phonics, p. 9; Spelling, p. 10
TRB 1.5: Phonics, p. 9; Spelling, p. 10

Oral Language pp. 18a, 41c

Build Oral Language

Expand Vocabulary: Identify and Use Multiple-Meaning Words

Writing pp. 10i, 41c–41d

Modeled Writing: Write About a Movie, Play, or TV Show

✓ **Grammar:** Adjectives (Describing Words)

PB 1.5: p. 11; **TRB 1.5:** p. 11; **GPB:** p. 42

Daily Writing Prompt: List things you could teach a friend.

Day 4

Reading pp. 42–43

Read Together Pupil Edition
READER RESPONSE *Test Prep*

Selection Test

PB 1.5: Selection Test, pp. 13–14
TRB 1.5: Selection Test, pp. 13–14

Review **Comprehension:** Plot

Fluency: Reread the MAIN SELECTION

Guided Reading Resources/Flexible Groups, pp. 18b; LR1–LR6
Leveled Readers 19A, 19B, 5C

Independent Reading
Self-Selected Reading, pp. 10d; AR24

Phonics pp. 43a–43b

✓ **Phonics:** Reteach Long *e: ea,* Inflected Ending *-ed*

Review Compound Words

Spelling: Partner Practice

High-Frequency Words: Review

PB 1.5: Phonics, p. 15; Spelling, p. 16
TRB 1.5: Phonics, p. 15; Spelling, p. 16

Oral Language pp. 44–45

Speaking: Talk About Adjectives

Writing pp. 10i, 44–45

✓ **Grammar:** Adjectives (Describing Words)

Writing: Identify Adjectives

TRB 1.5: pp. 17–18; **GPB:** p. 43

Daily Writing Prompt Write a list of words you see on the way home from school.

Day 5

Reading pp. 45a–45b

Assess Oral Reading: Oral Reading Checklist

Guided Reading Resources/Flexible Groups, pp. 18b; LR1–LR6
Leveled Readers 19A, 19B, 5C

Independent Reading
Self-Selected Reading, pp. 10d; AR24

Phonics p. 45c

✓ **Phonics:** Practice Long *e: ea,* Inflected Ending *-ed*

Apply Phonics: Read the PHONICS TAKE-HOME READER

Spelling: Inflected Ending *-ed* Words

Posttest

High-Frequency Words: Practice

Oral Language p. 45d

Speaking: Retell a Story

Writing pp. 10i, 45d

Interactive Writing: Poster *Portfolio*

Daily Writing Prompt: Write about your favorite place in the neighborhood.

Cross-Curricular Work Stations

Letters and Sounds

Neighborhood Signs 15 minutes

Materials: index cards, markers, butcher paper

Learning Styles Visual, Kinesthetic

Have children create a neighborhood on butcher paper using signs with *ea* words, such as *eat, teach, cream, treat,* and *dream* (for example: Ice Cream, Treats Here, We Teach, Eat Here). Write the *ea* words on index cards for children to use as models. After they finish, they can "take a walk" and read the signs in the neighborhood.

Writing

I Would Not See... 15 minutes

Materials: paper, crayons, pencils

Learning Styles Verbal, Kinesthetic

Ask children to think of something that they would NOT find in their neighborhood, draw a picture of it, and complete this sentence: "I would not see _____ in my neighborhood because _____." Place the pictures in a class book and read it together.

I would not see an elephant in my neighborhood because they live in Africa.

Social Studies

Neighborhood Walk Collage   15 minutes

Materials: drawing paper, chart paper, scissors, glue, markers

Learning Styles Visual, Kinesthetic, Social

Ask partners to imagine taking a neighborhood walk. Have them draw pictures of people, places, and signs they might see on their walk. Children can cut out their drawings and paste them on a large piece of chart paper to make a neighborhood walk collage. Have children write labels beneath each picture.

ESL Provide children with example pictures of signs they might see.

house mailman

sign library

 **INTERNET SAFETY** Establish guidelines for your students' safe and responsible use of the Internet. See the Scott Foresman Internet Guide for tips.

Technology

AstroWord 15 minutes

Learning Styles Individual, Visual

Have children use AstroWord to strengthen understanding of compound words. Children can work individually or in pairs to apply these skills in activities and games in the AstroWord Factory.

Reading Web Site 15 minutes

Learning Styles Individual, Kinesthetic

www Children can visit the Scott Foresman *Reading* Web site (sfreading.com) for current hyperlinks to relevant electronic texts that can be used for an Internet Workshop investigation of things around your neighborhood. Also see the Scott Foresman Internet Guide for additional information on the Internet Workshop method.

sfreading.com

Media

Is It Real? 15 minutes

Materials: chart paper and pencil

Learning Styles Logical, Visual

Have a small group discuss children's movies, videos, or television programs such as *Arthur*. Have the group divide the chart paper into columns headed Could Happen and Make-Believe. As the children discuss, they can fill in names of movies, videos, and programs in the appropriate columns.

Children with special knowledge of other cultures could share information about whether children's stories are mostly real or make-believe in other places around the world.

Math

Shapes in the Neighborhood   15 minutes

Materials: manila paper, colored construction-paper shapes, glue, crayons

Learning Styles Logical, Visual, Spatial

In small groups, have children discuss shapes they see in buildings around the neighborhood. Provide pictures of a school, a house, a store, or a tall building, and have them discuss the shapes of the buildings and windows. Give children cut-out squares, rectangles, triangles, ovals, and circles. Have them each create a neighborhood building with their shapes. When children have finished, they can discuss their buildings and the shapes they used.

Challenge Have children count how many of each shape they used in their building and show the results in a bar graph.

Daily Routines

Message Board

Day One

Today you will hear a book about rabbits. Tell me about rabbits or other animals in your neighborhood.

Encourage children to describe where they see animals and what the animals look like.

Have children find the high-frequency word *only*. Ask which word has the long *e* sound spelled *ea*. (*read*)

Day Two

Think about the girl who could not hear. She could only read signs. What will happen now that she can hear?

Have children find the high-frequency words *right* and *think*. Ask which words have the long *e* sound spelled *ea*. (*read, teach*)

Day Three

Right now you will find out what Arthur can't read. What do you think it will be? Maybe we could teach him.

Have children find the high-frequency word *or* and the spelling word *called*.

Day Four

Have you met Arthur before? What was the book or show called? Tell me about it.

Have children find the high-frequency word *buy* and the word with the inflected ending *-ed*. (*asked*) Have children find an adjective. (*yummy*)

Day Five

Arthur asked D.W. to read as they went to buy yummy ice cream. What have you seen when taking a walk?

Journal Writing

Day One
Write about a new place you went or a new thing you did.

Day Two
Write about a time someone helped you do something new.

Day Three
List things you could teach a friend.

Day Four
Write a list of words you see on the way home from school.

Day Five
Write about your favorite place in the neighborhood.

Family Times

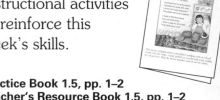

Send home the newsletter with daily instructional activities to reinforce this week's skills.

Practice Book 1.5, pp. 1–2
Teacher's Resource Book 1.5, pp. 1–2

Activate Prior Knowledge

▶ Assess Prior Knowledge

Discuss Around the Neighborhood
Describe things you see in your neighborhood and have children guess what you are describing. Then ask:

> **What is a neighborhood?**
>
> **What places or things are in your neighborhood?**
>
> **How do you find out about your neighborhood?**

Talk with children about how we can learn from the world around us. Tell children that this week they will be reading about different places. Ask:

> **How many places have you been to?**

Emphasize that even places we're very familiar with can teach us new things.

▶ Build Background

Preview the Big Book As you prepare to read aloud the Big Book *Rabbits & Raindrops,* invite children to talk about what animals they might see around their neighborhoods.

Then take children on a picture walk of the first few pages. Ask:

> **What do the pictures tell you about the rabbits' neighborhood?**

Help children set a purpose for listening, such as to get information about rabbits and to enjoy and appreciate animals and other things that are around their neighborhoods.

Read the Big Book As you read aloud the Big Book, invite children to talk about the different places the rabbits investigate in their neighborhood. Ask:

> **What do the rabbits learn about their neighborhood?**

Encourage children to think about how they respond to their neighborhoods. How do their responses compare to the rabbits'?

Return to the Big Book frequently throughout the unit to make connections between the topic, "Around the Neighborhood," and the unit's selections.

Big Book

Objectives

Children will

- activate prior knowledge of topic: Around the Neighborhood
- relate literature to experiences in their own life
- draw on experiences of others to form a broader perspective of the topic
- set a purpose for listening

Day
1

Long *e: ea*

▶ Develop Phonemic Awareness

CD 2/Tape 13, Side 1

Phonics Songs and Rhymes Audio

Sing or Read the Rhyme Chart Sing "Eat a Treat!" in a vaudeville "patter" tune or play the CD or tape. Ask children what they like about this song. Point to the pictures on the Rhyme Chart. Ask children to listen for the rhyming words.

Focus on the Long *e* Sound Say:

> The person in the song is gathering and selling food. What sound do you hear in the middle of *peach*? (/ē/)

Explain that *ea* stands for the long *e* sound. Have children repeat *peach* several times, listening for the long *e* sound.

Ask children to stand up each time they hear words with /ē/: *bean, tea, bake, jeans, home, please, read, time, tease.*

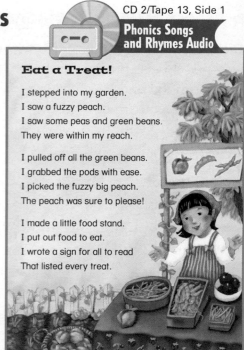

Eat a Treat!

I stepped into my garden.
I saw a fuzzy peach.
I saw some peas and green beans.
They were within my reach.

I pulled off all the green beans.
I grabbed the pods with ease.
I picked the fuzzy big peach.
The peach was sure to please!

I made a little food stand.
I put out food to eat.
I wrote a sign for all to read
That listed every treat.

Phonics Songs and Rhymes Chart 19

▶ Connect Sounds to Letters

Teach Point to and read the word *treat* on the chart. Say:

> The letters *ea* in *treat* stand for the sound /ē/.
> What do we call the sound /ē/? (the long *e* sound)

Blending Practice Have children blend the sounds /p/ /ē/ /ch/ to read *peach*. Have them continue decoding other *ea* words, such as *reach* and *beans.*

Make New Words Display the phonogram card *-eam.* Beginning with *team,* have children change the first letter to make new words. Children blend each new word. Repeat with *seat* and *seal.*

Then have children change final consonant letters to make the words *teach, beak,* and *beach.*

 Meeting Individual Needs

Intervention

Phonemic Awareness Say /t/ /r/ /ē/ /t/ slowly. Have children blend the sounds together and say the whole word. Say each of the following words slowly, sound by sound: *beach, mule, beans, please, use, eat, leap, blue, green.* Have children blend and say the whole word and then reach up with both hands when they say a word with the long *e* sound.

Phonics Generalization CVVC

When two vowels appear together in a word, the first one usually stands for its long vowel sound and the second is silent.

Inflected Ending -ed

▶ Teach Inflected Ending -ed

Explain to children that these sentences show something that is happening now. Have a volunteer change the sentences to show that these same events happened in the past. Help spell each word. Explain that sometimes the last letter in a base word is doubled before adding -ed. Have the doubled consonants identified.

I pick___ treats. (picked)

I stop___ near the treats. (stopped)

I grab___ a peach. (grabbed)

▶ Practice Inflected Ending -ed

Make New Words Write *pull, kick,* and *step* on the board. Have a volunteer come to the board and add -ed to these words and read them.

Spelling Inflected Ending -ed Words

Pretest Say the spelling word, use it in a sentence, repeat it, and allow children to write it. Have children check their pretests and correct misspelled words.

Work with the Spelling Pattern Write *ask, call,* and *clear* on the board. Have children read the words. Remind children that when -ed is added, it makes the word mean something that happened in the past.

Skills Trace	
🎯 Inflected Ending *-ed*	
Introduce/Teach	TE: 1.5 **10I**
Practice	PB: 1.5 4, 10
Reteach/Review	TE: 1.5 17c, 41a, 43a, 45c, 189a, AR11
Test	Skills Test, Unit 5 Benchmark Test, Unit 5

Day 1

Spelling Words

ask	asked
call	called
clean	cleaned

High-Frequency

think	only

Challenge

teach	neat

Word Wall

Introduce High-Frequency Words Use word cards for *buy, only, or, right,* and *think.* Point out the phonogram *-ink* in *think.* Ask children if they know of other *-ink* words, such as *pink* and *sink.*

Have children name the first letter of each word and ask a volunteer to attach each word to the Word Wall under the appropriate beginning letter.

Review Have children choose three Word Wall words and use all three in a silly sentence.

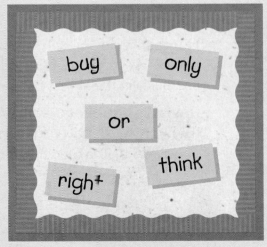

buy   only   or   think   right

Optional Resources

Waterford Early Reading Program
Level 2: Lessons 41, 43

Phonics
Phonics Workbook, pp. 126–128
Phonics Manipulatives Kit

High-Frequency Words
High-Frequency Word Cards
Phonics Sourcebook, pp. 90–99

Objectives

Children will

- learn selection vocabulary
- use sound-symbol relationships to read decodable text
- use prior knowledge to make predictions and make sense of texts
- draw conclusions

Day 1

A Real Gift

pp. 10–17

▶ Build Oral Language

Activate Prior Knowledge Have children discuss how they communicate with each other and with animals. Record their responses on a word web, or use Graphic Organizer Transparency 5 (Web 2).

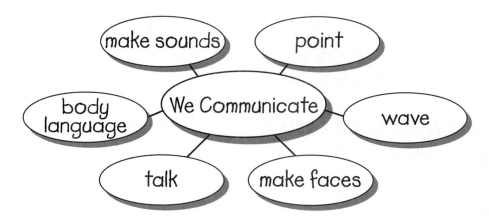

Build Background Write these sentences on index cards: *Don't sit there. I'm sad. Look out the window! I'm sleepy. Let's go outside. Where is my hat? Is this book yours?* Have a child select a card and pantomime the idea. Ask children how they know what the actor "said" without words.

▶ Vocabulary

Introduce Story Vocabulary Use Vocabulary Chart 36, or write sentences on the board using each word. Read each sentence aloud. Point out *signs*. Ask children for examples of signs they have seen. Frame *soft*. Ask children to provide synonyms and antonyms for the word.

people   signs   soft

Names Write *Nayeli Lopez* on the board. Help children pronounce the name. (Nä yé lē Lō´ pez) Tell children that *Nayeli* is the name of the main character in the story.

Review High-Frequency Words As you point to each of these words on the Word Wall, have children read the word. These words are also listed on page 228 of the Student Book.

buy   only   or   right   think

A Real Gift

1. Many <u>people</u> live and work in our neighborhood.
2. The <u>signs</u> on the shops tell what's for sale.
3. <u>Soft</u> music is playing in one shop.

Story Vocabulary Chart 36

— high-frequency/tested vocabulary

► Reading Strategies

Preview and Predict Read the title and the names of the author and photographer to children. Have children look at the pictures in the story. Be sure they recognize that the pictures are photographs and understand that the story could be nonfiction. Ask:

> **Do you think the selection is about a real person?**

> **Why do you think the story is about something that really happened?**

Picture Walk Have children do a picture walk, looking at all the photographs in the story. Ask children to predict what might happen in this story.

Set Purposes From the photographs, children know the story is about a girl named Nayeli. At the end of the story, she is in a doctor's office. Suggest that they read to find out why Nayeli went to the doctor.

Guide the Reading Have children read the first few pages of the selection, keeping their purposes in mind. Stop to check comprehension, using the questions provided. Have children read to page 13.

Phonics Story

A Real Gift
by Diane Hoyt-Goldsmith
photos by Lawrence Migdale

This is Nayeli Lopez.

She reads with her cat. She gives him something to eat too.

Selection Audio
CD 6/Tape21, Side 1

About the Author

Diane Hoyt-Goldsmith has a collection of Northwest Coast Indian carvings that inspired her first book, *Totem Pole.* She has collaborated with photographer Lawrence Migdale on a number of books. Other titles include *Pueblo Storyteller* and *Cherokee Summer.*

About the Photographer

Lawrence Migdale meets people from other backgrounds with his camera, and his partnership with author Diane Hoyt-Goldsmith continues to teach him about different cultures. His award-winning work appears in *Apache Rodeo* and *Arctic Hunter.*

Optional Resources

Reading
Adding English: ESL Teacher's Guide

Guiding Comprehension

Day
1

Recall and Retell/Literal

How does Nayeli speak?

She makes signs with her hands.

Drawing Conclusions/Inferential

Why is it hard for Nayeli to tell what people are saying?

It is hard for her because she can't hear very well.

Self-Monitoring Strategy

It doesn't say that Nayeli can't hear very well. How do you know?

She speaks sign language with her hands. Most people who use sign language are deaf or hard of hearing.

Predicting/Inferential

What do you think will happen in this story?

Children may say that Nayeli and her mother will go to a doctor or go shopping.

Connect Phonics to Reading

What does Nayeli do with her cat? She reads with her cat. **What vowel sound do you hear in that word?** You hear the long *e* sound in *reads*.

to the end of the story.

10–11   *Real Gift/Arthur's Race*

Phonics Story

A [ ] Gift

by Diane Hoyt-Goldsmith

photos by Lawrence Migdale

This is Nayeli Lopez.

She reads with her cat. She gives him something to eat too.

10

A Real Gift, page 10

Nayeli can speak with her hands. She knows how to make signs for words.

12 Phonics Story

A Real Gift, page 12

Nayeli lives in the country.

She rides the bus to school.

It is loud, but Nayeli does not mind.

For Nayeli, loud sounds are soft.

It's hard for her to tell what people

are saying.

Phonics Stcry **11**

A Real Gift, page 11

One day, Nayeli had something to
do. She met her mother right after
school. "We can go now," her
mother signed with her hands.

Phonics Story **13**

A Real Gift, page 13

Phonics Strategies

If... children have trouble reading *reads, eat,* and *speak,*

then... review the long *e* sound and have them segment and blend the sounds. **Decoding: Using Phonetic Analysis**

If... children need help reading *signed* on page 13,

then... tell them that *signed* is a tricky word in which not all the letters match the sounds. Point out that they can use the first and last letters and the picture on page 12 to help them read this word. **Consonants**

If... children have difficulty reading *it's,*

then... review the contraction for *it is.* **Decoding: Using Structural Analysis**

Reading Strategies

If... children are unable to explain how Nayeli speaks,

then... reread pages 12–13. Have children explain what it means to speak with your hands. Then have them tell why someone would use sign language. **Using Illustrations**

If... children can make a prediction,

then... ask them questions to help them further refine their prediction. **Refining Predictions**

Day **1**

▒▒▒ long *e: ea* and *-ed* endings
— high-frequency/tested vocabulary

Guiding Comprehension

pp. 14–17

Details/Literal

What things does Nayeli do after school?

Her mother takes her for a treat; they watch a soccer game, pet a puppy, and go to the doctor for a hearing aid.

Analyzing/Critical

How does Nayeli feel about going to the doctor? How do you know?

She is happy to go because the doctor will help her hear. You can tell because she's smiling.

Check Predictions

Did the story end as you thought it would?

Children are likely to say no—they did not guess that the doctor would help Nayeli hear.

Connect Phonics to Reading

Look at page 16. What did Nayeli do very fast? walked **Which two letters tell that this already happened?** the letters *ed*

Response Log Have children write questions to Diane Hoyt-Goldsmith about *A Real Gift*. Children may wish to share their questions with classmates.

They stopped to buy a treat.
Nayeli picked out a peach to eat.

Then they passed a soccer team.
They stopped to watch the game.
Nayeli wanted to stay,
but she had something to do.

14 Phonics Story

A Real Gift, **page 14**

Nayeli walked very fast.
They had only one more block to go.
She didn't want to be late.

16 Phonics Story

A Real Gift, **page 16**

Nayeli saw a dog.
It wanted to play or be petted.

"No," signed her mother.
"I think we have to go now."

Phonics Story **15**

A Real Gift, page 15

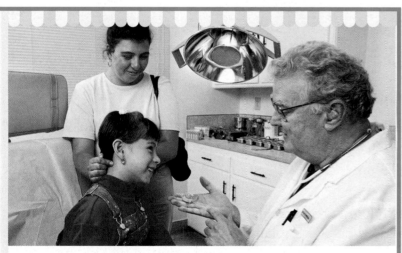

Now Nayeli had something to
help her. It fit just right.
The doctor's words sounded loud.

"Thank you" signed Nayeli
with her hands.

Phonics Story **17**

A Real Gift, page 17

Skills in Context

Day 1

Review
Draw Conclusions

Why did the doctor sound loud?

The doctor gave Nayeli something to help her hear better.

Ongoing Assessment

Draw Conclusions

If... children do not understand that Nayeli now has a hearing aid,	**then...** do the **Think Aloud** below to model the skill.

Model Your Thinking

EST TALK

I'll reread the words and look at the pictures. I see that the doctor puts something in Nayeli's ear. The words say: "It fit just right." Then the doctor's words sound loud. I think that the thing in her ear helps her hear.

Extend Language Arts

Thank-You Note

Have children imagine that they are Nayeli. Ask what they might write in a thank-you note to the doctor. Write an outline for children to follow:

> date
> Dear _____,
> Thank you for _____
> _____
> _____
> _____
>
> Your friend,
> _____

---

long *e: ea* and *-ed* endings
high-frequency/tested vocabulary

Real Gift/Arthur's Race **16–17**

Expand Vocabulary

▶ Discuss Multiple-Meaning Words

Remind children that in the story *A Real Gift* it was hard for Nayeli to hear. Explain that the word *hard* has more than one meaning. It can mean the opposite of *easy* as well as the opposite of *soft*.

Write the following chart on the board. Review with children the words, their multiple meanings, and the sentences using them. Then have children think of more sentences using each meaning of each word.

hard	opposite of easy	The puzzle was hard to do.
	opposite of soft	We sat on the hard floor.
batter	baseball player	The batter hit the ball.
	used to make cakes	We poured batter into the pan.
duck	put head down quickly	Duck your head.
	animal that quacks	Listen to the duck quack.

List

▶ Shared Writing

List Gifts You Appreciate Discuss with children how a gift isn't always something wrapped in a beautiful package. Sometimes it's something you deeply appreciate having, just as Nayeli appreciated having her hearing aid in *A Real Gift*.

Have children discuss gifts they appreciate having. List some of these on the board, such as those listed below. Explain that in a list, words are placed in a column, one under the other. Point out how you begin the first letter of one word directly under the first letter of the word above it, leaving space between the two words.

my cat	my eyeglasses
my best friend	seat belts
a rainbow	sunshine

Objectives

Children will

- use multiple-meaning words in sentences
- write about a gift
- practice handwriting

Day
1

Meeting Individual Needs

Challenge

Extended Vocabulary List
Encourage the use of words such as these.

bump	coast
cast	loaf
charge	stamp

Independent Writing Have each child choose a gift they appreciate having. They may choose a gift from the class list. Ask them to write at least two sentences about the gift they chose. Remind them to include specific details about it. Have them illustrate their sentences.

Handwriting Zz

Self-Selected Reading and Read Aloud D.E.A.R.

Read aloud from *Don't Tease the Guppies* by Pat Lowery Collins. Children choose new books for self-selected reading.

Day 1

Provide lined paper and handwriting models. Demonstrate how to write a capital *Z* and a lowercase *z* and have children practice writing a row of each letter.

Ask children to evaluate their handwriting by circling their best capital *Z* and their best lowercase *z*.

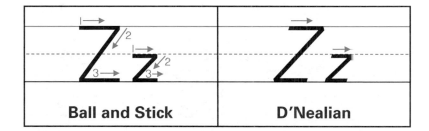

Ball and Stick	D'Nealian

Word Spacing Write these sentences on the board:

Zack and Zoe saw a zebra at the zoo.

A peach has fuzz.

As you write, explain that correct spacing makes your writing easier to read and that there is more space between words than between letters in a word.

Optional Resources

Oral Language
Adding English: ESL Teacher's Guide

Day
2

Objectives

Children will

- decode and build words with long *e: ea*
- use structural cues to decode and build words with inflected ending *-ed*
- use sound/symbol relationships as visual cues for decoding
- spell words with inflected ending *-ed*

Long *e: ea*
Inflected Ending *-ed*

▶ Phonics Practice Activities

Use the following activities and Practice Book pages to practice long *e: ea* and inflected ending *-ed*.

Phonics Songs and Rhymes Chart Children sing "Eat a Treat!" as you track the print. Children circle words with long *e: ea* or inflected ending *-ed*.

Make New Words Have children fold a sheet of paper into thirds. Ask them to write *peach, eat,* and *deal* as column heads. Working with a partner, have children use letter cards to build and then list as many rhyming words as they can in each column.

Long *e: ea*
Practice Book 1.5, p. 3
Teacher's Resource Book 1.5, p. 3

Inflected Ending *-ed*
Practice Book 1.5, p. 4
Teacher's Resource Book 1.5, p. 4

▶ Read the Phonics Reader

Tell children to use what they know about long *e: ea* and inflected ending *-ed* as they read *The Neat Green Cast.* Observe children's reading to determine their ability to transfer these phonics skills to a new selection. After reading, ask them to:
- identify their favorite character and explain why
- frame words with long *e* as they come across them, using a small leaf cutout

Phonics Reader

Optional Resources

Phonics
Phonics Workbook, pp. 126–128
Phonics Manipulatives Kit
Phonics Sourcebook, pp. 79–82, 100–123

High-Frequency Words
High-Frequency Word Cards
Phonics Sourcebook, pp. 90–99

Spelling Inflected Ending *-ed* Words

▶ Writing for Sounds

Have children write these sentences. Read the sentences. Then repeat words slowly, allowing children to hear each sound. Children may use the Word Wall to help in spelling high-frequency words. Proofread and correct completed sentences.

I called to ask you to clean your feet.
Mother asked me to call you.
Who cleaned the mule?

Spelling Words

ask	asked
call	called
clean	cleaned

High-Frequency

think	only

Challenge

teach	neat

Day 2

Word Wall

Practice High-Frequency Words

Choose ten words from the Word Wall, including this week's words. Include other *b*, *o*, and *t* words and words with three, four, and five letters.

Have partners write the words on slips of paper and sort them by beginning letter and then by number of letters.

buy   only   or   right   think

Pick a word from the box to finish each sentence. Write it on the line.

buy   only   or   right   think

1. Tom wants to **buy** a hat.
2. He can get **only** one hat.
3. Will he get this hat **or** that one?
4. He has to **think** a bit.
5. This hat fits just **right**.

Notes for Home: This week your child is learning to read the words *buy, only, or, right,* and *think*. **Home Activity:** Write each word on a slip of paper. Put all the slips in a bowl or hat. Ask your child to pick a word, say it aloud, and use it in a sentence.

High-Frequency Words
Practice Book 1.5, p. 5
Teacher's Resource Book 1.5, p. 5

Meeting Individual Needs

ESL	Intervention	Challenge	Other Ways to Learn
Put word cards for *jump, open, pull, stop, walk* in a pile. Have a volunteer choose one word, act it out, and use inflected *-ed* form of the word in a sentence, telling about the action. **(Word Study Support)** See also *Adding English.*	Use **Decodable Reader 33** and the teaching suggestions on p. AR1 to provide practice reading decodable text that includes words with long *e: ea* and inflected ending *-ed*. **(Phonics Support)**	Have children list the long *e: ea* words from *Eat a Treat!* and use as many of them as they can to tell a story about cooking. **(Tiered Assignments)**	Use Phonics Activity Mat 1 from the Phonics Manipulatives Kit for long *e* and Phonics Activity Mat 2 for inflected ending *-ed*. Instructions for using these games are on the back of the mats. **(Kinesthetic)**

Objectives

Children will

 make predictions

- listen critically to predict what will happen next
- read with fluency and understanding

Skills Trace

Predicting

Introduce	TE: 1.1 28–29	
Teach	Before	TE: 1.5 17e–17f
	During	TE: 1.5 18–19
	After	TE: 1.5 AR12
Practice	PB: 1.1 5; 1.2 38; 1.5 6	
Reteach/Review	TE: 1.2 AR15; 1.5 AR12	
Test	Skills Test, Unit 5 Benchmark Test, Unit 5	

Day 2

Building Systematic Instruction

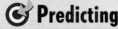 Predicting

LOOKING BACK

Kindergarten Children are able to talk about what might happen next in a selection.

Grade 1 Children predict accurately what will happen next in a story. Children identify the clues they used to make the prediction.

LOOKING AHEAD

Grade 2 Children rely on prediction when reading a story. Children verify their prediction based on clues in the story.

Predicting

▶ Develop Listening Comprehension

Read the following story aloud. Before you read the last paragraph, ask children to predict how Anna and Colleen solve the problem of the breakdown of the ice-cream truck.

Read Aloud

The Ice-Cream Problem

Anna and her sister Colleen loved to make and sell ice cream. Every day, Colleen made ice cream and Anna loaded up the truck to sell the ice cream in the city. Everyone loved the ice cream, so when the truck rang its bell, all the children and their parents ran to buy the delicious treat.

There was only one problem: Anna's truck began to break down once a week, usually on Friday.

The children who bought the ice cream were so disappointed when Anna did not show up on Fridays. Colleen was disappointed too, because no one could buy the ice cream she was making. Then one day Anna and Colleen had a great idea.

They sold the truck and opened an ice-cream parlor on the corner across from the Town Hall. Now people come from all over town to buy Colleen's delicious ice cream.

►Teach Predicting

Model the skill by telling children:

 Think ALOUD

The problem in this story was that the truck kept breaking down. There were some different things Anna and Colleen could have done to fix the problem. Thinking about the different possibilities to solve a problem is a good way to predict what happens next.

Ask children:

What do you think might happen now that they have set up an ice-cream parlor?

Practice Read a folktale such as "Stone Soup" or "The Brementown Musicians." As you read, pause every few pages and have children predict what they think will happen next. Later, discuss why they made each prediction.

Read the first sentence. Then read the pair of sentences.
Circle the sentence that tells what will happen next.
Draw a picture in the box that shows what will happen next.

1. Bob wakes up late.
   Bob will get to the bus on time.
   (Bob will miss the bus.)

2. Children's drawings may show a boy chasing after a bus.

3. Mom and Dad pack for a trip.
   Mom and Dad will buy a dog.
   (Mom and Dad will drive away.)

4. Children's drawings may show an adult couple driving down a road.

Look at the pictures.
Draw what will happen next.

5.

Children's drawings may show a dog chasing after a squirrel.

Notes for Home: Your child predicted what will happen next in a story and drew a picture to show this prediction. **Home Activity:** Read a story to your child. At several points in the story, stop and ask your child to predict what will happen next.

Predicting
Practice Book 1.5, p. 6
Teacher's Resource Book 1.5, p. 6

Day 2

Reread for Fluency

Attend to Punctuation Model fluent reading by reading aloud. Have children track the print as you read the punctuation, pausing for a comma, stopping at a period, and changing your tone of voice for dialogue.

Practice Reading Phrases Model how to use phrases to read a page from the book. Point out that some sentences are one phrase, and other sentences, such as *For Nayeli, loud sounds are soft*, contain two phrases. Then have partners take turns reading the story, phrase by phrase. Partners should reread the story, this time reading the phrases that their partners read the first time.

Phonics Story
A Real Gift
by Diane Hoyt-Goldsmith
photos by Lawrence Migdale

This is Nayeli Lopez.

She reads with her cat. She gives him something to eat too.

Leveled Practice for ⟳ Predicting

After children have read *Arthur's Reading Race,* use the appropriate leveled practice pictured on page 43 in this Teacher's Edition.

| Easy |
| On-Level |
| Challenge |

Meeting Individual Needs

ESL	Intervention	Challenge	Other Ways to Learn
Ask children to draw dark clouds. Help them to predict that rain likely is on the way. **(Skill Support)** See also *Adding English.* **ESL**	Before reading *That Is Right, Walrus, Texas Eggs,* or another book, have children predict what it will be about. Pause while reading to ask, "What do you think will happen next?" When finished, ask, "Were you right about ___?" **(Comprehension Support)**	Children write and illustrate a sentence that shows what Nayeli might do now that she has a hearing aid. **(Divergent Thinking)**	Children pantomime actions, such as blowing up a balloon, to a certain point and then stop. Let the class predict what might happen next. **(Kinesthetic)** Show pictures of sign language and have children predict each meaning. Tell children what the signs mean and have them tell whether their prediction was correct. **(Visual/Spatial)**

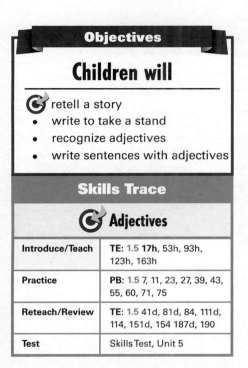

Objectives

Children will

- retell a story
- write to take a stand
- recognize adjectives
- write sentences with adjectives

Skills Trace

Adjectives

Introduce/Teach	TE: 1.5 **17h**, 53h, 93h, 123h, 163h
Practice	PB: 1.5 7, 11, 23, 27, 39, 43, 55, 60, 71, 75
Reteach/Review	TE: 1.5 41d, 81d, 84, 111d, 114, 151d, 154 187d, 190
Test	Skills Test, Unit 5

Day 2

Speaking: Retell a Story

▶ Discuss a Movie, Play, or TV Show

Model Retell to children the story of a movie, play, or TV show you've recently seen. You might retell the story of the play *Cinderella*.

> The story is about a girl named Cinderella who lives with her mean stepmother and two stepsisters. They all get invited to a ball given by the prince, but only the stepmother and stepsisters go. They leave Cinderella at home. While they are gone, Cinderella's fairy godmother comes and gives her a beautiful gown and a golden carriage so she can go to the ball. The fairy godmother warns Cinderella to leave the ball before midnight. At the ball the prince falls in love with Cinderella, but she runs off at midnight. The prince finds her glass slipper and asks every girl in the land to try it on. It fits Cinderella. The Prince and Cinderella get married and live happily ever after.

As you retell, model these behaviors:
- Give a clear beginning, middle, and ending of the story.
- Avoid unnecessary details.
- Speak clearly.
- Use enthusiasm in your voice.

Practice Have each child retell to a partner the story of a movie, play, or TV show they've recently seen. Remind them to give a clear beginning, middle, and ending of the story. Encourage them to tell what the story was mostly about in order to avoid unnecessary details.

Take a Stand

▶ Modeled Writing

Model Discuss with children issues they feel strongly about in their school or neighborhood. You might discuss a school rule or a neighborhood concern such as littering. Tell them you are going to have them each take a stand concerning one of these issues and then write about it. Explain that *taking a stand* means to stand up for something important.

> I feel very strongly about recycling. It makes me sad when I see people throwing newspapers and cans in the trash when these could be recycled. I'm going to take a stand about recycling.

▶ Write to Take a Stand

Model Write sentences to take a stand about a school or neighborhood issue such as a school rule or recycling. You may wish to model the sentences below.

> I will take a stand for recycling.
>
> Recycling helps keep Earth beautiful.
>
> People should recycle their newspapers and cans.

As you write, model these strategies:
- Give a brief and clear argument.
- Include at least one fact.
- Use correct letter formation.
- Use proper end punctuation.

Independent Writing Have each child choose an issue to take a stand about. Children should write at least three or four sentences that include supporting details to take a stand about their issue.

Author's Chair If time permits, allow children to share their writing.

Self-Selected Reading and Read Aloud D.E.A.R.

Read aloud *Not the Piano, Mrs. Medley* by Evan Levine. Children self-select books about journeys.

Day 2

Grammar: Adjectives (Describing Words)

Define Adjectives Write the sentence *We have a tall tree in our yard.* Explain that *tall* is an adjective that describes the word *tree.* An adjective is a describing word that tells more about a person, place, or thing.

Invite children to think of a person, place, or thing and an adjective that tells more about it. Write these on the board. Children might choose nouns and adjectives from their Oral Language or Writing activities, or they might choose new adjectives with nouns, such as *happy girl, big school,* or *crunchy snacks.*

Practice Write the following sentences on the board. Have children copy them on their own paper, filling in the blanks with adjectives.

> I like _____ pillows.
>
> I have a _____ shirt.
>
> Do you like _____ socks?

For further practice, have children identify adjectives they used in their writing.

Adjectives
Practice Book 1.5, p. 7
Teacher's Resource Book 1.5, p. 7

Day 3

Arthur's Reading Race

1. It was <u>almost</u> time to go to the pool.
2. I <u>bought</u> ice cream to eat on the way.
3. Mom said we <u>could</u> go swimming.
4. We stepped off the <u>curb</u> near the pool.
5. There were only <u>eight</u> people swimming.
6. A sign with wet <u>paint</u> said "Diving Contest Today."
7. I wanted to <u>prove</u> I could dive.
8. I <u>shook</u> with cold after I dived.
9. I could <u>spy</u> my mom watching me.

Story Vocabulary Chart 37

Pick a word from the box to match each clue.
Write the words in the puzzles.

| buy | eight | only | or | right | think |

1. Do you like cats ____ dogs?
2. not wrong
3. five, six, seven, ____
4. I have ____ one cat.
5. I ____ dogs are cute.
6. not sell

Notes for Home: Your child solved puzzles using words learned this week.
Home Activity: Work with your child to write a story using as many of these words as possible.

Tested Vocabulary
Practice Book 1.5, p. 8
Teacher's Resource Book 1.5, p. 8

Arthur's Reading Race
pp. 18–41

▶ Build Oral Language

Activate Prior Knowledge Ask children to discuss neighborhood sights and sounds.

> **What did Nayeli and her mother see as they walked?**
> **What might you see or hear on a walk in your neighborhood?**
> **What signs could you read in your neighborhood?**

Build Background Play the Background-Building audio segment, which presents a "listening race" in which children identify sounds they might hear on a road trip. Sounds include a car engine, radio, siren, parade, and an airplane. Ask children to name these sounds as you write their responses on a chart. After listening, ask children to name words they might see on signs during the same trip.

Background-Building Audio
CD 5/Tape 12, Side 1

▶ Vocabulary

Introduce Story Vocabulary List the selection vocabulary on the board. Use Vocabulary Chart 37 or write sentences using each word. Read the sentences aloud.

almost   bought   could   curb
eight   paint   prove   shook   spy

Point to *almost* in the list. Ask children to find it in a sentence. Have someone circle it and read it. Continue this routine with the rest of the selection vocabulary.

Point out the silent *gh* in the words *bought* and *eight*.

▶ Reading Strategies

Preview and Predict After reading the title of the story and the name of the author, have children do a picture walk. Encourage children to look for picture clues that help them read the words on the signs.

Set Purposes From the pictures, children know that the characters walk past many signs. Help children set a purpose for reading the selection. Suggest that children read to find out why the signs are important.

Guide the Reading Have children read the first few pages of the selection. Stop to check for comprehension, using the questions provided. Have children read to page 21.

Managing Flexible Groups

Intervention

Before reading, go over the words on the signs and discuss words that might be troublesome. Children listen to the selection audio and follow along in their books. After reading, children use the illustrations as cues to retell the story to a partner.

Selection Audio
CD 6/Tape 21, Side 1

To develop fluency and to practice high-frequency words, children can read **Leveled Reader 19A,** *That Is Right, Walrus.* Instructional support appears in this Teacher's Edition, pp. LR1–LR2.

Easy

Children can review the high-frequency words. Read the story aloud with children. Help children distinguish between narration and dialogue. Children join in to read the words on the signs. Use Guiding Comprehension to monitor understanding and Ongoing Assessment as appropriate.

To develop fluency and to practice high-frequency words, children can read **Leveled Reader 19B,** *Texas Eggs.* Instructional support appears in this Teacher's Edition, pp. LR4–LR5.

On-Level

Children can take turns reading the dialogue of the characters. Use Guiding Comprehension to monitor understanding and Ongoing Assessment to address reading difficulties.

To develop fluency and to practice high-frequency words, children can read **Leveled Reader 19B,** *Texas Eggs.* Instructional support appears in this Teacher's Edition, pp. LR4–LR5.

Challenge

Children can read the signs on the pages as well as the words of the story. Have them make predictions as they read and record them in their response logs. After reading, children think of another sign Arthur and D.W. might have seen, and draw a picture that includes the sign.

Children who have finished reading *Arthur's Reading Race* can read a selection in **Leveled Reader 5C.**

About the Author

Marc Brown
has written and illustrated over 30 Arthur stories since he first published *Arthur's Nose* in 1976. His grandmother encouraged him to take his drawing seriously, helping him through art school. He enjoys the creativity involved in creating children's books, often collaborating with his wife, writer Laurie Krasny Brown. They live in Hingham, Massachusetts, with their daughter, and also enjoy gardening at their summer home in Martha's Vineyard.

Optional Resources

Reading
Adding English: ESL Teacher's Guide

Guiding Comprehension

pp. 18–21

Plot/Literal

Where does Arthur read?

He reads in school, in the car, and in bed.

Drawing Conclusions/Inferential

Do you think Arthur likes to read?

Children are likely to say that Arthur likes to read because he reads everywhere. And he reads to his puppy and little sister.

Predicting/Inferential

What do you think the rest of this story is about?

Children are likely to say that the story is about how much Arthur likes to read. The story is about reading.

Read On...

to page 25.

Arthur's Reading Race, page 18

Arthur's Reading Race, page 20

Arthur's Reading Race, page 19

Reading Strategies

If... children successfully predict what the selection will be about,	**then...** tell them to read on for events that support their prediction. **Predicting**
If... children have trouble predicting,	**then...** talk about each page and ask, "What do you think you'll see on the next page? What makes you think so?" **Predicting**

Phonics Strategies

If... children say "reads at night" instead of "reads in bed,"	**then...** they may be overrelying on picture clues. Explain that "at night" does make sense in the sentence, but they need to look closely at the words. Draw attention to the initial and final sounds of *bed,* /b/ and /d/. **Decoding**

Day 3

Arthur's Reading Race, page 21

long *e*: *ea* and inflected ending *-ed*
— high-frequency/tested vocabulary

Guiding Comprehension

pp. 22–25

Summarizing/Inferential

What has happened so far in the story?

Arthur said he will teach D.W. to read, but she said she could already read. Arthur challenged her to read ten words.

Details/Literal

What is the first sign D.W. reads in the park?

D.W. reads the sign that says "Zoo."

Predicting/Inferential

What do you think will happen next?

Children are likely to say that Arthur and D.W. will keep walking, and D.W. will keep reading words.

Connect Phonics to Reading

What does Arthur promise to buy D.W. if she can read ten words? ice cream **Name another word on page 23 that has the same vowel sound as** *cream.* Children may say *read* or *deal.*

Read On…

to page 29

One day Arthur said,
"I can teach YOU to read too."

"I already know how to read,"
said D.W.

"You do not!" said Arthur.

"Do too!" said D.W.

Arthur's Reading Race, page 22

They raced to the park.
Arthur pointed to a sign.
"What's that say?" he asked.

"Zoo," said D.W.
"Easy as pie."

Arthur's Reading Race, page 24

"Prove it," said Arthur.
"Read ten words, D.W.,
and I'll buy you an ice cream."

D.W. stuck out her hand.
"It's a deal," she said.
"Let's go!"

23

Arthur's Reading Race, page 23

25

Arthur's Reading Race, page 25

Reading Strategies

If... children have trouble reading the text fluently,	**then...** go back and reread the pages, telling them that this is a conversation between Arthur and D. W. Ask children to read as though they were talking. **Fluency**
If... children successfully predict that D.W. will continue to read more words,	**then...** ask them what other signs they think D. W. and Arthur will see. **Predicting**

Phonics Strategies

If... children have trouble reading difficult words such as *prove, buy, pointed,* or *sign,*	**then...** tell them to look at the beginning letters and think carefully about the word that would sound correct in the sentence. **Decoding, Context Clues**

Day 3

Content Connection: Social Studies

SOCIAL STUDIES CONNECTION

The Detroit Zoo is located just outside Detroit in Royal Oak, Michigan. When the Detroit Zoo opened in 1928, it was the first zoo in the United States to extensively use exhibits without bars. Today the zoo provides a natural habitat for more than 1,250 animals. Some of its major exhibits include polar bears, giraffes, Siberian tigers, and African lions.

long *e*: *ea* and inflected ending *-ed*
high-frequency/tested vocabulary

Guiding Comprehension

pp. 26–29

Details/Literal

Arthur spies three words and D.W. reads them. What are these words?

The words are *taxi, gas,* and *milk.*

Summarizing/Inferential

Why did D.W. tell Arthur to look out?

He stepped off the curb when the sign said, "Don't Walk." She told him he could get hit by a car.

Predicting/Inferential

Do you think D.W. will read more words? Find sentences in the story to support your prediction.

D.W. is doing very well reading words on signs. She probably has a good chance of reading more words. Children may point to the sentences on page 27 or page 28 to show how well D.W. is reading.

Read On...

to page 33.

Arthur's Reading Race, page 26

Arthur's Reading Race, page 28

"Me too," said D.W.

"Taxi, gas, milk."

27

Arthur's Reading Race, page 27

Reading Strategies

If... children cannot remember what three words D.W. reads,	**then...** have them look at the pictures again and reread page 27 to find out. **Reread, Details**
If... children have trouble reading a word,	**then...** tell them to read through the entire sentence first and then go back to the word to see if they can figure it out. **Context Clues**
If... children read the sentence "Look out!" with expression,	**then...** acknowledge their understanding of the exclamation mark, which tells them how to read the word. **Matching Spoken to Printed Words**

Day **3**

DON'T WALK

29

Arthur's Reading Race, page 29

long *e*: *ea* and inflected ending *-ed*
high-frequency/tested vocabulary

Real Gift/Arthur's Race   **28–29**

Guiding Comprehension

pp. 30–33

Drawing Conclusions/Inferential

Why does D.W. tell Arthur he'd better get off the grass?

D.W. sees the sign that says, "Keep off the Grass," and thinks the police might say something to Arthur.

Compare and Contrast/Critical

What is the difference between the kind of bank D.W. has at home and the one she points to?

D.W. probably has a small bank at home where she keeps coins, but the one she points to is a big building where many people keep their money.

Predicting/Inferential

Where else do you think D.W. and Arthur will go?

Children are likely to say that they will go to the ice cream shop, because D.W. has already read eight words and needs to read only two more for Arthur to buy her an ice cream.

to page 37.

"All right, Miss Smarty-Pants, what's that say?" asked Arthur.

30

Arthur's Reading Race, page 30

"Bank," said D.W. "I have a bank.

32

Arthur's Reading Race, page 32

"Police," said D.W.
"And you better
keep off the grass
or the police will get you."

31

Arthur's Reading Race, page 31

I hide my money in it
so you can't find it.
Bank makes eight words."

33

Arthur's Reading Race, page 33

Skills In Context

Predicting

Do you think D.W. will read ten words by the end of the story?

Children are likely to answer that she will, because she's done such a good job with reading so far.

Ongoing Assessment

Predicting

If... children are unable to make a prediction,	**then...** do the **Think Aloud** below to model the skill.

Model Your Thinking

I know that D.W. has already read many words on the signs and is good at reading them. I also know she doesn't have too many more words to read before she has ten words. I think she'll continue and read ten words by the end of the story.

Have children return to the story to point out specific examples that support the idea that D.W. will read ten words by the end of the story. Then have children predict whether D.W. will also get the ice cream Arthur promised her. Ask children to tell you why they might make such a prediction.

Day
3

long *e*: *ea* and inflected ending *-ed*
high-frequency/tested vocabulary

Guiding Comprehension

pp. 34–37

Day

3

Drawing Conclusions/Inferential

What does D.W. mean when she says, "Hold your horses"?

She is telling Arthur to wait because she might still read ten words.

Self-Monitoring Strategy
Reread

It doesn't say that "hold your horses" means "wait." How do you know what these words mean?

If you "hold your horses," you are not letting them move forward. D.W. is telling Arthur to wait before he thinks he has won the bet because the walk is not over yet.

Hypothesizing/Inferential

How do you think Arthur felt about D.W. reading all ten words?

He seemed happy for her. They ran to the ice cream store together and got two big ice cream cones. Arthur had a big smile on his face as he watched D.W. eat her ice cream cone.

Predicting/Inferential

Do you think D.W. will read more words in this story? Why or why not?

Possible responses: She will read more words because she likes to read. She won't read more words because she has already read ten, and Arthur has already bought her an ice cream cone as promised.

to the end of the story.

"We're almost home," said Arthur. "Too bad. You only read eight words. No ice cream for you today."

Arthur's Reading Race, **page 34**

pizza chip   shoe lace
Bumpy road   moose ripple
frog chip
egg shell

D.W. and Arthur ran to the ice cream store. Arthur bought two big cones.

Arthur's Reading Race, **page 36**

"Hold your horses," said D.W.

"I spy . . . ice cream.

Hot dog! I read ten words.

Let's eat!"

35

Arthur's Reading Race, page 35

Strawberry for D.W.
and chocolate for himself.
"Yummy," said D.W.

37

Arthur's Reading Race, page 37

Reading Strategies

If... children have difficulty understanding the idiom *hold your horses,*

then... go back and reread pages 34–35 and discuss the unusual use of words to make sure children understand the meaning of the words in the story. **Drawing Conclusions, Context Clues**

If... children are able to draw conclusions about how Arthur feels,

then... recognize their use of the text and pictures, as well as their prior knowledge to figure out how Arthur feels. **Finding Meaning**

Phonics Strategies

If... children have difficulty reading the words *strawberry* and *chocolate* on page 37,

then... tell them to look at the beginning sounds, look at the picture for clues, and think about words that would make sense in that sentence. **Using Picture Clues, Decoding**

Day
3

long *e: ea* and inflected ending *-ed*
high-frequency/tested vocabulary

Guiding Comprehension

pp. 38–41

Making Inferences/Critical

Why do you think D.W. laughs after Arthur sits on the bench?

D.W. laughs because Arthur did not read the "Wet Paint" sign on the bench and he keeps telling her he is such a good reader.

Check Predictions

Did D.W. read any more words? Did the story end the way you thought it would? Explain your answer.

Children are likely to say they weren't surprised that D.W. read more words, but they were surprised that Arthur sat in wet paint.

Day 3

Critical Thinking
Reading Across Texts

How are *Arthur's Reading Race* and *A Real Gift* alike?

Both stories take place in neighborhoods. In *Arthur's Reading Race*, Arthur and D.W. read the words they see in the neighborhood. In *A Real Gift*, Nayeli and her mother walk through town to the doctor's office. In both stories, the children get a treat to eat.

Response Log Have children write a diary entry for Arthur or D.W. They should include important events from the story and feelings of the character.

Arthur sat down.
"Sit down with me," said Arthur,
"and I'll read you my book."

"No," said D.W.
"I'll read YOU the book."

38

Arthur's Reading Race, page 38

"Now I can teach you
two words that you don't know,"
said D.W.
"WET PAINT!"

40

Arthur's Reading Race, page 40

Arthur shook his head.
"I don't <u>think</u> so," he said.
"There are too many words
that you don't know."

D.W. laughed.
"Get up, Arthur."

WET PAINT

39

***Arthur's Reading Race,* page 39**

About the Author and Illustrator

Marc Brown

Arthur is a very famous
aardvark! Arthur first appeared
years ago. Marc Brown's son
wanted to hear a bedtime story.
Mr. Brown told one about an
aardvark. Now there are more
than thirty books about Arthur
and D.W. You may have even
seen Arthur on TV.

SOCCER

BEARS

41

***About the Author,* page 41**

Day
3

Oral Language: Environmental Print

Point out the signs in the story.

What kinds of signs do we see in our school?

Children may mention exit signs, restroom
signs, classroom numbers or signs with
teachers' names, office sign, nurse's office
sign, and a sign for the gym. Children who
speak other languages may know other
words for some signs.

Discuss why signs are important and how signs help keep
us safe.

Tell children as they move around their neighborhood to
take notice of different signs that they see. Invite them to
share their findings with the class.

long *e: ea* and inflected ending *-ed*

— high-frequency/tested vocabulary

Day 3

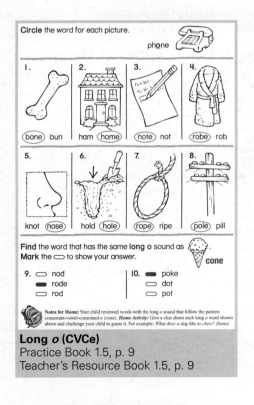

Circle the word for each picture.

phone

1. bone bun
2. ham home
3. note not
4. robe rob
5. knot nose
6. hold hole
7. rope ripe
8. pole pill

Find the word that has the same **long o** sound as
Mark the ⬭ to show your answer.

cone

9. ⬭ nod
   ⬛ rode
   ⬛ rod
10. ⬛ poke
    ⬭ dot
    ⬭ pot

Notes for Home: Your child reviewed words with the long *o* sound that follow the pattern consonant-vowel-consonant-*e (cone)*. **Home Activity:** Give a clue about each long *o* word shown above and challenge your child to guess it. For example: *What does a dog like to chew? (bone)*

Long *o* (CVCe)
Practice Book 1.5, p. 9
Teacher's Resource Book 1.5, p. 9

Long *e: ea*
Inflected Ending *-ed*

▶ Phonics Practice Activities

Careful observation of these activities will provide a basis for the Ongoing Assessment on page 41b.

Group Activity Write the following story on the board and read it aloud. Ask volunteers to circle words with long *e: ea* and underline words with inflected ending *-ed*.

> I <u>cooked</u> green (beans)
> I <u>peeled</u> a (peach)
> I <u>boiled</u> water for (tea)
> When do we (eat)?

Have the group paint a mural of cooks making the meal described in the story.

Partners Draw a tick-tack-toe grid on the board. Let each player choose one long *e: ea* phonogram, such as *-eam, -eat, -eal, -eak*. Have the first player write a word using the phonogram in one of the squares. The second player writes a word using his or her phonogram in a square. The first player to write three rhyming words in a row wins.

	seal	
	meal	
deal	beam	team

Reread for Fluency

Echo Reading Have children reread *The Neat Green Cast* to gain fluency. Read each sentence aloud with expression, and have children echo you.

Phonics Reader

Review

Long *o* (CVCe)

▶ Long *o* Riddles

Write the words *home, cone, pole, bone, nose, rose, note,* and *rope* on word cards and place them in a box. Have children choose a word card and give clues to the rest of the class to guess the long *o* word. Repeat for the remaining cards.

After completing the game, add cards with words *not, frog, on, rock,* and *pod* to the box. Have children sort the words by vowel sound.

Spelling Inflected Ending -ed Words

► Practice with Writing

Have children write the following words on index cards: *ask, call,* and *clean.*
Tell children to add the inflected ending *-ed* and write sentences for the words.

Look at each word. Say it.
Listen for the -ed ending.

		Write each word.	Check it.
1.	ask	ask	ask
2.	call	call	call
3.	clean	clean	clean
4.	asked	asked	asked
5.	called	called	called
6.	cleaned	cleaned	cleaned

Word Wall Words
Write each word.

7.	think	think	think
8.	only	only	only

Notes for Home: Your child spelled words with and without the ending *-ed,* as well as two frequently-used words: *think, only.* **Home Activity:** Have your child use each spelling word in a sentence. Check that your child uses *-ed* words to describe actions in the past.

Spelling
Practice Book 1.5, p. 10
Teacher's Resource Book 1.5, p. 10

Word Wall

Practice High-Frequency Words

Read to the Beat Say a word from the Word Wall. Then, say the first letter of the word. Use your hand to "beat" the number of letters in the word. For example, say *think.* Then say *t* and tap out four beats for *h, i, n,* and *k.* Ask a volunteer to spell the word aloud. Repeat for other Word Wall words.

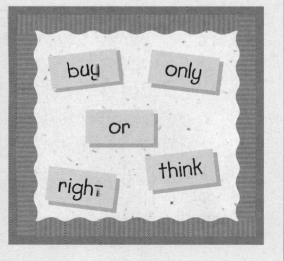

Optional Resources

Phonics
Phonics Workbook, pp. 126–129
Phonics Manipulatives Kit
Phonics Sourcebook, pp. 1–82

High-Frequency Words
High-Frequency Word Cards
Phonics Sourcebook, pp. 90–99

ORAL LANGUAGE

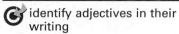

Children will

- identify adjectives in their writing
- use multiple-meaning words
- write about a movie, play, or TV show

Day 3

Expand Vocabulary

▶ Identify and Use Multiple-Meaning Words

Return to *Arthur's Reading Race* on page 22. Read to children the sentence *I can teach YOU to read too.* Write the word *can* on the board. Explain that this word has two meanings: "being able" and "a kind of container."

Have children say sentences with the word *can,* such as *I can read a book,* and *I opened the soup can.*

Write the following multiple-meaning words along with their meanings on the board. Have children say sentences using the words with their different meanings. (Possible sentences: The <u>school</u> of fish swam away. I go to <u>school</u> each day. Wear your seatbelt to keep <u>safe</u>. I put my money in a <u>safe</u>.)

<u>school</u>	<u>safe</u>
a group of fish	away from danger
place where you learn	a place to keep money

WRITING

Write About a Movie, Play, or TV Show

▶ Modeled Writing

Tell children you're going to ask them to write a report about the movie, play, or TV show they told about in yesterday's Oral Language activity.

Model Write four or five sentences, such as those below, telling about a movie, play, or TV show you've seen.

> I went to see the play <u>Cinderella</u>. I enjoyed it because the costumes were beautiful. The story was about a sweet girl with a mean stepmother and stepsisters. There was a handsome prince who throws a huge ball. He marries Cinderella at the end.

As you write, model these strategies:
- Give an opinion.
- Give a brief story synopsis.
- Keep sentences simple.
- Use adjectives.

Independent Writing Have children write at least three or four sentences about the movie, play, or TV show they told about yesterday in Oral Language.

Peer Conference Have partners read to each other their sentences about a movie, play, or TV show. Suggest they tell one another what they liked best about each other's writing.

You may wish to bind children's work into a class book.

Writer's Checklist

Did you . . .

✓ give an opinion?
✓ keep the story part brief?
✓ use adjectives?
✓ use proper end punctuation?

Self-Selected Reading and Read Aloud · D.E.A.R. · *Drop Everything And Read*

Read aloud *Night City* by Monica Wellington. After reading, discuss with children what they liked or disliked about the book.

Grammar: Adjectives

Review Adjectives Write the word *big* on the chalkboard. Explain that *big* is an adjective because it can describe a person, place, or thing. Have children suggest sentences with the word *big*, such as *The big dog barked*, and write these on the board.

Make an Adjective List Have children return to their writing about a movie, play or TV show. Ask them to fill in a chart, such as the one below, with adjectives and nouns they used.

Adjectives (describing words)	Nouns (person, place, thing)
beautiful	costumes
sweet	girl
mean	stepmother
handsome	prince
huge	ball

Pick the adjective from the box that matches each picture. Write it on the line.

sad   black   three   tall   small

1. **tall** man
2. **black** cat
3. **sad** doll
4. **small** dog
5. **three** ducks

Notes for Home: Your child used adjectives to describe objects. *Home Activity:* Say an adjective that describes color, shape, size, kind, or number (*white, round, small, happy,* or *five*). Have your child use that adjective to describe a person or object.

Adjectives
Practice Book 1.5, p. 11
Teacher's Resource Book 1.5, p. 11

Day 3

❄ Meeting Individual Needs

ESL	Intervention	Challenge	Other Ways to Learn
Show children objects in the classroom that can all be described with the same adjective, such as *long pencil, long ruler,* and *long string.* Point out that adjectives in sentences in English often come directly before the noun, but never directly after. Have children use the phrases in sentences. **(Skill Support)**	Write sentences with adjectives on chart paper. Read these aloud to children. Have children use colored pencils to circle the adjectives. **(Skill Support)**	Children reread *Arthur's Reading Race* looking for sentences where they can add an adjective. Children write the sentences with the added adjectives on sentence strips, including the page number of the original sentence. They can share and compare their sentences. **(Differentiated Learning Centers)**	Write adjectives such as *red, smooth, light,* and *soft* on index cards. Place each index card on a counter or some other place in the classroom. Have children find objects in the classroom that the adjectives describe and place the proper index card by the object. **(Kinesthetic)**

Reader Response

Student Book, pp. 42–43

Let's Talk

Personal Response You can begin the discussion using your own response. For example, say:

On page 18, I see the word *Jump* written on the book Arthur is reading.

Continue as children share their responses.

Let's Think

Critical Response Children may say that D. W. really can read because she reads the ten words, or that she can't read because she reads only the words on the signs. Children may say that D. W. can tell what the signs say because of the signs' color, shape, or location.

Test Prep

Let's Write

Written Response Discuss with children how to play the game "I Spy." Choose an object or a picture in the classroom and play a round of "I Spy" with a volunteer. For example, say *I spy something round. It is red and juicy.* (an apple)

After children finish writing their clues, organize them in small groups to read their clues aloud and play "I Spy."

Features for this writing product are listed below 4 in the Scoring Rubric.

Go on a Word Hunt

Creative Response Have children find and sort words from old magazines and newspapers. To make the words easier to handle, you may provide index cards and tape so that children can tape each word to a card. Tell children to look for words for at least two or three different kinds of things.

After children finish sorting their words, have them go through each pile, reading the words aloud.

Use the **Selection Test** in Practice Book 1.5, pages 13–14 or Teacher's Resource Book 1.5, pages 13–14.

Arthur's Reading Race, page 42

Scoring Rubric for Written Response	
4	**3**
• clearly focuses on the chosen object • gives strong clues for the object • expresses clues in complete sentences • begins sentences with capital letters and ends with correct punctuation	• focuses on the chosen object • gives fairly strong clues for the object • expresses most clues in complete sentences • may have poorly formed capital letter at beginning or incorrect punctuation at end of one or two sentences
2	**1**
• attempts to focus on the chosen object • gives minor clues for the object • may be missing parts of some clues • may be missing capital letter at beginning or punctuation at end of some sentences	• is unclear about the chosen object • uses irrelevant clues • clues are made up of disconnected words or phrases • lacks both capital letters and end punctuation

Day 4

Go on a Word Hunt

Arthur and D.W. hunted for words.
You and a partner can too. Here's how:

1. Look in magazines and newspapers for words you can sort. They might be words for colors, foods, cities, names, and animals.
2. Cut out the words and mix them up.
3. Take turns picking a word and putting it in the right pile.

43

Arthur's Reading Race, page 43

Skills in Context

Review Plot

Tell children that all stories have a plot, and the plot is what happens in the story. Then have three children stand at the front of the room with cards reading *beginning, middle,* and *end.* Stand behind the child with the beginning card and ask someone to tell what happened at the beginning of *Arthur's Reading Race.* Repeat for *middle* and *end.* Children may also record the beginning, middle, and end of the story in a short paragraph or in a chart story.

Reread for Fluency

Selection Audio Have children listen to the CD or tape of *Arthur's Reading Race* as they follow along in their books.

CD 6/Tape 21, Side 1

Partner Reading Have partners reread *Arthur's Reading Race,* taking the roles of Arthur and D.W. Tell children to read carefully, reading only those lines that belong to their character. Then have them read the story again, switching roles.

Day
4

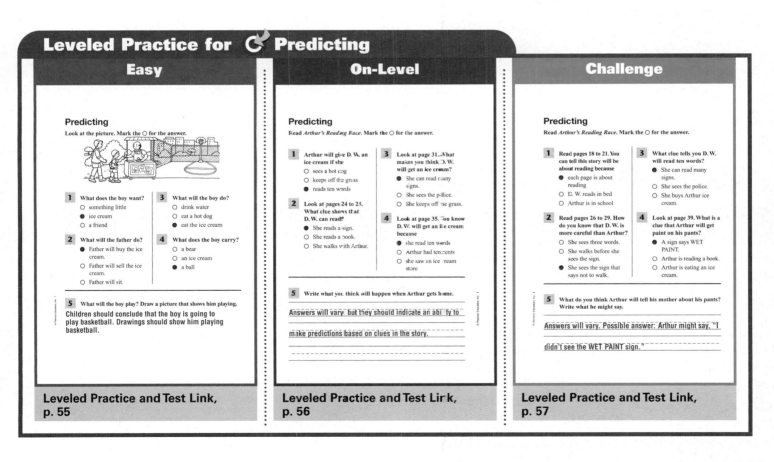

Leveled Practice for Predicting

Easy

Predicting

Look at the picture. Mark the ○ for the answer.

1. What does the boy want?
   ○ something little
   ● ice cream
   ○ a friend

2. What will the father do?
   ● Father will buy the ice cream.
   ○ Father will sell the ice cream.
   ○ Father will sit.

3. What will the boy do?
   ○ drink water
   ○ eat a hot dog
   ● eat the ice cream

4. What does the boy carry?
   ○ a bear
   ○ an ice cream
   ● a ball

5. What will the boy play? Draw a picture that shows him playing.
Children should conclude that the boy is going to play basketball. Drawings should show him playing basketball.

Leveled Practice and Test Link, p. 55

On-Level

Predicting

Read *Arthur's Reading Race.* Mark the ○ for the answer.

1. Arthur will give D. W. an ice cream if she
   ○ sees a hot dog
   ○ keeps off the grass
   ● reads ten words

2. Look at pages 24 to 25. What clue shows that D. W. can read?
   ● She reads a sign.
   ○ She reads a book.
   ○ She walks with Arthur.

3. Look at page 31. What makes you think D. W. will get an ice cream?
   ● She can read many signs.
   ○ She sees the police.
   ○ She keeps off the grass.

4. Look at page 35. You know D. W. will get an ice cream because
   ● she read ten words
   ○ Arthur had ten cents
   ○ she saw an ice cream store

5. Write what you think will happen when Arthur gets home.
Answers will vary, but they should indicate an ability to make predictions based on clues in the story.

Leveled Practice and Test Link, p. 56

Challenge

Predicting

Read *Arthur's Reading Race.* Mark the ○ for the answer.

1. Read pages 18 to 21. You can tell this story will be about reading because
   ● each page is about reading
   ○ D. W. reads in bed
   ○ Arthur is in school

2. Read pages 26 to 29. How do you know that D. W. is more careful than Arthur?
   ○ She sees three words.
   ○ She walks before she sees the sign.
   ● She sees the sign that says not to walk.

3. What clue tells you D. W. will read ten words?
   ● She can read many signs.
   ○ She sees the police.
   ○ She buys Arthur ice cream.

4. Look at page 39. What is a clue that Arthur will get paint on his pants?
   ● A sign says WET PAINT.
   ○ Arthur is reading a book.
   ○ Arthur is eating an ice cream.

5. What do you think Arthur will tell his mother about his pants? Write what he might say.
Answers will vary. Possible answer: Arthur might say, "I didn't see the WET PAINT sign."

Leveled Practice and Test Link, p. 57

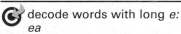

Children will

- decode words with long *e: ea*
- decode compound words
- spell words with inflected ending *-ed*
- recognize high-frequency words

Skills Trace

Compound Words

Introduce/Teach	TE: 1.4 168l; 1.5 156l
Practice	PB: 1.4 84; 1.5 15, 68; 1.6 31
Reteach/Review	TE: 1.4 175c, AR19; 1.5 **43a,** 163c, 187a, 189a, 191c, AR17; 1.6 73a
Test	Skills Test, Unit 6 Benchmark Test, Unit 6

Long *e: ea*
Inflected Ending *-ed*

►Reteach

Write *leaf, seat, beach, back, tune, neat, meal, rain, read* on the board. Remind children that long *e* can be spelled *ea*. Ask children to blend the listed words and raise their hands when they say a word with long *e*.

Write the following math sentences on the board: *pick + ed, ask + ed, call + ed, jump + ed.* Tell children to "add" the ending to each word and say the answer.

See page AR11 of this Teacher's Edition for additional **reteach activities.**

Review
Compound Words

Reread the Big Book *Rabbits & Raindrops* or a book of your choice with the class. Ask children to listen for compound words. Remind children that these words are two words put together to make one word. As you read the book, have children come up to the board and write the compound word and its two parts.

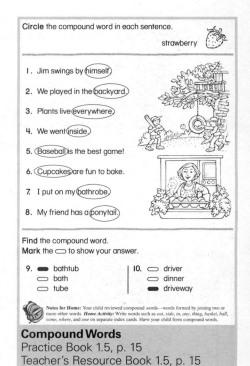

Compound Words
Practice Book 1.5, p. 15
Teacher's Resource Book 1.5, p. 15

❄ Meeting Individual Needs

ESL	Intervention	Challenge	Other Ways to Learn
Provide picture/word cards of *ea* words such as *peach, leaf, seat, beat, east.* Help children underline the *ea* and read each word. Then mix the cards, cover the pictures, and have children read each word. **(Phonics Support)** See also *Adding English.* ESL	Make a peach out of orange construction paper and write *each* on it. Show how adding letter card *p* makes the word *peach.* Have children add these letter cards to *each* and read the words: *b, t, r.* Repeat the activity using a cutout of a piece of meat for *eat: b, f, h, m, n, s.* **(Phonics Support)**	Children work in teams to complete three-column charts in which they collect words with the *-ed* endings: no changes, drop silent *e,* double final consonant. **(Tiered Assignments)**	Children work together to create a collage of magazine pictures of foods that contain the sound of long *e* (peach, bean, cream, meat, treat). **(Visual/Spatial)**

Day 4

Spelling Inflected Ending *-ed* Words

▶ Partner Spelling Practice

Children work in pairs. Supply each pair with cards in the shape of a telephone. One spelling word is written on each card. One child says, "Ring, ring," and reads the word. The partner says, "You called," and spells the word. After children switch roles, they check the words spelled against their cards and correct any mistakes.

Spelling
Practice Book 1.5, p. 16
Teacher's Resource Book 1.5, p. 16

Day 4

Word Wall

Review High-Frequency Words

Word Wall Conversations Invite children to pretend to be either Arthur or D.W. and use this week's words in a conversation as they are taking a neighborhood walk. Example sentences might include: "We can buy ice cream today!" or "D.W., what do you think that sign says?"

Optional Resources

Phonics
Phonics Workbook, pp. 126–128, 130
Phonics Manipulatives Kit
Phonics Sourcebook, pp. 1–78
Reading Road Show
AstroWord CD-ROM, Compound Words

High-Frequency Words
High-Frequency Word Cards
Phonics Sourcebook, pp. 90–99

Language Arts

Student Book, pp. 44–45

Adjectives

Have children read aloud with you the definitions of *adjective* and *noun*. Have the three example sentences read. After each sentence, identify the highlighted word in dark type as the adjective, or word that tells more about the noun that follows it.

Talk

Read aloud the directions with children. Have them name the people, places, animals, and things in the library picture. For each noun mentioned, children should suggest one or two adjectives that describe it.

Write

Guide children as they copy the sentences and underline the adjectives. When everyone has finished, review the responses and have children correct their mistakes.

Have children write sentences of their own that include adjectives. Remind them that adjectives can tell more about the size, color, or shape of something. Children may want to illustrate their sentences.

Use the Teacher's Resource Book 1.5 pages 17–18 for **reteaching** and extra practice for adjectives.

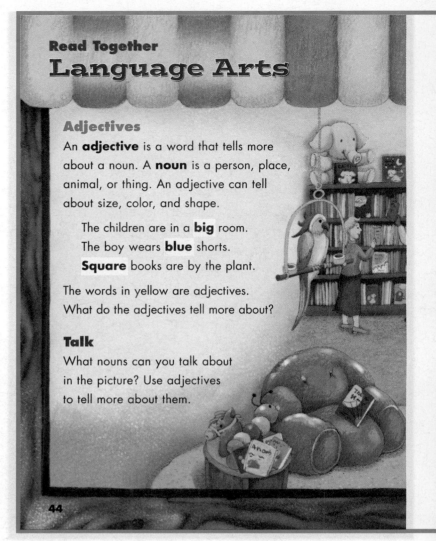

Read Together
Language Arts

Adjectives

An **adjective** is a word that tells more about a noun. A **noun** is a person, place, animal, or thing. An adjective can tell about size, color, and shape.

The children are in a **big** room.
The boy wears **blue** shorts.
Square books are by the plant.

The words in yellow are adjectives. What do the adjectives tell more about?

Talk

What nouns can you talk about in the picture? Use adjectives to tell more about them.

44

Arthur's Reading Race, **page 44**

Day 4

Write

Write the sentences. Draw a line under each adjective.

1. **The green parrot talks.**
2. **The girl wears a striped sweater.**
3. **Toys are on low tables.**

Write your own sentences. Use an adjective in each one. Draw a line under the adjectives.

45

Arthur's Reading Race, page 45

Study Skill

Map

On chart paper, draw and label a simple map of Arthur and D.W.'s neighborhood. Remind children that a map shows where places are located and how to get from one place to another. Read aloud the street signs and names of places and then model how to interpret the map.

Model Your Thinking

 On this map, I can trace the route that Arthur and D.W. took, starting at their house and ending at the ice-cream shop. The map shows me the places they passed and the names of the streets they walked along.

Have children describe the route by noting the names of the locations and streets. Then have them tell where each location is in relation to a few others.

Practice Ask partners to make their own maps of real or imaginary neighborhoods. Circulate to monitor how well children understand maps.

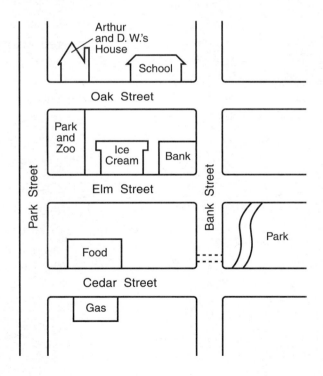

Day
4

Objectives

Children will

- make predictions about a story
- use sound-symbol relationships to read decodable text
- recognize high-frequency words
- read with fluency and understanding

Meeting Individual Needs

ESL

To prepare children for the oral reading assessment, choose one or two pages from the text. Ask children to tell you what is happening on those pages. Have children read the pages independently or do a paired reading.

Assess Oral Reading

▶ Prepare for the Assessment

Materials Children may choose from *A Real Gift, Arthur's Reading Race*, or any stories or books they've read this week. Have children prepare for the assessment by rereading the selection of their choice independently.

▶ Listen to Individual Readers

Have children read aloud to you. Use the chart on the following page to track children's abilities. The blank column is for any additional skills you want to assess.

Check Comprehension To assess children's ability to make predictions about a story, ask a question such as:

How did you know that D.W. would read ten words?

See page AR12 of this Teacher's Edition to **reteach** predicting.

You may prefer to assess only a portion of your class each week, perhaps half the class one week, and the other half the next.

▶ While You Assess

While you work with individuals, other children may choose from the following activities or the activities listed in the Cross-Curricular Work Stations on pages 10g–h.

Before They Read to You

Children should reread the chosen book, practicing until they feel they can read it well.

Children may listen to the CD or tape of *Arthur's Reading Race* or *A Real Gift* to hear a model of fluent reading.

Selection Audio

CD 6/Tape 21, Side 1

After They Read to You

Children can complete a Reading Log like the one shown or use Practice Book 1.5 page 98, or the Teacher's Resource Book 1.6 page 112.

Children can also complete the phonics activities on page 45c.

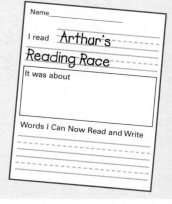

Name_____

I read *Arthur's Reading Race*

It was about

Words I Can Now Read and Write

Optional Resources

Assessment
The Assessment Handbook has information on running records.

Day 5

Oral Reading Checklist

Student Name	Reads Long e Words (ea)	Reads Words with -ed Endings	Uses Decoding Strategies	Reads High-Frequency Words	Makes Predictions	Reads with Expression	Demonstrates Reading for Meaning	Comments
1								
2								
3								
4								
5								
6								
7								
8								
9								
10								
11								
12								
13								
14								
15								
16								
17								
18								
19								
20								
21								
22								
23								
24								
25								

Day
5

Long *e: ea*
Inflected Ending *-ed*

▶ Phonics Practice Activities

Word Sea Have children color a large sheet of paper light blue and decorate it with sea creatures and plants. Tell children to write long *e* spelled *ea* words and inflected ending *-ed* words from this week's stories in their "sea."

Phonics Take-Home Reader Have children practice reading the book with a partner before taking it home.

The Neat Green Cast

by Dona R. McDuff
illustrated by Clive Scruton

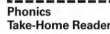

Phonics Take-Home Reader

Spelling Test

Have children number their papers. Read the underlined word, read the sentence, then repeat the underlined word.

1. I must <u>clean</u> my room.
2. We <u>asked</u> him to go with us to the park.
3. Birds <u>call</u> to one another.
4. We <u>cleaned</u> up after art class.
5. I always <u>ask</u> lots of questions.
6. I <u>called</u> to my friend.

High-Frequency Words

7. I <u>think</u> hard at school.
8. She has <u>only</u> five cents.

Challenge Words

9. I will <u>teach</u> my sister to read.
10. I like to keep my desk <u>neat</u>.

Word Wall

Practice High-Frequency Words

Write and Draw Dictate the following sentences. Say the words slowly so children have time to locate them on the Word Wall and write them.

I think I will buy milk today.
Do I turn right or left?
I have only one sister.

Have children draw pictures to illustrate their sentences.

buy only or think right

Day 5

ORAL LANGUAGE

Speaking: Retell a Story

Have children retell to the whole class the story they told their partners on Day 2 of Oral Language. Have classmates guess the title of the movie, play, or TV show.

WRITING

Poster

▶ Interactive Writing

In this method of writing, you and children work together. While you write on the board, children write on their own papers. As you write, draw out the sounds in the words and encourage children to name the letters that stand for the sounds.

Make a Poster Children will make a poster to advertise their movie, play, or TV show. Begin a poster of the movie, play, or TV show you told children about on Day 2 of Oral Language. Use Interactive Writing techniques as you write. You may wish to make your poster similar to the one shown. Before children begin their own posters you might want to brainstorm with them a list of adjectives they could use. Write these on the board.

Independent Writing Have children write the title of their movie, play, or TV show on a poster. Tell them to include at least three adjectives and an illustration. If you wrote a list of adjectives on the board during Interactive Writing, remind them to use the list. You might display posters in the classroom.

 Portfolio Children may wish to select a piece of writing from this week to put in their portfolios.

Objectives

Children will

 retell a story of a movie, play, or TV show
- write using adjectives

Speaker's Checklist

Did you . . .

✓ give a clear beginning, middle, and ending of the story?
✓ tell only the important parts?
✓ speak clearly with enthusiasm?
✓ use good eye contact?

Self-Selected Reading and Read Aloud   D.E.A.R.

Have children select a new book or reread an old favorite. Read aloud the children's posters.

Day
5

Optional Resources

High-Frequency Words
High-Frequency Word Cards
Phonics Sourcebook, pp. 90–99

Oral Language
Adding English: ESL Teacher's Guide

Assessment
The Assessment Handbook has information on informal assessment and grading.

Lesson Overview

Phonics Story

A Big Day for Jay
pages 46–53

Selection Audio

The **Phonics Story** . . .

- introduces 🔄 **Long *a*: *ai*, *ay*** and **Contractions**

- introduces the high-frequency words

  don't from hear live when

- builds fluency

- builds decoding skills

> **Use the Phonics Story to prepare children for reading the Main Selection.**

Main Selection

Lost!
pages 54–81

Selection Audio

The **Main Selection** . . .

- introduces 🔄 **Compare and Contrast**

- practices 🔄 **Long *a*: *ai*, *ay*** and **Contractions**

- practices the high-frequency words

  don't from hear live when

TEST Format

Leveled Practice
in Test Format
for *Lost!*

 TARGET SKILL

Compare and Contrast

Lost!
David McPhail

Leveled Readers

 TARGET SKILL

Compare and Contrast
Tested Vocabulary

Easy	On-Level	Challenge
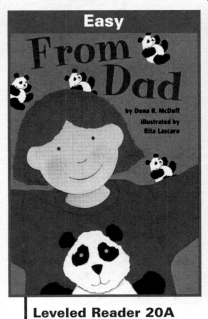 From Dad — by Dena R. McDuff, illustrated by Rita Lascaro	 House of Wood House of Snow — by Barbara Gannett, illustrated by Robin Moro	Take Me There

| **Leveled Reader 20A** | **Leveled Reader 20B** | **Leveled Reader 5C** |

For Guided Reading
see Teacher's Edition,
pp. LR7–LR12.

For instruction and leveled practice answers, see Teacher's Edition, pp. LR39–LR45.

Easy

Compare and Contrast
Look at the picture. Mark the ○ for the answer.

1 Who rides a big bike?
● a big bear
○ a girl
○ a little bear

3 Where is the little bear?
○ with the big bear
● with the girl
○ on the big bike

2 Who rides a small bike?
○ a little bear
● a girl
○ a big bear

4 How are the girl and big bear the same?
○ They are big.
○ They play ball.
● They ride bikes.

5 Draw two bears that are alike.
Children should draw two bears similar in size and features.

On-Level

Compare and Contrast
Read *Lost!* Mark the ○ for the answer.

1 How are the bear's home and the park alike?
● Both have trees.
○ Both have big buildings.
○ Both have friendly people.

3 How is the bear in the story like a real bear?
○ He rides a bus.
● He lives in a forest.
○ He talks to a boy.

2 How is the city different from the bear's home?
○ The city has more trees.
○ The city has more water.
● The city has many people.

4 The bear and the boy both
○ live in the city
● get lost
○ are big

5 Think about the bear's home and the boy's home. How are they the same?

Answers will vary, but children should compare their own home to a forest. Students might note that the boy's home is smaller, has walls and different rooms, and is protected from bad weather.

Practice for Leveled Readers

Easy

Compare and Contrast

Read the story *From Dad.* Then answer Numbers 1 through 5.

1 When the girl was five, her dad gave her
○ a panda.
○ a hug.
● a T-shirt.

3 How old is the girl at the end of the story?
○ five
● six
○ seven

2 How were things ALIKE each year?
● The girl wore the T-shirt.
○ The girl wore blue shoes.
○ The girl is little.

4 The T-shirt does not fit. What does the girl do?
○ She gives it to her sister.
● She puts it on her panda.
○ She throws it in the trash.

5 Look at page 3. Then look at page 11. How is the girl DIFFERENT? Use words from the story in your answer.

She is bigger.

Teacher's Edition, p. LR9

On-Level

Compare and Contrast

Read the story *House of Wood, House of Snow.* Then answer Numbers 1 through 5.

1 BOTH houses have
○ walls, sinks, stoves, tables.
● windows, doors, lamps, beds.
○ steps, tables, lamps, tubs.

3 How long does it take to make an igloo?
○ six hours
○ three days
● three hours

2 Who makes the igloo?
○ the father
○ the mother
● everyone

4 How does the girl feel about the two houses?
○ She likes to live in both houses.
○ She likes the igloo best.
● She wants one more wood house.

5 How are the two houses ALIKE? Use words from the story in your answer.

Both are full of friends.

Teacher's Edition, p. LR12

Challenge

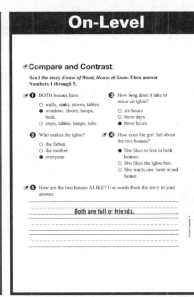

What's Happening?

Many things happened to Gunnar and Balto on their trip to Nome in 1925. But people did not find out about their trip right away. News did not travel as fast as it does today. Today news travels in many ways. Can you think of ways that you find out the news? Pretend you are a reporter. What would you write about Balto and Gunnar's trip to Nome? Answer these questions:

When you are finished writing, read your story to your class. What questions do they have?

Leveled Reader 5C, p. 13

Challenge

Compare and Contrast
Read *Lost!* Mark the ○ for the answer.

1 How are the bear's home and the city the same?
● They both have trees and water.
○ They both have buildings and many people.
○ They both have boats.

3 Both the bear and boy
○ read books
○ ride in a truck
● get lost

2 How is the city not like the bear's home?
○ The city has big trees and a lot of water.
● The city has big buildings and many people.
○ The city has a big forest.

4 The bear and the boy both feel
○ afraid of the forest
○ sleepy at the end
● afraid when they get lost

5 How are the bear and the boy not the same?

Answers will vary, but they should contrast the bear and the boy.

Children may mention that the boy is smaller and is a human being, while the bear is larger and an animal.

Leveled Practice and Test Link, pp. 58–60, *Lost!*

Additional Leveled Resources

Phonics Resources

Phonics Reader 26

Phonics Take-Home Readers in Reproducible Format

Book 26

Decodable Readers 34 and 35

Waterford Early Reading Program
Level 2
Lessons 13, 44

Language Support

Adding English
pp. 169–176

Ten Important Sentences
p. 32

Trade Books for Self-Selected Reading

Easy

Hide and Seek
by Neil Morris.
Little, Brown,
1982

The Hat
by Jan Brett.
Putnam,
1997

Where Are You Going, Little Mouse?
by Robert Kraus.
Greenwillow,
1986

On-Level

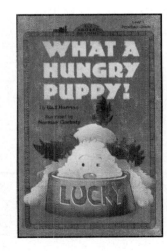

This Is the Way We Go to School
by Edith Baer.
Scholastic,
1992
Trade Book Library Title

The Big Hello
by Janet Schulman.
Mulberry,
1990

What a Hungry Puppy!
by Gail Herman.
Price Stern Sloan,
1993

Challenge

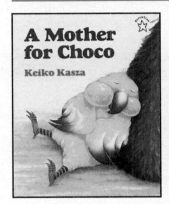

A Mother for Choco
by Keiko Kasza.
Paper Star,
1996
Trade Book Library Title

Lost
by Paul Brett Johnson and Celeste Lewis.
Orchard Books,
1996

The Day the Dog Said, "Cock-a-Doodle-Doo!"
by David McPhail.
Scholastic,
1997

Self-Selected Reading

- Allow 10–20 minutes per day for self-selected reading.
- For additional titles and for a read-aloud suggestion, see pp. AR24–AR25.
- For daily self-selected reading suggestions, see the 5-Day Planner, pp. 46e–46f.
- For activity ideas and management tips, see p. AR25.

- Have children select materials to read for pleasure, such as favorite books and stories.

Developmental Reading Assessment (DRA) from Celebration Press, an imprint of Pearson Learning, helps teachers by providing and documenting students' development as readers over time.

5-Day Planner

Reading

Comprehension

Vocabulary

Fluency

Independent Reading

Phonics/Word Study

Phonemic Awareness

Phonics

Spelling

High-Frequency Words

Oral Language

Speaking, Listening, Viewing

Oral Vocabulary

Writing

Grammar, Usage, Mechanics

Your State Standards

 Customize your week with the Teacher's Resource Planner CD-ROM!

Day 1

Activate Prior Knowledge, p. 46j

Phonics pp. 46k–46l

Phonemic Awareness: Long *a: ai, ay*

✓ **Phonics:** Introduce Long *a: ai, ay;* Contractions
PHONICS SONGS AND RHYMES CHART "Oh, What a Day!"

Spelling: Long *a: ai, ay*
 Pretest
Work with Spelling Pattern

High-Frequency Words: Introduce
don't, from, hear, live, when

Reading pp. 46m–53

Story Vocabulary

Read Pupil Edition PHONICS STORY:
A Big Day for Jay

Independent Reading
Self-Selected Reading, pp. 46d; AR24

Oral Language pp. 46m, 53a

Build Oral Language

Expand Vocabulary: Discuss Words That Have Opposite Meanings

Writing pp. 46i, 53a–53b

Shared Writing: List

Handwriting: *Yy*

Daily Writing Prompt: Make a sign about a lost pet.

Day 2

Phonics pp. 53c–53d

✓ **Phonics:** Practice Long *a: ai, ay;* Contractions

Apply Phonics: Read the
PHONICS READER *Who Rang the Bell?* or
DECODABLE READER 34

Spelling: Writing for Sounds

High-Frequency Words: Practice

PB 1.5: Phonics, pp. 19, 20; High-Frequency Words, p. 21
TRB 1.5: Phonics, pp. 21, 22; High-Frequency Words, p. 23

Reading pp. 53e–53f

✓ **Comprehension:** Compare and Contrast
READ ALOUD "Do Animals Get Lost?"

Fluency: Reread the PHONICS STORY: *A Big Day for Jay*

PB 1.5: Compare and Contrast, p. 22
TRB 1.5: Compare and Contrast, p. 24

Independent Reading
Self-Selected Reading, pp. 46d; AR24

Oral Language p. 53g

 Speaking: Discuss How to Solve a Problem

Writing pp. 46i, 53g–53h

Modeled Writing: Interesting Sentences

✓ **Grammar:** Adjectives That Tell Color and Shape

PB 1.5: p. 23; **TRB 1.5:** p. 25

Daily Writing Prompt: Write about the sights and sounds at a fair or outdoor party.

 Target Skill    **Review Skill**    **Assessment**

PB Practice Book
TRB Teacher's Resource Book

pp. 58–60

Leveled Practice and Test Link in
TerraNova, SAT9, or ITBS format

Target Skills of the Week

Reading Compare and Contrast
Phonics Long *a: ai, ay*; Contractions
Oral Language Discuss How to Solve a Problem
Writing Adjectives That Tell Color and Shape

Day 3

Reading pp. 54a–81

Story Vocabulary

Read Pupil Edition MAIN SELECTION:
Lost!

✓ **Comprehension:** Compare and Contrast

Guided Reading Resources/Flexible Groups, pp. 54b; LR7–LR12
Leveled Readers 20A, 20B, 5C

PB 1.5: Vocabulary, p. 24
TRB 1.5: Vocabulary, p. 26

Independent Reading
Self-Selected Reading, pp. 46d; AR24

Phonics pp. 81a–81b

✓  **Phonics:** Practice Long *a: ai, ay*; Contractions

(Review) Long Vowels (CVCe)

Fluency: Reread the PHONICS READER
Who Rang the Bell? or DECODABLE
READER 35

Spelling: Practice with Writing

High-Frequency Words: Practice

PB 1.5: Phonics, p. 25; Spelling, p. 26
TRB 1.5: Phonics, p. 27; Spelling, p. 28

Oral Language pp. 54a, 81c

Build Oral Language

Expand Vocabulary: Antonyms

Writing pp. 46i, 81c–81d

Modeled Writing: Description of a Story Illustration

✓ **Grammar:** Adjectives That Tell Color and Shape

PB 1.5: p. 27; **TRB 1.5:** p. 29; **GPB:** p. 44

Daily Writing Prompt: List things to do if you get lost.

Day 4

Reading pp. 82–83

Read Together Pupil Edition
READER RESPONSE *Test Prep*

 Selection Test

PB 1.5: Selection Test pp. 29–30
TRB 1.5: Selection Test, pp. 31–32

(Review) **Comprehension:** Setting

Fluency: Reread the MAIN SELECTION

Guided Reading Resources/Flexible Groups, pp. 54b; LR7–LR12
Leveled Readers 20A, 20B, 5C

Independent Reading
Self-Selected Reading, pp. 46d; AR24

Phonics pp. 83a–83b

✓ **Phonics:** Reteach Long *a: ai, ay*; Contractions

(Review) Initial Digraphs

Spelling: Partner Practice

High-Frequency Words: Review

PB 1.5: Phonics, p. 31; Spelling, p. 32
TRB 1.5: Phonics, p. 33; Spelling, p. 34

Oral Language pp. 84–85

Speaking: Talk About Adjectives

Writing pp. 46i, 84–85

✓ **Grammar:** Adjectives That Tell Color and Shape

Writing: Identify Adjectives That Tell Color and Shape

TRB 1.5: pp. 35–36; GPB: p. 45

Daily Writing Prompt: Write about the place where you live.

Day 5

Reading pp. 85a–85b

 Assess Accuracy and Comprehension: Accuracy and Comprehension Assessment

Guided Reading Resources/Flexible Groups, pp. 54b; LR7–LR12
Leveled Readers 20A, 20B, 5C

Independent Reading
Self-Selected Reading, pp. 46d; AR24

Phonics p. 85c

✓ **Phonics:** Practice Long *a: ai, ay*; Contractions

Apply Phonics: Read the PHONICS
TAKE-HOME READER

Spelling: Long *a: ai, ay*

 Posttest

High-Frequency Words: Practice

Oral Language p. 85d

Speaking: Discuss How to Solve a Problem

Writing pp. 46i, 85d

Interactive Writing: Postcard
Portfolio

Daily Writing Prompt: How would your family describe you if you got lost? Write what they would say.

Cross-Curricular Work Stations

Letters and Sounds

Find Your Way to Long *a* 15 minutes

Materials: outline of an *-ai* trail and an *-ay* way

Learning Styles Individual, Visual, Verbal

Provide an outline of an *-ai* trail and an *-ay* way for each child to use. Invite children to follow the trail to *ai*, or go all the way to *ay*, by writing long *a* words in the appropriate spaces so the spaces create a path leading from each sign to the correct destination.

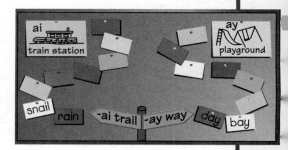

Career Link

Ideas for bringing the school and community together

Field Experiences
walk in town
hike in woods or state park
police department

Guest Speakers
police officer
park ranger or trail leader

Math

Find Your Way 15 minutes

Materials: game board, index cards, pencils, game markers

Learning Styles Logical, Social, Visual

Draw a game board, such as the one shown. Distribute one copy to each pair of children, along with 7 index cards. Have partners work together to write addition and subtraction problems on each card. Then have them shuffle the cards and put them facedown in a pile. Children take turns choosing a card and finding the answer and moving that number of spaces. The first player to reach the end is the winner.

Media

Solving Problems 15 minutes

Materials: paper and pencils

Learning Styles Social, Verbal

The bear in *Lost!* asks the child to help him solve a problem. Characters in TV and movie stories have problems too. Have partners describe a movie, video, or TV story in which a character has help solving a problem. Have them draw and label a picture of the character and the helper.

 ESL One child can act out a helping scene as a partner narrates the action.

Establish guidelines for your students' safe and responsible use of the Internet. See the Scott Foresman Internet Guide for tips.

INTERNET SAFETY

Technology

AstroWord   15 minutes

Learning Styles Visual, Social

Have students use AstroWord to strengthen understanding of initial digraphs. Children can work individually or in groups to apply these skills in activities and games in the AstroWord Factory.

Reading Web Site  15 minutes

Learning Styles Visual, Individual

Children can visit the Scott Foresman *Reading* Web site (sfreading.com) for current hyperlinks to relevant electronic texts that can be used for an Internet Workshop investigation of finding one's way. Also see the Scott Foresman Internet Guide for additional information on the Internet Workshop method.

sfreading.com

Art

Finding Help   15 minutes

Materials: paper, markers

Learning Styles Linguistic, Kinesthetic, Visual

Have small groups brainstorm things they could use to help them find their way, such as flashlights, street signs, or maps. Have children choose one of the items to draw and write a sentence about how the object can help someone find his or her way. When finished, children can share their artwork with the group and read their sentences.

flashlight

A flashlight helps you see in the dark.

Science

Follow Directions 15 minutes

Materials: compass, paper, pencils

Learning Styles Logical, Visual, Spatial

Label the walls in the room *north, east, south*, and *west* and demonstrate how a compass is used. Small groups can then play a guessing game, taking turns giving others in their group clues that include the directions. Children could also write their clues and have others pick them at random to solve.

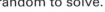 You may also want to label the four directions in Spanish and help all the children pronounce the words: *norte* (north), *sur* (south), *este* (east), *oeste* (west).

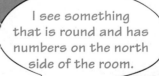

I see something that is round and has numbers on the north side of the room.

Daily Routines

Message Board

Day One

Today you will hear a song about a lost dog. Do you know someone who lost a pet?

Have children share personal experiences or those of others they know.

Have children find the high-frequency word *don't* and have them tell which word is an adjective. *(scared)* Have children find the contraction. *(don't)*

Day Two

You read a story about a boy who gets lost. Don't you think he was scared?

Day Three

Now you will hear a story about a bear far away from home. Don't you want to hear it? When were you far from home?

Have children find the high-frequency words *from, when,* and *hear.* Ask children to find a long *a* word spelled with *ay.* *(away)*

Have children find the high-frequency word *when* and the spelling word *play.* Have them tell which words are adjectives. *(little, brown, new)*

Day Four

The little boy helps when the brown bear is lost. They also play. What would you play with a new friend?

Day Five

Someone lost his way in these stories. How could you help if someone lost his or her way near where you live?

Have children find the high-frequency word *live* and the spelling word *way.*

Journal Writing

Day One
Make a sign about a lost pet.

Day Two
Write about the sights and sounds at a fair or outdoor party.

Day Three
List things to do if you get lost.

Day Four
Write about the place where you live.

Day Five
How would your family describe you if you got lost? Write what they would say.

Family Times

Send home the newsletter with daily instructional activities to reinforce this week's skills.

Practice Book 1.5, pp. 17–18
Teacher's Resource Book 1.5, pp. 19–20

Activate Prior Knowledge

▶ Assess Prior Knowledge

Discuss Finding Our Way Have children recall a time when someone they know was lost. Talk about a time when you or a family member was lost too. Begin the discussion with these questions:

What would it feel like to be lost?

What would you do?

▶ Build Background

Read Aloud

Preview the Song Discuss with children how a dog might get lost. Then help them set a purpose for listening. Ask:

What things could you do to find the dog?

Read the Song Sing this song for children and have them pretend they need to find a lost dog. They can predict where he may be.

Objectives

Children will

- activate prior knowledge of topic: Finding Our Way
- relate literature to experiences in their own life
- draw on experiences of others to form a broader perspective of the topic
- set a purpose for listening

Day 1

Read Aloud

Oh Where, Oh Where Has My Little Dog Gone?

Oh where, oh where has my little dog gone?
Oh where, oh where can he be?
With his ears cut short and his tail cut long;
Oh where, oh where can he be?

Long *a: ai, ay*

▶ Develop Phonemic Awareness

Sing or Read the Rhyme Chart Sing "Oh, What a Day!" to the tune of "The Goat," or play the CD or tape.

Focus on the Long *a* Sound Say:

The word *day* in the title ends with the /ā/ sound. This is the long *a* sound.

Repeat the song, singing one line at a time as children listen for words with the sound of long *a* they hear in *day*.

▶ Connect Sounds to Letters

Teach Point to *day* on the chart and have it read. Say:

The letters *ay* in *day* stand for the sound /ā/. What do we call the sound /ā/? (the long *a* sound)

CD 2/Tape 13, Side 2
Phonics Songs and Rhymes Audio

Oh, What a Day!

It's Saturday . . .
We swim all day . . .
We like to play . . .
Down by the bay . . .

It starts to rain . . .
And we can't stay . . .
We waddle home . . .
But lose our way . . .

A kind gray snail . . .
Shows us the way . . .
We'll soon be home . . .
Oh, what a day!

Phonics Songs and Rhymes Chart 20

Have children repeat the sound /ā/ several times, stretching the sound as they say it. Follow a similar procedure with *rain* and the letters *ai*. You may want to review the long *a* CVCe pattern in words such as *take*.

Blending Practice Have children blend the sounds /b/ /ā/ to read *bay* and /s/ /n/ /ā/ /l/ to read *snail*. Have them continue decoding other *ai*, *ay* words such as *rain* and *play*.

Make New Words Write the words *day, rain,* and *snail* across the top of chart paper. Challenge children to name words that rhyme with these words and write their suggestions below the correct word. Have children decode the words on the chart. Add the words *bay* and *snail* to the chunking wall.

day	rain	snail
say	gain	pail
lay	pain	tail
pay	train	rail

Then have children change vowel letters to make words *sea, pea,* and *real.*

Day
1

Objectives

Children will

- ◉ identify and decode words with the sound of long *a: ai, ay*
- ◉ use structural cues to recognize contractions
- • spell words with long *a:* digraphs *ai, ay*
- • recognize high-frequency words

Skills Trace

◉ Long *a: ai, ay*

Introduce/Teach	TE: 1.5 46k
Practice	PB: 1.5 19, 58
Reteach/Review	TE: 1.5 53c, 81a, 83a, 85c, 151a, AR12
Test	Skills Test, Unit 5 Benchmark Test, Unit 5

❄ Meeting Individual Needs

Intervention

Phonemic Awareness Say /w/ /ā/ slowly. Have children blend the sounds together. Say each set of words slowly, sound by sound: *rain, peal, pain; hay, day, sea.* Have children blend each word and then say the word. Have them identify rhyming words in each set.

Phonics Generalization CVVC

When two vowels appear together in a word, the first one usually stands for its long vowel sound and the second is silent.

Phonics Generalization CVV

The letters *ay* usually stand for the long *a* sound.

Contractions

▶ Teach Contractions

Write the following on the board:

> He is sad.   He's sad.

Have children read both sentences and tell how they are different. Explain that the word *he's* in the second sentence is a shorter way of writing and saying two words. Let volunteers identify the two words in the first sentence *he's* replaces. *(he is)* Point out the apostrophe, explaining that it stands for no sound but shows that a letter or letters were left out to form the contraction.

▶ Make New Words

List these contractions on the board: *I'm, aren't, let's, don't.* Then write four sentences, each containing two words that can be replaced with one of the contractions. Have children read the sentences and replace two words in each sentence with one contraction.

Spelling Long *a: ai, ay*

Pretest Say the spelling word, use it in a sentence, repeat it, and allow children to write it. Have children check their pretests and correct misspelled words.

Work with the Spelling Pattern List the spelling words. Have children read the words and underline the letters that spell the long *a* sound. Have children use each word in a sentence.

Skills Trace

G Contractions

Introduce/Teach	TE: 1.3 162I; 1.5 **46I**
Practice	PB: 1.3 84; 1.4 47; 1.5 20, 63
Reteach/Review	TE: 1.3 169c, 181a, 183a, 185c, AR19; 1.4 107a; 1.5 53c, 81a, 83a, 85c, 153a, AR13
Test	Skills Test, Unit 5

Day 1

Spelling Words

say	way
play	wait
may	rain

High-Frequency

when	from

Challenge

don't	I'm

Word Wall

Introduce High-Frequency Words

Use word cards for *don't, from, hear, live,* and *when.* Invite volunteers to hold up a word card and make up a sentence for it. Then have children attach each word to the Word Wall under the appropriate beginning letter.

Review Have children make up a riddle whose answer is a word from the Word Wall.

don't   from

hear

when

live

Optional Resources

Waterford Early Reading Program
Level 2: Lessons 13, 44

Phonics
Phonics Workbook, pp. 131–133
Phonics Manipulatives Kit

High-Frequency Words
High-Frequency Word Cards
Phonics Sourcebook, pp. 90–99

 **A Big Day For Jay**

pp. 46–53

► Build Oral Language

Activate Prior Knowledge Have children share experiences from cultural gatherings or festivals. Ask:

> **What can you do to keep from getting lost in a crowd?**

Create a word web with children's responses, or use Graphic Organizer Transparency 5 (Web 2).

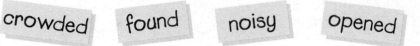

```
  have a              hold hands
meeting place
              How to Keep from
               Getting Lost
  have a              stay put
   buddy
```

Build Background Invite a police officer to visit the class and discuss ways to stay together in a crowd.

► Vocabulary

Introduce Story Vocabulary Use Vocabulary Chart 38, or write sentences on the board using each word. Read each sentence aloud.

crowded   **found**   **noisy**   **opened**   **knew**

Frame *knew.* Cover the *k* and have children read the word. Write *new* underneath it. Discuss the meanings of the homonyms.

Have children discuss the meanings of the words *crowded* and *found.*

Review High-Frequency Words Have children read each word as you point to it on the Word Wall. Have children identify the word that is a contraction. These words are also listed on page 228 of the Student Book.

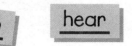

don't   **from**   **hear**   **live**   **when**

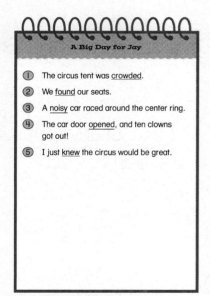

A Big Day for Jay

① The circus tent was <u>crowded</u>.

② We <u>found</u> our seats.

③ A <u>noisy</u> car raced around the center ring.

④ The car door <u>opened</u>, and ten clowns got out!

⑤ I just <u>knew</u> the circus would be great.

Story Vocabulary Chart 38

— high-frequency/tested vocabulary

▶ Reading Strategies

Preview and Predict Read the title and the name of the author and illustrator to children. Help children identify Jay and his family as they look at the first four pages.

> **Where are Jay and his family? How do you know?** (They are at a fair. There are rides, animals, foods, and lots of people.)

Have children support their answers with picture details.

Picture Walk Invite children to do a picture walk through all the pages of the story. Ask children what might happen in the story.

Set Purposes From the pictures and the title, children know the story is about a boy named Jay. Children may want to read to find out what happens to him.

Guide the Reading Have children read the first few pages of the selection, keeping their purposes in mind. Stop and check comprehension, using the questions provided. Have children read to page 49.

Phonics Story

A Big Day for Jay
by Lily Hong

It was noisy and crowded. Jay tugged at his dad. "When can we ride the Fire Dragon?" asked Jay. "I can't wait and I'm not afraid." His dad didn't hear him.

Selection Audio
CD 6/Tape 22, Side 1

About the Author and Illustrator

Lily Hong always knew she would write and illustrate children's books. She studied art in college and worked as a greeting-card artist before she became a freelance illustrator. Her first book, *How the Ox Star Fell from Heaven,* was an expanded college art assignment and was chosen as one of Parenting's Ten Best Books of 1991.

Optional Resources

Reading
Adding English: ESL Teacher's Guide

Guiding Comprehension

pp. 46–49

Details/Literal

Where are Jay and his family?

They are at a country fair.

Character/Inferential

Is Jay having fun? How do you know?

Children are likely to answer no, because he wants to ride the Fire Dragon and his family wants to do other things.

Predicting/Inferential

What do you think will happen?

Based on the picture walk, children may say that Jay gets lost.

Connect Phonics to Reading

Look at page 46. Who is talking? Jay **Name another word on page 46 that has the same vowel sound as _Jay._** Children may say _wait_ or _afraid._

to the end of the story.

A Big Day for Jay, page 46

48 Phonics Story

A Big Day for Jay, page 48

He tugged at his mom. "This isn't fun, Mom. All the jars look the same. Don't you want to see the Fire Dragon?"

All she said was, "Okay, we'll go soon."

Phonics Story **47**

A Big Day for Jay, page 47

They walked from the tent to the Fire Dragon. People were everywhere. They were going this way and that. A girl with a big gray dog bumped into Jay.

Phonics Story **49**

A Big Day for Jay, page 49

Phonics Strategies

If... children have difficulty reading the words *Okay, way, gray,* and *Jay,*	**then...** remind children that the long *a* sound can be spelled *ai* or *ay,* and have them segment and blend any problem words. **Decoding: Using Phonetic Analysis**

Reading Strategies

If... children have difficulty drawing conclusions about how Jay feels,	**then...** reread the first two pages. Ask children to tell what Jay wants to do. Then have them name the things his family does. **Drawing Conclusions: Inferential**
If... children have difficulty reading *can't, I'm,* and *isn't,*	**then...** review contractions for *cannot, I am,* and *is not.* **Decoding: Contractions**
If... children read these pages fluently,	**then...** have them read on to the end. **Fluency**

Day 1

long *a* spelled *ai, ay* and contractions
high-frequency/tested vocabulary

Guiding Comprehension

pp. 50–53

Drawing Conclusions/Inferential

How does Jay get lost?

Jay becomes separated from his family because there are so many people going in different directions.

Making Judgments/Critical

Jay acts bravely, but how do you think he feels?

Children may say he feels scared, worried, or upset.

Self-Monitoring Strategy

The story doesn't say how Jay feels about being lost. How do you know?

When I read, I think about how I would feel or what I would do if I were the character. I ask myself, "If that were me, what would I do? What would I feel?" I use my experiences in life to answer the questions.

Check Predictions

Did the story end as you predicted?

Most children will say yes, because most lost children find their families.

Connect Phonics to Reading

Where is the Lost and Found? It's by the train. **What two words does the contraction *It's* stand for?** *It is.*

Response Log Have children write a new title for *A Big Day for Jay*. Ask them to explain why they like their title. Remind children to keep in mind the main idea of the story.

"Mom, Dad," said Jay. No one called back. Jay knew where he was. But where was his family?

50

A Big Day for Jay, page 50

"Let's go to the Lost and Found," said the police officer. "It's by the train. We can wait for your family there. Okay?"

52 Phonics Story

A Big Day for Jay, page 52

Then Jay spotted a police officer. He acted brave. "I'll be okay," he said. "I'll tell her my name and where I <u>live</u>."

Phonics Story **51**

***A Big Day for Jay,* page 51**

Skills in Context

Review
Plot

What happens to Jay in the story?

Jay wants to ride the Fire Dragon at the fair. He gets separated from his family. A police officer takes him to the Lost and Found office. After his family finds him, Jay gets to ride the Fire Dragon.

Ongoing Assessment

Plot

If... children have difficulty identifying the plot,

then... do the **Think Aloud** below to model the skill.

Model Your Thinking

TEST TALK

After I read a story, I think about all the things that happened. I can review what happened by going back to the story and by looking at the pictures and retelling the story to myself.

Ask children if this story reminds them of any other story they have read.

"Did you get lost today too?" Jay asked the little pup at the Lost and Found.

Then the door opened.

"Dog!" said Kate.

"Jay!" said Mother.

"Now let's find the Fire Dragon!" smiled Father.

Phonics Story **53**

Extend Language Arts

Writing: Personal Information

Create an identification card for children. The information on the card should include full name, address, and phone number (with area code). Have children read the information on their cards aloud, until they know it by memory. Have them write their phone number and address legibly an a separate sheet for practice. Be sure all information is in correct left-to-right sequence.

Have children talk about times when it is a good idea to carry their ID.

long *a* spelled *ai, ay* and contractions
high-frequency/tested vocabulary

***A Big Day for Jay,* page 53**

Day 1

Meeting Individual Needs

Challenge

Extended Vocabulary List
Encourage the use of words such as these.

appear	disappear
arrive	depart
sunrise	sunset

Expand Vocabulary

▶ Discuss Words That Have Opposite Meanings

Have children recall *A Big Day for Jay* and have them think about the animals Jay sees in the story. Discuss how the cow toward the beginning of the story was *huge* and the dog at the end was *tiny*. Record these words on a chart, such as the one below, and encourage children to use the story to think of more words with opposite meanings.

huge	tiny
noisy	quiet
smooth	bumpy

List

▶ Shared Writing

List Ways to Stay Safe Brainstorm with children ways to stay safe at places such as the grocery store and zoo. Record their responses in a list on the chalkboard, such as the one below.

As you write, remind children that for a list each item begins on a new line.

Staying Safe at the Grocery Store

Stay close to the adult you are with.

Keep your hands off the shelves.

Don't talk to strangers.

You might point out certain words in the list and have children give their opposite meaning. (stay/go; close/far; adult/child; off/on; don't/do; strangers/friends)

Independent Writing Have children write at least one sentence about staying safe at a place such as the zoo or shopping mall. Ask them to illustrate their work and to give it a title. Assemble all the papers into a newsletter on how to stay safe.

Handwriting *Yy*

Provide lined paper and handwriting models. Demonstrate how to write a capital Y and a lowercase y and have children practice writing a row of each letter.

Ask children to evaluate their handwriting by circling with a red crayon their best capital Y and their best lowercase y.

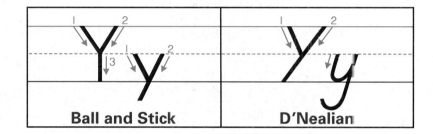

| Ball and Stick | D'Nealian |

Print Direction Write these sentences on the board:

Yes, you may play today.

Yolanda's yo-yo is yellow.

As you write, explain that letters and words in English are written and read from left to right.

Self-Selected Reading and Read Aloud D.E.A.R.

Read aloud *First Flight* by David McPhail. For independent reading, children can choose a book about getting lost.

Day **1**

Optional Resources

Oral Language
Adding English: ESL Teacher's Guide

Long *a: ai, ay* Contractions

▶ Phonics Practice Activities

Make New Words Have pairs of children use letter and phonogram cards *-ail, -ain,* and *-ay* to build long *a* words. Then have them build contractions with contraction cards *'s, n't, 'll,* and *'m* and high-frequency word cards *he, do, they, there,* and *I.* Have partners list the words they make according to their spelling or structural pattern.

Play Phonics Games Use Phonics Activity Mat 3 from the Phonics Manipulatives Kit for long *a*; use Phonics Activity Mat 2 for contractions, or make copies from the Phonics Sourcebook.

Instructions for using these games with long *a* and contractions are on the back of the mats.

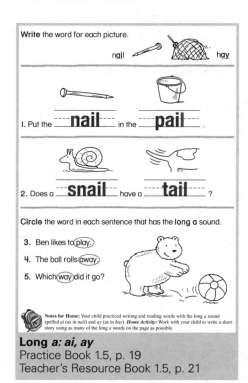

Long *a: ai, ay*
Practice Book 1.5, p. 19
Teacher's Resource Book 1.5, p. 21

Contractions
Practice Book 1.5, p. 20
Teacher's Resource Book 1.5, p. 22

▶ Read the Phonics Reader

Remind children to use what they know about long *a* words and contractions as they read *Who Rang the Bell?* Observe children's reading to determine their ability to transfer these phonics skills to a new selection. After reading, have them:
- draw pictures to show the beginning, middle, and end of the story
- list the rhyming long *a* words from the story

Phonics Reader

Day
2

Objectives

Children will

🎯 decode and build words with long *a: ai, ay*

🎯 use structural cues to recognize contractions

- use sound/symbol relationships as visual cues for decoding
- spell words with long *a: ai, ay*

Decodable Readers 33–41

Decodable Reader 34,
Roy's Fire Bell

Optional Resources

Phonics
Phonics Workbook, pp. 131–133
Phonics Manipulatives Kit
Phonics Sourcebook, pp. 79–82, 86–88, 100–123

High-Frequency Words
High-Frequency Word Cards
Phonics Sourcebook, pp. 90–99

53c Phonics • Spelling

Spelling Long *a* Words

▶Writing for Sounds

Have children write these sentences. Read the sentences. Then repeat words slowly, allowing children to hear each sound. Children may use the Word Wall to help in spelling high-frequency words. Proofread and correct completed sentences.

I can say that I like to play in the rain.
May I wait for you?
Can you find the way home?

Spelling Words

say	way
play	wait
may	rain

High-Frequency

when	from

Challenge

don't	I'm

Day 2

Word Wall

Practice High-Frequency Words

Play "Twenty Questions" using words from the Word Wall. Choose a word and invite children to guess the word by asking questions to which you may only answer yes or no. Examples of questions are: "Does it have two vowels?" "Does it rhyme with *dear?*"

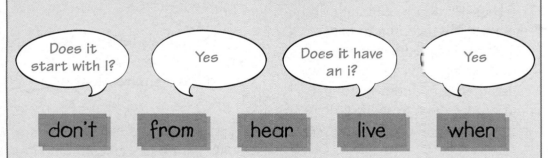

Does it start with l?	Yes	Does it have an i?	Yes

don't	from	hear	live	when

Pick a word from the box to finish each sentence. Write it on the line.

don't	from	hear	live	when

1. I __hear__ the mail truck beep.
2. I got a note __from__ my friend.
3. My friend used to __live__ here.
4. Now I __don't__ see him anymore.
5. I am glad __when__ he writes to me!

Notes for Home: This week your child is learning to read the words don't, from, hear, live, and when. Home Activity: Encourage your child to tell you a story using these words. Make a picture book of the completed story. Help your child write a caption for each picture.

High-Frequency Words
Practice Book 1.5, p. 21
Teacher's Resource Book 1.5, p. 23

Meeting Individual Needs

ESL	Intervention	Challenge	Other Ways to Learn
Provide pictures of a snail, a train, a sail (boat), and a jay. One at a time, have a child hold up a picture, name it, and say a word that rhymes with its name. For example, *This is a snail.* Tail *rhymes with* snail. **(Phonics Support)** See also *Adding English.* **ESL**	Use **Decodable Reader 34** and the teaching suggestions on p. AR2 to provide practice reading decodable text that includes words with long *a: ai, ay* and contractions. **(Phonics Support)**	Reread "Oh, What a Day!" with children. Have them circle the rhyming words. Then, working in small groups, let children write rhyming couplets for the phonemes *-ain, -ail,* and *-aid.* **(Divergent Thinking)**	Have children form three groups. Assign each group one verse from "Oh, What a Day!" Let each group pantomime its verse. Then have it identify the words with long *a: ai, ay* and contractions in its verse. **(Kinesthetic)**

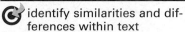

Children will

- identify similarities and differences within text
- listen critically to recognize how things are alike and different in a selection
- read with fluency and understanding

Skills Trace

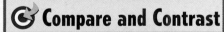

Compare and Contrast

Introduce		TE: 1.3 17e–17f
Teach	Before	TE: 1.5 53e–53f
	During	TE: 1.5 60–61
	After	TE: 1.5 AR13
Practice		PB: 1.3 6; 1.5 22
Reteach/Review		TE: 1.3 AR12; 1.5 AR13; 1.6 73
Test		Skills Test, Units 4, 5 Benchmark Test, Units 4, 5

Day **2**

Building Systematic Instruction

Compare and Contrast

LOOKING BACK

Kindergarten Children compare how things are like each other.

- - - - - - - - - - - - - - - - - - - -

Grade 1 Children understand that *alike* means telling how things are the same and *different* means telling how things are not the same.

LOOKING AHEAD

Grade 2 Children are introduced to the terms *compare* and *contrast*. Children use clue words to make comparisons and contrasts.

Compare and Contrast

▶ Develop Listening Comprehension

Read the following story aloud. Ask children to think about how the animals in the story are alike and how they are different.

Read Aloud

Do Animals Get Lost?

Do creatures that fly ever lose their way? Sometimes they do, but most flying animals have special ways to find their way home.

Bats are blind, but many find their way by listening to the echoes of sounds they make while flying. This special ability helps them find their next meal and guides them to their dark home at the end of the night.

Scientists think that bees find their way home by using their sense of smell. They also can smell their hive from far away, and that odor helps them find their way home.

How do geese know where to go in the summer and fall?

No one knows for sure. We do know that geese learn how to fly by following the actions of their mothers.

Flying creatures hardly ever get lost. Nature has given them all a different special ability so they can find their way home—wherever that home is!

▶ Teach Compare and Contrast

Model the skill by telling children:

All the animals in the story are able to find their way home. That's how they are alike. But bats use their ears and bees use their sense of smell to get home. That's how they are different.

Practice Consider the flying creatures in the story. Ask children to think about other ways they are alike and different. Add children's ideas to a chart. Consider things such as whether the animals have fur or feathers, how they live, what they eat, and how they build their homes.

Reread for Fluency

Read with Expression Model fluent reading by reading the selection aloud as children follow along in their books. Ask children:

Do you hear a difference in my voice when a character is talking?

Remind students to read the words a character says in a way that shows the character's feelings.

Paired Reading Have children read the selection with a partner. Each partner should read one page. Then partners should switch order and read the story again, so each partner has the opportunity to read each page.

Look at both pictures.
Write sentences to tell how the pictures are the same and different.

Same — Possible answers given.

1. Rex and Pip are dogs.
2. Rex and Pip have hats.

Different

3. Rex is a big dog.
4. Rex has big feet.
5. Pip has long fur.

Notes for Home: Your child used pictures to tell how two things are alike and different. *Home Activity:* Point out two objects to your child. Encourage your child to tell you how they are the same and how they are different.

Compare and Contrast
Practice Book 1.5, p. 22
Teacher's Resource Book 1.5, p. 24

Day 2

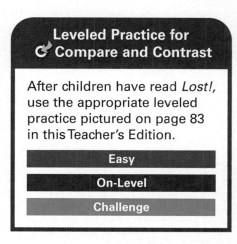

Leveled Practice for ↻ Compare and Contrast

After children have read *Lost!*, use the appropriate leveled practice pictured on page 83 in this Teacher's Edition.

| Easy |
| On-Level |
| Challenge |

❄ Meeting Individual Needs

ESL	Intervention	Challenge	Other Ways to Learn
Ask children to draw a big green ball and a little blue ball. Help them identify specifics as they compare and contrast the two. **(Skill Support)** See also *Adding English.* ESL	After reading *From Dad, House of Wood, House of Snow*, or another book, ask questions that require children to compare and contrast characters, setting, or plot events. **(Comprehension Support)**	Children plan and make a display that contrasts the setting of *A Big Day for Jay* with other busy settings, such as a bustling street or a crowded department store. **(Analogy)**	Children demonstrate with facial expressions how Jay felt before getting lost, while lost, and after he was found. **(Kinesthetic)** Children create a comparison web to contrast the different rides at the fair. Have them draw the rides and label each drawing with at least one descriptive word. **(Visual/ Spatial)**

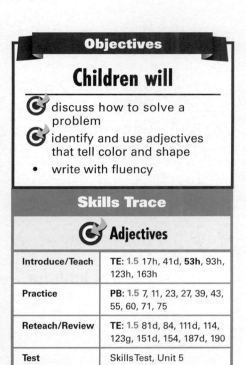

Objectives

Children will

◉ discuss how to solve a problem

◉ identify and use adjectives that tell color and shape

• write with fluency

Skills Trace	
◉ Adjectives	
Introduce/Teach	TE: 1.5 17h, 41d, **53h**, 93h, 123h, 163h
Practice	PB: 1.5 7, 11, 23, 27, 39, 43, 55, 60, 71, 75
Reteach/Review	TE: 1.5 81d, 84, 111d, 114, 123g, 151d, 154, 187d, 190
Test	Skills Test, Unit 5

Day
2

Speaking: Discuss How to Solve a Problem

► What Should You Do When You Get Lost?

Model Remind children that yesterday they read a story about Jay, who gets lost at a fair. Have children use this story as a reference to find information about things they can do if they get lost. Tell them that being lost is a problem and that you'd like to discuss with them solutions to this kind of problem. Present a scenario, such as the one below.

> **Anitra loved going to the amusement park with Grandma. She loved all the rides and especially the carousel. Anitra would always find her favorite horse on the carousel and wave at Grandma each time she rode by where Grandma was sitting. But when the ride was over, Anitra couldn't find her grandma. What would you have done if you were Anitra?**

Discuss these problem-solving techniques with children:

• Review all the problem information.
• Think about what you already know.
• Try a solution.
• Think of another solution in case the first one doesn't work.

Practice Assign partners. Have them discuss what they would do if they were Anitra. Remind them to use the problem-solving techniques you discussed with them. (**information:** Anitra can't find her Grandma; **what you already know:** Grandma will be looking for Anitra. She knows Anitra is by the carousel. Anitra should only talk to someone safe, such as a person who works at the park; **a solution:** wait for Grandma by the carousel; **another solution:** ask someone who works at the park to bring you to the lost and found.)

WRITING

Interesting Sentences

► Modeled Writing

Model Tell children it's important to write interesting sentences for their readers. Explain that you're going to write two sets of sentences about getting lost. Have them determine which set is more interesting.

Think ALOUD For my set of interesting sentences I'm going to make sure none are too long or short. I'm also going to make sure they don't all begin with the same word. That would make them sound pretty dull.

▶ Write About Getting Lost

Model Write two sets of sentences about getting lost. You might use those listed below.

I was in the park and I played on the swings and I played on the slide.	I played in the park all day.
I got lost.	On the way home I got lost.
I was scared.	The dark streets scared me.

As you write the second set of sentences, model these strategies:

- Avoid run-ons.
- Avoid sentences that are too short.
- Begin each with a different word.
- Read your sentences aloud to hear how they sound.

Independent Writing Have children write three sentences that tell about getting lost. They might write about getting lost at the beach or a museum. Remind children to model their work after your second set of sentences.

Author's Chair If time permits, allow children to share their writing.

Self-Selected Reading and Read Aloud D.E.A.R. Drop Everything And Read

Read aloud *Angus, Lost* by Marjorie Flack. Children self-select books by David McPhail.

Day 2

Grammar: Adjectives That Tell Color and Shape

Define Adjectives Show children an object such as a green, square block. Write on the board color and shape words that describe the object, such as *green* and *square*. Tell children that these words are describing words, or adjectives. Remind them that adjectives describe people, places, and things. Write another sentence on the board, such as *The brown cookie was round.* Ask children to identify the adjectives. *(brown, round)*

Practice Create a chart such as the one below. Ask children to describe objects or pictures that you provide. Write the adjectives in the correct column.

	Color Words	Shape Words
ball	red	round
block	yellow	square

For further practice, have children identify adjectives they used in their writing and add them to the chart.

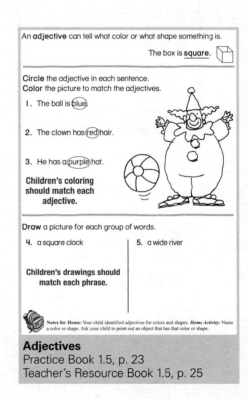

An **adjective** can tell what color or what shape something is.

The box is **square**.

Circle the adjective in each sentence.
Color the picture to match the adjectives.

1. The ball is blue.

2. The clown has red hair.

3. He has a purple hat.

Children's coloring should match each adjective.

Draw a picture for each group of words.

4. a square clock   5. a wide river

Children's drawings should match each phrase.

Notes for Home: Your child identified adjectives for colors and shapes. *Home Activity:* Name a color or shape. Ask your child to point out an object that has that color or shape.

Adjectives
Practice Book 1.5, p. 23
Teacher's Resource Book 1.5, p. 25

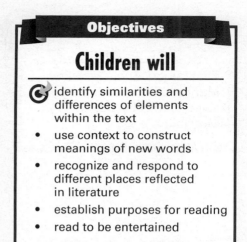
Day 3

Lost!

1. I <u>worry</u> about my cat.
2. She <u>disappears</u> from home a lot.
3. This time she ran <u>across</u> the street.
4. I think she went in one of the school <u>buildings</u>.
5. The <u>library</u> door is open.
6. I hear <u>crying</u> from inside.
7. I hope she did not <u>hurt</u> herself.
8. I run <u>through</u> the halls until I find her.
9. She has <u>climbed</u> onto a shelf, and she is fine!

Story Vocabulary Chart 39

Pick a word from the box to finish each sentence. **Write** it on the line.

| don't | from | hear | hurt | live | when |

1. I **hear** a pup.
2. Are you **hurt**, pup?
3. You **don't** look hurt.
4. Where do you **live**?
5. You are not **from** this block.
6. You will be glad **when** I find your home.

Notes for Home: Your child used new vocabulary words to complete a story. Home Activity: Read the vocabulary words aloud. Ask your child to write each word and explain its meaning.

Tested Vocabulary
Practice Book 1.5, p. 24
Teacher's Resource Book 1.5, p. 26

Lost!
pp. 54–81

▶ Build Oral Language

Activate Prior Knowledge Ask children to discuss being lost.

> How did Jay get lost?
> What would you do if you met a lost child?
> How can people help lost animals?

Build Background Play the Background-Building audio segment, an interview with author David McPhail. He tells why he likes to draw bears and shares how he wrote *Lost!* while living in Boston. Many of the scenes in the story are places in Boston, and he says a reader could actually follow where the bear and the boy go. After listening, you might want to discuss safety precautions to avoid becoming lost or what children should know if they become lost. You may wish to have children recite their home addresses and phone numbers.

Background-Building Audio

CD 5/Tape 12, Side 2

▶ Vocabulary

Introduce Story Vocabulary List the selection vocabulary. Use Vocabulary Chart 39 or write sentences using each word. Read the sentences aloud.

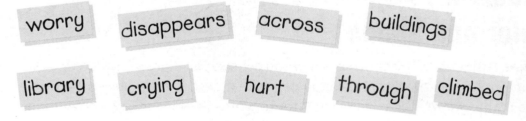

worry   disappears   across   buildings

library   crying   hurt   through   climbed

Point to the word *worry* in the list. Ask children to find it in a sentence. Talk about the meaning of *worry* in the sentence. Continue the procedure for the remaining words.

Point out *buildings* and the ending *-s.* Write *building.* Show children that by adding *-s,* they can make *buildings,* which means "more than one building."

Point out *climbed* and the ending *-ed.* Mask the ending and read the base word *climb.* Uncover the *-ed* and read *climbed* once more. Repeat with the word *crying* and the ending *-ing.*

▶ Reading Strategies

Preview and Predict Before reading the title, point out the exclamation point and explain that it indicates a word or phrase is to be read with expression. Have children read the title and the name of the author/illustrator. Explain that the same person wrote the story and drew the pictures. Then have children take a picture walk through the story. Children might use words from the story to describe the pictures.

Set Purposes Ask children if they would expect to see a bear in a city. Then have children set their own purposes for reading the story. Ask:

What do you want to find out as you read this story?

Guide the Reading Have children read the first few pages of the story, keeping their purposes in mind. Stop to check comprehension, using the questions provided. Have children read to page 57.

Managing Flexible Groups

Intervention

Children listen to the selection audio and follow along in their books. After reading, children retell the story using the pictures. Then reread the story, having children point to exclamation points in the text and show how they can read those sentences with expression.

Selection Audio
CD 6/Tape 22, Side 1

To develop fluency, children can read **Leveled Reader 20A,** *From Dad,* and/or **Decodable Reader 35.** Instructional support appears in this Teacher's Edition, pp. LR7–LR8 and AR3.

Easy

Children can review the high-frequency words. Read the story aloud with children. Help children distinguish between narration and dialogue. Children join in to read the bear's dialogue. Use Guiding Comprehension to monitor understanding and Ongoing Assessment as appropriate.

To develop fluency and to practice high-frequency words, children can read **Leveled Reader 20B,** *House of Wood, House of Snow.* Instructional support appears in this Teacher's Edition, pp. LR10–LR11.

On-Level

Have children take turns reading the dialogue of the characters. Use Guiding Comprehension to monitor understanding and Ongoing Assessment to address reading difficulties.

To develop fluency and to practice high-frequency words, children can read **Leveled Reader 20B,** *House of Wood, House of Snow.* Instructional support appears in this Teacher's Edition, pp. LR10–LR11.

Challenge

Fluent readers can note each thing the boy does to help the bear and think about whether they would do anything differently. They can record their ideas in their response logs. After reading, children write what they think might happen next as the bear helps the lost boy.

Children who have finished reading *Lost!* can read a selection in **Leveled Reader 5C.**

About the Author and Illustrator

David McPhail
writes and illustrates his books in an attic office in his Newburyport, Massachusetts home. He never thought drawing would lead to a career; growing up, he didn't think "fun" and "work" went together. After art school, he learned that drawing could be work as well as fun and has published numerous children's books, including *Pigs Ahoy!* and *Sisters.*

Day **3**

Decodable Reader 35,
Let's Play

Optional Resources

Reading
Adding English: ESL Teacher's Guide

Guiding Comprehension

pp. 54–57

Setting/Inferential

Where does most of this story take place?

Most of the story takes place in a city.

Using Illustrations/Inferential

How do you think the bear ends up in the city?

It looks as if he rides in the back of a truck.

Identifying Character/Literal

How does the bear feel? Why does he feel that way?

The bear feels afraid because he is lost. He is frightened by the tall buildings and the number of people.

Predicting/Inferential

What do you think will happen next?

Possible responses: The boy will try to help the bear. The boy will take the bear home. The bear will run away and cause trouble.

Connect Phonics to Reading

Look at page 57. How does the bear look? He looks lost and afraid. **What vowel sound do you hear in the middle of *afraid*?** You hear the long *a* sound in the middle of *afraid*.

to page 61.

Lost! page 54

I am walking down the street when I hear someone crying.

56

Lost! page 56

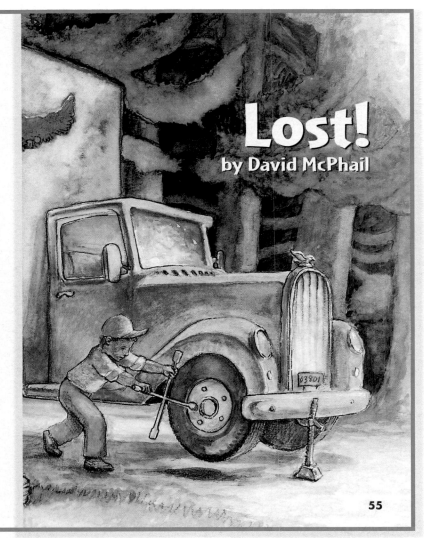

Lost!
by David McPhail

55

Lost! page 55

It's a bear!
He looks lost and afraid.
The tall buildings scare him.
And he's never seen so many people.

57

Lost! page 57

Fiction Genre: Fantasy

To help children identify *Lost!* as a fantasy, remind them of another fantasy your class has heard or read. Explain, for example, that *Winnie the Pooh* is make-believe because it tells about something that could never happen—the bear talks and acts like a person.

Ask children whether they think *Lost!* is make-believe, or if it could really happen. Have them give reasons for their answers. Possible reasons include: Bears don't cry or talk. A child would not lead a loose bear around the city.

Day
3

long *a: ai, ay;* contractions
high-frequency/tested vocabulary

Guiding Comprehension
pp. 58–61

Summarizing/Inferential
What has happened so far?
A boy finds a lost bear in the city, and he comforts the bear and tries to help it find its home. The bear says he lives where there are trees and water, but the places with trees and water the boy shows him are not his home.

Identifying Plot/Inferential
What is the problem in this story?
The bear and the boy want to find the bear's home.

Drawing Conclusions/Inferential
Where do you think the bear lives? Why do you think that?
The bear probably lives in a forest, because that's where bears live.

Predicting/Inferential
What do you think the boy will do now?
Possible responses: He will look for another place with trees and water. He will ask an adult for help. He will look for a forest.

Read On...

to page 65.

"Don't worry," I tell him.
"The buildings won't hurt you,
  and most of the people are friendly."

58

Lost! **page 58**

"There are trees where I live,"
  he tells me.
  So we find some trees.
  "More trees," he says, "and water!"

60

Lost! **page 60**

Day **3**

"How did you get here?" I ask.

"I climbed in to have a nap," he explains, "and when I woke up, I was *lost!*"

"I'll help you. Tell me where you live."

59

Lost! page 59

I take him to a place where there are more trees—and water too. "No," he says. "This is not it either."

61

Lost! page 61

Skills in Context

Compare and Contrast

Name two ways that the city and the bear's home are alike. How are the two places different?

The city and the bear's home are alike because there are trees and water in both places. They are different because in the forest there are more trees; water does not come from fountains; and there are no tall buildings and not many people.

Ongoing Assessment

Compare and Contrast

| **If...** children are unable to identify similarities and differences, | **then...** do the **Think Aloud** below to model the skill. |

Model Your Thinking

TEST TALK

I know from the story that both the city and the forest have trees and water because the boy finds trees and water for the bear in the city park. But forests have more trees than cities do, and forest water doesn't come from fountains. That's how forests and cities are different.

Create a simple feature list such as the one below. Help children identify other ways the city and the forest are the same or different and add their ideas to the list.

City and Forest

Alike	Different
trees	forest has more trees
water	city has tall buildings

long *a: ai, ay;* contractions
high-frequency/tested vocabulary

Guiding Comprehension

pp. 62–65

Drawing Conclusions/Inferential

Why does the boy take the bear to the top of a tall building?

From the top of the building, the bear can see the whole city. If the bear's home is there, he will see it.

Analyzing/Critical

Why is the bear looking through the telescope? What do you think he sees?

The telescope makes faraway things look closer. The bear probably sees lots of buildings and people and cars. The round circle shows that he sees the park through the telescope.

Predicting/Inferential

Do you think the park will turn out to be the bear's home? Why or why not?

Children are likely to say that the park is not the bear's home because there are not enough trees and water in a park, and bears do not live in city parks unless they are in a zoo.

to page 69.

I have an idea. "Follow me!" I say.

I take him to a tall building.

62

Lost! page 62

From up here we can see the whole city. "Look!" I say.

"Now we can find your home."

"There it is!" he says, pointing.

64

Lost! page 64

We go inside, get on the elevator, and ride all the *way* to the top.

63

Lost! page 63

Down we go, across three streets and into the park.

65

Lost! page 65

Reading Strategies

If... children do not understand why the bear is using the telescope,	**then...** have them remember a time when they looked at something far away. Remind them how small far-off objects can appear and explain that a telescope works something like eyeglasses to make things look closer. **Prior Knowledge, Using Illustrations**
If... children are able to identify antonyms in the story,	**then...** recognize their accomplishment. Tell them that good readers use words they have heard to help them read words. **Context Clues, Antonyms**

Phonics Strategies

If... children have trouble reading a word,	**then...** ask them to look at the first letter of the word and say the sound it stands for. Then say, "Look at the picture and think of a word that begins with that sound and that would make sense here." **Decoding, Picture Clues**

Day **3**

long *a: ai, ay;* contractions
high-frequency/tested vocabulary

Guiding Comprehension

pp. 66–69

Sequence/Literal

What do the boy and the bear do first at the park? What do they do next? What do they do after that?

First, they go for a boat ride. Next, they have lunch. Then they go to the playground.

Compare and Contrast/Literal

How are the bear's feelings on these pages different from his feelings at the beginning of the story?

The bear likes the park. He is not afraid anymore. He feels happy.

Predicting/Inferential

What do you think the boy and the bear will do next?

Possible responses: They will have more fun in the park. They will stop playing and look for the bear's home.

Read On...

to page 73.

Day 3

The park is not the bear's home after all—but he likes it there.

66

Lost! page 66

we have lunch,

68

Lost! page 68

We go for a boat ride,

67

Lost! page 67

and we go to the playground.

69

Lost! page 69

Reading Strategies

If... children cannot contrast the bear's present emotions with his feelings at the beginning of the story,

then... have them reread the first two pages of the story. Ask: "How do you think the bear felt when he realized he was lost in the city? Now how do you think he feels after spending time in the park?" Help children recognize the differences in the bear's feelings. **Compare and Contrast**

If... children misread a difficult word and then go back and self-correct,

then... acknowledge their achievement, saying, "Good readers know when they have made a mistake and figure out what went wrong." **Fix-Up Strategy**

Phonics Strategies

If... children have difficulty reading the word *playground*,

then... tell them *playground* is a word made up of two smaller words. If they cannot decode the word on their own, suggest that they ask a classmate for help. **Decoding/Seek Help from Other People**

Day
3

long *a: ai, ay*; contractions
high-frequency/tested vocabulary

Guiding Comprehension

pp. 70–73

Hypothesizing/Critical

Why do you think the bear does not stay in the park?

Children are likely to say that even though the park is fun, the park is not his home, and the bear wants to go home.

Plot/Literal

What happens after the boy and the bear leave the park?

They go to the library and look through books. The bear finds a picture of his home. They find the place on a map and leave the library.

Making Judgments/Critical

Do you think going to the library was a good idea? Why or why not?

Children are likely to say it was a good idea because there are books and maps to help the bear find his home.

Drawing Conclusions/Inferential

Why do you think the boy and the bear hurry outside?

Children are likely to say that it is getting late and they want to get the bear home.

Read On...
to page 77.

We are having a good time.
But it is getting late, and the
bear is still lost.

70

Lost! page 70

Inside the library we look
through lots of books.
The bear sees a picture that
looks like his home.

72

Lost! page 72

"Let's try the library," I tell him.

"We can find out anything here!"

71

We find the place on a map and hurry outside.

73

Reading Strategies

If... children are unable to judge whether going to the library was a good idea,

then... have them recall things they have found in the library. Ask whether they think the library might have information that can help the bear. If so, it was a good idea. **Prior Knowledge**

Phonics Strategies

If... children look at the picture and then read *lion* instead of *library*,

then... tell them to read to the end of the page and then go back and try again. Prompt cross-checking of letter cues and word meaning. **Decoding**

If... children say *globe* instead of *map*,

then... they may be relying too much on picture clues. Explain that while *globe* makes sense, they need to look closely at the letters in the word. Ask them to try again and think of a word that begins with *m* and also makes sense. **Decoding**

Day
3

Content Connection: Art

The illustrator of this story, David McPhail, likes to draw a first sketch in pencil, copied over by waterproof ink. Then he adds colors by using watercolor paints. His original painting is reproduced so that many books can be made.

long *a: ai, ay;* contractions

high-frequency/tested vocabulary

A Big Day for Jay/Lost! **72–73**

Guiding Comprehension

pp. 74–77

Summarizing/Inferential

What do the boy and bear do after they leave the library?

They catch a bus and ride it for a long time until they get to the forest. The bear hugs the boy, thanks him, and goes into the forest.

Character/Inferential

What kind of person do you think the boy is?

Possible responses include helpful, kind, smart, and brave.

Self-Monitoring Strategy
Reread

I didn't read any of the words you used to describe the boy. How do you know he is helpful (or kind, or smart, and so on)?

Children are likely to cite some of the boy's actions, such as helping the bear or going to the library, as reasons for their answers.

Predicting/Inferential

What do you think will happen now?

Possible responses: The boy will take the bus back to the city. He will get lost in the forest.

Read On...

to the end of the story.

A bus is leaving.

74

Lost! page 74

Finally, we are there.
"*This* is where I <u>live</u>!" says the bear.

76

Lost! page 76

We get on the bus and
ride for a long time.

75

Lost! page 75

He gives me a hug and
thanks me again for my help.
Then he waves good-bye and
disappears into the forest.

77

Lost! page 77

Reading Strategies

If... children are unable to describe the boy's character,	**then...** go back through the story and have them recall the boy's actions. Ask: "What kind of person would do this?" Some children may need help getting beyond the label *nice* to more descriptive words. **Character**
If... children read "*This* is where I live!" with appropriate expression and inflection,	**then...** acknowledge that they used italics and punctuation to help them read. **Text Features**

Phonics Strategies

If... children stop at a new word,	**then...** ask: "What starts with those letters? What word would sound right?" Prompt cross-checking of context clues with phonics clues. **Decoding**

Structural Analysis: Prefixes

Write the word *disappears* on the board and underline *dis-*. Read the word with children and have them tell what the word means. Erase the prefix *dis-* and read the word. Have children tell what the new word means and use it in a sentence. Ask a volunteer to add the prefix *dis-* to the word and tell how the meaning changes.

long *a: ai, ay;* contractions
— high-frequency/tested vocabulary

A Big Day for Jay/Lost! **76–77**

Guiding Comprehension

pp. 78–80

Compare and Contrast/Inferential

TEST TALK **How are the boy and the bear in this story alike? How are they different? Find sentences in the story to show you are right.**

They are alike because they both get lost, and they each help the other find the way home. They are different because the bear is afraid of tall buildings in the city, while the boy is afraid of the tall trees in the forest. Children may point to the sentences on pages 57 and 79 to show they both were lost.

Confirm Predictions

Did the story end the way you thought it would? Why or why not?

Children may have predicted that the boy would get lost, but they may be surprised that the boy needs the bear's help.

Drawing Conclusions/Inferential

After reading aloud page 81 with children, ask: What does David McPhail mean when he says, "It feels as if I'm about to win something?"

He means he has a happy feeling or he feels as if he's going to have a nice surprise.

Critical Thinking
Reading Across Texts

READING ACROSS TEXTS **How are *Lost!* and *A Big Day for Jay* alike/different?**

In *Lost!* a bear and a boy are lost. In *A Big Day for Jay*, a boy gets lost. *Lost!* is a funny, make-believe story that could not happen. *A Big Day for Jay* is not funny, and what happened to Jay could really happen to someone.

The trees are so tall, and there aren't any people. "Wait!" I call to the bear, "come back!"

78

Lost! page 78

"I will help you."

80

Lost! page 80

Day 3

"I think I'm lost!" I tell him.

"Don't worry," he says.

79

Lost! page 79

About the Author and Illustrator

David McPhail spends more time doing his artwork than he does writing his stories. When he gets an idea for a story, Mr. McPhail says, "It feels as if I'm about to win something." Do you feel that way about good ideas too?

81

About the Author/Illustrator, page 81

Reading Strategies

If... children are able to compare and contrast the boy and the bear,

then... tell them good readers are able to think about likenesses and differences to help them understand what they read. **Compare and Contrast**

Phonics Strategies

If... children have difficulty reading contractions,

then... have them cover the second part of the contraction and read the first word. Uncover the rest and direct children to use both the sentence and the letter sounds to read the whole contraction. **Structural Analysis**

Mechanics: Exclamation Point

Point out the exclamation points on the last few pages of the story. Remind children that an exclamation point shows that a sentence is to be read with expression. Model this by reading the sentences aloud.

Now write the following: *Get the dog. Get the dog!* Ask a volunteer to read each sentence with the appropriate expression. Repeat with other sentences. Tell children that when they read another story, they can look to see if the author chooses to use exclamation points to show excitement.

▓ long *a: ai, ay;* contractions
— high-frequency/tested vocabulary

Day 3

Objectives

Children will

- decode and build words with long *a: ai, ay*
- use structural cues to decode and build contractions
- review long vowels with final *e*
- spell words with long *a: ai, ay*
- recognize high-frequency words

Skills Trace

Long Vowels with Final *e*

Introduce/Teach	TE: 1.4 10k, 80k, 110k, 140k
Practice	PB: 1.4 3, 19, 35, 41, 51, 67, 74; 1.5 25
Reteach/Review	TE: 1.4 AR11, AR14, AR15, AR17; 1.5 81a
Test	Skills Test, Unit 4 Benchmark Test, Unit 4

Day 3

Long *a: ai, ay* Contractions

▶ Phonics Practice Activities

Careful observation of these activities will provide a basis for the Ongoing Assessment on page 81b.

Group Activity Give children a couple of minutes to list four long *a: ai, ay* words. Then have them read their words aloud. Record their words on the board, putting a check mark by each word when it is repeated. Put the words in order from those used most often to only once. Repeat the activity with contractions.

Partners Set word cards for *he'll, she's, don't, let's,* and *I'm* facedown. The first child draws a card and gives clues that describe the word's meaning. The partner guesses. Children take turns giving clues and guessing the word. After all cards have been drawn, children can sort them according to their spelling pattern.

Reread for Fluency

Practice Reading Phrases Model the difference between reading word-by-word and grouping words in phrases as you read. Help children gain fluency by rereading *Who Rang the Bell?* with attention to phrasing.

Phonics Reader

Review

Long Vowels with Final *e*

▶ Build Long Vowel Words with Final *e*

Write the following words, leaving out the vowels: *place, wave, ride, time, woke, whole, home,* and *use.* Give children letter cards for the missing vowels. Read a word and invite children with the appropriate vowel cards to come up and complete the word. Then have children read the words together.

$$pl\_c\_ \quad w\_v\_ \quad r\_d\_$$

Allow children to see that some words have more than one right answer. (*wave, wove*)

rake   Pete   bike   home   cube

Circle the word for each picture.

1. spice (space)
2. (kite) kit
3. (cane) can
4. (rose) rise
5. get (gate)
6. nice (nose)
7. (hive) have
8. tub (tube)

Find the word that has the **long vowel** sound. **Mark** the ⬯ to show your answer.

9. ● late
   ○ plan
   ○ man

10. ● bite
    ○ bit
    ○ brick

Notes for Home: Your child reviewed long vowel sounds in words ending with *e*. **Home Activity:** Write the words *Tim, rat, kit, can, rid,* and *rob* on a piece of paper. Ask your child to say each word. Then add *e* to the end of each word. Ask your child to say each new word.

Long Vowels with Final *e*
Practice Book 1.5, p. 25
Teacher's Resource Book 1.5, p. 27

Spelling Long *a: ai, ay* Words

▶ Practice with Writing

Have children choose two rhyming words from the spelling list and write a rhyme, such as "I say, Let's play!" They can then take turns reading a partner's sentences aloud.

<table>
<tr><td colspan="2" align="center">**Ongoing Assessment**</td></tr>
<tr><td colspan="2" align="center">**Phonics/Spelling**</td></tr>
<tr>
<td>**If...** children have difficulty decoding words with long *a*,</td>
<td>**then...** provide more word-building activities using the phonograms -*ay*, -*ain*, and -*ail* and have children write the words they build in their word study books. Also use the ESL activity, Day 4, page 83a.</td>
</tr>
<tr>
<td>**If...** children have difficulty identifying contractions,</td>
<td>**then...** have them look for a familiar word within each contraction and circle it. Ask them to think about what letter or letters the apostrophe replaces in the remaining word. Also use the Intervention activity, Day 4, page 83a.</td>
</tr>
<tr>
<td>**If...** children have difficulty spelling words with long *a*,</td>
<td>**then...** remind them that the spelling words with long *a* in the middle are spelled *ai*, and the words with long *a* at the end are spelled *ay*.</td>
</tr>
<tr>
<td>**If...** children have difficulty spelling the challenge words *don't* and *I'm*,</td>
<td>**then...** give them letter cards *d, o, n, o, t, I, a, m,* and two apostrophe cards. Have them form the phrases *do not* and *I am*. Then let them knock out the letters they do not use to spell *don't* and *I'm* and replace those letters with apostrophes.</td>
</tr>
</table>

Look at each word. Say it. Listen for the long **a** sound in ···· train

Write each word. | Check it.
1. say — **say** | **say**
2. play — **play** | **play**
3. may — **may** | **may**
4. way — **way** | **way**
5. wait — **wait** | **wait**
6. rain — **rain** | **rain**

Word Wall Words
Write each word.

7. when — **when** | **when**
8. from — **from** | **from**

Notes for Home: Your child spelled words in which the long *a* sound is spelled *ai* and *ay* and two frequently-used words: *when, from. Home Activity:* Say each spelling word. Ask your child to spell the word, and then use it in a sentence. Together, draw pictures for the sentences.

Spelling
Practice Book 1.5, p. 26
Teacher's Resource Book 1.5, p. 28

Day 3

Word Wall

Practice High-Frequency Words

Lost Words Tell children you have lost some words and ask them to find them for you on the Word Wall. Write the first letter of one of this week's words on the board and say a sentence leaving out a word that begins with that letter. Repeat with the rest of this week's words.

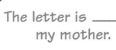

The letter is _____ my mother.

don't   from
hear
when
live

Optional Resources

Phonics
Phonics Workbook, pp. 131–134
Phonics Manipulatives Kit
Phonics Sourcebook, pp. 1–82, 89

High-Frequency Words
High-Frequency Word Cards
Phonics Sourcebook, pp. 90–99

Expand Vocabulary

▶ Antonyms

Recall *Lost!* Write a list of the following words from the story on the board. As you write each word, have children tell you its opposite. Record antonyms next to each word.

down	up	inside	outside
tall	short	on	off
many	few	good-bye	hello
lost	found		

After you've listed the words, you might want to read the story with the antonyms in place of the original words for a silly story time.

Description of a Story Illustration

▶ Modeled Writing

Revisit with children the title page of *Lost!* on page 55 of their books. Examine the picture together and ask children to use adjectives to tell about the colors and shapes they see. Remind them that an adjective is a word that describes a person, place, or thing.

Model Write two sentences such as those listed below to describe the picture. Draw a line under the describing words.

> I see a <u>yellow</u> truck.
>
> The <u>black</u> tire is <u>round</u>.
>
> The boy is wearing a <u>blue</u> hat.

As you write, model these strategies:
- Use color and shape words.
- Use correct punctuation.
- Separate words by spaces.
- Write words from left to right and sentences from top to bottom.
- Keep the left margin straight.

Day
3

Independent Writing Tell children to write two sentences to describe an illustration in *Lost!* Tell them to use shape and color words.

Peer Conference Have partners read their sentences to each other. Suggest they think of antonyms for words in each other's sentences.

Writer's Checklist

Did you . . .

- ✓ use color and shape words?
- ✓ use correct punctuation?
- ✓ separate words by spaces?
- ✓ write words from left to right?
- ✓ keep the left margin straight?

Self-Selected Reading and Read Aloud D.E.A.R. Drop Everything And Read

Read aloud *Mrs. Potter's Pig* by Phyllis Root or a book about losing something. After reading, discuss with children what they've learned from the story.

Grammar: Adjectives That Tell Color and Shape

Review Adjectives Show an object with a distinct color and shape, such as a red ball. List words for the color and shape of the object. Remind children that describing words tell about people, places, or things and are called *adjectives*.

Make Color and Shape Cards Have children take out crayons and a pencil. Provide each child with three cards and give instructions for them to follow, such as the following:

> Draw a red, round ball.
> Draw a blue, square house.

Have children label their pictures using color and shape words.

red, round ball   blue, square house

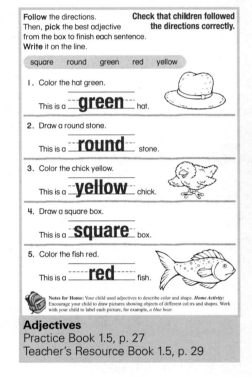

Follow the directions. Then, **pick** the best adjective from the box to finish each sentence. **Write** it on the line.

Check that children followed the directions correctly.

| square | round | green | red | yellow |

1. Color the hat green.
   This is a **green** hat.
2. Draw a round stone.
   This is a **round** stone.
3. Color the chick yellow.
   This is a **yellow** chick.
4. Draw a square box.
   This is a **square** box.
5. Color the fish red.
   This is a **red** fish.

Notes for Home: Your child used adjectives to describe color and shape. *Home Activity:* Encourage your child to draw pictures showing objects of different colors and shapes. Work with your child to label each picture, for example, *a blue bear.*

Adjectives
Practice Book 1.5, p. 27
Teacher's Resource Book 1.5, p. 29

Day 3

Meeting Individual Needs

ESL	Intervention	Challenge	Other Ways to Learn
Provide round and square objects of several colors and shapes. Have children describe each using color and shape words. **(Skill Support)**	Write a list of color words and a list of shape words on a chart. Write a sentence using a word from each list and have children underline the color and shape words. Then have them write their own sentences using words from the chart. **(Skill Support)**	Provide books that include shape and color adjectives. Number the books. Children hunt for color and shape adjectives in the books. They write these down along with the nouns they describe and the number of the book. The child with the most adjectives wins the hunt. **(Differentiated Learning Centers)**	Call out a color or shape. Have children find, point out, and name something in the classroom that matches the adjective you called out. **(Kinesthetic)**

Reader Response

Student Book, pp. 82–83

Let's Talk

Personal Response Encourage children to explain why they would or would not help the bear by modeling your own response.

I wouldn't help the bear because I would be afraid of a talking bear. I would find a police officer to help him.

Let's Think

Critical Response Children are likely to say that the bear climbed into a truck to have a nap and the truck took him away. They may say that the boy lives in a city, so when he got to the forest, he didn't know how to get out.

Test Prep

Let's Write

Written Response If possible, read aloud a brief, appropriate news article. Point out that a news story clearly reports something that happened. Have children write their news stories individually or with a partner. Remind children to tell events in their news stories in the order in which they happened.

Features for writing news stories are listed below 4 in the Scoring Rubric.

Make a Map

Creative Response Have each child make a map of the way to school from home.

Encourage children to share their maps. Model asking polite questions to clarify information on the maps, raising your hand and asking, for example:

I'm not sure what the big white building is. Do you go past the library?

Use the **Selection Test** in Practice Book 1.5, pages 29–30 or Teacher's Resource Book 1.5, pages 31–32.

Lost! page 82

Read Together

Reader Response

Let's Talk
Would you help the bear? Why or why not?

Let's Think
How does the bear get lost? Why is the boy lost? Look back at the story and pictures.

Test Prep
Let's Write
Write a news story. Tell about the lost bear. Tell how the boy helps him.

82

Scoring Rubric for Written Response	
4	**3**
• clearly focuses on the main events of the story • events are in an order that makes sense • expresses ideas in complete sentences • begins sentences with capital letters and ends with correct punctuation	• focuses on the main events • events are mostly in order • expresses most ideas in complete sentences • may have poorly formed capital letter at beginning or incorrect punctuation at end of one or two sentences
2	**1**
• attempts to focus on the main events • has a few events that are out of order • may be missing parts of some sentences • may be missing capital letter at beginning or punctuation at end of some sentences	• is not clearly focused on the events • has no order of events • is made up of disconnected words or phrases • lacks both capital letters and end punctuation

Make a Map

Think about the way you go
to school from your home.
Make a map.

1. Draw your home at one end of
   the paper. Draw your school at the
   other end.
2. Draw a path from your home to your
   school. Use → → →.
3. Show some things you see along the
   way. Is there a park? Are there stores?
4. Share your map with your class.

Lost! page 83

Skills in Context

Setting

Ask children where most of the story *Lost!* takes
place. Help them see how the setting influences
the story's problem and plot by playing "What If?"
Ask: "What if the bear had found himself in the
desert? How would the story be different? What if he
were lost in another part of the forest? What would
be different then?" Discuss ways in which the setting
determines the characters' actions and the solution
to the story's problem.

Reread for Fluency

Selection Audio Have children
listen to the CD or tape of
Lost! as they follow along in
their books.

CD 6/Tape 22, Side 1

Attend to Punctuation Have children reread *Lost!*
with a partner. Remind them to "read the punctuation"
as well as the words.

Day
4

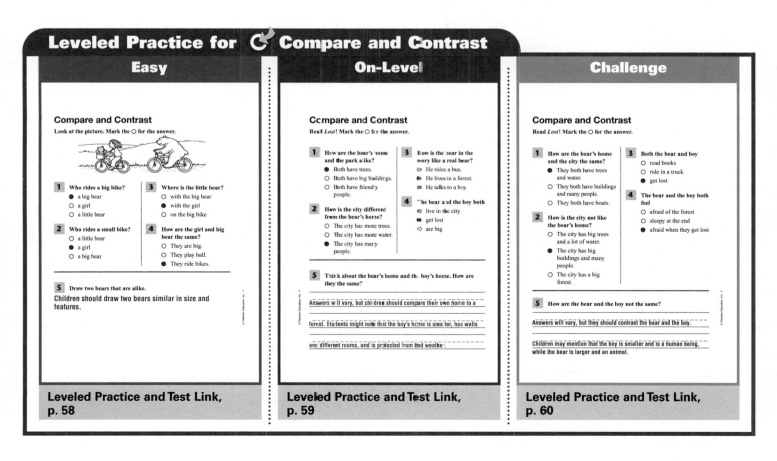

Leveled Practice for C Compare and Contrast

Easy

Compare and Contrast
Look at the picture. Mark the ○ for the answer.

1 Who rides a big bike?
● a big bear
○ a girl
○ a little bear

3 Where is the little bear?
○ with the big bear
● with the girl
○ on the big bike

2 Who rides a small bike?
○ a little bear
● a girl
○ a big bear

4 How are the girl and big
bear the same?
○ They are big.
○ They play ball.
● They ride bikes.

5 Draw two bears that are alike.
Children should draw two bears similar in size and
features.

**Leveled Practice and Test Link,
p. 58**

On-Level

Compare and Contrast
Read *Lost!* Mark the ○ for the answer.

1 How are the bear's home
and the park alike?
● Both have trees.
○ Both have big buildings.
○ Both have friendly
people.

3 How is the bear in the
story like a real bear?
○ He rides a bus.
● He lives in a forest.
○ He talks to a boy.

2 How is the city different
from the bear's home?
○ The city has more trees.
○ The city has more water.
● The city has many
people.

4 The bear and the boy both
○ live in the city
● get lost
○ are big

5 Think about the bear's home and the boy's home. How are
they the same?

Answers will vary, but children should compare their own home to a

forest. Students might note that the boy's home is smaller, has walls

and different rooms, and is protected from bad weather.

**Leveled Practice and Test Link,
p. 59**

Challenge

Compare and Contrast
Read *Lost!* Mark the ○ for the answer.

1 How are the bear's home
and the city the same?
● They both have trees
and water.
○ They both have buildings
and many people.
○ They both have boats.

3 Both the bear and boy
○ read books
○ ride in a truck
● get lost

2 How is the city not like
the bear's home?
○ The city has big trees
and a lot of water.
● The city has big
buildings and many
people.
○ The city has a big
forest.

4 The bear and the boy both
feel
○ afraid of the forest
○ sleepy at the end
● afraid when they get lost

5 How are the bear and the boy not the same?

Answers will vary, but they should contrast the bear and the boy.

Children may mention that the boy is smaller and is a human being,
while the bear is larger and an animal.

**Leveled Practice and Test Link,
p. 60**

Long *a: ai, ay* Contractions

►Reteach

Tell children that *ai* and *ay* both stand for /ā/, the long *a* sound. Review with children that when two vowels such as *ai* come together, the first one usually has its long vowel sound and the second is silent. Write *gain, pay, tail, lay, hail,* and *rain* on the board. Have volunteers read the words aloud and identify the pairs that rhyme.

Write *I* + *am* on the board and explain that *I'm* is a shorter way of writing and saying the two words. Point out the apostrophe that stands for the missing letter *a.* Have children write contractions for the following.

do + not   did + not   can + not
she + is   I + will   let + us

See pages AR12 and AR13 of this Teacher's Edition for additional **reteach activities.**

Review Initial Digraphs

Write the following digraphs on the board: *ch, sh, th, wh.* Give each child a card with one of the following words: *think, thank, this, there, when, where, chain, chair, ship, show.* Have children listen as you say words beginning with one of the digraphs. Children who have a word with the same initial digraph may stand.

Initial Digraphs
Practice Book 1.5, p. 31
Teacher's Resource Book 1.5, p. 33

Meeting Individual Needs

| ESL | Intervention | Challenge | Other Ways to Learn |

ESL

Display items (or pictures) such as *pail, mail, train, chain, paint.* Help children say each name, then label each item. Help children circle the *ai* and read each word. Then mix up the cards and have children read them. **(Phonics Support)** See also *Adding English.* **ESL**

Intervention

Use Phonics Activity Mat 3 from the Phonics Manipulatives Kit for long *a.* Use Phonics Activity Mat 2 for contractions. Instructions for using these games are on the back of the mats. **(Word Study Support)**

Challenge

Make six letter cubes: *ay, ai, ay, ai, ay, ai; b, d, g, h, j, l; m, p, r, s, w, cl; gr, pl, pr, spr, st, str; sw, tr, f, qu, a, i.* Children roll all six cubes and arrange them into words. Letters can be used more than once by arranging words across and down. **(Application of Different Symbol Systems)**

Other Ways to Learn

Children cut out magazine pictures illustrating long *a* words and arrange them in a collage. Using color coordinated cards, they label each picture according to its spelling pattern. **(Visual/Spatial)**

Day 4

Spelling Long *a: ai, ay* Words

▶ Partner Spelling Practice

Children work in pairs. Provide each pair with word cards with the spelling words. Have children place the cards facedown in a pile. One child takes the top card and reads it, and the other child writes the word. The first child shows the word and spells it aloud, allowing the writer to correct any mistakes. The card is returned to the bottom of the pile, and children switch roles until all the words have been spelled correctly.

say play may way wait rain

Write four words from the box that rhyme with **day**.

1. **say**   2. **play**

3. **may**   4. **way**

Write the word from the box that rhymes with each word below.

5. bait **wait**   6. main **rain**

Pick a word from the box to finish each sentence. Write it on the line.

7. We like to **play** games.

8. **Wait** for me to hide.

Write the word from the box that has the same beginning sound as the picture.

when from

9. frog **from**   10. wheel **when**

Notes for Home: Your child spelled words in which the long *a* sound is spelled *ai* and *ay*, as well as two frequently-used words: *when, from*. **Home Activity:** Challenge your child to write other words with *ai* and *ay* that have a long *a* sound.

Spelling
Practice Book 1.5, p. 32
Teacher's Resource Book 1.5, p. 34

Word Wall

Review High-Frequency Words

Write Around Organize the class into groups of four. Give paper and a pencil to one child in each group. Call out a word from the Word Wall and have the first child in each group write the first letter, then pass the paper and pencil to the next child. Each child in turn adds a letter until the word is completed. When a group has written a word, they can say the word and chant the spelling together. Repeat for other words.

don't from

hear

I've when

Day 4

Optional Resources

Phonics
Phonics Workbook, pp. 131–133, 135
Phonics Manipulatives Kit
Phonics Sourcebook, pp. 100–123
AstroWord CD-ROM, Consonant Digraphs

High-Frequency Words
High-Frequency Word Cards
Phonics Sourcebook, pp. 90–99

A Big Day For Jay/ Lost! **83b**

Language Arts

Student Book, pp. 84–85

Adjectives That Tell Color and Shape

Have children read aloud with you the information about adjectives. Ask them to name an adjective that tells color and an adjective that tells what shape something is.

Have the example sentences read. Ask children to identify the adjective and the noun that it modifies in each example sentence.

Talk

Have children describe things they see in the picture. Prompt them to use adjectives that describe color and shape. List on the board the adjectives they mention. Use one column for adjectives describing color and another for adjectives describing shape.

Write

Guide children as they copy the sentences and underline the adjectives. When everyone has finished, review the responses and have children correct their mistakes.

Then have children write sentences that include adjectives that describe color and shape, and underline those adjectives. Encourage them to refer to the lists on the board.

Use the Teacher's Resource Book 1.5 pages 35–36 for **reteaching** and extra practice for adjectives of color and shape.

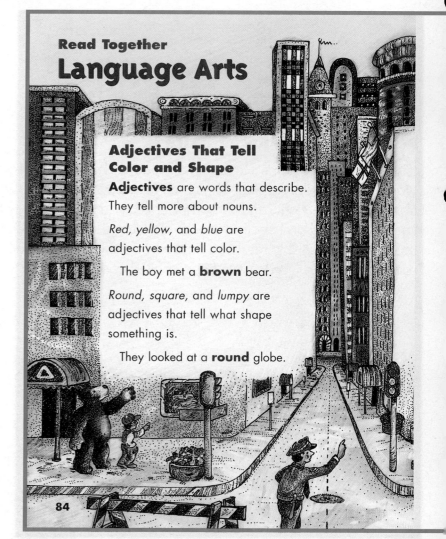

Read Together
Language Arts

Adjectives That Tell Color and Shape

Adjectives are words that describe. They tell more about nouns.

Red, yellow, and *blue* are adjectives that tell color.

The boy met a **brown** bear.

Round, square, and *lumpy* are adjectives that tell what shape something is.

They looked at a **round** globe.

84

Lost!, page 84

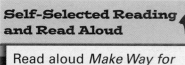

Self-Selected Reading and Read Aloud D.E.A.R. Drop Everything And Read

Read aloud *Make Way for Ducklings* by Robert McCloskey. Children choose a fiction or nonfiction book about growing or learning.

Day 4

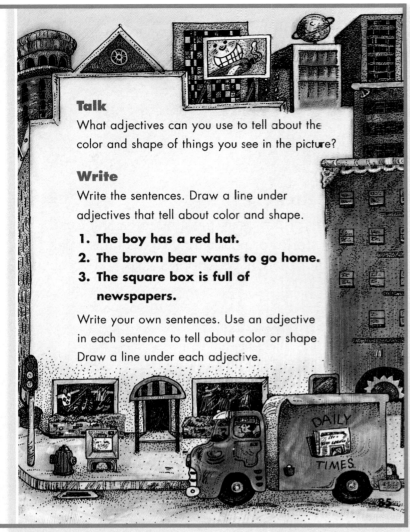

Lost!, page 85

Study Skill

Glossary: Guide Words

Have children turn to the beginning of the Glossary on page 232 in their books. Read aloud the heading at the top of the page. Help children recall that a glossary is a short, alphabetized dictionary at the back of some books and that it contains definitions of some words in the book. Review the terms *entry word, definition,* and *picture* by having children discuss the entry word *crowded.* Then have them turn to page 234 and model how to use guide words.

Model Your Thinking

Think ALOUD When I want to locate an entry word, I look at the two guide words in dark type at the top of each page. The guide words tell the first and last word on a page. The first word on this page is *dinosaur* and the last word is *fooling,* so I know that entry words starting with the letters *d, e,* and *f* are located here. If I'm looking for the word *disappears,* I know it will be on this page because it starts with the letter *d.*

Continue modeling, next locating *library.* Then call on children to locate the entry words *otter, ponies,* and *spy* and explain how they find them.

Practice List several glossary words on the board and have children work in pairs to locate the words. Ask children to read the entry words and definitions and study the pictures. In addition to the glossary, you may also want children to work with a dictionary.

Day
4

READING

Objectives

Children will

 compare and contrast
- use sound-symbol relation-ships to read decodable text
- recognize high-frequency words
- read with accuracy and comprehension

Meeting Individual Needs

ESL

To get children prepared for the assessment, make a poster with pictures and labels of different animals found on a ranch, such as horses and mules. Talk about the features of each animal.

Assess Accuracy and Comprehension

▶ Prepare for the Assessment

Materials Have children prepare for the assessment by rereading *Lost!*, *A Big Day for Jay*, or any other stories or books they've read this week. The assessment selection on page 85b reviews phonics skills and vocabulary previously introduced.

▶ Listen to Individual Readers

Ask children to read the selection on page 85b aloud.

- If the child cannot read three or more words in the first sentence, discontinue the reading assessment. Read the passage aloud to the child and label the test as Listening Comprehension.

- If the child reads the passage independently, keep the passage in front of the child as you ask the five questions. Label the test as Reading Comprehension. Read aloud the comprehension questions to children and have them answer them.

See page AR13 in this Teacher's Edition to **reteach** compare and contrast.

▶ While You Assess

While you work with individuals, other children may choose from the following activities or the activities listed in the Cross-Curricular Work Stations on pages 46g–h.

Before They Read to You

Children should reread the chosen story with a partner and then ask each other questions about the story.

Children may listen to the CD or tape of *Lost!* or *A Big Day for Jay* to hear a model of fluent reading.

Selection Audio

CD 6/Tape 22, Side 1

After They Read to You

Children can complete a Reading Log like the one shown or use Practice Book 1.5 page 99, or the Teacher's Resource Book 1.6 page 112.

Children can also complete the phonics activities on page 85c.

Name_____

I read *Lost!*

It was about

Words I Can Now Read and Write

Day 5

Optional Resources

Assessment
The Assessment Handbook has information on running records.

Accuracy and Comprehension Assessment

Name _____

Mark type of assessment. ☐ Listening Comprehension
                          ☐ Reading Comprehension

Number of Words Miscalled _____
Frustrational (below 90%: 6 or more miscalled)
Instructional (91–97%: 2–5 miscalled)
Independent (98% and above: 0–1 miscalled)

	Correct	Incorrect
1. Main Idea/Literal **What is the answer to this riddle?** The answer is *a mule*.		
2. Monitoring Comprehension/Critical **When did you figure out the answer to the riddle?** Some children may say that they didn't figure out the answer until they read it.		
3. Details/Literal **How would you describe a mule?** A mule is almost the same size as a horse, and it is brown and big.		
4. Compare and Contrast/Inferential **How is a mule like a horse? How is it different?** A mule is smaller and not as fast as a horse. You can ride both animals.		
5. Hypothesize/Inferential **What might a mule do on a ranch?** Possible answer: A mule could carry people or loads on its back.		

Scoring: Score 1 point for each correct answer. Number correct (Literal) _____ Number correct (Inferential/Critical)_____

- -

A Riddle

I have a hoof at the end of each leg.

I am big and brown and have a long black tail.

I am almost as big as a horse.

But I am not as fast as a horse.

Some cowboys like to ride me.

You can find me on a ranch.

What animal am I?

(a mule)

Day
5

Long *a: ai, ay* Contractions

▶ Phonics Practice Activities

Write a Sentence Together, list the long *a* words and contractions children have learned. Have each child write a sentence using at least one long *a* word and one contraction. Children can share their sentences.

Phonics Take-Home Reader Have children practice reading the book with a partner before taking it home.

Who Rang the Bell?

by Sydnie Meltzer Kleinhenz
Illustrated by George Ulrich

Phonics Take-Home Reader

Spelling Test

Have children number their papers. Read the underlined word, read the sentence, then repeat the underlined word.

1. It looks like it will <u>rain</u> soon.
2. Which <u>way</u> did he go?
3. You <u>may</u> have dessert now.
4. What did your mom <u>say</u>?
5. We will <u>wait</u> for the bus.
6. We can <u>play</u> at the park.

High-Frequency Words

7. Let me know <u>when</u> you are ready.
8. We got a card <u>from</u> our uncle.

Challenge Words

9. You <u>don't</u> have to go yet.
10. <u>I'm</u> so glad you are here.

Word Wall

Practice High-Frequency Words

Word Wall Cheers Invite a volunteer to call out the letters of one of the words on the Word Wall, and have the rest of the class respond as if performing a cheer. For example,

"Give me an *f!*"　　"F!"
"Give me an *r!*"　　"R!"

and so on.

Ask different children to lead cheers using the rest of this week's Word Wall words.

don't　from
hear
live　when

ORAL LANGUAGE

Speaking: Discuss How to Solve a Problem

Tell children a story that includes a problem such as the following. Have them listen so they can discuss the problem and possible solutions afterward.

> Bear is visiting her cousin's house in a faraway forest. She goes for a walk and sees a bush with big, red berries. She loves berries and eats a few. She wanders off some more, exploring. After a few hours a few inches of snow pile up, and Bear doesn't recognize anything familiar. She feels lost. How might Bear find her way back to her cousin's house?

In small groups have children discuss the problem and possible solutions. (They might say Bear should follow her footprints in the snow, look for the berry bush, or climb to the top of a tree looking for her cousin's house.)

WRITING

Postcard

▶ Interactive Writing

In this method of writing, you and the children work together. While you write on the board, children write on their own papers. As you write, point out the punctuation and how it affects the meaning of the sentence.

Write a Postcard Children will write a postcard from Bear to her friend Marty about getting lost in the woods. Begin the postcard using Interactive Writing techniques. You may wish to make your postcard similar to the one shown below. Leave a blank line for children to write how Bear solves her problem.

Dear Marty,

I got lost in the woods! Do you know what I did? I

_____

_____

Love,

Bear

Independent Writing Have children finish the letter. They might use a solution that was discussed in Oral Language. Invite children to decorate their postcards with markers or stickers. Place these around the classroom.

Portfolio Children may wish to select a piece of writing from this week to put in their portfolios.

Speaker's Checklist

Did you . . .

✓ speak clearly?
✓ think about what you already know?
✓ suggest more than one solution?

Self-Selected Reading and Read Aloud **D.E.A.R.**

Have children select a new book or read an old favorite. Read aloud children's postcards.

Optional Resources

Phonics
Phonics Workbook, pp. 131–133

High-Frequency Words
High-Frequency Word Cards
Phonics Sourcebook, pp. 90–99

Oral Language
Adding English: ESL Teacher's Guide

Assessment
The Assessment Handbook has information on informal assessment and grading.

Lesson Overview

Phonics Story

Baby Otter Grows Up

by Susan McCloskey
illustrated by Anna Vojtech

This is a baby otter. A baby otter is called a kit. This kit is three months old and still growing.

The kit rides on his mom's back. He is holding on to her coat to keep from slipping.

Phonics Story

Baby Otter Grows Up
pages 86–93

Selection Audio

The **Phonics Story** . . .

- introduces ⟳ **Long** *o: oa, ow* and **Inflected Ending** *-ing* (**with and without spelling changes; doubling final consonants**)

- introduces the high-frequency words

    around her new old show

- builds fluency

- builds decoding skills

> **Use the Phonics Story to prepare children for reading the Main Selection.**

SEE HOW THEY GROW

FOAL

Main Selection

Foal
pages 94–109

Selection Audio

The **Main Selection** . . .

- introduces ⟳ **Sequence**

- practices ⟳ **Long** *o: oa, ow* and **Inflected Ending** *-ing* (**with and without spelling changes; doubling final consonants**)

- practices the high-frequency words

    around her new old show

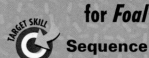
Leveled Practice
in Test Format
for *Foal*

SEE HOW THEY GROW
FOAL

TARGET SKILL **Sequence**

Leveled Readers

TARGET SKILL

Sequence

Tested Vocabulary

Easy

"Mary" Goes Walking

by Anne Phillips
illustrated by Shelley Dieterichs

Leveled Reader 21A

On-Level

Desert Fox

by Nat Gabriel
·
illustrated by
Sally Wern Comport

Leveled Reader 21B

For Guided Reading
see Teacher's Edition,
pp. LR13–LR18.

Challenge

Take Me There

Collected Readings

Leveled Reader 5C

For instruction and leveled
practice answers, see Teacher's
Edition, pp. LR39–LR45.

Easy

Sequence
Look at the pictures. Mark the ○ for the answer.

1   2   3

1 Who likes trash?
- ○ a friend
- ● a dog
- ○ a woman

2 What does the dog do first?
- ○ The dog runs.
- ● The dog finds the trash.
- ○ The trash falls over.

3 What happens after the dog finds the trash?
- ○ The dog eats.
- ○ The woman yells.
- ● The trash falls over.

4 What happens last?
- ● The woman yells at the dog.
- ○ The woman plays with the dog.
- ○ The dog finds the trash.

5 Draw a picture that shows what will happen next.
Pictures will vary, but they should make a prediction based on the three preceding pictures. The dog or the woman or perhaps both may be pictured cleaning up the trash.

On-Level

Sequence
Read *Foal*. Mark the ○ for the answer.

1 What is a newborn foal like?
- ○ It stands tall.
- ● Its legs are wobbly.
- ○ It is as big as its mother.

2 What happens just after the foal is born?
- ● The mother feeds it milk.
- ○ It stands tall.
- ○ It runs and plays.

3 What happens just after the foal drinks milk?
- ● It feels stronger.
- ○ It has wobbly legs.
- ○ It grows bigger.

4 What happens after the foal is two weeks old?
- ○ It gets teeth.
- ○ It is as tall as its mother.
- ○ It eats apples.

5 What does a foal do when it is eight weeks old?

Possible answers: gallops, runs, jumps, eats apples

Practice for Leveled Readers

Easy

Sequence of Events

Read the story *Mary Goes Walking*. Then answer Numbers 1 through 5.

1 What happens FIRST in the story?
- ● Mary gets dressed up.
- ○ Mary goes out to play.
- ○ Mary plays with her cat.

2 What happens AFTER Mary gets dressed up?
- ○ Mary goes to a dance.
- ● Mary goes for a walk.
- ○ Mary goes shopping.

3 Why does Mary lean over the water?
- ● to get a drink
- ○ to see her cat
- ○ to see how she looks

4 What happens when Mary leans over the water?
- ○ Mary sees a bug in the water.
- ● Mary falls in the water.
- ○ Mary jumps over the water.

5 What happens LAST in the story? Use words from the story in your answer.

Possible answer: Mary gets wet. Mary goes home.

Teacher's Edition, p. LR15

On-Level

Sequence of Events

Read the book *Desert Fox*. Then answer Numbers 1 through 5.

1 This book tells you about
- ○ a fox in a cage.
- ○ a fox in a zoo.
- ● a fox in the desert.

2 What does the fox need?
- ● food and water
- ○ rocks and plants
- ○ mom and dad

4 What does the fox do when the sun goes down?
- ○ She goes to sleep.
- ● She wakes up.
- ○ She drinks some water.

3 The old fox sees a lizard. What does she do FIRST?
- ○ She calls the lizard.
- ● She looks and waits.
- ○ She runs around.

5 What happens LAST in the book? Use words from the book in your answer.

Possible answers: The fox gets the lizard.

The fox eats the lizard.

Teacher's Edition, p. LR18

Challenge

The eight checkpoints are Kaltag, Unalakleet, Shaktoolik, Koyuk, Elim, Golovin, White Mountain, and Safety. Look at the chart. Answer these questions using the chart:
* Which two checkpoints have the most miles between them?
* Which two checkpoints have the least miles between them?
* How many miles are there between Golovin and Safety?

Checkpoints	Distance Between Checkpoints
Kaltag to Unalakleet	90 miles
Unalakleet to Shaktoolik	40 miles
Shaktoolik to Koyuk	58 miles
Koyuk to Elim	48 miles
Elim to Golovin	28 miles
Golovin to White Mountain	18 miles
White Mountain to Safety	55 miles
Safety to Nome	22 miles

Make up your own math problems using the chart. Ask your classmates to solve them.

Take Me There **15**

Leveled Reader 5C, p. 14–15

Challenge

Sequence
Read *Foal*. Mark the ○ for the answer.

1 What happens just after the foal gets milk?
- ○ It wobbles.
- ● It can stand up tall.
- ○ It runs and plays in the meadow.

2 What happens by the time the foal is two weeks old?
- ● It gets new teeth.
- ○ It has sturdy legs.
- ○ It is full-grown.

3 When does the foal begin to run and play games?
- ○ when it is two weeks old
- ○ when it is a newborn
- ● when it is five weeks old

4 When is the foal almost as tall as its mother?
- ○ when it is two months old
- ● when it is four months old
- ○ when it is five weeks old

5 What is something a foal does before it grows as tall as its mother?

Answers will vary, but they should show that the child

understands the sequence of the story.

Leveled Practice and Test Link, pp. 61–63, *Foal*

Unit Theme Take Me There   **Lesson Topic** Growing Up

Additional Leveled Resources

Phonics Resources

Phonics Reader 27

Phonics Take-Home Readers in Reproducible Format

Book 27

Decodable Reader 36

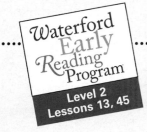

Waterford Early Reading Program Level 2 Lessons 13, 45

Language Support

Adding English pp. 177–184

Ten Important Sentences p. 33

Trade Books for Self-Selected Reading

Easy

Ducks Fly
by Lydia Dabcovich. Dutton, 1990

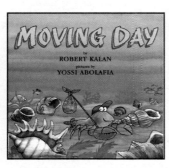

Moving Day
by Robert Kalan. Greenwillow, 1996

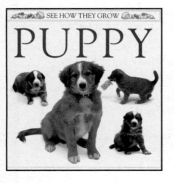

Puppy
photographed by Jane Burton. Dutton, 1991

On-Level

This Is the Way We Go to School
by Edith Baer. Scholastic, 1992
Trade Book Library Title

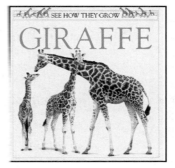

Giraffe
by Mary Ling. Dorling Kindersley, 1993

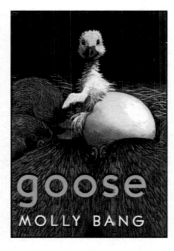

Goose
by Molly Bang. Scholastic, 1996

Challenge

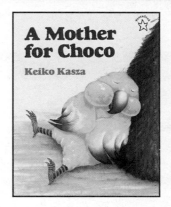

A Mother for Choco
by Keiko Kasza. Paper Star, 1996
Trade Book Library Title

Pitschi
by Hans Fischer. North-South Books, 1996

Stellaluna
by Janell Cannon. Harcourt Brace, 1993

Self-Selected Reading

- Allow 10–20 minutes per day for self-selected reading.
- For additional titles and for a read-aloud suggestion, see pp. AR24–AR25.
- For daily self-selected reading suggestions, see the 5-Day Planner, pp. 86e–86f.
- For activity ideas and management tips, see p. AR25.

- Have children select materials to read for pleasure, such as favorite books and stories.

Developmental Reading Assessment (DRA) from Celebration Press, an imprint of Pearson Learning, helps teachers by providing and documenting students' development as readers over time.

5-Day Planner

Reading

Comprehension

Vocabulary

Fluency

Independent Reading

Phonics/Word Study

Phonemic Awareness

Phonics

Spelling

High-Frequency Words

Oral Language

Speaking, Listening, Viewing

Oral Vocabulary

Writing

Grammar, Usage, Mechanics

Your State Standards

 Customize your week with the Teacher's Resource Planner CD-ROM!

Day 1

Activate Prior Knowledge, p. 86j

Phonics pp. 86k–86l

Phonemic Awareness: Long *o: oa, ow*

✓ **Phonics:** Introduce Long *o: oa, ow;* Inflected Ending *-ing*
PHONICS SONGS AND RHYMES CHART **"I See a Foal"**

Spelling: Inflected Ending *-ing*
  Pretest
  Work with Spelling Pattern

High-Frequency Words: Introduce **around, her, new, old, show**

Reading pp. 86m–93

Story Vocabulary

Read Pupil Edition PHONICS STORY: *Baby Otter Grows Up*

Independent Reading
  Self-Selected Reading, pp. 86d; AR24

Oral Language pp. 86m, 93a

Build Oral Language

✓ **Expand Vocabulary:** Discuss Unfamiliar Words

Writing pp. 86i, 93a–93b

Shared Writing: Award

Handwriting: *Gg*

Daily Writing Prompt: Write what you were like when you were a baby.

Day 2

Phonics pp. 93c–93d

✓ **Phonics:** Practice Long *o: oa, ow;* Inflected Ending *-ing*

Apply Phonics: Read the PHONICS READER *Duck Gets a New Coat* OR DECODABLE READER 36

Spelling: Writing for Sounds

High-Frequency Words: Practice

PB 1.5: Phonics, pp. 35, 36; High-Frequency Words, p. 37
TRB 1.5: Phonics, pp. 39, 40; High-Frequency Words, p. 41

Reading pp. 93e–93f

 Comprehension: Sequence
READ ALOUD "The Nightcrawler Hunt"

Fluency: Reread the PHONICS STORY: *Baby Otter Grows Up*

PB 1.5: Sequence, p. 38
TRB 1.5: Sequence, p. 42

Independent Reading
  Self-Selected Reading, pp. 86d; AR24

Oral Language p. 93g

 Listening: Listen for the Main Idea

Writing pp. 86i, 93g–93h

Modeled Writing: Write Facts

✓ **Grammar:** Adjectives That Tell Size

PB 1.5: p. 39; **TRB 1.5:** p. 43

Daily Writing Prompt: Draw a picture of how you look today. Write a sentence telling about the picture.

 Target Skill    **Review Skill**    **Assessment**

PB Practice Book
TRB Teacher's Resource Book

Target Skills of the Week

Reading Sequence
Phonics Long *o: oa, ow*; Inflected Ending *-ing*
Oral Language Listen for the Main Idea
Writing Adjectives That Tell Size

Day 3

Reading pp. 94a–111

Story Vocabulary

Read Pupil Edition MAIN SELECTION: *Foal*

 Comprehension: Sequence

Guided Reading Resources/Flexible Groups, pp. 94b; LR13–LR18
Leveled Readers 21A, 21B, 5C

PB 1.5: Vocabulary, p. 40
TRB 1.5: Vocabulary, p. 44

Independent Reading
Self-Selected Reading, pp. 86d; AR24

Phonics pp. 111a–111b

✓ 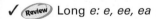 **Phonics:** Practice Long *o: oa, ow*; Inflected Ending *-ing*

✓ (Review) Long *e: e, ee, ea*

Fluency: Reread the PHONICS READER *Duck Gets a New Coat*

Spelling: Practice with Writing

High-Frequency Words: Practice

PB 1.5: Phonics, p. 41; Spelling, p. 42
TRB 1.5: Phonics, p. 45; Spelling, p. 46

Oral Language pp. 94a, 111c

Build Oral Language

✓ **Expand Vocabulary:** Understand Unfamiliar Words

Writing pp. 86i, 111c–111d

Modeled Writing: Animal Fact Cards

✓ **Grammar:** Adjectives That Tell Size

PB 1.5: p. 43; **TRB 1.5:** p. 47; **GPB:** p. 46

Daily Writing Prompt: Write a list of action words that tell what babies can do.

Day 4

Reading pp. 112–113

Read Together Pupil Edition
READER RESPONSE *Test Prep*

 Selection Test

PB 1.5: Selection Test, pp. 45–46
TRB 1.5: Selection Test, pp. 49–50

(Review) **Comprehension:** Setting

Fluency: Reread the MAIN SELECTION

Guided Reading Resources/Flexible Groups, pp. 94b; LR13–LR18
Leveled Readers 21A, 21B, 5C

Independent Reading
Self-Selected Reading, pp. 86d; AR24

Phonics pp. 113a–113b

✓ **Phonics:** Reteach Long *o: oa, ow*; Inflected Ending *-ing*

(Review) Single and Double Medial Consonants

Spelling: Partner Practice

High-Frequency Words: Review

PB 1.5: Phonics, p. 47; Spelling, p. 48
TRB 1.5: Phonics, p. 51; Spelling, p. 52

Oral Language pp. 114–115

Speaking: Talk About Adjectives

Writing pp. 86i, 114–115

✓ **Grammar:** Adjectives That Tell Size

Writing: Identify Adjectives That Tell Size

TRB 1.5: pp. 53–54; **GPB:** p. 47

Daily Writing Prompt: Write what you learned about a baby otter or a baby horse.

Day 5

Reading pp. 115a–115b

 Assess Oral Reading: Oral Reading Checklist

Guided Reading Resources/Flexible Groups, pp. 94b; LR13–LR18
Leveled Readers 21A, 21B, 5C

Independent Reading
Self-Selected Reading, pp. 86d; AR24

Phonics p. 115c

✓ **Phonics:** Practice Long *o: oa, ow*; Inflected Ending *-ing*

Apply Phonics: Read the PHONICS TAKE-HOME READER

Spelling: Inflected Ending *-ing*

 Posttest

High-Frequency Words: Practice

Oral Language p. 115d

 Listening: Listen for the Main Idea

Writing pp. 86i, 115d

Interactive Writing: Journal Entry *Portfolio*

Daily Writing Prompt: Write why you would like an otter or a horse for a pet.

Cross-Curricular Work Stations

Career Link

Ideas for bringing the school and community together

Field Experiences
horse farm or stables
pet shop

Guest Speakers
veterinarian
horse trainer

Letters and Sounds

Charades 15 minutes

Learning Styles Social, Verbal, Kinesthetic, Spatial

Children play charades with *-ing* verbs that tell what the foal learned to do. Write these words on cards: *jumping, running, galloping, grazing, roaming, neighing, wobbling, standing, staring, kicking, playing, walking.* Each child in turn chooses a card and acts out the word until it is correctly guessed. The child who guesses the word correctly chooses the next word to act out.

ESL Encourage children to participate in the pantomimes. Have pairs of children work together to act them out.

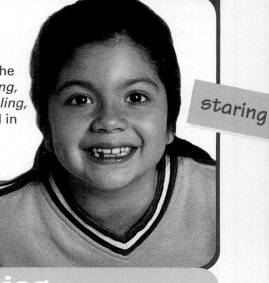
staring

Social Studies

Helping Chart 15 minutes

Materials: paper, markers or crayons

Learning Styles Visual, Verbal

Ask children to draw a picture that shows something they can do now that they couldn't do when they were in kindergarten. Then have children write a sentence that suggests a way that first graders could help kindergartners.

Math

How Much Have You Grown?   15 minutes

43	Tanya	Nyla
42		
41		
40		

Materials: yardstick, chart paper, markers

Learning Styles Kinesthetic, Visual, Spatial

Create a wall-size measuring stick with inches marked. Have small groups of children measure one another and mark the heights and label them with each child's name. Then have children create a bar graph showing the different heights.

Challenge Have children find out from an adult at home how long they were at birth. Then in class, children can use a calculator to determine how many inches each has grown.

INTERNET SAFETY Establish guidelines for your students' safe and responsible use of the Internet. See the Scott Foresman Internet Guide for tips.

Technology

Multimedia Presentation 15 minutes for five days

Learning Styles Visual, Verbal

Have each child bring one old and one recent photograph of himself or herself. Discuss ways the photographs are similar and different. Use Multimedia Studio to create and print out a presentation using the photographs (if possible) and the children's comparisons.

Reading Web Site 15 minutes

Learning Style Individual

Children can visit the Scott Foresman *Reading* Web site (sfreading.com) for current hyperlinks to relevant electronic texts that can be used for an Internet Workshop investigation of growing up. Also see the Scott Foresman Internet Guide for additional information on the Internet Workshop method.

sfreading.com

Art

Animal Family Painting 15 minutes

Materials: mural paper, tempera, paintbrushes, paint smocks

Learning Styles Visual, Spatial, Kinesthetic

One pair at a time chooses an animal and its baby to paint as part of a class mural. Some children may choose to paint a farm background with a barn, house, and fields. When reviewing the finished mural, ask pairs to describe what they think it might be like for their animal growing up.

Science

Animal Babies 15 minutes

Materials: index cards, drawing paper, paper punch, yarn, markers

Learning Styles Social, Verbal

Provide index cards with the names of adult and baby animals written on them, such as cow-calf, butterfly-caterpillar, goat-kid, hen-chick, bear-cub, frog-tadpole. Have children pick a card, write the name of the two animals at the bottom of a sheet of drawing paper, and illustrate them. When finished, make a class booklet to display.

Have children pronounce the Spanish names for animals and their babies. Examples include gato/gatito (*cat/kitten*); perro/perrito (*dog/puppy*).

Daily Routines

Message Board

Day One

Today you will hear a poem about a baby horse. What baby animals have you seen?

Have children describe baby animals and how the young animals are similar to and different from their parents.

Have children find the high-frequency words *show, her, new,* and *old* and the spelling word *float*.

Day Two

You read what an old otter can show her new baby. The baby can float! What have you learned from an adult?

Day Three

Today you will read about a foal. Have you ever been around large or small horses?

Have children find the high-frequency word *around*. Have them identify a long *o* word spelled with *oa*. (*foal*) Ask children to find two adjectives that tell about the size of horses. (*large, small*)

Have children find the spelling word *grow*. Have them find another word with the long *o* sound spelled *ow*. (*grows*)

Day Four

We read about how a foal grows and changes. Have you seen other animals grow and change? Tell me about them.

Day Five

These stories are about growing up. You are also getting older. How have you changed?

Have children find the spelling word *growing* and another word with the -*ing* ending. (*getting*)

Journal Writing

Day One
Write what you were like when you were a baby.

Day Two
Draw a picture of how you look today. Write a sentence telling about the picture.

Day Three
Write a list of action words that tell what babies can do.

Day Four
Write what you learned about a baby otter or a baby horse.

Day Five
Write why you would like an otter or a horse for a pet.

Family Times

Send home the newsletter with daily instructional activities to reinforce this week's skills.

Practice Book 1.5, pp. 33–34
Teacher's Resource Book 1.5, pp. 37–38

Activate Prior Knowledge

Objectives

Children will

- activate prior knowledge of topic: Growing Up
- relate literature to experiences in their own life
- visualize as they hear a selection read aloud
- set a purpose for listening

Day
1

▶ Assess Prior Knowledge

Discuss Growing Up Talk with children about experiences they have had with baby animals. Ask:

What do baby animals look like when they are just born?

What kinds of things do baby animals know how to do when they are born and what do they have to learn how to do?

How do baby animals change as they get older?

▶ Build Background

Read Aloud

Preview the Poem Discuss with children the sound a horse makes. Explain that the sound is called *neigh* or *whinny*. The word *whinny* is used in the poem. Help children set a purpose for listening such as to enjoy the picture the poem paints of the foal.

Read the Poem Share this poem with children. Ask:

How are foals similar to or different from their parents?

How do foals become more like their parents as they grow up?

Read Aloud
Foal

by Mary Britton Miller

Come trotting up
Beside your mother,
Little skinny.

Lay your neck across
Her back, and whinny,
Little foal.

You think you're a horse
Because you can trot—
But you're not.

Your eyes are so wild,
And each leg is as tall
As a pole;

And you're only a skittish
Child, after all,
Little foal.

PHONICS

Day 1

Objectives

Children will

- ⟳ identify the sound of long *o* spelled *oa, ow*
- ⟳ identify words with inflected ending *-ing*
- spell words with inflected ending *-ing*
- recognize high-frequency words

Skills Trace

⟳ **Long *o: oa, ow***

Introduce/Teach	TE: 1.5 86k
Practice	PB: 1.5 35; 1.6 9
Reteach/Review	TE: 1.5 93c, 111a, 113a, 115c, AR14; 1.6 31a
Test	Skills Test, Unit 5

Meeting Individual Needs

Intervention

Phonemic Awareness Say *coat.* Have children segment the word and repeat it very slowly, /k/ /ō/ /t/. Say *boat, goat, nail, pail, train, hose, rose,* and *rain.* Have children segment each word and sort their picture cards beneath the letters *o* and *a.*

Phonics Generalization CVVC

When two vowels appear together in a word, the first one usually stands for its long vowel sound and the second is silent.

Phonics Generalization

The letters *ow* can stand for the long *o* sound or for the diphthong sound /ou/.

Long *o: oa, ow*

▶ Develop Phonemic Awareness

Sing or Read the Rhyme Chart Tell children that as the CD or tape of this song is played, they should listen for words that have the same vowel sound as *foal.*

Focus on the Long *o* Sound Say:

> The rhyme is about a foal. When I say /f/ /ō/ /l/, I hear the long *o* sound in the middle of the word.

Explain that *oa* and *ow* can stand for /ō/, the long *o* sound. Have children say *foal* and *grow,* emphasizing the long *o* sound.

Then have children make an *o* shape with their thumb and forefinger when they hear words with /ō/: *coach, foal, snail, toast, boat, beat, way, grow, row, teach, road, tail.*

CD 2/Tape 14, Side 1
Phonics Songs and Rhymes Audio

I See a Foal

I see a foal with a shiny coat.
I see a foal playing with a goat.

I see a foal roaming all around.
I see a foal jumping on the ground.

I see a foal looking at a crow.
I see a foal running in the snow.

Phonics Songs and Rhymes Chart 21

▶ Connect Sounds to Letters

Teach Write the word *foal* on the board and have it read. Say:

> The letters *oa* in *foal* stand for the sound /ō/. /ō/ is the long *o* sound.

Have children repeat the sound /ō/ several times, stretching the sound as they say it. Follow a similar procedure with *snow* and the letters *ow.*

Blending Practice Have children blend the sounds /s/ /n/ /ō/ together to read *snow.* Have them continue decoding other *oa, ow* words the same way.

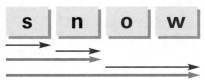

Make New Words Write *crow* on the board and have it read. Have children suggest rhyming words and tell how the words might be spelled. Write suggested words on the board. Then have children blend the words.

> crow   bow   low
> mow   row   sow   grow

Have children change *ow* to *ay* to make the rhyming words *bay, lay, may, ray, say,* and *gray.*

Inflected Ending *-ing*

▶ Teach Inflected Ending *-ing*

Write *walk* and *walking* on the board, circling the *-ing* ending. Remind children that *-ing* can be added to a base word such as *walk*. Using *hop* and *hopping*, have children tell how the base word changes when *-ing* is added. (another *p* was added)

▶ Make New Words

Have children brainstorm words that can have an *-ing* ending. List them in columns to show whether or not a spelling change is needed before *-ing* is added.

No Spelling Change	Spelling Change
spelling	hopping
walking	running
jumping	sitting

Spelling Inflected Ending *-ing*

Pretest Say the spelling word, use it in a sentence, repeat it, and allow children to write it. Have children check their pretests and correct misspelled words.

Work with the Spelling Pattern List the spelling words. Have children read the words, identify the letters in each word that spell the long *o* sound, and name the words that have the ending *-ing*. Have children use each word in a sentence.

<table>
<tr><th colspan="2">Skills Trace</th></tr>
<tr><th colspan="2">🎯 Inflected Ending -ing</th></tr>
<tr><td>Introduce/Teach</td><td>TE: 1.5 86l</td></tr>
<tr><td>Practice</td><td>PB: 1.5 36, 79</td></tr>
<tr><td>Reteach/Review</td><td>TE: 1.5 93c, 111a, 113a, 115c, 189a, AR14</td></tr>
<tr><td>Test</td><td>Skills Test, Units 2, 5 Benchmark Test, Units 2, 5</td></tr>
</table>

Day 1

Spelling Words

grow	growing
float	floating
show	showing

High-Frequency

around	old

Challenge

coat	yellow

Word Wall

Introduce High-Frequency Words

Use word cards for *around*, *her*, *new*, *old*, and *show*. Help children identify each word and use it in a sentence. As you attach each word under its beginning letter on the Word Wall, have children chant its spelling.

Review Ask children to read Word Wall words that have the long *o* sound.

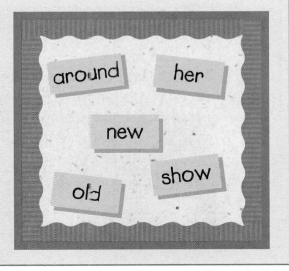

Optional Resources

Waterford Early Reading Program
Level 2: Lessons 13, 45

Phonics
Phonics Workbook, pp. 136–138
Phonics Manipulatives Kit

High-Frequency Words
High-Frequency Word Cards
Phonics Sourcebook, pp. 90–99

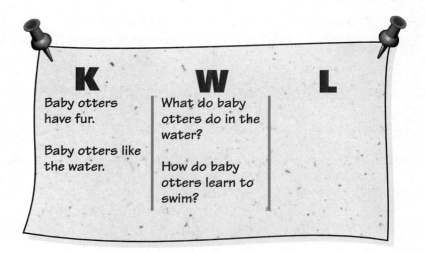

Objectives

Children will

- use context to develop meanings of new words
- use sound-symbol relationships to read decodable text
- identify the implied main idea of a selection
- use prior knowledge to make predictions about texts

Day 1

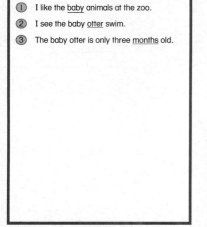

Baby Otter Grows Up

① I like the <u>baby</u> animals at the zoo.

② I see the baby <u>otter</u> swim.

③ The baby otter is only three <u>months</u> old.

Story Vocabulary Chart 40

Phonics Story **Baby Otter Grows Up**

pp. 86–93

▶ Build Oral Language

Activate Prior Knowledge Display a picture of a baby otter. Have children tell what they know and what they would like to learn about baby otters. Make a K-W-L chart to show their comments. You may use Graphic Organizer Transparency 7 (K-W-L Chart).

K	W	L
Baby otters have fur.	What do baby otters do in the water?	
Baby otters like the water.	How do baby otters learn to swim?	

Build Background Invite children to look through fiction and nonfiction picture books about otters and their babies.

▶ Vocabulary

Introduce Story Vocabulary List selection vocabulary words on the board. Use Vocabulary Chart 40, or write sentences on the board, using each vocabulary word. Read each sentence aloud.

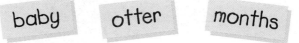

baby   otter   months

Frame *otter* in the sentence. Ask children to read the word. Ask children what they know about the otter from the sentence. Continue similarly for the other words.

Review High-Frequency Words As you point to each of these words on the Word Wall, have children read the word. Ask children to identify the words with the long o sound. (*old, show*) These words are also listed on page 228 of the Student Book.

around   her   new   old   show

— high-frequency/tested vocabulary

▶ Reading Strategies

Preview and Predict Read the title and the names of the author and illustrator to children. Ask children to find the baby otter in the picture on the first page of the story.

> **Whose back do you think the baby otter is on?** (It's on its mother's back.)
>
> **Why do you think the baby otter is on its mother's back?** (That's how the baby otter gets from one place to another. The mother otter can protect the baby.)

Picture Walk Have children do a picture walk, looking at all the pictures in the story. Ask children what they think they will learn about baby otters in the selection.

Set Purposes Have children set purposes for reading the selection based on their predictions. They may want to find out why the baby otter stays on its mother's back while she swims.

Guide the Reading Have children read the first few pages of the selection, keeping their purposes in mind. Stop and check comprehension, using the questions provided. Have children read to page 89.

Phonics Story

Baby Otter Grows Up
by Susan McCloskey
illustrated by Anna Vojtech

This is a baby otter. A baby otter is called a kit. This kit is three months old and still growing. The kit rides on his mom's back. He is holding on to her coat to keep from slipping.

Selection Audio
CD 6/Tape 23, Side 1

About the Author

Susan McCloskey lives in Portland, Maine. A few of her children's titles include *The Yard Sale, Sally's Spaceship,* and *The Hunt for a Cold Nose.* In addition to publishing several children's books, she contributes to many children's magazines.

Optional Resources

Reading
Adding English: ESL Teacher's Guide

Guiding Comprehension

pp. 86–89

Drawing Conclusions/Inferential

Why does the mother otter go in and out of the water with the kit on her back?

She wants the kit to get used to the water and learn how to swim.

Self-Monitoring Strategy

I don't see where it says that the mother is trying to get the baby used to the water by taking it on her back. How did you know that?

Possible answer: Moms try to teach babies. This mom is trying to teach the kit how to swim and not to be afraid by going in and out of the water.

Organizing Information/Critical

What have you learned about baby otters?

Baby otters are called kits. A baby otter holds on to its mother while she swims. At first it is afraid and then the kit gets used to her going in and out of the water. Add children's responses to the K-W-L chart.

Making Judgments/Critical

Why do you think the mother otter swims into deep water?

Possible answer: The mother otter swims into deep water to get the baby otter used to it.

Connect Phonics to Reading

What does the author compare the kit's mom to? a small boat **What sound do you hear in the middle of that word?** You hear the long o sound. Help children blend the word: /b/ /ō/ /t/.

Read On... to the end of the story.

Phonics Story

Baby Otter Grows Up

by Susan McCloskey
illustrated by Anna Vojtech

This is a baby otter. A baby otter is called a kit. This kit is three months old and still growing.

The kit rides on his mom's back. He is holding on to her coat to keep from slipping.

86

Baby Otter Grows Up, page 86

Soon the kit's mom comes out of the water. Then she slides in again. This time, her kit likes sailing on her back. Mom is like a small boat.

88 Phonics Story

Baby Otter Grows Up, page 88

One day, his mom slips into the water. This is something <u>new</u>!
The kit is afraid. But his mom does not go back to the land. She keeps swimming <u>around</u> in the water.

Phonics Story **87**

***Baby Otter Grows Up,* page 87**

One day the kit's mom swims into deep water. The little kit is holding on to <u>her</u> back. He seems to like floating <u>around</u>.

89

***Baby Otter Grows Up,* page 89**

Phonics Strategies

If... children read the word *growing,* | **then...** ask them how they figured out the word. **Self-Monitoring**

If... children have difficulty reading *floating,* | **then...** remind them that *-ing* is an ending added to a word. Cover the ending and have children read the base word. Then have children read the word with the ending. Ask children to find other words on pages 86–89 that have the *-ing* ending. *(growing, holding, slipping, swimming, sailing)* **Decoding Using Structural Analysis: Inflected Endings**

Reading Strategies

If... children have difficulty tracking from one line of text to the next, | **then...** have them use a card to mask the text so that only one line of text is revealed at a time. Encourage children to move the card so that their eyes track ahead of the words they are reading. **Adjusting Reading Rate**

If... children are unable to tell what they have learned about baby otters in the selection so far, | **then...** have them look at the pictures and tell what is happening in each. **Using Illustrations**

▓ long *o* and inflected ending *-ing*
— high-frequency/tested vocabulary

Guiding Comprehension

pp. 90–93

Day 1

Sequence/Literal

Tell in order what has happened to the kit since its mother began taking it into the water.

The mother otter went in and out of the water, then she went into deep water and sank below the kit. The kit learned it could swim. The kit grew up, and now it swims, floats on its back, and plays with other otters.

Making Judgments/Critical

Why is the mother otter a good mother?

Possible answer: She lets the kit hold on to her back so it can stay with her. She teaches the kit to swim.

Organizing Information/Critical

What else would you like to learn about baby otters that the selection didn't tell you?

Possible answers: What do baby otters eat? What do baby otters do before they learn to swim? Add responses to the K-W-L chart and help them find the answers.

Connect Phonics to Reading

What is happening to the kit's mother? The kit's mom is sinking. **Identify the base word.** *sink* **Does the base word change?** No

 **Response Log** Have children imagine themselves to be otters and create movements to show how they move in the water.

Look! The kit's mom is sinking! What will happen to the kit? Will he sink or float?

90

Baby Otter Grows Up, page 90

Now the kit is almost grown. He swims well. He swims around the slow ducks. He can float on his back too.

92 Phonics Story

Baby Otter Grows Up, page 92

The kit will float. He can swim!
But his mom had to show him that
he could.

Phonics Story **91**

Baby Otter Grows Up, page 91

Best of all, he can play in the
water with his friends.

93

Baby Otter Grows Up, page 93

Skills in Context

Review
Main Idea

What is the story *Baby Otter Grows Up* all about: a duck, a mother otter, or a baby otter?

It tells about a baby otter.

Ongoing Assessment
Main Idea
If... children are unable to tell what the selection is about, / **then...** do the **Think Aloud** below to model the skill.

Model Your Thinking

TEST TALK

The name of this story is *Baby Otter Grows Up*, so I know the story is not about ducks, although I see some in the pictures. The mother otter is important because she takes care of the baby otter. But I think the selection is mostly about the baby otter. It tells what happens as the baby otter learns to swim.

Have children tell what the picture on page 92 is all about—the ducks, the kit, or the mother otter.

Extend Language Arts
Grammar: Asking and Telling Sentences

Lead children in a choral reading of one asking sentence on page 90. Have children make the mark that shows it is an asking sentence in the air with their hands. Repeat with a telling sentence from the selection and a gesture to show a period.

Have partners take turns finding and reading examples of telling and asking sentences in other books. Invite them to make the end mark in the air.

▨ long *o* and inflected ending *-ing*
▬ high-frequency/tested vocabulary

Day 1

Expand Vocabulary

▶ Discuss Unfamiliar Words

Recall *Baby Otter Grows Up.* Have children turn to page 90 and follow along as you read, "Look! The kit's mom is sinking!" Ask, "How would you figure out the meaning of the word *sinking?*" Elicit responses such as:

- Look at words, phrases, and sentences nearby.
- Look at the picture.
- Use alphabetical order to find words in a picture dictionary.
- Ask a teacher or friend.

WRITING

Award

▶ Shared Writing

Create an Award Remind children that they read about the baby otter, or kit, growing up. Tell them they will create a growing-up award for the kit. Ask children to give ideas about what the kit has learned. You may wish to reread the story with children to refresh their memories.

As you write children's responses on the chalkboard, point out the left-to-right and top-to-bottom direction of the writing. Point out the spaces between letters and the spaces between words. Continue writing phrases until all phrases below appear on the chalkboard.

riding on his mother's back

floating in the water

floating on his back

sailing on his mother's back

swimming in the water

playing in water with friends

Independent Writing Cut out large circles of light-colored construction paper. Tape or glue ribbon to the bottom of each. Have each child create an award for the baby otter. Tell children to draw a picture that shows something the baby otter did as he grew up and have children write a phrase to describe the picture. Suggest they use phrases on the chalkboard for ideas.

Self-Selected Reading and Read Aloud D.E.A.R.

Read aloud *Verdi* by Janell Cannon. Children choose a book about baby animals for independent reading.

Day 1

Handwriting *Gg*

Provide lined paper and handwriting models. Demonstrate how to write a capital G and a lowercase g and have children practice writing a row of each letter.

Ask children to evaluate their handwriting by circling with a red crayon their best capital G and their best lowercase g.

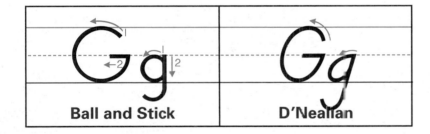

Ball and Stick	D'Nealian

Letter Names Write these sentences on the board:

> Goldie grows green grass.
> Grams got a gray goat.

As you write, point out that letters have names. Name the letters as you write them.

Optional Resources

Oral Language
Adding English: ESL Teacher's Guide

Objectives

Children will

- decode words with long *o* spelled *oa, ow* and with the inflected ending *-ing*
- spell words with inflected ending *-ing*
- build words with long *o* spelled *oa, ow*
- recognize high-frequency words

Day
2

Decodable Readers 33–41

Decodable Reader 36,
Duck's Coat

Optional Resources

Phonics
Phonics Workbook, pp. 136–138
Phonics Manipulatives Kit
Phonics Sourcebook, pp. 79–82, 100–123

High-Frequency Words
High-Frequency Word Cards
Phonics Sourcebook, pp. 90–99

93c Phonics • Spelling

Long *o: oa, ow* Inflected Ending *-ing*

▶ Phonics Practice Activities

Use the following activities and Practice Book pages to practice long *o* and inflected ending *-ing*.

Phonics Songs and Rhymes Chart Children sing "I See a Foal" as you track the print. Have volunteers draw lines from long *o* words to their pictures on the chart. Other children can list the words according to spelling pattern. Then ask volunteers to find a word with an *-ing* ending and read that line aloud.

Make New Words Pairs of children use letter cards *o, a, b, d, e, g, l, m, r, s, t,* and *w* to make long *o* words. Remind them that *oa* and *ow* can stand for the long *o* sound. Have each partner choose one word, write the word, and draw a picture that illustrates it.

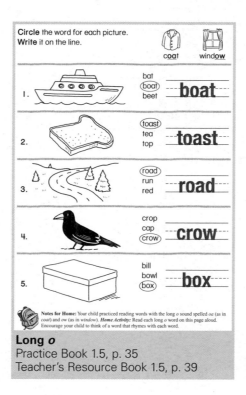

Long *o*
Practice Book 1.5, p. 35
Teacher's Resource Book 1.5, p. 39

Inflected Ending *-ing*
Practice Book 1.5, p. 36
Teacher's Resource Book 1.5, p. 40

▶ Read the Phonics Reader

Remind children to use what they know about long *o* spelled *oa* or *ow* and words with the *-ing* ending as they read *Duck Gets a New Coat*. Observe children's reading to determine their ability to transfer these phonics skills to a new selection. After reading, have children:

- draw a picture that tells the story
- write the base words for all *-ing* words in the story

Phonics Reader

Spelling Words with Long *o* and *-ing*

▶ Writing for Sounds

Have children write these sentences. Read the sentences. Then repeat words slowly, allowing children to hear each sound. Children may use the Word Wall to help in spelling high-frequency words. Proofread and correct completed sentences.

Let me show you what is growing in the ground.
They are showing how to float it.
A floating boy can grow.

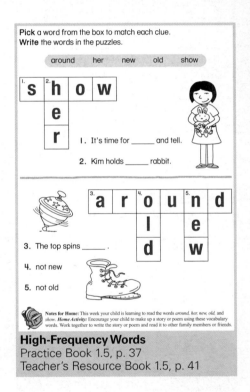

Spelling Words

grow	growing
float	floating
show	showing

High-Frequency

around	old

Challenge

coat	yellow

Day 2

Pick a word from the box to match each clue.
Write the words in the puzzles.

around   her   new   old   show

1. It's time for _____ and tell.
2. Kim holds _____ rabbit.

3. The top spins _____ .
4. not new
5. not old

Notes for Home: This week your child is learning to read the words *around, her, new, old,* and *show. Home Activity:* Encourage your child to make up a story or poem using these vocabulary words. Work together to write the story or poem and read it to other family members or friends.

High-Frequency Words
Practice Book 1.5, p. 37
Teacher's Resource Book 1.5, p. 41

Word Wall

Practice High-Frequency Words

Choose 10 words from the Word Wall. Have children write them on slips of paper. Invite children to find different ways to sort the words. For example, by initial or final letters, vowel sounds, number of letters, or those that can take an *-ing* ending. Discuss the importance of alphabetical order.

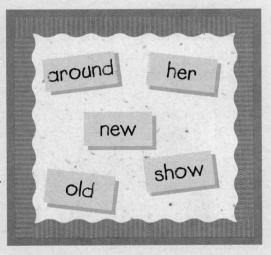

around   her   new   show   old

Meeting Individual Needs

ESL	Intervention	Challenge	Other Ways to Learn
Have children compare the vowel sounds, spellings, and the meanings of the following word pairs: *coat/cot, goat/got, soak/sock, road/rod, bloat/blot.* **(Phonics Support)** See also *Adding English.*	Use **Decodable Reader 36** and the teaching suggestions on p. AR4 to provide practice reading decodable text that includes words with long *o: oa, ow* and inflected ending *-ing.* **(Phonics Support)**	Make word cards for *toast, boat, road, toad, crow,* and *snow.* Have children take turns giving and using clues to identify words. For example, *This word rhymes with* roast *and is something you eat for breakfast.* **(Divergent Thinking)**	Use Phonics Activity Mat 6 from the Phonics Manipulatives Kit for long *o.* Use Phonics Activity Mat 1 for inflected ending *-ing.* Instructions for using these games are on the back of the mats. **(Kinesthetic)**

Objectives

Children will

- listen to determine the stated sequence of events in a story
- understand that events in a story happen in an ordered sequence
- read with fluency and understanding

Skills Trace

Sequence

Introduce	TE: 1.1 164	
Teach	Before	TE: 1.5 **93e–93f**
	During	TE: 1.5 108–109
	After	TE: 1.5 AR15
Practice	PB: 1.1 77; 1.5 38; 1.6 6	
Reteach/Review	TE: 1.5 AR15; 1.6 17e–17f, 28–29, 33, AR12	
Test	Skills Test, Units 2, 6	
	Benchmark Test, Units 2, 6	

Day 2

Building Systematic Instruction

Sequence

LOOKING BACK

Kindergarten Children understand that something happens first, next, and at the end of a story.

- - - - - - - - - - - - - - - - - -

Grade 1 Children talk about what happens first, next, and at the end of a story. Children begin to rely on clue words to signal the order of events.

LOOKING AHEAD

Grade 2 Children read to find what happens first, next, and at the end of a story, and understand that clue words indicate sequence.

Sequence

►Develop Listening Comprehension

Read the following story aloud. Ask children to listen to find out what happens first, next, and at the end of the story.

Read Aloud

The Nightcrawler Hunt

Jacob knew that it was a perfect evening to hunt for nightcrawlers. There had been a thunderstorm around dinner time. Not a big storm, just enough to cool things off and dampen the ground.

First, Jacob had waited for the sun to sink low on the horizon. He got his bucket, sat down on the grass, and waited for the moon to appear.

Next, as the moon was rising, he saw his first nightcrawler, a brown worm, shining between the blades of grass. He reached out and grabbed it between two fingers. He saw another and then another shining in the moonlight. He picked each one up, and soon his bucket was full.

Finally, Jacob went home and got into bed. He had wonderful dreams of the fishing he would have tomorrow after his successful night of nightcrawler hunting!

▶ Teach Sequence

Model the skill by telling children:

I can tell when things happen in the story by listening for clue words. First, Jacob sat on the grass and waited for the moon to appear. Next, he saw nightcrawlers, picked them up, and filled his bucket. Finally, he went to bed and dreamed about fishing.

Practice Have children create story maps to show their understanding of sequence. You can use Graphic Organizer Transparency 10 (Plot/Story Sequence) to help children get started.

Beginning	Middle	End
Jacob waits for night.	He catches nightcrawlers.	He dreams about fishing.

Sequence
Practice Book 1.5, p. 38
Teacher's Resource Book 1.5, p. 42

Day 2

Reread for Fluency

Attend to Punctuation Model fluent reading by reading aloud. Have children listen as you read complete sentences and pause for periods, question marks, and exclamation points, even though the line of type may continue or the sentence continues to the next line.

Paired Reading Have children find the beginning and end of each sentence on a page and have a different child read each sentence. Continue this way through the story. Then have pairs of children reread alternate pages of the story. Pairs should read the story again, this time reading the other pages.

Leveled Practice for ↻ Sequence

After children have read *Foal,* use the appropriate leveled practice pictured on page 113 in this Teacher's Edition.

Easy
On-Level
Challenge

❄ Meeting Individual Needs

ESL	Intervention	Challenge	Other Ways to Learn
Draw simple pictures of each of the following, one scene on each sheet of paper: seedling sprouting, small tree, huge mature tree. Mix up and then ask children to place the pictures in order. **(Skill Support)** See also *Adding English.* 🅔🅢🅛	Use another familiar selection to reinforce sequence of events. For *Mary Goes Walking,* have children order two pictures—one of Mary in clean clothes and one of Mary in dirty clothes. For *Desert Fox,* have children tell what the fox does first, next, and last each day. **(Comprehension Support)**	Children create a comic strip of *Baby Otter Grows Up* by drawing and labeling pictures of selection events in order. **(Application of Different Symbol Systems)**	Children make finger puppets and use them to show the sequence of events in *Baby Otter Grows Up.* **(Kinesthetic)** Children fold paper into thirds and draw the steps it took for the otter to learn to swim. **(Visual/Spatial)**

ORAL LANGUAGE

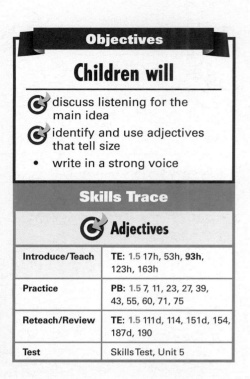

Objectives

Children will

◎ discuss listening for the main idea

◎ identify and use adjectives that tell size

• write in a strong voice

Skills Trace

◎ Adjectives

Introduce/Teach	**TE:** 1.5 17h, 53h, **93h**, 123h, 163h
Practice	**PB:** 1.5 7, 11, 23, 27, 39, 43, 55, 60, 71, 75
Reteach/Review	**TE:** 1.5 111d, 114, 151d, 154, 187d, 190
Test	Skills Test, Unit 5

Day 2

Listening: Listen for the Main Idea

► Discuss Growing Up

Model Tell children you will read a page from *Baby Otter Grows Up*. Ask children to listen so they can tell what this part of the story is all about. Read page 88.

Ask questions, such as:

> **What is the big picture?**
> **What is this part of the story mostly about?**
> **How did you decide what this part of the story is mostly about?**

As you ask questions and help children with responses, model these behaviors:

• Listen for details, such as Mom being like a small boat, and use them to make pictures in your mind.

• Show that little bits of information, or little pictures, help to build the big picture.

• Try to use one sentence or phrase to state the main idea.

Practice Assign partners. Have one partner read a page from a favorite book. The other partner should listen closely and then tell what that part of the story is all about. Partners can then switch roles.

WRITING

Write Facts

► Modeled Writing

Model Review the awards children created for the baby otter on Day 1. Tell children that they will write two sentences about what the baby sea otter learned. Demonstrate how to expand children's facts into sentences with a strong voice, a voice that sounds as though children are excited about the writing.

Think ALOUD I want to write about things the kit learned in a way that sounds just like me. As I write my sentences, I want to think about who will be reading them.

▶ Write About Growing Up

Model Write two sentences about the baby sea otter growing up.

> The baby sea otter quickly learned to swim.
> The playful kit can float on his back.

As you write the sentences, model these strategies:
- Use natural-sounding formal language (no slang).
- Use language and sentence structure that the audience will understand and find interesting.
- Provide accurate information.
- Show enthusiasm.
- Use correct end punctuation.
- Form letters correctly.

Independent Writing Have children write two sentences about things the baby otter learned while growing up. Remind them to write sentences that show their excitement about the baby otter and the things he learned. Have them look up the correct spelling of words they guessed at.

Author's Chair If time permits, allow children to share their writing.

Self-Selected Reading and Read Aloud D.E.A.R.

Read aloud *Hermit Crab Moves House* by Linda Hartley. Children self-select books about animals.

Day 2

Grammar: Adjectives That Tell Size

Define Adjectives Write the words *small* and *large* on the chalkboard. Ask volunteers to use their hands to show what the two words mean. Explain that *small* and *large* are adjectives. Remind children that adjectives describe people, places, and things. Point out that children already know adjectives that tell color and shape, and now they are going to think about adjectives, such as *small* and *large,* that tell size.

Practice Provide books and articles that include size adjectives. Discuss with children words they find in the books to describe size. Create a word web on a chart to record children's responses.

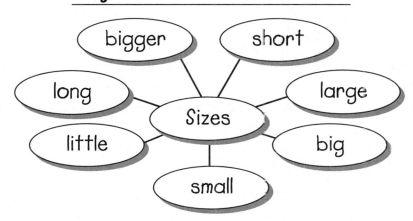

Adjectives That Tell Size

(word web: Sizes — bigger, short, long, large, little, big, small)

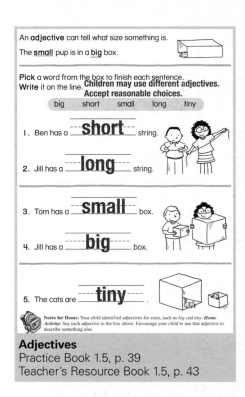

An **adjective** can tell what size something is.
The **small** pup is in a **big** box.

Pick a word from the box to finish each sentence. **Children may use different adjectives.**
Write it on the line. **Accept reasonable choices.**

| big | short | small | long | tiny |

1. Ben has a **short** string.
2. Jill has a **long** string.
3. Tom has a **small** box.
4. Jill has a **big** box.
5. The cats are **tiny**

Notes for Home: Your child identified adjectives for sizes, such as *big* and *tiny*. **Home Activity:** Say each adjective in the box above. Encourage your child to use that adjective to describe something else.

Adjectives
Practice Book 1.5, p. 39
Teacher's Resource Book 1.5, p. 43

For further practice, have children identify adjectives they used in their writing and add them to the web.

Day 3

Foal

1. The <u>ponies</u> are in the barn.
2. A <u>newborn</u> is a baby that was just born.
3. The newborn horse curled <u>beneath</u> its mother.
4. It was a <u>struggle</u> to reach the milk.
5. Milk makes baby horses <u>stronger</u>.
6. The baby horse's legs were <u>wobbly</u> at first.
7. The horses eat grass in the <u>field</u>.
8. One horse kicked its <u>hooves</u> into the air.
9. Did you hear the horse <u>neigh</u>?

Story Vocabulary Chart 41

Pick a word from the box to finish each sentence.
Write it on the line.

around   her   new   old   ponies   show

1. Look at the **ponies**
2. One pony has a **new** baby foal.
3. The foal looks **around** for its mother.
4. The mother is close to **her** foal.
5. The foal is new, but the mother is **old** .
6. I want to **show** the foal to my dad!

Notes for Home: Your child used newly-learned words to finish a story. *Home Activity:* Spell each of the vocabulary words aloud. Ask your child to name each word.

Tested Vocabulary
Practice Book 1.5, p. 40
Teacher's Resource Book 1.5, p. 44

Foal

pp. 94–109

▶ Build Oral Language

Activate Prior Knowledge Ask children to discuss what parents teach their children.

> **What does the baby otter learn to do?**
> **What have you learned from your parents?**
> **What other things do human and animal babies learn from their parents?**

Build Background Play the Background-Building audio segment, an interview with a horse breeder. After listening, create a K-W-L chart about foals or use Graphic Organizer 7 (K-W-L Chart). List the things that children know about foals and things they would like to find out. Say that they will return to the chart to record what they learn.

Background-Building Audio
CD 5/Tape 13, Side 1

▶ Vocabulary

Introduce Story Vocabulary List the selection vocabulary on the board. Use Vocabulary Chart 41 or write sentences using each word. Read the sentences aloud.

ponies   newborn   beneath   struggle

stronger   wobbly   field   hooves   neigh

Point to the word *beneath* in the list. Have children find it in one of the sentences. Have a volunteer circle the word, read it to the class, and tell what it means. Continue similarly with the remaining words.

▶ Reading Strategies

Preview and Predict Have children read the title of the story and the author's name. Explain that the pictures in this story are photographs taken by Gordon Clayton. As children do a picture walk, discuss what they think is happening in the photographs. Have them use the photographs and captions on pages 104–105 along with their knowledge about baby animals to make predictions about the selection.

Set Purposes Have children set a purpose for reading *Foal.* They may want to read to find out what happens to the foal as it grows up.

Guide the Reading Have children read the first two pages of the story, keeping their purposes in mind. Then, point out the chapter title at the top of page 96. Have children find each chapter title (on every left-hand page) and ask them why they think the author chose that title. Then ask children which chapter title they would use to find out what a newborn foal is like ("Newborn").

Stop to check comprehension, using the questions provided. Have children read to page 97.

Managing Flexible Groups

Intervention

Children listen to the selection audio and follow along in their books. After reading, children can use the pictures to retell the story of the foal's growth.

To develop fluency and to practice high-frequency words, children can read **Leveled Reader 21A**, *Mary Goes Walking.* Instructional support appears in this Teacher's Edition, pp. LR13–LR14.

Selection Audio

CD 6/Tape 23, Side 1

Easy

Children can review the high-frequency words. Read the story aloud with children. Call children's attention to section titles and to their purpose. Children echo-read each section title and each sentence. Help children with unfamiliar words such as *graze*. Use Guiding Comprehension to monitor understanding and Ongoing Assessment as appropriate.

To develop fluency and to practice high-frequency words, children can read **Leveled Reader 21B**, *Desert Fox.* Instructional support appears in this Teacher's Edition, pp. LR16–LR17.

On-Level

Have children read aloud the section titles and discuss what they think each section will be about. Have them pause after each section and tell what they learned about the foal. Use Guiding Comprehension to monitor understanding and Ongoing Assessment to address reading difficulties.

To develop fluency and to practice high-frequency words, children can read **Leveled Reader 21B**, *Desert Fox.* Instructional support appears in this Teacher's Edition, pp. LR16–LR17.

Challenge

Tell children to pay attention to the text and illustrations to see how the foal changes from page to page. After reading, children retell the stages of the foal's life to a partner.

Children who have finished reading *Foal* can read a selection in **Leveled Reader 5C**.

Day 3

Optional Resources

Reading
Adding English: ESL Teacher's Guide

Guiding Comprehension

pp. 94–97

Using Illustrations/Critical

What do the pictures show about how the foal changes after having its milk? Why do you think the mother's milk is important?

The pictures show that before having milk, the foal is wobbly. After having milk, the foal stands up strong and tall. Most children will use prior knowledge and say that just like children, foals need milk to grow.

Recall and Retell/Literal

What does the foal like to do in the meadow?

It cuddles close to its mother, and it loves to feel the soft grass beneath its hooves.

Organizing Ideas and Information/Critical

The foal can use its legs to stand. What do you think it will learn to do next?

Possible responses: The foal will walk. It will learn to run like its mother. If children have other questions, have them add their questions to the second column of the K-W-L chart.

Connect Phonics to Reading

Look at page 96. What word tells where the foal spends its days? What letters stand for /ō/ at the end of meadow?

The foal spends its days in the meadow. The letters *ow* stand for /ō/ at the end of *meadow*.

Read On...

to page 101.

Day 3

FOAL

by Mary Ling
photos by Gordon Clayton

Newborn

I am a foal, a newborn pony. My legs are very wobbly.

My mother feeds me her warm milk as soon as I struggle to my feet.

94

Foal, page 94

In the meadow

I am one week old.
I grow bigger every day.

I spend my days
in the meadow
with my mother.

96

Foal, page 96

I feel stronger
after my milk.
I can stand up tall.

95

Foal, page 95

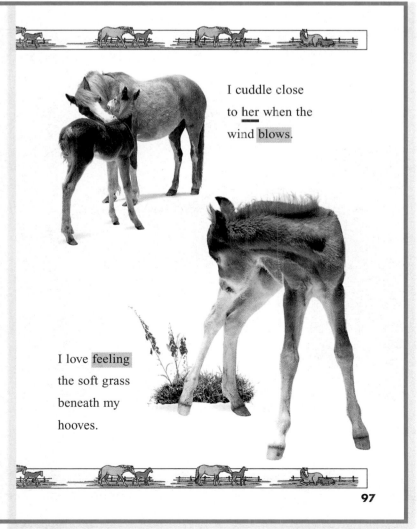

I cuddle close
to her when the
wind blows.

I love feeling
the soft grass
beneath my
hooves.

97

Foal, page 97

Explain to children that fiction tells stories of imaginary people and events. Nonfiction tells information about the real world. Help children understand that *Foal* is nonfiction, even though the foal is talking, because it gives facts about real horses. The selection tells about an event. Ask:

What event does *Foal* tell about? (a foal growing up)

Have children recite the facts they have learned so far about how a foal grows up.

Day
3

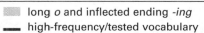

Content Connection: Art

Horses have been depicted in images since prehistoric times on cave walls. Today, horses are popular animals to showcase in paintings and in photographs. Photographers called equestrian photographers take pictures of horses as a career.

▒ long *o* and inflected ending *-ing*
▬ high-frequency/tested vocabulary

Guiding Comprehension

pp. 98–101

Day 3

Main Idea and Supporting Details/Inferential

What does the foal do to have fun?

The foal's friend comes to play games and run around the field. They eat fresh grass.

Drawing Conclusions/Inferential

How do you know that the foal likes to be with other foals?

The foal has fun playing with a friend.

Self-Monitoring Strategy
Use Illustrations

I didn't read, "The foal likes other foals." How do you know this?

Possible responses: The text tells that when the foal has a friend come to play, it will be a fun day. I know that if the foal did not like other foals, it would not play games and run with the other foal. The pictures show they like each other too.

Organizing Ideas and Information/Critical

What have you learned so far about foals?

Children are likely to say that they have learned that foals have wobbly legs when they are first born and drink milk from their mothers. The foal grows quickly and spends days in the meadow, gets new teeth, and plays with other foals. Add children's responses to the L column of the K-W-L chart.

Read On...

to page 105.

Looking for Mommy

I am two weeks old.
I have two new teeth.
I want to show my mother.

Where is she?
I neigh loudly to her.

98

Foal, page 98

Come and play

I am five weeks old.

Today will be a fun day!
A friend has come to play.

100

Foal, page 100

I hope she
hears me.

Soon my mother
comes. She is never
very far away.

99

Foal, page 99

We play our
games and run
around the field.

When we are
tired, we graze
together.
The fresh grass
tastes sweet.

101

Foal, page 101

Reading Strategies

If... children have trouble identifying that the foal is growing and changing,	**then...** ask them to look at the illustrations. Prompt them to talk about how the foal looks and what it is doing from one illustration to another. What can it do when it is five weeks old that it could not do when it was one week old? **Compare and Contrast, Using Illustrations**
If... children stop at an unknown word,	**then...** ask them to read on to the end of the sentence and predict what the word might be. Encourage children to use illustrations and what they know about letters and sounds to figure out the word. **Picture Clues, Context Clues, Decoding**

Phonics Strategies

If... children have difficulty decoding *show*,	**then...** remind them that the letters *ow* can stand for /ō/. **Decoding**

Day
3

▨ long *o* and inflected ending *-ing*
— high-frequency/tested vocabulary

Guiding Comprehension

pp. 102–105

Drawing Conclusions/Inferential

Why is the foal curious about the apples?

The foal is hungry and thinks the apples might be yummy.

Sequence/Inferential

TEST TALK **How do you think the foal has changed since it was born? Find sentences in the selection to support your answer.**

Children may point to the sentences on pages 94 and 102 to show how the foal has changed.

Summarizing/Inferential

What is the foal like at age four months?

Its coat is chestnut brown, its legs are sturdy, and it is almost as tall as its mother.

Day 3

Connect Phonics to Reading

The foal likes to run and jump. Look at page 102. What ending has been added to those words? How do the base words change?

The ending *-ing* has been added to those words. In the base word *run*, the last letter, *n*, is doubled before adding *-ing*. The base word *jump* does not change before the ending is added.

Read On...

to the end of the selection.

Crunchy apples

I am eight weeks old.
I gallop around the
fields every day.

Running and jumping
makes me very hungry.

102

Foal, page 102

Long legs

I am four months old.
My coat is chestnut brown now.

My long legs are sturdy.
I do not wobble anymore.

104

Foal, page 104

Look at these crunchy red apples. They smell yummy. I wonder if I can eat one?

103

Foal, page 103

Reading Strategies

If... children cannot explain why the foal is curious about the apples,	**then...** ask children to think about how they might have felt the first time they saw and smelled an apple. **Prior Knowledge**
If... children can explain how the foal is changing,	**then...** congratulate them on remembering what they read. **Recall and Retell**

Phonics Strategies

If... children have trouble reading the words *running*, *jumping*, and *growing*,	**then...** frame and have children read the base word first, then the entire word with the *-ing* ending. **Decoding**

I am growing taller every day.
I am almost as tall as my mother.

105

Foal, page 105

long *o* and inflected ending *-ing*
— high-frequency/tested vocabulary

Day **3**

Guiding Comprehension

pp. 106–109

Recall and Retell/Literal

How old is the foal when it is nearly full-grown?

It is five months old.

Compare and Contrast/Inferential

Do you think you were like the foal in any way when you were five months old? How were you different?

Children are likely to say that they were learning new things every day when they were five months old, but they were not grown up. They could not walk, talk, or go off to play with other babies by themselves.

Day 3

Organizing Ideas and Information/Critical

Which of your questions have been answered?

Have children add their answers to the *L* column of the K-W-L chart. Invite children to check the *W* column of the K-W-L chart to find out if their questions have been answered and to add other questions they have.

Critical Thinking
Reading Across Texts

READING ACROSS TEXTS **What things are the same about a kit and a foal? What things are different?**

They are the same because they both have mothers who take care of them and teach them. They are different because a kit has to learn to swim in the water and a foal has to learn to gallop and jump on land.

Response Log Have a group discussion comparing the two selections of the week. Discuss animals, topic, and theme.

In the field

I am five months <u>old</u> and nearly full-<u>grown</u>.

106

Foal, page 106

See how I grew

Newborn   One week <u>old</u>

Two weeks <u>old</u>   Five weeks <u>old</u>   Eight weeks <u>old</u>

108

Foal, page 108

Soon I will be big enough to join the other ponies in the field.

107

Foal, page 107

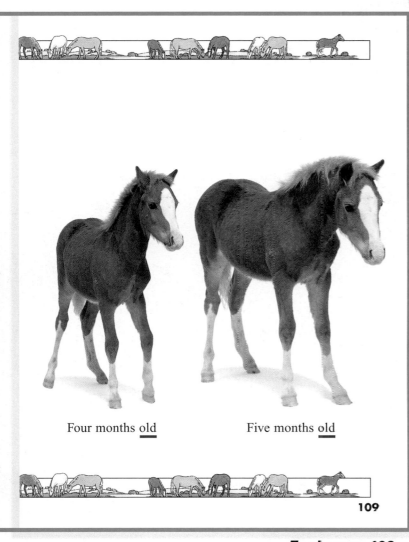

Four months <u>old</u>   Five months <u>old</u>

109

Foal, page 109

Skills in Context

Sequence

How does the foal grow and change in five months?

First, the foal drinks milk and stands. Next, it gets new teeth and eats grass in the field. Then, the foal grows a new coat. In the end, the foal can join the other ponies in the field.

Ongoing Assessment

Sequence

If... children are unable to recall the sequence of events,	**then...** do the **Think Aloud** below to model the skill.

Model Your Thinking

TEST TALK

When I look back at the selection, I can see from the pictures that the foal was much smaller as a newborn and that with each picture it grew a little bigger. It learned to do new things as it got bigger, and those happened in a certain order. Those things must be the way that it grew and changed.

Have children look at pages 108–109 and recall in sequential order the things the foal learned to do at each stage. As children contribute facts, write them in random order on the board. Have them put the events in the correct order.

Day 3

Extend Language Arts

Writing: Sentence Completion

Track the sentence on page 107 as children read the sentence aloud with you. Discuss what other things the foal may soon be big enough to do. Then write this sentence on the board:

Soon I will be big enough to _____.

Have children write the sentence and complete it with something they will soon be big enough to do. Invite them to draw a picture to accompany the text.

▓ long *o* and inflected ending *-ing*
— high-frequency/tested vocabulary

"Everything Grows," page 110

Selection
Audio

CD 6/Tape 23, Side 2

2. Food on the farm, fish in the sea,
   Birds in the air, leaves on the tree.
   Everything grows, anyone knows,
   That's how it goes.

3. That's how it goes, under the sun.
   That's how it goes, under the rain.
   Everything grows, anyone knows.
   That's how it goes.

111

"Everything Grows," page 111

Reading Poetry

▶ Model Reading Aloud

Guide children to understand that this song has a chorus and three verses. The first verse begins after the number 1 on page 110. Have children point to the first verse. The second and third verses are on page 111. Each verse is followed by the chorus.

Sing "Everything Grows" or play the CD or tape. Children can follow along in their books. Encourage them to join in the chorus.

▶ Discuss the Song

Making Judgments/Critical

Do you agree with the words in the song that say "Everything grows"?

Some children will say yes because all living things get bigger as they get older. Others may say no because rocks and pencils and stuffed animals don't grow.

Rhythm and Cadence/Literal

What words repeat in the chorus?

The repeated words in the chorus are *Everything grows and grows* and *. . . do . . . too* and *Everything grows.*

▶ Choral Singing

Have a volunteer point to the three verses in the text. Remind them when they sing a song, they sing each verse and then sing the chorus. Play the CD or tape and have children take turns singing the song. Divide the class into three groups. Have each group sing a verse and the whole class sing the chorus.

Critical Thinking
Reading Across Texts

Ask children to think about *Foal, Baby Otter Grows Up,* and "Everything Grows." Have them draw a picture of an animal when it is small and a picture of that animal when it is grown up.

PHONICS

Objectives

Children will

- decode words with long *o* spelled *oa, ow* and with inflected ending *-ing*
- spell words with inflected ending *-ing*
- build words with long *e* spelled *e, ee, ea*
- recognize high-frequency words

Skills Trace

Long *e*: *e, ee, ea*

Introduce/Teach	TE: 1.4 168k; 1.5 17c
Practice	PB: 1.4 83; 1.5 3, 41
Reteach/Review	TE: 1.4 AR18; 1.5 **111a**, AR11
Test	Skills Test, Unit 4 Benchmark Test, Unit 4

Day 3

Long *o*: *oa, ow*
Inflected Ending *-ing*

▶ Phonics Practice Activities

Careful observation of these activities will provide a basis for the Ongoing Assessment on page 111b.

Group Activity Play a word game by having children listen as you say three words. Have them tell what sound is the same in all three words. Use *coal, boat, oak; foal, coat, road; jumping, feeling, wishing; show, grow, blow; running, spitting, hopping.*

Independent Brainstorm with children a list of words with long *o*: *oa, ow*. Have children reread the rhyme chart "I See a Foal" and then each complete the sentence *I see a foal…* using words from the brainstormed list. Let each child read aloud his or her sentence.

Reread for Fluency

Express Characterization Have children reread *Duck Gets a New Coat* aloud. Encourage children to use their voices to bring the characters to life. You may wish to let volunteers read the parts of different characters in the book. Record their oral reading for children to listen to later.

Phonics Reader

Review

Long *e*: *e, ee, ea*

▶ Sort Long *e* Words

Write four headings: "*e—be*," "*ee—tree*," "*ea—meat*," "*e—red*" on chart paper. Remind children that the long *e* sound can be spelled in different ways and that short *e* is usually spelled *e*. Have children say the words on the chart. Then read aloud the words *me, feel, she, weep, seed* and ask volunteers to write the word in the correct column. Invite volunteers to suggest long *e* words spelled *ea*, such as *mean* or *neat*, and short *e* words, such as *met* or *yes*. Invite children to add to the list as they encounter long *e* words in their reading and writing this week.

e—be	ee—tree	ea—meat	e—red
me	feel	mean	met
she	weep	neat	yes
	seed		

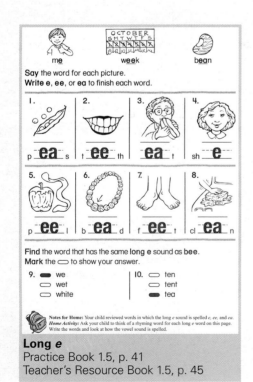

Say the word for each picture.
Write e, ee, or ea to finish each word.

1. p**ea**s 2. t**ee**th 3. **ea**t 4. sh**e**
5. p**ee**l 6. b**ea**d 7. f**ee**t 8. cl**ea**n

Find the word that has the same **long e** sound as **bee**.
Mark the ⊂⊃ to show your answer.

9. ⬤ we 10. ◯ ten
   ◯ wet   ◯ tent
   ◯ white   ⬤ tea

Notes for Home: Your child reviewed words in which the long e sound is spelled *e, ee,* and *ea*.
Home Activity: Ask your child to think of a rhyming word for each long e word on this page.
Write the words and look at how the vowel sound is spelled.

Long *e*
Practice Book 1.5, p. 41
Teacher's Resource Book 1.5, p. 45

Spelling Inflected Ending -*ing*

▶Practice with Writing

Have children write a few sentences about the foal in the story *Foal* using at least three of their spelling words. Allow them to share their sentences with the class.

Look at each word. Say it.
Listen for the **long o** sound in 🚢 boat

		Write each word.	Check it.
1.	grow	**grow**	**grow**
2.	float	**float**	**float**
3.	show	**show**	**show**
4.	growing	**growing**	**growing**
5.	floating	**floating**	**floating**
6.	showing	**showing**	**showing**

Word Wall Words
Write each word.

7.	around	**around**	**around**
8.	old	**old**	**old**

Notes for Home: Your child spelled words with and without the ending -*ing*, and two frequently-used words: *around, old*. **Home Activity:** Challenge your child to add -*ing* to other action words such as *jump, look, see,* and *help*.

Spelling
Practice Book 1.5, p. 42
Teacher's Resource Book 1.5, p. 46

Day
3

Word Wall

Practice High-Frequency Words

Drop Off Say one of this week's words in a sentence but drop off the first or last letter(s) in the word.

I want to __ow you my picture.

Call on a volunteer to say the word and spell the word aloud.

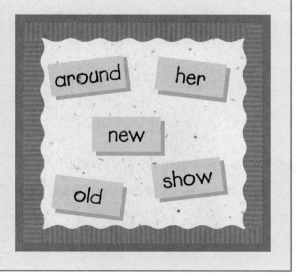

around   her
new
old   show

Optional Resources

Phonics
Phonics Workbook, pp. 136–138, 139
Phonics Manipulatives Kit

High-Frequency Words
High-Frequency Word Cards
Phonics Sourcebook, pp. 90–99

Expand Vocabulary

▶ Understand Unfamiliar Words

Recall the story *Foal*. Point out that there were new words for children to read in *Foal*, such as *graze* and *crunchy*. Ask them to think about how they figured out the meanings of the words. Write the passage below on the board.

> I crawled as an <u>infant</u>. I was just a baby when I crawled! Soon, I could <u>control</u> my legs. I could make my legs do what I wanted them to. Then I walked! My family <u>measured</u> my height often. We wanted to know how much I had grown.

Discuss how children can figure out the meaning of each underlined word. Have them use pictures, reread nearby words and sentences, or use a beginning picture dictionary to locate words in alphabetical order.

Animal Fact Cards

▶ Modeled Writing

Provide books and articles about animals. Give each child two index cards. Tell children they will write an animal fact on each card. Explain that a fact does not tell what someone thinks or feels. Instead, it tells information that is true and correct.

Model Write two sentences, such as those below, to tell animal facts.

> A baby sea otter can swim.
> A foal eats apples.

As you write, model these strategies:
• Write true and correct information.
• Do not write about your feelings.
• Track print from left to right.
• Form letters correctly.

Independent Writing Tell children to look through the books and articles you have provided. Have them write one animal fact on each of their two index cards.

Objectives

Children will

- identify and use adjectives that tell size
- identify and understand unfamiliar words
- generate ideas before writing
- write facts

Peer Conference Have partners read the sentences on their index cards to each another. Suggest they read clearly to their partners.

Writer's Checklist

Did you . .

✓ tell only facts?
✓ not tell your feelings?
✓ form letters correctly?
✓ leave spaces between words?

Self-Selected Reading and Read Aloud D.E.A.R. *Drop Everything And Read*

Read aloud *Every Autumn Comes the Bear* by Jim Arnosky. Children self-select nonfiction books about animal growth. After reading, discuss with children how animals are alike and how they are different.

Grammar: Adjectives That Tell Size

Review Adjectives Ask children to look through *Foal* with you to find adjectives that describe size. Remind children that adjectives are describing words that tell about people, places, and things.

Make an Adjective Chart Write the following sentence on a chart.

I see a _____ foal.

Invite children to complete the sentence with an adjective from *Foal* that tells size. Have children read the sentence aloud. Then invite them to suggest other size adjectives for the chart.

bigger	tiny
taller	huge
big	small

Follow the directions. Then, **pick** the best adjective from the box to finish each sentence. **Write** it on the line. Use each word only once.

Check that children followed the directions correctly.

thin long big fat little

1. Color the big dog.
   Rover is a **big** dog.

2. Color the long rope.
   The **long** rope has a knot.

3. Color in the paws on the little pup.
   Boots is a **little** pup.

4. Draw a hat on a fat cat.
   This **fat** cat has a hat.

5. Circle the thin line.
   This line is **thin**.

Notes for Home: Your child used adjectives to describe size. Home Activity: Go for a walk with your child. Encourage him or her to describe the objects and people you see using size adjectives, such as *big, small, tall,* and *short, huge, tiny.*

Adjectives
Practice Book 1.5, p. 43
Teacher's Resource Book 1.5, p. 47

Day 3

 # Meeting Individual Needs

ESL	**Intervention**	**Challenge**	**Other Ways to Learn**
Provide pictures of a giraffe and a dog. Ask children to point out the tall animal and the short animal. Have them repeat these descriptive phrases. **(Skill Support)** See also *Adding English.* (ESL)	Provide a huge box and a small box. Write the following phrases on index cards: *huge box, small box, big box, little box.* Have children circle the adjective on each card and place the cards next to the correct box. **(Comprehension Support)**	Help children understand the relativity of size. Have them compare and contrast objects that might all be labeled big when compared to one thing but small when compared to another—an elephant and a ship; a fire truck and a bicycle. Let children illustrate their findings. **(Tiered Assignments)**	Call out each of these adjectives, one at a time: *tall, short, huge, tiny.* Have children pantomime the adjective you have called out. **(Kinesthetic)**

Reader Response

Student Book, pp. 112–113

Let's Talk

Personal Response Direct children to consider all the stages, not just the newborn foal. Ask children who have small brothers or sisters to tell what the babies could do when they were five months old.

Let's Think

Critical Response Children may answer that they like this kind of writing because they feel as though they know the foal. Other children may say that they do not like it because foals can't really talk.

Test Prep

Let's Write

Written Response Have children brainstorm names of animals. Encourage children to tell the special word used for the babies of each animal if they know it. List the animals and their babies' names on the chalkboard.

Tell children to choose a young animal that they know a lot about, list facts to include, and then write their report. Remind them that the facts make their report interesting to others.

Features for writing reports are listed below 4 in the Scoring Rubric.

Make an Album

Creative Response Have each child make a picture album. If appropriate, send notes home requesting that children bring in photos of themselves at ages one, two, three, four, and five. You may provide the following: construction paper, glue, yarn, and a hole punch.

When children finish their albums, arrange them in groups and have them share their pictures.

Use the **Selection Test** in Practice Book 1.5, pages 45–46 or Teacher's Resource Book 1.5, pages 49–50.

Foal, page 112

Scoring Rubric for Written Response	
4	**3**
• clearly focuses on one young animal • includes several facts • writes in complete sentences • begins sentences with capital letters and ends with correct punctuation	• focuses on one young animal • includes a few facts • writes mostly in complete sentences • may have poorly formed capital letter at beginning or incorrect punctuation at end of one or two sentences
2	**1**
• attempts to focus on one young animal • includes one fact • may be missing parts of some sentences • may be missing capital letters at beginning or punctuation at end of some sentences	• is not focused on one animal • includes no facts • is made up of disconnected words or phrases • lacks both capital letters and end punctuation

Day 4

Make an Album

1. Bring in or draw a picture of yourself when you were little.

2. Under the picture write something you could do at that age.

3. Make more pictures. Tie your pictures into an album.

I could walk at 1.

113

Foal, page 113

Skills in Context

Review
Setting

Remind children that the setting of a story is where and when it takes place. Open the Big Book *Rabbits and Raindrops* to pages 4–5. Ask children to find the words that tell where the rabbits are. (by the nest, under a hedge, at the edge of the green lawn) Have children point out picture clues for the setting.

Have volunteers find the words on pages 10–11 that tell where the rabbits are now. Discuss picture clues on these pages.

Reread for Fluency

Selection Audio Have children listen to the CD or tape of *Foal* as they follow along in their books.

CD 6/Tape 23, Side 1

Use an Appropriate Pace

Tell children that when they read nonfiction, they should read smoothly, but slowly enough for listeners to understand the facts. Have partners reread pages 100–101 of *Foal* aloud three to five times for practice.

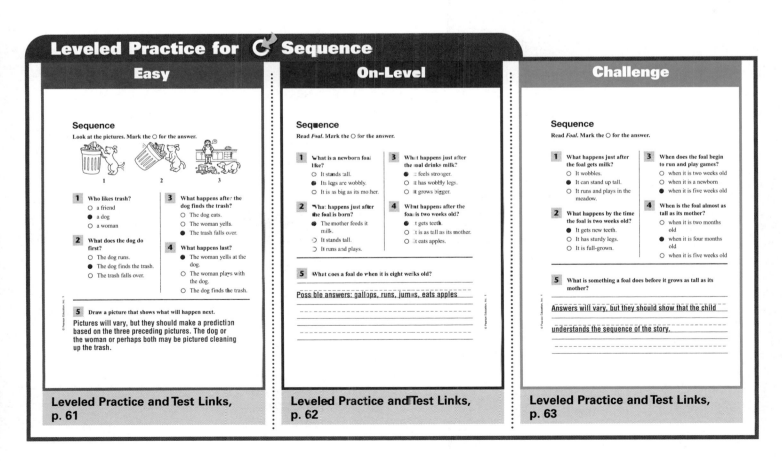

Leveled Practice for ☾ Sequence

Easy

Sequence
Look at the pictures. Mark the ○ for the answer.

1   2   3

1 Who likes trash?
○ a friend
● a dog
○ a woman

2 What does the dog do first?
○ The dog runs.
● The dog finds the trash.
○ The trash falls over.

3 What happens after the dog finds the trash?
○ The dog eats.
○ The woman yells.
● The trash falls over.

4 What happens last?
● The woman yells at the dog.
○ The woman plays with the dog.
○ The dog finds the trash.

5 Draw a picture that shows what will happen next.
Pictures will vary, but they should make a prediction based on the three preceding pictures. The dog or the woman or perhaps both may be pictured cleaning up the trash.

Leveled Practice and Test Links, p. 61

On-Level

Sequence
Read *Foal.* Mark the ○ for the answer.

1 What is a newborn foal like?
○ It stands tall.
● Its legs are wobbly.
○ It is as big as its mother.

2 What happens just after the foal is born?
● The mother feeds it milk.
○ It stands tall.
○ It runs and plays.

3 What happens just after the foal drinks milk?
● It feels stronger.
○ It has wobbly legs.
○ It grows bigger.

4 What happens after the foal is two weeks old?
● It gets teeth.
○ It is as tall as its mother.
○ It eats apples.

5 What does a foal do when it is eight weeks old?
Possible answers: gallops, runs, jumps, eats apples

Leveled Practice and Test Links, p. 62

Challenge

Sequence
Read *Foal.* Mark the ○ for the answer.

1 What happens just after the foal gets milk?
○ It wobbles.
● It can stand up tall.
○ It runs and plays in the meadow.

2 What happens by the time the foal is two weeks old?
● It gets new teeth.
○ It has sturdy legs.
○ It is full-grown.

3 When does the foal begin to run and play games?
○ when it is two weeks old
○ when it is a newborn
● when it is five weeks old

4 When is the foal almost as tall as its mother?
○ when it is two months old
● when it is four months old
○ when it is five weeks old

5 What is something a foal does before it grows as tall as its mother?
Answers will vary, but they should show that the child understands the sequence of the story.

Leveled Practice and Test Links, p. 63

Day **4**

PHONICS

Objectives

Children will

- decode words with long *o* spelled *oa, ow* and with inflected ending *-ing*
- decode words with medial consonants
- spell words with inflected ending *-ing*
- recognize high-frequency words

Skills Trace

Medial Consonants

Introduce/Teach	TE: 1.4 110l; 1.6 106l, 132l
Practice	PB: 1.4 52, 95; 1.5 47; 1.6 52, 68
Reteach/Review	TE: 1.4 AR16; 1.5 **113a**; 1.6 111c, 127a, 129a, 131c, 157a, 159a, 161c, AR16, AR17
Test	Skills Test, Unit 4 Benchmark Test, Unit 4

Long *o: oa, ow*
Inflected Ending *-ing*

►Reteach

Write *boat, soap,* and *goat* on the board. Ask children to blend the words. Then, write *bow* and *mow* on the board and explain that long *o* is sometimes spelled *ow*. Have children blend the *ow* words. Distribute picture cards for *boat, soap,* and *goat*. Have children hold up the picture card if they hear the long *o* sound in the following words: *oak, roast, beat, know, he, foam*.

Write *skipping, singing, floating, snowing,* and *hopping* on the board. Have children circle the *-ing* ending on each word and then use it in a sentence.

See page AR14 of this Teacher's Edition for additional **reteach activities.**

Review
Single and Double Medial Consonants

Write the words *ne_er* and *ga_ _op* on chart paper. Read this sentence.

> **Never stand on a horse that likes to gallop.**

Ask children the sound they hear in the middle of *never*. Then write the missing letter. Do the same for *gallop* and remind them that two consonants can stand for one sound. Continue with words with medial digraphs: *mother, teacher, bushel, cricket.*

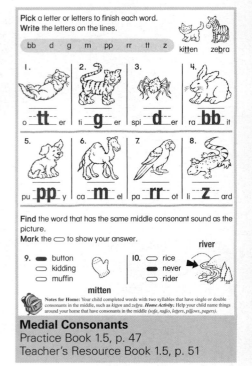

Medial Consonants
Practice Book 1.5, p. 47
Teacher's Resource Book 1.5, p. 51

Day 4

Meeting Individual Needs

ESL	**Intervention**	**Challenge**	**Other Ways to Learn**
Put word cards for *jump, clean, fish, float,* and *drum* in a pile. Have a volunteer choose one word, read it, act it out, and use it in a sentence. Then write words with the *-ing* ending and have children read them aloud. **(Word Study Support)** See also *Adding English.* **ESL**	Use long *o* word cards and help children read them. Then display all cards and give clues until children are able to guess the word. For example: I make the grass shorter. (mow) I am a bird. (crow) **(Phonics Support)**	Use letter cards that will make two long *o* words: one *oa* word and one *ow* word: for example, *g, o, a, t, m, o, w* (goat, mow). Place letter cards in envelopes at a center. Children unscramble them to make the two words. Have children write their words on the board. **(Tiered Assignments)**	Use word cards and ending cards for *-ing* and *-ed*. Children add the endings, read the new words, and use each in a sentence. **(Visual/Spatial)**

Spelling Inflected Ending *-ing*

▶ Partner Spelling Practice

Create two trains with an engine and three cars. Write "Long o" on one engine and "Long o with -ing" on the other. Have space on each of the cars for children to write spelling words. Duplicate. Pairs take turns reading a word and writing it on the correct train. Children can trade trains and check each other's work.

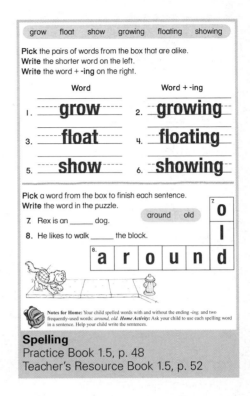

Spelling
Practice Book 1.5, p. 48
Teacher's Resource Book 1.5, p. 52

Day 4

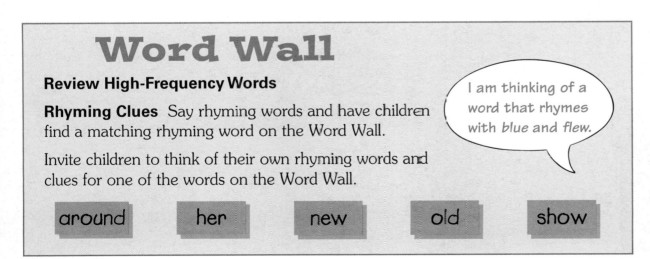

Word Wall

Review High-Frequency Words

Rhyming Clues Say rhyming words and have children find a matching rhyming word on the Word Wall.

Invite children to think of their own rhyming words and clues for one of the words on the Word Wall.

> I am thinking of a word that rhymes with *blue* and *flew.*

| around | her | new | old | show |

Optional Resources

Phonics
Phonics Workbook, pp. 136–138, 140
Phonics Manipulatives Kit
Phonics Sourcebook, pp. 79–82, 83–84

High-Frequency Words
High-Frequency Word Cards
Phonics Sourcebook, pp. 90–99

Baby Otter Grows Up/Foal **113b**

Language Arts

Adjectives That Tell Size

Have children read aloud with you the statements about adjectives and look at the two examples. Identify the adjective and noun in each example.

Talk

Have children read aloud the directions with you. Discuss the pictures and then ask children to each make a list of adjectives that describe the pictures.

Write

Guide children as they copy the sentences and underline the adjectives. When everyone has finished, review the responses and have children correct their mistakes.

Then have children write sentences that include adjectives from their lists. Children may want to illustrate their sentences.

Use the Teacher's Resource Book 1.5 pages 53–54 for **reteaching** and extra practice for adjectives of size.

Day 4

Foal, **page 114**

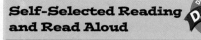

Self-Selected Reading and Read Aloud

Read aloud *Cheetah* by Taylor Morrison. Children choose a fiction or nonfiction book about animals growing.

Write

Write the sentences. Draw a line under the adjectives.

1. **Big cows stand in the barn.**
2. **A tall boy feeds the chickens.**
3. **A small puppy runs.**

Write your own sentences. Use adjectives from your list. Draw a line under the adjectives.

115

Foal, page 115

Study Skill

Illustrations and Captions

Have children turn to pages 94–95 in their books. Read the title and captions aloud as children look at the photographs. Explain that many nonfiction books and stories have detailed illustrations that give information. The words below the illustrations help us understand them. Have children point to the corresponding photos as you model how to interpret them.

Model Your Thinking

Think ALOUD **To understand the information on these pages, I look at the first photograph with the word *Newborn* next to it. Details in the photo show that when a foal is a newborn, it is very thin with long legs and a short tail. It looks like it might fall over. I can compare this photo to the photos with the words *Five weeks old* on pages 100–101. I see that the foal is a little taller and has larger hooves. Now it looks stronger and steadier.**

Continue modeling until children understand the concept. Reinforce that both the photos and the captions provide information about a foal at various ages.

Practice Divide children into two groups. The first group will study the otter and the second will study the horse. Children can refer to the appropriate selection to make a detailed drawing of the animal at a specific stage or age. Circulate and encourage children to write captions for their drawings. Make a display of each group's work.

Day 4

Objectives

Children will

- identify sequence of events in a story
- use sound-symbol relationships to read decodable text
- recognize high-frequency words
- read with fluency and understanding

Meeting Individual Needs

ESL

To prepare children for oral reading assessment, choose key sentences from the selection. Ask children to read the sentences to a partner and explain what they mean. Have children read the sentences aloud together.

Assess Oral Reading

▶ Prepare for the Assessment

Materials Children may choose from *Baby Otter Grows Up, Foal,* or any stories or books they've read this week. Have children prepare for the assessment by rereading the selection of their choice independently.

▶ Listen to Individual Readers

Have children read aloud to you. Use the chart on the following page to track children's abilities. The blank column is for any additional skills you want to assess.

Check Comprehension To assess children's ability to identify sequence of events in a story, ask a question such as:

> **How did the foal change from when it was first born to when it was four months old?**

See page AR15 in this Teacher's Edition to **reteach** sequence.

You may prefer to assess only a portion of your class each week, perhaps half one week, and the other half the next.

▶ While You Assess

While you work with individuals, other children may choose from the following activities or the activities listed in the Cross-Curricular Work Stations on pages 86g–h.

Before They Read to You

Children should reread the chosen book, practicing until they feel they can read it well.

Children may listen to the CD or tape of *Foal* or *Baby Otter Grows Up* to hear a model of fluent reading.

Selection Audio

CD 6/Tape 23, Side 1

After They Read to You

Children can complete a Reading Log like the one shown or use Practice Book 1.5 page 101, or the Teacher's Resource Book 1.6 page 112.

Children can also complete the phonics activities on page 115c.

Name _____

I read *Foal*

It was about

Words I Can Now Read and Write

Optional Resources

Assessment
The Assessment Handbook has information on running records.

Day
5

Oral Reading Checklist

May be reproduced for classroom use.

Student Name	Reads Long o Words (oa, ow)	Reads Words with __ing Endings	Uses Decoding Strategies	Reads High-Frequency Words	Identifies Sequence	Reads with Expression	Demonstrates Reading for Meaning	Comments
1								
2								
3								
4								
5								
6								
7								
8								
9								
10								
11								
12								
13								
14								
15								
16								
17								
18								
19								
20								
21								
22								
23								
24								
25								

Day 5

Long *o: oa, ow*
Inflected Ending *-ing*

▶ Phonics Practice Activities

Long *o* Words with *-ing* Endings Have children listen to and write these long *o* words with *-ing* endings: *rowing, soaking, blowing.*

Phonics Take-Home Reader Have children practice reading the book with a partner before taking it home.

Phonics
Take-Home Reader

Spelling Test

Have children number their papers. Read the underlined word, read the sentence, then repeat the underlined word.

1. I like to <u>grow</u> flowers in my garden.
2. I want to <u>show</u> you where I live.
3. It looks like the clouds are <u>floating</u> through the sky.
4. My flowers are <u>growing</u>.
5. I like to <u>float</u> my toy boat in the water.
6. The second graders are <u>showing</u> us their dinosaur project.

High-Frequency Words

7. Have you seen my <u>old</u> sneakers?
8. I rode my bike <u>around</u> the block.

Challenge Words

9. Josh wore his warm <u>coat</u>.
10. I painted the sun in my picture <u>yellow</u>.

Word Wall

Practice High-Frequency Words

Word Sort Have children sort the words according to the following categories.

- words that begin with a vowel *(around, old)*

- words that are opposites *(new, old)*

- the number of letters in two words adds up to 10 *(around, show)*

Day 5

ORAL LANGUAGE

Listening: Listen for the Main Idea

Ask children to listen as you tell a story. Tell them you will be asking them what the story is mostly about, the big picture.

> A foal lived on a farm. The foal was afraid to trot up the hill. One day, a soft rain began to fall. One of the foal's friends called from the top of the hill. "Help, I'm stuck in the mud!" The foal felt scared, but she forced herself to trot up the hill. She helped her friend. She wasn't afraid anymore.

Have children tell what the story is mostly about. (a foal that stops feeling scared) Encourage children to see the big picture.

WRITING

Journal Entry

▶ Interactive Writing

In this method of writing, you and the children work together. While you write on the board, children write on their own papers. As you write, point out that the spaces between words are larger than the spaces between letters.

Write a Journal Entry Children will write a journal entry about the things they have learned as they have grown up. Leave blanks in the journal entry for children to complete. Ask children to discuss how they might fill in the blanks.

> I have learned many things. I can _____, and I can _____. The best thing about growing up is _____.

Independent Writing Have children write in the missing words independently. Remind them to think about their own experiences. Have children illustrate their journal entries. Ask children if they would like to share what they have written in their journals.

 Portfolio Children may wish to select a piece of writing from this week to put in their portfolios.

Objectives

Children will

- listen for the main idea
- contribute ideas during a group writing activity

Listener's Checklist

Did you . . .

✓ listen closely?
✓ look for the big picture?
✓ think of what the story was mostly about?

Self-Selected Reading and Read Aloud D.E.A.R.

Read aloud *Fox*. Ask children to self-select a new book or reread an old favorite. After reading, discuss with children what they like and dislike about the book they chose.

Optional Resources

Phonics
Phonics Workbook, pp. 136–138

High-Frequency Words
High-Frequency Word Cards
Phonics Sourcebook, pp. 90–99

Oral Language
Adding English: ESL Teacher's Guide

Assessment
The Assessment Handbook has information on informal assessment and grading.

Day
5

Lesson Overview

What a Sight!

by Carolyn Crimi

illustrated by
Darryl Ligasan

Nicky and Jim were playing together
with Nicky's game.
"We're going to the museum!"
Dad said.
"Right now?" asked Jim.
"I'll tell Mom first," said Dad.

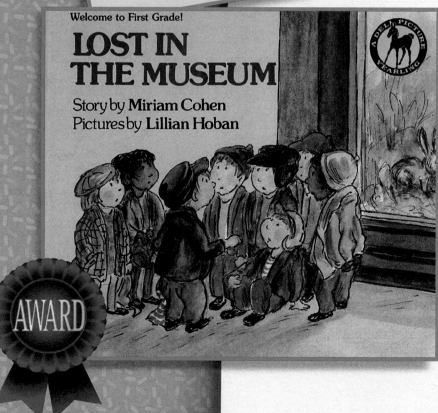

Welcome to First Grade!

LOST IN THE MUSEUM

Story by **Miriam Cohen**
Pictures by **Lillian Hoban**

A DELL PICTURE YEARLING

AWARD

Phonics Story

What a Sight!
pages 116–123

Selection Audio

The **Phonics Story** . . .

• introduces ⟳ **Long *i: igh, ie*** and **Singular Possessives**

• introduces the high-frequency words

    been first found start together

• builds fluency

• builds decoding skills

Use the Phonics Story to prepare children for reading the Main Selection.

Main Selection

Lost in the Museum
pages 124–151

Selection Audio

The **Main Selection** . . .

• introduces ⟳ **Cause and Effect**

• practices ⟳ **Long *i: igh, ie*** and **Singular Possessives**

• practices the high-frequency words

    been first found start together

Leveled Readers

TARGET SKILL

Cause and Effect
Tested Vocabulary

Easy
Leveled Reader 22A

On–Level
Leveled Reader 22B

For Guided Reading
see Teacher's Edition,
pp. LR19–LR24.

Challenge
Leveled Reader 5C

For instruction and leveled
practice answers, see Teacher's
Edition, pp. LR39–LR45.

Easy

Cause and Effect

Look at the pictures. Mark the ○ for the answer.

1 Bob wants a drink. What does he do?
- ● He gets water.
- ○ He catches a ball.
- ○ He trips.

2 Why is Bob thirsty?
- ● He played baseball.
- ○ He walked his dog.
- ○ He fell down.

3 What does Bob do with the water?
- ● He spills it.
- ○ He drinks it.
- ○ He laughs at it.

4 Why does Bob trip?
- ○ He is going fast.
- ● He steps on a toy car.
- ○ He is funny.

5 Think about a hot day. What can you do to be cool?
Answers will vary, but they should include a way to cool
off during a hot day.

On–Level

Cause and Effect

Read *Lost in the Museum.* Mark the ○ for the answer.

1 Why do Danny and Jim not stay with the class?
- ○ They want to eat.
- ● They want to see dinosaurs.
- ○ They want to see some art.

2 Why do Anna Marie and Sara run after the other children?
- ○ They want to get hot dogs at the cafeteria.
- ● They want them to come back.
- ○ They want to see dinosaurs.

3 Jim follows a red coat because
- ○ he thinks it is pretty
- ○ he thinks he sees his mother
- ● he thinks he sees Margaret

4 Why do the children get lost?
- ○ They like dinosaurs.
- ● They don't stay together.
- ○ They listen to the teacher.

5 What happens when the children go to see the dinosaur?

Answers will vary, but they should mention that when the

children go to see the dinosaur, they get lost.

Practice for Leveled Readers

Easy

Cause and Effect

Read the story *All Together Now!* Then answer Numbers 1 through 5.

1 Look at page 2. Where is the family going?
- ○ They are going camping.
- ○ They are going on a trip.
- ● They are going on a walk.

2 What happens when the family sees bugs?
- ● They slap the bugs.
- ○ They spray the bugs.
- ○ They catch the bugs.

3 Look at pages 14 and 15. Why does the family run away?
- ○ They see a bear.
- ● They see a skunk.
- ○ They see tracks.

4 The family does NOT see
- ● a snake on the walk.
- ○ a deer on the walk.
- ○ a hawk on the walk.

5 Look at page 7. Why does the sister hold her brother's arm? Use words from the story in your answer.

She helps him climb a rock.

Teacher's Edition, p. LR21

On–Level

Cause and Effect

Read the story *How Bill Found Rain.* Then answer Numbers 1 through 5.

1 Why does the family need rain?
- ○ The animals drank all the water.
- ● It has been too hot and dry.
- ○ Sis has a new raincoat.

2 Why does Bill look for a big black cloud?
- ● Rain comes from big black clouds.
- ○ He can not pull a white cloud home.
- ○ Bill only likes black clouds.

3 Look at page 15. Bill pulls hard on the rope. What happens?
- ○ The dog starts to bark.
- ○ Mom starts to laugh.
- ● It starts to rain.

4 What could NOT happen?
- ○ It could be hot and sunny.
- ○ People could not find lots of rope.
- ● A boy could not catch a cloud with a rope.

5 Look at page 16. Why is everyone dancing? Use words from the story in your answer.

Possible answers: They are dancing because they have rain.

They are dancing because the are happy.

Teacher's Edition, p. LR24

Challenge

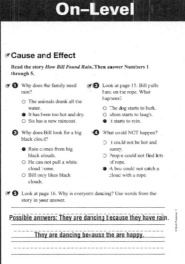

to Go!

Learn more about ways to travel. Look in books. Then, try one or more of these ideas.

- Find five different ways to travel. Draw pictures on note cards. Put your cards in order from the slowest way to travel to the fastest. Show them to a classmate.
- Make up a new way to travel. Draw a picture. Write about your idea.
- Make a board game about ways to travel. Use what you learned about travel. Draw pictures and write a title for your game.

Leveled Reader 5C, pp. 16–17

Challenge

Cause and Effect

Read *Lost in the Museum.* Mark the ○ for the answer.

1 Why do Danny and Jim not stay with the class?
- ○ They want to see the fish.
- ● They want to see the dinosaurs.
- ○ They want to eat lunch.

2 What does Paul do when Jim gets scared?
- ○ He says it is silly.
- ○ He tells the teacher about the dinosaur.
- ● He puts his arm around Jim.

3 Jim goes to find the teacher because he doesn't want to
- ● stay all night with the dinosaur
- ○ eat lunch
- ○ see Danny

4 Because he is scared to see the dinosaur, Jim
- ○ eats a hot dog
- ● squeezes his eyes shut
- ○ finds the teacher

5 Imagine you get lost in a museum. What would you tell your teacher about how it happened?

Answers will vary. Possible answer: I would say that I

stopped to get a drink at the water fountain and when I

looked up, everyone was gone.

Leveled Practice and Test Link,
pp. 64–66, *Lost in the Museum*

Additional Leveled Resources

Phonics Resources

Phonics Reader 28

Phonics Take-Home Readers in Reproducible Format

Book 28

Decodable Readers 37 and 38

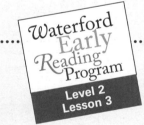

Waterford Early Reading Program
Level 2
Lesson 3

Language Support

Adding English
pp. 185–192

Ten Important Sentences
p. 34

Trade Books for Self-Selected Reading

Easy

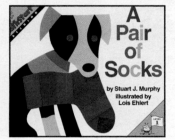

A Pair of Socks
by Stuart J. Murphy. HarperCollins, 1996

Train Song
by Harriet Ziefert. Orchard Books, 2000

Where's My Hat?
by Neil Morris. Little, Brown, 1982

On-Level

This Is the Way We Go to School
by Edith Baer. Scholastic, 1992
Trade Book Library Title

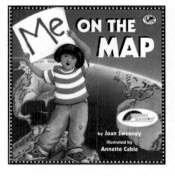

Me on the Map
by Joan Sweeney. Crown, 1996

See You in Second Grade!
by Miriam Cohen. Greenwillow, 1989

Challenge

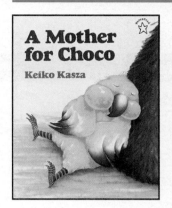

A Mother for Choco
by Keiko Kasza. Paper Star, 1996
Trade Book Library Title

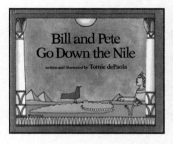

Bill and Pete Go Down the Nile
by Tomie dePaola. Putnam, 1987

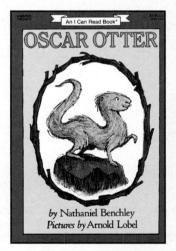

Oscar Otter
by Nathaniel Benchley. Harper Trophy, 1966

Self-Selected Reading

- Allow 10–20 minutes per day for self-selected reading.
- For additional titles and for a read-aloud suggestion, see pp. AR24–AR25.
- For daily self-selected reading suggestions, see the 5-Day Planner, pp. 116e–116f.
- For activity ideas and management tips, see p. AR25.

- Have children select materials to read for pleasure, such as favorite books and stories.

Developmental Reading Assessment (DRA) from
Celebration Press, an imprint of Pearson Learning, helps teachers by providing and documenting students' development as readers over time.

Links to Reading First 1.5, pp. 32–41

5-Day Planner

Reading

Comprehension

Vocabulary

Fluency

Independent Reading

Phonics/Word Study

Phonemic Awareness

Phonics

Spelling

High-Frequency Words

Oral Language

Speaking, Listening, Viewing

Oral Vocabulary

Writing

Grammar, Usage, Mechanics

Your State Standards

 Customize your week with the Teacher's Resource Planner CD-ROM!

Day 1

Activate Prior Knowledge, p. 116j

Phonics pp. 116k–116l

Phonemic Awareness: Long *i: igh, ie*

✓ **Phonics:** Introduce Long *i: igh, ie;* Singular Possessives
PHONICS SONGS AND RHYMES CHART **"Dwight the Knight"**

Spelling: Long *i* Words
 Pretest
Work with Spelling Pattern

High-Frequency Words: Introduce **been, first, found, start, together**

Reading pp. 116m–123

Story Vocabulary

Read Pupil Edition PHONICS STORY: *What a Sight!*

Independent Reading
Self-Selected Reading, pp. 116d; AR24

Oral Language pp. 116m, 123a

Build Oral Language

Expand Vocabulary: Discuss Place Names

Writing pp. 116i, 123a–123b

Shared Writing: List

Handwriting: *Jj*

Daily Writing Prompt: Write a list of things you would like to see in a museum.

Day 2

Phonics pp. 123c–123d

✓ **Phonics:** Practice Long *i: igh, ie;* Singular Possessives

Apply Phonics: Read the PHONICS READER *Dad's Gift* or DECODABLE READER 37

Spelling: Writing for Sounds

High-Frequency Words: Practice

PB 1.5: Phonics, pp. 51, 52; High-Frequency Words, p. 53
TRB 1.5: Phonics, pp. 57, 58; High-Frequency Words, p. 59

Reading pp. 123e–123f

✓ **Comprehension:** Cause and Effect
READ ALOUD "Goldilocks and the Three Bears"

Fluency: Reread the PHONICS STORY: *What a Sight!*

PB 1.5: Cause and Effect, p. 54
TRB 1.5: Cause and Effect, p. 60

Independent Reading
Self-Selected Reading, pp. 116d; AR24

Oral Language p. 123g

 Speaking: Large Group Discussion

Writing pp. 116i, 123g–123h

Modeled Writing: Ad

✓ **Grammar:** Adjectives

PB 1.5: p. 55; **TRB 1.5:** p. 61

Daily Writing Prompt: Make a cartoon. Show an animal in a museum.

 Target Skill   Review Review Skill   Assessment   PB Practice Book   TRB Teacher's Resource Book

pp. 64–66

Leveled Practice and Test Link in
TerraNova, SAT9, or ITBS format

Target Skills of the Week

Reading Cause and Effect
Phonics Long *i: igh, ie*; Singular Possessives
Oral Language Large Group Discussion
Writing Adjectives

Day 3

Reading pp. 124a–151

Story Vocabulary

Read Pupil Edition MAIN SELECTION:
Lost in the Museum

✓ **Comprehension:** Cause and Effect

Guided Reading Resources/Flexible Groups, pp. 124b; LR19–LR24
Leveled Readers 22A, 22B, 5C

PB 1.5: Vocabulary, p. 56
TRB 1.5: Vocabulary, p. 62

Independent Reading
Self-Selected Reading, pp. 116d; AR24

Phonics pp. 151a–151b

✓ **Phonics:** Practice Long *i: igh, ie*; Singular Possessives

✓ (Review) **Phonics:** Long *a: ai, ay*

Fluency: Reread the PHONICS READER
Dad's Gift or DECODABLE READER 38

Spelling: Practice with Writing

High-Frequency Words: Practice

PB 1.5: Phonics, p. 58; Spelling, p. 59
TRB 1.5: Phonics, p. 64; Spelling, p. 65

Oral Language pp. 124a, 151c

Build Oral Language

Expand Vocabulary: Name Items Found in Specific Places

Writing pp. 116i, 151c–151d

Modeled Writing: My Favorite Trip

✓ **Grammar:** Adjectives

PB 1.5: p. 60; TRB 1.5: p. 66; GPB: p. 48

Daily Writing Prompt: Write about your favorite class trip this year.

Day 4

Reading pp. 152–153

Read Together Pupil Edition
READER RESPONSE *Test Prep*

Selection Test

PB 1.5: Selection Test, pp. 61–62
TRB 1.5: Selection Test, pp. 67–68

(Review) Character

Fluency: Reread the MAIN SELECTION

Guided Reading Resources/Flexible Groups, pp. 124b; LR19–LR24
Leveled Readers 22A, 22B, 5C

Independent Reading
Self-Selected Reading, pp. 116d; AR24

Phonics pp. 153a–153b

✓ **Phonics:** Reteach Long *i: igh, ie*; Singular Possessives

✓ (Review) Contractions

Spelling: Partner Practice

High-Frequency Words: Review

PB 1.5: Phonics, p. 63; Spelling, p. 64
TRB 1.5: Phonics, p. 69; Spelling, p. 70

Oral Language pp. 154–155

Speaking: Talk About Adjectives

Writing pp. 116i, 154–155

✓ **Grammar:** Adjectives

Writing: Identify Adjectives That Tell What Kind

TRB 1.5: pp. 71–72; GPB: p. 49

Daily Writing Prompt: Write about where you would like to go on a class trip.

Day 5

Reading pp. 155a–155b

Assess Word Reading: Word Recognition Checklist

Guided Reading Resources/Flexible Groups, pp. 124b; LR19–LR24
Leveled Readers 22A, 22B, 5C

Independent Reading
Self-Selected Reading, pp. 116d; AR24

Phonics p. 155c

✓ **Phonics:** Practice Long *i: igh, ie*; Singular Possessives

Apply Phonics: Read the PHONICS TAKE-HOME READER

Spelling: Long *i* Words
Posttest

High-Frequency Words: Practice

Oral Language p. 155d

Speaking: Large Group Discussion

Writing pp. 116i, 155d

Interactive Writing: Thank-You Note
Portfolio

Daily Writing Prompt: Draw a map of a museum. Write labels on the map to show what is in the museum.

Cross-Curricular Work Stations

Career Link

Ideas for bringing the school and community together

Field Experiences
museum
zoo

Guest Speakers
museum curator or docent
archaeologist/paleon-tologist

Letters and Sounds

Going to My Store 15 minutes

Materials: paper, pencils

Learning Styles Visual, Linguistic

Write these sentences on a large piece of paper: *Hi! My name is___. We are going to___'s store. You can buy___.* Children copy the sentences and fill in their name in the first two blanks. Then they write names of items that begin with the same letter as their name in the last blank.

Challenge Invite children to choose items from five different "stores" and write them in alphabetical order.

Hi! My name is Barry.

We are going to Barry's store.

You can buy bolts, balls, bats, bread, and boxes.

Writing

Travel Poster 15 minutes

Materials: poster board, crayons, markers

Learning Styles Visual, Kinesthetic

Have children make signs advertising a place they have visited. They should draw pictures and write the name of the place and interesting facts about it. Have children pay particular attention to the layout of their sentences.

It is sunny.
You can swim.
There is sand.
You can find shells.

Math

How Much? Count by Twos 15 minutes

Materials: paper or play money, 10 marker chips

Learning Styles Logical, Auditory, Kinesthetic

Partners decide how much it will cost for people to enter a museum at $2 per person. For every marker that one child shows, the other child displays two dollar bills. Children write their findings as 1 person = $2, 2 people = $4,… until they reach 10 markers.

ESL Before you begin, go over with children the numbers 1 through 10.

1 person = $2
2 people = $4

INTERNET SAFETY Establish guidelines for your students' safe and responsible use of the Internet. See the Scott Foresman Internet Guide for tips.

Technology

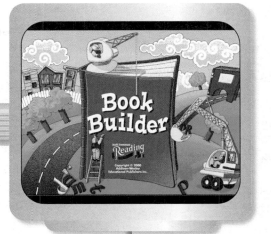

Book Builder Activity 🚶 ⏱ 15 minutes

Learning Style Individual

Have children create their own museum book. Remind children that they can use the graphics provided in the program or draw their own illustrations. They will also type the text. Children can also add audio to their book presentation.

Reading Web Site 🚶 ⏱ 15 minutes

Learning Styles Visual, Individual, Kinesthetic

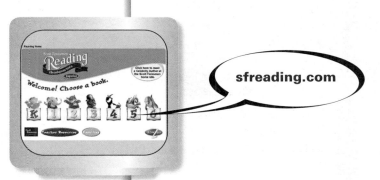

sfreading.com

WWW Children can visit the Scott Foresman *Reading* Web site (sfreading.com) for current hyperlinks to relevant electronic texts that can be used for an Internet Workshop investigation of places to go. Also see the Scott Foresman Internet Guide for additional information on the Internet Workshop method.

Social Studies

We Go Everywhere! 👥 ⏱ 15 minutes

Materials: chart paper, travel magazines, tape, markers, scissors

Learning Styles Visual, Kinesthetic

Have children draw or cut out pictures of places they have visited or would like to visit, such as museums, factories, zoos, and so on. Encourage children to write the place names under their pictures.

Ask children to bring in photos from other countries they have visited. Have children write the place names under their photos and display them.

Science

My Museum 🚶 ⏱ 15 minutes

Materials: paper, pencils, markers

Learning Styles Logical, Kinesthetic

After children understand that museums can show scientific collections like dinosaurs, space equipment, and rocks, have them think about what they would like to see in a museum and draw a picture of what would be in that exhibit. Have children label their pictures.

Daily Routines

Message Board

Day One

Today you will hear a poem about a visit to a museum. Have you ever been to a museum? What did you see?

Have children share their observations about museum visits.

Have children find the high-frequency word *first*. Ask why there is an apostrophe in *cat's*. (to show belonging)

Day Two

You read about a cat's first trip to the museum. Should pets go to a museum? Why?

Day Three

You will read a story about a class trip. What trips have we been on? Why do we stay together from the start?

Have children find the high-frequency words *been*, *together*, and *start*.

Have children find the high-frequency word *found* and the spelling word *right*. Have children find long *i* words with *igh*. (right, might) Then ask which words describe the whale. (great, gray)

Day Four

Jim found the teacher right by the great gray whale. How might you find something that is lost?

Day Five

We read about sights in a museum. Is day or night the best time to visit a museum? Why?

Have children find the spelling word *night*. Ask which letters stand for the long *i* sound in *sights* and *night*. (igh)

Journal Writing

Day One
Write a list of things you would like to see in a museum.

Day Two
Make a cartoon. Show an animal in a museum.

Day Three
Write about your favorite class trip this year.

Day Four
Write about where you would like to go on a class trip.

Day Five
Draw a map of a museum. Write labels on the map to show what is in the museum.

Family Times

Send home the newsletter with daily instructional activities to reinforce this week's skills.

Practice Book 1.5, pp. 49–50
Teacher's Resource Book 1.5, pp. 55–56

Activate Prior Knowledge

▶ Assess Prior Knowledge

Discuss Everywhere We Go Talk with children about experiences they have had visiting a museum. Share your experiences too. Ask:

> What kinds of things did you see in the museum?
>
> What are some of the rules you remember about what to do in museums?

▶ Build Background

Read Aloud

Preview the Poem Explain that items on display in a museum are often priceless. Point out that *priceless* means very, very valuable. Help children set a purpose for listening, such as to discover what priceless things are behind the museum door.

Read the Poem Share this poem with children. Invite children to talk about the items mentioned in the poem. Ask:

> What does each of the items make you think of?
>
> What might you learn if you visited a museum that had these items in it?

Objectives

Children will

- activate prior knowledge of topic: Everywhere We Go
- relate literature to experiences in their own life
- draw on experiences of others to form a broader perspective of the topic
- set a purpose for listening

Day **1**

Read Aloud

Behind the Museum Door

by Lee Bennett Hopkins

What's behind the museum door?

Ancient necklaces,
African art,
Armor of knights,
A peasant cart;

Pioneer wagons,
Vintage cars,
A planetarium

    ceilinged

    with stars;

Priceless old coins.
A king's golden throne,
Mummies in linen,

And

A dinosaur bone.

Objectives

Children will

- ◎ identify and decode words with long *i* spelled *igh* and *ie*
- ◎ use structural cues to identify and decode singular possessives
- • spell words with long *i*: *igh*, *ie*
- • recognize high-frequency words

Skills Trace

◎ **Long *i*: *igh*, *ie***

Introduce/Teach	TE: 1.5 116k
Practice	PB: 1.5 51, 73
Reteach/Review	TE: 1.5 123c, 151a, 153a, 155c, 187a, AR15
Test	Skills Test, Unit 5

Day 1

Phonemic Awareness Say /f/ /ī/ /t/. Have children blend the sounds. Repeat the following words slowly, sound by sound: *high, light, soak, toast, tie, pie, sigh, load, right,* and *road.* Have children blend and then say each word.

Phonics Generalization

When *i* is followed by *gh,* the *i* usually stands for its long sound and *g* and *h* are silent.

Phonics Generalization CVVC

When two vowels appear together in a word, the first one usually stands for its long vowel sound and the second is silent.

Long *i*: *igh*, *ie*

▶ Develop Phonemic Awareness

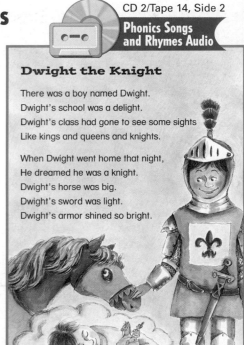

CD 2/Tape 14, Side 2
Phonics Songs and Rhymes Audio

Dwight the Knight

There was a boy named Dwight.
Dwight's school was a delight.
Dwight's class had gone to see some sights
Like kings and queens and knights.

When Dwight went home that night,
He dreamed he was a knight.
Dwight's horse was big.
Dwight's sword was light.
Dwight's armor shined so bright.

Phonics Songs and Rhymes Chart 22

Sing or Read the Rhyme Chart Sing "Dwight the Knight" to the tune of "Farmer in the Dell" or play the CD or tape.

Focus on the Long *i* Sound Say:

> The class goes to see some sights. What sound do you hear in the middle of *sight?* (/ī/)

Explain that /ī/ is the long *i* sound. Have children repeat *sight* several times, listening to the long *i* sound as they say it.

Ask children to raise their hands each time they hear the long *i* sound in one of these words: *tie, high, kid, light, lie, led, might, toast, night.*

▶ Connect Sounds to Letters

Teach Point to *sight* on the chart and have it read. Say:

> The letters *igh* in *sight* stand for the sound /ī/. /ī/ is the long *i* sound.

Have children repeat the sound /ī/ several times, stretching the sound as they say it. Follow a similar procedure with *tie* and the letters *ie.*

Blending Practice Frame the word *night.* Model blending /n/ /ī/ /t/ to read *night* as you run your hand beneath the letters. Repeat with several other long *i* spelled *igh* words.

Make New Words Write the words *sight* and *tie* on the board in two columns. Ask a volunteer to read them. Have children name rhyming words and suggest their spelling. Record the words under the correct column. Have children go back to decode the words on each list. Add *night* to the chunking wall.

sight	tie
night	lie
flight	pie
might	die

Then have children change vowel letters to make the words *seat, neat, meat,* and *lay, pay, day.*

Singular Possessives

▶ Teach Singular Possessives

Write the following on the board:

Dwight___ horse is big.
Dad___ garden is pretty.

Ask children to read the first sentence and think about what is missing. Have a volunteer add 's to *Dwight* and then read the sentence. Repeat for *Dad*. Point out that the 's shows that something belongs to someone.

▶ Make New Words

Return to the Chart Tell children that Dwight has five things that belong to him. Have children underline the names of things that are Dwight's.

Practice Possessives Write the words *friend, dog,* and *Sam* on the board. Have volunteers add 's to each word and write a sentence.

Spelling Long *i* Words

Pretest Say the spelling word, use it in a sentence, repeat it, and allow children to write it. Have children check their pretests and correct misspelled words.

Work with the Spelling Pattern Write *igh* and *ie* on chart paper. Write the *igh* and *ie* spelling words on index cards with double-stick tape on the back. Place the cards on a table with the words facing down and have volunteers pick a word and stick it below the correct heading.

Skills Trace

◯ Singular Possessives

Introduce/Teach	TE: 1.5 116I
Practice	PB: 1.5 52; 1.6 63
Reteach/Review	TE: 1.5 123c, 151a, 153a, 155c, AR16; 1.6 129b
Test	Skills Test, Unit 6
Benchmark Test, Unit 6

Day
1

Spelling Words

lie	night
pie	light
tie	right

High-Frequency

been	found

Challenge

cat's	dog's

Word Wall

Introduce High-Frequency Words Use word cards for *been, first, found, start,* and *together.* Help children identify each word and use it in a sentence.

Review Read and chant the spellings of other *b, f, s,* and *t* words.

been   first
found
start   together

Optional Resources

Waterford Early Reading Program
Level 2: Lesson 3

Phonics
Phonics Workbook, pp. 141–143
Phonics Manipulatives Kit

High-Frequency Words
High-Frequency Word Cards
Phonics Sourcebook, pp. 90–99

Objectives

Children will

- learn selection vocabulary
- use sound-symbol relationships to read decodable text
- use prior knowledge to make predictions and make sense of texts
- make predictions

Day 1

Phonics Story # What a Sight!
pp. 116–123

▶ Build Oral Language

Activate Prior Knowledge Ask children to tell what they know about museums. As children give ideas, create a word web to show what people can do in museums. You might want to use Graphic Organizer Transparency 5 (Web 2).

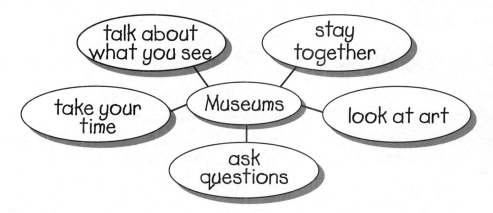

Build Background Provide books that show pictures from inside art museums.

▶ Vocabulary

Introduce Story Vocabulary Use Vocabulary Chart 42, or write sentences on the board, using each word. Read each sentence aloud.

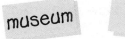

museum   fur

Frame *museum* in the sentence. Ask children to read the word and tell about their favorite parts of a museum.

Frame *fur* and ask children to read it. Have them share names of animals that have fur.

Review High-Frequency Words Have children read each word as you point to it on the Word Wall. These words are also listed on page 228 of the Student Book.

 been   first   found   start    together

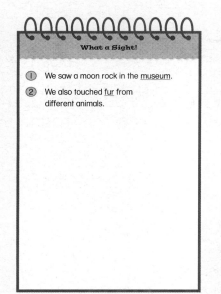

What a Sight!

① We saw a moon rock in the museum.

② We also touched fur from different animals.

Story Vocabulary Chart 42

— high-frequency/tested vocabulary

▶ Reading Strategies

Preview and Predict Read the title and the names of the author and illustrator with children. Ask them to identify Nicky, Jim, and Tiger in the first picture.

> **What can you tell about the children and their cat from the pictures on the first two pages?** (The children do things together. Their cat likes to be with them.)

Picture Walk Have children do a picture walk, looking at all the pictures in the story. Children might use words from the story to describe the pictures. Have children predict what might happen in the story.

Set Purposes From the pictures, children know that Tiger sneaks into the museum in Jim's backpack. Suggest that children read to find out whether Tiger gets into trouble.

Guide the Reading Have children read the first few pages of the selection, keeping their purposes in mind. Stop and check comprehension, using the questions provided. Have children read to page 119.

Phonics Story

What a Sight!

by Carolyn Crimi

Illustrated by Darryl Ligasan

Nicky and Jim were playing together with Nicky's game.

"We're going to the museum!" Dad said.

"Right now?" asked Jim.

"I'll tell Mom first," said Dad.

Selection Audio

CD 7/Tape 24, Side 1

Day 1

About the Author

Carolyn Crimi has published several books for children as well as stories and articles for children's magazines. She is the Program Director for the Society of Children's Book Writers and Illustrators in Illinois. She and her husband Al live in a 100-year-old house in Evanston, Illinois, with their two cats, Oscar and Mama.

About the Illustrator

Darryl Ligasan was raised in the Philippines. He teaches at the School of Visual Arts in New York City, where he now lives. He also works as a designer and illustrator. He has illustrated two other books for children, *Caravan* and *Allie's Basketball Dream*.

Optional Resources

Reading
Adding English: ESL Teacher's Guide

Guiding Comprehension

pp. 116–119

What a Sight!, page 116

Day 1

Details/Literal

Why don't Nicky and Jim think Tiger should go to the museum?

They think museums are not for cats.

Making Judgments/Critical

Do you agree with Nicky that museums are not for cats? Explain your answer.

Children are likely to say that museums are not for cats because cats might bother other people in the museum, or they might get lost or cause other kinds of problems.

Drawing Conclusions/Inferential

Do Nicky and Jim know that Tiger is in the museum? How do you know?

Nicky and Jim do not know that Tiger is in the museum because they didn't see Tiger hide in Jim's backpack. Also, since they felt that cats shouldn't be in museums, Nicky and Jim would probably take Tiger out if they knew he was there.

> ### Connect Phonics to Reading
>
> **What does Tiger sneak into?** Jim's backpack
> **How do you know that the backpack belongs to Jim?** The *'s* after the name *Jim* shows that the backpack belongs to Jim.

to the end of the story.

Phonics Story

What a Sight!

by Carolyn Crimi

illustrated by
Darryl Ligasan

Nicky and Jim were playing together with Nicky's game.
"We're going to the museum!" Dad said.
"Right now?" asked Jim.
"I'll tell Mom first," said Dad.

116

Jim and Nicky got dressed to go to the museum. They didn't see Tiger sneak into Jim's backpack. Tiger hid right inside.

118 Phonics Story

What a Sight!, page 118

Nicky petted Tiger's fur and sighed. "I wish we could bring Tiger. He might like to go. But I guess museums are not for cats."

"I think you're right," said Jim.

Phonics Story **117**

What a Sight!, page 117

Dad, Nicky, and Jim walked down the museum's halls. They looked at the bright paintings hanging high on the walls. Tiger looked out of Jim's backpack.

Phonics Story **119**

What a Sight!, page 119

Skills in Context

Predict

What do you think will happen next?

Reasonable predictions are that Tiger will be discovered, that Tiger will try to run away, or that Tiger will cause problems in the museum.

Ongoing Assessment

Predict

If... children are unable to use picture and text clues to predict what will happen next,	**then...** do the **Think Aloud** below to model the skill.

Model Your Thinking

TEST TALK

When I look at page 119, I can see that Tiger is peeking out of the backpack, so I think that Nicky and Jim will find out that Tiger is in the museum with them. Tiger seems to be a mischievous cat, which makes me think that maybe Tiger will try to run away or cause some problem, and the children will try to stop him.

Have children discuss their ideas about what will happen in the story. Ask them to give reasons for their predictions.

Day **1**

■ long *i*: *igh, ie,* and *'s* possessives
— high-frequency/tested vocabulary

Guiding Comprehension

pp. 120–123

Character/Inferential

How does Jim feel about Tiger at the end?

Jim is a little angry, but he also understands that Tiger had fun.

Self-Monitoring Strategy

It doesn't say that Jim is angry, or that he understands that Tiger had fun. Why do you think this?

Jim calls Tiger a bad kitty, which shows he might be a little angry. But he also says, "I bet you had fun!"

Evaluating/Critical

Would you like to have Tiger as your pet? Why or why not?

Children are likely to say they would like a pet like Tiger; the cat is cute and curious. Or they may not want Tiger as a pet because he causes trouble.

Check Predictions

Did the story end the way you thought it would?

Children who used picture clues are likely to say yes.

> **Connect Phonics to Reading**
>
> **Look at page 122. What did Tiger give one man?** a fright **Name another word on page 122 that has that same vowel sound as** *fright.* Children should say *sight.*

Response Log Ask children to write and illustrate a new ending for *What a Sight!*

They saw an apple pie and a lion that liked to lie in the shade. Tiger seemed to like the lion the best.

120 Phonics Story

***What a Sight!*, page 120**

Together, Nicky and Jim ran after Tiger. He gave one man a fright. Soon everyone ran after Tiger. What a sight! Jim found him at last.

122

***What a Sight!*, page 122**

Then Tiger saw a painting of a very big dog. It made him start to move around. He jumped out of Jim's backpack!

"Tiger!" Nicky called. "Is that you?"

Phonics Story **121**

What a Sight!, page 121

Ongoing Assessment

Phonics Strategies

If... children need help reading *right* on page 123,	**then...** tell them that *right* is a tricky word in which all the letters don't match the sounds. They can use the first and last letters to help them read this word. **Consonants**
If... children have difficulty reading *Jim's* and *Dad's,*	**then...** review how to form possessives. **Decoding: Using Structural Analysis**

Reading Strategies

If... children are unable to tell how Jim is feeling,	**then...** have them reread what Jim says on page 123. Ask what he might be feeling when he says, "You've been a bad kitty." Ask how he feels when he says, "But I bet you had fun!" **Rereading, Character**

Day 1

Dad's face was red from running. "Tiger, it isn't right to sneak into a museum," he said.

"You've been a bad kitty," said Jim. "But I bet you had fun!"

Phonics Story **123**

What a Sight!, page 123

Extend Language Arts

Writing: Making Comparisons

Have children look at page 120 in the story. Ask why they think Tiger liked the painting of the lion the best. Discuss some of the ways Tiger and the lion are the same. Write the children's ideas on the board.

Now have children write several sentences telling how Tiger and the lion in the painting are alike. They may use some of the ideas on the board and add some of their own. Remind children to use complete sentences and to begin each sentence with a capital letter and end it with a period. Encourage children to share their sentences with the rest of the class.

Suggest that when children read another story they look for ways that characters or situations in that story are alike.

▨	long *i: igh, ie,* and *'s* possessives
▬	high-frequency/tested vocabulary

Day 1

Objectives

Children will

- expand vocabulary
- name places
- write about places
- practice handwriting

Meeting Individual Needs

Challenge

Extended Vocabulary List
Encourage the use of words such as these.

aquarium	greenhouse
carnival	lighthouse
community	monument

Expand Vocabulary

▶ Discuss Place Names

Ask children to think about favorite places they have been in your community and favorite places where they have gone on vacation. As they answer, ask why they chose the places as favorites.

WRITING

List

▶ Shared Writing

List Places Explain that you want to write a list of places in your community. Ask children to name places in your community. Record children's responses in a list and save the list for use later.

As you write, point out that words are written from left to right. Call attention to the spaces between words.

post office	movie theater
mall	park
school	market

Independent Writing Distribute drawing paper folded in half. On each half, have children draw a picture of a place chosen from the list. Tell them to write the names of the places on their papers. Have children save the writing for use on Day 2.

Show children how they can use the list for ideas.

Self-Selected Reading and Read Aloud D.E.A.R.

Read aloud *Bill and Pete Go Down the Nile* by Tomie dePaola. Children can choose a book about museums for independent reading.

Day 1

Handwriting *Jj*

Provide lined paper and handwriting models. Demonstrate how to write a capital *J* and a lowercase *j* and have children practice writing a row of each letter.

Ask children to evaluate their handwriting by circling with a red crayon their best capital *J* and their best lowercase *j*.

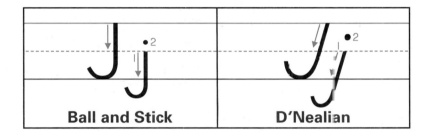

Ball and Stick	D'Nealian

Print Direction Write these sentences on the board:

Jim and John like to jog.
Jean eats jelly and jam.

As you write, point out that you begin writing on the left and move to the right.

Optional Resources

Oral Language
Adding English: ESL Teacher's Guide

Objectives

Children will

- decode and build words with long *i: igh, ie* and singular possessives
- use sound/symbol relationships as visual cues for decoding
- spell words with long *i: igh, ie*
- recognize high-frequency words

Day 2

Decodable Reader 37,
It's Just Right

Optional Resources

Phonics
Phonics Workbook, pp. 141–143
Phonics Manipulatives Kit
Phonics Sourcebook, pp. 100–123

High-Frequency Words
High-Frequency Word Cards
Phonics Sourcebook, pp. 90–99

123c   Phonics • Spelling

Long *i: igh, ie*
Singular Possessives

►Phonics Practice Activities

Use the following activities and Practice Book pages to practice long *i* and singular possessives.

Phonics Songs and Rhymes Chart Children sing "Dwight the Knight" as you track the print. Have them point to pictures and words on the chart that have long *i: igh, ie,* and words that are possessives.

Play "Concentration" Children work with a partner. Each child writes the following words on index cards: *lie, pie, tie, die, right, light, sight, might,* and *night.* Mix the cards up and have children turn them over in a 3-by-3 array. Matched pairs with the same /ī/ spelling are picked up and unmatched cards are returned to their original position. When the game is finished, partners can sort words according to their spelling pattern.

Long *i: igh, ie*
Practice Book 1.5, p. 51
Teacher's Resource Book 1.5, p. 57

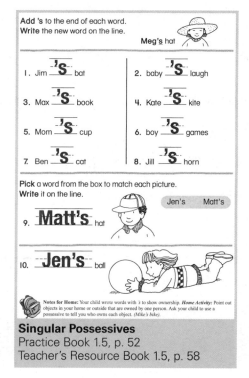

Singular Possessives
Practice Book 1.5, p. 52
Teacher's Resource Book 1.5, p. 58

►Read the Phonics Reader

Tell children to use what they know about *'s* and long *i* spelled *igh* and *ie* as they read *Dad's Gift*. Observe children's reading to determine their ability to transfer these phonics skills to a new selection. After reading, have them:
- describe their favorite character
- do a word hunt for *igh* and *ie* words

Phonics Reader

Spelling Long *i* Words

▶ Writing for Sounds

Have children write these sentences. Read the sentences. Then repeat words slowly, allowing children to hear each sound. Children may use the Word Wall to help in spelling high-frequency words. Proofread and correct completed sentences.

I cannot lie, I ate the pie.
Carry a light at night.
Put the tie around the right box.

Spelling Words

lie	night
pie	light
tie	right

High-Frequency

been	found

Challenge

cat's	dog's

Day **2**

Word Wall

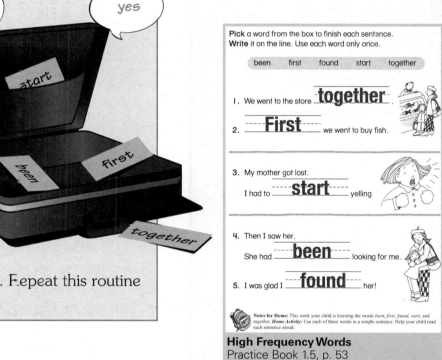

Does it begin with b?

yes

Practice High-Frequency Words
Write this week's words on the board. Tell children to choose one of the words and say the following:

I'm going on a trip and taking a word with me.

Have other children ask yes or no questions about the word. Give examples such as:

Does it begin with *b*? Is it an action word?

Let children ask questions until the word is guessed. Repeat this routine for the other words.

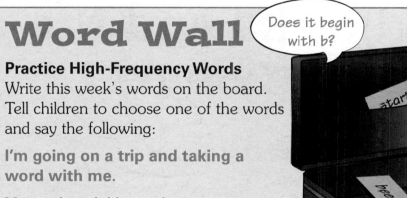

Pick a word from the box to finish each sentence. Write it on the line. Use each word only once.

been	first	found	start	together

1. We went to the store **together**.
2. **First** we went to buy fish.
3. My mother got lost. I had to **start** yelling.
4. Then I saw her. She had **been** looking for me.
5. I was glad I **found** her!

Notes for Home: This week your child is learning the words *been, first, found, start,* and *together.* **Home Activity:** Use each of these words in a simple sentence. Help your child read each sentence aloud.

High Frequency Words
Practice Book 1.5, p. 53
Teacher's Resource Book 1.5, p. 59

 ## Meeting Individual Needs

ESL	Intervention	Challenge	Other Ways to Learn
Practice blending sounds using word cards for *igh* and *ie* words. First, say it slowly, such as /n/ /ī/ /t/. Then, have children repeat it, blending the sounds. Finally, repeat the word slowly with children standing straight and tall like the letter *i* each time they hear the long *i* sound. **(Phonics Support)** See also *Adding English.* **ESL**	Use **Decodable Reader 37** and the teaching suggestions on p. AR5 to provide practice reading decodable text that includes words with long *i*: *igh, ie* and singular possessives. **(Phonics Support)**	Draw a sound box with four sections on the board. As you say each word, point to a box for each sound. Ask children how many sounds they hear in each word and which sound is the long *i*. Demonstrate with *lie* (2 sounds, last sound). Use *cried* (4, third), *tie* (2, last), *fries* (4, third), *pie* (2, last), *died* (3, second). **(Tiered Assignments)**	Use Phonics Activity Mat 4 from the Phonics Manipulatives Kit for long *i*. Use Phonics Activity Mat 2 for singular possessives. Instructions for using these games are on the back of the mats. **(Kinesthetic)**

Objectives

Children will

- ⊙ identify implied cause and effect in a story
- listen critically to understand cause and effect
- read with fluency and understanding

Skills Trace

⊙ Cause and Effect

Introduce		TE: 1.1 76
Teach	Before	TE: 1.5 **123e–123f**
	During	TE: 1.5 146–147
	After	TE: 1.5 AR16
Practice		PB: 1.2 22, 86; 1.5 54, 86
Reteach/Review		TE: 1.2 AR13, AR19; 1.5 189, 199e–199f, 210–211, AR16, AR19
Test		Skills Test, Units 2, 6 Benchmark Test, Units 2, 6

Day 2

Building Systematic Instruction

⊙ Cause and Effect

LOOKING BACK

Kindergarten Children understand what happened in a story and why.

Grade 1 Children identify what happened in a story and why. Children rely on clue words to identify cause and effect.

LOOKING AHEAD

Grade 2 Children identify cause and effect by name.

Cause and Effect

▶ Develop Listening Comprehension

Read the following story aloud. Ask children to listen and think about what happened in the story and why it happened.

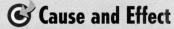

Goldilocks and the Three Bears

A little girl named Goldilocks was taking a walk in the woods. Along the way she saw a small house, and she stopped there because she was tired and hungry.

Goldilocks knocked on the door, but no one was home. She smelled something delicious, so she went in. On the kitchen table were three bowls of oatmeal. She discovered that the big bowl was too hot, the medium-size bowl was too cold, and the little bowl was just right. So she ate all of the oatmeal from that bowl.

Goldilocks was sleepy after she ate, so she went upstairs to take a nap. The big bed was too hard, the medium-size bed was too soft, but the little bed was just right. So she fell asleep on the little bed.

As she was sleeping, the Bear family came home from a walk. Baby Bear noticed right away that his oatmeal was gone. Then the Bears went upstairs.

Baby Bear screamed when he saw Goldilocks sleeping in his bed. When she heard the scream, Goldilocks woke up, looked at the Bears, and then ran as fast as she could out of their house.

▶ Teach Cause and Effect

Model the skill by telling children:

Think ALOUD

I can tell some things that happened in this story and I can also tell why they happened. Goldilocks stopped at the Bear's house because she was tired and hungry. She ate Baby Bear's oatmeal because it wasn't too hot or too cold.

Say this sentence and ask children to identify what happened and why it happened:

Goldilocks ran out of the house after Baby Bear screamed.

Practice Make two columns on a poster board, one with the heading "What Happened?" and the other with the heading "Why?" Reread the story and help children fill in the chart with story events.

Reread for Fluency

Paired Reading Read aloud the first page to model fluent reading. Have children reread the story with a partner until they feel their reading "sounds like talking."

Use an Appropriate Pace In the book or on an overhead, slide a card over the text as children read together. This encourages children's pace to move a bit more quickly. Then have pairs of children choose two pages from the story and reread them at least three times, focusing on reading at an appropriate pace.

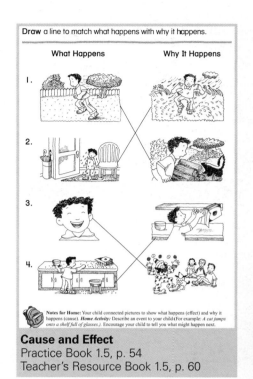

Draw a line to match what happens with why it happens.

What Happens	Why It Happens

Notes for Home: Your child connected pictures to show what happens (effect) and why it happens (cause). **Home Activity:** Describe an event to your child (For example: *A cat jumps onto a shelf full of glasses.*). Encourage your child to tell you what might happen next.

Cause and Effect
Practice Book 1.5, p. 54
Teacher's Resource Book 1.5, p. 60

Day 2

Leveled Practice for ↻ Cause and Effect

After children have read *Lost in the Museum,* use the appropriate leveled practice pictured on page 153 in this Teacher's Edition.

Easy
On-Level
Challenge

Meeting Individual Needs

ESL	Intervention	Challenge	Other Ways to Learn
Invite student to blow a feather or other lightweight object to make it move. Ask: "Why did the feather move?" **(Skill Support)** See also *Adding English.* **ESL**	Use a familiar selection to reinforce cause and effect. For *All Together Now!,* ask, "What happened on the walk? Could the family see these things if they didn't go for a walk?" For *How Bill Found Rain,* ask why it rained. **(Comprehension Support)**	Children use the word *because* in a written sentence that explains why Tiger jumped out of the backpack. Have them illustrate both parts of their sentence. **(Application of Different Symbol Systems)**	Children demonstrate what the cat did when it saw the painting of the tiger, how the man reacted when Tiger flew by, and how Dad looked when Tiger was loose at the museum. **(Kinesthetic)**

Day
2

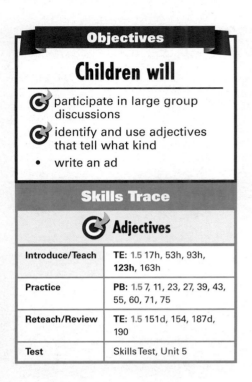

Objectives

Children will

- participate in large group discussions
- identify and use adjectives that tell what kind
- write an ad

Skills Trace

Adjectives

Introduce/Teach	TE: 1.5 17h, 53h, 93h, **123h**, 163h
Practice	PB: 1.5 7, 11, 23, 27, 39, 43, 55, 60, 71, 75
Reteach/Review	TE: 1.5 151d, 154, 187d, 190
Test	Skills Test, Unit 5

Speaking: Large Group Discussion

▶ Discuss Places to Learn

Model Explain that many people enjoy big talks, or discussions, to share their ideas. Tell children they will share ideas about places to shop. Ask children to suggest rules people should follow in a big discussion. Elicit responses similar to those in the chart below as you record children's answers. Save the list of rules for use on Day 5.

Rules

Raise your hand and wait your turn to speak.

Let everyone have a chance to speak.

Be polite and listen to each speaker.

Leave the chart where it can be seen and begin a brief discussion of places to learn. Prompt children with questions such as:

Where do you go to learn things?
What can you learn there?

Children will probably name school, library, museum, and so on.

Practice Divide the class into two or three groups. Assign one of these topics to each group: school, museum, library. Have children follow the rules on the chart as they discuss the topics. Discussion might touch on
- what the place is like
- what you can learn there
- who works there

Ad

▶ Modeled Writing

Model Tell children they are getting ready to write an ad about a special place in their town. Explain that the ad should make people want to come and visit. Ask children what kinds of things they might say about the special place in town.

I want people to come visit our museum, so I will think about what I like about the museum. I'll tell them about the dinosaur bones and the birds' eggs. I'll be sure to stay on the topic and tell only important things.

►Write an Ad for a Special Place

Model Write these sentences on the chalkboard.

> Come to the museum in our town. You'll love seeing the dinosaur bones and the birds' eggs. You'll have fun!

As you write the sentences, model these strategies:
- Focus on the topic—getting people to come to the museum.
- Tell only information about the museum.
- Grab the reader's attention at the beginning and end.
- Make sure all sentences fit together.
- Use correct end punctuation.
- Note spaces between words.

Independent Writing Have children write their own ads. They may write an ad for a museum, or they may write an ad for one of the places in their writing from Day 1. Tell them to give specific details and to make their ads exciting. Ask children to illustrate their writing.

Author's Chair If time permits, allow children to share their writing.

Grammar: Adjectives

Define Adjectives That Tell What Kind Provide a basin with water and two washcloths. Show children the dry washcloth as you say, "dry." Dip the other washcloth into the water as you say, "wet." Explain that these adjectives tell what kind of washcloth. Remind children that adjectives describe people, places, and things. Point out that children already know about adjectives that tell color, shape, and size. Explain that they will now work with adjectives that tell what kind.

Practice Show the following, and prompt children to say the describing phrases as you show each one: full glass and empty glass, happy face and sad face, clean dish and dirty dish, new toy and old toy. Write the phrases on a chart as children say them.

empty glass   full glass   new toy   old toy

happy face sad face   clean dish   dirty dish

For further practice, have children identify adjectives they used in their writing and add them to the chart.

Self-Selected Reading and Read Aloud D.E.A.R.

Read aloud a suspense story. For independent reading, children can self-select books about special places.

Day **2**

Some **adjectives** tell what kind. **Wet** tells what kind of day it is.

It is a **wet** day.

Circle an adjective in ( ) to finish each sentence.

1. This is a (funny/**yummy**) cake.

2. What a (hard/**soft**) bed!

3. The dog is (**wet**/dry).

4. He has a (**neat**/messy) place.

5. I read a (sad/**funny**) book.

Notes for Home: Your child identified adjectives that tell what kind, such as *wet* or *soft*. **Home Activity:** Point out objects to your child. Encourage your child to name an adjective telling what kind of object each one is.

Adjectives
Practice Book 1.5, p. 55
Teacher's Resource Book 1.5, p. 61

Objectives

Children will

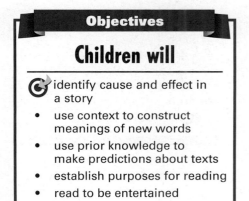

- identify cause and effect in a story
- use context to construct meanings of new words
- use prior knowledge to make predictions about texts
- establish purposes for reading
- read to be entertained

Day 3

Lost in the Museum

1. We ate in the museum <u>cafeteria</u>.
2. A waiter asked, "What <u>else</u> would you like?"
3. We saw a <u>dinosaur</u> at the museum.
4. The dinosaur looked <u>fierce</u>.
5. The dinosaur bones <u>scared</u> me.
6. We also saw many birds, even some <u>penguins</u>.
7. When we were <u>fooling</u> around, our class left.
8. Guess what <u>happened</u> next?
9. We <u>hurried</u> to catch up with our teacher.

Story Vocabulary Chart 43

Pick a word from the box that is the opposite of each word below. Write it on the line.

| been | first | found | start | together |

1. stop **start**
2. last **first**
3. lost **found**
4. apart **together**

Write a sentence with the word *been*. **Possible answer given.**

5. **I have been good.**

Notes for Home: Your child identified opposites and wrote a sentence using words learned this week. *Home Activity:* Encourage your child to make up a song or poem using as many of these words as possible.

Tested Vocabulary
Practice Book 1.5, p. 56
Teacher's Resource Book 1.5, p. 62

Lost in the Museum
pp. 124–151

▶ Build Oral Language

Activate Prior Knowledge Ask children to discuss museums.

> How did Tiger surprise Nicky, Jim, and Dad?
> What do you like about going to museums?
> Why is it easy to get lost in a museum?

Build Background Play the Background-Building audio segment, which takes listeners to the "Idea Factory" exhibit at Chicago's Museum of Science and Industry. After listening, ask children to share their own museum experiences. As a class, develop a list of rules for appropriate behavior in a museum.

Background-Building Audio

CD 5/Tape 13, Side 2

▶ Vocabulary

Introduce Story Vocabulary List the selection vocabulary on the board. Use Vocabulary Chart 43 or write sentences using each word. Read the sentences aloud.

cafeteria   else   dinosaur   fierce   scared

penguins   fooling   happened   hurried

Point to *cafeteria* in the list. Have someone circle it, read it, and use it in a sentence. Continue this routine with the rest of the selection vocabulary.

Names Write *Jim's* and *Danny's* on the board. Remind students the *'s* shows that something belongs to Jim and Danny.

▶ Reading Strategies

Preview and Predict After reading the title of the story and the name of the author, have children page through the story and discuss what they think is happening in the pictures. During the picture walk, have children pay attention to the looks on the children's faces and ask them to analyze how they think the children are feeling.

Set Purposes Once children realize that the children in the story have become separated from their teacher and are lost in the museum, suggest that they read to find out how the characters solve their problem. Ask children to be thinking about why the characters got lost.

Guide the Reading Have children read the first few pages of the story, keeping their purposes in mind. Stop to check comprehension, using the questions provided. Have children read to page 127.

Managing Flexible Groups

Intervention

Before reading, review the names of the characters, helping children pronounce them. Read and discuss difficult words, such as *museum, dinosaur, fierce, hurried, some-body,* and *every-body.* Children listen to the selection audio and follow along in their books. After reading the story once, reread it, having children point to exclamation points in the text and show how they can read those sentences with expression.

Selection Audio
CD 7/Tape 24, Side 1

To develop fluency, children can read **Leveled Reader 22A,** *All Together Now!,* and/or **Decodable Reader 38.** Instructional support appears in this Teacher's Edition, pp. LR19–LR20 and AR6.

Easy

Children can review the high-frequency words. Read the story aloud with children. Help children pronounce the names of the characters. Children join in to read the dialogue. Use Guiding Comprehension to monitor understanding and Ongoing Assessment as appropriate.

To develop fluency and to practice high-frequency words, children can read **Leveled Reader 22B,** *How Bill Found Rain.* Instructional support appears in this Teacher's Edition, pp. LR22–LR23.

On-Level

Ask children to be ready to tell you what happened that caused the characters to get lost. Children can take turns reading characters' dialogue. Use Guiding Comprehension to monitor understanding and Ongoing Assessment to address reading difficulties.

To develop fluency and to practice high-frequency words, children can read **Leveled Reader 22B,** *How Bill Found Rain.* Instructional support appears in this Teacher's Edition, pp. LR22–LR23.

Challenge

Children can buddy-read with a partner. Have them think about what happens and what causes each event to happen. They can record their observations in a response log. After reading, children write a short story about a time when they got lost, telling why it happened and what they did.

Children who have finished reading *Lost in the Museum* can read a selection in **Leveled Reader 5C.**

About the Author

Miriam Cohen
grew up in Newburgh, New York, where all she ever wanted to do was read. Though she even read while walking to school, it never occurred to her to become a writer. She wrote her first book after her first child was born and walked it over to the closest publisher. She has written many books for young readers, including *When Will I Read?* and *See You in Second Grade!*

Day **3**

About the Illustrator

Lillian Hoban
grew up in a family of readers and realized early on that she wanted to be an illustrator for children's books. She likes to work in pen and ink and says that drawing and painting bring her comfort. In addition to illustrating other authors' books, she has written many of her own, including *Mr. Pig and Family.*

Decodable Readers 33–41

Decodable Reader 38,
Night Sights

Optional Resources

Reading
Adding English: ESL Teacher's Guide

What a Sight!/Lost **124b**

Guiding Comprehension

pp. 124–127

Setting/Literal

Where does the story take place?

The story takes place in a large museum.

Summarizing/Inferential

What has happened so far in the story?

The teacher told the children to stay together, but Danny left the group to show some of the children a dinosaur.

Predicting/Inferential

What do you think will happen to the children in the story?

Children are likely to say that the children in the story will get lost or get into trouble for leaving the teacher.

to page 131.

Lost in the Museum

by Miriam Cohen

illustrated by Lillian Hoban

"This is a big place,"
the teacher told the <u>first</u> grade.

124

Lost in the Museum, page 124

Danny said to Jim,
"I know where the dinosaur is.
Come on, I'll show you!"

126

Lost in the Museum, page 126

"But if we all stay together,
nobody will get lost in the museum."

125

Lost in the Museum, page 125

Fiction Genre: Realistic Fiction

Invite two volunteers to tell stories. Take the volunteers aside and give the following instructions:

Tell a story about a dinosaur who comes to school and sits in class with the children, and you can tell the class what happened in *Lost in the Museum.*

After volunteers tell their stories, ask children if either story really happened. (no) Then ask if either story *could* happen.

Help children recognize that *Lost in the Museum* is realistic fiction. It *could* happen, even though it really didn't. Tell children the story about the dinosaur visiting the classroom is not realistic fiction. Ask them why. (It couldn't really happen because dinosaurs don't exist anymore.)

Jim had never seen a dinosaur.
He ran after Danny.
And Willy and Sammy,
Paul, and George did too.

127

Lost in the Museum, page 127

Day
3

     long *i: igh, ie* and singular possessives
— high-frequency/tested vocabulary

Guiding Comprehension

pp. 128–131

Day 3

Drawing Conclusions/Inferential

Why do the children follow Danny and not stay with their teacher?

They want to see a dinosaur too, and when Danny invites them to follow him, they forget about the teacher's directions.

Analyzing/Critical

Why do you think Willy says, "That is some big chicken!"?

Willy has probably never seen a dinosaur skeleton before and thinks it looks like a huge chicken.

Predicting/Inferential

What do you think will happen next?

Children are likely to say that the characters will wander farther and farther from the class.

Read On...

to page 135.

Anna Maria and Sara started after them. "Come back! You'll get lost!" they called.

128

Lost in the Museum, page 128

But Jim stopped.
He put his head way back.
He looked up.

130

Lost in the Museum, page 130

Danny slid down the hall very fast.
He slid into a room at the end.
Willy and Sammy, Paul, George, Jim,
Anna Maria, and Sara ran after him.

129

Lost in the Museum, page 129

Jim heard Willy say,
"That is some big chicken!"

"It's the dinosaur!" shouted Danny.

131

Lost in the Museum, page 131

Ongoing Assessment

Reading Strategies

If... children have trouble reading the names in the text,

then... tell them to ask a classmate for help if they can't decode it themselves. **Seek Help from Other People**

If... children cannot draw conclusions about why the children left their teacher,

then... ask children to think about how they might feel when they are visiting a fun place with their friends. Point out that they may be so excited that they could forget their teacher's directions. **Using Prior Knowledge**

If... children fail to read sentences with exclamation points expressively,

then... reread the dialogue, pointing out the exclamation point at the end of each sentence. Remind children that the exclamation point tells the reader to change voice tone and read with excitement. **Fluency**

Day 3

long *i: igh, ie* and singular possessives
— high-frequency/tested vocabulary

Guiding Comprehension

pp. 132–135

Using Illustrations/Inferential

How do you know Jim is frightened?

Possible answers: The dinosaur is large and scary looking. Jim runs away. Jim looks frightened.

Recall and Retell/Literal

What do the other children do to help Jim?

They use words to tell Jim not to be frightened. Paul puts his arm around Jim.

Predicting/Inferential

George says, "Come on, let's find the others." What do you think will happen now?

Possible responses: All the children will go look for the others. Some of the children will stay in one place while a few go to look for the others.

Jim came around the corner.
The dinosaur had his arms up over
Jim's head. The dinosaur's teeth
were smiling a fierce smile.

132

Lost in the Museum, page 132

Read On...

to page 139.

The kids came running after Jim.
"Don't worry. He won't hurt you," said Sammy.

"That's right," Willy told Jim.
"They don't have dinosaurs anymore."

134

Lost in the Museum, page 134

Day 3

Paul said, "Look out, Jim!
He's going to get you!"

Jim turned and ran as fast as he could.
"Jim, stop! I was only fooling," Paul called.

133

Lost in the Museum, **page 133**

Reading Strategies

If... children hesitate in making a prediction,	**then...** point out that the museum is a big place. Lead children to see that the children in the story could either find their teacher or have something else happen to them in the museum. **Predicting**
If... children easily tell details about the story,	**then...** acknowledge their close attention to detail, which helps them understand what is happening. **Comprehension**

Phonics Strategies

If... children have trouble reading *he's, don't, that's, it's,* and *let's,*	**then...** point out the apostrophes in these words. Reread the words, reminding children that these words are really two words put together, and the apostrophe shows that letters are left out. **Decoding: Contractions**

Day 3

Content Connection: Science

For many years, it was hard to find dinosaurs in museums. Scientists worked hard to find out how to make copies of skeletons. They had to take apart the entire skeleton and lay aside each bone. Then they copied each bone and made many more dinosaurs. The new dinosaurs weighed less, and their bones held together better. Museums all over the world now have dinosaur skeletons, real and simulated.

Paul put his arm around Jim.
Anna Maria said, "It's silly to be scared."
Jim knew it was silly.
He wished he could be brave.

"Come on, let's find the others," George said.

135

Lost in the Museum, **page 135**

long *i: igh, ie* and singular possessives
high-frequency/tested vocabulary

Guiding Comprehension

pp. 136–139

Day 3

Making Judgments/Inferential

Why do you think Jim volunteers to go look for the teacher?

Possible responses: He is worried about staying in the museum all night. He wants to show the others he can be brave. He wants to help his friends.

Drawing Conclusions/Inferential

Why is Jim so excited when he sees a red coat down the hallway?

He thinks the coat belongs to his classmate Margaret.

Self-Monitoring Strategy
Use Text Features

I didn't read, "Jim was excited about seeing the red coat." How do you know this?

He must be excited, because when he sees the girl in the red coat, he runs down the hall after her. Also, there are exclamation points at the end of the sentences.

Predicting/Inferential

What do you think will happen to Jim next?

He will stay lost. The teacher will find him. He will find his teacher.

Connect Phonics to Reading

What could Jim do with his eyes if he saw the dinosaur? What sound do you hear in the middle of the word *tight*?

He could shut them tight. You hear the long *i* sound in the middle of *tight*.

Read On...

to page 143.

"I think we are lost," said Sara.

"I know where to go," Danny said.

They all hurried after him down the big hall. But there were too many rooms.

"You got us lost," Anna Maria said to Danny.

"My toe hurts," said George.

"Maybe we will have to stay here all night," Paul said.

136

Lost in the Museum, **page 136**

A big boy was looking at birds' eggs.
Jim said, "Have you seen my teacher?"
Before the big boy could answer,
Jim saw a red coat way down the hall.

138

Lost in the Museum, **page 138**

Jim thought about staying all night with the dinosaur.
"I will go find the teacher," he said.
"You stay here in case she comes."

Jim went into many rooms. He kept his eyes shut a little. If he saw the dinosaur, he could shut them tight.

137

Lost in the Museum, page 137

Reading Strategies

If... children have trouble analyzing why Jim volunteered to look for his teacher,

then... go back and discuss the part of the story where Jim is frightened. Then prompt children to tell you why Jim might want to now do something brave. **Critical Thinking: Analyzing**

Phonics Strategies

If... children have difficulty decoding *night* and *tight,*

then... remind them that the letters *igh* can stand for /ī/. **Decoding**

If... children self-correct when reading a difficult word,

then... acknowledge their strength in realizing how to figure out what the word is. **Decoding: Strategies**

Margaret had a red coat! Jim ran to see. But somebody else was wearing Margaret's coat!

139

Lost in the Museum, page 139

long i: *igh, ie* and singular possessives
high-frequency/tested vocabulary

Guiding Comprehension

pp. 140–143

Recall and Retell/Literal

What are some of the things Jim sees in the museum while he tries to find his teacher?

He sees penguins, a deer family, and a large gray whale.

Character/Inferential

What kind of person is Jim?

Possible responses: He is fearful. He is brave. He is a good thinker.

Predicting/Inferential

Do you think Jim will find the teacher and other children soon?

Jim has been looking for his teacher for a while, so children are likely to say that Jim will soon find his teacher.

to page 147.

Jim was so tired.
He had to find the teacher!
He had to bring her back to the kids!
He ran on.

140

***Lost in the Museum,* page 140**

Jim stopped to rest.
The room was dark.
At <u>first</u> he couldn't see.

142

***Lost in the Museum,* page 142**

Day
3

Jim saw penguins playing in the snow like
first graders. He saw a mother, father, and
a child deer. The father stood with one
foot in the air.

141

Lost in the Museum, page 141

Ongoing Assessment

Reading Strategies

If... children have difficulty telling what Jim is like,	**then...** prompt them to give you characteristics by retelling several of the incidents of the story involving Jim. **Story Elements: Character**
If... children stop when they come to a difficult word,	**then...** allow them to go back and read the sentence again and try to figure out the word. **Rereading**
If... children are able to predict that Jim will find his teacher soon,	**then...** acknowledge their use of text and information they have learned in the story to make a good prediction. **Predicting**

Day 3

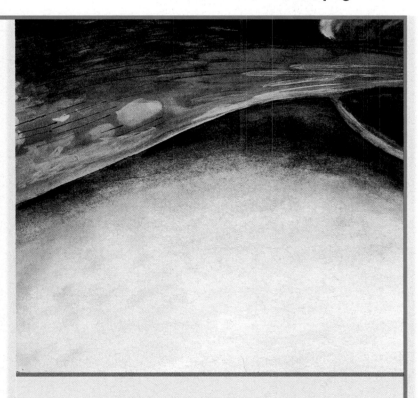

Then a great gray whale swam over
his head. He winked at Jim as if
he had something nice to tell him.
Jim looked all the way to the whale's tail.

143

Lost in the Museum, page 143

long *i: igh, ie* and singular possessives
— high-frequency/tested vocabulary

Guiding Comprehension

pp. 144–147

Summarizing/Inferential

What has happened so far in the story?

Jim and the children have gotten lost. Jim has found his teacher. Jim has taken his teacher back to the other children.

Cause and Effect/Inferential

The children leave their classmates at the beginning of the story to see the dinosaur. What is the effect of this action? Find sentences in the story to show you are right.

When they leave to see the dinosaur, they get separated from their classmates and teacher and get lost. Children may point to the sentences on page 136 to show how they got lost.

Day
3

Predicting/Inferential

How do you think the story will end?

Children are likely to say that Jim and the children will continue their museum trip.

Read On...

to the end of the story.

A lady was there with many children.
"Jim!" everybody called. "Oh, Jim!
We have <u>been</u> looking for you!"

144

Lost in the Museum, page 144

Jim <u>started</u> back.
He went past the penguins, past the deer.
This way? No! That way!
There they were—George, Willy and Sammy,
Anna Maria, Danny, Paul, and Sara.

146

Lost in the Museum, page 146

The teacher said, "Where have you been? Where are the other children?"

"I'll take you there," Jim said.

145

Lost in the Museum, page 145

When they saw their teacher,
George and Sara began to cry.
She hugged them.
"If we had stayed together, this
wouldn't have happened," she said.

147

Lost in the Museum, page 147

Skills in Context

TARGET SKILL ◎ Cause and Effect

What happens when Jim and his friends leave their classmates and teacher to see the dinosaur?

Jim and his friends get lost.

Ongoing Assessment

◎ Cause and Effect

If... children are unable to tell the effect of the children leaving the group,	**then...** do the **Think Aloud** below to model the skill.

Model Your Thinking

TEST TALK

I know from the story that when the children left their classmates and teacher to see the dinosaur, they got lost. When they got back together with their teacher, she said to them, "If we had stayed together, this wouldn't have happened."

Have children return to the story and discuss what happened when Jim told the children to stay in one place. Help children understand that one action often results in another. When they stayed in one place, the lost children were more easily found by Jim and the teacher.

Day
3

▓ long *i: igh, ie* and singular possessives
— high-frequency/tested vocabulary

Guiding Comprehension

pp. 148–151

Check Predictions

Did the story end the way you thought it would? Why or why not?

Children are likely to say they thought the lost children would find their teacher.

Making Judgments/Critical

After reading aloud page 151 with children, ask: If Jim is like the author's sons, how would you describe her children?

Children may answer that they are brave, curious, fearful, and smart.

Critical Thinking
Reading Across Texts

How is the problem in *What a Sight!* like the problem in *Lost in the Museum*? How are the problems different?

In both stories, the problem is caused by someone doing what he wasn't supposed to do. Tiger sneaks into the museum, even though it's not a good place for cats. Danny and Jim and the other children forget to stay with their teacher, wander off, and get lost.

Response Log Have children create a mural that illustrates the story line from beginning to end.

Willy and Sammy said, "Jim was brave. He went to find you!"

"Yes," the teacher said, "Jim was very brave. But next time, remember—IF WE ALL STAY TOGETHER, NOBODY WILL GET LOST."

148

Lost in the Museum, page 148

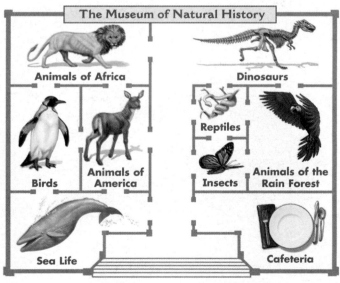

Museum Map

Here is a map of the museum the first grade visited. Some children got lost. This map might have helped them. It shows the rooms in the museum.

The Museum of Natural History

Animals of Africa

Dinosaurs

Reptiles

Birds

Animals of America

Insects

Animals of the Rain Forest

Sea Life

Cafeteria

Let's Talk
Where did Jim find his teacher?
What could you see in this museum?

150

Study Skill, page 150

They were so glad to be <u>found</u>!
Everybody went to have <u>lunch</u> in the cafeteria.
You could choose chicken and dumplings,
crisp fried fish, or beef stew with two vegetables.
But they all chose hot dogs.

149

Lost in the Museum, page 149

About the Author and the Illustrator

Miriam Cohen

Miriam Cohen wrote eighteen books about Jim and the other first graders. Ms. Cohen says that Jim is based on her three sons. She says Jim is a "rolling and patting together of Adam, Gabe, and Jem into one little guy."

Author

Lillian Hoban

Do you like to visit museums? Lillian Hoban did when she was your age. Those visits may have given her ideas for the pictures in *Lost in the Museum.*

Ms. Hoban also loved to draw and read as a child. Now she draws the pictures for all of Miriam Cohen's books.

Illustrator

151

About the Author/Illustrator, page 151

Skills in Context

Study Skill: Map

What does the map tell you about the museum?

It shows the rooms in the museum and tells what you would find in each room.

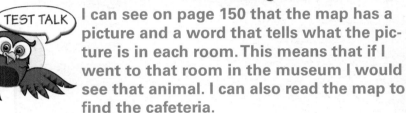

Ongoing Assessment

Map

If... children are unable to interpret the map,

then... do the **Think Aloud** below to model the skill.

Model Your Thinking

TEST TALK

I can see on page 150 that the map has a picture and a word that tells what the picture is in each room. This means that if I went to that room in the museum I would see that animal. I can also read the map to find the cafeteria.

Ask children to place a finger on the front steps of the museum on the map. Then have them trace a route with their finger as you tell them what room to visit. Ask children to locate where Jim got lost from his teacher (the dinosaur room). For additional practice with maps use Practice Book 1.5 page 57 (Teachers Resource Book 1.5 page 63).

Day 3

Extend Language Arts

Writing: Rules for a Field Trip

Make three columns on chart paper with these heads: "Rules," "Results if Rules Followed," "Results if Rules Not Followed." Have children suggest rules for a safe and happy field trip. Write their responses in the first column. Ask what will happen if each rule is followed. Write children's responses in the second column. Ask what will happen if each rule is not followed. Write responses in the third column.

▓ long *i: igh, ie* and singular possessives
— high-frequency/tested vocabulary

Long *i: igh, ie*
Singular Possessives

►Phonics Practice Activities

Careful observation of these activities will provide a basis for the Ongoing Assessment on page 151b.

Group Activity Write the following words in rows on the board and have them read. Ask volunteers to identify what the words in a row have in common.

lie	pie	tie	die
high	sigh	thigh	nigh
Tran's house	dog's house	Katie's house	bird's house
tight	might	right	fright

Independent Have children make a "night" bug. Cut circles from construction paper. On one circle, have children draw a bug's face and add antennae. Tell them this is a "night" bug. Ask them to write words with the phonogram *-ight* in the other circles. Then, have them make a baby bug with smaller circles and words with the phonogram *ie* in each circle.

Reread for Fluency

Use an Appropriate Pace Have children reread *Dad's Gift*. To gain fluency, have them practice reading aloud the same short passage at least 3–5 times to focus on achieving an appropriate reading rate.

Phonics Reader

Review

Long *a: ai, ay*

►Build Long *a* Words

Have children fold a sheet of paper in half. Ask them to write *tail* and *stay* as column heads. Working with a partner, have them write as many *ai* and *ay* words as they can in ten minutes. After the time is up, let children alternate reading the words they made.

tail	stay
laid	jay
raid	lay
hail	play
main	say

After reading the words, have children change the *ai* in words to *ea* or *ee* and read the new words.

Day 3

Long *a: ai, ay*
Practice Book 1.5, p. 58
Teacher's Resource Book 1.5, p. 64

Spelling Long *i: igh, ie* Words

▶ Practice with Writing

Write *lie, pie, tie, night, right,* and *light* on the board. Have pairs of children write and illustrate a sentence for each of the words.

Ongoing Assessment

Phonics/Spelling

If... children have difficulty decoding words with *-igh,*	**then...** have them practice blending words with the phonogram *-ight.* Also use Intervention activity, Day 4, page 153a.
If... children can easily write the possessive *cat's* and *dog's,*	**then...** give them a class list and ask them to write the possessive forms of their classmates' names. Also use Challenge activity, Day 4, page 153a.
If... children have difficulty spelling *lie, tie,* and *pie,*	**then...** have them work with a partner to read and practice writing these words.
If... children can easily write this week's spelling words,	**then...** write the following cloze activity on the board. Have children complete the sentences with the correct spelling words.

I cannot ____. *(lie)*
I ate all the ____. *(pie)*
I ate it at ____. *(night)*
I need a ____. *(light)*
I know it wasn't ____. *(right)*

Look at each word. Say it.
Listen for the long *i* sound in ⚔ **knight**

Write each word. | Check it.
1. lie — **lie** — **lie**
2. pie — **pie** — **pie**
3. tie — **tie** — **tie**
4. night — **night** — **night**
5. light — **light** — **light**
6. right — **right** — **right**

Word Wall Words
Write each word.
7. been — **been** — **been**
8. found — **found** — **found**

Notes for Home: Your child spelled words with the long *i* sound spelled *ie* and *igh,* and two frequently-used words: *been, found.* **Home Activity:** Work with your child to write a story that includes the spelling words about getting lost in a bakery.

Spelling
Practice Book 1.5, p. 59
Teacher's Resource Book 1.5, p. 65

Day 3

Word Wall

Practice High-Frequency Words

Going Places Start an oral class story with this sentence:

Jack and I have been to the museum together.

Then ask volunteers to add sentences to the story using this week's Word Wall words and also review words. List the Word Wall words on the board as they are used and then choral read the words when the story is finished.

been   first
found
start   together

Optional Resources

Phonics
Phonics Workbook, pp. 141–143, 144
Phonics Manipulatives Kit

High-Frequency Words
High-Frequency Word Cards
Phonics Sourcebook, pp. 90–99

Expand Vocabulary

► Name Items Found in Specific Places

Recall the list of places in your community from Day 1. Tell children that they will choose one of those places and name things people could find there. With children, create lists similar to the ones below.

Post Office	Mall
letters	stores
stamps	movie theaters
mailboxes	clothes

WRITING

My Favorite Trip

► Modeled Writing

Tell children they are going to write about a favorite trip. It could be a vacation trip or just a trip to a place in their neighborhood. Explain that children should write about things that can be found in the place they select. Begin by talking about a favorite trip of your own.

Model Write sentences such as these about a trip you have taken.

> My trip to the ocean was wonderful. The waves rolled to the shore. Birds flew in the sky. It was the best trip ever!

As you write, model these strategies:
- Focus on the topic—a trip you have taken.
- Begin and end in a way to grab the reader.
- Make sentences fit together in a way that makes sense.
- Track print from left to right.

Independent Writing Tell children to write about a personal experience while on a special trip. Have them illustrate their writing.

Conference As children read their sentences to you, note their success in writing something about their own experience.

Did you tell about something you saw or did? Is there anything you would like to add to your writing? What is it? Where could you add it?

Writer's Checklist

Did you . . .

✓ stay on one topic?
✓ begin and end in a way to grab the reader?
✓ write your sentences in an order that made sense?
✓ move smoothly from one sentence to another?
✓ form letters correctly?

Self-Selected Reading and Read Aloud D.E.A.R.

Read aloud *My Map Book* by Sara Fanelli. After listening, children discuss which map they liked best and why.

Grammar: Adjectives

Review Adjectives That Tell What Kind Remind children that adjectives tell about people, places, or things. Show children a full box and an empty box. Write the phrases *full box* and *empty box,* one on each of two index cards. Have children match each index card to the correct box.

Make an Adjective Board Divide paper vertically into three sections. Have children draw a picture to show each of the following, one picture in each section: hot day, cold night, soft cat. Have children write a phrase below each picture to describe it and underline the word that tells what kind. Have children tape or glue their papers to a piece of cardboard to make an adjective board.

Pick the best adjective from the box to finish each sentence. Write it on the line.

soft   clean   wet   old   full

1. This is a __full__ box.
2. This is an __old__ home.
3. This kitten is __soft__.
4. The __wet__ dog shakes.
5. I need a __clean__ dish to use.

Notes for Home: Your child used adjectives that tell what kind of object something is, such as *full box* or *wet dog*. Home Activity: Play *I Spy* with your child. Encourage your child to describe an object using adjectives for kind, and see if you can guess what object he or she is talking about.

Adjectives
Practice Book 1.5, p. 60
Teacher's Resource Book 1.5, p. 66

 # Meeting Individual Needs

ESL	Intervention	Challenge	Other Ways to Learn
Provide a full cup and an empty cup. Say the phrase to describe each and have children point out the correct cup. Have children repeat each phrase while pointing to the cup. **(Skill Support)** See also *Adding English.* **ESL**	Write the phrases below on sentence strips. Have children highlight each adjective. Then help children hang the sentence strips to make a mobile. Use phrases such as: *messy room, yummy apple, old sock.* **(Comprehension Support)**	Write the following adjectives on cards and at the bottom of drawing paper. Children use the cards to write phrases or sentences with the adjective and use the drawing paper to draw a picture and label the picture with a sentence using the adjective. **(Tiered Assignments)**	Say each of the following phrases with adjectives, one at a time: *happy child, scary monster, full stomach.* Have children pantomime to show an understanding of each phrase. **(Kinesthetic)**

Reader Response

Student Book, pp. 152–153

Let's Talk

Personal Response You can guide discussion through modeling. For example, say:

I would want to see the Animals of Africa exhibit, and if I got lost I would look for someone who worked at the museum to help me.

Have children share their responses.

Let's Think

Critical Response Children may say that Jim thinks the museum is fun because of all the interesting things to see, or they may say he thinks it is scary because of the huge creatures. Some children may say that Jim thinks the museum is both fun and scary because there are both interesting and frightening things to see.

Test Prep
Let's Write

Written Response Ask children who have been on field trips before to tell where they went and what they did there. Then tell children to choose a place they would like to go with the class and to write about it. Remind them to support their preference with detailed reasons.

Features for this writing product are listed below 4 in the Scoring Rubric.

Readers Theater

Creative Response Have children act out *Lost in the Museum* as a play. You may want to organize the class into two groups to present the story to each other. Remind children to speak clearly and loudly enough for others to hear and understand.

Use the **Selection Test** in Practice Book 1.5, pages 61–62 or Teacher's Resource Book 1.5, pages 67–68.

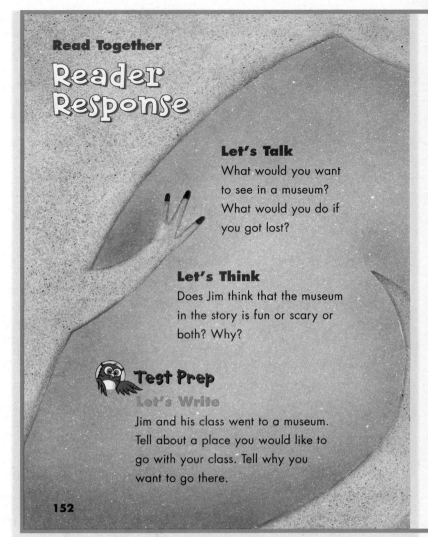

Read Together

Reader Response

Let's Talk
What would you want to see in a museum? What would you do if you got lost?

Let's Think
Does Jim think that the museum in the story is fun or scary or both? Why?

Test Prep
Let's Write
Jim and his class went to a museum. Tell about a place you would like to go with your class. Tell why you want to go there.

152

Lost in the Museum, page 152

Scoring Rubric for Written Response	
4	**3**
• clearly focuses on a special place • includes strong reasons for preference • expresses ideas in logical order • begins sentences with capital letters and ends with correct punctuation	• focuses on a special place • includes reasons for preference • is mostly in logical order • may have poorly formed capital letter at beginning or incorrect punctuation at end of one or two sentences
2	**1**
• attempts to focus on a special place • names a place but does not give reasons • is slightly out of order • may be missing a capital letter at beginning or punctuation at end of some sentences	• is unfocused • does not name a place and give reasons • lacks order • lacks both capital letters and end punctuation

Day 4

Readers Theater

Read and act out the story as a play.

1. One person reads what the teacher says.
2. Choose who will read the parts of Jim, Anna Maria, Sara, Danny, Paul, Willy, Sammy, and George.
3. Choose other children to play the rest of the first-grade class.

153

Lost in the Museum, **page 153**

Skills in Context

Review Character

Tell children that by reading a text and looking at pictures, they can learn about how story characters think and act.

Return to *Lost in the Museum* and ask children to tell you all the things they know about the main character, Jim. List children's suggestions on the board.

Have children draw a picture of Jim and write several sentences telling what he is like.

Reread for Fluency

Selection Audio Have children listen to the CD or tape of *Lost in the Museum* as they follow along in their books.

Selection Audio

CD 7/Tape 24, Side 1

Read with Feeling Have children reread *Lost in the Museum.* Then have each child choose a favorite part of the story to read aloud to a small group of classmates. Remind children to picture themselves taking a field trip and getting lost. How would they feel? What would their voices sound like?

Day 4

Leveled Practice for ℃ Cause and Effect

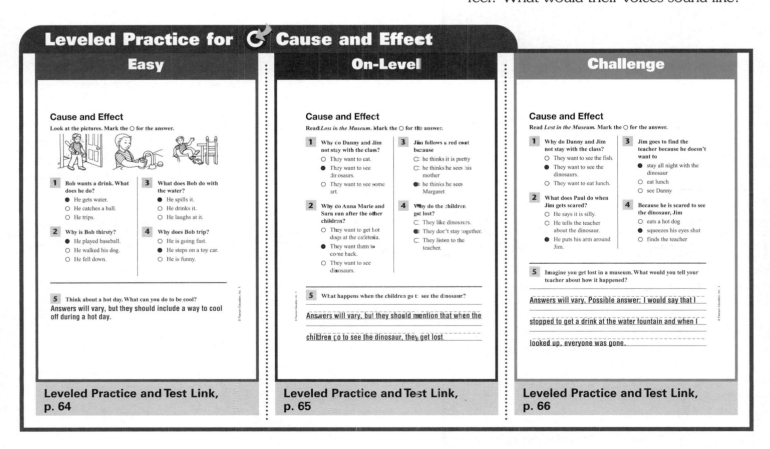

Easy

Cause and Effect

Look at the pictures. Mark the ○ for the answer.

1 Bob wants a drink. What does he do?
- ● He gets water.
- ○ He catches a ball.
- ○ He trips.

2 Why is Bob thirsty?
- ● He played baseball.
- ○ He walked his dog.
- ○ He fell down.

3 What does Bob do with the water?
- ● He spills it.
- ○ He drinks it.
- ○ He laughs at it.

4 Why does Bob trip?
- ○ He is going fast.
- ○ He steps on a toy car.
- ○ He is funny.

5 Think about a hot day. What can you do to be cool?
Answers will vary, but they should include a way to cool off during a hot day.

Leveled Practice and Test Link, p. 64

On-Level

Cause and Effect

Read *Lost in the Museum.* Mark the ○ for the answer.

1 Why do Danny and Jim not stay with the class?
- ○ They want to eat.
- ● They want to see dinosaurs.
- ○ They want to see some art.

2 Why do Anna Marie and Sara run after the other children?
- ○ They want to get hot dogs at the cafeteria.
- ● They want them to come back.
- ○ They want to see dinosaurs.

3 Jim follows a red coat because
- ○ he thinks it is pretty.
- ○ he thinks he sees his mother.
- ● he thinks he sees Margaret.

4 Why do the children get lost?
- ○ They like dinosaurs.
- ● They don't stay together.
- ○ They listen to the teacher.

5 What happens when the children go to see the dinosaur?
Answers will vary, but they should mention that when the children go to see the dinosaur, they get lost

Leveled Practice and Test Link, p. 65

Challenge

Cause and Effect

Read *Lost in the Museum.* Mark the ○ for the answer.

1 Why do Danny and Jim not stay with the class?
- ○ They want to see the fish.
- ● They want to see the dinosaurs.
- ○ They want to eat lunch.

2 What does Paul do when Jim gets scared?
- ○ He says it is silly.
- ○ He tells the teacher about the dinosaur.
- ● He puts his arm around Jim.

3 Jim goes to find the teacher because he doesn't want to
- ● stay all night with the dinosaur
- ○ eat lunch
- ○ see Danny

4 Because he is scared to see the dinosaur, Jim
- ○ eats a hot dog
- ● squeezes his eyes shut
- ○ finds the teacher

5 Imagine you get lost in a museum. What would you tell your teacher about how it happened?
Answers will vary. Possible answer: I would say that I
stopped to get a drink at the water fountain and when I
looked up, everyone was gone.

Leveled Practice and Test Link, p. 66

Objectives

Children will

 decode words with long *i: igh, ie,* and with singular possessives
- decode contractions
- spell words with long *i: igh, ie*
- recognize high-frequency words

Skills Trace

Contractions

Introduce/Teach	TE: 1.3 162l; 1.5 46l
Practice	PB: 1.3 84; 1.4 47; 1.5 20, 63
Reteach/ Review	TE: 1.3 AR19; 1.5 **153a,** AR13
Test	Skills Test, Unit 5 Benchmark Test, Unit 5

Day 4

Long *i: igh, ie*
Singular Possessives

►Reteach

Explain that when *i* is followed by *gh,* the *gh* is usually silent and the *i* stands for the long *i* sound. Also explain that the letters *ie* stand for the long *i* sound. Point out that the second vowel *e* is silent. Write *light, lie, sigh, high, pie, right, bright, might,* and *tie* on the board. Let volunteers cross out the silent letter or letters in each word. Then have them blend each word.

Explain that *'s* on a word usually shows that something belongs to someone. Write *Dwight's horse, Amy's coat, Dean's skates, Mom's pie, Dad's tie* on the board. Have volunteers circle the *'s* in each phrase and read the phrase.

See pages AR15 and AR16 of this Teacher's Edition for additional **reteach activities.**

Review Contractions

Review with children that a contraction is made by putting two words together using an apostrophe to make one new word. Have children read the following pairs of words and write the contractions for them.

would not (wouldn't)
do not (don't)
you will (you'll)
could not (couldn't)

Have children check their answers with another child's to see if they wrote the word correctly.

Write the contraction for each pair of words.

1. I + am =	**I'm**
2. you + will =	**you'll**
3. is + not =	**isn't**
4. they + are =	**they're**
5. could + not =	**couldn't**
6. she + had =	**she'd**
7. do + not =	**don't**
8. would + not =	**wouldn't**

Find the contraction.
Mark the ⊂⊃ to show your answer.

9. ⬤ it's 10. ⊂⊃ were
   ⊂⊃ hits   ⬤ we're
   ⊂⊃ its   ⊂⊃ worry

Notes for Home: Your child reviewed contractions—words made up of two words and an apostrophe. **Home Activity:** Write the words *it, is, did, not, I, am, we,* and *are* on separate index cards. Ask your child to see how many different contractions he or she can form.

Contractions
Practice Book 1.5. p. 63
Teacher's Resource Book 1.5, p. 69

❋ Meeting Individual Needs

ESL	Intervention	Challenge	Other Ways to Learn
Prepare picture cards for *pie, tie, lie, cries, dries.* Say each word and use it in a sentence. Have children repeat the words. Distribute the cards. Then give a simple clue. The child with the card that answers the clue says the word. **(Phonics Support)** See also *Adding English.* **ⓔⓢⓛ**	Provide phonogram card *-ight* and letter cards *f, t, l, m, n, r, s.* Show children how to make the word *tight* by placing the *t* in front of *-ight.* Then have them make the words *fight, light, might, night, right, sight.* **(Phonics Support)**	Write the following words in two columns on the board: *Margaret's, whale's, Jim's, dinosaur's; tail, head, claws, coat.* Children write four sentences by pairing a word from each column. Each sentence should make sense. **(Divergent Thinking)**	Read sentences that contain words with long *i,* such as "Ana turned on the light last night." Partners give each other a high-five each time they hear a long *i* word. **(Kinesthetic)**

Spelling Words with Long *i: igh, ie*

▶ Partner Spelling Practice

Children work in pairs. Have children take turns drawing pictures of their spelling words and then labeling them on a piece of drawing paper. Have pairs exchange their papers and check for spelling errors.

Spelling
Practice Book 1.5, p. 64
Teachers Resource Book 1.5, p. 70

Word Wall

Review High-Frequency Words

Missing Word Say a sentence and leave out one of this week's words. Ask children to find a word on the Word Wall to fill in the missing word. For example:

Scientists _____ dinosaurs that lived long ago.

If children are unable to guess the word *found*, then give them a clue such as, "The word begins with the letter *f*." Repeat the routine for the rest of this week's words.

Optional Resources

Phonics
Phonics Workbook, pp. 141–143, 145
Phonics Manipulatives Kit
Phonics Sourcebook, pp. 1–82, 86–88

High-Frequency Words
High-Frequency Word Cards
Phonics Sourcebook, pp. 90–99

Language Arts

Student Book, pp. 154–155

Adjectives That Tell What Kind

Have children read aloud with you the statements about adjectives at the top of the page. Have the example sentence read and identify *scary* as the adjective and *story* as the noun.

Talk

Read aloud the directions with children. Discuss the pictures and labels. Then have children each make a list of adjectives that describe the books.

Write

Guide children as they copy the sentences and underline the adjectives. When everyone has finished, review the responses and have children correct their mistakes.

Then have children write a sentence and underline the adjective in the sentence. Encourage children to refer to their lists for possible adjectives.

Use the Teacher's Resource Book 1.5 pages 71–72 for **reteaching** and extra practice for adjectives of kind.

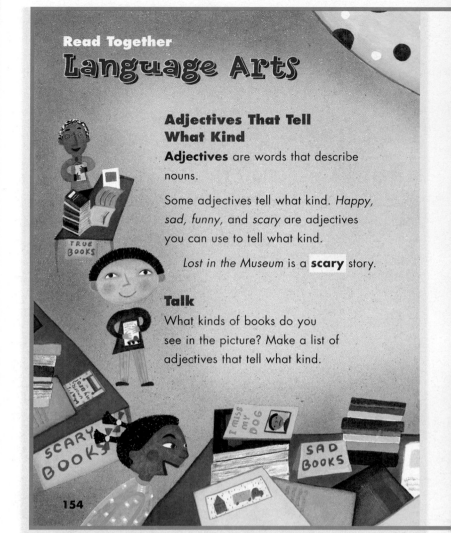

Lost in the Museum, page 154

Day 4

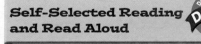

Self-Selected Reading and Read Aloud

Read aloud *My Visit to the Aquarium* by Aliki. Children choose a book about visiting a museum.

Write

Write the sentences. Draw
a line under the adjectives that tell what kind.

1. *Glasses for D.W.* has a happy ending.
2. *Mama and Papa Have a Store* tells
   a true story.
3. *John Willy and Freddy McGee* is a
   funny story.

Write your own sentence about a book you like.
Use an adjective that tells what kind of book it s.
Draw a line under the adjective.

155

Lost in the Museum, page 155

Study Skill

Map

Help children recall that a map shows where places
are located and how to get from one place to another.
On chart paper, draw a simple map of your school
community. Label a few streets, some significant
buildings, and other locations. Read aloud the labels
on your map and then model how to interpret it.

Model Your Thinking

Think ALOUD **This map shows where our school is
located, the name of the street that it
is on, and some streets and places
around it. If I want to go from our
school to another place I can use my finger to
trace the route.**

Continue modeling and then have children refer to
the map to give the street names of various locations
and to describe how they would get from one place
to another.

Practice Have partners draw maps of the interior of
your school. Help them by drawing and labeling the
main school entrance, your classroom, and the
corridor between the two. Children can draw and
label other locations and classrooms. Circulate to
monitor how well children understand maps.

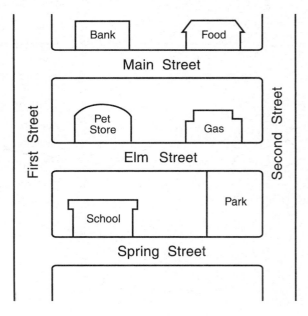

Meeting Individual Needs

ESL

To prepare children for the word recognition assessment, make sure that they understand the meanings of the words. Have them add drawings for troublesome words. Then they can practice reading the words with a partner.

Day
5

Optional Resources

Assessment
The Assessment Handbook has information on running records.

Assess Word Reading

▶ Prepare for the Assessment

Materials Children may choose high-frequency word cards from the Phonics Kit or make words with this unit's sounds using phonogram, letter, and *-ed, -ing,* and *'s* cards.

Have children prepare for the assessment by working with a partner. Each child writes words on index cards from the high-frequency cards or words made from this week's sounds. Children mix up the cards and read them aloud together.

▶ Listen to Individual Readers

Have individual children read the words on the following page. Use the scoring sheet on the page to track the words children can read.

Check Comprehension To assess children's ability to recognize cause and effect, ask a question such as:

> **What causes Jim and his classmates to get lost in the museum?**

See page AR16 in this Teacher's Edition to **reteach** cause and effect.

You may prefer to assess only a portion of the class each week, perhaps half the class one week, and the other half the next.

▶ While You Assess

While you work with individuals, other children may choose from the following activities or the activities listed in the Cross-Curricular Work Stations on pages 116g–h.

Before They Read to You

Children should reread the chosen words from the high-frequency cards or the words they made from the Phonics Kit cards. They should practice rereading the words independently or with a partner.

Selection Audio

CD 7/Tape 24, Side 1

After They Read to You

Children can complete a Reading Log like the one shown or use Practice Book 1.5 page 103, or the Teacher's Resource Book 1.6 page 112.

Children can also complete the phonics activities on page 155c.

Word Recognition Checklist

Name _____

Mark correct response.   Mark correct response.

buy	☐	leap	☐
only	☐	beach	☐
right	☐	begged	☐
don't	☐	rain	☐
from	☐	tray	☐
live	☐	can't	☐
around	☐	low	☐
her	☐	patting	☐
been	☐	right	☐
first	☐	Jean's	☐

Day
5

Scoring: Score 1 point for each correct answer.

Total correct _____

Long *i: igh, ie*
Singular Possessives

▶ Phonics Practice Activities

Word Ties Make a large necktie and let children trace around it to make their own construction paper ties. Have them label their tie at the top with their name, in this form: *(Jenny's) Word Tie*. Then they can write on their ties words with long *i: igh, ie* and singular possessives that they learned this week.

Phonics Take-Home Reader Have children practice reading the book with a partner before taking it home.

Dad's Gift

by Judy Veramendi
illustrated by Jackie Urbanovic

Phonics Take-Home Reader

Spelling Test

Have children number their papers. Read the underlined word, read the sentence, then repeat the underlined word.

1. We had pizza for dinner last <u>night</u>.
2. My aunt made a yummy apple <u>pie</u>.
3. I can <u>tie</u> my shoes!
4. I use my <u>right</u> hand.
5. Our porch <u>light</u> shines brightly.
6. Cats like to <u>lie</u> in the sun.

High-Frequency Words

7. I have <u>been</u> on an airplane.
8. I <u>found</u> a dollar bill yesterday.

Challenge Words

9. The <u>cat's</u> whiskers were wet.
10. The <u>dog's</u> tail wagged.

Word Wall

Practice High-Frequency Words

Dinosaur Cartoons Have children draw pictures of dinosaur skeletons in a museum. Then ask them to draw a speech bubble coming from the dinosaur's mouth and write a sentence using one of this week's Word Wall words. Have children brainstorm ideas about what their dinosaurs might say before they begin.

I hope they put me together the right way!

been	first	found	start	together

Day 5

ORAL LANGUAGE

Speaking: Large Group Discussion

Tell children to discuss the place where they would most like to take a vacation. Display the rules for a discussion they wrote earlier in the week and remind children to follow them. After the discussion, have children place check marks next to each entry on the Discussion Group chart to show which rules they observed.

Thank-You Note

▶ Interactive Writing

In this method of writing, you and the children work together. While you write on the board, children write on their own papers. As you write, point out that spaces between words are larger than spaces between letters.

Thank a Farmer Children will write a note to thank a farmer for a make-believe class trip to the farm. Leave blanks in the note for children to complete. Ask children to discuss how they might fill in the blanks.

October 20, 2002

Dear Farmer,

Thank you for showing us your farm. My favorite part was _____. I especially liked the sounds of the _____ and the _____.

Thanks again,

_____

Independent Writing Have children write in the missing words independently. Suggest that they include words that tell what kind and remind them to include their names at the end of the note.

Portfolio Children may wish to select a piece of writing from this week to put in their portfolios.

Day **5**

Lesson Overview

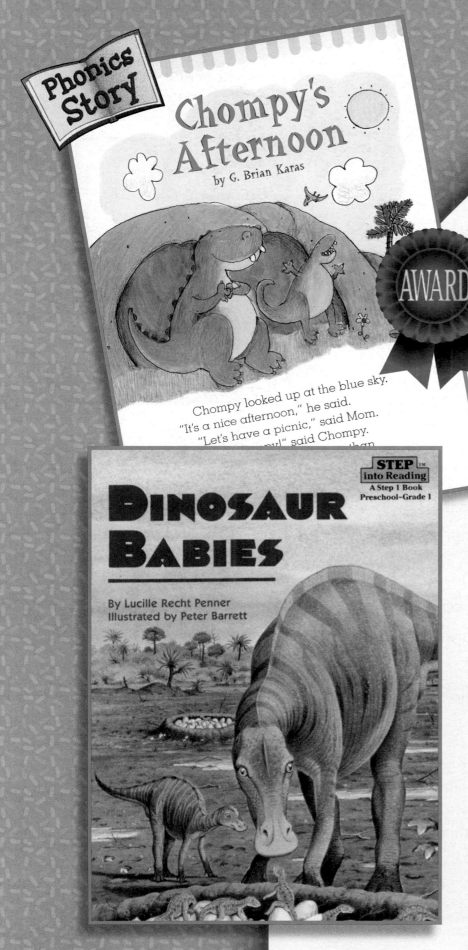

Chompy's Afternoon
by G. Brian Karas

AWARD

Chompy looked up at the blue sky.
"It's a nice afternoon," he said.
"Let's have a picnic," said Mom.
"_____ !" said Chompy. _____ than

STEP into Reading
A Step 1 Book
Preschool–Grade 1

DINOSAUR BABIES

By Lucille Recht Penner
Illustrated by Peter Barrett

Phonics Story

Chompy's Afternoon
pages 156–163

 Selection Audio

The **Phonics Story** . . .

- introduces 🔄 **Vowel Sounds of *y*** and **Compound Words**

- introduces the high-frequency words

  animals even heard most their

- builds fluency

- builds decoding skills

> **Use the Phonics Story to prepare children for reading the Main Selection.**

Main Selection

Dinosaur Babies
pages 164–185

 Selection Audio

The **Main Selection** . . .

- introduces 🔄 **Main Idea**

- practices 🔄 **Vowel Sounds of *y*** and **Compound Words**

- practices the high-frequency words

  animals even heard most their

Leveled Readers

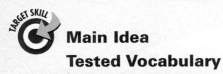
Main Idea
Tested Vocabulary

Easy

Pandas

by Kimberlee Mason

Leveled Reader 23A

On-Level

What Lilly Pup Heard

by Judy Nayer

illustrated by Rick Stromoski

Leveled Reader 23B

For Guided Reading

see Teacher's Edition, pp. LR25–LR30.

Challenge

Take Me There

Leveled Reader 5C

For instruction and leveled practice answers, see Teacher's Edition, pp. LR39–LR45.

Practice for Leveled Readers

Easy

Main Idea

Read the book *Pandas*. Then answer Numbers 1 through 5.

1 This book tells about
- ○ teddy bears.
- ○ *The Three Bears.*
- ● real pandas.

2 Where do pandas live?
- ● in China
- ○ in water
- ○ on a farm

3 Look at page 5. What does the word *habits* mean?
- ○ what an animal family looks like
- ● things an animal does again and again
- ○ the places where animals live

4 What BEST tells what this book is about?
- ● things pandas like to do
- ○ how pandas like to sleep
- ○ things pandas like to eat

5 What do pandas like to do? Write about one thing they do. Use words from the book in your answer.

Students may write about one of the following habits:

Pandas like to climb, hide, swim, slide, sit, play,

eat, roll, creep, or sleep.

Teacher's Edition, p. LR27

On-Level

Main Idea

Read the story *What Lilly Pup Heard*. Then answer Numbers 1 through 5.

1 What BEST tells what this story is about?
- ● Lilly Pup can not find a quiet place to read at home.
- ○ Lilly Pup gets lost in the woods.
- ○ Lilly Pup wants her mother to read.

2 Where does Lilly Pup go to read?
- ○ to her school
- ○ to her grandma's house
- ● to a quiet spot

3 What happens AFTER Lilly Pup reads most of her book?
- ○ She goes back home.
- ○ She goes to sleep.
- ● She plays a game.

4 Why does Lilly Pup wake up?
- ● She hears her family looking for her.
- ○ She hears her dog bancing.
- ○ She hears a bird tweeting.

5 What does Lilly Pup like to do MOST? Use words from the story in your answer.

Lilly Pup likes to read.

Teacher's Edition, p. LR30

Challenge

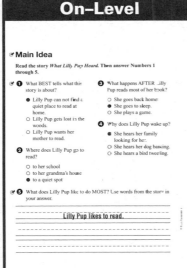

Earth Roars

Build Your Own Volcano
Make a model of a volcano. Show what a volcano looks like when the earth roars.

What You Need
a small plastic bottle, dirt or sand, clay, a plastic plate, red or orange paint, glue, a paper cup

What You Do

1 Fill most of the bottle with dirt or sand. Leave the cap off. Use clay to make a hill around the bottle.

2 Mix some paint and glue in a cup. Pour the paint mix into the top of the bottle. Keep filling until the mix spills over the top.

Use What You Learn
3 When your lava is dry, share your volcano with the class. What do you think would happen if lava kept coming out of your volcano? Draw a picture.

Take Me There **31**

Leveled Reader 5C, pp. 30–31

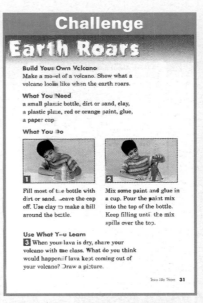

Easy

Main Idea
Look at the picture. Mark the ○ for the answer.

1 The picture is mostly about
- ○ trees growing
- ○ plants growing
- ● dinosaurs eating

2 What are the animals doing?
- ○ talking to each other
- ● eating
- ○ fighting

3 What do the dinosaurs eat?
- ● plants
- ○ other dinosaurs
- ○ fish

4 What is the best name for the picture?
- ● Plant-Eating Dinosaurs
- ○ Meat-Eating Dinosaurs
- ○ All About Dinosaurs

5 Draw a picture for this title.

Mother Dinosaur Feeds Her Babies

Drawing should show a mother dinosaur feeding her babies.

On-Level

Main Idea
Read *Dinosaur Babies*. Mark the ○ for the answer.

1 What have dinosaur hunters found?
- ● footprints, teeth, bones, and eggs
- ○ the sound of a baby dinosaur
- ○ feathers, fur, and skin

2 Read pages 168 and 169. What are they mostly about?
- ● one kind of dinosaur mother
- ○ eggs breaking from a heavy dinosaur
- ○ chickens sitting on eggs

3 Read page 173. What is it mostly about?
- ○ how dinosaur babies had big teeth
- ● what dinosaur babies looked like
- ○ what human babies look like

4 What is *Dinosaur Babies* mostly about?
- ● how dinosaurs lived and grew up
- ○ what baby dinosaurs ate
- ○ how dinosaurs walked

5 What is the main thing you learned in this story?

Answers will vary, but they should mention the way

dinosaur babies lived.

Challenge

Main Idea
Read *Dinosaur Babies*. Mark the ○ for the answer.

1 The title tells us this story is all about
- ○ dinosaur bones
- ● dinosaur babies
- ○ dinosaur mothers

2 Read page 167. What is it mostly about?
- ○ dinosaur bones
- ● the size of dinosaur eggs
- ○ big dinosaur eggs

3 What did baby dinosaurs look like?
- ● They had big heads and big eyes.
- ○ They looked like human babies.
- ○ They were born without any teeth.

4 Read page 176. What is it mostly about?
- ○ Dinosaur babies hunted for food alone.
- ● Dinosaur babies had to hide from enemies.
- ○ Dinosaurs babies liked to run and hide.

5 What is *Dinosaur Babies* all about?

Answers will vary, but they should indicate an

understanding of the main idea.

Leveled Practice and Test Link, pp. 67–69, *Dinosaur Babies*

Additional Leveled Resources

Phonics Resources

Phonics Reader 29

Phonics Take-Home Readers in Reproducible Format

Book 29

Decodable Reader 39

Waterford Early Reading Program
Level 2
Lesson 25

Language Support

Adding English
pp. 193–200

Ten Important Sentences
p. 35

Trade Books for Self-Selected Reading

Easy

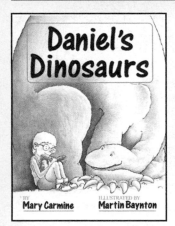

Daniel's Dinosaurs
by Mary Carmine. Scholastic, 1990

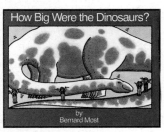

How Big Were the Dinosaurs?
by Bernard Most. Harcourt Brace, 1994

Mrs. Toggle and the Dinosaur
by Robin Pulver. Four Winds Press, 1991

On-Level

This Is the Way We Go to School
by Edith Baer. Scholastic, 1992
Trade Book Library Title

Dinosaur Dinners
by Lee Davis. Dorling Kindersley, 1998

What Happened to the Dinosaurs?
by Franklyn M. Branley. Crowell, 1989

Challenge

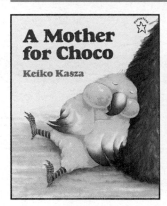

A Mother for Choco
by Keiko Kasza. Paper Star, 1996
Trade Book Library Title

Dinosaur Bones
by Aliki. Crowell, 1988

Dinosaurs and Their Young
by Russell Freedman. Holiday House, 1983

Self-Selected Reading

- Allow 10–20 minutes per day for self-selected reading.
- For additional titles and for a read-aloud suggestion, see pp. AR24–AR25.
- For daily self-selected reading suggestions, see the 5-Day Planner, pp. 156e–156f.
- For activity ideas and management tips, see p. AR25.

- Have children select materials to read for pleasure, such as favorite books and stories.

Developmental Reading Assessment (DRA) from Celebration Press, an imprint of Pearson Learning, helps teachers by providing and documenting students' development as readers over time.

Links to Reading First 1.5, pp. 42–51

5-Day Planner

Reading

Comprehension

Vocabulary

Fluency

Independent Reading

Phonics/Word Study

Phonemic Awareness

Phonics

Spelling

High-Frequency Words

Oral Language

Speaking, Listening, Viewing

Oral Vocabulary

Writing

Grammar, Usage, Mechanics

Your State Standards

Customize your week with the Teacher's Resource Planner CD-ROM!

Day 1

Activate Prior Knowledge, p. 156j

Phonics pp. 156k–156l

Phonemic Awareness: Vowel Sounds of *y*

✓ **Phonics:** Introduce Vowel Sounds of *y*, Compound Words **PHONICS SONGS AND RHYMES CHART** "I'm a Baby Dinosaur"

Spelling: Vowel Sounds of *y*

Pretest
Work with Spelling Pattern

High-Frequency Words: Introduce **animals, even, heard, most, their**

Reading pp. 156m–163

Story Vocabulary

Read Pupil Edition PHONICS STORY: *Chompy's Afternoon*

Independent Reading
Self-Selected Reading, pp. 156d; AR24

Oral Language pp. 156m, 163a

Build Oral Language

Expand Vocabulary: Create Homonym Titles

Writing pp. 156i, 163a–163b

Shared Writing: Word Bank

Handwriting: *Bb*

Daily Writing Prompt: Draw a picture of an animal inside an egg. Write about it.

Day 2

Phonics pp. 163c–163d

✓ **Phonics:** Practice Vowel Sounds of *y*, Compound Words

Apply Phonics: Read the **PHONICS READER** *My Mail* or **DECODABLE READER** 39

Spelling: Writing for Sounds

High-Frequency Words: Practice

PB 1.5: Phonics, pp. 67, 68; High-Frequency Words, p. 69
TRB 1.5: Phonics, pp. 75, 76; High-Frequency Words, p. 77

Reading pp. 163e–163f

✓ **Comprehension:** Main Idea **READ ALOUD** "No Escape!"

Fluency: Reread the **PHONICS STORY:** *Chompy's Afternoon*

PB 1.5: Main Idea, p. 70
TRB 1.5: Main Idea, p. 78

Independent Reading
Self-Selected Reading, pp. 156d; AR24

Oral Language p. 163g

 Speaking: Tell an Original Story in Order

Writing pp. 156i, 163g–163h

Modeled Writing: Choose Vivid Words

✓ **Grammar:** Adjectives

PB 1.5: p. 71; **TRB 1.5:** p. 79

Daily Writing Prompt: List things you would take on a picnic.

 **Target Skill** Review **Review Skill** **Assessment**

PB Practice Book
TRB Teacher's Resource Book

Target Skills of the Week

Reading	Main Idea
Phonics	Vowel Sounds of *y*, Compound Words
Oral Language	Tell an Original Story in Order
Writing	Adjectives

Day 3

Reading pp. 164a–187

Story Vocabulary

Read Pupil Edition MAIN SELECTION:
Dinosaur Babies

Read Pupil Edition POEMS

✓ **Comprehension:** Main Idea

Guided Reading Resources/Flexible Groups, pp. 164b; LR25–LR30
Leveled Readers 23A, 23B, 5C

PB 1.5: Vocabulary, p. 72
TRB 1.5: Vocabulary, p. 80

Independent Reading
Self-Selected Reading, pp. 156d; AR24

Phonics pp. 187a–187b

✓ **Phonics:** Practice Vowel Sounds of *y*, Compound Words

✓ *Review* Long *i*: *igh, ie*

Fluency: Reread the PHONICS READER
My Mail

Spelling: Practice with Writing

High-Frequency Words: Practice

PB 1.5: Phonics, p. 73; Spelling, p. 74
TRB 1.5: Phonics, p. 81; Spelling, p. 82

Oral Language pp. 164a, 187c

Build Oral Language

Expand Vocabulary: Name Types of Dinosaurs

Writing pp. 156i, 187c–187d

Modeled Writing: Dinosaur Description

✓ **Grammar:** Adjectives

PB 1.5: p. 75; **TRB 1.5:** p. 83; **GPB:** p. 50

Daily Writing Prompt: Write one real thing and one make-believe thing about dinosaurs.

Day 4

Reading pp. 188–189

Read Together Pupil Edition
READER RESPONSE *Test Prep*

✓ Selection Test

PB 1.5: Selection Test, pp. 77–78
TRB 1.5: Selection Test, pp. 85–86

✓ *Review* **Comprehension:** Cause and Effect

Fluency: Reread the MAIN SELECTION

Guided Reading Resources/Flexible Groups, pp. 164b; LR25–LR30
Leveled Readers 23A, 23B, 5C

Independent Reading
Self-Selected Reading, pp. 156d; AR24

Phonics pp. 189a–189b

✓ **Phonics:** Reteach Vowel Sounds of *y*, Compound Words

✓ *Review* Endings *-ed* and *-ing*

Spelling: Partner Practice

High-Frequency Words: Review

PB 1.5: Phonics, p. 79; Spelling, p. 80
TRB 1.5: Phonics, p. 87; Spelling, p. 88

Oral Language pp. 190–191

Speaking: Talk About Adjectives

Writing pp. 156i, 190–191

✓ **Grammar:** Adjectives

Writing: Identify Adjectives That Tell How Many

TRB 1.5: pp. 89–90; **GPB:** p. 51

Daily Writing Prompt: Write how you would take care of a baby dinosaur.

Day 5

Reading pp. 191a–191b

✓ **Assess Accuracy and Comprehension:** Accuracy and Comprehension Assessment

Guided Reading Resources/Flexible Groups, pp. 164b; LR25–LR30
Leveled Readers 23A, 23B, 5C

Independent Reading
Self-Selected Reading, pp. 156d; AR24

Phonics p. 191c

✓ **Phonics:** Practice Vowel Sounds of *y*, Compound Words

Apply Phonics: Read the PHONICS TAKE-HOME READER

Spelling: Vowel Sounds of *y*

✓ Posttest

High-Frequency Words: Practice

Oral Language p. 191d

Speaking: Tell an Original Story in Order

Writing pp. 156i, 191d

Interactive Writing: E-mail Note
Portfolio

Daily Writing Prompt: Write some new things you learned about dinosaurs.

Cross-Curricular Work Stations

Career Link

Ideas for bringing the school and community together

Field Experiences
natural history museum
science museum
zoo

Guest Speakers
paleontologist
model builder/preparator
  for museum of natural
  history

Letters and Sounds

Baby Dinosaur Names 15 minutes

Materials: drawing paper, scissors, crayons or markers

Learning Styles Auditory, Visual, Kinesthetic

Provide a list of names that contain *y* (long *e,* long *i*), such as *Bryan, Byron, Cyrus, Tyler, Mylet, Myles, Tory, Larry, Cathy, Suzy, Nancy, Randy, Bradley, Danny, Mikey, Kerry, Terry, Sherry, Mary.* Children choose one name and write it on a drawing of a baby dinosaur coming out of its egg. Then children color and cut out their baby dinosaurs.

Larry

Writing

Dear Park Ranger 15 minutes

Materials: paper, crayons, pencils

Learning Style Verbal

Children can use word processors, if available, to write a letter to a park ranger at Dinosaur National Monument in Colorado and Utah or to a curator at a nearby museum. Explain that their letters should ask the park ranger or curator questions about dinosaurs.

Dear Park Ranger,

I like dinosaurs. Did dinosaurs swim? Please write back with the answer.

Thank you,
Kitty Dawkins

Science

I Hatch from an Egg Too! 15 minutes

Materials: old children's science magazines, scissors, egg cartons

Learning Styles Visual, Kinesthetic

Children cut out (or draw) pictures of animals that hatch from eggs, as dinosaurs did. You might first want to brainstorm with children a list of animals that hatch from eggs, such as chickens, robins, snakes, iguanas, turtles. Each pair works until they have filled an egg carton—one animal in each section.

ESL Ask children to tell a partner about the animals in their egg carton.

Technology

AstroWord 15 minutes

Learning Styles Visual, Social

Have children use AstroWord to strengthen understanding of compound words. Children can work individually or in groups to apply these skills in activities and games in the AstroWord Factory.

Reading Web Site 15 minutes

Learning Styles Visual, Individual

Children can visit the Scott Foresman *Reading* Web site (sfreading.com) for current hyperlinks to relevant electronic texts that can be used for an Internet Workshop investigation of dinosaur days. Also see the Scott Foresman Internet Guide for additional information on the Internet Workshop method.

sfreading.com

Social Studies

Dinos on the Map   15 minutes

Materials: United States map, stencils of dinosaurs, pencils, construction paper, scissors, pins or tape

Learning Styles Visual, Kinesthetic, Spatial

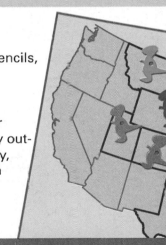

Display a map of the United States that shows Dinosaur National Monument in Utah and Colorado, with a heavy outline drawn around the states of Connecticut, New Jersey, Texas, Montana, Wyoming, Utah, and Colorado. Explain that scientists have found dinosaur bones or tracks in these states. Children trace and cut out dinosaurs, then stick them to the map where they have been found.

Math

Giant Steps 15 minutes

Materials: masking tape, adding-machine tape (optional)

Learning Styles Visual, Kinesthetic, Logical, Spatial

Place strips of masking tape on the floor that are the actual lengths of several dinosaurs: coelophysis, 10 feet; compsognathus, 2 feet; stegosaurus, 20 feet. Write the names of the dinosaurs on each strip. Have partners measure the lengths using giant steps. One child steps while the partner counts steps. Have partners alternate roles.

Challenge Give children the lengths of other dinosaurs and have them use a yardstick or ruler to cut strips of adding-machine tape that equal the lengths.

Compsognathus, 2 feet

Daily Routines

Message Board

Day One

Today you will hear a poem about a baby dinosaur. What other animals do you know of that come from eggs?

Have children discuss what they know about dinosaurs and other animals that hatch from eggs.

Have children find the spelling word *funny* and a word that tells how many. *(three)* Have children find words with the long *e* sound spelled *y*. *(story, scary, funny)*

Day Two

The story with the three dinosaurs was scary and funny. Tell about a time someone helped you when you were scared.

Day Three

You will read even more about baby dinosaurs. The next story is about real dinosaurs. How do you think the mothers cared for their babies?

Have children find the high-frequency words *even* and *their* and the spelling word *baby*. Ask what sound the *y* in *baby* stands for. *(long e)*

Have children find the high-frequency words *most, animals,* and *heard*.

Day Four

Dinosaurs are one of the most interesting kinds of animals. What have you heard about them?

Day Five

Is there something you want to know about dinosaurs? How could you find out more?

Have children identify the words that make up the compound word *something*.

Journal Writing

Day One
Draw a picture of an animal inside an egg. Write about it.

Day Two
List things you would take on a picnic.

Day Three
Write one real thing and one make-believe thing about dinosaurs.

Day Four
Write how you would take care of a baby dinosaur.

Day Five
Write some new things you learned about dinosaurs.

Family Times

Send home the newsletter with daily instructional activities to reinforce this week's skills.

Practice Book 1.5, pp. 65–66
Teacher's Resource Book 1.5, pp. 73–74

Activate Prior Knowledge

▶ Assess Prior Knowledge

Discuss Dinosaur Days Talk with children about what they know about dinosaurs. Share your knowledge too. Ask:

What were some of the different kinds of dinosaurs?

What do you know about different dinosaurs' behavior: what they ate, how they acted?

▶ Build Background

Read Aloud

Preview the Poem Explain that words such as *tap* and *puff* actually sound like what they mean. Help children set a purpose for listening, such as listening for other words that sound like what they mean.

Read the Poem Share this poem with children. Lead them in discussing how the words that sound like what they mean help them figure out where the baby dinosaur was at the beginning of the poem.

Read Aloud
A Dinosaur Baby

by Pamela Conn Beall, Susan Hagen Nipp, and
Nancy Spence Klein

Tap, tap, chip-chip, ow!
Thud, thud, oomph-oomph, wow!
There's the light, I'm almost through,
One more shove and that should do!

Puff, puff, eek, my snout!
Cr-rr-ack, I'm out!
That eggshell was tough, it's great to be free,
And look all around, there's so much to see,
Could that be my sister?
No, maybe my brother,
And look over there, that must be my mother!

This new life is great,
I want to learn more,
I'm a dinosaur baby and ready to explore.

Vowel Sounds of *y*

▶ Develop Phonemic Awareness

Sing or Read the Rhyme Chart Sing the rhyme "I'm a Baby Dinosaur" to the tune of "Yankee Doodle," or play the CD or tape.

Focus on the Sounds of *y* Say:

> **What sound do you hear at the end of *baby*?** (/ē/) **What sound do you hear at the end of *my*?** (/ī/)

Explain that when *y* is at the end of a word, it can stand for the long *e* sound /ē/ or the long *i* sound /ī/. Have children repeat *baby* and *my* several times, listening for the long vowel sound.

Ask children to raise their hands when you come to a word with the long *e* or long *i* sound at the end as you reread the rhyme.

CD 2/Tape 15, Side 1

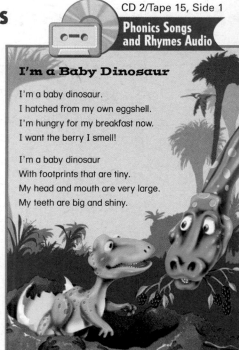
Phonics Songs and Rhymes Audio

I'm a Baby Dinosaur

I'm a baby dinosaur.
I hatched from my own eggshell.
I'm hungry for my breakfast now.
I want the berry I smell!

I'm a baby dinosaur
With footprints that are tiny.
My head and mouth are very large.
My teeth are big and shiny.

Phonics Songs and Rhymes Chart 23

▶ Connect Sounds to Letters

Teach Point to *baby* on the chart and have it read. Say:

> **The letter *y* in *baby* stands for /ē/, the long *e* sound.**
> **The letter *y* in *my* stands for /ī/, the long *i* sound.**

Have children repeat the sound /ē/ several times. Follow a similar procedure with *my* and the letter *y* with the vowel sound /ī/.

Blending Practice Have children blend the sounds /m/ /ī/ to read *my* and /b/ /ā/ /b/ /ē/ to read *baby*. Have them continue decoding several other *y* as long *e* or long *i* words.

Make New Words Write *baby* and *cry* as column heads on the board. Using word cards for *carry, happy, why, funny, my, many, only, by, pretty, very,* have children sort the words into the appropriate column.

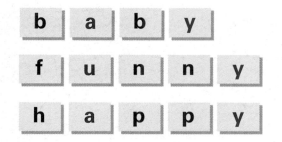

Have children list other words with medial sounds /ē/ and /ī/ and then underline the letters that spell those sounds.

Compound Words

▶ Teach Compound Words

Write the following on the board.

egg + shell = eggshell

tip + toe =

sun + set =

Explain to children that two small words such as *egg* and *shell* can be put together to make a new word—*eggshell*. Work with children to blend the words *egg* and *shell* to say *eggshell*. Repeat the process for *tiptoe, sunset, nearby,* and *inside.*

▶ Make New Words

Return to the Rhyme Chart Point to the word *eggshell* in "I'm a Baby Dinosaur." Have a volunteer read the word and then draw a line between the two words that make the compound word. Ask volunteers to find other compound words (*breakfast, footprints*) and predict their meaning by examining the individual words that make them up.

Spelling Vowel *y* Words

Pretest Say the spelling word, use it in a sentence, repeat it, and allow children to write it. Have children check their pretests and correct misspelled words.

Work with the Spelling Pattern List the spelling words on the board. Have children read the words, identify the letter at the end of each word that spells /ē/ or /ī/, and name the rhyming words.

Skills Trace

⟳ **Compound Words**

Introduce/Teach	TE: 1.4 168l; 1.5 **156l**
Practice	PB: 1.4 84; 1.5 15, 68; 1.6 31
Reteach/Review	TE: 1.4 AR19; 1.5 163c, 187a, 189a, 191c, AR17; 1.6 73a
Test	Skills Test, Unit 6 Benchmark Test, Unit 6

Day 1

Spelling Words

baby	my
funny	why
many	fly

High-Frequency

| even | most |

Challenge

| without | nobody |

Word Wall

Introduce High-Frequency Words Use the word cards for *animals, even, heard, most,* and *their.* Then say a sentence and leave out a high-frequency word for volunteers to fill in, such as: *Dinosaurs are _____ that lived a long time ago.*

Have children name the first letter of each word, and ask a volunteer to attach each word to the Word Wall under the appropriate beginning letter.

Review Have children read the other Word Wall words that begin with the same letters.

animals · even · heard · their · most

Optional Resources

Waterford Early Reading Program
Level 2: Lesson 25

Phonics
Phonics Workbook, pp. 146–148
Phonics Manipulatives Kit
Phonics Sourcebook, pp. 83–84
Reading Road Show

High-Frequency Words
High-Frequency Word Cards
Phonics Sourcebook, pp. 90–99

Objectives

Children will

- learn selection vocabulary
- use sound-symbol relationships to read decodable text
- use prior knowledge to make predictions and make sense of a selection
- distinguish realism from fantasy

Day 1

Phonics Story

Chompy's Afternoon

pp. 156–163

▶ Build Oral Language

Activate Prior Knowledge Ask children to think about their experiences with picnics. Ask:

What do you need to have a picnic?

Create a word web to show children's responses. You may want to use Graphic Organizer Transparency 5 (Web 2).

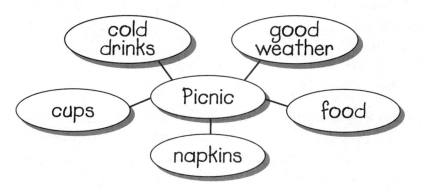

Build Background Fill a backpack with real foods or pictures of foods people might take on a picnic. Invite children to pull foods out of the backpack and discuss why they would be good to bring on a picnic.

▶ Vocabulary

Introduce Story Vocabulary Use Vocabulary Chart 44, or write sentences on the board, using the words. Read each sentence aloud.

Frame *thought* in the sentences. Ask children to read the word aloud and tell what the word means. Repeat with the word *roar*.

Review High-Frequency Words Have children read each word as you point to it on the Word Wall. These words are also listed on page 229 of the Student Book.

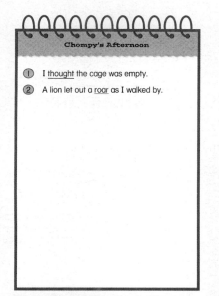

Story Vocabulary Chart 44

—— high-frequency/tested vocabulary

156m Reading • Comprehension • Vocabulary

▶ Reading Strategies

Preview and Predict Read the title and the name of the author and illustrator to children. Ask them to identify Chompy and his mom in the first picture.

> **What can you tell about Chompy from the pictures on the first two pages?** (He looks happy. He seems to like food.)

Picture Walk Have children do a picture walk, looking at all the pictures in the story. Children might use words from the story to describe the pictures. Ask children what might happen in the story.

Set Purposes From the pictures, children know that Chompy walks off alone during the picnic. Have children set their own purposes for reading. They may want to read to find out why he goes off without his mother.

Guide the Reading Have children read the first few pages of the selection, keeping their purposes in mind. Stop and check comprehension, using the questions provided. Have the children read to page 159.

Chompy looked up at the blue sky. "It's a nice afternoon," he said. "Let's have a picnic," said Mom. "I'm so happy!" said Chompy. Chompy loved picnics more than anything.

Selection Audio
CD 7/Tape 25, Side 1

About the Author and Illustrator

G. Brian Karas is author and illustrator of over 50 books. An aspiring artist at age five, he continued to combine drawing with his passion for reading while in art school. His college teachers, many of whom were children's book illustrators, introduced him to publishing. *Like Butter on Pancakes, Saving Sweetness,* and *Elevator Dreams* are a few of his award-winning titles.

Optional Resources

Reading
Adding English: ESL Teacher's Guide

Guiding Comprehension

pp. 156–159

Character/Literal

How does Chompy feel when his mom suggests a picnic?

He feels happy.

Hypothesizing/Critical

Why do you think Chompy loves picnics more than anything?

Children are likely to say that Chompy loves picnics because he likes to eat, or because it's fun to eat outside.

Recall and Retell/Literal

What does Mom pack instead of the watermelons?

She puts cupcakes in the backpack.

Predicting/Inferential

What do you think Chompy will do next?

Reasonable predictions are that Chompy will eat more or that he will go on a hike.

Connect Phonics to Reading

What did Chompy and his mom sit down by to have their picnic? They sat down by a waterfall. **What word has been added to the word *water*?** *fall* **What new word does it make?** *waterfall* **What does *waterfall* mean?** a stream of water that falls from a high place

---

Read On...

to the end of the story.

Phonics Story

Chompy's Afternoon
by G. Brian Karas

Chompy looked up at the blue sky. "It's a nice afternoon," he said.
"Let's have a picnic," said Mom.
"I'm so happy!" said Chompy. Chompy loved picnics more than anything.

156

Chompy's Afternoon, **page 156**

"My, my, Chompy. This is too much food," said Mom.
"I'll try to carry it," said Chompy. Chompy couldn't carry it all.
So Mom put most of the food back. Then she packed two cupcakes.

158 Phonics Story

Chompy's Afternoon, **page 158**

Chompy packed yummy food. He
packed everything he could find. "I'll
even pack these huge watermelons,"
he said.
Chompy was very hungry.

Phonics Story **157**

***Chompy's Afternoon,* page 157**

Chompy and his mom walked up
the pathway to a hilltop. They sat
down by a waterfall.
"It's very pretty here," said Mom.
They ate most of their food.

Phonics Story **159**

***Chompy's Afternoon,* page 159**

Phonics Strategies

If... children have trouble reading *yummy*,	**then...** have them segment /y/ /u/ /m/ /ē/ as they point to the letters in *yummy*. **Decoding**
If... children hesitate at compound words such as *afternoon, anything, watermelons,* and *hilltop*,	**then...** have them break the word into its smaller words and read each word separately before combining them. **Decoding: Using Structural Analysis**

Reading Strategies

If... children are unable to hypothesize why Chompy loves picnics,	**then...** have them think about what they enjoy about picnics and tell which of those reasons could apply to Chompy. **Prior Knowledge**
If... children stop at a difficult word,	**then...** have them read on to the end of the sentence and then go back and try again. Encourage cross-checking of letter cues against meaning. **Decoding; Context Clues**

Day 1

▢ vowel sounds of *y* and compound words
— high-frequency/tested vocabulary

Guiding Comprehension

pp. 160–163

Day 1

Confirming Predictions

Did the story end the way you thought it would?
Children who used picture clues are likely to say yes.

Drawing Conclusions/Inferential

Why does Chompy bite the big dinosaur's tail?
He thinks it's something good to eat.

Self-Monitoring Strategy

It doesn't say Chompy bites the dinosaur's tail because he thinks it's something good to eat. How do you know?
Chompy was thinking about food when he saw the dinosaur's tail. Chompy takes a bite of what he thinks is a nice little treat.

Evaluating/Critical

Do you think Chompy is a good name for the young dinosaur? Why or why not?
Children are likely to say that Chompy is a good name because the character spends a lot of time eating or looking for food to eat.

Connect Phonics to Reading

Why does Chompy take a little walk? He's still hungry. **What sound is at the end of hungry?** You hear the /ē/ sound.

Response Log Have children create a story map that includes setting, characters, and story solution.

"I'm still hungry. I think I'll take a little walk," Chompy thought. Chompy looked around for more food.
"There has to be something to eat somewhere!" he thought.

160 Phonics Story

Chompy's Afternoon, page 160

Chompy heard a big roar.
"I'm not so lucky!" yelled Chompy.
He ran as fast as he could.
Mom heard Chompy cry. "Go away, you big bully!" she roared.

162 Phonics Story

Chompy's Afternoon, page 162

"I'm so lucky," said Chompy. "Here is a nice little treat." He took a big bite.

But it was not nice or little or a treat. It was a huge, mean animal.

Phonics Story **161**

***Chompy's Afternoon,* page 161**

The animal ran far away. Chompy and his mom went back to the hilltop.

"Here is a little treat, Chompy," said Mom. "And it won't bite back."

Chompy was very happy now.

163

***Chompy's Afternoon,* page 163**

Skills in Context

Review

Realism and Fantasy

Do you think *Chompy's Afternoon* could really happen, or do you think it's make-believe? Explain your answer.

The story is make-believe because dinosaurs didn't go on picnics or talk.

Day 1

Ongoing Assessment

Realism and Fantasy

If... children are unable to identify the story as fantasy,	**then...** do the **Think Aloud** below to model the skill.

Model Your Thinking

A make-believe story is one that could not really happen. When I reread, I think *Chompy's Afternoon* is make-believe because dinosaurs haven't been around for millions of years. When they were alive, they didn't live in houses, talk, go on picnics, or eat cupcakes.

Have children return to the story to name other details that could not really happen, supporting the story's classification as a fantasy.

Extend Language Arts

Grammar: Adjectives

Have children look at page 156. Ask them to find the words that describe the sky and the afternoon. Write *blue* and *nice* on the board. Now have them find the word that Chompy uses to describe himself. Write *happy* on the board. Explain that these describing words are adjectives. They tell what something is like: its size, color, taste, and so on.

Go through the story and have children identify the adjectives on each page. Write the words on the board. Invite children to write an adjective and something it could describe, then illustrate the phrase. For example, a child might write *blue chair.*

vowel sounds of *y* and compound words
high-frequency/tested vocabulary

Objectives

Children will

- expand vocabulary
- identify and use homonyms
- create a word bank
- practice handwriting

Day
1

Expand Vocabulary

▶ Create Homonym Titles

Remind children that homonyms are words that sound the same but are spelled differently and have different meanings. Write *tale/tail* on the board and ask volunteers to tell you what each means.

Then write *A Tale of a Dinosaur Tail* on the board. Circle the homonym pair in the title and tell what each means. Then explain that children will work in small groups to think up homonym titles from the list you provide. When a group has a title with both homonyms in it, record the title on the board. Have a volunteer circle the homonyms and tell what each means.

son/sun	tow/toe
road/rode	whole/hole
sale/sail	blue/blew

Word Bank

▶ Shared Writing

Dinosaur Days Word Bank Tell children they will create a word bank of things they might have seen during dinosaur days. Suggest they look at the illustrations in *Chompy's Afternoon,* as well as those in encyclopedias and other classroom resources, to help them think of ideas. Record their ideas on a chart.

As you write, call attention to the connection between the spoken words and the letters you are writing.

Dinosaur Days

sunshine	trees
volcanoes	waterfalls
dinosaurs	plants

Independent Writing Have children choose a word from the word bank and write two sentences that include the word. Ask children to illustrate their writing.

Handwriting *Bb*

Provide lined paper and handwriting models. Demonstrate how to write a capital *B* and a lowercase *b,* and have children practice writing a row of each letter.

Ask children to evaluate their handwriting by circling with a red crayon their best capital *B* and their best lowercase *b.*

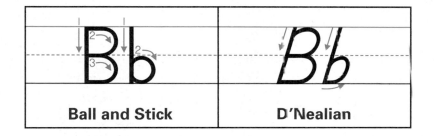

| Ball and Stick | D'Nealian |

Word Spacing Write these sentences on the board:

Bobby is my baby brother.
My dog Buster barks.

As you write, explain that correct spacing makes your writing easier to read. Point out that there is more space between words than between letters in each word.

Self-Selected Reading and Read Aloud

Read aloud a book about dinosaurs. Children can choose more books about dinosaurs for independent reading.

Day
1

Optional Resources

Oral Language
Adding English: ESL Teacher's Guide

Day 2

Vowel Sounds of *y* Compound Words

▶ Phonics Practice Activities

Use the following activities and Practice Book pages to practice vowel sounds of *y* and compound words.

Phonics Songs and Rhymes Chart Have children chant "I'm a Baby Dinosaur" as they track the print. Children can circle words that have the long *e* sound of *y* as in *bunny.* Then have children find the words with the long *i* sound of *y.*

Have children come to the poster to find compound words and circle both words in each compound word.

Make New Words Pairs of children use letter cards *a, b, b, f, l, m, n, u,* and *y* to build *y* words with long *e* and long *i* sounds. Have them list the words they make, sorting according to final vowel sound.

Vowel Sound of *y*
Practice Book 1.5, p. 67
Teacher's Resource Book 1.5, p. 75

Compound Words
Practice Book 1.5, p. 68
Teacher's Resource Book 1.5, p. 76

Decodable Readers 33–41

Decodable Reader 39,
My Mail

▶ Read the Phonics Reader

Tell children to use what they know about vowel sounds of *y* and compound words as they read *My Mail.* Observe children's reading to determine their ability to transfer these phonics skills to a new selection. After reading, have them:

- take turns retelling the story with a partner
- find and use compound words in sentences

Phonics Reader

Spelling Vowel *y* Words

▶ Writing for Sounds

Have children write these sentences. Read the sentences. Then repeat words slowly, allowing children to hear each sound. Children may use the Word Wall to help in spelling high-frequency words. Proofread and correct complete sentences.

My puppy does funny tricks.
Many baby ducks floated on the pond.
Why can't a kitten fly?

Spelling Words

baby	my
funny	why
many	fly

High-Frequency

even	most

Challenge

without	nobody

Word Wall

Practice High-Frequency Words

Say a word from the Word Wall. Then say the first letter of the word and toss a beanbag to a child who says the next letter. Have children pass the beanbag until the word has been spelled. The last child to get the beanbag should use the word in a sentence. Have children chant the spelling together after it is used in a sentence.

animals   even

heard   most   their

Even.
e

v

e

n

Even I can catch.

Pick a word from the box to finish each sentence. Write it on the line.

animals	even	heard	most	their

1. Last night I **heard** something outside.
2. I know that **animals** live in our backyard.
5. **Most** of them come out at night.
4. I can **even** see them if I look outside.
5. I see **their** faces looking at me!

Notes for Home: This week your child is learning to read the words *animals, even, heard, most,* and *their. Home Activity:* Work with your child to write a story using these new words. Help your child read the story to you when he or she is done.

High-Frequency Words
Practice Book 1.5, p. 69
Teacher's Resource Book 1.5, p. 77

❄ Meeting Individual Needs

ESL	Intervention	Challenge	Other Ways to Learn
Write *happy* on the board and read it, clapping once for each syllable. Then write the following words and guide children to clap the syllables they hear as they read the words with you: *funny, pretty, berry, hungry, tiny,* and *daddy.* **(Word Study Support)** See also *Adding English.* (ESL)	Use **Decodable Reader 39** and the teaching suggestions on p. AR7 to provide practice reading decodable text that includes words with sounds of *y* and compounds. **(Phonics Support)**	Use word cards for *happy, puppy, penny, fly, sky,* and *baby* to play a partner riddle game. Let each partner choose a word card and make up a riddle, such as *My y stands for the long e sound and I'm the same as one cent* (penny). Then the guesser draws a picture and labels it. Partners take turns making up riddles. **(Divergent Thinking)**	Use Phonics Activity Mat 3 from the Phonics Manipulatives Kit for *y* sounds and Phonics Activity Mat 1 for compounds. Instructions for using these games are on the back of the mats. **(Kinesthetic)**

Main Idea

▶ Develop Listening Comprehension

Read the following selection aloud. Ask children to listen and to find out what this selection is about.

Read Aloud

No Escape!

The tyrannosaurus was the fiercest—and largest— meat-eating creature ever to walk the earth. And the tyrannosaurus probably never went hungry! When it hunted for its next meal, there weren't many dinosaurs that could escape the grip of its sharp, pointy teeth.

The ornithomimus (or ni tho MY mus) was probably fast enough to make a quick getaway. This long-necked creature was very fast! It could scramble away and hide until a tyrannosaurus passed.

Slower dinosaurs, like the triceratops, used their own hard skin to protect them from becoming the tyrannosaurus's next meal.

And some dinosaurs, like the ankylosaurus, may have fought the tyrannosaurus for their lives. Their big tails could be used as a kind of club to fight off attackers.

Fighting back and running away were the only ways to avoid becoming tyrannosaurus's next meal. And even then, the mighty tyrannosaurus usually won.

▶ Teach Main Idea

Model the skill by telling children:

Think ALOUD This story is all about dinosaurs and how some of them protected themselves from the tyrannosaurus.

Elicit details from the story. (Ornithomimus was fast. Triceratops had hard skin. Ankylosaurus had a big tail.) Explain that these details are small parts of the story but not what it is all about. You may wish to record children's responses on Graphic Organizer Transparency 15.

Practice Have children read together a story they have previously read. Then give them three main ideas to choose from, with only one of them being correct. Have children select the main idea from the three choices.

Reread for Fluency

Attend to Punctuation Model fluent reading by reading aloud pages 160–163. Point out how you use the punctuation, as well as what you know about the story, to give your voice expression.

Paired Reading Have partners practice reading these four pages. Remind them to use the punctuation and words such as *yelled* and *roared* to add expression to their reading. Partners should read alternate pages. When they reread the story, they should read the other pages.

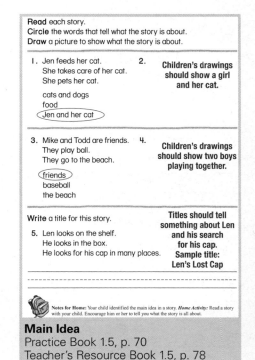

Main Idea
Practice Book 1.5, p. 70
Teacher's Resource Book 1.5, p. 78

Day 2

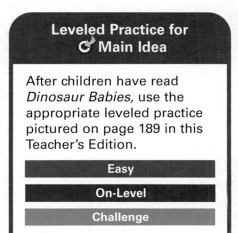

Leveled Practice for ↻ Main Idea

After children have read *Dinosaur Babies,* use the appropriate leveled practice pictured on page 189 in this Teacher's Edition.

| Easy |
| On-Level |
| Challenge |

❄ Meeting Individual Needs

ESL	Intervention	Challenge	Other Ways to Learn
Display an interesting photograph or illustration. Have children tell what they see, and then help them identify the main idea in the picture. Then read a short story with children. Help them recognize the "big picture." **(Skill Support)** See also *Adding English.* **ESL**	Use *Pandas, What Lilly Pup Heard,* or another familiar selection to discuss main idea. Help children formulate an answer to the question: "What are these readers all about?" **(Comprehension Support)**	Children use self-stick notes to write a main idea for each page in *Chompy's Afternoon.* **(Divergent Thinking)**	Children meet in small groups to discuss what *Chompy's Afternoon* is all about. They can record their responses on audiotape. **(Social/Interpersonal)** Children draw pictures of what Chompy ate in the order that he ate it. Then they use the pictures to retell the story. **(Visual/Spatial)**

Objectives

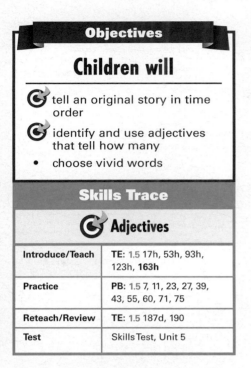

Children will

- ◎ tell an original story in time order
- ◎ identify and use adjectives that tell how many
- • choose vivid words

Skills Trace

◎ Adjectives

Introduce/Teach	TE: 1.5 17h, 53h, 93h, 123h, **163h**
Practice	PB: 1.5 7, 11, 23, 27, 39, 43, 55, 60, 71, 75
Reteach/Review	TE: 1.5 187d, 190
Test	Skills Test, Unit 5

Day
2

Speaking: Tell an Original Story in Order

► Discuss a Dinosaur Story

Model Invite children to tell a dinosaur story they have created. Explain that the events in the story should be told in time order. Tell a short dinosaur story of your own, such as the one below.

> Dina Dinosaur couldn't find her lunch. First, she raced past the hot volcano. Then, she climbed the tall tree. Next, she looked behind a hill. Hooray! She finally found her lunch near a leafy plant.

As you tell your story, model these behaviors:
- • Use time-order words.
- • Speak clearly.
- • Speak loud enough for all to hear.
- • Make eye contact with listeners.

Practice Assign partners. Have each tell an original story to the other, modeling the above behaviors. Tell partners to point out good use of time order words, as well as what they liked about each other's story.

Choose Vivid Words

► Modeled Writing

Model Review the Dinosaur Days word bank created on Day 1. Choose a word from the word bank as you demonstrate how children can create strong and interesting word pictures.

If I wanted to tell about a volcano in a story, I could just say, "There was a volcano," but that wouldn't paint a strong word picture. Instead, I could say, "Lava bubbled out of a steamy volcano." The second sentence would paint a stronger word picture.

▶Write About Dinosaur Days

Model Write both volcano sentences from the Think Aloud on page 163g:

> There was a volcano.
> Lava bubbled out of a steamy volcano.

As you write, model these strategies:
• Choose vivid words.
• Use strong verbs.
• Include facts and details.

Independent Writing Invite children to choose a word from the word bank and use it in two sentences of their own. (Some children may benefit from drawing a picture first and then writing about it.) The first sentence should paint a weak word picture. The second sentence should paint a strong word picture. You might want to provide adjective charts from previous weeks for children to use.

Grammar: Adjectives

Define Adjectives That Tell How Many Remind children that adjectives describe people, places, and things. Point out that children already know about adjectives that tell color, shape, size, and what kind. Explain that they will now work with adjectives that tell how many.

Practice Organize small blocks or similar objects into groups of one, three, four, and six. Write the word *block* on the chalkboard four times. Place a blank in front of each word. Choose a group of blocks and ask a child to tell how many are in it. Then have the child write the word for the numeral in the blank. You may wish to extend this activity by having children tell how many candles, how many watermelons, and how many dinosaurs they see on page 158 of *Chompy's Afternoon*.

For further practice, have children identify adjectives they used in their writing.

Self-Selected Reading and Read Aloud — D.E.A.R.

Read aloud *Dinosaur Bob and His Adventures with the Family Lizardo* by William Joyce. For independent reading, children self-select books about dinosaurs or museums.

Day 2

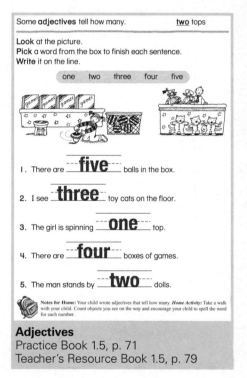

Some **adjectives** tell how many.   **two** tops

Look at the picture.
Pick a word from the box to finish each sentence.
Write it on the line.

| one | two | three | four | five |

1. There are **five** balls in the box.
2. I see **three** toy cats on the floor.
3. The girl is spinning **one** top.
4. There are **four** boxes of games.
5. The man stands by **two** dolls.

Notes for Home: Your child wrote adjectives that tell how many. *Home Activity:* Take a walk with your child. Count objects you see on the way and encourage your child to spell the word for each number.

Adjectives
Practice Book 1.5, p. 71
Teacher's Resource Book 1.5, p. 79

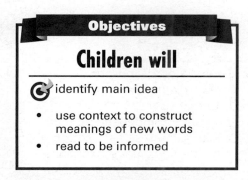
Day 3

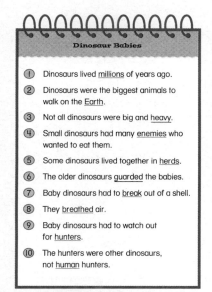

Dinosaur Babies

1. Dinosaurs lived <u>millions</u> of years ago.
2. Dinosaurs were the biggest animals to walk on the <u>Earth</u>.
3. Not all dinosaurs were big and <u>heavy</u>.
4. Small dinosaurs had many <u>enemies</u> who wanted to eat them.
5. Some dinosaurs lived together in <u>herds</u>.
6. The older dinosaurs <u>guarded</u> the babies.
7. Baby dinosaurs had to <u>break</u> out of a shell.
8. They <u>breathed</u> air.
9. Baby dinosaurs had to watch out for <u>hunters</u>.
10. The hunters were other dinosaurs, not <u>human</u> hunters.

Story Vocabulary Chart 45

Pick a word from the box to finish each sentence.
Write it on the line.

| animals | even | heard | heavy | most | their |

1. Many **animals** live on my dad's ranch.
2. I **heard** the sheep say "baa."
3. **Most** of our sheep are black.
4. We cut **their** hair twice a year.
5. The big sheep are **heavy**.
6. Some are **even** as heavy as my dad.

Notes for Home: Your child completed a story using words learned this week.
Home Activity: Encourage your child to write a poem or song using as many of these words as possible.

Tested Vocabulary
Practice Book 1.5, p. 72
Teacher's Resource Book 1.5, p. 80

Dinosaur Babies
pp. 164–185

▶ Build Oral Language

Activate Prior Knowledge Ask children to discuss animal mothers.

> How does Chompy's mom help him?
> How do other animal mothers help their babies?
> What might real dinosaur mothers do to help their babies?

Build Background Play the Background-Building audio segment, which takes listeners on an "electronic field trip." A class of "Time Spies" asks a museum expert questions about dinosaurs. After listening, help children recall what they learned about dinosaurs. Ask what questions they would have for the expert.

Background-Building Audio
CD 5/Tape 14, Side 1

▶ Vocabulary

Introduce Story Vocabulary List the selection vocabulary on the board. Use Vocabulary Chart 45 or write sentences using each word. Read the sentences aloud.

millions   Earth   heavy   enemies   herds

guarded   break   breathed   hunters   human

Frame the word *millions* in the list. Ask children to find it in the sentences. Have a volunteer find the word, read it to the class and tell what it means. Continue for the remaining words.

Remind children that some words have an ending *-s* to mean more than one. Ask children which words mean more than one. (*enemies, herds, hunters, millions*)

▶ Reading Strategies

Preview and Predict After reading the title of the selection and the names of the author and illustrator, children can do a picture walk through the first few pages of the selection. Ask children if they think that this selection gives true information about dinosaurs.

Set Purposes After children have looked at the first few pages, have them brainstorm questions about dinosaur babies. Read aloud the list of questions that children have.

Guide the Reading Have children read the first few pages of the selection, keeping their purposes in mind. Stop to check comprehension, using the questions provided. Have children read to page 167.

DINOSAUR BABIES

into Reading
A Step 1 Book
Preschool–Grade 1

By Lucille Recht Penner
Illustrated by Peter Barrett

Managing Flexible Groups

Intervention

Children listen to the selection audio and follow along in their books. After reading, children make a concept web about baby dinosaurs. The web might include where dinosaur babies came from, who cared for them, what they ate, what they looked like, and so on. Have children use illustrations from the selection to recall important details.

Selection Audio
CD 7/Tape 25,
Side 1

To develop fluency and to practice high-frequency words, children can read **Leveled Reader 23A,** *Pandas.* Instructional support appears in this Teacher's Edition, pp. LR25–LR26.

Easy

Children can review the high-frequency words. Read the story aloud with children. Have them echo-read the names of the dinosaur species. Children join in to read the questions in the text. Use Guiding Comprehension to monitor understanding and Ongoing Assessment as appropriate.

To develop fluency and to practice high-frequency words, children can read **Leveled Reader 23B,** *What Lilly Pup Heard.* Instructional support appears in this Teacher's Edition, pp. LR28–LR29.

On-Level

Before reading, preview the names of the dinosaur species and other unfamiliar words. Use Guiding Comprehension to monitor understanding and Ongoing Assessment to address reading difficulties.

To develop fluency and to practice high-frequency words, children can read **Leveled Reader 23B,** *What Lilly Pup Heard.* Instructional support appears in this Teacher's Edition, pp. LR28–LR29.

Challenge

Children can look for the main idea on each spread. Have them write each main idea in their response logs. After reading, children choose one kind of baby dinosaur and make a poster for a class display. Each poster should show what the child learned about the baby dinosaur.

Children who have finished reading *Dinosaur Babies* can read a selection in **Leveled Reader 5C.**

Optional Resources

Reading
Adding English: ESL Teacher's Guide

Guiding Comprehension

pp. 164–167

Text Features/Inferential

The dinosaurs in each illustration have a name written near their pictures. What does the author do to make it easy to say the names?

The author shows how to say each name below the name for each dinosaur.

Inferring/Critical

Why do you think no one has ever heard or seen a dinosaur?

No people were alive at the time of the dinosaurs. They lived millions of years ago.

Drawing Conclusions/Inferential

The dinosaur hunters found baby dinosaur bones in the nests. How did the bones get there?

The mother dinosaur built the nest to protect her babies. Then something went wrong, and the babies in the nest died.

Organizing Ideas and Information/Critical

What other information do you hope to find out about dinosaur babies?

Possible responses: what they eat, how big they get, where they lived.

Read On…

to page 171.

by Lucille Recht Penner
illustrated by Peter Barrett

Apatosaurus
(a–PAT–uh–sor–us)

Squeak! Squeak!
Is that the sound of a baby
dinosaur calling to its mother?

164

***Dinosaur Babies*, page 164**

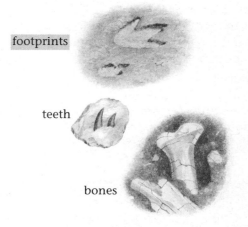

All the dinosaurs died millions of years ago.
But we know a lot about them from what
dinosaur hunters have found . . .

footprints

teeth

bones

They have found small baby bones in nests.

166

***Dinosaur Babies*, page 166**

Nobody knows.

Nobody has ever heard

a baby dinosaur.

Nobody has seen one.

165

Dinosaur Babies, page 165

They have even found dinosaur eggs.

Most dinosaurs were very big.

But their eggs were small.

The smallest was only as big as a quarter.

The biggest was about the size

of a football!

167

Dinosaur Babies, page 167

Skills in Context

Genre: Expository Nonfiction

Does this selection give facts about real dinosaurs, or is it make-believe?

The selection gives facts about dinosaurs that really lived on Earth.

Model Your Thinking

TEST TALK

I think that *Dinosaur Babies* gives real facts, because on pages 166 and 167 are footprints and eggs that dinosaur hunters have found. The pictures of dinosaurs look like real animals, not make-believe ones.

As they read, children can look for further evidence that the selection gives facts about real baby dinosaurs.

Day 3

Develop Literary Skills

Genre: Expository Nonfiction

Tell students that *Dinosaur Babies* gives us information and facts. Facts are statements that are true. Have children work together to make a list of facts they are reading in *Dinosaur Babies*. Begin your list with these facts:

1. Dinosaurs died millions of years ago.
2. Most dinosaurs were very big.
3. Dinosaur eggs were small.
4. The smallest egg was only as big as a quarter.

Have children add to the list as you continue reading *Dinosaur Babies*.

 vowel sound of *y* (long *e* and long *i*) and compound words
— high-frequency/tested vocabulary

Guiding Comprehension

pp. 168–171

Text Features/Inferential

What kind of dinosaur was a good mother? What kind of dinosaur liked to eat dinosaur eggs?

The Maiasaura was a good mother. Troödons tried to eat the eggs.

Making Judgments/Critical

Do you agree with the author that the Maiasaura was a good mother? Why or why not?

Possible response: Yes, she was a good mother because she protected her babies by making a nest, keeping the eggs warm, and keeping the other dinosaurs away.

Drawing Conclusions/Inferential

What is the mother dinosaur doing in the picture on pages 168 and 169?

She is putting leaves on the eggs to keep them warm.

Organizing Ideas and Information/Critical

What have you learned so far about baby dinosaurs? What questions about dinosaurs would you like to add to your K-W-L chart?

Possible answer: I learned that baby dinosaurs hatched from eggs, that mother dinosaurs took care of the nests, and that other dinosaurs liked to eat dinosaur eggs. I would like to know what baby dinosaurs looked like when they were born.

Read On...

to page 175.

Were dinosaurs good mothers?
This kind of dinosaur was.
She made a nest of mud and
laid her eggs in it.
Chickens sit on their eggs.

168

Dinosaur Babies, page 168

The mother watched the nest.
Lots of animals liked to eat dinosaur eggs!
She kept them away.

170

Dinosaur Babies, page 170

But this dinosaur did not.
She was too heavy.
The eggs would break!
She put leaves on the eggs
to keep them warm.

Maiasaura
(my–uh–SOR–uh)

169

Dinosaur Babies, **page 169**

Inside the eggs the babies grew.
They breathed through tiny holes
in the eggshells.

Troödon
(TRO–o–don)

171

Dinosaur Babies, **page 171**

Ongoing Assessment

Reading Strategies

If... children are unable to relate what they have learned so far about baby dinosaurs,

then... have them go back and "read" the selection by looking at the pictures. **Using Illustrations**

Phonics Strategies

If... children have trouble decoding words with final *y* as the long *e* or long *i* sound,

then... explain that *y* at the end of a word has the sound of long *e* or long *i*. Have children write the words *baby* and *cry* on bookmarks and illustrate each word. Children can refer to the bookmark when they come to a word with *y*. **Decoding**

If... children are able to use structural cues to decode compound words,

then... acknowledge their good reading and ask them to explain how they figured out the compound words. **Self-Monitoring**

Day **3**

vowel sound of *y* (long *e* and long *i*) and compound words
high-frequency/tested vocabulary

Chompy/Dinosaur Babies   **170–171**

Guiding Comprehension

pp. 172–175

Day
3

Visualizing/Inferential

What did baby dinosaurs look like when they hatched?

They looked like their mothers. They had big heads, big eyes, and lots of teeth.

Compare and Contrast/Inferential

How are dinosaur babies and human babies the same? How are they different?

Possible responses: Both dinosaur babies and human babies are fed by their mothers. Dinosaur babies hatch from eggs, but human babies do not.

Recall and Retell/Literal

What did baby dinosaurs eat?

Some kinds ate leaves and berries and seeds. Some kinds ate little animals and bugs.

Organizing Ideas and Information/Critical

What else would you like to learn about baby dinosaurs?

Possible responses: How long it took them to grow up, how big they got, what they did for fun. Have children write their questions into the *W* column of the K-W-L chart.

Connect Phonics to Reading

How did the little baby dinosaurs feel after they came out of their eggs? Find another word on page 172 that has the same ending sound as *hungry*.

They were hungry. Children may say *baby* or *maybe*.

to page 179.

One day the eggs cracked!
Little baby dinosaurs came out.
They were hungry.
Maybe they squeaked.

The mother dinosaur brought them food.
The babies ate and ate all day long.

172

Dinosaur Babies, **page 172**

Apatosaurus
(a–PAT–uh–sor–us)

What did baby dinosaurs eat?
Some kinds ate leaves and berries and seeds.

174

Dinosaur Babies, **page 174**

Dinosaur babies had big heads and big eyes.
They could see and hear well.

Human babies are born without any teeth.
Not dinosaur babies! They had lots of teeth.

Tyrannosaurus
(tie–RAN–uh–SOR–us)

173

Dinosaur Babies, page 173

Some kinds ate little animals
and bugs.

Deinonychus
(die–NON–ee–kus)

175

Dinosaur Babies, page 175

Content Connection: Social Studies

Dinosaurs used to live all over the world. In the United States, scientists have found dinosaur bones or tracks in Connecticut, New Jersey, Texas, Montana, Wyoming, Utah, Colorado, and many other states. Dinosaur bones also have been found in China, Siberia, South America, Africa, India, and Australia. A good place to see dinosaur bones is Dinosaur National Monument in Utah and Colorado.

vowel sound of *y* (long *e* and long *i*) and compound words
high-frequency/tested vocabulary

Guiding Comprehension

pp. 176–179

Day 3

Cause and Effect/Literal

Why wasn't it safe for baby dinosaurs to look for food on their own?

Enemies were all around. Baby dinosaurs were not big enough to fight or to run away.

Context Clues/Inferential

How can you tell what the word *herds* means on page 179?

The sentence just before it tells that the baby dinosaurs were never alone. So herds must be groups of dinosaurs.

Self-Monitoring Strategy
Use Illustrations

How do you know that *herd* means "a group of dinosaurs" rather than "listened to something"?

Possible responses: I can see the group of dinosaurs in the picture, so I know the word means "a group of animals." Also, the other words in the sentence are not about listening.

Organizing Ideas and Information/Critical

What have you learned about baby dinosaurs so far?

Baby dinosaurs hatched from eggs. There were many different kinds of dinosaurs. Encourage children to record their answers in the *L* column of the K-W-L chart.

Read On...

to page 183.

Was it safe for baby dinosaurs to hunt for food alone? No! Enemies were all around. And baby dinosaurs could not fight or run fast. They could only hide.

Psittacosaurus
(SIT–uh–ko–SOR–us)

176

Dinosaur Babies, page 176

Triceratops
(try–SER–uh–tops)

178

Dinosaur Babies, page 178

Tyrannosaurus
(tie–RAN–uh–SOR–us)

177

Dinosaur Babies, page 177

Reading Strategies

If... children stumble on unfamiliar words and struggle with decoding,	**then...** suggest that they reread a sentence to the end, skipping the hard word. Then have them go back and use the meaning of other words in the sentence, letter cues, and prior experience to help them identify the word. **Context Clues**
If... children do not use appropriate expression when reading the interrogative, exclamatory, and declarative sentences on page 176,	**then...** point out the different ending punctuation and model how to read the sentences. Have children read the sentences after you, modeling your pace and expression. **Fluency**
If... children are able to recall and interpret what they have read,	**then...** recognize them for their good comprehension. **Recall and Retell/Analyzing**

Day 3

Some baby dinosaurs were lucky.
They were never alone.
They lived in herds.

179

Dinosaur Babies, page 179

vowel sound of *y* (long *e* and long *i*) and compound words
— high-frequency/tested vocabulary

Guiding Comprehension

pp. 180–183

Recall and Retell/Literal

How did adult dinosaurs in a herd protect baby dinosaurs?

Big adult dinosaurs formed a circle around little baby dinosaurs and guarded the outside.

Summarizing/Inferential

What are the sentences on pages 180 and 181 all about?

The herd protects the babies by putting them in the middle of a circle.

Analyzing/Critical

Why do you think the dinosaurs are sleeping among the trees?

Possible response: They are probably there because they can hide and be protected by the trees.

Organizing Ideas and Information/Critical

Think about what you wanted to know about baby dinosaurs. What have you learned? What questions do you still have?

Possible responses: I learned that baby dinosaurs hatched from eggs, that their mothers protected them, and that they may have traveled in herds. I still want to know exactly how big these dinosaurs were and how long it took for baby dinosaurs to become adults.

Read On...

to the end of the selection.

Even then enemies tried to grab the babies and eat them!

180

Dinosaur Babies, page 180

Babies were safe in the
dinosaur herd.
The dinosaurs walked and
ate and slept together.

182

Dinosaur Babies, page 182

So the dinosaurs made a circle.

Little ones stayed on the inside.

Big ones guarded the outside.

181

Dinosaur Babies, page 181

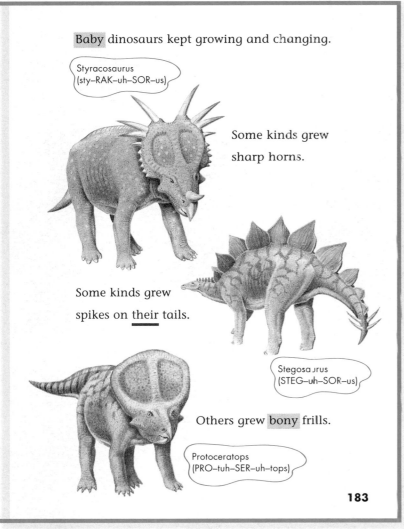

Baby dinosaurs kept growing and changing.

Styracosaurus
(sty–RAK–uh–SOR–us)

Some kinds grew
sharp horns.

Some kinds grew
spikes on their tails.

Stegosaurus
(STEG–uh–SOR–us)

Others grew bony frills.

Protoceratops
(PRO–tuh–SER–uh–tops)

183

Dinosaur Babies, page 183

Skills in Context

 Main Idea

What is *Dinosaur Babies* all about—why dinosaurs died, where dinosaurs lived, or how baby dinosaurs lived and grew?

It is about how baby dinosaurs lived and grew.

Model Your Thinking

TEST TALK

When I read the story, I learned that baby dinosaurs hatched from eggs, but that is just a small part of *Dinosaur Babies*. *Dinosaur Babies* is all about how dinosaurs lived and grew up.

Have children return to the selection to find other details. Discuss how each detail is just a part of the selection.

Day
3

▒ vowel sound of *y* (long *e* and long *i*) and compound words
— High-frequency/tested vocabulary

Guiding Comprehension

pp. 184–187

Text Features/Literal

What kind of dinosaur is pictured on these pages?

Brachiosaurus.

Summarizing/Inferential

Describe the life of a baby dinosaur.

A baby dinosaur hatched from an egg. Its mother helped feed it and keep it safe.

Return to the K-W-L Chart

Ask children to look at the *W* column of the K-W-L chart and notice if any of the questions they had about baby dinosaurs have been answered. Then help children fill in the *L* column of the chart to record what they have learned. Have children consider other ways they can find answers to their questions.

Day
3

Critical Thinking
Reading Across Texts

What did you learn in *Dinosaur Babies* that helps explain some of the action in *Chompy's Afternoon*?

Dinosaur babies ate all day long, which is why Chompy seemed always to be hungry. It wasn't safe for dinosaur babies to hunt for food alone because they had many enemies and couldn't protect themselves. They needed adult dinosaurs to protect them. Chompy went alone to look for more food and got chased by a bigger dinosaur. His mother protected him.

Dinosaur Babies, page 184

Something Big Has Been Here

by Jack Prelutsky

Something big has been here,
what it was, I do not know,
for I did not see it coming,
and I did not see it go,
but I hope I never meet it,
if I do, I'm in a fix,
for it left behind its footprints,
they are size nine-fifty-six.

186

"Something Big Has Been Here," page 186

They grew until they weren't
babies anymore.
Some grew to be the biggest
animals ever to walk the Earth!
And some had dinosaur babies
of their own.

135

Dinosaur Babies, page 185

Unfortunately
by Bobbi Katz

Dinosaurs lived so long ago
they never had a chance to know
how many kids would love to get
a dinosaur to be their pet!

187

"Unfortunately," page 187

Reading Poetry

▶ Model Reading Aloud

Read aloud the poems in a playful tone.

▶ Discuss the Poems

Main Idea/Inferential

Who do you think made the huge footprints in "Something Big Has Been Here"? A dinosaur.

Making Judgments/Critical

Which poem is your favorite? Why?

Some children may prefer "Something Big Has Been Here," because it is fun to think about finding huge tracks. Others may prefer "Unfortunately" because it is fun to think about having a dinosaur for a pet.

▶ Oral Reading

Have volunteers choose one poem to read aloud. Encourage them to speak loudly and clearly. Remind them to pause after commas and speak with excitement when they see an exclamation point.

Connect Across Texts

READING ACROSS TEXTS

Ask children to think about what they learned about dinosaurs in *Dinosaur Babies*. Then ask: "Is it possible to find a dinosaur's footprint? Would it be possible to have a dinosaur for a pet?" Have them explain their answers.

Day 3

Selection Audio

CD 7/Tape 25, Side 2

▨ vowel sound of y (long *e* and long *i*) and compound words
▬ high-frequency/tested vocabulary

PHONICS

Objectives

Children will

- identify, decode, and build words with the vowel sounds of *y* (long *e* and long *i*)
- use structural cues to decode and build compound words
  - review long *i*: *igh, ie*
  - spell words with vowel *y* (long *e* and long *i*)
  - recognize high-frequency words

Skills Trace

Long *i*: *igh, ie*

Introduce/Teach	TE: 1.5 116k
Practice	PB: 1.5 51, 73
Reteach/Review	TE: 1.5 187a, AR15
Test	Skills Test, Unit 5

Day 3

Long *i*: *igh, ie*
Practice Book 1.5, p. 73
Teacher's Resource Book 1.5, p. 81

Vowel Sounds of *y* Compound Words

▶ Phonics Practice Activities

Careful observation of these activities will provide a basis for the Ongoing Assessment on page 187b.

Group Activity Divide compound words into two words and write each word on a separate strip of paper. Put the strips in a bag and have each child choose one and search for its partner.

| in | side | bed | room | rain | drop |

Partners Partners reread "I'm a Baby Dinosaur." Give each pair a list of several /ē/ /ī/ *y* words and compound words to find and circle on the chart. Each pair can use a different color to circle their words. Then sing the rhyme together as a class, pausing for each pair to say the words they found and circled.

Reread for Fluency

Readers Theater Have children reread *My Mail,* each taking the part of a story character. One child may read the part of narrator.

Phonics Reader

Review

Long *i*: *igh, ie*

▶ Long *i* Words

Ask children to listen for /ī/ as you reread the Big Book, *Rabbits & Raindrops.* Ask children to raise their hands each time they hear the long *i* sound. After reading the story, turn to page 6 and point out the words *bright* and *sunlight.* Write the words on the board and ask a volunteer to read them. Have volunteers circle the letters that stand for the long *i* sound. Remind children that /ī/ can also be spelled *ie* as in *die.* Write *die* on the board. Have children name words that rhyme with *bright* and *die* and suggest the spelling for each. Then have children find *rain* in the book. Have children name words that rhyme with *rain* and suggest the spelling for each.

Spelling Vowel *y* Words

▶ Practice with Writing

Have pairs of children write the spelling words on separate pieces of paper and put each word in a bag. Have one child pull a spelling word from the bag and pantomime its meaning. When the partner guesses the word, both children can write sentences telling what was acted out. Have children take turns until all words are used.

Ongoing Assessment

Phonics/Spelling

If... children have difficulty decoding /ē/ /ī/ *y* words,	**then...** write and say two similar words—one with the long *e* or *i* sound of *y* and one without, such as *flo/fly* or *bun/bunny*. Ask children to point to, spell aloud, and say the words with *y*. Also use the ESL and Intervention activities, Day 4, page 189a.
If... children have difficulty using structural cues to decode compound words,	**then...** use word cards for each of the separate words in the compounds. Be sure children can read the words individually before putting them together as compounds.
If... children can easily decode words with the vowel sounds of *y*,	**then...** have them go back to the Big Book, *Rabbits and Raindrops,* or a book of your choice and find words with the long *e* and long *i* sounds of *y*. Children can list these words in their word study books.
If... children can easily spell this week's spelling words,	**then...** have them use the spelling word patterns to spell rhyming words, such as *sunny* and *try*.

Spelling
Practice Book 1.5, p. 74
Teacher's Resource Book 1.5, p. 82

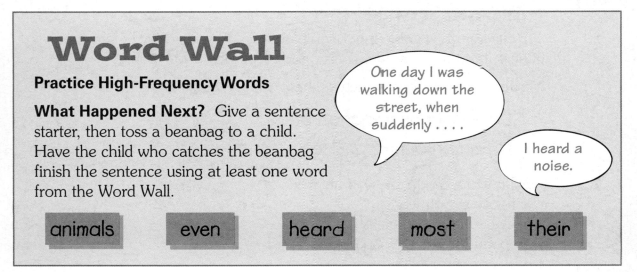

Word Wall

Practice High-Frequency Words

What Happened Next? Give a sentence starter, then toss a beanbag to a child. Have the child who catches the beanbag finish the sentence using at least one word from the Word Wall.

> One day I was walking down the street, when suddenly . . . .

> I heard a noise.

animals · even · heard · most · their

Optional Resources

Phonics
Phonics Workbook, pp. 146–148, 149
Phonics Manipulatives Kit
Phonics Sourcebook, pp. 83–85
AstroWord CD–Rom, Compound Words
Reading Road Show

High-Frequency Words
High-Frequency Word Cards
Phonics Sourcebook, pp. 90–99

Day **3**

Chompy/Dinosaur Babies   **187b**

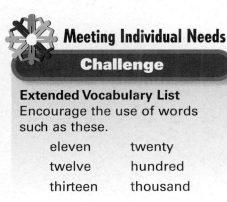

Expand Vocabulary

► Name Types of Dinosaurs

Recall *Dinosaur Babies*. Tell children that many kinds of dinosaurs walked the Earth and that the story names some of them.

Write each of these dinosaur names on a separate index card: *psittacosaurus, maiasaura, deinonychus, stegosaurus.* Then organize clues in a chart like the one below. Have children open their copies of *Dinosaur Babies*. Then read clues aloud. As groups look through the story and correctly point to each dinosaur, give the correct index card to a volunteer, and have the volunteer tape it to the chart.

Kinds of Dinosaurs

Clues	Dinosaur Name
small, no horns, walked on all fours, no scales on back	psittacosaurus
huge, heavy, did not sit on her eggs	maiasaura
ate bugs, walked on two legs	deinonychus
spikes on tail, walked on all fours	stegosaurus

Dinosaur Description

► Modeled Writing

Tell children they are going to write about a dinosaur. Have them choose either a dinosaur from the chart or one from *Dinosaur Babies*.

Model Write sentences such as these about a dinosaur.

> Deinonychus munched bugs.
> It ran on only two feet.

As you write, model these strategies:
- Choose strong words.
- Include facts and details.
- Separate words with spaces.
- Use correct punctuation.

Independent Writing Tell children to write a dinosaur description. Invite them to use *Dinosaur Babies* and other classroom resources, such as encyclopedias. Have children illustrate their writing.

Peer Conference Have partners read descriptions to one another. Have children tell their partners one thing they liked about the dinosaur description.

Writer's Checklist

Did you . . .

✓ choose strong words?
✓ include facts and details?
✓ separate words with spaces?
✓ use correct punctuation?

Self-Selected Reading and Read Aloud D.E.A.R.

Read aloud *I Met a Dinosaur* by Jan Wahl. After reading, have children discuss what they liked and disliked about the book.

Grammar: Adjectives

Review Adjectives That Tell How Many Remind children that adjectives tell about people, places, or things. Show children three balls of different sizes. Ask them to give an adjective that tells *how many* to describe the balls. Check to see that children respond with a number, rather than a color, size, or shape.

Guess How Many
Provide buttons and similar objects that children can organize into groups. One partner chooses a specific number of objects and places the objects on the table. The other partner must then give an adjective to tell how many.

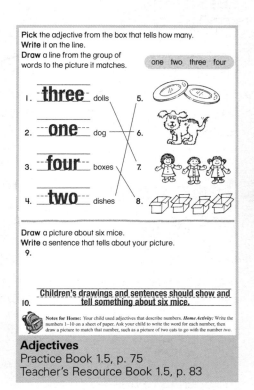

Adjectives
Practice Book 1.5, p. 75
Teacher's Resource Book 1.5, p. 83

Day
3

❄ Meeting Individual Needs

ESL	Intervention	Challenge	Other Ways to Learn
Provide two books and six pencils. Have children say phrases to tell how many they see of each. **(Skill Support)** See also *Adding English*. ESL	Write the phrases below on sentence strips. Have children circle each adjective: *three cats, five dogs, eight balls.* **(Comprehension Support)**	Have pairs of children use the Challenge Words for larger numbers in oral sentences. They may also write the Challenge Words and corresponding numbers on separate cards and then match them. **(Application of Different Symbol Systems)**	Ask children, "How many eyes do you have? How many noses? How many ears? How many toes?" Have children point to the body part and then hold up the correct numbers of fingers to show the answer as they answer aloud in phrases. **(Kinesthetic)**

Reader Response

Student Book, pp. 188–189

Let's Talk

Personal Response Guide discussion about dinosaur facts through modeling. For example, say:

I learned that baby dinosaurs were born with teeth. I was surprised to learn that some dinosaurs ate bugs.

Encourage children to share their responses.

Let's Think

Critical Response Children may mention differences such as: dinosaurs hatch from eggs, but a foal does not; dinosaur babies are born with teeth, but a foal takes time to grow teeth. Children may mention likenesses such as: both need someone to take care of them; both get bigger.

Test Prep

Let's Write

Written Response Brainstorm with the class what they think life was like in the days of the dinosaurs. List their responses on the chalkboard. Then have children write about what they would like and not like about living in the days of the dinosaurs.

Features for this writing product are listed below 4 in the Scoring Rubric.

Make a Dinosaur

Creative Response Have children make a dinosaur diorama. You may provide the following materials: shoe boxes, modeling clay, construction paper, scissors, tape, art supplies, and natural materials such as rocks, twigs, and pinecones.

When children finish making their dinosaurs and dinosaur homes, set them up as a dinosaur exhibit.

Use the **Selection Test** in Practice Book 1.5, pages 77–78 or Teacher's Resource Book 1.5, pages 85–86.

Read Together

Reader Response

Let's Talk

What did you learn about dinosaurs? What surprised you?

Let's Think

Look back at the stories "Foal" and "Dinosaur Babies." How is a baby dinosaur different from a foal? How are they the same?

Test Prep
Let's Write

Pretend that you lived in the days of the dinosaurs. Write sentences. Tell what would you have liked most about it. Tell what would you have liked least about it.

188

Dinosaur Babies, page 188

Scoring Rubric for Written Response	
4	**3**
• clearly expresses personal preferences • is arranged in an order that makes sense • expresses a complete idea in each sentence • begins all sentences with capital letters and ends with correct punctuation	• expresses personal preferences • is mostly in a logical order • expresses most ideas in complete sentences • may have a poorly formed capital letter at beginning or incorrect punctuation at end of one or two sentences
2	**1**
• attempts to express personal preferences • is slightly out of order • may be missing parts of some sentences • may be missing a capital letter at beginning or punctuation at end of some sentences	• does not express personal preferences • is confusing or out of order • consists of scattered words or phrases • lacks both capital letters and end punctuation

Make a Dinosaur

You know a lot about how dinosaurs lived and how they looked. You can make a dinosaur of your own.

1. Get what you need.
2. Shape a dinosaur out of clay.
3. Make a home for your dinosaur. Put it inside.
4. Write the dinosaur's name on the top of the box.

189

Dinosaur Babies, page 189

Skills in Context

Review

Cause and Effect

Reread pages 172, 180, and 181 in *Dinosaur Babies.* Ask children why the mother dinosaur brought the babies food. (The mother brought food because the babies were too small to get it on their own.) Then ask why the dinosaurs made a circle and put the babies on the inside. (Enemies tried to grab the babies and eat them. The baby dinosaurs were safe inside the circle.)

Reread for Fluency

Selection Audio Have children listen to the CD or tape of *Dinosaur Babies* as they follow along in their books.

CD 7/Tape 25, Side 1

Read with Expression Have children work in pairs to reread the selection by alternating pages. Remind children to read the lines as if they were talking.

Day 4

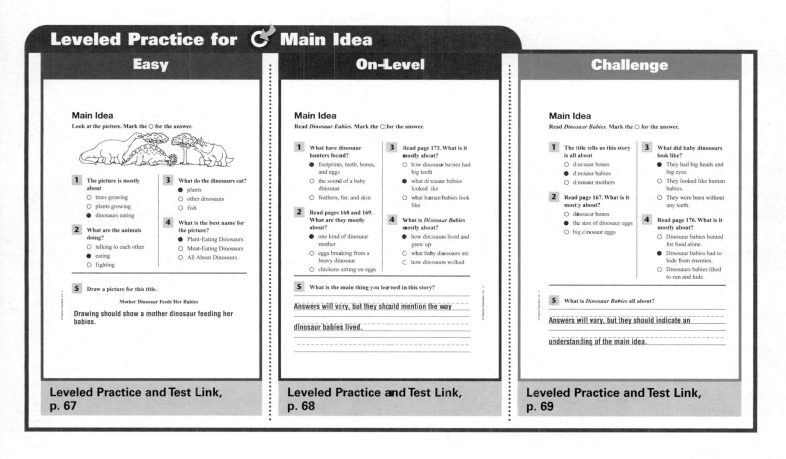

Vowel Sounds of *y*
Compound Words

▶Reteach

Write *funny* and *sunny*. Tell children that *y* stands for the long *e* sound. Ask children to name words that rhyme with *funny* and *sunny*. List them on the board. Then write *my* and *why*. Tell children that *y* can stand for the long *i* sound. Have children name rhyming words for *my* and *why*. Say words that end in *y* (both /ē/ and /ī/). Have children identify the final sound as /ē/ or /ī/.

List *redbird, snowflake, rainbow, rosebud,* and *baseball* on the board. Have volunteers read the words and identify the two words that form them.

See page AR17 of this Teacher's Edition for additional **reteach activities.**

Review Endings -*ed* and -*ing*

Make bingo cards that have two columns of five boxes. On each card, randomly place five words ending with -*ed* and five words ending with -*ing*. Write each word on a separate index card. Pass out the bingo cards. Call out the words on the index cards and have children put a marker on each word you call. Children call "Bingo!" when they have a whole column covered.

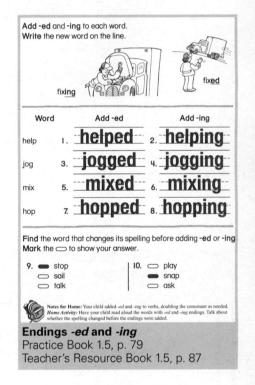

Add -ed and -ing to each word.
Write the new word on the line.

Word	Add -ed	Add -ing
help	1. **helped**	2. **helping**
jog	3. **jogged**	4. **jogging**
mix	5. **mixed**	6. **mixing**
hop	7. **hopped**	8. **hopping**

Find the word that changes its spelling before adding -ed or -ing
Mark the ⊂⊃ to show your answer.

9. ● stop   10. ⊂⊃ play
⊂⊃ sail   ⊂⊃ snap
⊂⊃ talk   ● ask

Notes for Home: Your child added -*ed* and -*ing* to verbs, doubling the consonant as needed. **Home Activity:** Have your child read aloud the words with -*ed* and -*ing* endings. Talk about whether the spelling changed before the endings were added.

Endings -*ed* and -*ing*
Practice Book 1.5, p. 79
Teacher's Resource Book 1.5, p. 87

Day 4

 Meeting Individual Needs

ESL	Intervention	Challenge	Other Ways to Learn
Make slide word cards. On the horizontal strip of paper, write -*y*. On the vertical strip write *b, m, cr, fl, sk, dr, tr*. Read each word, using pantomime when needed to help children understand meaning. Have children repeat each word. Then have them read the words with a partner. **(Phonics Support)** See also *Adding English*. **ESL**	Prepare word cards for *happy, messy, funny, foggy, skinny, muddy*. Read the words together. Point to the *y* in each word and have children say the sound it stands for. Then mix the cards and using them as flash cards, have children read the words on their own. **(Phonics Support)**	Children look through books to list compound words. They use as many of the words as they can in a rap song about compound words. **(Application of Different Symbol Systems)**	Provide word cards for both long *e* and long *i* spelled *y*. Children sort the cards according to the vowel sound of *y*. **(Visual/Spatial)**

Spelling Vowel *y* Words

▶ Partner Spelling Practice

Children work in pairs. Have each child make a set of cards with one spelling word per card. Give each pair a generic game board and a spinner or number cube. Players take turns asking each other to spell a word from his or her deck. If the player spells the word correctly, the player spins or rolls and moves that number of spaces on the board.

Spelling
Practice Book 1.5, p. 80
Teacher's Resource Book 1.5, p. 88

Word Wall

Review High-Frequency Words

Crosswords Prepare a crossword puzzle using five Word Wall words. Write the puzzle on a board or on a transparency for a whole group activity, or on separate sheets of paper for pairs to complete. Give clues for each word.

Optional Resources

Phonics
Phonics Workbook, pp. 146–148, 150
Phonics Manipulatives Kit
AstroWord CD-ROM, Compound Words
Reading Road Show

High-Frequency Words
High-Frequency Word Cards
Phonics Sourcebook, pp. 90–99

Language Arts

Student Book, pp. 190–191

Adjectives That Tell How Many

Have children read aloud with you the information about adjectives. Ask children to tell words for numbers.

Have the two example sentences read. Ask children to identify the adjective and noun in each example sentence.

Talk

Have children describe the pictures. Encourage them to use number adjectives in their descriptions.

Write

Guide children as they copy the sentences and circle the adjectives that tell how many. When everyone has finished, review the responses and have children correct their mistakes.

Then ask children to write sentences that include adjectives that tell how many. Have children circle the adjectives.

Use the Teacher's Resource Book 1.5 pages 89–90 for **reteaching** and extra practice for adjectives of number.

Day 4

Dinosaur Babies, page 190

Self-Selected Reading and Read Aloud D.E.A.R.

Read aloud *An Alphabet of Dinosaurs* by Peter Dodson. Children choose a fiction or nonfiction book about dinosaurs.

Write

Write the sentences. Circle the adjectives that tell how many.

1. **Some footprints show four toes.**
2. **One nest has ten eggs in it.**
3. **Tyrannosaurus ran on two legs.**

Write your own sentences.
Use adjectives that tell how many.
Circle the adjectives.

191

Dinosaur Babies, **page 191**

Study Skill

Take Notes

Have children turn to the nonfiction selection *Dinosaur Babies* on page 164 in their books. Ask them to page through the selection to recall facts. Then explain that one way to remember important facts is to write them down. Print the heading *How Baby Dinosaurs Stayed Safe* on the board and read aloud pages 176–182. Model how to take notes by listing facts under the heading.

Model Your Thinking

Think ALOUD **I want to remember how some baby dinosaurs stayed safe from predators. In the pages I read, the author mentions a few facts about this. I will use my own words to write the facts. First, I'll write *Baby dinosaurs hid*. Next, I'll write *Triceratops babies lived in herds* and *Triceratops babies stayed safe in the middle of a circle of adults*. Finally, I can reread my list to remember how some baby dinosaurs stayed safe.**

Practice Children can work in small groups to read pages of *Dinosaur Babies* and take notes. Assign topics such as these: *How We Know About Dinosaurs* (pages 166–167); *Facts About Dinosaur Nests and Eggs* (pages 168–171); *What Baby Dinosaurs Looked Like* (page 173); *What Baby Dinosaurs Ate* (pages 174–175). Circulate to monitor how well children understand how to take notes. Have groups read their completed notes to the class.

Day 4

Objectives

Children will

- identify main idea
- use sound-symbol relationships to read decodable text
- recognize high-frequency words
- read with accuracy and comprehension

Meeting Individual Needs

ESL

To help children prepare, choose several key phrases from the story and record them on tape. Have children listen to these phrases over and over again until they can read them on their own.

Optional Resources

Assessment
The Assessment Handbook has information on running records.

191a Reading

Assess Accuracy and Comprehension

▶ Prepare for the Assessment

Materials Have children prepare by rereading *Dinosaur Babies, Chompy's Afternoon,* or other stories or books they've read this week. The assessment selection on page 191b reviews phonics skills and vocabulary previously introduced.

▶ Listen to Individual Readers

Ask children to read the selection on page 191b aloud.

- If the child cannot read three or more words in the first sentence, discontinue the reading assessment. Read the story aloud to the child and label the test as Listening Comprehension.

- If the child reads the story independently, keep the story in front of the child as you ask the five questions. Label the test as Reading Comprehension. Read aloud the comprehension questions to children and have them answer them.

See page AR18 in this Teacher's Edition to **reteach** main idea.

▶ While You Assess

While you work with individuals, other children may choose from the following activities or the activities listed in the Cross-Curricular Work Stations on pages 156g–h.

Before They Read to You

Children should reread the chosen book with a partner and then ask each other questions about the book.

Children may listen to the CD or tape of *Dinosaur Babies* or *Chompy's Afternoon* to hear a model of fluent reading.

Selection Audio

CD 7/Tape 25, Side 1

After They Read to You

Children can complete a Reading Log like the one shown or use Practice Book 1.5 page 105, or the Teacher's Resource Book 1.6 page 112.

Children can also complete the phonics activities on page 191c.

Name_____

I read *Dinosaur Babies*

It was about

Words I Can Now Read and Write

Accuracy and Comprehension Assessment

Name _____

Mark type of assessment. ☐ Listening Comprehension
                          ☐ Reading Comprehension

Number of Words Miscalled _____
Frustrational (below 90%: 8 or more miscalled)
Instructional (91–97%: 2–7 miscalled)
Independent (98% and above: 0–1 miscalled)

	Correct	Incorrect
1. Main Idea/Inferential **What is this story all about?** Jeff saw a dinosaur.		
2. Cause and Effect/Literal **Why does Ana say it is impossible that Jeff saw a dinosaur?** The last dinosaurs died out a long time ago.		
3. Hypothesize/Critical **What do you think made the heavy steps that Ana and Jeff heard?** Possible answer: It could be other children running to see the dinosaur.		
4. Details/Literal **Where does Jeff take Ana?** Jeff takes Ana across the street.		
5. Drawing Conclusions/Inferential **What kind of dinosaur do you think Ana and Jeff saw?** Possible answers: A balloon, a kite, a cloud, or perhaps a blimp.		

Scoring: Score 1 point for each correct answer. Number correct (Literal) _____ Number correct (Inferential/Critical)_____

✂ -

"Ana! Over there!" yelled Jeff. "Look at that dinosaur!"

"Where?" said Ana. "I don't think you saw a dinosaur!"

"Yes, I did! It is across the street around those shops!"

"I don't think so," said Ana. "There are no dinosaurs."

"I'll prove it!" said Jeff. "Follow me." Jeff and Ana went

across the street. Then they heard heavy steps.

Ana looked up and saw a fierce dinosaur in the sky.

"You were not fooling, were you?" said Ana.

Day
5

Vowel Sounds of *y*
Compound Words

▶ Phonics Practice Activities

Story Ask children to make up a group story using words with the long *e* and long *i* sounds of *y* as well as compound words they learned this week.

Phonics Take-Home Reader Have children practice reading the book with a partner before taking it home.

My Mail

by Kathy Mormile
illustrated by George Ulrich

Phonics Take-Home Reader

Objectives

Children will

- spell words with vowel *y* (long *e* and long *i*)
- use sound/symbol relationships as visual cues for decoding
- recognize high-frequency words

Spelling Test

Have children number their papers. Read the underlined word, read the sentence, then repeat the underlined word.

1. That joke about dinosaurs is <u>funny</u>.
2. <u>Why</u> did all the dinosaurs die?
3. A <u>baby</u> dinosaur hatched from an egg.
4. <u>My</u> favorite dinosaur is the tyrannosaurus rex.
5. <u>Many</u> dinosaurs ate plants.
6. Some dinosaurs could <u>fly</u> like birds.

High-Frequency Words

7. Scientists <u>even</u> found dinosaur eggs still in the nest.
8. <u>Most</u> dinosaurs had long tails.

Challenge Words

9. <u>Nobody</u> knows what dinosaurs sounded like.
10. Dinosaurs couldn't live <u>without</u> food and water.

Word Wall

Practice High-Frequency Words

Secret Code Tell children that you are going to name a child in the room using a secret code. The code is that the first letter of each high-frequency word you say is also the first letter of a child's name.

Say the "secret word" and the child's name. Have children stand up as they figure out the code.

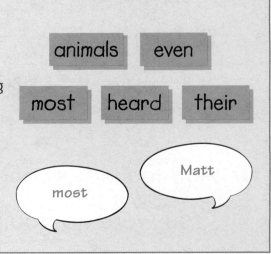

animals   even

most   heard   their

most   Matt

Day 5

ORAL LANGUAGE

Speaking: Tell an Original Story in Order

Tell children to pretend that they have traveled in a time machine to Chompy's world. Have them make up a story all their own about their adventures with Chompy. Remind children to tell what happens in their story in time order. Have children tell their stories to the class. Suggest that listeners raise their hands when they hear a time-order word or phrase, such as *first, next, then, last,* or *at the end.*

E-mail Note

► Interactive Writing

In this method of writing, you and the children work together. If possible, provide the e-mail note below as a computer print-out. If time and equipment allow, key the e-mail note into the computer as children participate in the activity. While you create your note, children write on their own papers. As you write, point out the importance of correct end punctuation.

E-mail a Friend Children will write an e-mail message to tell a friend about a time-travel trip to visit Chompy. Leave blanks in the message for children to complete. Ask children to discuss how they might fill in the blanks.

> Dear José,
>
>   I'm visiting a dinosaur! His name is Chompy. I saw _____ yesterday, and I rode on a _____. You wouldn't believe the size of the _____! I have to go now. I will see you soon.
>
>   Your friend,
>
>   _____

Independent Writing Have children write in the missing words independently. Remind them to write interesting information and to sign the note. Allow those children who are comfortable with and knowledgeable about e-mail and typing to write their messages directly on the computer.

Portfolio Children may wish to select a piece of writing from this week to put in their portfolios.

Objectives

Children will

- tell an original story in time order
- contribute ideas during a group writing activity

Speaker's Checklist

Did you . . .

✓ use time-order words?
✓ speak clearly?
✓ speak loud enough for all to hear?
✓ make eye contact with listeners?
✓ make the story interesting?

Self-Selected Reading and Read Aloud

Ask children to name a favorite book you have shared with them. Read it aloud. After reading, discuss with children their likes and dislikes about the book.

Optional Resources

Phonics
Phonics Workbook, pp. 146–148

High-Frequency Words
High-Frequency Word Cards
Phonics Sourcebook, pp. 90-99

Oral Language
Adding English: ESL Teacher's Guide

Assessment
The Assessment Handbook has information on informal assessment and grading.

Day
5

Lesson Overview

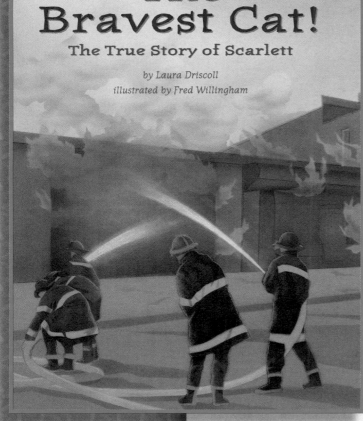

Phonics Story

*The True Story
of Abbie Burgess*
pages 192–199

Selection Audio

The **Phonics Story** . . .

- introduces ⟳ **Vowel Pattern** *ew, ue* and **Inflected and Plural** *-es*

- introduces the high-frequency words

    because better give people put

- builds fluency

- builds decoding skills

> **Use the Phonics Story to prepare children for reading the Main Selection.**

Main Selection

*The Bravest Cat!
The True Story of Scarlett*
pages 200–221

Selection Audio

The **Main Selection** . . .

- introduces ⟳ **Cause and Effect**

- practices ⟳ **Vowel Pattern** *ew, ue* and **Inflected and Plural** *-es*

- practices the high-frequency words

    because better give people put

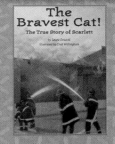

TEST Format

Leveled Practice
in Test Format
for *The Bravest Cat! The True Story of Scarlett*

TARGET SKILL **Cause and Effect**

Leveled Readers

TARGET SKILL
Cause and Effect
Tested Vocabulary

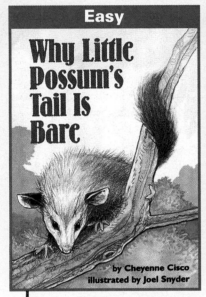

Easy

Why Little Possum's Tail Is Bare

by Cheyenne Cisco
illustrated by Joel Snyder

Leveled Reader 24A

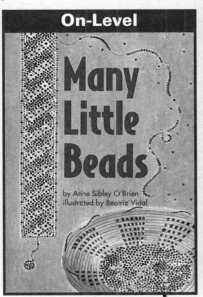

On-Level

Many Little Beads

by Anne Sibley O'Brien
illustrated by Beatriz Vidal

Leveled Reader 24B

For Guided Reading
see Teacher's Edition,
pp. LR31–LR36.

Challenge

Take Me There

Collected Readings

Leveled Reader 5C

For instruction and leveled practice answers, see Teacher's Edition, pp. LR39–LR45.

Practice for Leveled Readers

Easy

Cause and Effect

Read the story *Why Little Possum's Tail Is Bare.* Then answer Numbers 1 through 5.

1 This is a make-believe story that tells

- ○ why possums run from cats.
- ● why bees sting.
- ○ why possums have bare tails.

2 This story teaches us that

- ● we should listen to our mothers.
- ○ we should stay away from possums.
- ○ we should try to see everything.

3 Little Possum gets too close to the fire. What happens?

- ○ The fire goes out.
- ● The fire burns his tail.
- ○ The fire burns his ears.

4 The story tells us that all possums have bare tails because

- ○ Little Possum had to see the bees.
- ○ Little Possum listened to his mother.
- ● Little Possum got too close to the fire.

5 Little Possum puts his nose in the beehive. What happens? Use story words in your answer.

Little Possum gets a bee sting.

Teacher's Edition, p. LR33

On-Level

Cause and Effect

Read the story *Many Little Beads.* Then answer Numbers 1 through 5.

1 Who made Robin's bracelet?

- ○ a girl who works at the mall
- ● a girl who lives far away
- ○ a woman who lives down the street

2 Look at pages 6 and 7. Why does the woman buy the bracelet?

- ○ She wants to wear it.
- ○ She wants to sell it.
- ● She likes the many little beads.

3 What does the woman do with the bracelet?

- ● She sends it to Robin.
- ○ She keeps it in a bag.
- ○ She wears it every day.

4 Who sent the bracelet to Robin?

- ● her mother's sister
- ○ her mother
- ○ her dad

5 What happens when Robin looks at her bracelet? Use words from the story in your answer.

Robin smiles. Robin thinks of the girl far away.

Teacher's Edition, p. LR36

Challenge

Reader Response

Think About a Question
1 Where will we go? How will we grow? Both Gunnar and the farmer went to new places. Think of new places you have been. What did you learn? Write your answer.

Ask a Question
2 Write five questions that you might ask Gunnar about doing his job.

Use New Words
3 Look for new words in *The Bravest Dog Ever.* Act out the words for a friend. Can they guess the meaning of each word?

Correct What You Read
4 Think about the people in the stories. How are they the same? How are they different? Write about your ideas.

Take a Careful Look
5 What was the problem in each story? Tell what Gunnar and the farmer did to fix the problem.

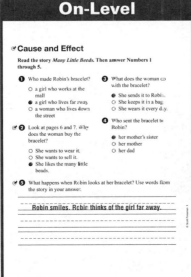

32 Take Me There

Leveled Reader 5C, p. 32

Easy

Cause and Effect

Look at the picture. Mark the ○ for the answer.

1 Who is in the tree?
- ○ a man
- ● a cat
- ○ a dog

2 Why is the dog barking?
- ○ to help the cat
- ● to scare the cat
- ○ to scare the man

3 Why is the cat in the tree?
- ● to get away from the dog
- ○ to get away from the man
- ○ to get a drink of water

4 Why does the man come?
- ○ to get the dog
- ○ to cut the tree down
- ● to get the cat

5 What will happen to the cat next? Write words and draw a picture.

Answers will vary, but words and drawings should conclude that the man will get the cat out of the tree.

On-Level

Cause and Effect

Read *The Bravest Cat!* Mark the ○ for the answer.

1 Why do the firefighters come?
- ○ They are in Brooklyn.
- ● There is a fire.
- ○ There is a cat in a building.

2 Read page 205. Why does the cat go back?
- ○ She is running away from the fire.
- ○ She wants to find a new safe place.
- ● She has to get more kittens.

3 Why does the firefighter take the cats to a hospital?
- ○ They are hungry.
- ● They need a doctor.
- ○ They need a home.

4 People think the mother cat is brave because
- ○ she has five kittens.
- ● she saves her kittens.
- ○ she sees a fire.

5 Why do you think the mother cat saved her kittens?

Answers will vary. Possible answer: She saves them because she loves them and doesn't want them to be hurt.

Challenge

Cause and Effect

Read *The Bravest Cat!* Mark the ○ for the answer.

1 Why are no people hurt in the fire?
- ○ The cat saves them.
- ● No people live in the garage.
- ○ The firemen save them.

2 The mother cat cannot see, so she
- ○ cries for the firemen
- ● counts her kittens with her nose
- ○ runs back into the fire

3 The doctors call the cat Scarlett because
- ● it means red and she has red burns
- ○ it is the firemen's favorite name
- ○ it was the name on her collar

4 Why is Karen a good person to care for Scarlett?
- ○ She was the first person to say she wanted Scarlett.
- ● She knows what Scarlett went through.
- ○ She wrote a letter.

5 Why do you think so many people wrote letters?

Answers will vary. Possible answer: People wanted to give the cats a good home because they felt sorry for them.

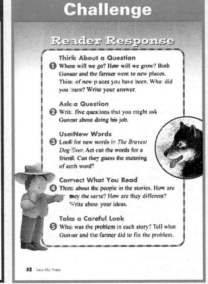

Leveled Practice and Test Link, pp. 70–72, *The Bravest Cat!*

192b

Additional Leveled Resources

Phonics Resources

Phonics Reader 30

Phonics Take-Home Readers in Reproducible Format

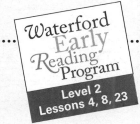

Book 30

Decodable Readers 40 and 41

Waterford
Early
Reading
Program
Level 2
Lessons 4, 8, 23

Language Support

Adding English
pp. 201–208

Ten Important Sentences
p. 36

Trade Books for Self-Selected Reading

Easy

Come Along, Daisy!
by Jane Simmons. Little, Brown, 1998

Good Dog, Carl
by Alexandra Day. Simon & Schuster, 1985

Hide and Seek in the Yellow House
by Agatha Rose. Puffin, 1995

On-Level

This Is the Way We Go to School
by Edith Baer. Scholastic, 1992
Trade Book Library Title

Where's That Cat?
by Eve Merriam and Pam Pollack. Margaret K. McElderry Books, 2000.

If You Were a Cat
by S. J. Calder. Silver, 1989

Challenge

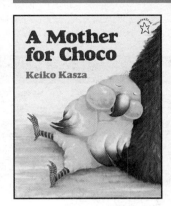

A Mother for Choco
by Keiko Kasza. Paper Star, 1996
Trade Book Library Title

Cat Poems
selected by Myra Cohn Livingston. Holiday House, 1987

My New Kitten
by Joanna Cole. William Morrow, 1995

Self-Selected Reading

- Allow 10–20 minutes per day for self-selected reading.
- For additional titles and for a read-aloud suggestion, see pp. AR24–AR25.
- For daily self-selected reading suggestions, see the 5-Day Planner, pp. 192e–192f.
- For activity ideas and management tips, see p. AR25.

- Have children select materials to read for pleasure, such as favorite books and stories.

Developmental Reading Assessment (DRA) from Celebration Press, an imprint of Pearson Learning, helps teachers by providing and documenting students' development as readers over time.

5-Day Planner

Reading

Comprehension

Vocabulary

Fluency

Independent Reading

Phonics/Word Study

Phonemic Awareness

Phonics

Spelling

High-Frequency Words

Oral Language

Speaking, Listening, Viewing

Oral Vocabulary

Writing

Grammar, Usage, Mechanics

Your State Standards

Customize your week with the Teacher's Resource Planner CD-ROM!

Day 1

Activate Prior Knowledge, p. 192j

Phonics pp. 192k–192l

Phonemic Awareness: Vowel Patterns *ew, ue*

✓ **Phonics:** Introduce Vowel Patterns *ew, ue*; Inflected Ending *-es* and Plural *-es*
PHONICS SONGS AND RHYMES CHART "Bluey and Dewey"

Spelling: *ew, ue* Words
Pretest
Work with Spelling Pattern

High-Frequency Words: Introduce **because, better, give, people, put**

Reading pp. 192m–199

Story Vocabulary

Read Pupil Edition PHONICS STORY:
The True Story of Abbie Burgess

Independent Reading
Self-Selected Reading, pp. 192d; AR24

Oral Language pp. 192m, 199a

Build Oral Language

Expand Vocabulary: Discuss Comparatives

Writing pp. 192i, 199a–199b

✓ **Writing Process:** Class Research Report *Prewrite*

Handwriting: *Pp*

Daily Writing Prompt: Write a list of ways you help at home.

Day 2

Phonics pp. 199c–199d

✓ **Phonics:** Practice Vowel Patterns *ew, ue*; Inflected Ending *-es* and Plural *-es*

Apply Phonics: Read the **PHONICS READER** *Sue Blew a Big Bubble* **OR DECODABLE READER** 40

Spelling: Writing for Sounds

High-Frequency Words: Practice

PB 1.5: Phonics, pp. 83, 84;
High-Frequency Words, p. 85
TRB 1.5: Phonics, pp. 93, 94;
High-Frequency Words, p. 95

Reading pp. 199e–199f

✓ **Comprehension:** Cause and Effect
READ ALOUD "The Accidental Hero"

Fluency: Reread the **PHONICS STORY:**
The True Story of Abbie Burgess

PB 1.5: Cause and Effect, p. 86
TRB 1.5: Cause and Effect, p. 96

Independent Reading
Self-Selected Reading, pp. 192d; AR24

Oral Language p. 199g

Speaking: Small Group Discussion

Writing pp. 192i, 199g–199h

✓ **Writing Process:** Class Research Report *Draft*

✓ **Grammar:** Adjectives

PB 1.5: p. 87; **TRB 1.5:** p. 97

Daily Writing Prompt: Write about a time when you were brave.

 **Target Skill**  **Review Skill**   **Assessment**

PB Practice Book
TRB Teacher's Resource Book

pp. 70–72

Reading

Leveled Practice and Test Link in TerraNova, SAT9, or ITBS format

Target Skills of the Week

Reading Cause and Effect

Phonics Vowel Patterns *ew, ue*; Inflected Ending *-es* and Plural *-es*

Oral Language Small Group Discussion

Writing Adjectives

Day 3

Reading pp. 200a–223

Story Vocabulary

Read Pupil Edition MAIN SELECTION: *The Bravest Cat!*

Read Pupil Edition POEM

Comprehension: Cause and Effect

Guided Reading Resources/Flexible Groups, pp. 200b; LR31–LR36 Leveled Readers 24A, 24B, 5C

PB 1.5: Vocabulary, p. 88
TRB 1.5: Vocabulary, p. 98

Independent Reading
Self-Selected Reading, pp. 192d; AR24

Phonics pp. 223a–223b

✓ **Phonics:** Practice Vowel Patterns *ew, ue*; Inflected Ending *-es* and Plural *-es*

✓ Review **Vowel Sounds of** *y*

Fluency: Reread the PHONICS READER *Sue Blew a Big Bubble* or DECODABLE READER 41

Spelling: Practice with Writing

High-Frequency Words: Practice

PB 1.5: Phonics, p. 89; Spelling, p. 90
TRB 1.5: Phonics, p. 99; Spelling, p. 100

Oral Language pp. 200a, 223c

Build Oral Language

✓ **Expand Vocabulary:** Unfamiliar Words

Writing pp. 192i, 223c–223d

✓ **Writing Process:** Class Research Report *Revise, Edit*

✓ **Grammar:** Adjectives

PB 1.5: pp. 91, 97, 92; **TRB 1.5:** pp. 101, 109, 102; **GPB:** p. 52

Daily Writing Prompt: Write a list of things you should do in a fire.

Day 4

Reading pp. 224–225

Read Together Pupil Edition
READER RESPONSE *Test Prep*

Selection Test

PB 1.5: Selection Test, pp. 93–94
TRB 1.5: Selection Test, pp. 103–104

✓ Review **Comprehension:** Main Idea

Fluency: Reread the MAIN SELECTION

Guided Reading Resources/Flexible Groups, pp. 200b; LR31–LR36 Leveled Readers 24A, 24B, 5C

Independent Reading
Self-Selected Reading, pp. 192d; AR24

Phonics pp. 225a–225b

✓ **Phonics:** Reteach Vowel Patterns *ew, ue*; Inflected Ending *-es* and Plural *-es*

Review **Final Digraphs** *-ng, -nk*

Spelling: Partner Practice

High-Frequency Words: Review

PB 1.5: Phonics, p. 95; Spelling, p. 96
TRB 1.5: Phonics, p. 105; Spelling, p. 106

Oral Language pp. 226–227

Speaking: Talk About Adjectives

Writing pp. 192i, 226–227

✓ **Grammar:** Adjectives

Writing: Identify Adjectives

TRB 1.5: pp. 107–108; **GPB:** p. 53

Daily Writing Prompt: Write a letter telling why you would give Scarlett a good home.

Day 5

Reading pp. 227a–227b

Assess Oral Reading: Oral Reading Checklist

Guided Reading Resources/Flexible Groups, pp. 200b; LR31–LR36 Leveled Readers 24A, 24B, 5C

Independent Reading
Self-Selected Reading, pp. 192d; AR24

Phonics p. 227c

✓ **Phonics:** Practice Vowel Patterns *ew, ue*; Inflected Ending *-es* and Plural *-es*

Apply Phonics: Read the PHONICS TAKE-HOME READER

Spelling: *ew, ue* Words

Posttest

High-Frequency Words: Practice

Oral Language p. 227d

Speaking: Small Group Discussion

Writing pp. 192i, 227d

✓ **Writing Process:** Class Research Report *Publish Portfolio*

Daily Writing Prompt: Write why someone you know is a hero.

Cross-Curricular Work Stations

Letters and Sounds

Pantomime 15 minutes

Materials: index cards

Learning Styles Visual, Kinesthetic, Spatial

On each index card, write an *ew, ue* word that can be acted out, such as *glue, blew, chew, drew, flew, grew,* and *threw.*

Have small groups place cards face down on a table. One child takes a card and reads it silently. Then the child acts out the meaning of the word while group members figure out which *ew, ue* word it is.

 ESL Preview with children the pronunciations and meanings of the words on the index cards.

Writing

Scarlett's Headline 15 minutes

Materials: newspaper and magazine headlines, paper, crayons, pencils, or word processing program (optional)

Learning Style Verbal

Provide examples of newspaper headlines. Explain that headlines usually contain only important words and are not whole sentences. Have children write a headline for an article about a human or animal hero. They may illustrate their headlines if they want. Children might choose to create their headlines using a word processing function.

Challenge Invite children to write an article to go with their headline. Suggest that they write about what the hero did and why he, she, or it is a hero.

Media

Our Heroes 15 minutes

Materials: newspaper and magazine photos, paper, pencils

Learning Styles Visual, Linguistic, Social

Provide current newspaper and magazine photographs that show firefighters, police officers, paramedics, and community service workers helping others. Ask partners to write a caption about the photo. Suggest that they focus their viewpoint on either the helper or the person being helped.

INTERNET SAFETY Establish guidelines for your students' safe and responsible use of the Internet. See the Scott Foresman Internet Guide for tips.

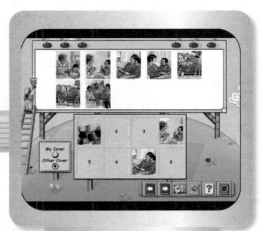

Technology

Book Builder Activity 🚶 ⏱ 15 minutes

Learning Style Individual

Have children create their own heroes book. Remind children that they can use the graphics provided in the program or draw their own illustrations. Children can also add audio to their book presentation.

Reading Web Site 🚶 ⏱ 15 minutes

Learning Style Individual

sfreading.com

WWW Children can visit the Scott Foresman *Reading* Web site (sfreading.com) for current hyperlinks to relevant electronic texts that can be used for an Internet Workshop investigation of heroism. Also see the Scott Foresman Internet Guide for additional information on the Internet Workshop method.

Math

Measure Up! 🚶🚶 ⏱ 15 minutes

Materials: paper, rulers, pencils

Learning Styles Logical, Visual, Spatial

Explain to children that full-grown cats are about 8 to 10 inches tall from the floor to their shoulders. Allow partners to estimate and then measure objects in the classroom that are about 8 to 10 inches in one direction. Have children make a sketch of the objects and record the estimate and the actual measure.

Estimate: 8 inches
Actual: 10 inches

Science

What Do Cats Need to Grow? 🚶🚶 ⏱ 15 minutes

Materials: paper, markers or crayons, scissors, glue, magazines

Learning Styles Visual, Logical, Kinesthetic

Have children create "Healthy Cats" collages. Pictures should show cats and examples of things that keep them healthy and happy, such as water, food, exercise, toys, and lots of love.

CROSSING CULTURES Have children plot on a map or globe the places where certain breeds of cats were first bred.

Type of Cat	Origin
Abyssinian	Abyssinia (now Ethiopia)
Siamese	Siam (now Thailand)
Burmese	Burma (now Myanmar)
Persian	Persia (now Iran) and Afghanistan

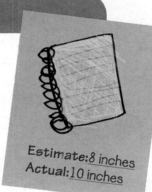

Daily Routines

Message Board

Day One

Today you will hear a story about a lion and a mouse. Do you think even someone little can be a helper?

Have children discuss ways they could help someone bigger than themselves.

Have children find the high-frequency words *put* and *people*. Which word tells about *nights*? *(many)*

Day Two

You read about Abbie Burgess. She put a lamp in the lighthouse for many nights. How did the lamp help people?

Have children find the high-frequency words *put* and *because*. Have children find the spelling word *true* and tell which letters stand for the vowel sound in *true* and *news*. *(ue, ew)*

Day Three

You will read a true story about a cat. She was put on the news because she was a hero. How could a cat be a hero?

Have children find the high-frequency words *better* and *give* and the spelling word *new*. Have children find the describing words. *(many, new, better, good)*

Day Four

Many people wanted to give Scarlett a new and better home. What makes a good home for a cat?

Day Five

You read about some heroes this week. What other things can heroes do to help people?

Have children find the high-frequency word *people*. Then ask which letters show the plural ending of *heroes*. *(es)*

Journal Writing

Day One
Write a list of ways you help at home.

Day Two
Write about a time when you were brave.

Day Three
Write a list of things you should do in a fire.

Day Four
Write a letter telling why you would give Scarlett a good home.

Day Five
Write why someone you know is a hero.

Family Times

Send home the newsletter with daily instructional activities to reinforce this week's skills.

Practice Book 1.5, pp. 81–82
Teacher's Resource Book 1.5, pp. 91–92

Activate Prior Knowledge

▶ Assess Prior Knowledge

Discuss Stories of Heroes Talk with children about what they think a hero is. Share your ideas too. Ask:

What do you think it takes to be a hero?

Can anybody be a hero? Can a pet be a hero? Tell why.

What stories about heroes have you read or heard?

▶ Build Background

Read Aloud

Preview the Fable Explain that this fable is about a mouse who saves a lion. Help children set a purpose for listening, such as to learn how "little" friends can be "big" heroes.

Read the Fable Share this fable with children. Invite children to tell a story about a time when they were heroes—when they did something to help someone else.

Objectives

Children will

- activate prior knowledge of topic: Stories of Heroes
- relate literature to experiences in their own life
- draw on experiences of others to form a broader perspective of the topic
- set a purpose for listening

Day
1

Read Aloud

The Lion and the Mouse

An Aesop Fable retold by Sandra Corniels

One day a lion fell asleep outside his cave. By accident, a tiny mouse bumped into the lion. In a flash the lion woke up and caught the mouse in his paw.

"Please spare me," begged the mouse. "If you let me go, I will pay you back someday. I will help you. After all, one good turn deserves another."

The lion laughed at the idea of a mouse helping him, but he let the mouse go. "You wouldn't make much of a meal," the lion said. Then he went back to sleep. The lion slept so soundly that he did not hear the hunters. They caught the lion and tied him to a tree with strong ropes. Then they went to get a cage.

The lion roared in fear and anger and tugged at the ropes, but he could not get free. Suddenly the mouse appeared and started to chew the ropes with her sharp teeth. Soon the ropes fell away, and the lion was free.

"Thank you," said the lion. "You saved my life. You helped me just as you said you would. I learned my lesson. Little friends can be the best friends."

Vowel Patterns *ew, ue*

CD 2/Tape 15, Side 2

► Develop Phonemic Awareness

Chant the Rhyme Chart Chant "Bluey and Dewey" or play the CD or tape.

Focus on the /ü/ Sound Say:

> **Bluey and Dewey are both birds. What sound do you hear in the middle of *Bluey* and *Dewey*? (/ü/)**

Have children repeat the sound /ü/ several times, stretching the sound as they say it.

Ask children to clap each time they hear /ü/ in "Bluey and Dewey."

► Connect Sounds to Letters

Teach Point to *Bluey* on the chart and have it read. Say:

> **The letters *ue* in *Bluey* stand for the sound /ü/.**

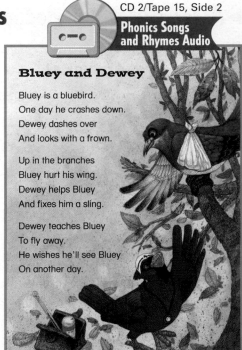

Phonics Songs and Rhymes Chart 24

Have children repeat *Bluey* several times, stretching /ü/ as they say it. Follow a similar procedure with *Dewey* and the letters *ew*. Point out that usually the letters *ue* and *ew* stand for the sound /ü/.

Blending Practice Write *blue* and ask children to blend it. Repeat with *dew*.

| b | l | u | e | | d | e | w |

Make New Words Write the words *dew* and *blue* in separate columns on the board. Ask children to think of rhyming words. Write each word in the appropriate column. Have children go back to decode the words on the board. Add the words *blue* and *dew* to the chunking wall.

dew	blue
stew	true
new	Sue
grew	glue

Then have children change vowel patterns to make *day, stay, gray, tray,* and *say*.

Objectives

Children will

- ⦿ identify and decode words with the vowel patterns *ew* and *ue*
- ⦿ use structural cues to identify and decode words with inflected ending *-es* and plural *-es*
- build words with phonograms *ew* and *ue*, inflected endings and plural *-es*
- spell words with vowel patterns *ew* and *ue*
- recognize high-frequency words

Skills Trace

⦿ **Vowel Patterns *ew, ue***

Introduce/Teach	TE: 1.5 192k
Practice	PB: 1.5 83; 1.6 73
Reteach/Review	TE: 1.5 199c, 223a, 225a, 227c, AR18; 1.6 157a
Test	Skills Test, Unit 5 Benchmark Test, Unit 5

Day 1

 **Meeting Individual Needs**

Intervention

Phonemic Awareness Say /b/ /l/ /ü/. Have children blend the sounds. Repeat the following words slowly, sound by sound: *flew, clue, bright, true, fly, bluebird, dew, die,* and *drew*. Have children blend and then say each whole word. Have them hold up a blue crayon each time they say a word that rhymes with *blue*.

Phonics Generalization

The letters *ew* and *ue* can stand for the sounds /ü/ or /yü/.

Bluey and Dewey

Bluey is a bluebird.
One day he crashes down.
Dewey dashes over
And looks with a frown.

Up in the branches
Bluey hurt his wing.
Dewey helps Bluey
And fixes him a sling.

Dewey teaches Bluey
To fly away.
He wishes he'll see Bluey
On another day.

Inflected Ending -*es* and Plural -*es*

▶ Teach Inflected Ending -*es*

In "One day he crashes down," the word *crash* has an ending. Explain that when the ending -*es* is added to a word, it adds an extra syllable. Ask:

What sound do the letters -*es* stand for? (/ez/)

Repeat the process for *branch* and *branches,* pointing out that the ending -*es* can also mean more than one.

▶ Make New Words

Practice Inflected Ending -*es* and Plural -*es* Write these words on the board: *bush, ranch, march, rush, fish, reach, push.* Read the words aloud with the class. Have volunteers add -*es* to each word. Read the new word aloud with the class.

bush<u>es</u>	march<u>es</u>
ranch<u>es</u>	reach<u>es</u>

Spelling *ew, ue* Words

Pretest Say the spelling word, use it in a sentence, repeat it, and allow children to write it. Have children check their pretests and correct misspelled words.

Work with the Spelling Pattern List the spelling words on the board. Have children read the words, identify the letters in each word that spell /ü/, and name the rhyming words. If including *fixes* and *washes,* point out the ending -*es* in each. Then use each word in a sentence.

Skills Trace

🎯 **Inflected Ending -*es*, Plural -*es***

Introduce/Teach	TE: 1.5 **192I**
Practice	PB: 1.5 84
Reteach/Review	TE: 1.5 199c, 223a, 225a, 227c, AR19
Test	Skills Test, Unit 5 Benchmark Test, Unit 5

Day 1

Spelling Words

new	blue
grew	true
drew	glue

High-Frequency

give	put

Challenge

fixes	washes

Word Wall

Introduce High-Frequency Words Use word cards for *because, better, give, people,* and *put.* Help children read the words and have volunteers make up a sentence for each. Have volunteers name the first letter of each word and attach each word to the Word Wall under the appropriate beginning letter.

Review Have children read the other Word Wall words that begin with the same letters.

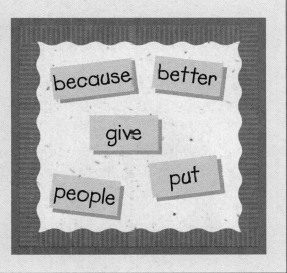

because better
give
put
people

Optional Resources

Waterford Early Reading Program
Level 2: Lessons 4, 8, 23

Phonics
Phonics Workbook, pp. 151–153
Phonics Manipulatives Kit

High-Frequency Words
High-Frequency Word Cards
Phonics Sourcebook, pp. 90–99

Objectives

Children will

- use context to develop meanings of new words
- use sound-symbol relationships to read decodable text
- describe the setting in a story
- use prior knowledge to make predictions of texts

Day 1

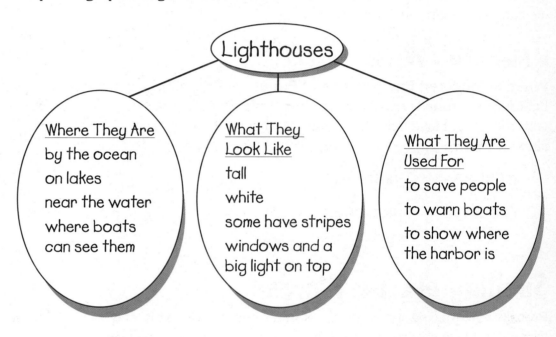

Phonics Story

The True Story of Abbie Burgess

pp. 192–199

▶ Build Oral Language

Activate Prior Knowledge Display a picture of a lighthouse. Have children tell what they know about lighthouses. Record their answers in a semantic map or a graphic organizer like the one below.

Lighthouses

Where They Are
- by the ocean
- on lakes
- near the water
- where boats can see them

What They Look Like
- tall
- white
- some have stripes
- windows and a big light on top

What They Are Used For
- to save people
- to warn boats
- to show where the harbor is

Build Background Turn on a flashlight and point the light at yourself. Slowly, turn the light to face children. Explain the similarity to a lighthouse.

▶ Vocabulary

Introduce Story Vocabulary List the selection vocabulary on the board. Use Vocabulary Chart 46, or write your own sentences on the board for each vocabulary word. Read each sentence aloud.

Frame *safely*. Ask children to read the word. Have children talk about how to do something safely, such as ride a bike. Repeat the process with *hero*.

Review High-Frequency Words Have children read each word as you point to it on the Word Wall. These words are also listed on page 229 of the Student Book.

Story Vocabulary Chart 46

192m   **Reading • Comprehension • Vocabulary**

— high-frequency/tested vocabulary

►Reading Strategies

Preview and Predict Read the title and the names of the author and illustrator to children. Have children look at the first picture in the story. Ask:

> **Who do you think is waving?** (It is Abbie Burgess.)

Picture Walk Have children do a picture walk, looking at all the pictures in the story. Ask children where they think this story takes place. Have them predict what might happen.

Set Purposes Have children use their predictions to set purposes for reading the selection. They may want to find out what happens when the storm comes.

Guide the Reading Have children read the first few pages of the selection, keeping their purposes in mind. Stop and check comprehension, using the questions provided. Have children read to page 195.

Phonics Story

The True Story of Abbie Burgess
by Fay Robinson
illustrated by Lane DuPont

Abbie Burgess watches her dad leave. While he is away, she'll do his job.

Selection Audio
CD 7/Tape 26, Side 1

About the Author

Fay Robinson says she writes for children because she still remembers her childhood interests and curiosities. Before she began writing, she worked as a teacher and then as a textbook editor. Some of her titles for early readers are *Where Did All the Dragons Go?*, *Real Bears and Alligators,* and *Rhymes We Like.*

Optional Resources

Reading
Adding English: ESL Teacher's Guide

Day 1

Guiding Comprehension

pp. 192–195

Summarizing/Literal

What has happened to Abbie Burgess so far?

Abbie and her father live at a lighthouse. Her dad
went away. She stayed and will do his job. A storm
comes up, and she goes to light the lamps.

Drawing Conclusions/Inferential

What is Abbie's dad's job?

Her dad is the lighthouse keeper. He lights the lamps
in the lighthouse so people in boats can see the
rocks nearby.

Self-Monitoring Strategy

**The story doesn't say exactly what Abbie's
dad's job is. How did you know what it is?**

The story says that Abbie will do her dad's job, and
then it tells that she will light the lamps. That must
mean that lighting the lamps in the lighthouse is her
dad's job.

Predicting/Inferential

How do you think the selection will end?

Possible answer: Abbie will light the lamps, and all
the boats will be safe in the storm.

> **Connect Phonics to Reading**
>
> **Look at page 194. What word tells what
> the wind blew into the blue water?** branches
> **What ending has been added to the word
> *branch*?** the ending *-es* **What does this
> ending tell you?** The ending *-es* tells that there
> is more than one branch.

to the end of the story.

Abbie Burgess watches her dad
leave. While he is away, she'll do
his job.

192

The True Story of Abbie Burgess, page 192

Abbie looks out at the sea.
She puts out her hand. She
feels a few raindrops. The
wind blows branches into
the blue water and tosses
the boats around. A big
storm is on its way!

194

The True Story of Abbie Burgess, page 194

She'll light the lamps in the lighthouse. The lamps help <u>people</u> in boats see the rocks <u>better</u>.

Phonics Story **193**

The True Story of Abbie Burgess, page 193

Abbie knows she must light the lamps right away. She dashes up the steps. Rain washes over the lighthouse.

Phonics Story **195**

The True Story of Abbie Burgess, page 195

Skills in Context

Review

Setting

When and where does this story take place?

The story takes place long ago in a lighthouse by the ocean.

Ongoing Assessment
Setting
If... children are unable to identify the setting of the story, **then...** do the **Think Aloud** below to model the skill.

Model Your Thinking

TEST TALK

When I look back at the pictures in the story, I can tell by looking at the clothes that Abbie and her father are wearing that this story took place long ago. I can also tell in the illustrations that the story is taking place near the ocean because there are lots of rocks and waves at the edge of the water. I can tell it is happening at a lighthouse because the words in the story tell me Abbie is at a lighthouse, and I can see a picture of a lighthouse.

Ask children to look at the illustration on page 195 and tell where this part of the story is taking place. (It is on the stairs in the lighthouse.)

▨ vowel pattern *ew, ue* and ending *-es*
— high-frequency/tested vocabulary

Guiding Comprehension

pp. 196–199

Cause and Effect/Literal

Why does Abbie light the lamps?

She lights the lamps so that boat crews can see the rocks and keep their boats away.

Character/Critical

How do you think Abbie feels during the storm?

Children are likely to say that she feels tired, worried, and excited because of keeping the lights lit.

Synthesizing/Critical

Do you agree with the author that Abbie was a hero? Explain your answer.

Possible answer: Yes, I think she's a hero because a hero does things to save other people even though she is scared and could be hurt herself. Abbie helped all the people in boats who could have hit the rocks.

Confirming Predictions

Did the story end the way you thought it would? Explain.

Possible answer: Yes, I thought that Abbie would light the lamps and keep the boats safe, and that's just what she did. I didn't expect that the storm would go on for days and that she'd be alone.

> **Connect Phonics to Reading**
>
> **Who does Abbie light the lamps for?** the boat crews **What sound do you hear in the middle of _crews_?** the /ü/ sound

Abbie lights the lamps one by one. Now boat crews can see the rocks, and they can keep their boats away. Abbie watches as a boat passes by safely.

196 Phonics Story

The True Story of Abbie Burgess, **page 196**

But her dad can't come back because it is still raining!

Night after night, Abbie lights the lamps. Again and again, boats go around the rocks safely.

198 Phonics Story

The True Story of Abbie Burgess, **page 198**

All night, Abbie rushes up the steps to check the lights. They must stay lit. She doesn't sleep at all. She won't give up. At last, the night is over. Abbie's dad will be back soon.

Phonics Story **197**

The True Story of Abbie Burgess, page 197

At last, the storm is over. Abbie's dad comes back. He gives Abbie a hug. He knew she could do the job! Abbie Burgess helped a lot of people. She was a true hero.

199

The True Story of Abbie Burgess, page 199

Ongoing Assessment

Phonics Strategies

If... children have difficulty reading *crews* or *true,*

then... remind them that the letters *ew* and *ue* stand for /ü/, as in *blue.* Have them blend the sounds to read the words. **Decoding: Using Phonetic Analysis**

If... children have difficulty decoding the inflected ending *watches, passes,* and *rushes,*

then... cover the *-es* endings and have children read the base words. Have them blend the sounds to read the words. **Decoding: Using Structural Analysis**

Reading Strategies

If... children have difficulty understanding what Abbie is doing and why it is important,

then... point out the rocks and the waves in the illustrations. Explain that lighthouses are put in places where there are rocks so boats won't crash into them in the dark or in a storm. The boat captains look for the light in the lighthouse to help them stay away from the rocks. **Using Illustrations**

Day **1**

Extend Language Arts

Writing: Write a News Story

Tell children that at the time of this story, there was no television news to report the story. The report was written in the newspaper instead. Tell children that they will be news reporters telling how Abbie Burgess helped a lot of people during the storm.

Remind children that a good news story gives the facts. It tells *who, what, where, when, why,* and *how.* Ask:

Whom is the news story about?

When and where did it take place?

What happened? How did it turn out?

Encourage children to dictate the answers to the questions and record their responses on a chart. Have the class work together to organize the news story in an order that makes sense.

▨ vowel pattern *ew, ue* and ending *-es*
— high-frequency/tested vocabulary

ORAL LANGUAGE

Expand Vocabulary

▶ Discuss Comparatives

Have children recall where Abbie Burgess lived. (a lighthouse) Ask these questions, stressing the underlined words.

> **Was Abbie's lighthouse a <u>tall</u> building?**
> **Is our school a <u>taller</u> building than the lighthouse?**
> **What is the <u>tallest</u> building you've seen?**

Explain that the words *taller* and *tallest* are used to compare tall things. Have children use their knowledge of suffixes *-er* and *-est* to find the meaning of the words. Continue by asking:

> **Was *The True Story of Abbie Burgess* a <u>good</u> story?**
> **Was *Chompy's Afternoon* a <u>better</u> story than *Abbie Burgess?***
> **What was the <u>best</u> story in your book?**

Explain that the words *better* and *best* are used to compare good things.

Continue the activity by comparing other things from the story or from the classroom. Prompt children to supply the comparative forms. Use examples such as these: a <u>large</u> boat (larger, largest), a <u>brave</u> girl (braver, bravest), a <u>bad</u> storm (worse, worst).

WRITING

STEP 1 Writing Process
Prewrite

▶ Class Research Report

Describe a Report Tell children that this week the class will research and write a report. To research is to find information using books and other sources. Their report will tell facts about one animal that they find interesting.

Brainstorm a Topic Invite children to suggest an animal and tell why that animal would be fun to research. List their suggestions. Help them choose an animal for which books, magazines, or multimedia materials will be accessible.

snake   lion   dinosaur   kangaroo
seal   eagle   whale   caterpillar

Day 1

Meeting Individual Needs

Challenge

Extended Vocabulary List
Encourage the use of words such as these.

gentle   wild
gentler   wilder
gentlest   wildest

Brainstorm Questions Have children brainstorm questions about the animal to be answered in their report. You may want to write each question on a card. The class also may consider the questions on Writing Process Transparency 7.

Work with children to find out what they already know about the chosen animal. Record their ideas on Writing Transparency 7.

Organize small groups. Help each group choose a question to research. Help children find classroom or media center books and materials that may serve as information sources about the animal. Encourage them to use audiovisual software. If possible, contact someone whom they can interview for information to add to their report.

Thinking Like a Writer

Suggest that children think about all the different things that they would like to tell someone about a certain animal.

- What if that animal were a pet? What things would the children in the family need to know?

- What if that animal lived in a zoo? What things would the zookeeper need to know?

Self-Selected Reading and Read Aloud

Read aloud a story about bravery such as *Hazel's Amazing Mother* by Rosemary Wells. Children may choose a book about a hero animal to read.

Day 1

Handwriting *Pp*

Provide lined paper and handwriting models. Demonstrate how to write a capital *P* and a lowercase *p* and have children practice writing a row of each letter.

Ask children to evaluate their handwriting by circling with a purple crayon their best capital *P* and their best lowercase *p*.

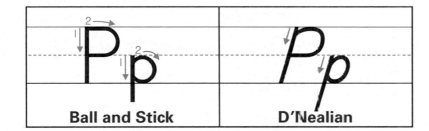

| Ball and Stick | D'Nealian |

Paragraph Form Write these sentences in paragraph form on the chalkboard:

People pick pink poppies. Purple poppies are pretty too.

As you write, model how to indent the paragraph and use appropriate sentence spacing.

Optional Resources

Oral Language
Adding English: ESL Teacher's Guide

Day 2

Vowel Patterns *ew, ue*
Inflected Ending *-es* and
Plural *-es*

▶ Phonics Practice Activities

Use the following activities and Practice Book pages to practice vowel patterns *ew* and *ue* and inflected endings -*es* and plural ending -*es*.

Phonics Songs and Rhymes Chart Have children chant "Bluey and Dewey" as you track the print. Have children draw blue circles around *ew* and *ue* words. Have children read the rhyme again and pantomime the action words *crashes, dashes, fixes, teaches,* and *wishes.*

Make New Words Tell each child to use letter cards *b, c, d, e, g, l, n, r, s, t, u,* and *w* to build *ew, ue* /ü/ words. Have them list the words according to spelling pattern as they make them.

Vowel Patterns *ew, ue*
Practice Book 1.5, p. 83
Teacher's Resource Book 1.5, p. 93

Inflected Ending/Plural -*es*
Practice Book 1.5, p. 84
Teacher's Resource Book 1.5, p. 94

Decodable Reader 40,
What's New with Sue?

▶ Read the Phonics Reader

Tell children to use what they know about vowel patterns *ew* and *ue* and inflected ending -*es* and plural -*es* as they read *Sue Blew a Big Bubble.* Observe children's reading to determine their ability to transfer these phonics skills to a new selection. After reading, ask them to:

• tell the main idea of the story

• work with a partner to find all vowel patterns *ew* and *ue* and inflected ending -*es* and plural -*es* words

Phonics Reader

Spelling *ew, ue* Words

▶ Writing for Sounds

Have children write these sentences. Read the sentences. Then repeat words slowly, allowing children to hear each sound. Children may use the Word Wall to help in spelling high-frequency words. Proofread and correct completed sentences.

> **I got a new blue bike.**
> **It is true that glue will help your picture.**
> **I drew a picture of something that grew in the ground.**

Day
2

Spelling Words

new	blue
grew	true
drew	glue

High-Frequency

give	put

Challenge

fixes	washes

Word Wall

Practice High-Frequency Words

Say a word from the Word Wall. Then begin to spell the word. Substitute claps for several letters. Have a volunteer tell which letters are missing.

After each word is identified, have children chant the spelling while clapping for each letter. Together they chant b-e-t-t-e-r.

because	better
people	give
	put

> better
> b-e-t-(clap) -(clap)-(clap)

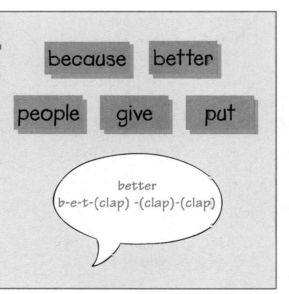

Pick a word from the box to finish each sentence.
Write it on the line.

because	better	give	people	put

1. I like to ride my bike **because** it is fun.
2. Some **people** like skating.
3. I like riding **better** than skating.
4. I **give** my baby sister a ride!
5. I always **put** my bike away.

Notes for Home: This week your child is learning to read the words *because, better, give, people,* and *put.* **Home Activity:** Write each word on a separate slip of paper. Put the slips of paper in a bowl or hat. Ask your child to pick one word and use it in a sentence.

High-Frequency Words
Practice Book 1.5, p. 85
Teacher's Resource Book 1.5, p. 95

 ## Meeting Individual Needs

ESL	**Intervention**	**Challenge**	**Other Ways to Learn**
Using word cards for *blew, baby, chew, fly, glue, few,* and *tie,* have one partner pick a card and pantomime the word. The other partner guesses the word. If the word has the /ü/ sound, they should list it on paper with a blue crayon. Pairs compare lists with other children. **(Phonics Support)** See also *Adding English.*	Use **Decodable Reader 40** and the teaching suggestions on p. AR8 to provide practice reading decodable text that includes words with vowel patterns *ew, ue* and inflected ending *-es* and plural ending *-es.* **(Phonics Support)**	Have children write a group recipe for Sue to follow to make Silly Stew. Encourage them to use *glue, true, new, chew, few, grew,* and words with endings *-es* in their recipe. Children may want to illustrate the recipe. **(Divergent Thinking)**	Use Phonics Activity Mat 5 from the Phonics Manipulatives Kit for vowel patterns *ew, ue* and Phonics Activity Mat 2 for *-es* endings. Instructions for using these games are on the back of the mats. **(Kinesthetic)**

Objectives

Children will

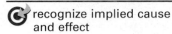

🎯 recognize implied cause and effect

- read with fluency and understanding

Skills Trace

🎯 **Cause and Effect**

Introduce	TE: 1.1 76	
Teach	Before	TE: 1.5 199e–199f
	During	TE: 1.5 210–211
	After	TE: 1.5 AR19
Practice	PB: 1.2 22, 86; 1.5 54, 86	
Reteach/Review	TE: 1.2 AR13, AR19; 1.5 AR16, AR19	
Test	Skills Test, Units 2, 5 Benchmark Test, Units 2, 5	

Day 2

Building Systematic Instruction

🎯 **Cause and Effect**

LOOKING BACK

Kindergarten Children understand what happened in a story and why.

- -

Grade 1 Children identify what happened in a story and why. Children rely on clue words to identify cause and effect.

LOOKING AHEAD

Grade 2 Children cite examples of what happened in a story and why and identify clue words that suggest cause and effect.

Cause and Effect

▶ Develop Listening Comprehension

Read the following story aloud. Ask children to listen and think about what happened to Neta in the story and why.

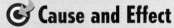

The Accidental Hero

Neta had just moved to Maple Street. She wasn't sure how to make friends, so she watched the kids from the tree in her front yard.

One day, as she perched on a branch, she heard a meow. She looked up. There was a tiny white kitten. It was shaking as Neta touched its fur.

"Don't worry, kitty," Neta said. "I'll get you down."

She reached up and grabbed the furry ball. Carefully, she held the kitten against her and climbed down.

All of a sudden she heard, "Snowball! You've found my kitten, Snowball!" a girl about Neta's size said. "She's been missing for two days. You're a real hero!"

Neta smiled. It felt good to be a hero, but it would feel better to be a friend. "My name's Neta," she said.

"Mine's April. Want to play tag with us?"

►Teach Cause and Effect

Model the skill by telling children:

Think ALOUD

When we read stories we can think about what happens and why it happens. In this story, one thing that happens is that Neta becomes a hero. When I ask myself why it happened, I can say it is because she saved the kitten.

Help children think of other things that happened in the story and tell why those things happened.

Practice Have children finish the sentences:

The cat was shaking because (it was frightened).
Neta removed the cat from the tree because (the cat needed help).
Neta made a new friend because (she rescued the girl's cat)

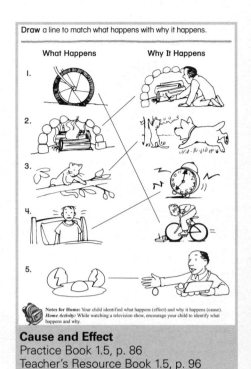

Draw a line to match what happens with why it happens.

What Happens   Why It Happens

1.
2.
3.
4.
5.

Notes for Home: Your child identified what happens (effect) and why it happens (cause). *Home Activity:* While watching a television show, encourage your child to identify what happens and why.

Cause and Effect
Practice Book 1.5, p. 86
Teacher's Resource Book 1.5, p. 96

Day 2

Reread for Fluency

Read with Feeling Model fluent reading by reading aloud. Emphasize the heroic sense of the story by reading the various passages with the feelings suggested by the text. Help children see that pages 192–193 state facts, while on pages 194–195 we begin to get a sense of the challenge facing Abbie. On pages 196–197 this challenge continues to the climax on page 198, when we learn that she must light the lamps for several nights. Page 199 shows the relief and the pride of a job well done. Have children reread the story in pairs, alternating reading and listening to each page. Remind them to read with feeling. Pairs should reread the story, this time reading different pages.

Phonics Story

The True Story of Abbie Burgess
by Fay Robinson
illustrated by Jane DuPont

Abbie Burgess watches her dad leave. While he is away she'll do his job.

Leveled Practice for ℭ Cause and Effect

After children have read *The Bravest Cat! The True Story of Scarlett,* use the appropriate leveled practice pictured on page 225 in this Teacher's Edition.

| Easy |
| On-Level |
| Challenge |

❄ Meeting Individual Needs

ESL	**Intervention**	**Challenge**	**Other Ways to Learn**
Crack an egg in a bowl. Ask children: "What made the egg slip out of the shell?" **(Skill Support)** See also *Adding English.* **ESL**	After reading *Why Little Possum's Tail Is Bare, Many Little Beads,* or another familiar selection, ask children what happened and why. **(Comprehension Support)**	Children brainstorm several causes and effects from *The True Story of Abbie Burgess* and discuss how they are similar to the causes and effects they listed for *What a Sight!* **Analogy)**	Children meet in small groups to discuss what Abbie did and why, how she felt during the storm, and how they would have felt if they were Abbie. **(Social/ Interpersonal)**

ORAL LANGUAGE

Speaking: Small Group Discussion

▶ Discuss the Class Report

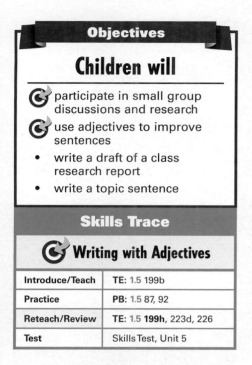
Help children identify classroom, media center, or other sources to find information. A media specialist or librarian may be able to help find suitable sources, especially audiovisual software.

Alternately, you may prefer to collect knowledge children already have.

Question	Where to find answer
Where do seals live?	<u>Cimru the Seal</u> on our bookshelf
What colors are seals?	children's encyclopedia

Model Tell children that they will discuss their group's question.

Assist them in recalling what they know about participating in discussions. Elicit responses such as those below.
- Wait your turn to speak. Don't interrupt.
- Raise your hand to speak.
- Let everyone have a chance to speak.
- Be polite. Face the speaker as you listen.
- Keep your voice just right—not too loud and not too soft.

Practice Ask children to return to their small groups. Help the groups use the children's knowledge or new information to answer their questions. Suggest that children record their ideas. Each piece of information might be noted on an index card.

Guide groups to share information they find that could help another group and to note new facts that are interesting but were not assigned to any group.

WRITING

STEP 2 Writing Process
Draft

▶ Class Research Report

Draft a Paragraph Have children review the facts they read and noted during the Oral Language activity. Encourage each group to organize its facts into an order that makes sense, with the most important idea first. Have each group draft a part of the class report. Encourage each group to write at least four sentences to answer their question.

Model Demonstrate how to write a topic sentence.

If my group is writing about how dogs help people, I want to begin with a sentence that tells the big idea. Our first sentence should tell the reader what our paragraph is all about. I would write, "Dogs help people in many ways."

Thinking Like a Writer

Just Write Give this advice to children: What's the most important thing you want to say? Get that sentence down on paper and then add the rest of the details. You can go back and fix any mistakes later.

Self-Selected Reading and Read Aloud D.E.A.R.

Read aloud a story of bravery. Have children select books about brave animals such as *Quick, Quack, Quick* by Marsha Arnold.

Day 2

Organize the Key Points Once each group has completed its draft, have a volunteer read it to the rest of the class. Organize the speakers from the groups into a logical order and have them read their drafts in order. Have children discuss whether this order makes sense and sounds good for their report.

Grammar: Adjectives

Use Adjectives to Improve Sentences Remind children that adjectives describe people, places, and things, and that adjectives can tell color, shape, size, what kind, and how many. Encourage them to use what they have learned about adjectives in their drafts to make their writing more interesting.

Ask questions such as these:
- What would your senses tell you about what the animal looks like, sounds like, smells like, or feels like?
- Is there a better way to describe it? Could you say "light gray" or "dark gray" instead of just "gray"?

Practice Encourage children to read their sentences aloud to their groups and have group members suggest adjectives that will make the facts more interesting.

An **adjective** tells more about a person, place, or thing. **Cute** tells more about Mary's cat.

Mary has a <u>cute</u> cat.

Pick a word from the box that helps each sentence tell more. Write it on the line.

| black | hot | tall | three | wet |

1. Dad sips a **hot** drink.

2. Tom is a **tall** man.

3. I have a **black** cat.

4. I have **three** sisters.

5. Take off your **wet** coat.

Notes for Home: Your child used adjectives to improve sentences. *Home Activity:* Make up simple sentences for your child. Encourage your child to add adjectives to make each sentence more interesting.

Writing with Adjectives
Practice Book 1.5, p. 87
Teacher's Resource Book 1.5, p. 97

The Bravest Cat!

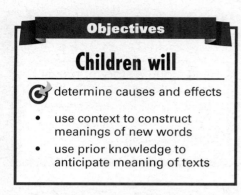

Objectives

Children will

- ⊙ determine causes and effects
- use context to construct meanings of new words
- use prior knowledge to anticipate meaning of texts

Day 3

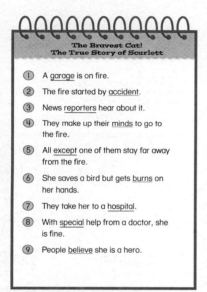

The Bravest Cat!
The True Story of Scarlett

① A <u>garage</u> is on fire.

② The fire started by <u>accident</u>.

③ News <u>reporters</u> hear about it.

④ They make up their <u>minds</u> to go to the fire.

⑤ All <u>except</u> one of them stay far away from the fire.

⑥ She saves a bird but gets <u>burns</u> on her hands.

⑦ They take her to a <u>hospital</u>.

⑧ With <u>special</u> help from a doctor, she is fine.

⑨ People <u>believe</u> she is a hero.

Story Vocabulary Chart 47

Pick a word from the box to finish each sentence.
Write it on the line.

because   better   burns   give   people   put

1. My dog barks **because** there is a fire!

2. His barking wakes up the sleeping **people**.

3. The firefighters **put** the fire out.

4. My dog has **burns** on his feet.

5. I will **give** my dog a big hug.

6. That will make him feel **better**.

Notes for Home: Your child used words learned this week to finish a story. *Home Activity:* Take turns reading each word from the box aloud and using it in a sentence.

Tested Vocabulary
Practice Book 1.5, p. 88
Teacher's Resource Book 1.5, p. 98

The Bravest Cat!
pp. 200–221

▶ Build Oral Language

Activate Prior Knowledge Ask children to discuss bravery.

> What brave thing did Abbie do?
> When have you been brave?
> Could a pet be brave? Explain how.

Build Background Play the Background-Building audio segment, in which Dr. Stephen Zawistowski of the American Society for the Prevention of Cruelty to Animals tells about animals that have rescued people. After listening, have children retell to a partner their favorite rescue story.

Background-Building Audio
CD 5/Tape 14, side 2

▶ Vocabulary

Introduce Story Vocabulary List the selection vocabulary on the board. Use Vocabulary Chart 47 or write sentences using each word. Read the sentences aloud.

garage   accident   reporters   minds   except

<u>burns</u>   hospital   special   believe

Frame *garage* in the list. Ask children to find it in a sentence. Have a volunteer circle the word, read the sentence, and tell what it means. Continue for the remaining words.

Ask children which two words name places. *(hospital, garage)*

Names Write *Scarlett* and *Karen Wellen* on the board. Explain that *Scarlett* is the name of the cat and *Karen Wellen* is the name of a real person in the story.

▶ Reading Strategies

Preview and Predict After reading the title of the story and the names of the author and illustrator, children can do a picture walk through the first few pages of the story. Explain to children that this story is nonfiction—a true story. Discuss illustrations that show that the story is about a cat that gets caught in a fire. Have children predict what they think will happen next.

— tested vocabulary

Set Purposes Have children set a purpose for reading the selection. Once children see that the cat gets her babies out of the fire, they may want to read to find out what happens to the cat after the fire.

Guide the Reading Have children read the first few pages of the story, keeping their purposes in mind. Stop to check comprehension, using the questions provided. Have children read to page 203.

Managing Flexible Groups

Intervention

Children listen to the selection audio and follow along in their books. After reading, children reread with partners. Have them stop at difficult words and sentences and look at the illustrations for clues that will help them figure out the text.

Selection Audio
CD 7/Tape 26, Side 1

To develop fluency, children can read **Leveled Reader 24A,** *Why Little Possum's Tail Is Bare,* and/or **Decodable Reader 41.** Instructional support appears in this Teacher's Edition, pp. LR31–LR32 and AR9.

Easy

Children can review the high-frequency words. Read the story aloud with children. Children join in to read exclamatory sentences. Help children with unfamiliar words. Use Guiding Comprehension to monitor understanding and Ongoing Assessment as appropriate.

To develop fluency and to practice high-frequency words, children can read **Leveled Reader 24B,** *Many Little Beads.* Instructional support appears in this Teacher's Edition, pp. LR34– LR35.

On-Level

Before reading, ask children to make predictions about what Scarlett will do and why she is called "The Bravest Cat!" Use Guiding Comprehension to monitor understanding and Ongoing Assessment to address reading difficulties.

To develop fluency and to practice high-frequency words, children can read **Leveled Reader 24B,** *Many Little Beads.* Instructional support appears in this Teacher's Edition, pp. LR34– LR35.

Challenge

Children look for answers to these questions: What happened? Why did it happen? After reading, children make a cause-and-effect chart, listing in the first column things that happened and explaining in the second column why they happened.

Children who have finished reading *The Bravest Cat! The True Story of Scarlett* can read a selection in **Leveled Reader 5C.**

About the Illustrator

Fred Willingham
has been drawing all his life. After he graduated from the Art Institute of Pennsylvania he began his career as a freelance illustrator. He enjoys working first in air brushing, then he finishes with pastels. A few of his books for children include *The Riches of Oseola McCarty* and *That's My Grandpa.* His latest and most favorite is *Busy Toes.* He now lives in Cleveland, Ohio.

Decodable Reader 41,
Ty's New Baseball

Optional Resources

Reading
Adding English: ESL Teacher's Guide

Day
3

Guiding Comprehension

pp. 200–203

Realism and Fantasy/Inferential

How can you tell that *The Bravest Cat!* is a true story?

The title is *The Bravest Cat! The True Story of Scarlett.* The title says it is a true story.

Summarizing/Literal

What is happening at the beginning of the story?

There is a fire in a garage. A cat carries a kitten out of the fire.

Drawing Conclusions/Inferential

Why is the cat carrying the kitten?

They are living in the garage. The kitten is too small and weak to walk by itself. The mother cat is saving her kitten from the fire.

Predicting/Inferential

What do you think will happen next in the story?

Possible responses: The firefighters will put out the fire. The firefighters will take the cat and the kitten to the fire station.

to page 207.

The Bravest Cat!
The True Story of Scarlett
by Laura Driscoll
illustrated by Fred Willingham

200

The Bravest Cat! page 200

Wait! Look!
What do the firefighters see?

202

The Bravest Cat! page 202

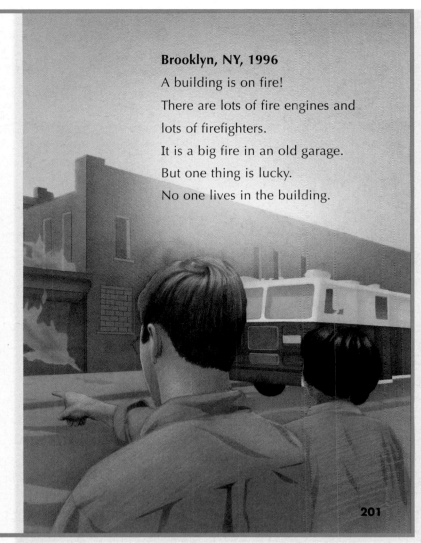

Brooklyn, NY, 1996

A building is on fire!

There are lots of fire engines and
lots of firefighters.

It is a big fire in an old garage.

But one thing is lucky.

No one lives in the building.

201

The Bravest Cat! page 201

It is a cat!

She runs out of the garage.

She is carrying something—
something small.

It is a tiny kitten!

203

The Bravest Cat! page 203

Ongoing Assessment

Reading Strategies

If... children have trouble reading the dateline at the beginning of the story,	**then...** explain that this dark type tells where and when this true story takes place. Point out that the first word is a city. NY is an abbreviation for the state the city is in. Then the year that the story happened follows it. **Using Text Features**
If... children are able to summarize the story,	**then...** acknowledge their good summaries. Tell them that good readers use the pictures and the words to help them remember the most important parts of the story. **Summarizing**

Phonics Strategies

If... children have trouble decoding *lucky, carrying,* and *tiny,*	**then...** explain that when *y* comes at the end of words with two vowel sounds, the *y* usually has the long *e* sound. **Decoding**

Day
3

vowel patterns *ew, ue,* and inflected and plural *-es*
high-frequency/tested vocabulary

Guiding Comprehension

pp. 204–207

Sequence/Literal

What happens after the cat runs back into the building?

The cat runs in and out to bring four more kittens out of the fire. The firefighters look at the kittens and see that the kittens are scared and that one has burns.

Using Illustrations/Inferential

Look at the pictures on page 206. Why does the cat look dirtier in the last picture?

The cat kept going in and out of the building to rescue her kittens. The dirt from the fire made her dirtier each time she went into the building.

Character/Inferential

How would you describe the mother cat? What is she like?

Children are likely to respond that she is brave and that she is a good mother to take such good care of her kittens.

Predicting/Inferential

What do you think will happen to the mother cat and the kittens now?

Possible responses: They will find a new place to live. The firefighters will feed the mother cat and kittens and take care of them. Someone will take the mother cat and kittens to the doctor.

Read On... to page 211.

The Bravest Cat! page 204

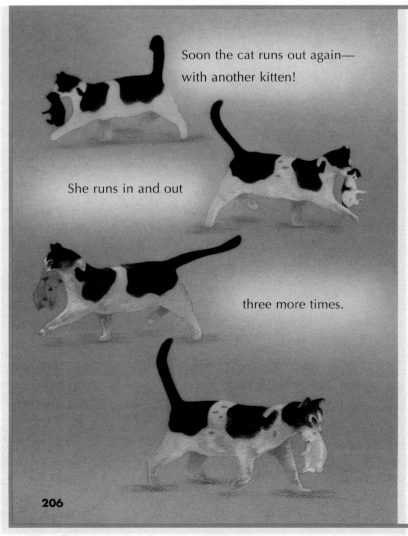

Soon the cat runs out again— with another kitten!

She runs in and out

three more times.

The Bravest Cat! page 206

The cat puts her kitten
in a safe place.
Then she runs back into the fire!
What is she doing?

205

The Bravest Cat! page 205

The firefighters cannot believe their eyes.
Now there is a pile of kittens!
They are tiny and scared.
One has burns on his little ears.

207

The Bravest Cat! page 207

Ongoing Assessment

Reading Strategies

If... children are unable to make predictions about what will happen to the mother cat and kittens,

then... ask them to tell what they would do for the mother cat and kittens if they were there on the day of the fire. **Reflecting and Responding**

Phonics Strategies

If... children hesitate before reading *cannot* on page 207,

then... ask them to find the two smaller words that make up the word. Then have them put the small words together to read the word *cannot*. **Decoding**

If... children have difficulty reading the word *believe* on page 207,

then... tell them that the long *e* sound is sometimes spelled with the letters *ie*. Have children frame and read each syllable and then put the syllables together to read the word. **Decoding**

Day
3

Content Connection: Science

A mother cat picks a dark place to give birth to her kittens because she wants to protect their eyes from bright light. Kittens' eyes are delicate and could be injured by bright light. Cats see better in dim light than humans or other animals. In bright light, a cat's irises close to tiny slits to shut out glare. The iris is the colored part of the eye. In darkness, the iris opens fully to let in all possible light.

▨ vowel patterns *ew, ue*, and inflected and plural *-es*
— high-frequency/tested vocabulary

Guiding Comprehension

pp. 208–211

Day 3

Context Clues/Inferential

What words in the story help you understand what the word *strays* means?

The sentence before has the words "do not belong to anyone." That helps me know that these cats don't have owners.

Making Judgments/Critical

Do you think Scarlett is a hero? Tell why you answered the way you did.

Most children will say yes, she is a hero. She could have gotten hurt, but she kept going back into the burning building until all her kittens were safe.

Predicting/Inferential

What do you think will happen to Scarlett and her kittens?

Reasonable responses: The doctors will make them well and a nice family will adopt them. The doctors will make them well and Scarlett and the kittens will live with the firefighters.

Connect Phonics to Reading

Look at page 211. What ran stories about Scarlett the brave cat? What letters stand for /ü/ in *newspapers*?

Newspapers ran stories about Scarlett. The letters *ew* stand for /ü/ in *newspapers*.

Read On... to page 215.

And the poor mother cat!
Her burns are bad.
Her eyes are hurt.
She cannot even see her kittens.
So she touches each kitten with her nose.
One, two, three, four, five.
They are all there.

208

The Bravest Cat! page 208

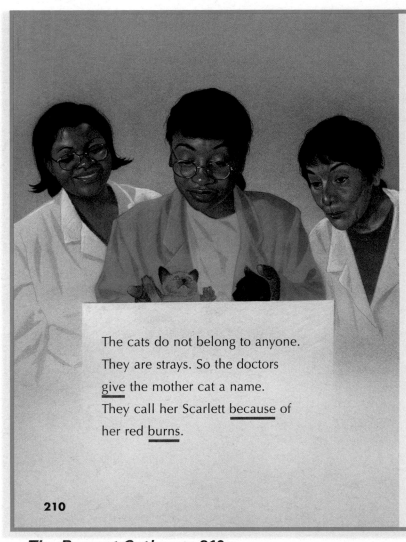

The cats do not belong to anyone.
They are strays. So the doctors give the mother cat a name.
They call her Scarlett because of her red burns.

210

The Bravest Cat! page 210

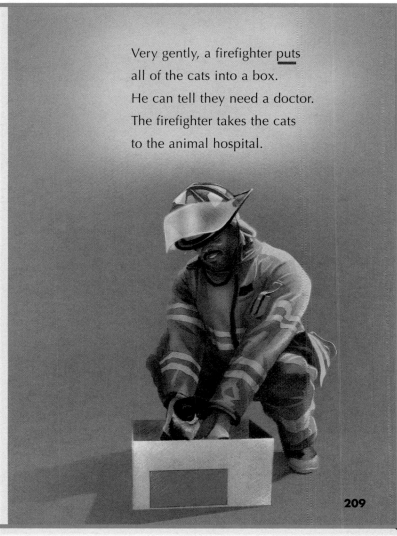

Very gently, a firefighter puts
all of the cats into a box.
He can tell they need a doctor.
The firefighter takes the cats
to the animal hospital.

209

The Bravest Cat! **page 209**

Soon lots of people
know about Scarlett.
Newspapers run stories.
People want her to be on TV.
She is a hero and a star.

211

The Bravest Cat! **page 211**

Skills in Context

TARGET SKILL

☞ Cause and Effect

Why does the cat touch each kitten with her nose?

She can't see her kittens so she makes sure they are all there by touching them.

Ongoing Assessment

☞ Cause and Effect

If... children are unable to determine causes and effects,	**then...** do the **Think Aloud** below to model the skill.

Model Your Thinking

TEST TALK

I know the cat went back into the building several times to get all her kittens out. I know that the cat got burned and that her eyes are hurt. That's the reason she can't see to tell if all her kittens are safe. She needs to touch and smell them to know she has them all.

Have children return to the story and determine the cause or effect of other story events, such as the reason that the doctors named the cat Scarlett, or the reason that Scarlett became famous. Guide children to understand that sometimes events are linked—one thing causes another to happen.

Day
3

▭ vowel patterns *ew*, *ue*, and inflected and plural *-es*
━ high-frequency/tested vocabulary

Abbie Burgess/Bravest Cat! **210–211**

Guiding Comprehension

pp. 212–215

Recall and Retell/Literal

Tell about all the things people do to help Scarlett and her kittens get well.

They keep Scarlett in a separate room so she can rest. They help the kittens by loving them, holding them, feeding them bottles, and giving them medicine.

Cause and Effect/Inferential

Why does one kitten die? Find sentences in the story to support your answer.

That kitten is the last one out. He is hurt the most. Children may point to the sentences on page 213 to explain why the kitten died.

Setting/Inferential

Look at pages 212 and 214. Where is this part of the story taking place? How can you tell?

They are at the animal hospital. There are doctors and nurses in the picture with Scarlett.

Predicting/Inferential

How do you think the doctors and nurses will choose a new home for Scarlett?

Children are likely to say that the doctors and nurses will read all the letters and then choose the person who wants Scarlett the most and will give her a good home.

Read On... to page 219.

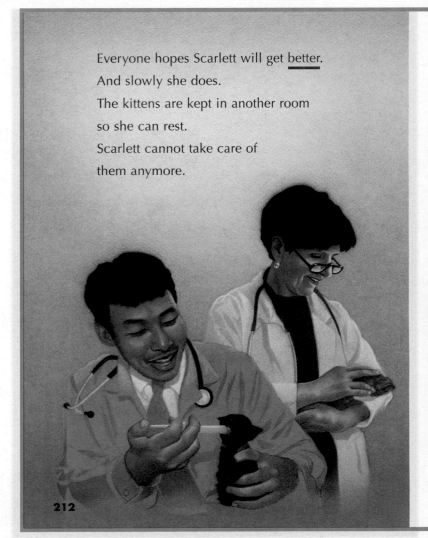

Everyone hopes Scarlett will get <u>better</u>.
And slowly she does.
The kittens are kept in another room
so she can rest.
Scarlett cannot take care of
them anymore.

212

The Bravest Cat! page 212

But the other kittens get new homes.
And what about Scarlett?
Letters for her come from all
over the world.
So many <u>people</u> want to <u>give</u> her
a good home.

214

The Bravest Cat! page 214

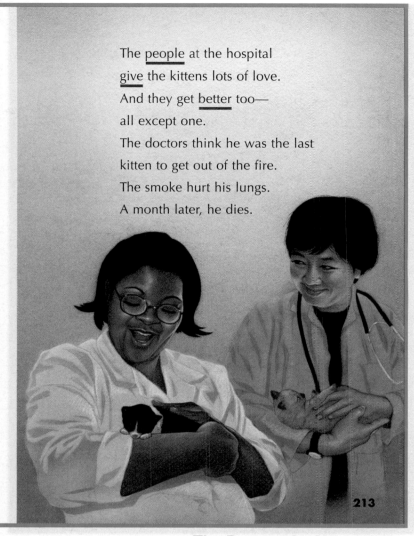

The people at the hospital
give the kittens lots of love.
And they get better too—
all except one.
The doctors think he was the last
kitten to get out of the fire.
The smoke hurt his lungs.
A month later, he dies.

213

The Bravest Cat! **page 213**

215

The Bravest Cat! **page 215**

Reading Strategies

If... children read at a choppy, uneven pace,	**then...** read a sentence or two and have them echo read the same passage using your reading as a model for pacing and expression. **Fluency**
If... children are able to determine the cause of given events,	**then...** recognize that they are careful readers and ask how they figured out the reasons the events happened. **Cause and Effect**

Phonics Strategies

If... children are unable to decode *ew* /ü/ words, such as *new*,	**then...** tell children that the letters *ew* in the word make it rhyme with *blew*. Have them use what they know about sounds to figure out the word. **Decoding**

Day 3

vowel patterns *ew*, *ue*, and inflected and plural -*es*
— high-frequency/tested vocabulary

Abbie Burgess/Bravest Cat! **214–215**

Guiding Comprehension

pp. 216–219

Plot/Inferential

Tell what happens at the beginning, the middle, and the end of the story.

The cat saves her five kittens from the burning garage. Then the doctors help the cat and kittens get better. People send letters wanting to take Scarlett because she is a hero. Karen Wellen adopts Scarlett.

Organizing Ideas and Information/Critical

What good things and what bad things happen to Scarlett in this story?

The good things are that she saves all of her kittens from the fire. The doctors make her better. She has a new home. The bad things are that her home, her kittens, and Scarlett are burned. One of her kittens dies. Children can place their answers in a two-column chart. You can use Graphic Organizer 24 (T-Chart).

Inferring/Critical

Why do so many people want Scarlett to find a good home?

Possible responses: The people care what happens to Scarlett because Scarlett is brave. They may feel she deserves a good home now because of her brave actions.

Self-Monitoring Strategy
Relate to Prior Knowledge

The story doesn't explain why people care so much about Scarlett. How do you know?

Children are likely to relate her heroic deed or refer to personal experiences.

Read On...

to the end of the selection.

The people at the hospital read more than 1,000 letters! They try to find the best home for Scarlett.

The Bravest Cat! page 216

In her letter, Karen wrote about her own accident— a car accident. Like Scarlett, it took a long time for Karen to get better. She knows what Scarlett has been through.

The Bravest Cat! page 218

At last, they make up their minds.
TV and newspaper reporters
come to hear the big news.
A woman named Karen Wellen
will care for Scarlett.

217

The Bravest Cat! page 217

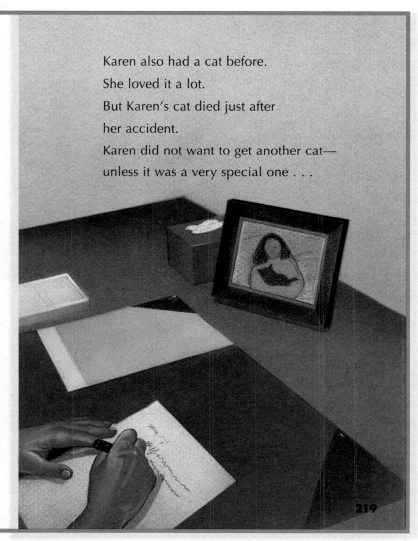

Karen also had a cat before.
She loved it a lot.
But Karen's cat died just after
her accident.
Karen did not want to get another cat—
unless it was a very special one . . .

219

The Bravest Cat! page 219

Ongoing Assessment

Reading Strategies

If... children cannot describe the plot of the story,

then... draw a story map with *beginning, middle,* and *end* or use Graphic Organizer 10 (Plot/Story Sequence). Guide children as they go through the story from the beginning. Have children use the picture clues to tell the main things that happened. **Plot**

If... children are able to identify the referent for the pronoun *they,*

then... acknowledge their careful attention to the sense and the setting of the story. Remind them that they sometimes have to go back and reread portions of a story for it to make sense. **Rereading**

Phonics Strategies

If... children have trouble decoding *try,*

then... remind them that the letter *y* can stand for /ī/. **Decoding**

Day
3

▨ vowel patterns *ew, ue,* and inflected and plural *-es*
— High-frequency/tested vocabulary

Guiding Comprehension

pp. 220–223

Day 3

Theme/Inferential

Who do you think are the heroes in this story? Explain why you think each is a hero.

Possible answers: Scarlett, because she saves her kittens; the firefighters, because they save the building and Scarlett and the kittens; and the doctors and nurses, because they save Scarlett and her kittens.

Confirm Predictions

Did the story end the way you thought it would? Explain.

Children are likely to say yes, because they thought Scarlett and her kittens would get well.

Confirm Predictions

After reading aloud page 221 with children, ask: On page 221, it says Fred Willingham uses photographs to make his drawings. If there are photographs, why does he make drawings of them?

Possible response: The photos are of individual people, animals, or things. Mr. Willingham puts them together to make pictures that help tell the story.

Critical Thinking
Reading Across Texts

How are Scarlett and Abbie Burgess alike? How are they different?

They are both heroes. They both saved someone. Abbie saved people in the boats from crashing on the rocks. Scarlett saved her kittens from a fire.

> **Response Log** Have children create a poster advertising the selection. It should include the title, author, and an important event from the story.

220–221   *Abbie Burgess/Bravest Cat!*

just like Scarlett!

220

The Bravest Cat! page 220

Kittens
by Myra Cohn Livingston

Our cat had kittens
weeks ago
when everything outside was snow.

So she stayed in
and kept them warm
and safe from all the clouds and storm.

But yesterday
when there was sun
she snuzzled on the smallest one

and turned it over
from beneath
and took its fur between her teeth

222

"Kittens," page 222

About the Illustrator

Fred Willingham

To make his drawings look real, Fred Willingham looks at photographs as he draws. Sometimes he takes the photographs. He uses his children and his friends as models. He used photos of cats in many poses when he drew the pictures for *The Bravest Cat!* He found those photos at the library. He knew just how to draw Scarlett because he saw a photograph of her.

221

***The Bravest Cat!* page 221**

and carried it
outside to see
how nice a winter day can be

and then our dog
decided he
would help her take the other three

and one by one
they took them out
to see what sun is all about

so when they're grown
they'll always know
to never be afraid of snow.

223

"Kittens," page 223

Reading Poetry

▶ Model Reading Aloud

Read aloud "Kittens" as children follow along. Ask them how many verses they see. (eight)

▶ Discuss the Poem

Rhyme/Literal

What words rhyme in this poem?

Rhyming words are *ago/snow, warm/storm, sun/one, beneath/teeth, see/be, he/three, out/about, know/snow.*

▶ Oral Reading

Tell children to pause after each verse they read. Then have them take turns reading a verse aloud.

Reading Across Texts

Ask children to think about *The Bravest Cat!* and "Kittens." Then ask: "How can you help an animal feel brave?" Ask children to illustrate their ideas.

Day 3

Extend Language Arts

Writing: Letter

Discuss with children the possible contents of Karen's letter asking to adopt Scarlett. Did she compare her accident to Scarlett's? Did Karen give reasons why she could provide a good home for Scarlett? Together as a class, write the letter that Karen might have written. Point out the parts of a letter as you write. Let children contribute sentences to the letter. When finished, help children read the letter.

Selection Audio

CD 7/Tape 26, Side 2

▓ vowel patterns *ew, ue,* and inflected and plural *-es*
▬ high-frequency/tested vocabulary

Abbie Burgess/Bravest Cat! **222–223**

Objectives

Children will

🎯 identify and decode words with vowel patterns *ew* and *ue*

🎯 use structural cues to decode and build words with inflected ending *-es* and plural *-es*

- review vowel sounds of *y*
- spell words with *ew, ue*
- recognize high-frequency words

Skills Trace

Vowel Sounds of *y*

Introduce/Teach	TE: 1.5 156k
Practice	PB: 1.5 67, 89
Reteach/Review	TE: 1.5 **223a**, AR17
Test	Skills Test, Unit 5

Day 3

Vowel Sounds of *y*
Practice Book 1.5, p. 89
Teacher's Resource Book 1.5, p. 99

Vowel Patterns *ew* and *ue*
Inflected Ending *-es* and
Plural *-es*

▶ Phonics Practice Activities

Careful observation of these activities will provide a basis for the Ongoing Assessment on page 223b.

Group Activity Give children digraph card *ch*, consonant blend cards *bl, cl, fl, gl, dr, gr, tr,* and *st,* and phonogram cards *ew* and *ue*. Share riddles with children and have them find the answers by making words with the cards.

Partners Children work in pairs reading alternate lines of "Bluey and Dewey." Have children underline words with *ew* and *ue* and circle *-es* endings. They can also look for rhyming words.

Reread for Fluency

Read with Feeling Have children reread *Sue Blew a Big Bubble* to gain fluency. Have them practice reading it with feeling and then read it to a partner, using the appropriate feeling as they read.

Phonics Reader

Review

Vowel Sounds of *y*

▶ Sort Words with Vowel Sounds of *y*

On separate slips of paper write words with long *i* spelled *y* and long *e* spelled *y*, such as *sky, cry, family, dry, city,* or *puppy*. Attach *y* /ī/ words to one coat hanger to make a mobile, and attach *y* /ē/ words to another. Children might like to illustrate the words.

Spelling *ew, ue* Words

▶ Practice with Writing

Have children write and illustrate three sentences about things they can see in the classroom. Each sentence should include at least two spelling words.

Phonics/Spelling

If... children have difficulty decoding *ew*, *ue* /ü/ words,

then... write *glue* and *few* on the board and have children name rhyming words. Write these under the correct spelling. Also use ESL and Intervention activities, Day 4, page 225a.

If... children have difficulty recognizing words with inflected ending *-es* or plurals with *-es*,

then... provide more phonemic awareness activities for discriminating words with and without their ending. Use word pairs such as *glass/glasses*, *fix/fixes*, *toss/tosses*, *patch/patches*.

If... children correctly spell words with *ew* and *ue*,

then... challenge them to spell other words with vowel patterns *ew* and *ue*, such as *dewdrop*, *bluegrass*, *newsletter*, and *blueberry*.

If... children have trouble spelling words with *ew* and *ue*,

then... give them individual envelopes containing letter cards for each spelling word. Have children use the cards in each envelope to spell and write a word.

Look at each word. **Say** it.
Listen for the vowel sound.

		Write each word.	Check it.
1.	new	**new**	**new**
2.	grew	**grew**	**grew**
3.	drew	**drew**	**drew**
4.	blue	**blue**	**blue**
5.	true	**true**	**true**
6.	glue	**glue**	**glue**

Word Wall Words
Write each word.

7.	give	**give**	**give**
8.	put	**put**	**put**

Notes for Home: Your child spelled words with *ew* and *ue* that stand for the same vowel sound, as well as two frequently-used words: *give*, *put*. **Home Activity:** Encourage your child to draw pictures for some of the spelling words. Help your child label each picture.

Spelling
Practice Book 1.5, p. 90
Teacher's Resource Book 1.5, p. 100

Word Wall

Practice High-Frequency Words

Be a Word Use the high-frequency word cards. Give each card to a volunteer. Say sentences that use one or more of those words, pointing to the appropriate child who says the word when you come to it in the sentence.

Optional Resources

Phonics
Phonics Workbook, pp. 151–153
Phonics Manipulatives Kit
Phonics Sourcebook, pp. 1–78, 86–89

High-Frequency Words
High-Frequency Word Cards
Phonics Sourcebook, pp. 90–99

Objectives

Children will

 use adjectives to improve sentences

- identify and understand unfamiliar words
- revise and edit a class research report

Day 3

Expand Vocabulary

►Unfamiliar Words

Ask children to think about *The Bravest Cat!* Say:

> **The fireman took the cats to the animal hospital to recover.**

Ask children how they can figure out what the word *recover* means. Encourage them to seek out clues by

- thinking about what a hospital is and why cats would need to be there
- remembering what happened in the story
- using a dictionary
- asking for help from a friend or teacher

Have children figure out the meanings of the underlined words in these sentences.

> **Karen Wellen was hurt in a <u>serious</u> accident.**
> **Scarlett was so <u>courageous</u> that she saved her kittens from the fire.**

WRITING

STEP 3 Writing Process
Revise

►Class Research Report

In their small groups, ask children to look at the sentences they wrote in their report and check for the following:

- Does the first sentence tell the big idea?
- Do the other sentences give more details?
- Do all the sentences answer your question?
- What adjectives could you add to make the sentences more interesting?

Encourage children to revise by adding or substituting text and using a caret. Have groups check their writing using the Revising Checklist on Writing Process Transparency 8.

After all groups have made their revisions, have a volunteer from each group read the parts of the report in order.

Thinking Like a Writer

Ask children if their reports have enough detail. If not, they can underline each noun and ask themselves some questions about it:

- How does it look?
- What color is it?
- What shape is it?
- What size is it?

Add adjectives to tell more about a person, place, or thing.

Jan has a dog.   Jan has a <u>small</u> dog.

What word describes the animal best?
Circle a word to finish each sentence.
Write it on the line. **Possible answer given.**

old (bushy) new
1. The pup has a **bushy** tail.

(long) sweet nice
2. What **long** legs the spider has!

square (shy) best
3. The **shy** mice hide in their cage.

fast fine (lazy)
4. The **lazy** cat sleeps all day.

Write about a frog.
Use an adjective to describe it.

5. **The wet frog jumps up.**

Notes for Home: Your child used adjectives (words that describe a person, place, or thing) to improve sentences. **Home Activity:** Write some simple sentences for your child. *(I saw a cow.)* Invite your child to improve the sentences with one or more adjectives. *(I saw a big, fat cow.)*

Revise
Practice Book 1.5, p. 91
Teacher's Resource Book 1.5, p. 101

STEP 4 Edit

▶ Class Research Report

Tell children that they are going to edit their reports by reading them and checking for the following:

- Does each sentence have a naming part and a verb?
- Does each sentence start with a capital letter and end with the correct mark?
- Are the words spelled correctly?
- Is the first word in the paragraph indented?

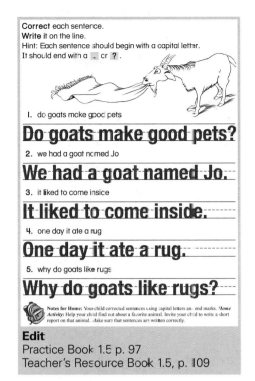

Correct each sentence.
Write it on the line.
Hint: Each sentence should begin with a capital letter.
It should end with a . or ? .

1. do goats make good pets

Do goats make good pets?

2. we had a goat named Jo

We had a goat named Jo.

3. it liked to come inside

It liked to come inside.

4. one day it ate a rug

One day it ate a rug.

5. why do goats like rugs

Why do goats like rugs?

Notes for Home: Your child corrected sentences using capital letters and end marks. **Home Activity:** Help your child find out about a favorite animal. Invite your child to write a short report on that animal. Make sure that sentences are written correctly.

Edit
Practice Book 1.5 p. 97
Teacher's Resource Book 1.5, p. 109

Self-Selected Reading and Read Aloud D.E.A.R. Drop Everything And Read

Have children read other books by Laura Driscoll, or read aloud Driscoll's *A Trip to the Firehouse.* After reading, children discuss what they like and dislike about the author's books.

Grammar: Adjectives

Review Using Adjectives to Improve Sentences Remind children that adjectives can make sentences better by telling color, shape, size, what kind, and how many. Ask children to think about what happened when they added adjectives to their report.

Giant Adjective Bank Gather all charts on which the class has listed adjectives. Invite children to brainstorm additional adjectives to make a giant adjective bank. Children can use the bank to improve sentences in their writing. Encourage children to include comparatives.

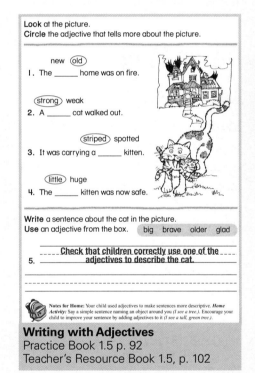

Look at the picture.
Circle the adjective that tells more about the picture.

new (old)
1. The _____ home was on fire.

(strong) weak
2. A _____ cat walked out.

(striped) spotted
3. It was carrying a _____ kitten.

(little) huge
4. The _____ kitten was now safe.

Write a sentence about the cat in the picture.
Use an adjective from the box. big brave older glad

5. _____ Check that children correctly use one of the adjectives to describe the cat.

Notes for Home: Your child used adjectives to make sentences more descriptive. **Home Activity:** Say a simple sentence naming an object around you (*I see a tree.*). Encourage your child to improve your sentence by adding adjectives to it (*I see a tall, green tree.*).

Writing with Adjectives
Practice Book 1.5 p. 92
Teacher's Resource Book 1.5, p. 102

Day 3

❄ Meeting Individual Needs

ESL	Intervention	Challenge	Other Ways to Learn
Provide a big red ball. Write the words *big* and *red* on self-stick notes. Have children stick the notes to the ball and repeat: *I have a big red ball.* Continue with other items and adjectives. **(Skill Support)** See also *Adding English.* (ESL)	Write on a sentence strip: *The cat ran.* Provide an index card with the word *big.* Have children cut the sentence strip and place the word *big* to modify *cat.* Tell children to read aloud the new sentence. Continue with other sentences. **(Skill Support)**	Ask small groups to work together as they create descriptions that include as many adjectives as possible. Others may illustrate the object being described, translating into their art as much of the written description as possible. **(Tiered Assignments)**	Write an assortment of adjectives on self-stick notes. Have children choose an adjective and walk around the room until they find a place to attach it. Then have them create sentences using the adjectives. **(Kinesthetic)**

Reader Response

Student Book, pp. 224–225

Let's Talk

Personal Response You can guide discussion by modeling your own responses. For example, say:

I think the doctors are heroes. They took the time to take care of the cat and the kittens.

Then have children share their responses.

Let's Think

Critical Response Children may mention the line "The True Story of Scarlett" below the title, the dateline at the beginning of the story, or the photo of Karen Wellen with Scarlett.

Test Prep

Let's Write

Written Response Tell children that the words and the pictures in *The Bravest Cat!* may help them think about what the day of the fire was like. They might want to make a chart with three columns labeled *See, Hear,* and *Smell* and list adjectives in each column to describe the day. Remind children to tell about the events of the day in order.

Features for this writing product are listed below 4 in the Scoring Rubric.

Make a Hero Award

Creative Response Have each child make an award ribbon for a hero. You may provide the following materials: construction paper, markers, scissors, and glue.

Create a "wall of fame" to display children's hero awards. Encourage volunteers to tell what their heroes did to win the award.

Use the **Selection Test** in Practice Book 1.5, pages 93–94 or Teacher's Resource Book 1.5, pages 103–104.

Read Together

Reader Response

Let's Talk
Scarlett is a hero. Who else in the story might be called a hero? Why?

Let's Think
"The Bravest Cat" is a true story. How do you know? Look back in the story for clues.

Test Prep
Let's Write
Pretend that you are Scarlett. Write in your journal about the day of the fire. What do you see, hear, and smell?

224

The Bravest Cat! page 224

Scoring Rubric for Written Response	
4	**3**
• clearly is written from Scarlett's point of view • tells events in order • uses strong descriptive words • begins all sentences with capital letters and ends with correct punctuation	• is written from Scarlett's point of view • has events mostly in order • uses some descriptive words • may have poorly formed capital letters at beginning or incorrect punctuation at end of one or two sentences
2	**1**
• attempts to write from Scarlett's point of view • has a few events out of order • uses one or two descriptive words • may be missing capital letters at beginning or punctuation at end of some sentences	• does not write from Scarlett's point of view • has unclear order of events • has no descriptive words • lacks both capital letters and end punctuation

Make a Hero Award

Would you like to make an award for
a hero?

1. Draw a picture of your hero.
2. Make an award ribbon.
3. Write the name of your
   hero on the ribbon.
4. Glue the ribbon to
   your picture.

The Bravest Cat! **page 225**

Skills in Context

Review
Main Idea

Reread pages 216–220. Ask children to decide which
of the following is the main idea of these pages:

• Karen Wellen was in an accident.

• Karen Wellen had a cat that died.

• Scarlett gets a home with someone who
  understands what she needs.

Help children understand that some of the details are
about Karen but the main idea is about Scarlett—that
she finds a good home. Ask children to suggest other
details from these pages.

Reread for Fluency

Selection Audio Have children
listen to the CD or tape of
The Bravest Cat! as they
follow along in their books.

CD 7/Tape 26, Side 1

Practice Reading Phrases Read aloud the second
sentence on page 218, using smooth, natural phrasing.
Remind children to read as they speak, without long
pauses. Have partners reread *The Bravest Cat!*

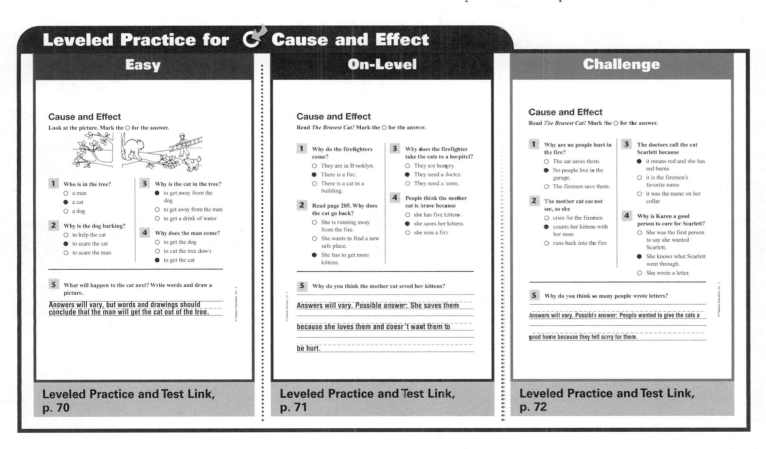

Leveled Practice for ◖ Cause and Effect

Easy

Cause and Effect
Look at the picture. Mark the ○ for the answer.

1 Who is in the tree?
   ○ a man
   ● a cat
   ○ a dog

2 Why is the dog barking?
   ○ to help the cat
   ● to scare the cat
   ○ to scare the man

3 Why is the cat in the tree?
   ● to get away from the dog
   ○ to get away from the man
   ○ to get a drink of water

4 Why does the man come?
   ○ to get the dog
   ○ to cut the tree down
   ● to get the cat

5 What will happen to the cat next? Write words and draw a picture.

Answers will vary, but words and drawings should
conclude that the man will get the cat out of the tree.

**Leveled Practice and Test Link,
p. 70**

On-Level

Cause and Effect
Read *The Bravest Cat!* Mark the ○ for the answer.

1 Why do the firefighters come?
   ○ They are in Brooklyn.
   ● There is a fire.
   ○ There is a cat in a building.

2 Read page 205. Why does the cat go back?
   ○ She is running away from the fire.
   ○ She wants to find a new safe place.
   ● She has to get more kittens.

3 Why does the firefighter take the cats to a hospital?
   ○ They are hungry.
   ● They need a doctor.
   ○ They need a home.

4 People think the mother cat is brave because
   ○ she has five kittens
   ● she saves her kittens
   ○ she sees a fire

5 Why do you think the mother cat saved her kittens?

Answers will vary. Possible answer: She saves them

because she loves them and doesn't want them to

be hurt.

**Leveled Practice and Test Link,
p. 71**

Challenge

Cause and Effect
Read *The Bravest Cat!* Mark the ○ for the answer.

1 Why are no people hurt in the fire?
   ○ The cat saves them.
   ● No people live in the garage.
   ○ The firemen save them.

2 The mother cat cannot see, so she
   ○ cries for the firemen
   ● counts her kittens with her nose
   ○ runs back into the fire

3 The doctors call the cat Scarlett because
   ● it means red and she has red burns
   ○ it is the firemen's favorite name
   ○ it was the name on her collar

4 Why is Karen a good person to care for Scarlett?
   ○ She was the first person to say she wanted Scarlett.
   ● She knows what Scarlett went through.
   ○ She wrote a letter.

5 Why do you think so many people wrote letters?

Answers will vary. Possible answer: People wanted to give the cats a

good home because they felt sorry for them.

**Leveled Practice and Test Link,
p. 72**

Day 4

Abbie Burgess/Bravest Cat! **225**

Objectives

Children will

- identify and decode words with the vowel pattern *ew* and *ue*
- use structural cues to identify and decode words with inflected ending *-es* and plural ending *-es*
- decode and build words with final digraphs *-ng* and *-nk*
- spell words with vowel pattern *ew, ue*
- recognize high-frequency words

Skills Trace

Final Digraphs *-ng, -nk*

Introduce/Teach	TE: 1.4 140I
Practice	PB: 1.4 68; 1.5 95; 1.6 15
Reteach/Review	TE: 1.4 AR17; 1.5 **225a**; 1.6 33a
Test	Skills Test, Unit 4 Benchmark Test, Unit 4

Vowel Patterns *ew, ue*
Inflected Ending *-es* and
Plural *-es*

▶ Reteach

Write the words *clue, fly, stew, steam, chew,* and *true*. Tell children to say each word and circle the word with the /ü/ sound. Point out the two spellings for /ü/.

Have children read the following sentences.

> Lee misses the ball.
> Sue catches the ball.

Have them circle the words with the *-es* ending. Tell children that /ez/ is spelled *es*. List the words children circled and have them tell the base word for each.

See pages AR18 and AR19 of this Teacher's Edition for additional **reteach activities.**

Review
Final Digraphs
-ng, -nk

Draw six ladders of three rungs each. On each of the three rungs within a ladder write one of the following phonograms: *-ang, -ank, -ing, -ink, -ong, -onk*.

Challenge children to climb the ladder by adding an initial consonant or consonant blend to each phonogram to make a word.

Final Digraphs *-ng, -nk*
Practice Book 1.5, p 95
Teacher's Resource Book 1.5, p. 105

Meeting Individual Needs

ESL	Intervention	Challenge	Other Ways to Learn
Use *ew* picture cards. Have children repeat the picture names after you. Mix the cards, say a word, and have a child choose that picture. Turn the cards over. Show children that the words all contain *ew* for /ü/. **(Phonics Support)** See also *Adding English.* **ESL**	Write as a list *due, hue,* and *Sue.* Begin a second list of non-*ue* words that begin with the same sounds, such as *dim, her, sand.* Then read other words from a list that contains both *ue* and non-*ue* words. Children tell to which list the word should be added. **(Phonics Support)**	Create a hidden word puzzle on an 8-by-8 grid using words that end in *-es,* such as *washes, dishes, fixes, glasses.* Also include *ue* and *ew* words. Fill empty blanks with random letters. Children circle the words they find and write them. **(Differentiated Learning Centers)**	Children sort word cards according to *ue* or *ew.* Then they read each group of cards with a partner. **(Visual/Spatial)**

Spelling *ew, ue* Words

▶ Partner Spelling Practice

Give each pair of children two sentences in which some spelling words are misspelled. The misspellings should show common spelling errors for those words. Ask children to "mark" the paper by checking the ones that are correct and fixing the ones that are incorrect. Have them tell what was wrong with each misspelled word.

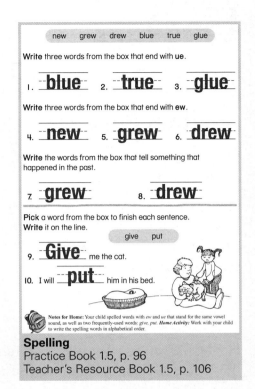

Spelling
Practice Book 1.5, p. 96
Teacher's Resource Book 1.5, p. 106

Day 4

Word Wall

Review High-Frequency Words

Word Race Have pairs stand by the Word Wall. One uses a ruler to point to words for the other child to read. The object is to point to and say ten words in 15 seconds. Tell children to point to this week's words as well as review words. You are the timekeeper.

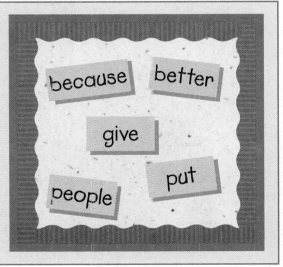

Optional Resources

Phonics
Phonics Workbook, pp. 151–153, 155
Phonics Manipulatives Kit

High-Frequency Words
High-Frequency Word Cards
Phonics Sourcebook, pp. 90–99

Abbie Burgess/Bravest Cat!   **225b**

Language Arts

Student Book, pp. 226–227

Adjectives Make Sentences Better

Have children read aloud with you the information about adjectives.

Have the four example sentences read. Ask children to identify the adjective and noun in each example sentence and to tell how the adjectives make the sentences better.

Talk

Have children use complete sentences to describe the pictures. Prompt them to use adjectives. After each child's sentence, have the child explain why the adjective makes the sentence better.

Write

Guide children as they copy the sentences and circle the adjectives. When everyone has finished, review the responses and have children correct their mistakes.

Then ask children to write sentences that include adjectives. Afterwards, they can tell partners how the adjectives improve the sentences.

Use the Teacher's Resource Book 1.5 pages 107–108 for **reteaching** and extra practice for adjectives.

The Bravest Cat!, page 226

Day 4

Write

Write the sentences. Circle the adjectives.

1. The fluffy cat has white feet.
2. The happy baby looks out of the blue buggy.
3. The black dog helps the man.

Write your own sentences. Use adjectives. Tell how the adjectives make your sentences better.

227

The Bravest Cat!, **page 227**

Study Skill

Periodicals

Have children turn to the selection *The Bravest Cat!* on page 200 in their books. Explain that true stories like *The Bravest Cat!* often appear in newspapers and magazines. Ask them to page through the selection to recall what the author wrote about Scarlett's rescue of her kittens and what happened after. Then model how to read such a work for information. As you raise the questions *Who?, What?, Where?, When?, Why?,* and *How?,* have children give the answers.

Model Your Thinking

Think ALOUD

When I read a story like *The Bravest Cat!,* I look first for details that tell who the story is about and what happened. I also want to know where and when the story events happened. Finally, I want to understand why the events happened and how everything turned out.

Practice Display and discuss several recent newspapers or children's periodicals such as *Ranger Rick* magazine. Read the titles of several articles of interest to children and explain that periodicals are available in the media center/library. Children can then work in small groups to study assigned articles and report what they learned to the class.

Day
4

READING

Objectives

Children will

 recognize cause and effect
- use sound-symbol relation-ships to read decodable text
- recognize high-frequency words
- read with fluency and understanding

Meeting Individual Needs

ESL

To prepare children for the oral reading assessment, choose a page from the story. Ask children to tell what is happening in the illustration. Then have them reread the page independently or with a partner.

Assess Oral Reading

►Prepare for the Assessment

Materials Children may choose from *The True Story of Abbie Burgess*, *The Bravest Cat!*, or any stories or books they've read this week. Have children prepare for the assessment by rereading the selection of their choice independently.

►Listen to Individual Readers

Have children read aloud to you. Use the chart on the following page to track children's abilities. The blank column is for any additional skills you want to assess.

Check Comprehension To assess children's ability to recognize cause and effect, ask a question such as:

> **Why did Scarlett run in and out of the burning building many times?**

See page AR19 in this Teacher's Edition to **reteach** cause and effect.

You may prefer to assess only a portion of your class each week, perhaps half one week, and the other half the next.

►While You Assess

While you work with individuals, other children may choose from the following activities or the activities listed in the Cross-Curricular Work Stations on pages 192g–h.

Before They Read to You

Children should reread the chosen book, practicing until they feel they can read it well.

Children may listen to the CD or tape of *The Bravest Cat!* or *The True Story of Abbie Burgess* to hear a model of fluent reading.

CD 7/Tape 26, Side 1

After They Read to You

Children can complete a Reading Log like the one shown or use Practice Book 1.5 page 107, or the Teacher's Resource Book 1.6 page 112.

Children can also complete the phonics activities on page 227c.

Day 5

Optional Resources

Assessment
The Assessment Handbook has information on running records.

Oral Reading Checklist

Student Name	Reads Long ue, ew /ü/ /yü/ Words	Reads Words with -es Ending and Plurals	Uses Decoding Strategies	Reads High Frequency Words	Recognizes Cause and Effect	Reads with Expression	Demonstrates Reading for Meaning	Comments
1								
2								
3								
4								
5								
6								
7								
8								
9								
10								
11								
12								
13								
14								
15								
16								
17								
18								
19								
20								
21								
22								
23								
24								
25								

Day 5

Day
5

Objectives

Children will

- spell words with *ew, ue*
- use sound/symbol relationships as visual cues for decoding
- recognize high-frequency words

Vowel Patterns *ew, ue* Inflected Ending *-es* and Plural *-es*

▶ Phonics Practice Activities

Story Have children make up a story about Sue and Lewis. Have children use other words with *ew* and *ue*. They can tape-record and illustrate their stories, labeling Sue, Lewis, and other *ew* and *ue* words.

Phonics Take-Home Reader Have children practice reading the book with a partner before taking it home.

Sue Blew a Big Bubble

by Myka-Lynne Sokoloff
illustrated by Andy Levine

Phonics Take-Home Reader

Spelling Test

Have children number their papers. Read the underlined word, read the sentence, then repeat the underlined word.

1. I <u>drew</u> a picture of my family.
2. That plant <u>grew</u> two inches this week.
3. My favorite color is <u>blue</u>.
4. I just got a <u>new</u> jacket.
5. Is it <u>true</u> that you are moving away?
6. I need <u>glue</u> to put this back together.

High-Frequency Words

7. Please <u>give</u> me your hand.
8. I <u>put</u> the spoon in the drawer.

Challenge Words

9. My dad <u>fixes</u> his own car.
10. Kate <u>washes</u> the dishes in the sink.

Word Wall

Practice High-Frequency Words

Make a Sentence Make up sentences with as many words as possible from the Word Wall. Give a word card to each child and ask children to arrange themselves in an order that makes one sentence.

Have the rest of the class read the sentence to make sure it makes sense. Repeat the routine for the remaining sentences.

because better

give

put

people

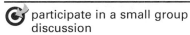

ORAL LANGUAGE

Speaking: Small Group Discussion

Invite children to discuss the most interesting facts they have learned while working on the report. Remind children to be polite, to allow each child a turn to speak, and to speak in a loud enough voice to be heard.

 WRITING

Writing Process

Publish

▶ Class Research Report

Have groups choose one person to make a clean copy of the group's report. Other members can create drawings. Ask one member of the group to write a "heading" that describes the section and post it on a bulletin board.

Where Seals Live

Seals live in cold oceans.

You can see seals on rocks.

They like clean harbors.

They stay near water.

Construct the class research report by placing the completed pages under the appropriate headings.

Conference Invite individuals to read their group's part of the report to you.

What does this part tell me about the animal?
What did you like best about your part of the report?

 Portfolio Before placing copies of the report in children's portfolios, ask them to point out the adjectives the group used in its report. Invite children to compare their writing to previous work.

Scoring Guide for Research Report
For 6-, 5-, and 3-point Scoring Rubrics, see pages AR44–AR47.

4	3	2	1
• group efforts/ideas well integrated • main idea clearly stated • ideas elaborated with rich detail • errors do not prevent understanding	• group efforts/ideas integrated • main idea clear • ideas elaborated with detail • errors may prevent understanding of some details	• group ideas may not be fully integrated • main idea unclear • limited elaboration of ideas • errors may prevent understanding	• little evidence of group effort • main idea not stated • lacks elaboration of ideas • errors prevent understanding

Objectives

Children will

* participate in a small group discussion
* present their group's part of the research report

Speaker's Checklist

Did you . . .

✓ wait your turn to speak?
✓ let everyone have a chance to speak?
✓ act politely and listen to each speaker without interrupting?
✓ keep your voice just right—not too loud and not too soft?

Self-Selected Reading and Read Aloud

Read aloud *Balto and the Great Race* by Elizabeth Cody Kimmel. After reading, children discuss what makes a person or an animal a hero.

Optional Resources

Phonics
Phonics Workbook, pp. 151–153

High-Frequency Words
High-Frequency Word Cards
Phonics Sourcebook, pp. 90–99

Oral Language
Adding English: ESL Teacher's Guide

Assessment
The Assessment Handbook has information on informal assessment and grading.

Day 5

Words I Know

Word Review

Review the words from the unit before children are tested on them. Have volunteers read through the lists and use activities to help children read and practice the words.

Remind children that they have already learned and practiced these words. Refer to the Word Wall and the stories to make that connection.

Words I Know, page 228

Words I Know, page 229

Working With Words

Climb the Ladder Use masking tape to make a ladder with three rungs on the classroom floor. Divide the word cards into three equal stacks and place them face down on each ladder rung. Player 1 picks the top word card from the bottom rung. He or she reads the word aloud. If the word is read correctly, the child keeps the card and advances to the next rung. Play continues until Player 1 has read the top card on all three rungs correctly or misreads a card. When a player is unable to read a word, he or she keeps any word cards already earned, and lets the next player take a turn. The game ends when there are no word cards left on the ladder. The player with the most cards wins.

Tick-tack-toe Show children how to make a tick-tack-toe grid. Have pairs decide who will be *X* and who will be *O*. Vary the traditional version of the game by placing the word cards face down in a pile next to the grid. Explain that each turn consists of a player taking the top word card and reading it aloud. If the player reads the word correctly, he or she keeps the card and places an *X* or an *O* on the grid. If the player reads the word incorrectly, he or she places the card on the bottom of the stack. Players continue taking turns in this manner until the grid has been filled or until tick-tack-toe occurs. Then players begin a new round. Continue until there are no word cards left. The player with the most cards at the end of the game wins.

Can You Remember? Have children select a story from the unit. Give them the word cards for their story. Tell children that they must use the words as they tell what happened in the beginning, middle, and end of their story. Have children hold up each word card as they use it in their retelling.

ABC Order Have children select five words, each of which begins with a different initial consonant. They write each word on a separate slip of paper and then exchange slips with a partner. Partners alphabetize the words. Have children repeat the activity for as long as time permits.

Test Talk

Objectives

Children will

- find key words in a test question
- use key words to choose the right answer

Read Together

Read the instructions aloud. Have children tell what they remember about *The Bravest Cat.* Remind children not to mark in their books. Read the question and answers aloud. Point out the key word *Who.* Tell children that *who* is an important word because it tells what the question is asking. *Who* lets them know that the answer will be a person. Allow children to practice asking each other *who* questions. Listen in on partners as they ask and answer questions to make sure they understand.

Check for Understanding

Read the thought balloon aloud.

What do you do to choose the right answer? (Find the important words and use them to choose the right answer.)

At this point children should focus on finding the key words rather than answering the question. The answer is A, a woman who wanted a special cat.

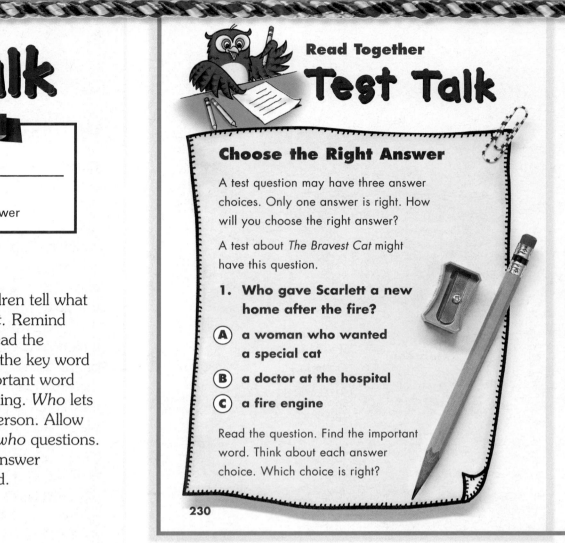

Test Talk, page 230

Building Test-Taking Strategies

Unit 2	**Taking a Test:** Fill in the Bubble	Test Talk pp. 204–205
Unit 3	**Understand the Question:** Find Key Words in the Question	Test Talk pp. 188–189
Unit 4	**Use Pictures:** Use Pictures to Answer Questions	Test Talk pp. 202–203
Unit 5	**Choose the Right Answer:** Use Key Words to Choose the Right Answer	Test Talk pp. 230–231
Unit 6	**Complete the Sentence:** Use Key Words to Locate Answers and Complete Sentences	Test Talk pp. 198–199

Here is how one girl chose her answer.

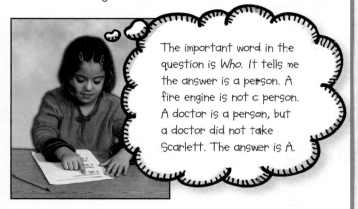

> The important word in the question is *Who*. It tells me the answer is a person. A fire engine is not a person. A doctor is a person, but a doctor did not take Scarlett. The answer is A.

Try it!

Use what you have learned to choose the right answer to this test question.

2. **Where was the fire that hurt Scarlett?**

(A) a firetruck

(B) in a garage

(C) in a house

231

Test Talk page 231

Model Using Test Talk Transparency

Read aloud the Try it! question. Have partners find the important words in the question.

Use Test Talk Transparency 7 to model how to understand test question 2 from the student book.

"Where was the fire that hurt Scarlett?" (Run your finger under the text as you read.) **This question must be about a place because it starts with *where*.** (Circle *where*.) **What place am I looking for? The place where Scarlett was hurt in a fire. A *firetruck* is not a place. A garage and a house are places. I remember from the story that the fire was in a garage. So B is the answer.**

Use Test Talk Transparency 8 for additional practice of this strategy. Answers to all of the questions are provided with the transparencies.

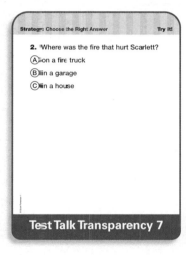

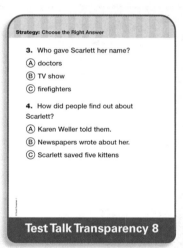

Unit 5 Assessment

Administer the Unit 5 Skills Test or the Unit 5 Benchmark Test to measure progress on
- reading and writing skills
- comprehension skills
- writing modes
- phonics skills

See the Unit Skills and Benchmark Test Teacher's Guides for directions, answer keys, and diagnostic scoring.

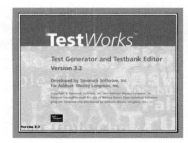

The TestWorks CD-ROM

- generates electronic versions of Skills Tests and Selection Tests
- customizes tests
- creates tests

Storytelling

Objectives

Children will

- listen responsively to accounts of true stories
- compare language patterns of true stories and fantasy stories
- prepare and tell a true story
- experiment with question stories (interviews)

True Stories

The Bravest Cat!

Different types of stories require different types of language. True stories are often told in a manner that distinguishes them from folk tales, fairy tales, fables, jokes, or poems. *The Bravest Cat!* is a true story about one cat's attempts to save her kittens. Have your students consider the following story beginnings:

Fairy tale: "Long, long ago and far, far away, seven little dwarves lived in a tiny house. . . . "

True Story *(The Bravest Cat!)*: "A building is on fire! There are lots of fire engines and lots of fire fighters. It is a big fire in an old garage . . . "

Discuss how the words used in these story beginnings sound different from one another and why these language differences are needed. These questions will help children think about the differences:

- What makes a true story different from a fairy tale? (Fairy tales are make-believe; news stories are true stories.)

- Are fairy tales told about recent events? (No, fairy tales tell about a time long ago.)

- Do fairy tales come from the same part of the world? (No, fairy tales come from many regions of the world.)

- Are news stories true stories about recent events? (Yes)

Continue reading *The Bravest Cat!* as students listen critically. Point out that this story will not sound like most children's stories. There are no rhymes or repeated lines in most true stories.

Telling a News Story

A Storyteller's Decision Ask your students to pretend they are television news reporters. Have them imagine that *The Bravest Cat!* happened in the neighborhood surrounding your school. Then ask students to present this as a news story that would take less than one minute to tell.

> **Example:** Good evening. Topping the news tonight, a cat named Scarlett made five trips into a burning building to save her kittens. Firefighters Fred Bates and Lee Smith watched as the cat went back into the building over and over again, each time returning with another of her kittens.

Students as Storytellers

Assign partners. Choose one of the following exercises.

Classroom News Team Have students select an event that has happened in your classroom or school. Ask them to share this event as a news story. Possible topics include

- the class Valentine's Day party
- a classroom visit from the mayor
- the school play
- the field trip to the zoo
- the time the fire alarm sounded

The Interview Story Have students ask one another these questions:

- If Scarlett could talk, what do you think she would tell these firefighters?
- What would Scarlett say to her kittens? to her owner?

Discuss some sample questions that someone might ask Scarlett, and write these on the chalkboard. Then let class members conduct a mock interview with Scarlett using these or other questions.

School-Home Connection

Suggest that students find family events that could be told as news stories. Have students prepare one of these events for a "family newscast" to be presented at home.

Presentation Tips

True Stories

When telling true stories, have students consider the following:

- Double-check information to make sure it is correct.
- Tell the story loudly enough so that everyone in the room can hear.
- Speak slowly enough that listeners can understand everything.

Project Wrap-Up

Presentation Options

Children should present their projects during the last week of the unit. They may choose a variety of ways to present their trips:

- class collection of brochures
- videotaped interviews
- multimedia presentation
- classroom display
- informative posters

School-Home Connection

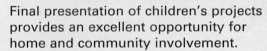

Final presentation of children's projects provides an excellent opportunity for home and community involvement.

- Invite family members who have visited some of the travel destinations to talk to the class and show photographs of the place.

- Encourage children to invite their families and community members to the travel presentations.

- If feasible, plan a culminating activity of a short train or bus trip with the class.

Project Assessment

Assess children's projects using the following rubric:

Scoring Rubric for Unit Project

4 Exemplary
- The presentation clearly tells many accurate facts about the destination.
- The presentation is attractive, with photographs or drawings that convey information about what to see and do at the destination.

3 Competent
- The brochure or other presentation gives some facts about the destination.
- The presentation is attractive, but the photographs or drawings need more detail to help understand the destination.

2 Developing
- The brochure contains few, if any, facts about the destination.
- The presentation is not very clear and does not convey much information about the destination.

1 Emerging
- The brochure does not clearly identify the travel destination.

Glossary

Words from Your Stories

Aa

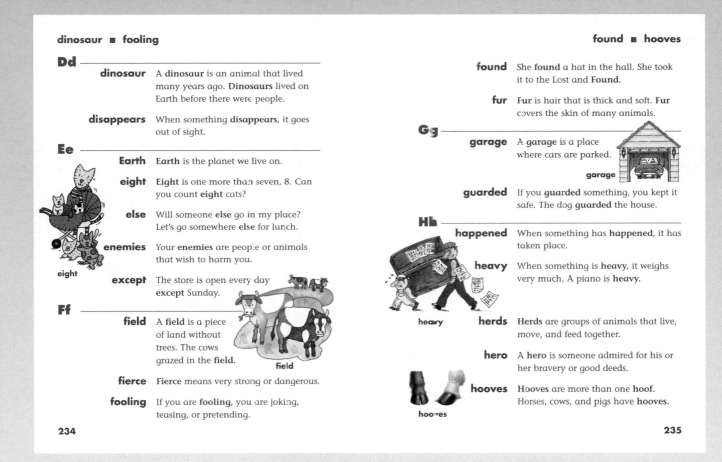

accident An **accident** is something bad that happens. We were in a car **accident**.

across He rode the bicycle **across** the tightrope.

across

almost I **almost** missed the bus. It is **almost** ten o'clock.

Bb

baby A **baby** is a very young child or animal. A **baby** cat is called a kitten.

believe When you **believe** something, you think it is true.

beneath **Beneath** means below or under. The dog's bone is **beneath** the bed.

beneath

bought He **bought** a new pair of shoes.

break If you **break** something, it comes apart or goes to pieces.

breathed If you **breathed**, you took in air through your nose or mouth.

232

buildings **Buildings** have walls and a roof. Schools and houses are **buildings**.

building

burns **Burns** are sores caused by too much heat. He got **burns** from the hot pan.

Cc

cafeteria A **cafeteria** is a place to eat in a school or other building. You choose your food and carry it to a table.

climbed If you **climbed**, you went up something. The squirrels **climbed** the post.

could Her brother said she **could** come. She **could** run very fast.

crowded **Crowded** means too full. The bus was very **crowded** this morning.

climbed

crowded

crying If you are **crying**, you have tears coming from your eyes.

curb A **curb** is the raised edge between the sidewalk and street.

233

Dd

dinosaur A **dinosaur** is an animal that lived many years ago. **Dinosaurs** lived on Earth before there were people.

disappears When something **disappears**, it goes out of sight.

Ee

Earth **Earth** is the planet we live on.

eight **Eight** is one more than seven, 8. Can you count **eight** cats?

else Will someone **else** go in my place? Let's go somewhere **else** for lunch.

enemies Your **enemies** are people or animals that wish to harm you.

eight

except The store is open every day **except** Sunday.

Ff

field A **field** is a piece of land without trees. The cows grazed in the **field**.

field

fierce **Fierce** means very strong or dangerous.

fooling If you are **fooling**, you are joking, teasing, or pretending.

234

found She **found** a hat in the hall. She took it to the Lost and **Found**.

fur **Fur** is hair that is thick and soft. **Fur** covers the skin of many animals.

Gg

garage A **garage** is a place where cars are parked.

garage

guarded If you **guarded** something, you kept it safe. The dog **guarded** the house.

Hh

happened When something has **happened**, it has taken place.

heavy When something is **heavy**, it weighs very much. A piano is **heavy**.

heavy

herds **Herds** are groups of animals that live, move, and feed together.

hero A **hero** is someone admired for his or her bravery or good deeds.

hooves **Hooves** are more than one **hoof**. Horses, cows, and pigs have **hooves**.

hooves

235

231d

hospital A **hospital** is a place where sick people are cared for.

human A **human** body is the body of a person.

hunters **Hunters** are people who kill wild birds or animals for food or for sport.

hurried If you **hurried**, you went very quickly. He **hurried** to catch the school bus.

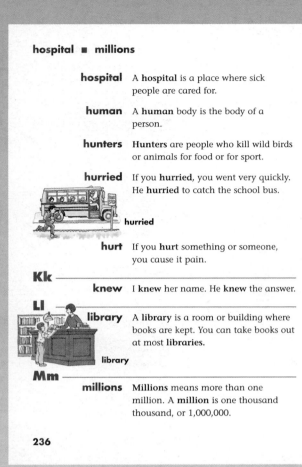

hurried

hurt If you **hurt** something or someone, you cause it pain.

Kk

knew I **knew** her name. He **knew** the answer.

Ll

library A **library** is a room or building where books are kept. You can take books out at most **libraries.**

library

Mm

millions **Millions** means more than one million. A **million** is one thousand thousand, or 1,000,000.

236

minds When people make up their **minds**, they decide about something.

months **Months** are parts of a year. There are twelve **months** in a year.

months

museum A **museum** is a building for keeping and showing interesting things.

Nn

neigh To **neigh** is to make the sound that a horse makes.

newborn **Newborn** means only just born.

noisy **Noisy** means full of noise. It is very **noisy** near the airport.

Oo

opened When something has been **opened**, people and things can get in or out of it. The cat **opened** the drawer.

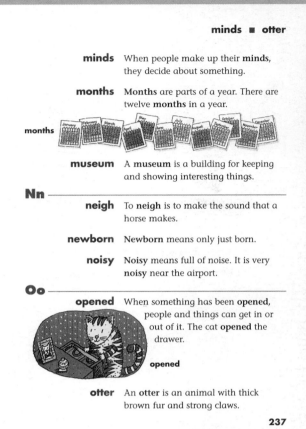

opened

otter An **otter** is an animal with thick brown fur and strong claws.

237

Pp

paint **Paint** is a liquid used to color things. **Paint** comes in many different colors.

penguins **Penguins** are sea birds that dive and swim but do not fly. **Penguins** live in very cold places.

penguins

people Men, women, and children are **people.**

ponies **Ponies** are small horses.

prove To **prove** something is to show that it is true.

Rr

reporters **Reporters** are people who write or tell news for a newspaper, magazine, or a radio or TV station.

roar A **roar** is a loud, deep sound. The lion's **roar** frightened us.

Ss

safely **Safely** means without harm or danger.

scared **Scared** means afraid.

shook If you **shook** your head, you moved it from side to side. It is a way to say no.

signs

signs **Signs** are marks or words used to tell you something. Cars stop at stop **signs.**

238

soft **Soft** means not loud.

special Something that is **special** is unusual or different.

spy When you **spy** something, you see it and notice it. Meg **spies** footprints.

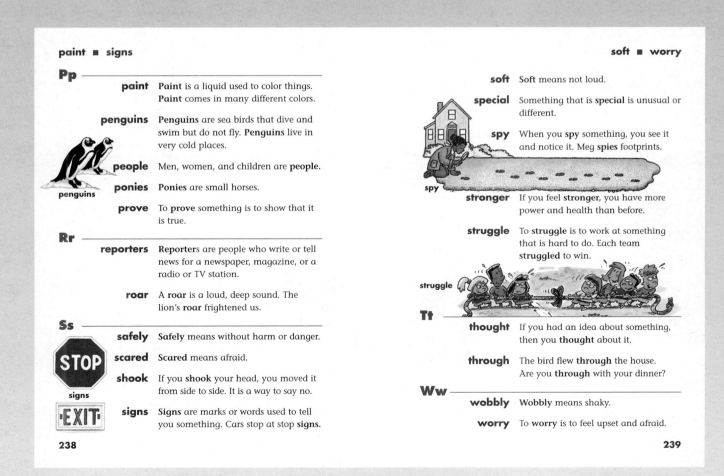

spy

stronger If you feel **stronger**, you have more power and health than before.

struggle To **struggle** is to work at something that is hard to do. Each team **struggled** to win.

struggle

Tt

thought If you had an idea about something, then you **thought** about it.

through The bird flew **through** the house. Are you **through** with your dinner?

Ww

wobbly **Wobbly** means shaky.

worry To **worry** is to feel upset and afraid.

239

231e

Tested Word List

A Real Gift
Arthur's Reading Race
buy
only
or
right
think

Baby Otter Grows Up
Foal
around
her
new
old
show

Chompy's Afternoon
Dinosaur Babies
animals
even
heard
most
their

A Big Day for Jay
Lost!
don't
from
hear
live
when

What a Sight!
Lost in the Museum
been
first
found
start
together

The True Story of
Abbie Burgess
The Bravest Cat! The
True Story of Scarlett
because
better
burns
give
people
put

Acknowledgments

Text
Page 18: *Arthur's Reading Race* by Marc Brown, pp. 2–23. Text and illustrations copyright © 1996 by Marc Brown. Reprinted by permission of Random House, Inc. Permission granted by Sunny Macmillan for Marc Brown and for Laurie Krasny Brown.
Page 54: *Lost!* by David McPhail. Copyright © 1990 by David McPhail. Reprinted by permission of Little, Brown and Company.
Page 94: *Foal* by Mary Ling, photographed by Gordon Clayton, pp. 6–21. Copyright © 1992 by Dorling Kindersley Limited, London. Reprinted by permission of Dorling Kindersley Publishing, Inc.
Page 110: "Everything Grows" Words by Raffi, D. Pike. Music by Raffi. © 1987 Homeland Publishing (CAPAC). A division of Troubadour Records Ltd. All rights reserved. Used by permission.
Page 124: *Lost in the Museum* by Miriam Cohen, pictures by Lillian Hoban. Text copyright © 1980 by Miriam Cohen. Used by permission of HarperCollins Publishers.
Page 164: *Dinosaur Babies* by Lucille Recht Penner, illustrated by Peter Barrett. Text copyright © 1991 by Lucille Recht Penner. Illustrations copyright © 1991 by Peter Barrett. Reprinted by permission of Random House, Inc.
Page 186: "Something Big Has Been Here" from *Something Big Has Been Here* poems by Jack Prelutsky, p. 7. Text copyright © 1990 by Jack Prelutsky. Used by permission of HarperCollins Publishers.
Page 187: "Unfortunately" by Bobbi Katz. Copyright © 1976. Renewed 1995. Reprinted with permission of the poet.
Page 200: Abridgment of *The Bravest Cat!* by

Laura Driscoll, illustrated by Dyanne DiSalvo-Ryan. Text copyright © Laura Driscoll, 1997. Illustrations copyright © Dyanne DiSalvo-Ryan, 1997. Published by arrangement with Grosset & Dunlap, an imprint of Penguin Putnam Books for Young Readers, a division of Penguin Putnam Inc.
Page 222: "Kittens" from *Worlds I Know and Other Poems* by Myra Cohn Livingston, p. 8. Reprinted with the permission of Margaret K. McElderry Books, an imprint of Simon & Schuster Children's Publishing Division from *Worlds I Know and Other Poems* by Myra Cohn Livingston. Copyright © 1985 Myra Cohn Livingston.
Selected text and images in this book are copyrighted © 2002.

Artists
Cover illustration © Maryjane Begin
Marc Brown, 18–41
Benrei Huang, 42–45
Lily Hong Hatch, 46–53
David McPhail, 4–5, 54–81, 253
Craig Brown, 82–85
Anna Vojtech, 86–93
Jack Wallen, 110
Ana Maria Guadalupe Ochoa, 112–115
Darryl Ligasan, 116–123
Lillian Hoban, 124–149
Walter Stuart, 150
Jo Ann Adinolfi, 152–155
G. Brian Karas, 6–7, 156–163, 255
Peter Barrett, 164–185
Claudia Sargent, (border) 164–165
Allan Eitzen, 186, 187
Randy Chewning, 188–189
Pamela Johnson, 190–191

Lane DuPon, 192–199
Fred Willingham, 200–219
Stephanie Britt, 222–223
Robert Alley, 224–227
Dan Sullivan, 228
Franklin Hammond, 230–231

Photographs
Every effort has been made to secure permission and provide appropriate credit for photographic material. The publisher deeply regrets any omission and pledges to correct, in subsequent editions, errors called to its attention.
Unless otherwise acknowledged, all photographs are the property of Scott Foresman, a division of Pearson Education. Page abbreviations are as follows: (t) top, (b) bottom, (l) left, (r) right, (ins) inset, (s) spot, (bk) background.
Page 41: Susan Cohen (TL) Courtesy Marc Brown
Page 81: Richard Hutchings (CL) Richard Hutchings
Page 66: (C. Alan D. Carey/Photo Researchers, Inc.
Page 53: (C) © Walter Chaodoha
Page 110: © Bruce McMillan
Page 111: (TL) © Bruce McMillan
Page 111: (C) © Bruce McMillan
Page 111: (TR) © Bruce McMillan
Page 151: William Morrow (BL) Courtesy William Morrow
Page 151: Miriam Cohen (T.) Courtesy Miriam Cohen
Page 220: (C) AP/Wide World

Glossary
The content of this glossary have been adapted from *Ivy First Dictionary*. Copyright © 2000 by Scott, Foresman and Company, a division of Addison Wesley Educational Publishers, Inc.

256

231g

Leveled Resources
Table of Contents

19A

That Is Right, Walrus

by Kana Riley
Leveled Reader 19A
Genre: Animal Fantasy
Level: Easy

Summary

Walrus is planning trips to the beach, a ranch, camping, and a visit to Grandma. She needs to figure out what is the correct thing to buy for each trip. For example, she wonders whether to buy a snowsuit or a bathing suit for a trip to the beach. Readers learn the correct choice for each trip. When it comes to getting a gift for her Grandma, Walrus discovers both ideas are right.

At a Glance

Links to the Student Edition

◉ **Comprehension Skill:** Predicting

Selection Vocabulary: *buy, or, right*

Program Theme: Journeys in Time and Space
Unit Theme: Take Me There

Going on a journey requires careful planning so you will be well prepared.

Before Reading

Motivating the Reader
Build Background About Packing for a Trip

Ask children to think of a trip they have taken. It could be a trip to a faraway place or a visit to someone nearby. Encourage children to talk about their travels. Guide them to relate the things they took with them to the needs of the trip. Then play a guessing game. Say:

> I'm going to the desert. Which will I need, a hair dryer or a water bottle?

Have the child who answers correctly make up another question.

Preview and Predict

Have children scan the cover, text, and illustrations to get an idea of what the book is about. Prepare children for reading by saying:

> Walrus needs help choosing what to take with her on some trips. As you read, try to think about what might happen if she makes the wrong choice. Then decide what is the right choice.

Draw pictures and write labels for each of Walrus's choices in a T-chart. Give each child a copy. As they read, children can circle the choice or choices they predict will be the right choice. Encourage them to read to find out if their predictions are correct.

Point out selection vocabulary and any unfamiliar words that are important to understanding the book, such as *walrus, beach, ranch,* and *camping.*

During Reading

Guiding Comprehension

Use the following questions to support children as they read.

- **Page 2** Where is Walrus going? (She is going to the beach.)

- **Page 3** What two things is Walrus thinking of buying? (She is buying either a snowsuit or a bathing suit.) **Which do you think is the better choice? Why?** (The bathing suit is the better choice because it is hot at the beach and you can swim there.)

- **Pages 4–5** Why is the snowsuit not a good choice for this trip? (The snowsuit is too hot for the beach.)

- **Pages 6–13** Ask similar questions as those above for each set of choices. Encourage children to use the story pattern to predict which choice is the best one.

- **Pages 14–15** Where is Walrus going now? (She is going to see her grandmother.) **What two things is Walrus thinking of buying?** (She is buying either a book or flowers.) **Which do you think Walrus will choose?** (Answers will vary. Some children will choose either the book or the flowers, and some may choose both.)

- **Page 16** What did Walrus buy for her grandmother? (She bought both a book and flowers.)

- **Page 16** When you are planning to buy something for a trip, what things should you think about to help you figure out what to buy? (Answers will vary. Possible answers include: temperature, weather, activities you can do, size of your suitcase or backpack)

Model Your Thinking

 Comprehension Skill: Predicting

As I read this book, it helps to think about what will happen next in the story. Walrus is going to the beach, and she has to choose what to take. She is thinking of buying a snowsuit or a bathing suit. I know beaches are hot, so buying a snowsuit isn't a good idea. I also know you can swim at a beach, so buying a bathing suit is a good idea. I keep reading to see if I was right. As I continue to read, I will think about what Walrus will buy for each of her trips. Thinking about each choice is a good way for me to tell what will happen next.

After Reading

Revisiting the Text

Comprehension Have children share the predictions they circled on the T-charts while reading. Discuss what clues children used to decide which choice or choices were right. Have pairs extend the story by showing another trip Walrus will take.

Predicting

Read the story *That is Right, Walrus*. Then answer Numbers 1 through 5.

1 Walrus does NOT go

- ○ to the playground.
- ○ to the beach.
- ○ to Grandma's house.

2 Look at page 7. Walrus should buy cowboy boots. Why?

- ○ She is going to a cold place.
- ○ She is going to a ranch.
- ○ She is going to the beach.

3 Look at page 11. Will Walrus think of the bed or the sleeping bag first?

- ○ She will think of the bed first.
- ○ She will think of the sleeping bag first.
- ○ She will ask her Grandma first.

4 What is the right gift for Grandma?

- ○ flowers
- ○ a book
- ○ a book and flowers

5 Look at page 2. How do you know Walrus will buy the bathing suit?

_____

_____

_____

_____

_____

19B

Texas Eggs

by Sydnie Meltzer Kleinhenz
Leveled Reader 19B
Genre: Realistic Story
Level: Easy/Average

Summary

A young girl visits her grandpa in Texas. Each day they eat eggs, and Grandpa saves the shells. Each day the girl asks why, but Grandpa won't tell her. When they have a party, the girl learns that Grandpa has filled the eggshells with confetti. They have fun breaking the eggs over each other's heads.

At a Glance

Links to the Student Edition

☞ **Comprehension Skill:** Predicting

Selection Vocabulary: *only, think*

Program Theme: Journeys in Time and Space
Unit Theme: Take Me There

It's always fun to travel and visit loved ones.

Before Reading

Motivating the Reader
Build Background About Visiting Grandparents

Ask children if they have ever visited a grandparent or other relative. Encourage them to tell whom they visited, where they traveled, and how they got there. Ask them to share special things that they did with their grandparents or relatives.

Preview and Predict

Have children scan the cover, text, and illustrations. Encourage them to use picture clues and familiar words to predict what the story is about. Prepare children for reading by saying:

> Where is the girl going? Whom is she visiting? What do you think she will learn about? As you read, pay attention to what the girl's grandfather does with the eggs.

As children read, encourage them to use a T-chart to record their predictions of what will happen next. They can write page numbers in the left column and draw pictures or write words to show their predictions in the right column.

Point out selection vocabulary and any unfamiliar words that are important to understanding the book, such as *Texas, Grandpa, eggs, shells,* and *party.*

During Reading

Guiding Comprehension

Use the following questions to support children as they read.

- **Pages 2–3** Where is the girl going? (She is going to Texas.) **Who is she visiting?** (She is visiting her grandfather.) **How does she get to Texas? How do you know?** (She flies in an airplane. I know because there is a sign that says, "Flight 360 from New York." Also there is a plane taking off in the background.)

- **Page 4** How does the girl feel about visiting her grandpa? (She likes being with him because he is funny.)

- **Page 6** Where did the shells come from? (They are the eggshells left over from the eggs the girl and her grandfather ate.)

- **Pages 6–7** What does the girl ask her grandpa? (She wants to know why he is keeping the eggshells.) **What is his answer?** (He says the shells are only for fun, and he puts one on his nose like a clown.)

- **Page 9** What do you think will happen next? Why? (They will eat more eggs. Grandpa will save the eggshells. When his granddaughter asks why, he will say, "Only for fun." This pattern has already happened twice, so I think it will happen again.)

- **Page 13** Why do you think the grandfather is saving the eggshells? (Answers will vary.)

- **Pages 14–15** What is the grandfather doing? What do you think he will do with the eggs now? (Grandpa is filling an eggshell with confetti. I think he will break the shells, and the confetti will come out.)

- **Page 16** How do the girl and her grandpa play with eggs? (When they break the eggs, colorful confetti falls out.)

Reading Strategies

If... a child reads slowly and with difficulty,	**Then...** call attention to the sentence pattern that starts on pages 6–7. Have the child note where the pattern recurs in the text.
If... a child has difficulty making accurate predictions,	**Then...** use **Model Your Thinking** below.

Model Your Thinking

 Comprehension Skill: Predicting

Think ALOUD

As I read this book, I keep wondering what will happen next. I think about what has happened already to try to figure out what will happen next. On page 5, when the girl says they eat eggs, I wonder why she tells us that. On page 7, I notice that Grandpa looks at her, and gives an answer that doesn't tell very much. "Only for fun," he says. What does that mean? On page 15, I can see that he is putting confetti, tiny colorful pieces of paper, in the eggs. I've seen people throw confetti at parties, and I know the characters are having a party. I predict that the eggs are for the party, maybe to break and get confetti over everyone. I read to see if I'm right. On page 16, the girl finally gets to play with the eggs herself and throw confetti all over Grandpa.

After Reading

Revisiting the Text

Comprehension Have children share the T-charts they completed to show the predictions they made while reading. Invite volunteers to read the book aloud. Have children tell the predictions they made as each page is read.

☞ Predicting

Read the story *Texas Eggs*. Then answer Numbers 1 through 5.

1 Look at pages 2 and 3. How did the girl get to Texas?

- ○ by boat
- ○ by plane
- ○ by car

☞ **2** Look at page 11. How do you know Grandpa will play with the shell next?

- ○ Grandpa played with the shells on the other days.
- ○ Grandpa likes to play with things to eat.
- ○ All grandpas use shells for fun.

3 Why does Grandpa save the shells?

- ○ He fills the shells with bits of paper.
- ○ He wants to give them to the cat.
- ○ He makes pictures with the shells.

4 The girl breaks the shell over Grandpa's head. What happens?

- ○ Grandpa gets mad.
- ○ The children stop playing.
- ○ The bits of paper fall on Grandpa.

☞ **5** The girl asks, **"Why do you want the shells?"** What will Grandpa say next? Write the words from the story.

_____

_____

_____

_____

_____

© Scott Foresman 1

20A
From Dad

by Dona R. McDuff
Leveled Reader 20A
Genre: Realistic Story
Level: Easy

Summary

A girl treasures a T-shirt that she receives from her dad. When she was little, the shirt was too big. But she wore it anyway. Then she was six and it fit just right. Now she is seven and the shirt is too small. Her dad gives her a new T-shirt. She finds a way to keep and use both the old T-shirt and the new one.

At a Glance

Links to the Student Edition

Comprehension Skill: Compare and Contrast

Selection Vocabulary: *don't, from, hear*

Program Theme: Journeys in Time and Space
Unit Theme: Take Me There

As we grow, some things, like favorite T-shirts, don't grow with us, but we still think they are special.

Before Reading

Motivating the Reader
Build Background About Favorite Clothes

Ask children to name a favorite item of clothing that they have had for a long time and tell a story about it. Have them describe what the item was like when it was new and what it is like now. Ask them why this item is special to them. Talk about how one feels about something old and dear and how it feels when it's too old or too small to wear. Ask if it is easy to throw such a thing away.

Preview and Predict

Have children scan the cover, text, and illustrations. Encourage them to use picture clues and familiar words to predict what the story is about. Prepare children for reading by saying:

> What do you think the story is about? Follow the girl through the story to see what happens to her. What do you think the girl's problem is?

Suggest children read to find out what problem the girl has and how she solves it.

Point out selection vocabulary and any unfamiliar words that are important to understanding the book, such as *T-shirt, years, looked, school, bigger, smaller,* and *give.*

During Reading

Guiding Comprehension

Use the following questions to support children as they read.

- **Pages 2–3** **What does the girl tell us about her T-shirt?** (She got the T-shirt from her father. She got it when she was little, and the shirt was big and long.)

- **Pages 4–6** **Where did the girl wear her shirt?** (on her swing, at the beach, in bed) **Do you see any patterns in the words?** (Yes. The last two sentences are the same on pages 4–6: "I was little. The shirt looked big.")

- **Page 7** **What happens when the girl turns six years old?** (She has grown bigger, so it made her shirt look smaller.) **Did the shirt really get smaller? How do you know?** (No. It stayed the same size, but the girl grew bigger. The word *looked* is a clue, and I know children outgrow their clothes as they grow bigger.)

- **Pages 8–9** **How did the girl's shirt fit her when she was six?** (It fit just right.)

- **Pages 8–10** **Now where does the girl wear her shirt?** (on her bike, at school, in a tree)

- **Page 11** **How old is the girl now?** (She is seven.) **How does her shirt fit now?** (It is too small for her.)

- **Pages 12–13** **What does the girl's father give her?** (He gives her a new T-shirt.)

- **Pages 14–15** **Does the girl want the new shirt? Why or why not?** (No. She does not want the new shirt. She likes her old shirt.)

- **Page 16** **What does the girl do with her old shirt?** (She puts it on her stuffed bear.) **Do you think this is a good solution to her problem? Why or why not?** (Yes. The girl can still keep and enjoy seeing the old T-shirt, and she can wear and learn to like the new one.)

Reading Strategies

If... a child hesitates on page 4 at *looked*,	**Then...** cover the suffix with your finger. Ask the child to read the base word first, and then add the *-ed*.
If... a child pronounces *give* on page 14 with a long *i* sound instead of a short *i* sound,	**Then...** have him or her read the entire sentence to determine the correct pronunciation.
If... a child has difficulty comparing and contrasting,	**Then...** use **Model Your Thinking** below.

Model Your Thinking

 Comprehension Skill: Compare and Contrast

This is a story about a girl and her favorite T-shirt. As I read about the girl when she was five, six, and then seven years old, I can tell how things are alike and different each year. One way things are alike is that the girl likes to wear her favorite T-shirt. However, as she grew, the shirt didn't fit as well. She is little at five years old but she is bigger at six and even bigger at seven. This is one way she is different each year. At five, the shirt is too big. At six, it is just right. At seven, it is too small. This is how the fit of the shirt is different each year.

After Reading

Revisiting the Text

Comprehension Have pairs reread the book and record details about the girl at ages five, six, and seven in a three-column chart, one column for each age. Have children draw pictures and/or write words about the girl's size, shirt, activities, and feelings. Have pairs use their charts to make statements about how things are alike and different among the ages.

☞ Compare and Contrast

Read the story *From Dad*. Then answer Numbers 1 through 5.

1 When the girl was five, her dad gave her

- ○ a panda.
- ○ a hug.
- ○ a T-shirt.

3 How old is the girl at the end of the story?

- ○ five
- ○ six
- ○ seven

☞ **2** How were things ALIKE each year?

- ○ The girl wore the T-shirt.
- ○ The girl wore blue shoes.
- ○ The girl is little.

4 The T-shirt does not fit. What does the girl do?

- ○ She gives it to her sister.
- ○ She puts it on her panda.
- ○ She throws it in the trash.

☞ **5** Look at page 3. Then look at page 11. How is the girl DIFFERENT? Use words from the story in your answer.

_____

— —

_____

_____

— —

_____

_____

— —

_____

20B

House of Wood, House of Snow

by Barbara Gannett
Leveled Reader 20B
Genre: Narrative Nonfiction
Level: Easy/Average

Summary

A child narrator enjoys living in two kinds of houses—a traditional wood house and an igloo. She points out similarities between the two dwellings. They both have windows and doors, lamps and beds. Perhaps most importantly, they can both be full of friends.

At a Glance

Links to the Student Edition

⊙ **Comprehension Skill:** Compare and Contrast

Selection Vocabulary: *live, when*

Program Theme: Journeys in Time and Space
Unit Theme: Take Me There

People who live in places with lots of snow build igloos to house visiting guests.

Before Reading

Motivating the Reader
Build Background About Igloos

Ask children to imagine they are out on a snowy day. There's nothing around but snow, snow, snow. Ask them whether they think they could make a house out of the snow. Invite a volunteer to show how he or she would do it. Encourage children to think about how they might build a house of snow and how they could use it. Use reference sources or the Leveled Reader book to show children examples of igloos.

Preview and Predict

Have students scan the cover, text, and illustrations. Encourage them to use picture clues and familiar words to make a prediction of what the story is about. Prepare students for reading by asking:

> The first word in this story is "I," so someone is telling the story. Look through the book. Who is telling the story? How do you know?

Suggest children read to find out how houses made of wood are like and unlike houses made of snow.

Point out selection vocabulary and any unfamiliar words, such as *igloo, door,* and *window,* that might be important to understanding the book.

During Reading

Guiding Comprehension

Use the following questions to support children as they read.

- **Pages 2–3** Look at these pictures. What do they show about where the people in this story live? (They live where it is very cold. They live in different kinds of houses.)

- **Pages 4–5** How are the windows in the houses alike? How are they different? (Both are used for seeing out. The window in the wood house is a rectangle. The igloo window looks like one half of a circle.)

- **Pages 5–6** How are the doors in the houses alike? How are they different? (Both can be used to get in and out of the houses. The wood house has a wooden door with a window in it. The igloo has a door made of snow. The shape of each door is different.)

- **Pages 7–8** What do you use lamps and beds for? (You use lamps for light and beds for sleeping.)

- **Pages 12–13** Why do you think the girl and her family make igloos when Grandpa or friends visit? (They are used as guest rooms.)

- **Pages 14–15** What does this story tell you about how igloos are made? Where can you find that information? (They are made from blocks of snow, piled in a circle that gets smaller at the top. The picture shows that.)

- **Page 15** There are two words in this book that the author uses when she tells how the houses are alike. One is always at the beginning of a sentence. The other is always at the end of a sentence. What are the words? (both, too)

- **Page 16** How does the girl feel about the two kinds of houses? (She likes both of them.) Do you think you would like to visit the girl and stay in an igloo? Why or why not? (It might be fun to stay in such a different house. It might be awkward getting in and out of the low door.)

Reading Strategies

If... a child reads *live* on page 2 with a long *i* sound instead of a short *i* sound,	**Then...** ask him or her to read the sentence again and discuss its meaning.
If... a child reads the question on page 12 with proper intonation,	**Then...** praise him or her for recognizing that the sentence is a question.
If... a child has difficulty comparing and contrasting,	**Then...** use **Model Your Thinking** below.

Model Your Thinking

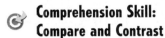 **Comprehension Skill: Compare and Contrast**

 Think ALOUD

This book is about two kinds of houses—a wood house and an igloo. In some ways, the two houses are the same, or alike. In other ways, they are different. As I read, I look for clues that tell me how the houses are alike and how they are different. On pages 6 and 7, I read that a wood house has a door and an igloo has a door too. That is one way they are alike. The word *too* at the end of a sentence is a clue that the sentence tells about how two things are alike. I also read that one of the doors is made of wood. The other is made of snow. That's a way the houses are different. Thinking about the ways the houses are alike and different helps me understand more about them.

After Reading

Revisiting the Text

Comprehension Ask pairs to reread the book. Have them use a T-chart to show how the two houses are alike and different. Have children draw the wood house on the left side and the igloo on the right. Children can use their charts as a prop and point out similarities and differences between the houses.

☙ Compare and Contrast

Read the story *House of Wood, House of Snow.* **Then answer Numbers 1 through 5.**

☙ **1** BOTH houses have

    ○ walls, sinks, stoves, tables.
    ○ windows, doors, lamps, beds.
    ○ steps, tables, lamps, tubs.

2 Who makes the igloo?

    ○ the father
    ○ the mother
    ○ everyone

3 How long does it take to make an igloo?

    ○ six hours
    ○ three days
    ○ three hours

☙ **4** How does the girl feel about the two houses?

    ○ She likes to live in both houses.
    ○ She likes the igloo best.
    ○ She wants one more wood house.

☙ **5** How are the two houses ALIKE? Use words from the story in your answer.

_____

_____

_____

_____

_____

_____

© Scott Foresman 1

21A
Mary Goes Walking

by Anne Phillips
Leveled Reader 21A
Genre: Realistic Story
Level: Easy

Summary

Little Mary plays dress up—putting on a pair of shoes, a dress, and a hat—and then goes walking outside. She comes to a puddle and admires her reflection in it. As she leans over to see more of her reflection, she falls in the puddle. In her wet clothes, Mary walks all the way home.

At a Glance

Links to the Student Edition

Comprehension Skill: Sequence

Selection Vocabulary: *her, new, show*

Program Theme: Journeys in Time and Space
Unit Theme: Take Me There

Even the shortest of journeys, such as a walk down the street, can have unexpected results.

Before Reading

Motivating the Reader
Build Background About New Clothes

Ask children what they do when they get new clothes. Ask them if they put them in a drawer or if they put them on and wear them right away. Discuss how they feel wearing new clothes. Invite children to pantomime opening a bag or box containing two items of new clothes, putting them on, and showing them off, as Mary does in the story.

Preview and Predict

Have children scan the cover, text, and illustrations. Encourage them to use picture clues and familiar words to predict what the story is about. Prepare children for reading by saying:

> Whom is this story about? Why do you think Mary goes walking? Read to find out what happens during her walk.

Point out selection vocabulary and any unfamiliar words that are important to understanding the book, such as *off, next, leans, sees,* and *wet.*

During Reading

Guiding Comprehension

Use the following questions to support children as they read.

- **Page 2** What is Mary doing? (She is putting on a pair of new blue shoes.)

- **Pages 2–3** What does Mary show off first? (She shows off her new shoes.) **What color are her shoes?** (They are blue.) **Do you think the shoes are Mary's? Why or why not?** (Possible answers: Yes. They are Mary's shoes because it says "Mary has new shoes." No. They are not Mary's shoes because they are too big and do not fit her feet.)

- **Pages 4–5** What happens next? (Mary puts on and shows off her new red dress.)

- **Page 5** What do you think will happen next? (Possible answers: She will put on and show off something else new. She will play or go walking in her new clothes.)

- **Pages 6–7** What does Mary show off now? (Mary shows off her new hat.) **What color is the hat?** (The hat is yellow.)

- **Pages 8–9** How do you think Mary feels in her new clothes? How can you tell? (Mary feels proud of her new clothes. I can tell by her smile and by the way she walks. She enjoys looking at herself in the puddle.)

- **Pages 10–11** Why do you think Mary leans over? (She leans over to see more of herself and her new clothes in the water.) **What does she see next?** (She sees her red dress next.)

- **Page 11** What do you think will happen next? (She will lean over some more, so she can see her new blue shoes.)

- **Page 13** What do you think will happen next? (Possible answers: Maybe she will continue on her walk. Mary will lean over too far and fall in the water.)

- **Page 16** Now how do you think Mary feels? Why? (Possible answers: She feels sad because her new clothes are wet. She feels silly because she fell in the water.)

Reading Strategies

If... a child has difficulty with new clothing and color words,	Then... support the child in working through the page slowly, using letter-sound knowledge and picture clues.
If... a child hesitates on page 8 at the word *walking*,	Then... cover the inflected ending. Have the child read the base word first, add the suffix, and then read the whole sentence.
If... a child has difficulty following the sequence of events,	Then... use **Model Your Thinking** below.

Model Your Thinking

 Comprehension Skill: Sequence

Think ALOUD

Good readers pay attention to the order in which things happen in a story. I look for clue words such as *first, next, then,* and *finally* to figure out the order of events. In this story, Mary first puts on her blue shoes. Next she puts on the dress. Then she puts on a hat. Then she goes walking. She sees a puddle. The first thing Mary sees in the puddle is her hat. Next she sees her dress. She sees her shoes last. Finally, Mary falls in the puddle and walks home with her wet clothes.

After Reading

Revisiting the Text

Comprehension Help children record the sequence of story events on a time line. They can draw pictures and/or write words to show the order of events. Then ask questions about the book using clue words such as *first, next,* and *then.* Children can use their charts to answer the questions.

↻ Sequence of Events

Read the story *Mary Goes Walking*. Then answer Numbers 1 through 5.

① What happens FIRST in the story?

- ○ Mary gets dressed up.
- ○ Mary goes out to play
- ○ Mary plays with her cat.

② What happens AFTER Mary gets dressed up?

- ○ Mary goes to a dance.
- ○ Mary goes for a walk.
- ○ Mary goes shopping.

③ Why does Mary lean over the water?

- ○ to get a drink
- ○ to see her cat
- ○ to see how she looks

④ What happens when Mary leans over the water?

- ○ Mary sees a bug in the water.
- ○ Mary falls in the water.
- ○ Mary jumps over the water.

⑤ What happens LAST in the story? Use words from the story in your answer.

_____

_____

_____

_____

21B

Desert Fox

by Nat Gabriel
Leveled Reader 21B
Genre: Narrative Nonfiction
Level: Easy/Average

Summary

In the desert of North Africa, a small desert fox sleeps to avoid the scorching heat of the sun. At night, when it is cooler, she comes out to hunt and finds a small lizard to eat.

At a Glance

Links to the Student Edition

☞ **Comprehension Skill:** Sequence

Selection Vocabulary: *old, around*

Program Theme: Journeys in Time and Space
Unit Theme: Take Me There

Stories can take us to faraway places that we've never been before. This book takes readers to a hot desert to see how a desert fox lives.

Before Reading

Motivating the Reader
Build Background About Deserts

Display books with photographs of deserts and desert animals, including the North African desert. Ask children what they think a desert is like. Record their responses in a word web on the chalkboard. Explain, if necessary, that deserts are usually hot during the day, but cool at night.

Preview and Predict

Have children scan the cover, text, and illustrations. Encourage them to use picture clues and familiar words to predict what the story is about. Prepare children for reading by saying:

> What kind of animal is this book about?
> Where does it live? What does it do?
> As you read, notice when the fox
> goes hunting and when she rests.

Point out selection vocabulary and any unfamiliar words that are important to understanding the book, such as *needs, finds, food, hunt, wakes, lizard, hides,* and *waits.*

During Reading

Guiding Comprehension

Use the following questions to support children as they read.

- **Pages 2–3** What do you see in this desert? (The sun is coming up. There are a few plants growing in the sand. I see a fox peeking out of a hole.)

- **Pages 4–5** Why do you think the fox is hot? (She is hot because the sun is out and it is very hot in the desert.)

- **Page 6** Why does the fox need water? (She is thirsty. She needs to find water to drink.)

- **Page 7** What food does the fox find? (a lizard)

- **Page 8** Why doesn't the fox hunt now? (It is too hot to run after the lizard.)

- **Page 9** What kind of spot does the fox find? How do you know? (She finds a dark spot out of the sun. The picture shows she is in a dark place.)

- **Pages 10–11** What time of day is it now? How do you know? (It is evening. The sun is going down.) Why does the fox come out now? (The fox comes out because it is cooler and she can hunt more easily.)

- **Pages 12–13** How does the fox find the lizard? (She uses her ears and eyes to find the lizard.)

- **Pages 13–15** What does she do to catch the lizard? (First she hides. Then she looks and waits. Next she runs after it. Then she jumps on it, catching it under her paw.)

- **Page 16** What time is it now? What will the fox do? (It is morning again. The fox will eat the lizard and then probably rest.)

Reading Strategies

If... a child successfully reads an unknown word,	Then... praise him or her and ask what clues he or she used to help figure out the word.
If... a child has difficulty following the sequence of events,	Then... use **Model Your Thinking** below.

Model Your Thinking

 Comprehension Skill: Sequence

Good readers pay attention to the order in which things happen in a story. I can use clue words such as *first, next,* and *then* to help me figure out the order of events. This story begins when the sun comes up. So it is daytime. The fox comes out and looks around. She drinks water. But it is too hot to hunt. She finds a cool place and sleeps. When the sun goes down and night comes, the fox wakes up and goes out. Now it is cool and she can hunt. When she sees the lizard, the first thing she does is hide. Then she looks and waits. Next she runs after it, and then jumps on it. At the end of the night, as the sun is rising, the fox takes the lizard back to her burrow to eat.

After Reading

Revisiting the Text

Comprehension Have children reread pages 13–15 and use clue words to list the sequence of events in a sequence chart. Children can use their charts to act out the fox hunting. Then conduct a book walk, inviting volunteers to tell what happens first, next, and at the end of the story.

☛ Sequence of Events

Read the story *Desert Fox*. Then answer Numbers 1 through 5.

❶ This story tells you about

- ○ a fox in a cage.
- ○ a fox in zoo.
- ○ a fox in the desert.

❷ What does the fox need?

- ○ food and water
- ○ rocks and plants
- ○ mom and dad

❸ What does the fox do when the sun goes down?

- ○ She goes to sleep.
- ○ She wakes up.
- ○ She drinks some water.

☛ **❹** The old fox sees a lizard. What does she do FIRST?

- ○ She calls the lizard.
- ○ She looks and waits.
- ○ She runs around.

☛ **❺** What happens LAST in the story? Use words from the story in your answer.

_____

_____

_____

_____

© Scott Foresman 1

22A
All Together Now!

by Susan Hood
Leveled Reader 22A
Genre: Realistic Story
Level: Easy

Summary

A family of five sets out together on a walk. They see a deer, a hawk, many bugs, a cave, and even a bat. They are interested in some paw prints until they discover the animal is a skunk! They quickly run away—together.

At a Glance

Links to the Student Edition

⊙ **Comprehension Skill:** Cause and Effect

Selection Vocabulary: *together, start*

Program Theme: Journeys in Time and Space
Unit Theme: Take Me There

Exploring the natural world around us can be more enjoyable when it's done as a family.

Before Reading

Motivating the Reader
Build Background About Hikes

Ask children if they have gone on a hike or for a walk in the woods. Invite children to share their experiences, telling what they brought with them and how they dressed. Ask what animals they saw. Then invite children to imagine they are setting off on a walk in some hills and woods. Have them imagine and describe the plants, animals, and other natural features they will see.

Preview and Predict

Have children scan the cover, text, and illustrations. Encourage them to use picture clues and familiar words to predict what the story is about. Prepare children for reading by saying:

> Who is going on a walk in this book? What do you think they mean by "All together now!"? Read to find out what adventure they have.

Point out selection vocabulary and any unfamiliar words that are important to understanding the book, such as *family, bright, climb, deep, brave,* and *tracks.*

During Reading

Guiding Comprehension

Use the following questions to support children as they read.

- **Page 2** Who are these people? What are they doing? (They are a family going for a walk.)

- **Page 3** Why are the children pointing? (They see a hawk in the sky.) What other animal did they see? (They saw a deer.)

- **Page 4** How did the family get wet? (They got wet crossing a stream.)

- **Page 5** How do the hugs make the family feel? How do you know? (The hugs make them feel good. They are smiling. I know I feel good when I give or get a hug.)

- **Page 5** What do you think they mean when they say, "All together now!"? (They mean that they are taking this walk together as a family.)

- **Page 6** What are the parents doing? (They are slapping at bugs.) Why do you think they are doing this? (The bugs may be biting them or buzzing too near them.)

- **Page 9** Why do you think the people feel brave? (The cave is deep and dark, but they are all together and look in anyway.)

- **Page 11** What does the family see near the cave? (They see a bat and some animal tracks.)

- **Pages 14–15** Why does the family run away? (They see a skunk and probably do not want to get sprayed with its bad smell.)

Reading Strategies

If... a child skips words or plural endings while reading,	Then... encourage the child to use his or her finger to track words and word endings.
If... a child reads unfamiliar words correctly,	**Then...** praise him or her for good word solving and checking skills.
If... a child cannot recognize cause-and-effect relationships,	**Then...** use **Model Your Thinking** below.

Model Your Thinking

 Comprehension Skill: Cause and Effect

When I read, I think about what happens in a story and why it happens. For example, in this story, I wonder what happened to make the family turn and run near the end. They see some animal tracks, so I think they turned around to find out what animal made the tracks. But then they see a skunk. I know that if a skunk is afraid or disturbed, it can spray you with a terrible smell that doesn't come out of your clothes and is hard to wash off. They did not want to have the skunk spray its smell on them, so that is why they ran.

After Reading

Revisiting the Text

Comprehension Have children reread the book as a group. Encourage them to talk about what happened to the family and the cause of each of these events. Record children's thoughts in a T-chart using as heads the questions: *What happens?* and *Why does it happen?* Then have children use the charts to draw pictures and write captions about a favorite story event.

☞ Cause and Effect

Read the story *All Together Now!* Then answer Numbers 1 through 5.

❶ Look at page 2. Where is the family going?

○ They are going camping.
○ They are going on a trip.
○ They are going on a walk.

☞ ❷ What happens when the family sees bugs?

○ They slap the bugs.
○ They spray the bugs.
○ They catch the bugs.

☞ ❸ Look at pages 14 and 15. Why does the family run away?

○ They see a bear.
○ They see a skunk.
○ They see tracks.

❹ The family does NOT see

○ a snake on the walk.
○ a deer on the walk.
○ a hawk on the walk.

☞ ❺ Look at page 7. Why does the sister hold her brother's arm? Use words from the story in your answer.

_____
_____
_____
_____
_____

© Scott Foresman 1

22B

How Bill Found Rain

by Susan McCloskey
Leveled Reader 22B
Genre: Tall Tale
Level: Easy/Average

Summary

Mom, Dad, and Sis all agree that it is just too hot and sunny. Bill collects pieces of rope from everyone and rides off to look for rain. Finally he finds a big black cloud. He ropes the cloud and brings it home, where it finally begins to rain.

At a Glance

Links to the Student Edition

Comprehension Skill: Cause and Effect

Selection Vocabulary: *first, been, found*

**Program Theme: Journeys in Time and Space
Unit Theme: Take Me There**

A young boy travels far and wide to find rain to bring back to his family's dry farmland.

Before Reading

Motivating the Reader
Build Background About the Weather

Ask children to imagine what it would be like if it was sunny and hot every day for a long time. Ask how people and animals would feel and what would happen to plants, trees, and crops. When children mention that rain would be needed, ask them about rain. Have children talk about rain and thunderstorms and share their experiences with rainy weather.

Preview and Predict

Have children scan the cover, text, and illustrations. Encourage them to use picture clues and familiar words to predict what the story is about. Prepare children for reading by saying:

> **The people in this book have a problem. Read to find out what the problem is, and what the boy, Bill, does about it.**

Point out selection vocabulary and any unfamiliar words that are important to understanding the book, such as *rain, rode, cloud, home,* and *kiss.*

During Reading

Guiding Comprehension

Use the following questions to support children as they read.

- **Pages 2–3 What problem does the family have? How do you know?** (It has been too hot and dry. The family says they need rain. The father shows a pail full of dust. The girl uses an umbrella to protect herself from the sun. She looks at wilted plants.)

- **Page 4 What does the family need to solve their problem?** (They need rain.)

- **Pages 5–7 Why does the family get rope?** (Bill said he would find rain, and he asked for rope.) **What do you think Bill will do with all the rope?** (Predictions will vary.)

- **Pages 8–9 What is Bill looking for?** (Bill is looking for a cloud.) **Why does Bill want to find a big, black cloud?** (Big, black clouds usually come before a rainstorm.) **What will Bill do next?** (He will use the rope to catch the cloud and bring it back to the family's farm.)

- **Pages 10–13 What does Bill do with the cloud?** (Bill throws his rope at the cloud and tries to lasso it. Then he pulls the cloud all the way home.)

- **Page 15 What does Bill do when he gets home?** (Bill pulls hard on the rope and then it begins to rain.)

- **Page 16 What things could really happen in this story?** (The weather could stay hot and sunny for a long time and cause problems for the family.) **What things could not really happen?** (A little boy could not catch a rain cloud with rope, bring it home, and make it rain.)

Reading Strategies

If... a child stumbles over the word *sunny*,	**Then...** guide the child to break the word into two smaller parts.
If... a child seems confused by *pulled* and *tugged*,	**Then...** ask the child what familiar word he or she sees in each one. Guide the child to understand that the suffix *-ed* means the action occurred in the past.
If... a child cannot recognize cause-and-effect relationships,	**Then...** use **Model Your Thinking** below.

Model Your Thinking

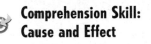 **Comprehension Skill: Cause and Effect**

As I read, I think about what happens in a story and why it happens. One thing that happens in this story is that Bill uses rope to catch a rain cloud and bring it to his family's farm. I ask myself: "Why does he do this?" I think the answer is at the beginning of the story. It is hot and dry, and it is very sunny. The family members say they need rain. That is why Bill went out to find a rain cloud.

After Reading

Revisiting the Text

Comprehension Have children take turns using the book's pictures to retell the story. A child should point to the picture and explain what is happening and why. Then have children extend the story by drawing pictures and writing words to show what effects the rain will have on the farm.

☞ Cause and Effect

Read the story *How Bill Found Rain*. Then answer Numbers 1 through 5.

☞ **1** Why does the family need rain?

- ○ The animals drank all the water.
- ○ It has been too hot and dry.
- ○ Sis has a new raincoat.

❭ Why does Bill look for a big black cloud?

- ○ Rain comes from big black clouds.
- ○ He can not pull a white cloud home.
- ○ Bill only likes black clouds.

☞ **3** Look at page 15. Bill pulls hard on the rope. What happens?

- ○ The dog starts to bark.
- ○ Mom starts to laugh.
- ○ It starts to rain.

4 What could NOT happen?

- ○ It could not be hot and sunny.
- ○ People could not find lots of rope.
- ○ A boy could not catch a cloud with a rope.

☞ **5** Look at page 16. Why is everyone dancing? Use words from the story in your answer.

_____

_____

_____

_____

23A
Pandas

by Kimberlee Mason
Leveled Reader 23A
Genre: Informational Article
Level: Easy

Summary

This book shows pandas engaging in some of their favorite activities, such as climbing, playing, eating, and sleeping.

At a Glance

Links to the Student Edition

◉ **Comprehension Skill:** Main Idea

Selection Vocabulary: *animals, their*

Program Theme: Journeys in Time and Space
Unit Theme: Take Me There

Take a journey to the mountains of China to learn about panda bears.

Before Reading

Motivating the Reader
Build Background About Pandas

Show a picture of a panda, and ask children what they know about pandas. Write their ideas in the first column of a large K-W-L chart. Then ask children what they would like to learn about pandas. Write children's questions in the second column of the chart. Keep the chart on display while children read the book. After reading, have a discussion in which children tell what they learned about pandas. Enter that information in the last column of the chart.

Preview and Predict

Have children scan the cover, text, and photographs. Encourage them to use picture clues and familiar words to predict what the story is about. Prepare children for reading by saying:

> What kind of animal is this? What do you think pandas like to do?

Review the questions listed in the K-W-L chart. Suggest children read to look for answers to their questions and other interesting facts about pandas.

Point out selection vocabulary and any unfamiliar words that are important to understanding the book, such as *fur, habits, hide, swim, sit, roll,* and *creep.*

During Reading

Guiding Comprehension

Use the following questions to support children as they read.

- **Page 2** *Who is telling about pandas?* (a girl named Su-Lin) *Is Su-Lin telling about something real or make-believe? How do you know?* (She is telling about something real. She gives facts about pandas, which are real animals.)

- **Pages 2–3** *Where do Su-Lin and pandas live?* (They both live in China.)

- **Page 3** *What colors does a panda's fur have?* (A panda's fur is black and white.)

- **Pages 5–6** *What do you think a habit is?* (Accept all reasonable responses, but guide children to read on, using the example on page 6 to figure out that a habit is a behavior that a person or animal does repeatedly.)

- **Pages 6–11** *What do pandas like to do?* (Pandas like to climb, hide, swim, slide, sit, and play.)

- **Pages 12–13** *Do you think pandas eat a lot? Why or why not?* (Yes. They eat a lot because it says they eat night and day. They are big animals, so they need a lot of food.)

- **Page 14** *Do you think pandas like to have fun? Why or why not?* (Yes. Rolling down a hill is fun. Earlier it said they like to swim, slide, and play—all fun activities.)

- **Page 15** *Look at the picture. What do you think creep means?* (It means "to crawl forward, low to the ground.")

- **Page 16** *What do you learn about pandas on this page?* (Pandas like to sleep.)

Reading Strategies

If... a child recognizes that some pages have words that rhyme and uses that to figure out some words,	**Then...** praise the child for finding helpful clues when reading.
If... a child appears to rely too heavily on the pictures to help them figure out unfamiliar words,	**Then...** point out that on pages 7 and 9, the pictures confirm a word, but they do not clearly tell what the word should be.
If... a child has difficulty identifying the book's main idea,	**Then...** use **Model Your Thinking** below.

Model Your Thinking

 **Comprehension Skill: Main Idea**

 Think ALOUD

Before I begin reading, I look at the words and pictures to try to figure out what the book is all about. All the pictures show a panda doing something different. Most of the sentences are about what pandas do—swim, eat, roll, sleep. So I know the book is all about what pandas like to do.

After Reading

Revisiting the Text

Comprehension Give students three choices of a main idea. Give them one correct choice and two choices of supporting details. Have children choose the main idea from these choices. Then have them tell what they learned about pandas from reading the book. Record their responses in the last column of the K-W-L chart they began before reading the book. Groups can use the chart to help them create fact file cards.

☞ Main Idea

Read the book *Pandas*. Then answer Numbers 1 through 5.

1 This book tells about

○ teddy bears.
○ *The Three Bears.*
○ real pandas.

2 Where do pandas live?

○ in China
○ in water
○ on a farm

3 Look at page 5. What does the word *habits* mean?

○ what an animal family looks like
○ things an animal does again and again
○ the places where animals live

☞ **4** What BEST tells what this story is about?

○ things pandas like to do
○ how pandas like to sleep
○ things pandas like to eat

☞ **5** What do pandas like to do? Write about one thing they do. Use words from the story in your answer.

_____

_____

_____

_____

_____

_____

© Scott Foresman 1

23B
What Lilly Pup Heard

by Judy Nayer
Leveled Reader 23B
Genre: Animal Fantasy
Level: Easy/Average

Summary

Lilly Pup can't read because everyone at home is making noise. So she finds a quiet spot to read and soon falls asleep. Then she hears a different noise—her family is looking for her! Last and best of all, Lilly Pup hears her mother reading to her as she falls asleep in bed.

At a Glance

Links to the Student Edition

☞ Comprehension Skill: Main Idea

Selection Vocabulary: *most, even, heard*

Program Theme: Journeys in Time and Space
Unit Theme: Take Me There

You don't have to travel far from home to go on a journey, and sometimes the best part of a journey is coming home.

Before Reading

Motivating the Reader
Build Background About Favorite Activities

Tell children that the character in this book really loves to read. Ask children to think of activities they especially enjoy and have individuals pantomime doing the activity or give word clues about it for the group to guess. Then discuss the fact that sometimes it's hard to do what you enjoy, and ask if anyone has experienced that problem.

Preview and Predict

Have children scan the cover, text, and illustrations. Encourage them to use picture clues and familiar words to predict what the story is about. Draw their attention to the book title and ask:

> **Whom is the book all about? What is Lilly Pup doing? What problem do you think she has?**

Suggest children read to find out what problem Lilly Pup has and how she tries to solve it.

Point out selection vocabulary and any unfamiliar words that are important to understanding the book, such as *started, something, read, baby, can't, quiet,* and *told.*

During Reading

Guiding Comprehension

Use the following questions to support children as they read.

- **Pages 2–3** **Why can't Lilly Pup read on her bed?** (The baby is making noise, so it is hard to read.)

- **Page 3** Point to the word *can't*. **What is this word?** (can't) **What does it mean?** (It means "cannot, not able to do something.")

- **Pages 4–5** **Why can't Lilly Pup read in the kitchen?** (Her father is making noise with a blender.)

- **Pages 6–7** **Why can't Lilly Pup read outside?** (Her mother is cutting the hedges.)

- **Page 7** **How do you think Lilly Pup is feeling? How do you know?** (She is feeling upset and frustrated because she can't find a quiet place to read. I see an exclamation mark after her words. I know I would be upset if there was something I wanted to do, but couldn't.)

- **Pages 8–9** **What is Lilly Pup's problem?** (She loves her family, but she also likes to read. She can't read because everyone at home is making noise.)

- **Pages 10–11** **What does Lilly Pup do to try to solve her problem?** (She walks in the woods to find a quiet spot to read.) **What happens next?** (She falls asleep after reading most of her book.)

- **Pages 12–13** **Why does Lilly Pup wake up?** (Lilly Pup hears her family calling her. They are looking for her.)

- **Page 16** **Why do you think Lilly Pup likes to hear her mother read?** (She likes hearing stories. She probably likes hearing her mother's voice, and she feels loved and cared for.)

- **Page 16** **What is this book all about?** (It is about a young pup who is having trouble finding a quiet place to read.)

Reading Strategies

If... a child hesitates at *started*, *walked*, or *liked*,	**Then...** cover the *-ed*, and ask the child to read the base word. Then have the child read the whole word.
If... a child uses picture clues to explain why Lilly Pup can't read at home,	**Then...** praise him or her for paying attention to pictures as well as words.
If... a child has difficulty identifying the book's main idea,	**Then...** use **Model Your Thinking** below.

Model Your Thinking

 Comprehension Skill: Main Idea

 Think ALOUD

As I read, I think about what the book is all about. I look at the sentences to see how they are alike. Most of them are about Lilly Pup trying to read, but she can't because of the noise. This book is all about a young pup who likes to read, but has trouble finding a quiet place to read.

After Reading

Revisiting the Text

Comprehension Give children three choices for a main idea, with only one correct choice. Have children select the main idea from one of the three choices and draw a picture to show the main idea. Invite children to share their pictures and explain them.

☞ Main Idea

Read the story _What Lilly Pup Heard._ Then answer Numbers 1 through 5.

☞ **1** What BEST tells what this story is about?

- ○ Lilly Pup can not find a quiet place to read at home.
- ○ Lilly Pup gets lost in the woods.
- ○ Lilly Pup wants her mother to read.

2 Where does Lilly Pup go to read?

- ○ to her school
- ○ to her grandma's house
- ○ to a quiet spot

3 What happens AFTER Lilly Pup reads most of her book?

- ○ She goes back home.
- ○ She goes to sleep.
- ○ She plays a game.

4 Why does Lilly Pup wake up?

- ○ She hears her family looking for her.
- ○ She hears her dog barking.
- ○ She hears a bird tweeting.

☞ **5** What does Lilly Pup like to do MOST? Use words from the story in your answer.

_____

_____

_____

_____

24A
Why Little Possum's Tail Is Bare

by Cheyenne Cisco
Leveled Reader 24A
Genre: Fable
Level: Easy

Summary

Little Possum is a very curious animal. Even though his mother warns him about getting into trouble, his curiosity gets the best of him. But Little Possum learns an important lesson when he goes to investigate a fire up close. A spark ignites the fur on his tail, and that is why possums have bare tails to this day.

At a Glance

Links to the Student Edition

Comprehension Skill: Cause and Effect

Selection Vocabulary: *burns, better, because*

**Program Theme: Journeys in Time and Space
Unit Theme: Take Me There**

Fables can tell stories about long ago that help us understand something about today's world, such as why possums have bare tails.

Before Reading

Motivating the Reader
Build Background About Safety Rules

Ask children to name dangers they have been warned about and what their parents, teachers, or others have said about them. Children may mention safety rules about traffic, electrical sockets and appliances, stairs, animals, matches, and fire. Have children dictate to you statements of things you should or shouldn't do in order to stay safe.

Preview and Predict

Have children scan the cover, text, and illustrations. Encourage them to use picture clues and familiar words to predict what the story is about. Prepare children for reading by saying:

> *What things does Little Possum see? What do you think his mother says about these things? What does Little Possum do?*

Explain that this story is a fable and that most fables teach a lesson. Suggest children read to find out what lesson Little Possum learns.

Point out selection vocabulary and any unfamiliar words that are important to understanding the book, such as *sting, those, light, glow, tail,* and *bare.*

During Reading

Guiding Comprehension

Use the following questions to support children as they read.

- **Pages 2–3** *What does Little Possum hear?* (He hears the buzz of a bee.) *What does Little Possum's mother tell him? What do you think she wants Little Possum to do?* (His mother tells him that bees sting. She wants him to stay away from them.)

- **Pages 4–5** *What does Little Possum do? Why do you think he does this?* (He peeks into the beehive because he is very curious.)

- **Page 5** *What do you think will happen next?* (Little Possum will get stung by a bee.)

- **Page 6** *What happened to Little Possum? Why did it happen?* (When he stuck his nose in the beehive, he got stung by a bee.)

- **Page 7** *What is Little Possum curious about now?* (a cat)

- **Page 8** *What does his mother tell him? Why does she tell him this?* (She tells him that cats bite. She wants him to stay away from the cat.)

- **Page 9** *What do you think will happen next?* (Little Possum will go close to the cat. The cat will bite or scratch him.)

- **Page 12** *What is Little Possum interested in now?* (He is curious about a fire.) *What does Mama Possum say?* (Mama Possum tells him that fire burns.)

- **Page 13** *What do you think will happen next? Why?* (Little Possum will investigate because he is too curious to listen to his mother. He will probably get hurt.)

- **Pages 14–15** *What happens to Little Possum?* (Little Possum didn't listen to his mother and went near the fire. A spark from the fire hit his tail.)

- **Page 16** *What do you think the lesson of this story is?* (The lesson is that we should always listen to our mothers.)

Reading Strategies

If... a child reads very slowly,	**Then...** have him or her reread the page to become familiar with the text. Then model fluent reading and have the child read the page again, following your model.
If... a child begins to pick up the rhythm of the verses,	**Then...** praise him or her for reading fluently and observing the rhythm of the text.
If... a child cannot recognize cause-and-effect relationships,	**Then...** use **Model Your Thinking** below.

Model Your Thinking

 Comprehension Skill: Cause and Effect

 Think ALOUD

As I read, I think about what happens in the story and why it happens. On page 6, I see Mama Possum hugging Little Possum. I ask myself: "What happened?" I read and find out that he got stung by a bee. Then I ask myself: "Why did this happen?" I look back at pages 4 and 5 and see Little Possum sticking his nose in a beehive with bees all around. I know bees will sting if you get too close to them. That is why Little Possum got stung.

After Reading

Revisiting the Text

Comprehension Have pairs reread the story to find out what happens and why. Label the columns in a T-chart *What happens?* and *Why?* Have children write words and/or draw pictures to show what happens to Little Possum and why it happens. Pairs can then use their charts and take turns retelling the story to one another.

☞ Cause and Effect

Read the story *Why Little Possum's Tail is Bare*. Then answer Numbers 1 through 5.

1 This is a make-believe story that tells

- ○ why possums run from cats.
- ○ why bees sting.
- ○ why possums have bare tails.

2 This story teaches us that

- ○ we should listen to our mothers.
- ○ we should stay away from possums.
- ○ we should try to see everything.

☞ **3** Little Possum gets too close to the fire. What happens?

- ○ The fire goes out.
- ○ The fire burns his tail.
- ○ The fire burns his ears.

☞ **4** The story tells us that all possums have bare tails because

- ○ Little Possum had to see the bees.
- ○ Little Possum listened to his mother.
- ○ Little Possum got too close to the fire.

☞ **5** Little Possum puts his nose in the beehive. What happens? Use story words in your answer.

_____

_____

_____

_____

_____

_____

© Scott Foresman 1

24B
Many Little Beads

by Anne Sibley O'Brien
Leveled Reader 24B
Genre: Realistic Story
Level: Easy/Average

Summary

A young American girl named Robin receives a bracelet. The book traces the story of this bracelet—from the girl in Africa who makes the bracelet from many little colored beads to Robin's aunt who buys the bracelet to send to Robin. The story ends as Robin imagines going to Africa to meet the girl who made the bracelet.

At a Glance

Links to the Student Edition

 Comprehension Skill: Cause and Effect

Selection Vocabulary: *people, put, give*

**Program Theme: Journeys in Time and Space
Unit Theme: Take Me There**

Even something as small as a bracelet can be part of a story about an amazing journey.

Before Reading

Motivating the Reader
Build Background About Gifts

Ask children if they have ever received gifts from a relative or friend from far away. You may wish to use a globe or world map to locate places from which children's gifts have come. Have volunteers act out someone making a gift to be sold, a person buying that gift and sending it to a friend or family member who lives far away, and that person opening the gift. Discuss why people make, buy, and give gifts, and how it feels to give or get a gift.

Preview and Predict

Have children scan the cover, text, and illustrations. Encourage them to use picture clues and familiar words to predict what the story is about. Prepare children for reading by saying:

> What do you think this book is about? Where do you think the bracelet was made? Look for the answer as you read.

Point out selection vocabulary and any unfamiliar words that are important to understanding the book, such as *woman, lady, sent, mail,* and *note.*

During Reading

Guiding Comprehension

Use the following questions to support children as they read.

- **Pages 2–3** What do you think you will find out in this book? (Possible answer: I'll find out how the bracelet got from the faraway girl to Robin.)

- **Page 4** How did the girl make a bracelet? (She put the colored beads on a string.)

- **Page 5** Why do you think the girl and the woman have so many baskets, bracelets, and necklaces? (They are selling them.)

- **Page 5** Which words keep getting repeated? ("Many little beads" and "white, yellow, blue, red, black" keep getting repeated.)

- **Pages 6–7** What does the woman in blue do? (She sees the bracelet, buys it, and takes a picture of the girl who made it.) Why does the woman buy the bracelet? (She likes the many little beads. She may want a gift for herself or someone else.)

- **Pages 8–9** What does the woman do with the bracelet? (She puts the bracelet in a box and sends it back home.)

- **Pages 10–11** How is the woman who sent the bracelet related to Robin? How do you know? (It is her aunt. Robin's mother tells her that her sister sent it.)

- **Page 14** How do you think Robin feels about the bracelet? How do you know? (She likes it. She puts it on. She smiles when she looks at it. I know I like getting pretty things as gifts.)

- **Page 16** What does the bracelet cause Robin to think about? (Robin thinks about the girl who made the bracelet, and she wonders if she will meet her one day.)

Model Your Thinking

Think ALOUD

 Comprehension Skill: Cause and Effect

As I read this book, I think about what happens and why it happens. One thing that happens is that a woman sees a bracelet with many little beads. She buys it because she likes the beads, and she wants to send a gift to her niece Robin. These are reasons why she buys the bracelet.

After Reading

Revisiting the Text

Comprehension Have children take turns reading the book aloud. As they read, have them pause at natural breaking points in the story to talk about what has happened and why it happened. Give children partial sentences to complete, such as: "The woman buys a bracelet because. . . ." When they have finished the book, work together to write a thank you letter from Robin to her aunt.

☛ Cause and Effect

Read the story *Many Little Beads*. Then answer Numbers 1 through 5.

1 Who made Robin's bracelet?

○ a girl who works at the mall

○ a girl who lives far away

○ a woman who lives down the street

☛ **2** Look at pages 6 and 7. Why does the woman buy the bracelet?

○ She wants to wear it.

○ She wants to sell it.

○ She likes the many little beads.

3 What does the woman do with the bracelet?

○ She sends it to Robin.

○ She keeps it in a bag.

○ She wears it every day.

4 Who sent the bracelet to Robin?

○ her mother's sister

○ her mother

○ her dad

☛ **5** What happens when Robin looks at her bracelet? Use words from the story in your answer.

_____

_____

_____

_____

_____

_____

© Scott Foresman 1

Answer Key for Leveled Practice A and B

Leveled Reader 19A
p. LR3

That Is Right, Walrus
⊙ Predicting

1. to the playground.
2. She is going to a ranch.
3. She will think of the bed first.
4. a book and flowers
5. She is going to the beach.

Leveled Reader 19B
p. LR6

Texas Eggs
⊙ Predicting

1. by plane
2. Grandpa played with the shells on the other days.
3. He fills the shells with bits of paper.
4. The bits of paper fall on Grandpa.
5. "Only for fun."

Leveled Reader 20A
p. LR9

From Dad
⊙ Compare and Contrast

1. a T-shirt.
2. The girl wore the T-shirt.
3. seven
4. She puts it on her panda.
5. She is bigger.

Leveled Reader 20B
p. LR12

House of Wood, House of Snow
⊙ Compare and Contrast

1. windows, doors, lamps, beds.
2. everyone
3. three hours
4. She likes to live in both houses.
5. Both are full of friends.

Leveled Reader 21A
p. LR15

Mary Goes Walking
⊙ Sequence of Events

1. Mary gets dressed up.
2. Mary goes for a walk.
3. to see how she looks
4. Mary falls in the water.
5. Possible answer: Mary gets wet. Mary goes home.

Leveled Reader 21B
p. LR18

Desert Fox
⊙ Sequence of Events

1. a fox in the desert.
2. food and water
3. She wakes up.
4. She looks and waits.
5. Possible answers: The fox gets the lizard. The fox eats the lizard.

Leveled Reader 22A   p. LR21

All Together Now!

⊙ Cause and Effect

1. They are going on a walk.
2. They slap the bugs.
3. They see a skunk.
4. a snake on the walk.
5. She helps him climb a rock.

Leveled Reader 22B   p. LR24

How Bill Found Rain

⊙ Cause and Effect

1. It has been too hot and dry.
2. Rain comes from big black clouds.
3. It starts to rain.
4. A boy could not catch a cloud with a rope.
5. Possible answers: They are dancing because they have rain. They are dancing because they are happy.

Leveled Reader 23A   p. LR27

Pandas

⊙ Main Idea

1. real pandas.
2. in China
3. things an animal does again and again
4. things pandas like to do
5. Students may write about one of the following habits: Pandas like to climb, hide, swim, slide, sit, play, eat, roll, creep, or sleep.

Leveled Reader 23B   p. LR30

What Lilly Pup Heard

⊙ Main Idea

1. Lilly Pup can not find a quiet place to read at home.
2. to a quiet spot
3. She goes to sleep.
4. She hears her family looking for her.
5. Lilly Pup likes to read.

Leveled Reader 24A   p. LR33

Why Little Possum's Tail Is Bare

⊙ Cause and Effect

1. why possums have bare tails.
2. we should listen to our mothers.
3. The fire burns his tail.
4. Little Possum got too close to the fire.
5. Little Possum gets a bee sting.

Leveled Reader 24B   p. LR36

Many Little Beads

⊙ Cause and Effect

1. a girl who lives far away
2. She likes the many little beads.
3. She sends it to Robin.
4. her mother's sister
5. Robin smiles. Robin thinks of the girl far away.

Take Me There

This collection of literature with related readings, activities, and a research project focuses on appreciating people and places in our world today and from the past. Children can use Leveled Reader 5C to expand their understanding of the unit theme and explore the questions: *Where will we go? How will we grow?*

Use the Unit at a Glance to find where skills from *Scott Foresman Reading* are practiced and reinforced in the Leveled Reader Resource Guide.

Unit at a Glance

Comprehension Skills

☞ **Sequence**
from The Bravest Dog Ever: The True Story of Balto

☞ **Cause and Effect**
from Hill of Fire

Research Skills

Using a Map
The Places I Go

Writing Skills

Expository Writing
What's Happening?

Cross-Curricular Connections

Mathematics
The Great Race

Social Studies
Way to Go!

Science
When the Earth Roars

Critical Thinking
Reader Response

Suggested Pacing Guide

Week 1	Week 2	Week 3	Week 4	Week 5
• Children read "Ode to My Shoes." • Discuss unit theme and preview Leveled Reader 5C. • Launch the research project, The Places I Go. • Children set goals in Unit and Research Project Planners.	• Children read from *The Bravest Dog Ever: The True Story of Balto.* • Children read about how news travels and write news articles. • Review steps and goals in planners with children.	• Children read about the Iditarod and devise math problems about it. • Children read about ways to travel. Then they make and sort travel card sets, invent new ways to travel, or create travel board games. • Check progress of research projects.	• Children read from *Hill of Fire.* • Children read about volcanoes and build volcano models. • Children conclude research projects.	• Children respond to literature. • Children present research projects.

© Scott Foresman 1

Page numbers refer to the Leveled Reader C Resource Guide.

Introduce the Leveled Reader

Activate Prior Knowledge

Use the poem "Ode to My Shoes," Leveled Reader 5C, page 2, to introduce the unit theme, Take Me There. Ask children to name places their shoes visit each day. Then ask children to think of places they have gone in the past and places they might go in the future. Record their responses. Lead children to conclude that over time they go many places and grow in many ways. Encourage children to look in the literature they will read for new places and examples of how story characters grow and change.

Preview and Predict

Have children scan Leveled Reader 5C, Take Me There. Point out the theme question in the table of contents, and encourage children to make predictions about how the literature, research project, and related activities will help them answer the theme questions. Use the Suggested Pacing Guide to help children set goals for reading the literature and doing the related activities. You may wish to distribute copies of the Unit Planner on page 45. Children can record their goals in the Unit Planner and track their progress each week.

Unit Planner

Leveled Reader Resource Guide, p. 45

Research Project Tips

Children can

- ask family members to provide three or four photographs representing themselves at various ages.
- plan a way to mount the drawings and writings.
- use clothespins to attach drawings to a classroom clothesline to form a time line.
- use Multimedia Studio and www.scottforesman.com to research and present projects.

Research Project Planner

Leveled Reader Resource Guide, p. 46

Research Project: The Places I Go

Leveled Reader 5C, p. 3

Summary Children look at where they have gone and think about where they might still go as they grow and change.

Research Skill: Using a Map

The Places I Go gives children an opportunity to expand their research skills in using maps. Children recall memories and collect facts about their lives. They look at a map to find where they were born and places they have been. Then children create a time line using drawings and writings about various stages of their lives: past, present, and future. Products might include photographs and/or multimedia presentations using interview recordings of family members.

Launching the Project

Have children read the steps of the research project, The Places I Go. Children can set weekly goals and record them in the Research Project Planner on page 46. Share with children the characteristics of an excellent research project and presentation, which are listed in the Research Project Scoring Guide. Encourage children to use these characteristics to help them set standards for their own work.

© Scott Foresman 1

Summary In this nonfiction selection, an Alaskan sled dog pulls his team 53 miles to bring much-needed medicine to the people of Nome.

© Scott Foresman 1

As children read from *The Bravest Dog Ever: The True Story of Balto,* they will learn about a famous sled dog and follow the sequence of events that resulted in saving the lives of many sick people. Use the Fact File to build background as needed.

Have children read the selection independently. After they have finished reading, review with children what they have learned about **sequence.**

- In a story, things happen in a certain order.

- Readers think about what happens first, next, and last.

☞ Comprehension Check: Sequence

Use the following questions to assess children's understanding of the selection and the target comprehension skill.

1. **Place these sentences in the order in which they happened in the story: a. Gunnar packed the sled; b. Balto raced through the night to get to Nome; c. Two children in Nome got very sick.** Children read or write sentences in order: c, a, and b.

2. **After Balto pulled into town, what happened first, next, and last in Nome.** First, Gunnar took the medicine to the doctor. Next, the doctor gave it to the sick people. Last, the people got well, and Nome was saved.

Fact File

The lead dog is very important to the success of a sled-dog team. The lead dog has to listen carefully to the spoken commands of the driver, or musher, because the other dogs are trained to follow only the leader. A good lead dog has to be able to outrun the other dogs, not get distracted, sense hidden dangers, and follow a trail, even in blizzard conditions.

Activity Tips

Children can

- review and discuss simple, high-interest newspaper articles.
- develop a method of recording and organizing answers to the questions.
- write a headline that will grab readers' attention.

What's Happening? Leveled Reader 5C, p. 13

 Summary Children read about how news travels and write news articles that tell about Balto and Gunnar's trip to Nome.

This activity provides an opportunity for children to retell the true story of Balto in a newspaper article format. Their writings will focus on answering who, what, where, when, and why questions. Children will expand their research and study skills by locating, organizing, and presenting information. **Expository Writing**

Activity Assessment

Before they begin, encourage children to use these characteristics as standards for their work.

> **An excellent news article**
> - tells facts about Balto and Gunnar's trip to Nome.
> - answers the questions *who?, what?, when?, where?,* and *why?.*
> - is clear and includes the most important information.

✓ Student Self-Assessment form appears on page 47.

Activity Tips

Children can

- plan a way to keep track of miles between checkpoints, such as making a photocopy of the map and labeling distances on it.
- review word problems in a math book to see how they are written.
- use calculators to solve the problems.
- write a separate answer key for their problems.
- go over their math problems and answers with a friend before asking others to solve them.

The Great Race Leveled Reader 5C, pp. 14–15

 Summary Children read about the Iditarod and solve math problems using a chart that provides information about Iditarod checkpoints. Then children make up their own problems using the chart.

In this activity, children learn about the dog-sled race that celebrates Balto's famous feat. They will expand their research and study skills by using a map to follow the last part of the race and using a chart to answer questions about the race. **Mathematics**

Answers To Activity Questions

- Kaltag and Unalakleet are the two check points with the most miles between them.
- Golovin and White Mountain are the two checkpoints with the fewest miles between them.
- There are 73 miles between Golovin and Safety (18 miles + 55 miles = 73 miles).

© Scott Foresman 1

Activity Assessment

Before they begin, encourage children to use these characteristics as standards for their work.

> **An excellent math problem**
> • can be solved by using the chart.
> • has enough information for classmates to be able to figure out the answer.
> • has a correct answer.

✓ Student Self-Assessment form appears on page 47.

○ ○

Way To Go! Leveled Reader 5C, pp. 16–17

Summary Children read about ways to travel and then create and sort travel cards, invent new ways to travel, or design travel board games.

In this activity, children learn more about ways people travel. They will expand their research and study skills by locating, collecting, and organizing information about ways people move from place to place. **Social Studies**

Activity Assessment

Before they begin, encourage children to use these characteristics as standards for their work.

> **An excellent travel card set, a new travel idea, or a travel board game**
> • includes pictures of five different ways to travel, sorted by speed. (travel card set)
> • includes a detailed drawing of a new way to travel and a written description of this traveling method. (new travel idea)
> • includes a game board that shows a variety of ways to travel, has a title, and has instructions for playing a game about traveling. (travel board game)

✓ Student Self-Assessment form appears on page 47.

© Scott Foresman 1

from Hill of Fire

Leveled Reader 5C, pp. 18–29

Summary Set in Mexico, this realistic story describes how villagers react to an erupting volcano.

Hill of Fire provides an opportunity for children to think about what happens in a story and why it happens. Use the Fact File to build background as needed.

Activity Tips

Children can

• find transportation books and books about other countries in the library.

• scan travel magazines and brochures.

• use self-sticking notes to mark interesting ways to travel in books, magazines, and brochures.

• use an encyclopedia to figure out average speeds for different methods of travel.

Fact File

Hill of Fire is based on the story of Dionisio Pulido, a farmer, who in 1943, was plowing his field near Parícutin, Mexico, when the ground began to shake and crack. He ran to the village to warn the people. The volcano that was being born kept growing until it covered Parícutin and another town too. Today, the volcano is a mountain more than 1,000 feet high, but the volcano is currently inactive.

Have children read the selection independently. After they have finished reading, review with children what they have learned about **cause and effect.**

- Readers think about things that happen in a story and why those things happen.

☞ Comprehension Check: Cause and Effect

Use the following questions to assess children's understanding of the selection and the target comprehension skill. Possible responses are provided.

1. What is happening in the picture on pages 22 and 23? Why does this happen? The farmer, Pablo, and the ox are running away. They are running because the earth opened, and fire, smoke, and lava came up from the ground.

2. Why do the people of the village have a great fiesta? They have a great fiesta because they have a new village that is far enough away from the volcano to be safe.

● ●

When the Earth Roars Leveled Reader 5C, pp. 30–31

READING ACROSS TEXTS

Summary Children read about volcanoes and make models of a volcano.

Children learn the scientific explanation for the birth of volcanoes. They will expand their research and study skills by interpreting photographs and following directions to make a volcano model. **Science**

Activity Assessment

Before they begin, encourage children to use these characteristics as standards for their work.

> **An excellent volcano model**
> - shows appropriate use of suggested materials.
> - can be used to explain how a volcano erupts.

✔ Student Self-Assessment form appears on page 47.

© Scott Foresman 1

Reader Response Leveled Reader 5C, p. 32

1. Places children write about can be unusual, such as a faraway vacation spot, or ordinary, such as a new playground, as long as the focus is on what they learned while there. **Drawing Conclusions**

2. Questions should be logical extensions of details given in the selection about Gunnar's actions, such as his use of a whip or his packing of the sled. **Divergent Questioning**

3. Actions should show that children understand the meanings of the words. **Vocabulary Building/Context Clues**

4. Responses should include details about the characters' likenesses and differences. For example, both the farmer and Gunnar survived something dangerous. **Compare and Contrast**

5. Gunnar and Balto had to get medicine to sick people in Nome, so they traveled as fast as they could in the cold and snow. The farmer was the first to notice the volcano eruption, so he ran to warn the people of the village. **Analyzing**

Student Assessment

Ask children to share what they have learned by having them choose one selection or activity and write a paragraph or two explaining why they liked it and what they learned from it. After children share their paragraphs with others, they can add them to their portfolios along with their completed work for the unit.

Presenting the Research Project

Have children share the results of their research projects with the class. Children can organize and prepare their own presentations using their Research Project Planners, pictures, writings, and the time lines they created. Review with children the characteristics of an excellent presentation. Allow time for the class to ask questions and give their own comments about the project.

Research Project Assessment

Assess the research project, The Places I Go, using the Research Project Scoring Guide at the right.

Research Project Scoring Guide

4 Excellent
- Child sets reasonable goals each week and makes steady progress during the project. Child follows each step of the project independently.
- Child's drawings are filled with vivid details. Child labels each picture with a well-thought out selection of facts and ideas about his or her life.
- Child effectively uses drawings and writings to create an accurate time line. Child shares life events, in order, in a cohesive style.

3 Good
- Child sets reasonable goals each week, but needs some reminders to maintain progress. Child requires some assistance to figure out certain steps.
- Child makes a consistent effort to include details in the drawings. Child elaborates each drawing with at least one fact or idea about his or her life.
- Child correctly uses drawings and writings to create a time line with events presented in the correct sequence. Child needs some assistance presenting and explaining the time line with classmates.

2 Fair
- Child needs help setting reasonable goals each week and maintaining progress during the project. Some steps are not done correctly or completely.
- Child completes only one or two drawings that are lacking in detail. Child exhibits a limited writing vocabulary and elaborates on the drawings in a general, rather than a personal, manner.
- Child does not have enough drawings to be sequenced in a time line. Child has difficulty sharing pictures and writings.

1 Poor
- Child does not set reasonable goals each week or maintain steady progress.
- Child's drawings are incomplete. Child does not attempt to write about drawings.
- Child cannot complete a time line and has difficulty describing life events.

✔ Student Self-Assessment form appears on page 47.

Grade 1 Leveled Resources

Unit 2 Take a Closer Look

Easy	On-Level	Challenge
1A Come Back!	**1B** Tex Has an Itch	**2C** Take a Closer Look
2A Come and Play	**2B** Paper Fun	
3A Who Went Up?	**3B** Go Away, Bugs!	
4A How Many on the Log?	**4B** With the Fish	
5A Jack and Jill	**5B** In and Out	
6A Stop! Eat!	**6B** Night Songs	

Unit 3 Let's Learn Together

Easy	On-Level	Challenge
7A Goal!	**7B** This Means Stop	**3C** Let's Learn Together
8A Hic! Hic! Hic!	**8B** Oh, Good!	
9A Jump Rope Time	**9B** Sleepy Pig	
10A Molly and Polly	**10B** The Zookeeper	
11A Wash Day	**11B** Looking for the Queen	
12A Do What I Do	**12B** Peas Please	

Unit 4 Favorite Things Old and New

Easy	On-Level	Challenge
13A Jump, Jump	**13B** Biff Helps After All	**4C** Favorite Things Old and New
14A Mother's Day	**14B** Where Bat Came From	
15A A Day for Dad	**15B** Karate Class	
16A Be There!	**16B** Zulu Dancer	
17A The Three Bears	**17B** Long Tom	
18A Knock-Knock Jokes	**18B** The First Day of Winter	

Unit 5 Take Me There

Easy	On-Level	Challenge
19A That Is Right, Walrus	**19B** Texas Eggs	**5C** Take Me There
20A From Dad	**20B** House of Wood, House of Snow	
21A Mary Goes Walking	**21B** Desert Fox	
22A All Together Now!	**22B** How Bill Found Rain	
23A Pandas	**23B** What Lilly Pup Heard	
24A Why Little Possum's Tail Is Bare	**24B** Many Little Beads	

Unit 6 Suprise Me!

Easy	On-Level	Challenge
25A Wish Faces	**25B** The Toymaker	**6C** Surprise Me!
26A Look at Him Go!	**26B** The Three Hares	
27A Which Is Which?	**27B** How Crayons Are Made	
28A Yes, But	**28B** Mr. Small	
29A Almost	**29B** Panda Picture	
30A The Move	**30B** Our Place	

Additional Resources
Table of Contents